THE TAVERN LAMPS ARE BURNING

ALSO BY CARL CARMER

Stars Fell on Alabama

Listen for a Lonesome Drum

Dark Trees to the Wind

The Hudson

The Susquehanna

Rivers of America, Editor

Regions of America, Editor

THE TAVERN LAMPS ARE BURNING

Literary Journeys Through Six Regions and Four Centuries of New York State Selected by

CARL CARMER

FORDHAM UNIVERSITY PRESS
New York
1996

LC 96-28634
ISBN 0-8232-1697-7 (hardcover)
ISBN 0-8232-1698-5 (paperback)

Published by arrangement with David McKay Company, Inc.

Library of Congress Cataloging-in-Publication Data

The tavern lamps are burning : literary journeys through six regions
and four centuries of New York State / selected by Carl Carmer.
p. cm.
Reprint. Originally published: New York : D. McKay Co., [1964]
Includes bibliographical references and index.
ISBN 0-8232-1697-7 (hardcover). — ISBN 0-8232-1698-5 (pbk.)
1. American literature—New York (State) 2. New York (State)—
Description and travel. 3. New York (State)—Literary collections.
I. Carmer, Carl Lamson, 1893–
PS548.N7T38 1996
810.8′032747—dc20 96-28634
CIP

Printed in the United States of America

To

AGNES AND LOUIS JONES

with deep affection

FOREWORD

THE COMPILING of an anthology is perforce a matter of personal taste. The compiler must be prepared for strong protests based on his choices and his omissions. On such matters I can only plead that I have not read everything ever written about the subject. I might admit the undeniable fact that my judgment is not infallible. I do not believe that my love for the land described in this volume may be challenged since I have devoted such a large proportion of my own writings to it.

Naturally in the course of following my profession I have sought to find out what other writers have had to say about my native country, widely known as "upstate," and I have borne in mind those passages that have most impressed me. Hence this volume is an accumulation made through decades of study of those paragraphs, chapters, or undefined gleanings which I have considered to interpret best those New York State areas that I love. I have long held that "York State" (as old-timers still call it) is a country, that its people have specific characteristics that make it distinctive, that it is not to be loosely gathered into a category called "the Mid-Atlantic States," nor is it to be regarded as a minor suburb of Yankeedom.

I have not the least doubt of my own prejudices in selecting the contents of this grouping of writings about this land north of Manhattan and west of New England. The book is meant to be a blast from a literary shotgun. Every pellet with which it is loaded is aimed at persuading those who exist within our nationwide pattern to believe in Upstate's unique, peculiar, and especial qualities. Whether the buckshot be Rudyard Kipling's essay on Buffalo's grain elevators, Paul Horgan's perceptive notes on Rochester, Mrs. Hall's descriptions of Albany society in the early nineteenth century, Theodore Dreiser's moody narrative of crime on Adirondack waters, or Artemus Ward's report of a criminal attack on the wax figure of Judas

Iscariot in a canalboat moored at Utica, I am hoping that the peppered reader will be convinced that there is an over-all, one-of-a-kind nonesuchness that separates Upstate from all other land-units of the world.

CARL CARMER

Octagon House
Irvington-on-Hudson, N.Y.
February, 1964

TABLE OF CONTENTS

BOOK V

WESTERN NEW YORK

A FOLIO OF PAINTINGS OF UPSTATE NEW YORK

To illustrate *The Tavern Lamps Are Burning,* a special group of forty-three paintings are selected from the collections of The New York State Historical Association by Agnes Halsey Jones, Assistant in Art Research at the Cooperstown Museum. The pictures portray New York scenes and people from the first third of the 18th Century to the period of the Civil War and later.

Illustrations appear between pages 234 and 235

☛ BOOK ONE ☚

The Hudson

The Catskills

The Taconics

Hudson River

INTRODUCTION TO BOOK I

IT WAS natural that the early writings about New York State should be about the Hudson. That doughty Elizabethan explorer, Henry Hudson, who named the wide stream "Great River of the Mountains," had the opportunity of observing the river and its native valley dwellers for many sunny and misty September days. Though his journal was lost, some quotations from it have remained in the writings of other men, and the journal of Robert Juet, who was one of the officers of Hudson's *The Half Moon,* offers several passages that indicate how impressed all of its crew were by the majestic scenery.

The early settlements on the riverbanks led to appreciative writings, and the Hudson still inspires a variety of poems and novels, essays and historical narrations.

The landscape of the Hudson Valley and the Catskill Mountains proved challenging to most of the American writers of the mid-nineteenth century. George William Curtis, Nathaniel Parker Willis, the Reverend Dr. Murdoch, Washington Irving, Willis Gaylord Clarke, William Cullen Bryant, and the Irish comedian, Tyrone Power, each took his turn at putting into words his personal impressions of the river and its mountain surroundings. From the Catskill Mountain House, which overlooked eighty miles of Hudson water, to the river's little tributaries, each bit of valley landscape seemed to have its own interpreter. The prose of the era was romantic, decorative, sentimental, paralleling the canvases of the Hudson River School painters, who were inspired by the European artists, Claude Lorraine and Salvatore Rosa. A hundred years later Oriana Atkinson painted with exciting words in her historical novel, *The Golden Season,* a prose canvas more like the work of an American Breughel. And her contemporary, Edmund Gilligan, created in his *Strangers in The Vly* a wild Catskill legend more imaginative than the tales Washington Irving had related in the previous century. Brooks Atkinson (husband of Oriana Atkinson), famous as a theatre critic, but an observant and poetic naturalist as well, wrote a detailed and realistic calendar of the Catskill year deserving of comparison with the essays of John Burroughs.

The Taconic Hills across the river from the Catskills and bordering on Connecticut's Berkshires have not presented as much subject matter for literary writings. The most sensitive and popular of the authors who wrote from these hills was the poet, Edna St. Vincent Millay. Her poems struck deep into the consciousness of the 1920's.

THE HUDSON

17TH CENTURY

ROBERT JUET

A Month of Fair Weather on the "Great River of the Mountains"

September, 1609

The second, in the morning close weather, the wind at South in the morning; from twelve until two of the clock we steered North North-west, and had sounding one and twenty fathoms, and in running one glass we had but sixteen fathoms, then seventeen, and so shallower and shallower until it came to twelve fathoms. We saw a great fire, but could not see the land, then we came to ten fathoms, whereupon we brought our tacks aboard, and stood to the Eastward East South-east, four glasses. Then the sun arose, and we steered away North again, and saw the land . . . all like broken islands, and our soundings were eleven and ten fathoms. Then we luffed in for the shore, and fair by the shore, we had seven fathoms. The course along the land we found to be North-east by North. From the land which we had first sight of, until we came to a great lake of water, as we could judge it to be, being drowned land, which made it to rise like islands, which was in length ten leagues. The mouth of that lake had many shallows, and the sea breaketh on them as it is cast out of the mouth of it. And from that lake or bay, the land lay North by East, and we had a great stream out of the bay; and from thence our sounding was ten fathoms, two leagues from the land. At five of the clock, we anchored, being little wind, and rode in eight fathoms

Excerpts from *The Journal of the Half Moon* (*1609*) by Robert Juet. First published in *Hakluytus Posthumus* by Samuel Purchas, B.D., London, 1625.

water, the night was fair ... this is a very good land to fall with, and a pleasant land to see.

The third, the morning misty until ten of the clock, then it cleared, and the wind came to the South South-east, so we weighed and stood to the Northward. The land is very pleasant and high, and bold to fall withall. At three of the clock in the after-noon, we came to three great rivers. So we stood along to the Northermost, thinking to have gone into it, but we found it to have a very shallow bar before it, for we had but ten foot water. Then we cast about to the Southward, and found two fathoms, three fathoms, and three and a quarter, till we came to the Souther side of them, then we had five and six fathoms, and anchored. So we sent in our boat to sound, and they found no less water than four, five, six, and seven fathoms, and returned in an hour and a half. So we weighed and went in, and rode in five fathoms, ooze ground, and saw many salmons, and mullets, and rays very great. The height is 40 degrees 30 minutes.

The fourth, in the morning as soon as the day was light, we saw that it was good riding farther up. So we sent our boats to sound, and found that it was a very good harbour; and four and five fathoms, two cables length from the shore. Then we weighed and went in with our ship. Then our boat went on land with our net to fish, and caught ten great mullets, of a foot and a half long a piece, and a ray as great as four men could haul into the ship. So we trimmed our boat and rode still all day. At night the wind blew hard at the North-west, and our anchor came home, and we drove on shore, but took no hurt, thanked be God, for the ground is soft sand and ooze. This day the people of the country came aboard of us, seeming very glad of our coming, and brought green tobacco, and gave us of it for knives and beads. They go in deer skins loose, well dressed. They have yellow copper. They desire clothes, and are very civil. They have great store of maize or Indian wheat, whereof they make good bread. The country is full of great and tall oaks.

The fifth, in the morning as soon as the day was light, the wind ceased and the flood came. So we heaved off our ship again into five fathoms water, and sent our boat to sound the bay, and we found that there was three fathoms hard by the Souther shore. Our man went on land there, and saw great store of men, women and children, who gave them tabacco at their coming on land. So they went up into the woods, and saw great store of very goodly oaks, and some currants. For one of them came aboard and brought some dried, and gave me some, which were sweet and good. This day many of the people came aboard, some in mantles of feathers, and some in skins of divers sorts of good furs. Some women also came to us with hemp. They had red copper tobacco pipes, and other things of copper they did wear about their necks. At night they went on land again, so we rode very quiet, but durst not trust them.

The sixth, in the morning was fair weather, and our master sent John Colman, with four other men in our boat to the North-side, to sound the other river, being four leagues from us. They found . . . very good riding for ships; and a narrow river to the westward between two islands. The lands they told us were as pleasant with grass and flowers, and goodly trees, as ever they had seen, and very sweet smells came from them. So they went in two leagues and saw an open sea, and returned; and as they came back, they were set upon by two canoes, the one having twelve, the other fourteen men. The night came on, and it began to rain, so that their match went out; and they had one man slain in the fight, which was an Englishman, named John Colman, with an arrow shot into his throat, and two more hurt. It grew so dark that they could not find the ship that night, but labored to and fro on their oars. They had so great a stream, that their grapnell would not hold them. . . .

The ninth, fair weather. In the morning, two great canoes came aboard full of men; the one with their bows and arrows, and the other in show of buying of knives to betray us; but we perceived their intent. We took two of them to have kept them, and put red coats on them, and would not suffer the other to come near us. So they went on land, and two other came aboard in a canoe; we took the one and let the other go; but he which we had taken, got up and leapt over-board. Then we weighed and went off into the channel of the river, and anchored there all night. . . .

The eleventh, was fair and very hot weather. At one of the clock in the after-noon, we weighed and went into the river, the wind at South Southwest, little wind. Our soundings were seven, six, five, six, seven, eight, nine, ten, twelve, thirteen, and fourteen fathoms. Then it shallowed again, and came to five fathoms. Then we anchored, and saw that it was a very good harbour for all winds, and rode all night. The people of the country came aboard of us, making show of love, and gave us tobacco and Indian wheat, and departed for that night; but we durst not trust them.

The twelfth, very fair and hot. In the after-noon at two of the clock we weighed, the wind being variable, between the North and the North-west. So we turned into the river two leagues and anchored. This morning at our first rode in the river, there came eight and twenty canoes full of men, women and children to betray us: but we saw their intent, and suffered none of them to come aboard of us. At twelve of the clock they departed. They brought with them oysters and beans, whereof we bought some. They have great tobacco pipes of yellow copper, and pots of earth to dress their meat in. It floweth South-east by South within....

The fifteenth, in the morning was misty until the sun arose: then it cleared. So we weighed with the wind at South, and ran up into the river twenty leagues, passing by high mountains. We had a very good depth, as six, seven, eight, nine, ten, twelve, and thirteen fathoms, and great store of salmons in the river. This morning our two savages got out of a port and swam away. After we were under sail they called to us in scorn. At night we came to other mountains, which lie from the river side. There we found very loving people, and very old men: where we were well used. Our boat went to fish, and caught great store of very good fish....

The eighteenth, in the morning was fair weather, and we rode still. In the after-noon our masters mate went on land with an old savage, a governor of the country; who carried him to his house, and made him good cheers....

The one and twentieth, was fair weather, and the wind all Southerly: we determined yet once more to go farther up into the river, to try what depth and breadth it did bear; but much people resorted aboard, so we went not this day. Our carpenter went on land, and made a foreyard. And our master and his mate determined to try some of the chief men of the country, whether they had any treachery in them. So they took them down into the cabin, and gave them so much wine and aqua vitae, that they were all merry: and one of them had his wife with him, which sat so modestly, as any of our country women would do in a strange place. In the end one of them was drunk, which had been aboard of our ship all the time that we had been there: and that was strange to them; for they could not tell how to take it. The canoes and folk went all on shore: but some of them came again, and brought strops of beads: some had six, seven, eight, nine, ten; and gave him. So he slept all night quietly.

The two and twentieth, was fair weather: in the morning our masters mate and four more of the company went up with our boat to sound the river higher up. The people of the country came not aboard till noon: but when they came, and saw the savages well, they were glad. So at three of the clock in the after-noon they came aboard, and brought tobacco, and more beads, and gave them to our master, and made an oration, and showed him all the country round about. Then they sent one of their company on land, who presently returned, and brought a great platter full of venison, dressed by themselves; and they caused him to eat with them: then they made him reverence, and departed all save the old man that lay aboard. This night at ten of the clock, our boat returned in a shower of rain from sounding of the river; and found it to be at an end for shipping to go in. For they had been up eight or nine leagues, and found but seven foot water, and unconstant soundings....

The six and twentieth was fair weather, and the wind at South a stiff gale, we rode still. In the morning our carpenter went on land with our masters mate, and four more of our company to cut wood. This morning, two canoes came up the river from the place where we first found loving people, and in one of them was the old man that had lain aboard of us at the other place. He brought another old man with him, which brought more strops of beads, and gave them to our master, and showed him all the country there about, as though it were at his command. So he made the two old men dine with him, and the old man's wife: for they brought two old women, and two young maidens of the age of sixteen or seventeen years with them, who behaved themselves very modestly. Our master gave one of the old men a knife, and they gave him and us tobacco. And at one of the clock they departed down the river, making signs that we should come down to them; for we were within two leagues of the place where they dwelt....

The nine and twentieth was dry close weather: the wind at South, and South and by West, we weighed early in the morning, and turned down three leagues by a low water, and anchored at the lower end of the long reach; for it is six leagues long. Then there came certain Indians in a canoe to us, but would not come aboard. After dinner there came the canoe with other men, whereof three came aboard us. They brought Indian wheat, which we bought for trifles. At three of the clock in the after-noon we weighed, as soon as the ebb came, and turned down to the edge of the mountains, or the Northermost of the mountains, and anchored: because the high land hath many points, and a narrow channel, and hath many eddy wids. So we rode quietly all night in seven fathoms water.

The thirtieth was fair weather, and the wind at South-east a stiff gale between the mountains. We rode still the after-noon. The people of the country came aboard us, and brought some small skins with them, which we bought for knives and trifles. This is a very pleasant place to build a town on. The road is very near, and very good for all winds, save an East North-east wind. The mountains look as if some metal or mineral were in them. For the trees that grow on them were all blasted, and some of them barren with few or no trees on them. The people brought a stone aboard like to emery (a stone used by glaziers to cut glass) it would cut iron or steel: yet being bruised small, and water put to it, it made a color like black lead glistening; It is also good for painters colors. At three of the clock they departed and we rode still all night.

The first of October, fair weather, the wind variable between the West and the North. In the morning we weighed at seven of the clock with the ebb, and got down below the mountains, which was seven leagues. Then it fell calm and the flood was come, and we anchored at twelve of the clock. The people of the mountains came aboard us, wondering at our ship and weapons. We bought some small skins of them for trifles. This after-noon, one canoe kept hanging under our stern with one man in it, which we could not keep from thence, who got up by our rudder to the cabin window, and stole out my pillow, and two shirts, and two bandoleers. Our masters mate shot at him, and struck him on the breast, and killed him. Whereupon all the rest fled away, some in their canoes, and so leapt out of them into the water. We manned our boat, and got our things again. Then one of them that swam got hold of our boat, thinking to overthrow it. But our cook took a sword, and cut off one of his hands, and he was drowned. By this time the ebb was come, and we weighed and got down two leagues, by that time it was dark. So we anchored in four fathoms water, and rode well.

The second, fair weather. At break of day we weighed, the wind being at North-west, and got down seven leagues; then the flood was come strong, so we anchored. Then came one of the savages that swam away from us at our going up the river with many other, thinking to betray us. But we perceived their intent, and suffered none of them to enter our ship. Whereupon two canoes full of men, with their bows and arrows shot at us after our stern: in recompense whereof we discharged six muskets, and killed two or three of them. Then about an hundred of them came to a point of land to shoot at us. There I shot a falcon [a small cannon] at them, and killed two of them: whereupon the rest fled into the woods. Yet they manned off another canoe with nine or ten men, which came to meet us. So I shot at it also a falcon, and shot it through, and killed one of them. Then our men with their muskets, killed three or four more of them. So they went their way, within a while after, we got down two leagues beyond that place, and anchored in a bay, clear from all danger of them on the other side of the river, where we saw a very good piece of ground: and hard by it there was a cliff, that looked of the color of a white green, as though it were either copper, or silver mine and I think it to be one of them, by the trees that grow upon it. For they be all burned, and the other places are green as grass, it is on that side of the river that is called Manna-hata. There we saw no people to trouble us: and rode quietly all night; but had much wind and rain....

The fourth, was fair weather, and the wind at North North-west, we weighed and came out of the river, into which we had run so far. Within a while after, we came out also of the great mouth of the great river, that runs up to the North-west, borrowing upon the Norther side of the same, thinking to have deep water: for we had sounded a great way with our boat at our first going in, and found seven, six and five fathoms. So we came out that way, but we were deceived, for we had but eight foot and a half water: and so to three, five, three, and two fathoms and an half. And then three, four, five, six, seven, eight, nine and ten fathoms. And by twelve of the clock we were clear of all the inlet. Then we took in our boat, and set our main-sail and sprit-sail, and our top-sails, and steered away East South-east, and South-east by East off into the main sea.

DANIEL DENTON

Along Hudson's River

Hudsons River runs by *New-York* northward into the Countrey, toward the Head of which is seated New-Albany, a place of great Trade with the *Indians,* betwixt which & New York, being above one hundred miles, is as good Corn-land as the world affords, enough to entertain hundreds of Families ... [Such] a League of Peace was made, & Friendship con-

From *A Brief Description of New York* by Daniel Denton, London, 1670. Published by the Press of the Historical Society of Pennsylvania, 1845, from the original in the British Museum.

cluded betwixt that Colony & the *Indians* that they have not resisted or disturbed any Christians there, in the settling or peaceable possessing of any Lands...but every man hath sate under his own Vine, & hath peaceably reapt and enjoyed the fruits of their own labours, which God continue....

To give some satisfaction to people that shall be desirous to transport themselves thither, (the Countrey being capable of entertaining many thousands,) how & after what manner people live, & how Land may be procured, &c. I shall answer, that the usual way is for a Company of people to joyn together either enough to make a Town, or a lesser number; These go with the consent of the Governor to view a Tract of Land, there being choice enough, and finding a place convenient for a town, they return to the Governor, who upon their desire admits them into the Colony, & gives them a Grant or Patent for the said Land, for themselves & associates. These persons being thus qualified, setle the place, & take in what inhabitants to themselves they shall see cause to admit of till their Town be full; these Associates thus taken in have equal priviledges with themselves, & they make a division of the Land suitable to every mans occasions, no man being debarr'd of such quantities as he hath occasion for, the rest they let lie in Common till they have occasion for a new division, never dividing their Pasture-land at all, which lies in common to the whole Town....For the manner how they get a livelihood, it is principally by Corn & Cattel, which will there fetch them any Commodities; likewise they sowe store of Flax which they make every one Cloth of for their own wearing, as also woollen Cloth, and Linsey-Woolsey, & had they more Tradesmen among them, they would in a little time live without the help of any other Countrey for their Clothing: For Tradesmen there is none but live happily there, as Carpenters, Blacksmiths, Masons, Tailors, Weavers, Shoemakers, Tanners, Brickmakers, & so any other Trade; them that have no Trade betake themselves to Husbandry, get land of their own, and live exceeding well.

Thus have I briefly given you a Relation of *New-York,* with the places therunto adjoyning;...if I have err'd, it is principally in not giving it its due commendation; for besides those earthly blessings where it is stor'd, Heaven hath not been wanting to open his Treasure, in sending down seasonable showers upon the Earth, blessing it with a sweet and pleasant air, and a continuation of such Influences as tend to the Health both of Man & Beast: and the Climate hath such an affinity with that of *England,* that it breeds ordinarily no alteration to those which remove thither; that the name of seasoning, which is common to some other Countreys hath never there been known; That I may say, & say truly, that if there be any terrestrial happiness to be had by people of all ranks, especially of an inferior rank, it must certainly be here: here any one may furnish himself with land, & live rent-free, yea, with such a quantity of Land, that he may weary himself with walking over his fields of Corn, and all sorts of Grain: & let his stock of Cattel amount to some hundreds, he needs not fear their want of pasture in the Summer or Fodder in the Winter, the Woods affording sufficient supply. For the *Summer*-season, where you have grass as high as a mans knees, nay, as high as his waste [sic], interlaced with Pea-vines and other weeds that Cattel much delight in, as much as a man can press through; and these woods also every mile or half-mile are furnished with fresh ponds, brooks or rivers, where all sorts of Cattel, during the heat of the day, do quench their thirst & cool themselves; these brooks and rivers being environed of each side with several sorts of trees & Grape-vines, the Vines, arbor-like, interchanging places and crossing these rivers, does shade and shelter them from the scorching beams of *Sols* fiery influence; Here those which Fortune hath frown'd upon in *England,* to deny them an inheritance amongst their Brethren, or such as by their utmost labors can scarcely procure a living, I say such may procure here inheritances of lands & possessions, stock themselves with all sorts of Cattel, enjoy the benefit of them whilst they live, & leave them to the benefit of their children when they die: here you need not trouble the Shambles for meats nor Bakers nor Brewers for Beer & Bread, nor run to a Linnen-Draper for a supply, every one making their own Linnen, & a great part of their woollen cloth for their ordinary wearing: And how prodigal, if I may so say, hath Nature been to furnish the Countrey with all sorts of wilde Beasts & Fowle, which every one hath an interest in, and may hunt at his pleasure: where besides the pleasure in Hunting, he may furnish his house with excellent fat Venison, Turkeys, Geese, Heath-Hens, Cranes, Swans, Ducks, Pidgeons & the like; & wearied with that, he may go a Fishing, where the Rivers are so furnished, that he may supply himself with Fish before he can leave off the Recreation: Where you may travel by Land upon the same Continent hundreds of miles, & passe through Towns & Villages, & never hear the least complaint for want, nor hear any ask you for a farthing; then you may lodge in the fields & woods, travel from one end of the Countrey to another, with as much security as if you were lockt within your own Chamber; And if you chance to meet with an *Indian*-Town, they shall give you the best entertainment they have, & upon your desire, direct you on your way: But that which adds happiness to all the rest is the Healthfulness of the place where many people in twenty years time never know what sickness is: where they look upon it as a great mortality if two or three die out of a towne in a years time; where besides the sweetness of the Air, the Countrey itself sends forth such a fragrant smell, that it may be perceived at Sea before they can make the Land; where no Air-fog or vapour doth no sooner appear but a North-west or Westerly winde doth immediately dissolve it, and drive it away: What shall I say more? you shall scarce see a house, but the South side is begirt with Hives of Bees, which increase after an incredible manner: That I must needs say, that if there be any terrestrial *Canaans,* 'tis surely here, where all the Land floweth with milk & Honey. The inhabitants are blest with Peace & plenty, blessed in their Countrey, blessed in their Fields, blessed in the Fruit of their bodies, in the fruit of their grounds, in the increase of their Cattel, Horses and Sheep, blessed in their Basket, & in their store; In a word, blessed in whatsoever they take in hand, or go about, the Earth yielding plentiful increases to all their painful labours.

Were it not to avoid prolixity I could say a great deal more, & yet say too little, how free are those parts of the world from that pride and oppression, with their miserable effects, which many, nay almost all parts of the world are troubled, with being ignorant of that pomp & bravery which aspiring Humours are servants to, & striving after almost every where: Where a Waggon or Cart gives as good content as a Coach; and a piece of their home-made Cloth, better than the finest Lawns or richest Silks: & though their low-roofed houses may seem to shut their doors against pride & luxury, yet how do they stand wide open to let charity in & out either to assist each other, or relieve a stranger, & the distance of place from other Nations, doth secure them from the envious frowns of ill-affected Neighbours, & the troubles which usually arise thence.

WASHINGTON IRVING

Knickerbocker's New York

It has already been mentioned, that, in the early times of Oloffe the Dreamer, a frontier post, or trading house, called Fort Aurania, had been established on the upper waters of the Hudson, precisely on the site of the present venerable city of Albany; which was at that time considered at the very end of the habitable world. It was, indeed, a remote possession, with which, for a long time, New Amsterdam held but little intercourse. Now

From *A History of New York, from the Beginning to the End of the Dutch Dynasty* by Diedrich Knickerbocker. Published by Inskeep and Bradford, New York, 1809.

and then the "Company's Yacht," as it was called, was sent to the fort with supplies, and to bring away the peltries which had been purchased of the Indians. It was like an expedition to the Indias, or the North Pole, and always made great talk in the settlement. Sometimes an adventurous burgher would accompany the expedition, to the great uneasiness of his friends; but, on his return, had so many stories to tell of storms and tempests on the Tappan Zee, of hobgoblins in the Highlands and at the Devil's Dans Kammer, and of all the other wonders and perils with which the river abounded in those early days, that he deterred the less adventurous inhabitants from following his example.

Matters were in this state, when, one day, as Walter the Doubter and his burgermeesters were smoking and pondering over the affairs of the province, they were roused by the report of a cannon. Sallying forth, they beheld a strange vessel at anchor in the bay. It was unquestionably of Dutch build; broad bottomed and high pooped, and bore the flag of their High Mightinesses at the mast-head.

After a while, a boat put off for land, and a stranger stepped on shore, a lofty, lordly kind of man, tall and dry, with a meagre face, furnished with huge moustaches. He was clad in Flemish doublet and hose, and an insufferably tall hat, with a cocktail feather. Such was the patroon Killian Van Rensselaer, who had come out from Holland to found a colony or patroonship on a great tract of wild land, granted to him by their High Mightinesses the Lords States General, in the upper regions of the Hudson.

Killian Van Rensselaer was a nine days' wonder in New Amsterdam; for he carried a high head, looked down upon the portly, short-legged burgomasters, and owned no allegiance to the governor himself; boasting that he held his patroonship directly from the Lords States General.

He tarried but a short time in New Amsterdam; merely to beat up recruits for his colony. Few, however, ventured to enlist for those remote and savage regions; and when they embarked, their friends took leave of them as if they should never see them more, and stood gazing with tearful eye as the stout, round-sterned little vessel ploughed and splashed its way up the Hudson, with great noise and little progress, taking nearly a day to get out of sight of the city.

And now, from time to time, floated down tidings to the Manhattoes of the growing importance of this new colony. Every account represented Killian Van Rensselaer as rising in importance and becoming a mighty patroon in the land. He had received more recruits from Holland. His patroonship of Rensselaerwick lay immediately below Fort Aurania, and extended for several miles on each side of the Hudson, beside embracing the mountainous region of the Helderberg. Over all this he claimed to hold separate jurisdiction, independent of the colonial authorities of New Amsterdam.

All these assumptions of authority were duly reported to Governor Van Twiller and his council, by dispatches from Fort Aurania; at each new report the governor and his counsellors looked at each other, raised their eyebrows, gave an extra puff or two of smoke, and then relapsed into their usual tranquillity.

At length tidings came that the patroon of Rensselaerwick had extended his usurpations along the river, beyond the limits granted him by their High Mightinesses; and that he had even seized upon a rocky island in the Hudson, commonly known by the name of Bearn or Bear's Island, where he was erecting a fortress, to be called by the lordly name of Rensselaerstein.

Wouter Van Twiller was roused by this intelligence. After consulting with his burgomasters, he dispatched a letter to the patroon of Rensselaerwick, demanding by what right he had seized upon this island, which lay beyond the bounds of his patroonship. The answer of Killian Van Rensselaer was in his own lordly style, *"By wapen recht!"*—that is to say, by the right of arms, or, in common parlance, by club-law. This answer plunged the worthy Wouter in one of the deepest doubts he had in the whole course of his administration; in the mean time, while Wouter doubted, the lordly Killian went on to finish his fortress of Rensselaerstein, about which I foresee I shall have something to record in a future chapter of this most eventful history....

About this time the testy little governor of the New Netherlands appears to have had his hands full, and with one annoyance and the other to have been kept continually on the bounce. He was on the very point of following up the expedition of Jan Jansen Alpendam by some belligerent measures against the marauders of Merryland, when his attention was suddenly called away by belligerent troubles springing up in another quarter, the seeds of which had been sown in the tranquil days of Walter the Doubter.

The reader will recollect the deep doubt into which that most pacific governor was thrown on Killian Van Rensselaer's taking possession of Bearn Island by *wapen recht*. While the governor doubted and did nothing, the lordly Killian went on to complete his sturdy little castellum of Rensselaerstein, and to garrison it with a number of his tenants from the Helderberg, a mountain region famous for the hardest heads and hardest fists in the province. Nicholas Koorn, a faithful squire of the patroon, accustomed to strut at his heels, wear his cast-off clothes, and imitate his lofty bearing, was established in this post as wacht-meester. His duty it was to keep an eye on the river, and oblige every vessel that passed, unless on the service of their High Mightinesses, to strike its flag, lower its peak, and pay toll to the lord of Rensselaerstein.

This assumption of sovereign authority within the territories of the Lords States General, however it might have been tolerated by Walter the Doubter, had been sharply contested by William the Testy on coming into office; and many written remonstrances had been addressed by him to Killian Van Rensselaer, to which the latter never deigned a reply. Thus, by degrees, a sore place, or, in Hibernian parlance, a *raw,* had been established in the irritable soul of the little governor, insomuch that he winced at the very name of Rensselaerstein.

Now it came to pass, that, on a fine sunny day, the Company's yacht, the Half-Moon, having been on one of its stated visits to Fort Aurania, was quietly tiding it down the Hudson. The commander, Govert Lockerman, a veteran Dutch skipper of few words but great bottom, was seated on the high poop, quietly smoking his pipe under the shadow of the proud flag of Orange, when, on arriving abreast of Bearn Island, he was saluted by a stentorian voice from the shore, "Lower thy flag, and be d——d to thee!"

Govert Lockerman, without taking his pipe out of his mouth, turned up his eye from under his broad-brimmed hat to see who had hailed him thus discourteously. There, on the ramparts of the fort, stood Nicholas Koorn, armed to the teeth, flourishing a brass-hilted sword, while a steeple-crowned hat and cock's tail-feather, formerly worn by Killian Van Rensselaer himself, gave an inexpressible loftiness to his demeanor.

Govert Lockerman eyed the warrior from top to toe, but was not to be dismayed. Taking the pipe slowly out of his mouth, "To whom should I lower my flag?" demanded he. "To the high and mighty Killian Van Rensselaer, the lord of Rensselaerstein!" was the reply.

"I lower it to none but the Prince of Orange and my masters the Lords States General." So saying, he resumed his pipe and smoked with an air of dogged determination.

Bang! went a gun from the fortress; the ball cut both sail and rigging. Govert Lockerman said nothing, but smoked the more doggedly.

Bang! went another gun; the shot whistled close astern.

"Fire, and be d——d," cried Govert Lockerman, cramming a new charge of tobacco into his pipe, and smoking with still increasing vehemence.

Bang! went a third gun. The shot passed over his head, tearing a hole in the "princely flag of Orange."

This was the hardest trial of all for the pride and patience of Govert Lockerman. He maintained a stubborn, though swelling silence; but his smothered rage might be perceived by the short vehement puffs of smoke emitted from his pipe, by which he might be tracked for miles, as he slowly floated out of shot and out of sight of Bearn Island. In fact he never gave vent to his passion until he got fairly among the highlands of the Hudson; when he let fly whole volleys of Dutch oaths, which are said to linger to this very day among the echoes of the Dunderberg, and to give particular effect to the thunder-storms in that neighborhood.

It was the sudden apparition of Govert Lockerman at Dog's Misery, bearing in his hand the tattered flag of Orange, that arrested the attention of William the Testy, just as he was devising a new expedition against the marauders of Merryland. I will not pretend to describe the passion of the little man when he heard of the outrage of Rensselaerstein. Suffice it to say, in the first transports of his fury, he turned Dog's Misery topsy-turvy; kicked every cur out of doors, and threw the cats out of the window; after which, his spleen being in some measure relieved, he went into council of war with Govert Lockerman, the skipper, assisted by Antony Van Corlear, the Trumpeter.

The eyes of all New Amsterdam were now turned to see what would be the end of this direful feud betwen William the Testy and the patroon of Rensselaerwick; and some, observing the consultations of the governor with the skipper and the trumpeter, predicted warlike measures by sea and land. The wrath of William Kieft, however, though quick to rise, was quick to evaporate. He was a perfect brush-heap in a blaze, snapping and crackling for a time, and then ending in smoke. Like many other valiant potentates, his first thoughts were all for war, his sober second thoughts for diplomacy.

Accordingly, Govert Lockerman was once more despatched up the river in the Company's yacht, the Goed Hoop, bearing Antony the Trumpeter as ambassador, to treat with the belligerent powers of Rensselaerstein. In the fulness of time the yacht arrived before Bearn Island, and Antony the Trumpeter, mounting the poop, sounded a parley to the fortress. In a little while the steeple-crowned hat of Nicholas Koorn, the wacht-meester, rose above the battlements, followed by his iron visage, and ultimately his whole person, armed, as before, to the very teeth; while, one by one, a whole row of Helderbergers reared their round burly heads above the wall, and beside each pumpkin-head peered the end of a rusty musket. Nothing daunted by this formidable array, Antony Van Corlear drew forth and read with audible voice a missive from William the Testy, protesting against the usurpation of Bearn Island, and ordering the garrison to quit the premises, bag and baggage, on pain of the vengeance of the potentate of the Manhattoes.

In reply, the wacht-meester applied the thumb of his right hand to the end of his nose, and the thumb of his left hand to the little finger of the right, and spreading each hand like a fan, made an aërial flourish with his fingers. Antony Van Corlear was sorely perplexed to understand this sign, which seemed to him something mysterious and masonic. Not liking to betray his ignorance, he again read with a loud voice the missive of William the Testy, and again Nicholas Koorn applied the thumb of his right hand to the end of his nose, and the thumb of his left hand to the little finger of the right, and repeated this kind of nasal weather-cock. Antony Van Corlear now persuaded himself that this was some short-hand sign or symbol, current in diplomacy, which, though unintelligible to a new diplomat, like himself, would speak volumes to the experienced intellect of William the Testy; considering his embassy therefore at an end, he sounded his trumpet with great complacency, and set sail on his return down the river, every now and then practising this mysterious sign of the wacht-meester, to keep it accurately in mind.

Arrived at New Amsterdam he made a faithful report of his embassy to the governor, accompanied by a manual exhibition of the response of Nicholas Koorn. The governor was equally perplexed with his embassy. He was deeply versed in the mysteries of freemasonry; but they threw no light on the matter. He knew every variety of windmill and weather-cock, but was not a whit the wiser as to the aërial sign in question. He had even dabbled in Egyptian hieroglyphics and the mystic symbols of the obelisks, but none furnished a key to the reply of Nicholas Koorn. He called a meeting of his council. Antony Van Corlear stood forth in the midst, and putting the thumb of his right hand to his nose, and the thumb of his left hand to the finger of the right, he gave a faithful facsimile of the portentous sign. Having a nose of unusual dimensions, it was as if the reply had been put in capitals; but all in vain: the worthy burgomasters were equally perplexed with the governor. Each one put his thumb to the end of his nose, spread his fingers like a fan, imitated the motion of Antony Van Corlear, and then smoked in dubious silence. Several times was Antony obliged to stand forth like a fugleman and repeat the sign, and each time a circle of nasal weather-cocks might be seen in the council chamber.

Perplexed in the extreme, William the Testy sent for all the soothsayers, and fortune-tellers and wise men of the Manhattoes, but none could interpret the mysterious reply of Nicholas Koorn. The council broke up in sore perplexity. The matter got abroad, and Antony Van Corlear was stopped at every corner to repeat the signal to a knot of anxious newsmongers, each of whom departed with his thumb to his nose and his fingers in the air, to carry the story home to his family. For several days, all business was neglected in New Amsterdam; nothing was talked of but the diplomatic mission of Antony the Trumpeter—nothing was to be seen but knots of politicians with their thumbs to their noses. In the meantime the fierce feud between William the Testy and Killian Van Rensselaer, which at first had menaced deadly warfare, gradually cooled off, like many other war-questions, in the prolonged delays of diplomacy.

Still to this early affair of Rensselaerstein may be traced the remote origin of those windy wars in modern days which rage in the bowels of the Helderberg, and have well nigh shaken the great patroonship of the Van Rensselaers to its foundation; for we are told that the bully boys of the Helderberg, who served under Nicholas Koorn the wacht-meester, carried back to their mountains the hieroglyphic sign which had so sorely puzzled Antony Van Corlear and the sages of the Manhattoes; so that to the present day the thumb to the nose and the fingers in the air is apt to be the reply of the Helderbergers whenever called upon for any long arrears of rent.

18TH CENTURY

HAROLD FREDERIC

I Go to a Famous Gathering at the Patroon's Manor House

We come to a soft, clear night in the Indian summer-time of 1774—a night not to be forgotten while memory remains to me.

There was a grand gathering and ball at the Manor House of the Patroons, and to it I was invited. Cadwallader Colden, the octogenarian lieutenant-governor, and chief representative of the Crown now that Tryon was away in England, had come up to Albany in state, upon some business which I now forget, and he was to be entertained at the Van Rensselaer mansion, and with him the rank, beauty, and worth of all the country roundabout. I had heard that a considerable number of invitations had been despatched to the Tory families in my old neighborhood, and that, despite the great distance, sundry of them had been accepted. Sir William Johnson had now been dead some months, and it was fitting that his successor, Sir John, newly master of all the vast estates, should embrace this opportunity to make his first appearance as baronet in public. In fact, he had arrived in town with Lady Johnson, and it was said that they came in company with others. I could not help wondering, as I attired myself, with more than ordinary care, in my best maroon coat and smallclothes and flowered saffron waistcoat, who it was that accompanied the Johnsons. Was I at last to meet Daisy?

Succeeding generations have discovered many tricks of embellishment and decoration of which we old ones never dreamed. But I doubt if even the

From *In the Valley* by Harold Frederic. Published by Charles Scribner's Sons, New York, 1890.

most favored of progressive moderns has laid eyes upon any sight more beautiful than that which I recall now, as the events of this evening return to me.

You may still see for yourselves how noble, one might say palatial, was the home which young Stephen Van Rensselaer built for himself, there on the lowlands at the end of Broadway, across the Kissing Bridge. But no power of fancy can restore for *you*—sober-clad, pre-occupied, democratic people that you are—the flashing glories of that spectacle: the broad, fine front of the Manor House, with all its windows blazing in welcome; the tall trees in front aglow with swinging lanterns and colored lights, hung cunningly in their shadowy branches after some Italian device; the stately carriages sweeping up the gravelled avenue, and discharging their passengers at the block; the gay procession up the wide stone steps—rich velvets and costly satins, powdered wigs and alabaster throats, bright eyes, and gems on sword-hilts or at fair breasts—all radiant in the hospitable flood of light streaming from the open door; the throng of gaping slaves with torches, and smartly dressed servants holding the horses or helping with my lady's train and cloak; the resplendent body of color, and light, and sparkling beauty, which the eye caught in the spacious hall within, beyond the figures of the widowed hostess and her son, the eight-year-old Patroon, who stood forth to greet their guests. No! the scene belongs to its own dead century and fading generation. You shall strive in vain to reproduce it, even in fancy.

The full harvest-moon, which hung in the lambent heavens above all, pictures itself to my memory as far fairer and more luminous than is the best of nowaday moons. Alas! my old eyes read no romance in the silvery beams now, but suspect rheumatism instead.

This round, lustrous orb, pendant over the Hudson, was not plainer to every sight that evening than was to every consciousness the fact that this gathering was a sort of ceremonial salute before a duel. The storm was soon to break we all felt it in the air. There was a subdued, almost stiff, politeness in the tone and manner when Dutchman met Englishman, when Whig met Tory, which spoke more eloquently than words. Beneath the formal courtesy, and careful avoidance of debatable topics, one could see sidelong glances cast, and hear muttered sneers. We bowed low to one another, but with anxious faces, knowing that we stood upon the thin crust over the crater, likely at any moment to crash through it.

It was my fortune to be well known to Madame Van Rensselaer, our hostess. She was a Livingston, and a patriot, and she knew me for one as well. "The Tories are here in great muster," she whispered to me, when I bowed before her; "I doubt not it is the last time you will ever see them under my roof. The Colonel has news from Philadelphia to-day. There is trouble brewing."

I could see Colonel Schuyler standing beside one of the doors to the left, but to reach him was not easy. First I must pause to exchange a few words with Dominie Westerlo, the learned and good pastor of the Dutch church, of whose intended marriage with the widow, our hostess, there were even then rumors. And afterward there was the mayor, Abraham Cuyler, whom we all liked personally, despite his weak leaning toward the English, and it would not do to pass him by unheeded.

While I still stood with him, talking of I know not what, the arrival of the lieutenant-governor was announced. A buzz of whispering ran round the hall. In the succeeding silence that dignitary walked toward us, a space clearing about him as he did so. The mayor advanced to meet him, and I perforce followed.

I knew much about this remarkable Mr. Colden. Almost my first English book had been his account of the Indian tribes, and in later years I had been equally instructed by his writings on astronomy and scientific subjects. Even in my boyhood I had heard of him as a very old man, and here he was now, eighty-six years of age, the highest representative in the Colony of English authority. I could feel none of the hostility I ought from his office to have felt, when I presently made my obeisance, and he offered me his hand.

It was a pleasant face and a kindly eye which met my look. Despite his great age, he seemed scarcely older in countenance and bearing than had Mr. Stewart when last I saw him. He was simply clad, and I saw from his long, waving, untied hair why he was called "Old Silver Locks." His few words to me were amiable commonplaces, and I passed to make room for others, and found my way now to where Schuyler stood.

"The old fox!" he said, smilingly nodding toward Colden. "One may not but like him, for all his tricks. If England had had the wit to keep that rude boor of a Tryon at home, and make Colden governor, and listen to him, matters would have gone better. Who is that behind him? Oh, yes, De Lancey."

Oliver de Lancey was chiefly notable on account of his late brother James, who had been chief justice and lieutenant-governor, and the most brilliant, unscrupulous, masterful politician of his time. Oliver was himself a man of much energy and ambition. I observed him curiously, for his mother had been a Van Cortlandt, and I had some of that blood in my veins as well. So far as it had contributed to shape his face, I was not proud of it, for he had a selfish and arrogant mien.

It was more satisfactory to watch my companion, as he told me the names of the Tories who followed in Colden's wake, and commented on their characters. I do not recall them, but I remember every line of Philip Schuyler's face, and every inflection of his voice. He was then not quite forty years of age, and almost of my stature—that is to say, a tall man. He held himself very erect, giving strangers the impression of a haughty air, which his dark face and eyes, and black lines of hair peeping from under the powder, helped to confirm. But no one could speak in amity with him without finding him to be the most affable and sweet-natured of men. If he had had more of the personal vanity and self-love which his bearing seemed to indicate, it would have served him well, perhaps, when New England jealousy assailed and overbore him. But he was too proud to fight for himself, and too patriotic not to fight for his country, whether the just reward came or was withheld.

Colonel Schuyler had been chosen as one of the five delegates of the Colony to attend the first Continental Congress, now sitting at Philadelphia, but ill-health had compelled him to decline the journey. He had since been to New York, however, where he had learned much of the situation, and now was in receipt of tidings from the Congress itself. By a compromise in the New York Assembly, both parties had been represented in our delegation, the Whigs sending Philip Livingston and Isaac Low, the Tories James Duane and John Jay, and the fifth man, one Alsopp, being a neutral-tinted individual to whom neither side could object. The information which Schuyler had received was to the effect that all five, under the tremendous and enthusiastic pressure they had encountered in Philadelphia, had now resolved to act together in all things for the Colonies and against the Crown.

"That means," said he, "that we shall all adopt Massachusetts's cause as our own. After Virginia led the way with Patrick Henry's speech, there was no other course possible for even Jay and Duane. I should like to hear that man Henry. He must be wonderful."

The space about Mr. Colden had shifted across the room, so that we were now upon its edge, and Schuyler went to him with outstretched hand. The two men exchanged a glance, and each knew what the other was thinking of.

"Your excellency has heard from Philadelphia," said the Colonel, more as a statement of fact than as an inquiry.

"Sad, sad!" exclaimed the aged politician, in a low tone. "It is a grief instead of a joy to have lived so long, if my life must end amid contention and strife."

"He is really sincere in deploring the trouble," said Schuyler, when he had rejoined me. "He knows in his heart that the Ministry are pig-headedly wrong, and that we are in the right. He would do justice if he could, but he is as powerless as I am so far as influencing London goes, and here he is in the hands of the De Lanceys. To give the devil his due, I believe Sir William Johnson was on our side, too, at heart."

We had talked of this before, and out of deference to my sentiments of liking and gratitude to Sir William, he always tried to say amiable things about the late baronet to me. But they did not come easily, for there was an old-time feud between the two families. The dislike dated back to the beginning of young Johnson's career, when, by taking sides shrewdly in a political struggle between Clinton and De Lancey, he had ousted John Schuyler, Philip's grandfather, from the Indian comissionership and secured it for himself. In later years, since the Colonel had come to manhood, he had been forced into rivalry, almost amounting to antagonism at times, with the baronet, in Colonial and Indian affairs; and even now, after the baronet's death, it was hard for him to acknowledge the existence of all the virtues which my boyish liking had found in Sir William. But still he did try, if only to please me.

As we spoke, Sir John Johnson passed us, in company with several younger men, pushing toward the room to the right, where the punch-bowl was placed.

"At least, *he* is no friend of yours?" said Schuyler, indicating the red-faced young baronet.

"No man less so," I replied, promptly. Two years ago I doubt I should have been so certain of my entire enmity toward Sir John. But in the interim all my accumulating political fervor had unconsciously stretched back to include the Johnstown Tories; I found myself now honestly hating them all alike for their former coolness to me and their present odious attitude toward my people. And it was not difficult, recalling all my boyish dislike for John Johnson and his steadily contemptuous treatment of me, to make him the chief object of my aversion.

We talked of him now, and of his wife, a beautiful, sweet-faced girl of twenty, who had been Polly Watts of New York. My companion pointed her out to me, as one of a circle beyond the fire-place. He had only soft words and pity for her—as if foreseeing the anguish and travail soon to be brought upon her by her husband's misdeeds—but he spoke very slightingly and angrily of Sir John. To Schuyler's mind there was no good in him.

"I have known him more or less since he was a boy and followed his father in the Lake George campaign. The officers then could not abide him, though some were submissive to him because of his father's position. So now, fifteen years afterward, although he has many toadies and flatterers, I doubt his having any real friends. Through all these score of years, I have yet to learn of any gracious or manly thing he has done."

"At least he did gallop from the Fort to the Hall at news of his father's death, and kill his horse by the pace," I said.

"Heirs can afford to ride swiftly," replied the Colonel, in a dry tone. "No: he has neither the honesty to respect the rights of others, nor the wit to enforce those which he arrogates to himself. Look at his management in the Mohawk Valley. Scarce two months after the old baronet's death—before he was barely warm in his father's bed—all the Dutch and Palatines and Cherry Valley Scotch were up in arms against him and his friends. I call that the work of a fool. Why, Tryon County ought, by all the rules, to be the Tories' strongest citadel. There, of all other places, they should be able to hold their own. Old Sir William would have contrived matters better, believe me. But this sulky, slave-driving cub must needs force the quarrel from the start. Already they have their committee in the Palatine district, with men like Frey and Yates and Paris on it, and their resolutions are as strong as any we have heard."

Others came up at this, and I moved away, thinking to pay my respects to friends in the rooms on the left. The fine hall was almost overcrowded. One's knee struck a sword, or one's foot touched a satin train, at every step. There were many whom I knew, chiefly Albanians, and my progress was thus rendered slow. At the door I met my kinsman, Dr. Teunis Van Hoorn.

"Ha! well met, Cousin Sobriety!" he cried. "Let us cross the hall, and get near the punch-bowl."

"It is my idea that you have had enough," I answered.

" 'Too much is enough,' as the Indian said. He was nearer the truth than you are," replied Teunis, taking my arm.

"No, not now! First let me see who is here."

"Who is here? Everybody—from Hendrik Hudson and Killian the First down. Old Centenarian Colden is telling them about William the Silent, whom he remembers very well."

"I have never heard any one speak of Teunis the Silent."

"Nor ever will! It is not my *métier,* as the French students used to say. Well, then, I will turn back with you; but the punch will all be gone, mark my words. I saw Johnson and Watts and their party headed for the bowl five-and-twenty minutes ago. We shall get not so much as a lemon-seed. But I sacrifice myself."

We entered the room, and my eyes were drawn, as by the force of a million magnets, to the place where Daisy sat.

For the moment she was unattended. She was very beautifully attired, and jewels glistened from her hair and throat. Her eyes were downcast—looking upon the waxed floor as if in meditation. Even to this sudden, momentary glance, her fair face looked thinner and paler than I remembered it—and ah, how well did I remember it! With some muttered word of explanation I broke away from my companion, and went straight to her.

She had not noted my presence or approach, and only looked up when I stood before her. There was not in her face the look of surprise which I had expected. She smiled in a wan way, and gave me her hand.

"I knew you were here," she said, in a soft voice which I scarcely recognized, so changed, I might say saddened, was it by the introduction of some plaintive, minor element. "Philip told me. I thought that sooner or later I should see you."

"And I have thought of little else but the chance of seeing you," I replied, speaking what was in my heart, with no reflection save that this was our Daisy, come into my life again.

She was silent for a moment, her eyes seeking the floor and a faint glow coming upon her cheeks. Then she raised them to my face, with something of the old sparkle in their glance.

"Well, then," she said, drawing aside her skirts, "sit here, and see me."

J. HECTOR ST. JOHN DE CRÈVECOEUR

What Is an American?

What attachment can a poor European emigrant have for a country where he had nothing? The knowledge of the language, the love of a few kindred as poor as himself, were the only cords that tied him: his country is now that which gives him land, bread, protection, and consequence: *Ubi panis ibi patria,* is the motto of all emigrants. What then is the American, this new man? He is either an European, or the descendant of an European, hence that strange mixture of blood, which you will find in no other country. I could point out to you a family whose grandfather was an Englishman, whose wife was Dutch, whose son married a French woman, and whose present four sons have now four wives of different nations. *He* is an American, who, leaving behind him all his ancient prejudices and manners, receives new ones from the new mode of life he has embraced, the new government he obeys, and the new rank he holds. He becomes an American

From the book *Letters from an American Farmer* by J. Hector St. John de Crèvecoeur. Dutton Paperback Edition. Reprinted by permission of E. P. Dutton & Co., Inc.

by being received in the broad lap of our great *Alma Mater*. Here individuals of all nations are melted into a new race of men, whose labours and posterity will one day cause great changes in the world. Americans are the western pilgrims, who are carrying along with them that great mass of arts, sciences, vigour, and industry which began long since in the east; they will finish the great circle. The Americans were once scattered all over Europe; here they are incorporated into one of the finest systems of population which has ever appeared, and which will hereafter become distinct by the power of the different climates they inhabit. The American ought therefore to love this country much better than that wherein either he or his forefathers were born. Here the rewards of his industry follow with equal steps the progress of his labour; his labour is founded on the basis of nature, *self-interest;* can it want a stronger allurement? Wives and children, who before in vain demanded of him a morsel of bread, now, fat and frolicsome, gladly help their father to clear those fields whence exuberant crops are to arise to feed and to clothe them all; without any part being claimed, either by a despotic prince, a rich abbot, or a mighty lord. Here religion demands but little of him; a small voluntary salary to the minister, and gratitude to God; can he refuse these? The American is a new man, who acts upon new principles; he must therefore entertain new ideas, and form new opinions. From involuntary idleness, servile dependence, penury, and useless labour, he has passed to toils of a very different nature, rewarded by ample subsistence.—This is an American....

There is no wonder that this country has so many charms, and presents to Europeans so many temptations to remain in it. A traveller in Europe becomes a stranger as soon as he quits his own kingdom; but it is otherwise here. We know, properly speaking, no strangers; this is every person's country; the variety of our soils, situations, climates, governments, and produce, hath something which must please everybody. No sooner does an European arrive, no matter of what condition, than his eyes are opened upon the fair prospect; he hears his language spoken, he retraces many of his own country manners, he perpetually hears the names of families and towns with which he is acquainted; he sees happiness and prosperity in all places disseminated; he meets with hospitality, kindness and plenty everywhere; he beholds hardly any poor, he seldom hears of punishments and executions; and he wonders at the elegance of our towns, those miracles of industry and freedom. He cannot admire enough our rural districts, our convenient roads, good taverns, and our many accommodations; he involuntarily loves a country where everything is so lovely. When in England, he was a mere Englishman; here he stands on a larger portion of the globe, not less than its fourth part, and may see the productions of the north, in iron and naval stores; the provisions of Ireland, the grain of Egypt, the indigo, the rice of China. He does not find, as in Europe, a crowded society, where every place is over-stocked; he does not feel that perpetual collision of parties, that difficulty of beginning, that contention which oversets so many. There is room for everybody in America; has he any particular talent, or industry? he exerts it in order to procure a livelihood, and it succeeds. Is he a merchant? the avenues of trade are infinite; is he eminent in any respect? he will be employed and respected. Does he love a country life? pleasant farms present themselves; he may purchase what he wants, and thereby become an American farmer. Is he a labourer, sober and industrious? he need not go many miles, nor receive many informations before he will be hired, well fed at the table of his employer, and paid four or five times more than he can get in Europe. Does he want uncultivated lands? thousands of acres present themselves, which he may purchase cheap. Whatever be his talents or inclinations, if they are moderate, he may satisfy them. I do not mean that every one who comes will grow rich in a little time; no, but he may procure an easy, decent maintenance, by his industry. Instead of starving he will be fed, instead of being idle he will have employment; and these are riches enough for such men as come over here. The rich stay in Europe, it is only the middling and the poor that emigrate. Would you wish to travel in independent idleness, from north to south, you will find easy access, and the most cheerful reception at every house; society without ostentation, good cheer without pride, and every decent diversion which the country affords, with little expense. It is no wonder that the European who has lived here a few years, is desirous to remain; Europe with all its pomp, is not to be compared to this continent, for men of middle stations, or labourers.

An European, when he first arrives, seems limited in his intentions, as well as in his views; but he very suddenly alters his scale; two hundred miles formerly appeared a very great distance, it is now but a trifle; he no sooner breathes our air than he forms schemes, and embarks in designs he never would have thought of in his own country. There the plenitude of society confines many useful ideas, and often extinguishes the most laudable schemes which here ripen into maturity. Thus Europeans become Americans.

But how is this accomplished in that crowd of low, indigent people, who flock here every year from all parts of Europe? I will tell you; they no sooner arrive than they immediately feel the good effects of that plenty of provisions we possess: they fare on our best food, and they are kindly entertained; their talents, character, and peculiar industry are immediately inquired into; they find countrymen everywhere disseminated, let them come from whatever part of Europe. Let me select one as an epitome of the rest; he is hired, he goes to work, and works moderately; instead of being employed by a haughty person, he finds himself with his equal, placed at the substantial table of the farmer, or else at an inferior one as good; his wages are high, his bed is not like that bed of sorrow on which he used to lie; if he behaves with propriety, and is faithful, he is caressed, and becomes as it were a member of the family. He begins to feel the effects of a sort of resurrection; hitherto he had not lived, but simply vegetated; he now feels himself a man, because he is treated as such; the laws of his own country had overlooked him in his insignificancy; the laws of this cover him with their mantle. Judge what an alteration there must arise in the mind and thoughts of this man; he begins to forget his former servitude and dependence, his heart involuntarily swells and glows; this first swell inspires him with those new thoughts which constitute an American. What love can he entertain for a country where his existence was a burthen to him; if he is a generous good man, the love of this new adoptive parent will sink deep into his heart. He looks around, and sees many a prosperous person, who but a few years before was as poor as himself. This encourages him much, he begins to form some little scheme, the first, alas, he ever formed in his life. If he is wise he thus spends two or three years, in which time he acquires knowledge, the use of tools, the modes of working the lands, felling trees, etc. This prepares the foundation of a good name, the most useful acquisition he can make. He is encouraged, he has gained friends; he is advised and directed, he feels bold, he purchases some land; he gives all the money he has brought over, as well as what he has earned, and trusts to the God of harvests for the discharge of the rest. His good name procures him credit. He is now possessed of the deed, conveying to him and his posterity the fee simple and absolute property of two hundred acres of land, situated on such a river. What an epocha in this man's life! He is become a freeholder, from perhaps a German boor—he is now an American, a Pennsylvanian, an English subject. He is naturalised, his name is enrolled with those of the other citizens of the province. Instead of being a vagrant, he has a place of residence; he is called the inhabitant of such a county, or of such a district, and for the first time in his life counts for something; for hitherto he has been a cypher. I only repeat what I have heard many say, and no wonder their hearts should glow, and be agitated with a multitude of feelings, not easy to describe. From nothing to start into being; from a servant to the rank of a master; from being the slave of some despotic prince, to become a free man, invested with lands, to which every municipal blessing is annexed! What a change indeed! It is in consequence of that change that he becomes an American. This great metamorphosis has a double effect, it extinguishes all his European prejudices, he forgets that mechanism of subordination, that servility of disposition which poverty had taught him; and sometimes he is apt to forget too much, often passing from one extreme to the other. If he is a good man, he forms schemes of future prosperity, he proposes to educate his children better than he has been educated himself; he thinks of future modes of conduct, feels an ardour to labour he never felt before. Pride steps in and leads him to everything that the laws do not forbid: he respects them; with a heart-felt gratitude he looks toward the east, toward that insular government from whose wisdom all his new felicity is derived, and under whose wings and protection he now lives. These reflections constitute him the good man and the good subject. Ye poor Europeans, ye, who sweat, and work for the great—ye, who are obliged to give so many sheaves to the church, so many to your lords, so many to your government, and have hardly any left for yourselves—ye, who are held in less estimation than favourite hunters or useless lap-dogs—ye, who only breathe the air of nature, because it cannot be withheld from you; it is here that ye can conceive the possibility of those feelings I have been describing; it is here the laws of naturalisation invite every one to partake of our great labours and felicity, to till unrented, untaxed lands!

WASHINGTON IRVING

The Legend of Sleepy Hollow

Found Among the Papers of the Late Diedrich Knickerbocker

A pleasing land of drowsy heat it was,
  Of dreams that wave before the half-shut eye;
And of gay castles in the clouds that pass,
  For ever flushing round a summer sky.

CASTLE OF INDOLENCE.

In the bosom of one of those spacious coves which indent the eastern shore of the Hudson, at that broad expansion of the river denominated by the ancient Dutch navigators the Tappan Zee, and where they

From *The Sketch Book* by Washington Irving. Published by G. P. Putnam's Sons, New York, 1822.

always prudently shortened sail, and implored the protection of St. Nicholas when they crossed, there lies a small market-town or rural port, which by some is called Greensburgh, but which is more generally and properly known by the name of Tarry Town. This name was given, we are told, in former days, by the good housewives of the adjacent country, from the inveterate propensity of their husbands to linger about the village tavern on market-days. Be that as it may, I do not vouch for the fact, but merely advert to it for the sake of being precise and authentic. Not far from this village, perhaps about two miles, there is a little valley, or rather lap of land, among high hills, which is one of the quietest places in the whole world. A small brook glides through it, with just murmur enough to lull one to repose; and the occasional whistle of a quail, or tapping of a woodpecker, is almost the only sound that ever breaks in upon the uniform tranquillity.

I recollect that, when a stripling, my first exploit in squirrel-shooting was in a grove of tall walnut-trees that shades one side of the valley. I had wandered into it at noon-time, when all nature is peculiarly quiet, and was startled by the roar of my own gun, as it broke the Sabbath stillness around, and was prolonged and reverberated by the angry echoes. If ever I should wish for a retreat, whither I might steal from the world and its distractions, and dream quietly away the remnant of a troubled life, I know of none more promising than this little valley.

From the listless repose of the place, and the peculiar character of its inhabitants, who are descendants from the original Dutch settlers, this sequestered glen has long been known by the name of **Sleepy Hollow,** and its rustic lads are called the Sleepy Hollow Boys throughout all the neighboring country. A drowsy, dreamy influence seems to hang over the land, and to pervade the very atmosphere. Some say that the place was bewitched by a high German doctor, during the early days of the settlement; others, that an old Indian chief, the prophet or wizard of his tribe, held his pow-wows there before the country was discovered by Master Hendrick Hudson. Certain it is, the place still continues under the sway of some witching power, that holds a spell over the minds of the good people, causing them to walk in a continual reverie. They are given to all kinds of marvellous beliefs; are subject to trances and visions; and frequently see strange sights, and hear music and voices in the air. The whole neighborhood abounds with local tales, haunted spots, and twilight superstitions; stars shoot and meteors glare oftener across the valley than in any other part of the country, and the nightmare, with her whole ninefold, seems to make it the favorite scene of her gambols.

The dominant spirit, however, that haunts this enchanted region, and seems to be commander-in-chief of all the powers of the air, is the apparition of a figure on horseback without a head. It is said by some to be the ghost of a Hessian trooper, whose head had been carried away by a cannon-ball, in some nameless battle during the Revolutionary War, and who is ever and anon seen by the country folk, hurrying along in the gloom of night, as if on the wings of the wind. His haunts are not confined to the valley, but extend at times to the adjacent roads, and especially to the vicinity of a church at no great distance. Indeed, certain of the most authentic historians of those parts, who have been careful in collecting and collating the floating facts concerning this spectre, allege that the body of the trooper, having been buried in the churchyard, the ghost rides forth to the scene of battle in nightly quest of his head; and that the rushing speed with which he sometimes passes along the Hollow, like a midnight blast, is owing to his being belated, and in a hurry to get back to the churchyard before daybreak.

Such is the general purport of this legendary superstition, which has furnished materials for many a wild story in that region of shadows; and the spectre is known, at all the country firesides, by the name of the Headless Horseman of Sleepy Hollow.

It is remarkable that the visionary propensity I have mentioned is not confined to the native inhabitants of the valley, but is unconsciously imbibed by every one who resides there for a time. However wide awake they may have been before they entered that sleepy region, they are sure, in a little time, to inhale the witching influence of the air, and begin to grow imaginative—to dream dreams, and see apparitions.

I mention this peaceful spot with all possible laud; for it is in such little retired Dutch valleys, found here and there embosomed in the great State of New-York, that population, manners, and customs, remain fixed; while the great torrent of migration and improvement, which is making such incessant changes in other parts of this restless country, sweeps by them unobserved. They are like those little nooks of still water which border a rapid stream; where we may see the straw and bubble riding quietly at anchor, or slowly revolving in their mimic harbor, undisturbed by the rush of the passing current. Though many years have elapsed since I trod the drowsy shades of Sleepy Hollow, yet I question whether I should not still find the same trees and the same families vegetating in its sheltered bosom.

In this by-place of nature, there abode, in a remote period of American history, that is to say, some thirty years since, a worthy wight of the name of Ichabod Crane; who sojourned, or, as he expressed it, "tarried," in Sleepy Hollow, for the purpose of instructing the children of the vicinity. He was a native of Connecticut; a State which supplies the Union with pioneers for the mind as well as for the forest, and sends forth yearly its legions of frontier woodsmen and country schoolmasters. The cognomen of Crane was not inapplicable to his person. He was tall, but exceedingly lank, with narrow shoulders, long arms and legs, hands that dangled a mile out of his sleeves, feet that might have served for shovels, and his whole frame most loosely hung together. His head was small, and flat at top, with huge ears, large green glassy eyes, and a long snipe nose, so that it looked like a weathercock, perched upon his spindle neck, to tell which way the wind blew. To see him striding along the profile of a hill on a windy day, with his clothes bagging and fluttering about him, one might have mistaken him for the genius of famine descending upon the earth, or some scarecrow eloped from a cornfield.

His school-house was a low building of one large room, rudely constructed of logs; the windows partly glazed, and partly patched with leaves of old copy-books. It was most ingeniously secured at vacant hours, by a withe twisted in the handle of the door, and stakes set against the window-shutters; so that, though a thief might get in with perfect ease, he would find some embarrassment in getting out; an idea most probably borrowed by the architect, Yost Van Houten, from the mystery of an eel-pot. The school-house stood in a rather lonely but pleasant situation, just at the foot of a woody hill, with a brook running close by, and a formidable birch tree growing at one end of it. From hence the low murmur of his pupils' voices, conning over their lessons, might be heard in a drowsy summer's day, like the hum of a beehive; interrupted now and then by the authoritative voice of the master, in the tone of menace or command; or, peradventure, by the appalling sound of the birch, as he urged some tardy loiterer along the flowery path of knowledge. Truth to say, he was a conscientious man, and ever bore in mind the golden maxim, "Spare the rod and spoil the child."—Ichabod Crane's scholars certainly were not spoiled.

I would not have it imagined, however, that he was one of those cruel potentates of the school, who joy in the smart of their subjects; on the contrary, he administered justice with discrimination rather than severity, taking the burthen off the backs of the weak, and laying it on those of the strong. Your mere puny stripling, that winced at the least flourish of the rod, was passed by with indulgence; but the claims of justice were satisfied by inflicting a double portion on some little, tough, wrong-headed, broad-skirted Dutch urchin, who sulked and swelled and grew dogged and sullen beneath the birch. All this he called "doing his duty by their parents"; and he never inflicted a chastisement without following it by the assurance, so consolatory to the smarting urchin, that "he would remember it, and thank him for it the longest day he had to live."

When school-hours were over, he was even the companion and playmate of the larger boys; and on holiday afternoons would convoy some of the smaller ones home, who happened to have pretty sisters, or good housewives for mothers, noted for the comforts of the cupboard. Indeed it behooved him to keep on good terms with his pupils. The revenue arising from his school was small, and would have been scarcely sufficient to furnish him with daily bread, for he was a huge feeder, and though lank, had the dilating powers of an anaconda; but to help out his maintenance, he was, according to country custom in those parts, boarded and lodged at the houses of the farmers, whose children he instructed. With these he lived successively a week at a time; thus going the rounds of the neighborhood, with all his worldly effects tied up in a cotton handkerchief.

That all this might not be too onerous on the purses of his rustic patrons, who are apt to consider the costs of schooling a grievous burden, and schoolmasters as mere drones, he had various ways of rendering himself both useful and agreeable. He assisted the farmers occasionally in the lighter labors of their farms; helped to make hay; mended the fences; took the horses to water; drove the cows from pasture; and cut wood for the winter fire. He laid aside, too, all the dominant dignity and absolute sway with which he lorded it in his little empire, the school, and became wonderfully gentle and ingratiating. He found favor in the eyes of the mothers, by petting the children, particularly the youngest; and like the lion bold, which whilom so magnanimously the lamb did hold, he would sit with a child on one knee, and rock a cradle with his foot for whole hours together.

In addition to his other vocations, he was the singing-master of the neighborhood, and picked up many bright shillings by instructing the young folks in psalmody. It was a matter of no little vanity to him, on Sundays, to take his station in front of the church-gallery, with a band of chosen singers; where, in his own mind, he completely carried away the palm from the parson. Certain it is, his voice resounded far above all the rest of the congregation; and there are peculiar quavers still to be heard in that church, and which may even be heard half a mile off, quite to the opposite side of the mill-pond, on a still Sunday morning, which are said to be legitimately descended from the nose of Ichabod Crane. Thus, by divers little makeshifts in that ingenious way which is commonly denominated "by hook and by crook," the worthy pedagogue got on tolerably enough, and was thought, by all who understood nothing of the labor of headwork, to have a wonderfully easy life of it.

The schoolmaster is generally a man of some importance in the female circle of a rural neighborhood; being considered a kind of idle gentleman-like personage, of vastly superior taste and accomplishments to the rough country swains, and, indeed, inferior in learning only to the parson. His appearance, therefore, is apt to occasion some little stir at the tea-table of a farm-house, and the addition of a supernumerary dish of cakes or sweet-meats, or peradventure, the parade of a silver tea-pot. Our man of letters, therefore, was peculiarly happy in the smiles of all the country damsels. How he would figure among them in the churchyard, between services on Sundays! gathering grapes for them from the wild vines that overrun the surrounding trees; reciting for their amusement all the epitaphs on the tomb-stones; or sauntering, with a whole bevy of them, along the banks of the adjacent mill-pond; while the more bashful country bumpkins hung sheep-ishly back, envying his superior elegance and address.

From his half itinerant life, also, he was a kind of travelling gazette, carrying the whole budget of local gossip from house to house; so that his appearance was always greeted with satisfaction. He was, moreover, esteemed by the women as a man of great erudition, for he had read several books quite through, and was a perfect master of Cotton Mather's "History of New England Witchcraft," in which, by the way, he most firmly and potently believed.

He was, in fact, an off mixture of small shrewdness and simple credulity. His appetite for the marvellous, and his powers of digesting it, were equally extraordinary; and both had been increased by his residence in this spell-bound region. No tale was too gross or monstrous for his capacious swallow. It was often his delight, after his school was dismissed in the afternoon, to stretch himself on the rich bed of clover, bordering the little brook that whimpered by his school-house, and there con over old Mather's direful tales, until the gathering dusk of the evening made the printed page a mere mist before his eyes. Then, as he wended his way, by swamp and stream and awful woodland, to the farm-house where he happened to be quartered, every sound of nature, at that witching hour, fluttered his excited imagination: the moan of the whip-poor-will * from the hill-side; the boding cry of the tree-toad, that harbinger of storm; the dreary hooting of the screech-owl, or the sudden rustling in the thicket of birds frightened from their roost. The fire-flies, too, which sparkled most vividly in the darkest places, now and then startled him, as one of uncommon brightness would stream across his path; and if, by chance, a huge blockhead of a beetle came wing-

* The whip-poor-will is a bird which is only heard at night. It receives its name from its note, which is thought to resemble those words.

ing his blundering flight against him, the poor varlet was ready to give up the ghost, with the idea that he was struck with a witch's token. His only resource on such occasions, either to drown thought, or drive away evil spirits, was to sing psalm-tunes; and the good people of Sleepy Hollow, as they sat by their doors of an evening, were often filled with awe, at hearing his nasal melody, "in linked sweetness long drawn out," floating from the distant hill, or along the dusky road.

Another of his sources of fearful pleasure was, to pass long winter evenings with the old Dutch wives, as they sat spinning by the fire, with a row of apples roasting and spluttering along the hearth, and listen to their marvellous tales of ghosts and goblins, and haunted fields, and haunted brooks, and haunted bridges, and haunted houses, and particularly of the headless horseman, or Galloping Hessian of the Hollow, as they sometimes called him. He would delight them equally by his anecdotes of witchcraft, and of the direful omens and portentous sights and sounds in the air, which prevailed in the earlier times of Connecticut, and would frighten them woefully with speculations upon comets and shooting stars; and with alarming fact that the world did absolutely turn round, and that they were half the time topsy-turvy!

But if there was a pleasure in all this, while snugly cuddling in the chimney-corner of a chamber that was all of a ruddy glow from the crackling wood-fire, and where, of course, no spectre dared to show his face, it was dearly purchased by the terrors of his subsequent walk homewards. What fearful shapes and shadows beset his path amidst the dim and ghastly glare of a snowy night!—With what wistful look did he eye every trembling ray of light streaming across the waste fields from some distant window!—How often was he appalled by some shrub covered with snow, which, like a sheeted spectre, beset his very path!—How often did he shrink with curdling awe at the sound of his own steps on the frosty crust beneath his feet; and dread to look over his shoulder, lest he should behold some uncouth being tramping close behind him!—and how often was he thrown into complete dismay by some rushing blast, howling among the trees, in the idea that it was the Galloping Hessian on one side of his nightly scourings!

All these, however, were mere terrors of the night, phantoms of the mind that walk in darkness; and though he had seen many spectres in his time, and been more than once beset by Satan in divers shapes, in his lonely perambulations, yet daylight put an end to all these evils; and he would have passed a pleasant life of it, in despite of the devil and all his works, if his path had not been crossed by a being that causes more perplexity to mortal man than ghosts, goblins, and the whole race of witches put together, and that was—a woman.

Among the musical disciples who assembled, one evening in each week, to receive his instructions in psalmody, was Katrina Van Tassel, the daughter and only child of a substantial Dutch farmer. She was a blooming lass of fresh eighteen; plump as a partridge; ripe and melting and rosy-cheeked as one of her father's peaches, and universally famed, not merely for her beauty, but her vast expectations. She was withal a little of a coquette, as might be perceived even in her dress, which was a mixture of ancient and modern fashions, as most suited to set off her charms. She wore the ornaments of pure yellow gold, which her great-great-grandmother had brought over from Saardam; the tempting stomacher of the olden time; and withal a provokingly short petticoat to display the prettiest foot and ankle in the country round.

Ichabod Crane had a soft and foolish heart towards the sex; and it is not to be wondered at that so tempting a morsel soon found favor in his eyes; more especially after he had visited her in her paternal mansion. Old Baltus Van Tassel was a perfect picture of a thriving, contented, liberal-hearted farmer. He seldom, it is true, sent either his eyes or his thoughts beyond the boundaries of his own farm; but within those everything was snug, happy, and well-conditioned. He was satisfied with his wealth, but not proud of it; and piqued himself upon the hearty abundance, rather than the style in which he lived. His stronghold was situated on the banks of the Hudson, in one of those green, sheltered, fertile nooks, in which the Dutch farmers are so fond of nestling. A great elm-tree spread its broad branches over it; at the foot of which bubbled up a spring of the softest and sweetest water, in a little well, formed of a barrel; and then stole sparkling away through the grass, to a neighboring brook, that bubbled along among alders and dwarf willows. Hard by the farm-house was a vast barn, that might have served for a church; every window and crevice of which seemed bursting forth with the treasures of the farm; the flail was busily resounding within it from morning to night; swallows and martins skimmed twittering about the eaves; and rows of pigeons, some with one eye turned up, as if watching the weather, some with their heads under their wings, or buried in their bosoms, and others swelling, and cooing, and bowing about their dames, were enjoying the sunshine on the roof. Sleek unwieldy porkers were grunting in the repose and abundance of their pens; whence sallied forth, now and then, troops of sucking pigs, as if to snuff the air. A stately squadron of snowy geese were riding in an adjoining pond, convoying whole fleets of ducks; regiments of turkeys were gobbling through the farm-yard, and guinea fowls fretting about it, like ill-tempered housewives, with their peevish discontented cry. Before the barn door strutted the gallant cock, that pattern of a husband, a warrior, and a fine gentleman, clapping his burnished wings, and crowing in the pride and gladness of his heart—sometimes tearing up the earth with his feet, and then generously calling his ever-hungry family of wives and children to enjoy the rich morsel which he had discovered.

The pedagogue's mouth watered, as he looked upon this sumptuous promise of luxurious winter fare. In his devouring mind's eye he pictured to himself every roasting-pig running about with a pudding in his belly, and an apple in his mouth; the pigeons were snugly put to bed in a comfortable pie, and tucked in with a coverlet of crust; the geese were swimming in their own gravy; and the ducks pairing cosily in dishes, like snug married couples, with a decent competency of onion sauce. In the porkers he saw carved out the future sleek side of bacon, and juicy relishing ham; not a turkey but he beheld daintily trussed up, with its gizzard under its wing, and peradventure, a necklace of savory sausages; and even bright chanticleer himself lay sprawling on his back, in a side-dish, with uplifted claws, as if craving that quarter which his chivalrous spirit disdained to ask while living.

As the enraptured Ichabod fancied all this, and as he rolled his great green eyes over the fat meadow-lands, the rich fields of wheat, of rye, of buckwheat, and Indian corn, and the orchards burthened with ruddy fruit, which surrounded the warm tenement of Van Tassel, his heart yearned after the damsel who was to inherit these domains, and his imagination expanded with the idea how they might be readily turned into cash, and the money invested in immense tracts of wild land, and shingle palaces in the wilderness. Nay, his busy fancy already realized his hopes, and presented to him the blooming Katrina, with a whole family of children, mounted on the top of a wagon loaded with household trumpery, with pots and kettles dangling beneath; and he beheld himself bestriding a pacing mare, with a colt at her heels, setting out for Kentucky, Tennessee, or the Lord knows where.

When he entered the house, the conquest of his heart was complete. It was one of those spacious farm-houses, with high-ridged, but lowly-sloping roofs, built in the style handed down from the first Dutch settlers; the low projecting eaves forming a piazza along the front, capable of being closed up in bad weather. Under this were hung flails, harness, various utensils of husbandry, and nets for fishing in the neighboring river. Benches were built along the sides for summer use; and a great spinning-wheel at one end, and a churn at the other, showed the various uses to which this important porch might be devoted. From this piazza the wondering Ichabod entered the hall, which formed the centre of the mansion and the place of usual residence. Here, rows of resplendent pewter, ranged on a long dresser, dazzled his eyes. In one corner stood a huge bag of wool ready to be spun; in another a quantity of linsey-woolsey just from the loom; ears of Indian corn, and strings of dried apples and peaches, hung in gay festoons along the walls, mingled with the gaud of red peppers; and a door left ajar gave him a peep into the best parlor, where the claw-footed chairs, and dark mahogany tables, shone like mirrors; and irons, with their accompanying shovel and tongs, glistened from their covert of asparagus tops; mock-oranges and conch-shells decorated the mantelpiece; strings of various colored birds' eggs were suspended above it; a great ostrich egg was hung from the centre of the room, and a corner-cupboard, knowingly left open, displayed immense treasures of old silver and well-mended china.

From the moment Ichabod laid his eyes upon these regions of delight, the peace of his mind was at an end, and his only study was how to gain the affections of the peerless daughter of Van Tassel. In this enterprise, he had more real difficulties than generally fell to the lot of a knight-errant of yore, who seldom had any thing but giants, enchanters, fiery dragons, and such like easily-conquered adversaries, to contend with; and had to make his way merely through gates of iron and brass, and walls of adamant, to the castle-keep, where the lady of his heart was confined; all which he achieved as easily as a man would carve his way to the centre of a Christmas pie; and then the lady gave him her hand as a matter of course. Ichabod, on the contrary, had to win his way to the heart of a country coquette, beset with a labyrinth of whims and caprices, which were forever presenting new difficulties and impediments; and he had to encounter a host of fearful adversaries of real flesh and blood, the numerous rustic admirers, who beset every portal to her heart; keeping a watchful and angry eye upon each other, but ready to fly out in the common cause against any new competitor.

Among these the most formidable was a burly, roaring, roistering blade, of the name of Abraham, or, according to the Dutch abbreviation, Brom Van Brunt, the hero of the country round, which rang with his feats of strength and hardihood. He was broad-shouldered and double-jointed, with short curly black hair and a bluff, but not unpleasant countenance, having a mingled air of fun and arrogance. From his Herculean frame and great powers of limb, he had received the nickname of **Brom Bones,** by which he was universally known. He was famed for great knowledge and skill in horsemanship, being as dexterous on horseback as a Tartar. He was foremost at all races and cockfights; and, with the ascendency which bodily strength acquires in rustic life, was the umpire in all disputes, setting his hat on one side, and giving his decisions with an air and tone admitting of no gainsay or appeal. He was always ready for either a fight or a frolic; but had more mischief than ill-will in his composition; and, with all his overbearing roughness, there was a strong dash of waggish good humor at bottom. He had three or four boon companions, who regarded him as their model, and at the head of whom he scoured the country, attending every scene of feud or merriment for miles round. In cold weather he was distinguished by a fur cap, surmounted with a flaunting fox's tail; and when the folks at a country gathering descried this well-known crest at a distance, whisking about among a squad of hard riders, they always stood by for a squall. Sometimes his crew would be heard dashing along past the farmhouses at midnight, with whoop and halloo, like a troop of Don Cossacks; and the old dames, startled out of their sleep, would listen for a moment till the hurry-scurry had clattered by, and then exclaim, "Ay, there goes Brom Bones and his gang!" The neighbors looked upon him with a mixture of awe, admiration, and good-will; and when any madcap prank, or rustic brawl, occurred in the vicinity, always shook their heads, and warranted Brom Bones was at the bottom of it.

This rantipole hero had for some time singled out the blooming Katrina for the object of his uncouth gallantries, and though his amorous toyings were something like the gentle caresses and endearments of a bear, yet it was whispered that she did not altogether discourage his hopes. Certain it is, his advances were signals for rival candidates to retire, who felt no inclination to cross a lion in his amours; insomuch, that when his horse was seen tied to Van Tassel's paling, on a Sunday night, a sure sign that his master was courting, or as it is termed, "sparking," within, all other suitors passed by in despair, and carried the war into other quarters.

Such was the formidable rival with whom Ichabod Crane had to contend, and, considering all things, a stouter man than he would have shrunk from the competition, and a wiser man would have despaired. He had, however, a happy mixture of pliability and perseverance in his nature; he was in form and spirit like a supple-jack—yielding, but tough; though he bent, he never broke; and though he bowed beneath the slightest pressure, yet, the moment it was away—jerk! he was as erect, and carried his head as high as ever.

To have taken the field openly against his rival would have been madness; for he was not a man to be thwarted in his amours, any more than that stormy lover, Achilles. Ichabod, therefore, made his advances in a quiet and gently insinuating manner. Under cover of his character of singing-master, he made frequent visits at the farm-house; not that he had any thing to apprehend from the meddlesome interference of parents, which is so often a stumbling-block in the path of lovers. Balt Van Tassel was an easy, indulgent soul; he loved his daughter better even than his pipe, and, like a reasonable man and an excellent father, let her have her way in every thing. His notable little wife, too, had enough to do to attend to her housekeeping and manage her poultry; for, as she sagely observed, ducks and geese are foolish things, and must be looked after, but girls can take care of themselves. Thus while the busy dame bustled about the house, or plied her spinning wheel at one end of the piazza, honest Balt would sit smoking his evening pipe at the other, watching the achievements of a little wooden warrior, who, armed with a sword in each hand, was most valiantly fighting the wind on the pinnacle of the barn. In the mean time, Ichabod would carry on his suit with the daughter by the side of the spring under the great elm, or sauntering along in the twilight,—that hour so favorable to the lover's eloquence.

I profess not to know how women's hearts are wooed and won. To me they have always been matters of riddle and admiration. Some seem to have but one vulnerable point, or door of access; while others have a thousand avenues, and may be captured in a thousand different ways. It is a great triumph of skill to gain the former, but a still greater proof of generalship to maintain possession of the latter, for the man must battle for his fortress at every door and window. He who wins a thousand common hearts is therefore entitled to some renown; but he who keeps undisputed sway over the heart of a coquette, is indeed a hero. Certain it is, this was not the case with the redoubtable Brom Bones; and from the moment Ichabod Crane made his advances, the interests of the former evidently declined; his horse was no longer seen tied at the palings on Sunday nights, and a deadly feud gradually arose between him and the preceptor of Sleepy Hollow.

Brom, who had a degree of rough chivalry in his nature, would fain have carried matters to open warfare, and have settled their pretensions to the lady, according to the mode of those most concise and simple reasoners, the knights-errant of yore—by single combat; but Ichabod was too conscious of the superior might of his adversary to enter the lists against him; he had overheard a boast of Bones, that he would "double the schoolmaster up, and lay him on a shelf of his own schoolhouse"; and he was too wary to give him an opportunity. There was something extremely provoking in this obstinately pacific system; it left Brom no alternative but to draw upon the funds of rustic waggery in his disposition, and to play off boorish practical jokes upon his rival. Ichabod became the object of whimsical persecution to Bones, and his gang of rough riders. They harried his hitherto peaceful domains; smoked out his singing-school, by stopping up the chimney; broke into the school-house at night, in spite of its formidable fastenings of withe and window-stakes, and turned every thing topsy-turvy: so that the poor schoolmaster began to think all the witches in the country held their meetings there. But what was still more annoying, Brom took all opportunities of turning him into ridicule in presence of his mistress, and had a scoundrel dog whom he taught to whine in the most ludicrous manner, and introduced as a rival of Ichabod's to instruct her in psalmody.

In this way matters went on for some time, without producing any material effect on the relative situation of the contending powers. On a fine autumnal afternoon, Ichabod, in pensive mood, sat enthroned on the lofty stool whence he usually watched all the concerns of his little literary realm. In his hand he swayed a ferule, that sceptre of despotic power; the birch of justice reposed on three nails, behind the throne, a constant terror to evildoers; while on the desk before him might be seen sundry contraband articles and prohibited weapons, detected upon the persons of idle urchins; such as half-munched apples, popguns, whirligigs, fly-cages, and whole legions of rampant little paper game-cocks. Apparently there had been some appalling act of justice recently inflicted, for his scholars were all busily intent upon their books, or slyly whispering behind them with one eye kept upon the master; and a kind of buzzing stillness reigned throughout the school-room. It was suddenly interrupted by the appearance of a Negro, in tow-cloth jacket and trousers, a round-crowned fragment of a hat, like the cap of Mercury, and mounted on the back of a ragged, wild, half-broken colt, which he managed with a rope by way of halter. He came clattering up to the school-door with an invitation to Ichabod to attend a merry-making or "quilting frolic," to be held that evening at Mynheer Van Tassel's; and having delivered his message he dashed over the brook, and was seen scampering away up the Hollow.

All was now bustle and hubbub in the late quiet school-room. The scholars were hurried through their lessons, without stopping at trifles; those who were nimble skipped over half with impunity, and those who were tardy, had a smart application now and then in the rear, to quicken their speed, or help them over a tall word. Books were flung aside without being put away on the shelves, inkstands were overturned, benches thrown down, and the whole school was turned loose an hour before the usual time, bursting forth like a legion of young imps, yelping and racketing about the green, in joy at their early emancipation.

The gallant Ichabod now spent at least an extra half-hour at his toilet, brushing and furbishing up his best, and indeed only, suit of rusty black, and arranging his looks by a bit of broken looking-glass, that hung up in the school-house. That he might make his appearance before his mistress in the true style of a cavalier, he borrowed a horse from the farmer with whom he was domiciliated, a choleric old Dutchman, of the name of Hans Van Ripper, and, thus gallantly mounted, issued forth, like a knight-errant in quest of adventures. But it is meet I should, in the true spirit of romantic story, give some account of the looks and equipments of my hero and his steed. The animal he bestrode was a broken-down plough-horse, that had outlived almost every thing but his viciousness. He was gaunt and shagged, with a ewe neck and a head like a hammer; his rusty mane and tail were tangled and knotted with burrs; one eye had lost its pupil, and was glaring and spectral; but the other had the gleam of a genuine devil in it. Still he must have had fire and mettle in his day, if we may judge from the name he bore of Gunpowder. He had, in fact, been a favorite steed of his master's, the choleric Van Ripper, who was a furious rider, and had infused, very probably, some of his own spirit into the animal; for, old and broken-down as he looked, there was more of the lurking devil in him than in any young filly in the country.

Ichabod was a suitable figure for such a steed. He rode with short stirrups, which brought his knees nearly up to the pommel of the saddle; his sharp elbows stuck out like grasshoppers'; he carried his whip perpendicularly in his hand, like a sceptre, and, as his horse jogged on, the motion of his arms was not unlike the flapping of a pair of wings. A small wool hat rested on the top of his nose, for so his scanty strip of forehead might be called; and the skirts of his black coat fluttered out almost to the horse's tail. Such was the appearance of Ichabod and his steed, as they shambled out of the gate of Hans Van Ripper, and it was altogether such an apparition as is seldom to be met with in broad daylight.

It was, as I have said, a fine autumnal day, the sky was clear and serene, and nature wore that rich and golden livery which we always associate with the idea of abundance. The forests had put on their sober brown and yellow, while some trees of the tenderer kind had been nipped by the frosts into brilliant dyes of orange, purple, and scarlet. Streaming files of wild ducks began to make their appearance high in the air; the bark of the squirrel might be heard from the groves of beech and hickory nuts, and the pensive whistle of the quail at intervals from the neighboring stubble-field.

The small birds were taking their farewell banquets. In the fulness of their revelry, they fluttered, chirping and frolicking, from bush to bush, and tree to tree, capricious from the very profusion and variety around them. There was the honest cockrobin, the favorite game of stripling sportsmen, with its loud querulous note; and the twittering blackbirds flying in sable clouds; and the golden-winged woodpecker, with his crimson crest, his broad black gorget, and splendid plumage; and the cedar bird, with its red-tipt wings and yellow-tipt tail, and its little monteiro cap of feathers; and the blue jay, that noisy coxcomb, in his gay light-blue coat and white underclothes; screaming and chattering, nodding and bobbing and bowing, and pretending to be on good terms with every songster of the grove.

As Ichabod jogged slowly on his way, his eye, ever open to every symptom of culinary abundance, ranged with delight over the treasures of jolly autumn. On all sides he beheld vast store of apples; some hanging in oppressive opulence on the trees; some gathered into baskets and barrels for the market; others heaped up in rich piles for the cider-press. Farther on he beheld great fields of Indian corn, with its golden ears peeping from their leafy coverts, and holding out the promise of cakes and hasty-pudding; and the yellow pumpkins lying beneath them, turning up their fair round bellies to the sun, and giving ample prospects of the most luxurious of pies; and anon he passed the fragrant buckwheat fields, breathing the odor of the bee-hive, and as he beheld them, soft anticipations stole over his mind of dainty slapjacks, well buttered, and garnished with honey or treacle, by the delicate little dimpled hand of Katrina Van Tassel.

Thus feeding his mind with many sweet thoughts and "sugared suppositions," he journeyed along the sides of a range of hills which look out upon some of the goodliest scenes of the mighty Hudson. The sun gradually wheeled his broad disk down into the west. The wide bosom of the Tappan Zee lay motionless and glassy, excepting that here and there a gentle undulation waved and prolonged the blue shadow of the distant mountain. A few amber clouds floated in the sky, without a breath of air to move them. The horizon was of a fine golden tint, changing gradually into a pure apple-green, and from that into the deep blue of the mid-heaven. A slanting ray lingered on the woody crests of the precipices that overhung some parts of the river, giving greater depth to the dark-gray and purple of their rocky sides. A sloop was loitering in the distance, dropping slowly down with the tide, her sail hanging uselessly against the mast; and as the reflection of the sky gleamed along the still water, it seemed as if the vessel was suspended in the air.

It was toward evening that Ichabod arrived at the castle of the Heer Van Tassel, which he found thronged with the pride and flower of the adjacent country. Old farmers, a spare leathern-faced race, in homespun coats and breeches, blue stockings, huge shoes, and magnificent pewter buckles. Their brisk withered little dames, in close crimped caps, long-waisted shortgowns, homespun petticoats, with scissors and pincushions, and gay calico pockets hanging on the outside. Buxom lasses, almost as antiquated as their mothers, excepting where a straw hat, a fine ribbon, or perhaps a white frock, gave symptoms of city innovation. The sons, in short square-skirted coats with rows of stupendous brass buttons, and their hair generally queued in the fashion of the times, especially if they could procure an eel-skin for the purpose, it being esteemed, throughout the country, as a potent nourisher and strengthener of the hair.

Brom Bones, however, was the hero of the scene, having come to the gathering on his favorite steed Daredevil, a creature, like himself, full of mettle and mischief, and which no one but himself could manage. He was, in fact, noted for preferring vicious animals, given to all kinds of tricks, which kept the rider in constant risk of his neck, for he held a tractable well-broken horse as unworthy of a lad of spirit.

Fain would I pause to dwell upon the world of charms that burst upon the enraptured gaze of my hero, as he entered the state parlor of Van Tassel's mansion. Not those of the bevy of buxom lasses, with their luxurious display of red and white; but the ample charms of a genuine Dutch country tea-table, in the sumptous time of autumn. Such heaped-up platters of cakes of various and almost indescribable kinds, known only to experienced Dutch housewives! There was the doughty doughnut, the tenderer oly koek, and the crisp and crumbling cruller; sweet cakes and short cakes, ginger-cakes and honey-cakes, and the whole family of cakes. And then there were apple-pies and peach-pies and pumpkin-pies; besides slices of ham and smoked beef; and moreover delectable dishes of preserved plums, and peaches, and pears, and quinces; not to mention broiled shad and roasted chickens; together with bowls of milk and cream, all mingled higgledy-piggledy, pretty much as I have enumerated them, with the motherly tea-pot sending up its clouds of vapor from the midst—Heaven bless the mark! I want breath and time to discuss this banquet as it deserves, and am too eager to get on with my story. Happily, Ichabod Crane was not in so great a hurry as his historian, but did ample justice to every dainty.

He was a kind and thankful creature, whose heart dilated in proportion as skin was filled with good cheer; and whose spirits rose with eating as some men's do with drink. He could not help, too, rolling his large eyes round him as he ate, and chuckling with the possibility that he might one day be lord of all this scene of almost unimaginable luxury and splendor. Then, he thought, how soon he'd turn his back upon the old school-house; snap his fingers in the face of Hans Van Ripper, and every other niggardly patron, and kick any itinerant pedagogue out-of-doors that should dare to call him comrade!

Old Baltus Van Tassel moved about among his guests with a face dilated with content and good humor, round and jolly as the harvest moon. His hospitable attentions were brief, but expressive, being confined to a shake of the hand, a slap on the shoulder, a loud laugh, and a pressing invitation to "fall to, and help themselves."

And now the sound of the music from the common room, or hall, summoned to the dance. The musician was an old gray-headed Negro, who had been the itinerant orchestra of the neighborhood for more than half a century. His instrument was as old and battered as himself. The greater part of the time he scraped on two or three strings, accompanying every movement of the bow with a motion of the head; bowing almost to the ground, and stamping with his foot whenever a fresh couple were to start.

Ichabod prided himself upon his dancing as much as upon his vocal powers. Not a limb, not a fibre about him was idle; and to have seen his loosely hung frame in full motion, and clattering about the room, you would have thought Saint Vitus himself, that blessed patron of the dance, was figuring before you in person. He was the admiration of all the Negroes; who having gathered, of all ages and sizes, from the farm and the neighborhood, stood forming a pyramid of shining black faces at every door and window, gazing with delight at the scene, rolling their white eyeballs, and showing grinning rows of ivory from ear to ear. How could the flogger of urchins be otherwise than animated and joyous? the lady of his heart was his partner in the dance, and smiling graciously in reply to all his amorous oglings; while Brom Bones, sorely smitten with love and jealousy, sat brooding by himself in one corner.

When the dance was at an end, Ichabod was attracted to a knot of the sager folks, who, with old Van Tassel, sat smoking at one end of the piazza, gossiping over former times, and drawing out long stories about the war.

This neighborhood, at the time of which I am speaking, was one of those highly favored places which abound with chronicle and great men. The British and American line had run near it during the war; it had, therefore, been the scene of marauding, and infested with refugees, cowboys, and all kinds of border chivalry. Just sufficient time had elapsed to enable each storyteller to dress up his tale with a little becoming fiction, and, in the indistinctness of his recollection, to make himself the hero of every exploit.

There was the story of Doffue Martling, a large blue-bearded Dutchman, who had nearly taken a Britich frigate with an old iron nine-pounder from a mud breastwork, only that his gun burst at the sixth discharge. And there was an old gentleman who shall be nameless, being too rich a mynheer to be lightly mentioned, who in the battle of White-plains, being an excellent master of defence, parried a musket ball with a small sword, insomuch that he absolutely felt it whiz round the blade, and glance off at the hilt; in proof of which, he was ready at any time to show the sword, with the hilt a little bent. There were several more that had been equally great in the field, not one of whom but was persuaded that he had a considerable hand in bringing the war to a happy termination.

But all these were nothing to the tales of ghosts and apparitions that succeeded. The neighborhood is rich in legendary treasures of the kind. Local tales and superstitions thrive best in these sheltered long-settled retreats; but are trampled under foot by the shifting throng that forms the population of most of our country places. Besides, there is no encouragement for ghosts in most of our villages, for they have scarcely had time to finish their first nap, and turn themselves in their graves, before their surviving friends have travelled away from the neighborhood; so that when they turn out at night to walk their rounds, they have no acquaintance left to call upon. This is perhaps the reason why we so seldom hear of ghosts except in our long-established Dutch communities.

The immediate cause, however, of the prevalence of supernatural stories in these parts, was doubtless owing to the vicinity of Sleepy Hollow. There was a contagion in the very air that blew from that haunted region; it breathed forth an atmosphere of dreams and fancies infecting all the land. Several of the Sleepy Hollow people were present at Van Tassel's, and, as usual, were doling out their wild and wonderful legends. Many dismal tales were told about funeral trains, and mourning cries and wailing heard and seen about the great tree where the unfortunate Major André was taken, and which stood in the neighborhood. Some mention was made also of the woman in white, that haunted the dark glen at Raven Rock, and was often heard to shriek on winter nights before a storm, having perished there in the snow. The chief part of the stories, however, turned upon the favorite spectre of Sleepy Hollow, the headless horseman, who had been heard several times of late, patrolling the country; and, it was said, tethered his horse nightly among the graves in the churchyard.

The sequestered situation of this church seems always to have made it a favorite haunt of troubled spirits. It stands on a knoll, surrounded by locust-trees and lofty elms, from among which its decent whitewashed walls shine modestly forth, like Christian purity beaming through the shades of retirement. A gentle slope descends from it to a silver sheet of water, bordered by high trees, between which, peeps may be caught at the blue hills of the Hudson. To look upon its grass-grown yard, where the sunbeams seem to sleep so quietly, one would think that there at least the dead might rest in peace. On one side of the church extends a wide woody dell, along which raves a large brook among broken rocks and trunks of fallen trees. Over a deep black part of the stream, not far from the church, was formerly thrown a wooden bridge; the road that led to it, and the bridge itself, were thickly shaded by overhanging trees, which cast a gloom about it, even in the daytime; but occasioned a fearful darkness at night. This was one of the favorite haunts of the headless horseman; and the place where he was most frequently encountered. The tale was told of old Brouwer, a most heretical disbeliever in ghosts, how he met the horseman returning from his foray into Sleepy Hollow, and was obliged to get up behind him; how they galloped over bush and brake, over hill and swamp, until they reached the bridge; when the horseman suddenly turned into a skeleton, threw old Brouwer into the brook, and sprang away over the tree-tops with a clap of thunder.

This story was immediately matched by a thrice marvellous adventure of Brom Bones, who made light of the galloping Hessian as an arrant jockey. He affirmed that, on returning one night from the neighboring village of Sing Sing, he had been overtaken by this midnight trooper; that he had offered to race with him for a bowl of punch, and should have won it too, for Daredevil beat the goblin horse all hollow, but, just as they came to the church bridge, the Hessian bolted, and vanished in a flash of fire.

All these tales, told in that drowsy undertone with which men talk in the dark, the countenances of the listeners only now and then receiving a casual gleam from the glare of a pipe, sank deep in the mind of Ichabod. He repaid them in kind with large extracts from his invaluable author, Cotton Mather, and added many marvellous events that had taken place in his native State of Connecticut, and fearful sights which he had seen in his nightly walks about Sleepy Hollow.

The revel now gradually broke up. The old farmers gathered together their families in their wagons, and were heard for some time rattling along the hollow roads, and over the distant hills. Some of the damsels mounted on pillions behind their favorite swains, and their light-hearted laughter, mingling with the clatter of hoofs, echoed along the silent woodlands, sounding fainter and fainter until they gradually died away—and the late scene of noise and frolic was all silent and deserted. Ichabod only lingered behind, according to the custom of country lovers, to have a *tête-à-tête* with the heiress, fully convinced that he was now on the high road to success. What passed at this interview I will not pretend to say, for in fact I do not know. Something, however, I fear me, must have gone wrong, for he certainly sallied forth, after no very great interval, with an air quite desolate and chop-fallen.—Oh these women! These women! Could that girl have been playing off any of her coquettish tricks?—Was her encouragement of the poor pedagogue all a mere sham to secure her conquest of his rival?—Heaven only knows, not I!—Let it suffice to say, Ichabod stole forth with the air of one who had been sacking a hen-roost, rather than a fair lady's heart. Without looking to the right or left to notice the scene of rural wealth on which he had so often gloated, he went straight to the stable, and with several hearty cuffs and kicks, roused his steed most uncourteously from the comfortable quarters in which he was soundly sleeping, dreaming of mountains of corn and oats, and whole valleys of timothy and clover.

It was the very witching times of night that Ichabod, heavy-hearted and crestfallen, pursued his travel homewards, along the sides of the lofty hills which rise above Tarry Town, and which he had traversed so cheerily in the afternoon. The hour was as dismal as himself. Far below him, the Tappan Zee spread its dusky and indistinct waste of waters, with here and there the tall mast of a sloop, riding quietly at anchor under the land. In the dead hush of midnight, he could even hear the barking of the watch-dog from the opposite shore of the Hudson; but it was so vague and faint as only to give an idea of his distance from this faithful companion of man. Now and then, too, the long-drawn crowing of a cock, accidentally awakened, would sound far, far off, from some farm-house away among the hills—but it was like a dreaming sound in his ear. No signs of life occurred near him, but occasionally the melancholy chirp of a cricket, or perhaps the guttural twang of a bull-frog, from a neighboring marsh, as if sleeping uncomfortably, and turning suddenly in his bed.

All the stories of ghosts and goblins that he had heard in the afternoon, now came crowding upon his recollection. The night grew darker and darker; the stars seemed to sink deeper in the sky, and driving clouds occasionally hid them from his sight. He had never felt so lonely and dismal. He was, moreover, approaching the very place where many of the scenes of the ghost stories had been laid. In the centre of the road stood an enormous tulip-tree, which towered like a giant above all the other trees of the neighborhood, and formed a kind of landmark. Its limbs were gnarled, and fantastic, large enough to form trunks for ordinary trees, twisting down almost to the earth, and rising again into the air. It was connected with the tragical story of the unfortunate André, who had been taken prisoner hard by; and was universally known by the name of Major André's tree. The common people regarded it with a mixture of respect and superstition, partly out of sympathy for the fate of its ill-starred namesake, and partly from the tales of strange sights and doleful lamentations told concerning it.

As Ichabod approached this fearful tree, he began to whistle; he thought his whistle was answered,—it was but a blast sweeping sharply through the dry branches. As he approached a little nearer, he thought he saw something white, hanging in the midst of the tree,—he paused and ceased whistling; but on looking more narrowly, perceived that it was a place where the tree had been scathed by lightning, and the white wood laid bare. Suddenly he heard a groan,—his teeth chattered and his knees smote against the saddle; it was but the rubbing of one huge bough upon another, as they were swayed about by the breeze. He passed the tree in safety, but new perils lay before him.

About two hundred yards from the tree a small brook crossed the road, and ran into a marshy and thickly wooded glen, known by the name of Wiley's swamp. A few rough logs, laid side by side, served for a bridge over this stream. On that side of the road where the brook entered the wood, a group of oaks and chestnuts, matted thick with wild grapevines, threw a cavernous gloom over it. To pass this bridge was the severest trial. It was at this identical spot that the unfortunate André was captured, and under the covert of those chestnuts and vines were the sturdy yeomen concealed who surprised him. This has ever since been considered a haunted stream, and fearful are the feelings of the schoolboy who has to pass it alone after dark.

As he approached the stream his heart began to thump; he summoned up, however, all his resolution, gave his horse half a score of kicks in the ribs, and attempted to dash briskly across the bridge; but instead of starting forward, the perverse old animal made a lateral movement, and ran broadside against the fence. Ichabod, whose fears increased with the delay, jerked the reins on the other side, and kicked lustily with the contrary foot: it was all in vain; his steed started, it is true, but it was only to plunge to the opposite side of the road into a thicket of brambles and alder bushes. The schoolmaster now bestowed both whip and heel upon the starveling ribs of old Gunpowder, who dashed forward, snuffling and snorting, but came to a stand just by the bridge, with a suddenness that had nearly sent his rider sprawling over his head. Just at this moment a plashy tramp by the side of the bridge caught the sensitive ear of Ichabod. In the dark shadow of the grove, on the margin of the brook, he beheld something huge, misshapen, black and towering. It stirred not, but seemed gathered up in the gloom, like some gigantic monster ready to spring upon the traveller.

The hair of the affrighted pedagogue rose upon his head with terror.

What was to be done? To turn and fly was now too late; and besides, what chance was there of escaping ghost or goblin, if such it was, which could ride upon the wings of the wind? Summoning up, therefore, a show of courage, he demanded in stammering accents—"Who are you?" He received no reply. He repeated his demand in a still more agitated voice. Still there was no answer. Once more he cudgelled the sides of the inflexible Gunpowder, and, shutting his eyes, broke forth with involuntary fervor into a psalm-tune. Just then the shadowy object of alarm put itself in motion, and, with a scramble and a bound, stood at once in the middle of the road. Though the night was dark and dismal, yet the form of the unknown might now in some degree be ascertained. He appeared to be a horseman of large dimensions, and mounted on a black horse of powerful frame. He made no offer of molestation or sociability, but kept aloof on one side of the road, jogging along on the blind side of old Gunpowder, who had now got over his fright and waywardness.

Ichabod, who had no relish for this strange midnight companion, and bethought himself of the adventure of Brom Bones with the Galloping Hessian, now quickened his steed, in hopes of leaving him behind. The stranger, however, quickened his horse to an equal pace. Ichabod pulled up, and fell into a walk, thinking to lag behind,—the other did the same. His heart began to sink within him; he endeavored to resume his psalm-tune, but his parched tongue clove to the roof of his mouth, and he could not utter a stave. There was something in the moody and dogged silence of this pertinacious companion that was mysterious and appalling. It was soon fearfully accounted for. On mounting a rising ground, which brought the figure of his fellow-traveller in relief against the sky, gigantic in height, and muffled in a cloak, Ichabod was horror-struck, on perceiving that he was headless!—but his horror was still more increased, on observing that the head, which should have rested on his shoulder, was carried before him on the pommel of the saddle: his terror rose to desperation; he rained a shower of kicks and blows upon Gunpowder, hoping, by a sudden movement, to give his companion the slip,—but the spectre started full jump with him. Away then they dashed, through thick and thin; stones flying, and sparks flashing at every bound. Ichabod's flimsy garments fluttered in the air, as he stretched his long lank body away over his horse's head, in the eagerness of his flight.

They had now reached the road which turns off to Sleepy Hollow; but Gunpowder, who seemed possessed with a demon, instead of keeping up it, made an opposite turn, and plunged headlong downhill to the left. This road leads through a sandy hollow, shaded by trees for about a quarter of a mile, where it crosses the bridge famous in goblin story, and just beyond swells the green knoll on which stands the whitewashed church.

As yet the panic of the steed had given his unskilful rider an apparent advantage in the chase; but just as he had got half-way through the hollow, the girths of the saddle gave way, and he felt it slipping from under him. He seized it by the pommel, and endeavored to hold it firm, but in vain; and he had just time to save himself by clasping old Gunpowder round the neck, when the saddle fell to the earth, and he heard it trampled under foot by his pursuer. For a moment the terror of Hans Van Ripper's wrath passed across his mind—for it was his Sunday saddle; but this was no time for petty fears; the goblin was hard on his haunches; and (unskilful rider that he was!) he had much ado to maintain his seat; sometimes slipping on one side, sometimes on another, and sometimes jolted on the high ridge of his horse's backbone with a violence that he verily feared would cleave him asunder.

An opening in the trees now cheered him with the hopes that the church-bridge was at hand. The wavering reflection of a silver star in the bosom of the brook told him that he was not mistaken. He saw the walls of the church dimly glaring under the trees beyond. He recollected the place where Brom Bones's ghostly competitor had disappeared. "If I can but reach that bridge," thought Ichabod, "I am safe." Just then he heard the black steed panting and blowing close behind him; he even fancied that he felt his hot breath. Another convulsive kick in the ribs, and old Gunpowder sprang upon the bridge; he thundered over the resounding planks; he gained the opposite side; and now Ichabod cast a look behind to see if his pursuer should vanish, according to rule, in a flash of fire and brimstone. Just then he saw the goblin rising in his stirrups, and in the very act of hurling his head at him. Ichabod endeavored to dodge the horrible missile, but too late. It encountered his cranium with a tremendous crash—he was tumbled headlong into the dust, and Gunpowder, the black steed, and the goblin rider, passed by like a whirlwind.

The next morning the old horse was found without his saddle, and with the bridle under his feet, soberly cropping the grass at his master's gate. Ichabod did not make his appearance at breakfast;—dinner-hour came, but no Ichabod. The boys assembled at the school-house, and strolled idly about the banks of the brook; but no schoolmaster. Hans Van Ripper now began to feel some uneasiness about the fate of poor Ichabod, and his saddle. An inquiry was set on foot, and after diligent investigation they came upon his traces. In one part of the road leading to the church was found the saddle trampled in the dirt; the tracks of horses' hoofs deeply dented in the road, and evidently at furious speed, were traced to the bridge, beyond which, on the bank of a broad part of the brook, where the water ran deep and black, was found the hat of the unfortunate Ichabod, and close beside it a shattered pumpkin.

The brook was searched, but the body of the schoolmaster was not to be discovered. Hans Van Ripper, as executor of his estate, examined the bundle which contained all his worldly effects. They consisted of two shirts and a half; two stocks for the neck; a pair or two of worsted stockings; an old pair of corduroy small-clothes; a rusty razor; a book of psalm-tunes, full of dogs' ears; and a broken pitchpipe. As to the books and furniture of the school-house, they belonged to the community, excepting Cotton Mather's "History of Witchcraft," a "New England Almanac," and a book of dreams and fortune-telling; in which last was a sheet of foolscap much scribbled and blotted in several fruitless attempts to make a copy of verses in honor of the heiress of Van Tassel. These magic books and the poetic scrawl were forthwith consigned to the flames by Hans Van Ripper; who from that time forward determined to send his children no more to school; observing, that he never knew any good come of this same reading and writing. Whatever money the schoolmaster possessed, and he had received his quarter's pay but a day or two before, he must have had about his person at the time of his disappearance.

The mysterious event caused much speculation at the church on the following Sunday. Knots of gazers and gossips were collected in the churchyard, at the bridge, and at the spot where the hat and pumpkin had been found. The stories of Brouwer, of Bones, and a whole budget of others, were called to mind; and when they had diligently considered them all, and compared them with symptoms of the present case, they shook their heads, and came to the conclusion that Ichabod had been carried off by the Galloping Hessian. As he was a bachelor, and in nobody's debt, nobody troubled his head any more about him. The school was removed to a different quarter of the Hollow, and another pedagogue reigned in his stead.

It is true, an old farmer, who had been down to New York on a visit several years after, and from whom this account of the ghostly adventure was received, brought home the intelligence that Ichabod Crane was still alive; that he had left the neighborhood, partly through fear of the goblin and Hans Van Ripper, and partly in mortification at having been suddenly dismissed by the heiress; that he had changed his quarters to a distant part of the country; had kept school and studied law at the same time, had been admitted to the bar, turned politician, electioneered, written for the newspapers, and finally had been made a justice of the Ten Pound Court. Brom

Bones too, who shortly after his rival's disappearance conducted the blooming Katrina in triumph to the altar, was observed to look exceedingly knowing whenever the story of Ichabod was related, and always burst into a hearty laugh at the mention of the pumpkin; which led some to suspect that he knew more about the matter than he chose to tell.

The old country wives, however, who are the best judges of these matters, maintain to this day that Ichabod was spirited away by supernatural means; and it is a favorite story often told about the neighborhood round the winter evening fire. The bridge became more than ever an object of superstitious awe, and that may be the reason why the road has been altered of late years, so as to approach the church by the border of the millpond. The school-house, being deserted, soon fell to decay, and was reported to be haunted by the ghost of the unfortunate pedagogue; and the ploughboy, loitering homeward of a still summer evening, has often fancied his voice at a distance, chanting a melancholy psalm-tune among the tranquil solitudes of Sleepy Hollow.

POSTSCRIPT

Found in the Handwriting of Mr. Knickerbocker

The preceding Tale is given, almost in the precise words in which I heard it related at a Corporation meeting of the ancient city of Manhattoes, at which were present many of its sagest and most illustrious burghers. The narrator was a pleasant, shabby, gentlemanly old fellow, in pepper-and-salt clothes, with a sadly humorous face; and one whom I strongly suspected of being poor,—he made such efforts to be entertaining. When his story was concluded, there was much laughter and approbation, particularly from two or three deputy aldermen, who had been asleep a greater part of the time. There was, however, one tall, dry-looking old gentleman, with beetling eyebrows, who maintained a grave and rather severe face throughout; now and then folding his arms, inclining his head, and looking down upon the floor, as if turning a doubt over in his mind. He was one of your wary men, who never laugh, but upon good grounds—when they have reason and the law on their side. When the mirth of the rest of the company had subsided and silence was restored, he leaned one arm on the elbow of his chair, and, sticking the other akimbo, demanded, with a slight but exceedingly sage motion of the head, and contraction of the brow, what was the moral of the story, and what it went to prove?

The story-teller, who was just putting a glass of wine to his lips, as a refreshment after his toils, paused for a moment, looked at his inquirer with an air of infinite deference, and, lowering the glass slowly to the table, observed that the story was intended most logically to prove:—

"That there is no situation in life but had its advantages and pleasures—provided we will but take a joke as we find it:

"That, therefore, he that runs races with goblin troopers is likely to have rough riding of it.

"Ergo, for a country schoolmaster to be refused the hand of a Dutch heiress is a certain step to high preferment in the state."

The cautious old gentleman knit his brows tenfold closer after this explanation, being sorely puzzled by the ratiocination of the syllogism; while, methought, the one in pepper-and-salt eyed him with something of a triumphant leer. At length, he observed that all this was very well, but still he thought the story a little on the extravagant—there were one or two points on which he had his doubts.

"Faith, sir," replied the story-teller, "as to that matter, I don't believe one-half of it myself."

D.K.

19TH CENTURY

MRS. BASIL HALL

Albany

Albany, September 15, 1827.

My Dearest Jane,

I do not remember whether I have described to you at any time the stiffness of an American party, at least as far as we had an opportunity of judging. We were last night at one at Mrs. Clinton's. Mr. Clinton, you know, is Governor of this State of which this place is the capital. Consequently the specimen we had may be clearly reckoned a sample of quite the *haut ton* of this part of the Union. We were invited to tea and went at eight o'clock. On entering the first drawing room both Basil and I started back, for we saw none but gentlemen, not a single lady, and we thought there must be some mistake in asking us in there, but in a moment the Governor came forward and giving me his arm hurried me into the adjoining room at the top of which sat Mrs. Clinton who placed me on the seat next to herself. Round the room were placed as many chairs as could be crammed in and a lady upon each, a most formidable circle, and I had to go through the not less formidable ordeal of an introduction to at least a dozen of those who were nearest me. In the course of the evening the gentlemen did venture into the room and stood for a short time talking to one or other of the ladies, but there was seldom a chair vacant for any of the males to seat themselves upon, and altho' occasionally the ladies had courage to cross the room and change places with each other I never saw any lady standing during the whole evening, and the Mistress of the House alone seemed to enjoy the privilege of moving at her ease about the rooms. We had abundance of refreshments with several editions of tea and cake, then came two servants, one with a tray full of beautiful, china plates of which he gave each lady one, another man followed bearing a tray covered with dishes of peaches and grapes which were in like manner handed round, then followed another course of plates and in their rear a magnificent pyramid of ice, supported on each side by preserved pineapple and other sweetmeats. Then came wine, and again more plates and more ice. In short, Mrs. Clinton seemed to be of the opinion of a lady of whom I have been told by some of my friends at home, that the easiest way to entertain her guests was to keep them eating. I was introduced to many persons during the course of the evening, the Chancellor of the State of New York, and Mr. Van Buren, one of the most eminent men in this State.

This house, Cruttenden's, is pretty well filled at present owing to the Extraordinary Meeting of the Legislature. The Ordinary Meeting is in winter, but they are at present assembled to revise the laws of the State. Our friend Mr. Granger belongs to the House of Assembly and lodges here, and there are also several other pleasant persons, and altogether they appear to be more sociably disposed at meal times than we have usually found them. In general instead of being questioned and cross-questioned as to whither we are going and whence we have come, as we were led to expect, we have great reason to complain of the extreme taciturnity of those at the public tables in spite of Basil's efforts to draw them into conversation, and you would think, were you to see us upon these occasions, that the curiosity belongs entirely to the English part of the company. The Americans are in such prodigious haste to get away from the table at all their meals that they have no time for opening their mouths except for the purpose of eating. Occasionally in a steamboat I have been asked various particulars as to my plans and calling, but quite as frequently by an Irish emigrant as by an American.

September 16:

...We dined yesterday at Governor Clinton's. Mrs. Clinton invited us to a family dinner, and so it strictly was, for the party consisted entirely of members of the family, namely the Governor and Mrs. Clinton, her mother Mrs. Jones, the two Miss Clintons, daughters of the Governor by a former marriage, and Mrs. Clinton's niece, Miss Allen. Perhaps you would like to know what is considered a family dinner in the first style at Albany, which you know is the capital of the State and the seat of government, so I took a more particular survey of the table than I am apt to do, and on the other page you will find a bill of fare. I must first premise that we had beautiful china and cut glass an inch thick. [A sketch made by Captain Hall of Mrs. Clinton's dinner table is inserted in the letter.]

Tarts, fruit, and cheese are always put on the table at the same time in this country, except at quite dress parties, when the fruit is a separate concern, but the ice is always along with the second course. The party was really very agreeable. Mr. Clinton is a very superior man, and Mrs. Clinton, tho' by no means elegant, is extremely good-natured and animated and amuses me very much by her strong aristocratic feelings, of which I believe she is quite unconscious. She has a little niece living with her, a child five months older than Eliza, who I was requested to take along with us yesterday. The little girl is a delicate little bit of a thing, by no means a match for my tomboy, which Miss Eliza soon found out, and when she discovers that any child is afraid of her, from that moment she tyrannises over her without mercy. So it was yesterday, and the poor little Livingstone was thoroughly frightened by Eliza's rough ways. We owe at least half our popularity in this country to Eliza; she is so perfectly at home with everyone, so ready to laugh and talk in her own fashion to those who will laugh and talk with her, that her good humour is quite irresistible, and altho' she is not what can strictly be called a pretty child there is something in her long, flowing hair, white skin, merry blue eyes, and broad shoulders that attracts the attention of all strangers.

We went from the Governor's to a party at General Solomon van Rensselaer's the Post Master. It was very much of the same kind as the night before, not so numerous, but the eatables were of the same quality and quantity. The attendance was not so good and was a very tolerable specimen of how ill that branch of polite society or at least of its accomplishment is understood. The first in the train was a black man in white trousers, next followed a lass in a black stuff dress and white apron with not a few holes, and last of all came a little girlie not more than ten or twelve years old. One of my correspondents remark that the ladies in America must be very stupid not to arrange their domestic concerns and their tables better, but it must be remembered that such a luxury as a good servant is not to be had, nothing but the very riff-raff of the Irish, and the ease of getting another place or doing for themselves in some way in case of dismissal, is so great that if you venture to find fault with your housemaid or butler they will tell you that you may suit yourself elsewhere....

MARGARET ARMSTRONG

Danskammer

1826—1859

He built a house of hewn stone, very stately and durable.

—Doctor Johnson

When Colonel William Armstrong made his visit to Newburgh under a flag of truce as a bearer of dispatches to General Washington from the British commander, he was not so overawed by Washington that he didn't have time to admire the beauty of the landscape. I daresay the mountains reminded him of his native Scotland. Anyway, when his son Edward married Sarah Ward of Carolina and began looking about for a country place, Colonel Armstrong suggested Newburgh. Edward explored that neighborhood—still wild and lovely and "unimproved"—on foot and on horseback; he found, at length, what he wanted, a level stretch of land on the Hudson six miles above Newburgh, a plateau overlooking Danskammer Point with a wide view to the south across Newburgh Bay to the Highlands. This, Edward decided, was the perfect spot. He bought it, hesitated for a while as to whether to call it "Gilknockie" after the old tower, or "Kirtleton" after the country place in Scotland, and at length wisely decided to keep the old name of "Danskammer."

The Dutch name "Teufels' Danskammer," or "Devils' Dance-Chamber," is one of the oldest in America. It appears on very ancient maps and was given, they say, by Henry Hudson when, sailing up the river in the *Half Moon,* he saw Indians dancing on the point that juts out into the water above Newburgh Bay. These figures in the twilight, leaping and dancing around their camp fire on the flat rock that tipped the point, must have added a spice of wild mystery to Hudson's calm voyage. Day after day of golden September weather, "under a very fair sun, shining and hot," the *Half Moon* slipped on up the still stream. Deer, moose, elk—all sorts of wild animals—went crashing up through the underbrush of the wooded slopes as the ship approached; in the bays, "swans in their season were so plenty that the shores seemed dressed in white drapery"; "...The land was very pleasant with grass and flowers and goodly trees, and very sweet smells came from them." It was, Hudson decided, "as pleasant a land as one need tread upon."...

The Indian village on the plateau which had been a stronghold in the war between Governor Stuyvesant and the Esopus Indians was gone when Edward Armstrong bought the place. No camp fires burned on the point. No ceremonial dances, such as Lieutenant Cowenhoven watched in 1663, alarmed the passing river craft—his description might be that of a modern Arizona tourist. Nothing was left of the Danskammer Indians but a vast quantity of arrow heads and pounders and spearheads; so many, that Indian relics are turned up to this day by the ploughshares of each succeeding spring.

But the full beauty of the landscape remained. The mountains were, for the most part, still thick with primeval forest; the bluffs unscarred by stone crushers; the river flats undefiled by brickyards. No railroads had straightened out the river's curves and obliterated bays and bathing beaches. Except that a few small towns dotted the shores, and a country house showed here and there among the trees, and white sails starred the water, the river had scarcely changed in the two centuries since Hudson first saw it.

And the river held its own for some years after Edward himself was dead and buried. It was not until 1848 that the decline began, with the building of the railroad along the eastern shore. Vanderbilt and the other promoters, proud of "opening up the country," were contemptuous when the Verplancks said they didn't want a railroad, amazed when they refused five thousand dollars for damages for their long beautiful water front, and punished them for their obstinacy by getting an appraisal of eighteen hundred and making them accept it....

The flat rock at the end of Danskammer Point still projected over the water until some forty years ago, and then the "dancing room" was broken off when the steamer *Cornell* ran aground on a foggy night. It lies in fragments now under water, and a lighthouse has been built there by the government.

But no railroads or lighthouses were imminent when Edward bought the place....The house he planned was to be the real thing; a Grecian temple built of granite, not an imitation classic affair of white wood like so many of those southern houses. It was to be stone outside and black walnut within —mahogany was not the fashion any more and Edward cared a lot about fashion. So barge after barge came up the river loaded to the waterline with slabs of dark gray granite from Breakneck, and pale gray granite from Quincy for the trim and the columns. The columns were so enormous that yokes of oxen sweated and grunted and tried in vain to haul them up the hill from the dock, until some bright workman drilled holes in the ends and made the columns into rollers and attached a tongue and rolled them up to the house. And the roads were rutted as if artillery had gone over them, and the lawns turned into sloughs of mud, and some good trees had to be cut down....

But, at last, the house stood on its eminence; a Grecian temple looking majestically across the bay to the Highlands—just missing a glimpse of Stony Point where Colonel Armstrong had once passed a bad quarter of an hour. A substantial rectangle of stone, flanked by an equally substantial and rectangular wing on each side; a veranda in front paved with blocks of stone and flanked by columns, with a flight of granite steps leading to the lawn. Not a graceful house, but Edward was delighted with it. That house would stay there overlooking the bay, Edward said to himself, as long as the temples of Greece had stood. Wind and rain could beat on those walls for a thousand years without making a dint. It would stand there for his remote descendants to see and admire, would remain as unchanged as the view itself....

...Mr. Downing, the famous landscape architect, helped to lay out the garden and plant all sorts of new shrubs and fruit trees, and suggested a double row of locusts along the avenue—locusts were the fashion. A shady road led down to the bathing beach—a lovely crescent of pure white sand until the next railroad came—and to the wharf, which ran out into water deep enough for big steamboats to stop. There was a fine stable, for Edward was passionately fond of horses, and a flock of Southdown sheep, for Edward considered fancy farming a part of the life of a country gentleman. Inside, there was a billiard room, for billiards were the fashion; and a gun room, for Edward was passionately fond of shooting....Of course there were large drawing-rooms and nice airy nurseries for the children—a great many children, mostly boys, arrived in a remarkably short time, for Edward approved of large families. And he added other farms to his original purchase until he owned two miles of river front. Everybody told him, with truth, that he had a very handsome estate.

And Edward was as handsome as his establishment. Family tradition has a great deal to say on the subject of Edward's good looks and personal charm. How, when he went to church in Charleston with his friend Lord

Stanley, the congregation, staring at the two young men in Colonel Ward's pew, made a mistake, whispered that it was even easier than they had supposed to tell an English nobleman from an ordinary American. But Edward had more than good looks. He wrote poetry, and drew, and played the violin, "had some knowledge of medicine," raised and drilled a local "train-band," was a good shot, rode like a centaur, and danced better than any other young gentleman between New York and Albany—old Mrs. Chrystie told me that she had never seen anybody who could cut a perfect *double* pigeon-wing except this grandfather of mine. "He was an adept in all manly arts, and up to all the sports of the time."

Edward's stables turned out many fine race-horses, chiefly sired by "Sir Henry," famous for his race with "Eclipse"; but his wife did not care for racing, so he never entered a horse for a race except once, and then not for money but only for "a pipe of wine." Many of the trotting horses of Orange County, celebrated for its trotters, are descended from Edward Armstrong's thoroughbred mares. And old people in the neighborhood used to speak of the fine figure he made on his favorite horse, a mahogany bay named Frank; my father remembered Frank, for the horse outlived his master.

HENRY CHRISTMAN

A Landed Aristocracy

Nowhere in the America of the late eighteen-thirties were the promises of the Declaration of Independence less fulfilled than in Albany, the capital of New York. Here was the seat of power of a landed aristocracy, the center of an island of semifeudalism in a nation that had, little more than half a century before, declared its common faith in democracy and free enterprise. Under the patroon system, flourishing as vigorously as it had in the days of the early seventeenth century, a few families, intricately intermarried, controlled the destinies of three hundred thousand people and ruled in almost kingly splendor over nearly two million acres of land.

In Albany class lines were sharp. Democracy was so little known that a veteran of the Revolution might be refused a seat on the Albany-Troy stage

From *Tin Horns and Calico: An Episode in the Emergence of American Democracy* by Henry Christman. Collier Books Paperback, 1961. Reprinted by permission of the author.

because he was shabbily dressed. Newspapers found it sufficiently important to report that cigar-smoking had lost its charm for the elite since almost every shop boy and dirty little urchin had taken it up. Society was geared to a round of pleasure matched only in Washington, and local politicians mapped the nation's political future over drinks at Eagle Tavern.

Workers left stranded at the completion of the railroad and the Erie Canal, demoralized by the panic of 1837, herded together in the poverty-ridden section on the city's edge known as the Pasture. They had begun to talk of organizing against low wages, unemployment, and unstable purchasing power. Most of all they were beginning to cry out for land—land through which to escape the vagaries of profits and wages. But almost no land within a radius of one hundred and fifty miles of Albany could belong to the people. The Hudson Valley gentry had owned it for generations, their ownership guaranteed by a charter which was a direct denial of the people's constitutional rights. The situation, in these unsettled times, was beginning to draw question: How long must this continue? Had it established a principle for the future in a nation rapidly expanding into the territories of the West?

Some of the Hudson Valley gentry bore British names—Livingston, Morris, Jay; others, descendants of Dutch settlers, were named Van Rensselaer, Hardenbergh, Verplanck, Van Cortlandt, and Schuyler. No other was so proud or so influential as the Van Rensselaer family, pioneers in American feudalism, who for more than two hundred years had been the owners of the largest estate in the region. Rensselaerwyck embraced all of Albany and Rensselaer counties and part of Columbia, and by 1838 was maintaining between sixty and one hundred thousand tenant farmers. Their overlord was Stephen Van Rensselaer III, who had become the sixth lord of the manor at the age of five, and was now an urbane old gentleman in his seventies, a former soldier and a former Congressman who rejoiced in the sobriquet of the Good Patroon and was adored by six sons, three daughters, and numerous grandchildren.

The patroon system which Stephen and his contemporaries inherited had been engrafted on America by Kiliaen Van Rensselaer in 1629, long after it had been discarded in Holland. An influential pearl-and-diamond merchant in the Dutch capital, Kiliaen joined with other crafty businessmen to obtain a charter for the Dutch West India Company, ostensibly to colonize the New World. However, their true purpose was to wage privateer war against Spanish ships carrying gold and silver from Peru and Mexico, and to re-establish Dutch command of the sea without violating the country's treaty of friendship with Spain. Armed fleets set sail with orders and authority to "conquer provinces and peoples and administer justice." Enormous riches returned to the company, and the prize of maritime supremacy kept the government complaisant until other interests, alarmed at the British challenge of Dutch claims in the New World, began to ask what had become of the projected colonization. Shrewdly, the directors explained that settlement of "such a wild and uncultivated country" called for more settlers than they could supply; important inducements would have to be offered before the undertaking could succeed.

It was relatively easy, therefore, for the directors to get authority to offer a grant of land, with absolute power as patroon, to any member of the company who would plant a colony of fifty persons in America within four years. The patroon would have baronial authority, with full property rights and complete civil and military control over the people, who would be bound by contract to fealty and military service as vassals.

Each tract was to be legally purchased from the Indians, and limited to a river frontage of sixteen miles, or if the land lay on both sides of a river, eight miles on each bank. But enterprising Kiliaen made his own laws. He had his agents give a basket of trinkets to the Indian chiefs for title to land stretching twenty-four miles along the Hudson River, with Fort Orange, a fur-trading settlement, as the approximate geographical center. Of six patroonships granted, his was the only one to survive the first six years, for although he never crossed the ocean to his dominions, he was as fortunate in choosing his deputies as he had been in selecting his location.

Tenants imported to secure his title were under absolute control of his agents. They were compelled to buy all supplies from the patroon's commissary at usurious prices, grind their grain at the patroon's mill, and pay over to him part of all crops and increase in livestock. Hobbled by such restraints, agricultural settlers were few, but the traffic in beaver skins flourished.

The Van Rensselaer empire stood at the gateway to the fur trade of the inland wilderness, and although the grant of patroonship specifically reserved this trade to the company, Kiliaen had a fort built on Barren Island at the southern end of his domain, and decreed that no ships should pass except those in his personal service. When the company protested that trade rights belonged equally to all members, Kiliaen declared he would enforce his edict "by weapon right," and from the watchmaster of Barren Island all ships got orders to "strike thy colors for the Lord Kiliaen and the staple right of Rensselaerwyck."

Peter Stuyvesant, the hot-tempered, peg-legged director general in New Amsterdam, took passage upriver to have it out with Van Rensselaer's agent at Fort Orange. When the boat docked, he stumped up the hill to the agent's house and ordered the soldiers to tear down the patroon's flag. That done, he laid out a town adjacent to Fort Orange, named it Beverwyck, and proclaimed it company property under the jurisdiction of three magistrates whom he himself appointed. Beyond that, the patroon's influence with the home government proved too strong even for the hotheaded governor.

As the land was cleared and farms became productive, the tribute paid by Kiliaen's slowly growing nucleus of settlers added measurably to his fortune. "I would not like to have my people get too wise and figure out their master's profit, especially in matters in which they themselves are somewhat interested," he wrote in 1629 to William Kieft, director of New Netherland.

After the British seized New Netherland in 1664, the changes were largely superficial. Fort Orange and Beverwyck were combined under the name of Albany, from the Scottish title of the Duke of York, afterward James II of England. Kiliaen's grandson, then in actual residence, was confirmed in his possession of Rensselaerwyck by provisional orders; in 1685 the governor granted a patent transforming the patroonship into an English manor and the patroon into the lord of the manor. His civil rights were restricted a bit, but there was no change in the relations between landlord and tenant.

The English almost outdid their predecessors in saddling the valley with big estates, for in addition to nine actual manors, they handed out millions of acres in patents to lesser members of the Hudson River aristocracy. It was regarded as good policy to place large tracts in the hands of gentlemen of weight and consideration, who would naturally farm out their lands to tenants, a method which would create subordination and, as the last of the colonial governors expressed it, "counterpoise in some measure the general levelling spirit that so prevails in some of His Majesty's governments."

Even the Revolution did not weaken the feudal hold of the big landowners. It merely stripped them of baronial honors and privileges. The rent-distressed tenants of New York State gave themselves and their supplies to the struggle; they fought at Saratoga, Oriskany, and Valley Forge for the right to be independent landholders. Side by side with men seeking freedom for capital enterprise to exploit the wealth of the New World, farmers and wage earners fought for the principles of individual political and economic freedom. With a common rallying cry, two wars were fought, one within the other—and one was lost. The farmers and the wage earners found themselves betrayed in victory, when the new government became a bulwark for the rich and the middle class against the "despised proletariat" and the rising tide of democracy.

L. MARIA CHILD

The Grave of Major André

August 4, 1842

Last week, for a single day, I hid myself in the green sanctuary of Nature; and from the rising of the sun till the going down of the moon, took no more thought of cities, than if such excrescences never existed on the surface of the globe. A huge wagon, traversing our streets, under the midsummer sun, bearing in immense letters, the words, ICE FROM ROCKLAND LAKE, had frequently attracted my attention, and become associated with images of freshness and romantic beauty. Therefore, in seeking the country for a day, I said our course should be up the Hudson to Rockland Lake. The noontide sun was scorching; and our heads were dizzy with the motion of the boat; but these inconveniences, so irksome at the moment, are faintly traced on the tablet of memory. She engraves only the beautiful in lasting characters; for beauty alone is immortal and divine.

We stopped at Piermont, on the widest part of Tappan bay, where the Hudson extends itself to the width of three miles. On the opposite side, in full view from the Hotel, is Tarrytown, where poor Andre was captured. Tradition says, that a very large white-wood tree, under which he was taken, was struck by lightning, on the very day that news of Arnold's death was received at Tarrytown. As I sat gazing on the opposite woods, dark in the shadows of moonlight, I thought upon how very slight a circumstance often depends the fate of individuals, and the destiny of nations. In the autumn of 1780, a farmer chanced to be making cider at a mill, on the east bank of the Hudson, near that part of Haverstraw Bay, called 'Mother's Lap'. Two young men, carrying muskets, as usual in those troubled times, stopped for a draught of sweet cider, and seated themselves on a log to wait for it. The farmer found them looking very intently on some distant object, and inquired what they saw. 'Hush! hush!' they replied; 'the red-coats are yonder, just within the Lap,' pointing to an English gun-boat, with twenty-four men, lying on their oars. Behind the shelter of a rock they fired into the boat, and killed two persons. The British returned a random shot; but ig-

From *Letters from New York* by L. Maria Child. Published by C. S. Francis & Co., New York, 1843.

norant of the number of their opponents, and seeing that it was useless to waste ammunition on a hidden foe, they returned whence they came, with all possible speed. This boat had been sent to convey Major Andre to the British sloop-of-war, Vulture, then lying at anchor off Teller's point. Shortly after, Andre arrived, and finding the boat gone, he, in attempting to proceed through the interior, was captured. Had not those men stopped to drink sweet cider, it is possible that Andre would not have been hung; the American revolution might have terminated in quite different fashion; men now deified as heroes, might have been handed down to posterity as traitors; our citizens might be proud of claiming descent from tories; and slavery have been abolished eight years ago, by virtue of our being British colonies. So much may depend on a draught of cider! But would England herself have abolished slavery, had it not been for the impulse given to free principles by the American revolution? Probably not. It is not easy to calculate the consequences involved even in a draught of cider; for no fact stands alone; each has infinite relations.

A very pleasant ride at sunset brought us to Orangetown, to the lone field where Major Andre was executed. It is planted with potatoes, but the plough spares the spot on which was once his gallows and his grave. A rude heap of stones, with the remains of a dead fir tree in the midst, are all that mark it; but tree and stones are covered with names. It is on an eminence, commanding a view of the country for miles. I gazed on the surrounding woods, and remembered that on this self-same spot, the beautiful and accomplished young man walked back and forth, a few minutes preceding his execution, taking an earnest farewell look of earth and sky. My heart was sad within me. Our guide pointed to a house in full view, at half a mile's distance, which he told us was at that time the head-quarters of General Washington. I turned my back suddenly upon it. The last place on earth where I would wish to think of Washington, is at the grave of Andre. I know that military men not only sanction, but applaud the deed; and reasoning according to the maxims of war, I am well aware how much can be said in its defence. That Washington considered it a duty, the discharge of which was most painful to him, I doubt not. But, thank God, the instincts of my childhood are unvitiated by any such maxims. From the first hour I read of the deed, until the present day, I never did, and never could, look upon it as otherwise than cool, deliberate murder. That the theory and practice of war commends the transaction, only serves to prove the infernal nature of war itself....

A few years ago, the Duke of York requested the British consul to send the remains of Major Andre to England. At that time, two thriving firs were found near the grave, and a peach tree, which a lady in the neighbourhood had planted there, in the kindness of her heart. The farmers, who came to witness the interesting ceremony, generally evinced the most respectful tenderness for the memory of the unfortunate dead; and many of the women and children wept. A few loafers, educated by militia trainings, and Fourth of July declamation, began to murmur that the memory of General Washington was insulted by any respect shown to the remains of Andre; but the offer of a treat lured them to the tavern, where they soon became too drunk to guard the character of Washington. It was a beautiful day: and these disturbing spirits being removed, the impressive ceremony proceeded in solemn silence. The coffin was in good preservation, and contained all the bones, with a small quantity of dust. The roots of the peach tree had entirely interwoven the skull with their fine network. His hair, so much praised for its uncommon beauty, was tied, on the day of his execution, according to the fashion of the times. When his grave was opened, half a century afterward, the ribbon was found in perfect preservation, and sent to his sister in England. When it was known that the sarcophagus, containing his remains, had arrived in New York, on its way to London, many ladies sent garlands, and emblematic devices, to be wreathed around it, in the memory of the 'beloved and lamented Andre.'...

Not far from the church [the Dutch Reformed Church in which Major Andre was tried and sentenced] is a small stone building, used as a tavern. Here they showed me the identical room where Andre was imprisoned. With the exception of new plastering, it remains the same as then. It is long, low, and narrow, and being without furniture or fireplace, it still has rather a jail-like look. I was sorry for the new plastering; for I hoped to find some record of prison thoughts cut in the walls. Two doves were cuddled together on a bench in one corner, and looked in somewhat melancholy mood. These mates were all alone in that silent apartment, where Andre shed bitter tears over the miniature of his beloved. Alas for mated human hearts! This world is too often for them a pilgrimage of sorrow.

The miniature, which Andre made such strong efforts to preserve, when everything else was taken from him, and which he carried next his heart till the last fatal moment, is generally supposed to have been a likeness of the beautiful, graceful, and highly-gifted Honora Sneyd, who married Richard Lovel Edgeworth, and thus became step-mother to the celebrated Maria Edgeworth. A strong youthful attachment existed between her and Major Andre; but for some reason or other they separated. He entered the army, and died the death of a felon. *Was* he a felon? No. He was generous, kind, and brave. His noble nature was perverted by the maxims of war; but the act he committed for the British army was what an American officer would have gloried in doing for his own. Washington *employed* spies; nor is it probable that he, or any other military commander, would have hesitated to *become* one, if by so doing he could get the enemy completely into his power. It is not therefore a sense of justice, but a wish to inspire terror, which leads to the execution of spies. War is a game, in which the devil plays at nine-pins with the souls of men.

MRS. (ANNE) GRANT

Breaking Up of the Ice on the Hudson River

Soon after this I witnessed, for the last time, the sublime spectacle of the ice breaking up on the river.... This noble object of animated greatness, for such it seemed, I never missed; its approach being announced, like a loud and long peal of thunder, the whole population of Albany were down at the river-side in a moment; and if it happened, as was often the case, in the morning, there could not be a more grotesque assemblage. No one who had a nightcap on waited to put it off; as for waiting for one's cloak, or gloves, it was a thing out of the question; you caught the thing next you, that could wrap round you, and ran. In the way you saw every door left open, and pails, baskets, &c., without number, set down in the street. It was a perfect saturnalia. People never dreamed of being obeyed by their slaves, till the ice was past. The houses were left quite empty; the meanest slave, the youngest child, all were to be found on the shore. Such as could walk, ran; and they that could not, were carried by those whose duty would have been to stay and attend them. When arrived at the *show-place,* unlike the audience collected to witness any spectacle of human invention, the multitude, with their eyes all bent one way, stood immoveable, and silent as death, till the tumult ceased, and the mighty commotion was passed by; then every one tried to give vent to the vast conceptions with which his mind

From *Memoirs of an American Lady,* published by D. Appleton & Co., New York, 1846.

had been distended. Every child, and every negro, was sure to say, "Is not this like the day of judgment?" and what they said every one else thought. Now to describe this is impossible; but I mean to account, in some degree, for it. The ice, which had been all winter very thick, instead of diminishing, as might be expected in spring, still increased, as the sunshine came, and the days lengthened. Much snow fell in February, which, melted by the heat of the sun, was stagnant for a day on the surface of the ice, and then by the night frosts, which were still severe, was added, as a new accession to the thickness of it, above the former surface. This was so often repeated, that, in some years, the ice gained two feet in thickness, after the heat of the sun became such as one would have expected should have entirely dissolved it. So conscious were the natives of the safety this accumulation of ice afforded, that the sledges continued to drive on the ice when the trees were budding, and everything looked like spring; nay, when there was so much melted on the surface that the horses were knee-deep in water while travelling on it, and portentous cracks on every side announced the approaching rupture. This could scarce have been produced by the mere influence of the sun till midsummer. It was the swelling of the waters under the ice, increased by rivulets, enlarged by melted snows, that produced this catastrophe; for such the awful concussion made it appear. The prelude to the general bursting of this mighty mass, was a fracture, lengthways, in the middle of the stream, produced by the effort of the imprisoned waters, now increased too much to be contained within their wonted bounds. Conceive a solid mass, from six to eight feet thick, bursting for many miles in one continued rupture, produced by a force inconceivably great, and, in a manner, inexpressibly sudden. Thunder is no adequate image of this awful explosion, which roused all the sleepers, within the reach of the sound, as completely as the final convulsion of nature, and the solemn peal of the awakening trumpet, might be supposed to do.... But when the bursting of the crystal surface set loose the many waters that had rushed down, swollen with the annual tribute of dissolving snow, the islands and low lands were all flooded in an instant; and the lofty banks, from which you were wont to overlook the stream, were now entirely filled by an impetuous torrent, bearing down, with incredible and tumultuous rage, immense shoals of ice; which, breaking every instant by the concussion of others, jammed together in some places, in others erecting themselves in gigantic heights for an instant in the air, and seeming to combat with their fellow-giants crowding on in all directions, and falling together with an inconceivable crash, formed a terrible moving picture, animated and various beyond conception; for it was not only the cerulean ice, whose broken edges, combating with the stream, refracted light into a thousand rainbows, that charmed your attention, lofty pines, large pieces of the bank torn off by the ice with all their early green and tender foliage, were driven on like travelling islands, amid this battle of breakers.

GEORGE WILLIAM CURTIS

The Hudson and the Rhine

July

Newburgh on the Hudson

Although the day was tropical, on which we left New York, the "Reindeer" ran with us as if we had been mere Laplanders, and our way a frozen plain, instead of the broad, blue river. It is only in the steamer that the Hudson can be truly perceived and enjoyed. In the Indian summer, the western shore, seen from the railroad, is a swiftly unrolling panorama of dreams; yet the rush, and roar, and sharp steam-shriek would have roused Rip Van Winkle himself, and the dust would have choked and blinded him as he opened his eyes. The railroad will answer to deliver legislators at Albany, although which "side up" is a little uncertain. But the traveller who loves the law of beauty and pursues pleasure, will take the steamer and secure silence, cleanliness, sufficient speed, and an unencumbered enjoyment of the landscape....

I know that romance is in the poet's heart, and not in the outward forms he sees. But there is a technical material of romance—the moonlight, a ruin, an Italian girl, for instance—which is useful in begetting a romantic mood of mind, as a quotation will often suggest verses that haunt you all day long. And it is in this material that the Rhine is so rich.

The Hudson, however, is larger and grander. It is not to be devoured in detail. No region without association, is, except by science. But its spacious and stately character, its varied and magnificent outline, from the Palisades to the Catskill, are as epical as the loveliness of the Rhine is lyrical. The Hudson implies a continent behind. For vineyards it has forests. For a belt of water, a majestic stream. For graceful and grain-goldened heights it has

From *Lotus-Eating: A Summer Book* by George William Curtis. Published by Harper and Brothers, New York, 1852.

imposing mountains. There is no littleness about the Hudson, but there is in the Rhine. Here every thing is boldly touched. What lucid and penetrant lights, what broad and sober shadows! The river moistens the feet, and the clouds anoint the heads, of regal hills. The Danube has, in parts, glimpses of such grandeur. The Elbe has sometimes such delicately pencilled effects. But no European river is so lordly in its bearing, none flows in such state to the sea.

Of all our rivers that I know, the Hudson, with this grandeur, has the most exquisite episodes. Its morning and evening reaches are like the lakes of dreams. Looking from this garden, at twilight, toward the huge hills, enameled with soft darkness, that guard the entrance of the Highlands, near West Point, I "would be a merman bold," to float on the last ray through that mysterious gate to the softest shadow in Cro' Nest, where, if I *were* a merman bold, I should know the culprit fay was sleeping. Out of that dim portal glide the white sails of sloops, like spectres; they loiter languidly along the bases of the hills, as the evening breeze runs after them, enamored, and they fly, taking my fascinated eyes captive, far and far away, until they glimmer like ghosts and strand my sight upon the distance.

These tranquil evening reveries are the seed of such beautiful and characteristic harvests as the Hudson tales of the Sketch Book and Knickerbocker's History. And rubbing those golden grains upon his eyes, Darley has so well perceived the spirit of the river, that in a few simple forms, in the vignette of his illustrations of Rip Van Winkle, he has seized its suggestions and made it visible. Nor will any lover of the Hudson forget its poet, Joseph Rodman Drake, who in his "Culprit Fay," shows that the spirits of romance and beauty haunt every spot upon which falls the poetic eye. If a man would touch the extremes of experience in a single day, I know not how it could be better done, than by stepping upon a steamer, after a long bustling morning in Wall-street, and reading the "Culprit Fay" by moonlight upon the piazza of the hotel at West Point, looking up the river to Cro' Nest.

It was a happy fortune for the beauty of the river that steam did not drive away the sails. It was feared that the steamers would carry all the freight, and so bereave the river of the characteristic and picturesque life of the white-sailed sloops. But economy was on the side of beauty this time, and it was found cheaper to carry heavy freights by sail, as of old. So the sloops doze and dream along, very beautiful to behold from the banks, and sometimes, awakened as they enter the Highlands by a sudden stoop from some saucy gust coquetting with the hills, they bend and dip, and come crowding toward us through the grim mountain gate, like a troop of white-winged pilgrims fluttering and flying from the Castle of Giant Despair.

You see I have heard the Hudson Syrens: perhaps some faint, far-off strain of that lullaby of silence that soothed old Rip to his mountain nap.... But when, leaving the garden, and sitting under the foliaged trellises of the piazza, we see the moon rise over the opposite mountains—the ghost of the summer day—drawing the outline of the Warwick vase more delicately in shadow upon the sward than ever the skilful artist carved it in marble, then a glimpse of Grecian beauty penetrates and purifies the night.

Saratoga

August

The romance of a watering-place, like other romance, always seems past when you are there. Here at Saratoga, when the last polka is polked, and the last light in the ball-room is extinguished, you saunter along the great piazza, with the "good night" of Beauty yet trembling upon your lips, and meet some old Habitué, or even a group of them, smoking in lonely arm-chairs, and meditating the days departed.

The great court is dark and still. The waning moon is rising beyond the trees, but does not yet draw their shadows, moonlight-mosaics, upon the lawn. There are no mysterious couples moving in the garden, not a solitary foot-fall upon the piazza. A few lanterns burn dimly about the doors, and the light yet lingering in a lofty chamber reminds you that some form, whose grace this evening has made memory a festival, is robing itself for dreams....

...As you cross the court, after breakfast, to the bowling alley, with a bevy so young and lovely, that age and mob-caps seem only fantastic visions of dyspepsia, and, of hearts that were never young, you will see them sitting, a solemn reality of "black manhood," along the western piazza, leaning back in arm-chairs, smoking perhaps, chatting of stocks possibly,—a little rounded in the shoulders, holding canes which are no longer foppish switches, but substantial and serious supports. They are the sub-bass in the various-voiced song, the prosaic notes to the pleasant lyric of Saratoga life....

Be assured, Saratoga is still a golden-clasped, illuminated romance for summer reading. Young men still linger, loth to fly, and when the trunk must be packed, they yet sit gossipping upon the edge of the bed.... Then, gorged with experience, blasé of the world, patronising and enduring life, the royal Arthurs, scorning the heaps of broken hearts they leave behind, transfer themselves and their boots to a new realm of conquest at Newport....

But while we laugh at Saratoga, its dancing, dressing, and flirtation, it is yet a "coign of vantage" for an observing eye. It is not all dress and dancing. Like every aspect of life, and like most persons, it is a hint and suggestion of something high and poetic. It is an oasis of repose in the desert of our American hurry. Life is leisurely there, and business is amusement.

It is perpetual festival. The "United States" is the nearest hit we Americans can make to Boccaccio's garden. It is a spacious house, admirably kept, with a stately piazza surrounding a smooth green lawn, constantly close-shaven, and shadowed with lofty trees. Along that stately piazza we pass to the ball-room, and cross that lawn under those trees to the bowling-alley, and the place of spirits. We rise and breakfast at any time. Then we chat a little and bowl till noon. If you choose, you may sit apart and converse, instead of bowling, upon metaphysics and morals. At noon, we must return to the parlor and practice the polka which we have not danced since yesterday midnight. There are sofas and comfortable chairs strewn around the room, and, if you have reached no metaphysical conclusion, in the bowling-alley, you may wish to continue your chat. We ladies must go shopping after the polka, and we mere men may go to the bath. Dinner then, in our semi-toilettes, feeing Ambrose and Anthony to get us something to eat, and watching the mighty Morris, in an endless frenzy of excitement, tearing his hair, whenever a plate, loud-crashing, shivers on the floor.

After dinner the band plays upon the lawn, and we all promenade upon the piazza, or in the walks of the court, or sit at the parlor windows. We discuss the new arrivals. We criticise dresses, and styles, and manners. We discriminate the arctic and antarctic Bostonians, fair, still, and stately, with a vein of scorn in their Saratoga enjoyment, and the languid, cordial, and careless Southerners, far from precise in dress or style, but balmy in manner as a bland southern morning. We mark the crisp courtesy of the New Yorker, elegant in dress, exclusive in association, a pallid ghost of Paris—without its easy elegance, its *bonhommie,* its gracious *savoir faire,* without the *spirituel* sparkle of its conversation, and its natural and elastic grace of style. We find that a Parisian toilette is not France, nor grace, nor fascination. We discover that exclusiveness is not elegance.

But while we mark and moralize, the last strain of Lucia or Ernani has died away, and it is 5 o'clock. A crowd of carriages throngs the street before the door, there is a flutter through the hall, a tripping up and down stairs, and we are bowling along to the lake. There is but one drive: every body goes to the lake. And no sooner have we turned by the Congress Spring, than we are in the depths of the country, in a long, level reach of pines, with a few distant hills of the Green Mountains rolling along the horizon. It is a city gala at the hotel, but the five minutes were magical, and among the pines upon the road we remember the city and its life as a winter dream.

The vivid and sudden contrast of this little drive with the hotel, is one of the pleasantest points of Saratoga life. In the excitement of the day, it is like stepping out on summer evenings from the glaring ball-room upon the cool and still piazza.

There is a range of carriages at the Lake. A select party is dining upon those choice trouts, black bass and young woodcock—various other select parties are scattered about upon the banks or on the piazza, watching the sails and sipping cobblers. The descent to the Lake is very steep, and the smooth water is dotted with a few boats gliding under the low, monotonous banks. The afternoon is tranquil, the light is tender, the air is soft, and the lapping of the water upon the pebbly shore is haply not so musical as words spoken upon its surface.

In the sunset we bowl back again to the hotel. I saw most autumnal sunsets at Saratoga, cold and gorgeous, like the splendor of October woods. They were still and solemn over the purple hills of the horizon, and their light looked strangely in at the windows of the hotel....

Music flows towards us from the ball-room in languid, luxurious measures, like warm, voluptuous arms wreathing around us and drawing us to the dance. When we enter the hall we find very few people, but at the lower end a sprinkling of New Yorklings are in their heaven.

Dancing is natural and lovely as singing. The court of youth and beauty—with the presence of brilliantly dressed women, and an air smoothed and softened with delicate and penetrating perfumes, and the dazzling splendor of lights, is a song unsung, a flower not blossomed, until you mingle in movement with the strain—until the scene is so measured by the music that they become one....

This is a day at Saratoga, and all days there. It is a place for pleasure. The original aim of a visit thither, to drink the waters, is now mainly the excuse of fathers and of the Habitués, to whom, however, summer and Saratoga are synonymous. It is our pleasant social exchange. There we step out of the worn and weary ruts of city society, and mingle in a broad field of various acquaintance....

If you seek health, avoid it if you can; or if you must drink the waters there, take rooms in some other house, not in the "United States," where you will be tortured with the constant vision of the carnival of the high health you have lost. Youth, health and beauty are still the trinity of Saratoga. No old belle ever returns. No girl who was beautiful and famous there, comes as a grandmother to that gay haunt. The ghosts of her blooming days would dance a direful dance around her in the moonlight of the court. Faces that grew sad, and cold, and changed, would look in at her midnight window. Phantoms of promenades, when the wish was spoken rather than the feeling, would make her shudder as she hurried along the piazza. The dull aching sense of youth passed forever would become suddenly poignant, as she glanced upon the gay groups, gay as she was gay, young and fair no more than she had been. Worst of all, if in some lonely path she met gray-haired, dull-eyed and tottering upon crutches, the handsome and graceful partner of her first Saratoga season.

Lake George

August

An hour upon the railroad brings you from Saratoga to the Moreau Station. Here you climb a stagecoach to roll across the country to Lake George. It is a fine strip of landscape variously outlined, and with glimpses of beautiful distance. The driver pointed out to us the tree under which Jane McCrea was murdered by the Indians—a lovely spot, meet for so sad a tradition. Between us and the dim-rolling outline of the Green Mountains were the windings of the Hudson, which here, in its infancy, is a stream of fine promise, and rolled our fancies forward to its beautiful banks below, its dark highlands, its glassy reaches, and the forms of friends on lawns and in gardens along its shores.

We dined at Glen's Falls, which we visited. They are oppressed by the petty tyranny of a decayed dynasty of saw-mills, and the vexed river rages and tumbles among channelled rocks, making a fine spectacle of the Trentonian character. Then we bowled along through a brilliant afternoon toward the Lake. The road is one of the pleasantest I remember. And particularly on that day the grain-fields and the mountains were of the rarest delicacy of tone and texture. Through the trees, an hour from Glen's Falls, I saw a sheet of water, and we emerged upon a fine view of the Lake.

An azure air, of which the water seemed only a part more palpable, set in hills of graceful figure and foliage, and studded with countless isles of romantic beauty—such a picture as imagination touches upon the transparent perfection of summer noons, was my fancy of Lake George.

It was but partly true.

Caldwell is a hamlet at the southern end of the Lake. It is named from an eccentric gentleman, (illiberal obstinacy is always posthumously beautified into eccentricity) who owned the whole region, built a hotel on the wrong spot, determined that no one else should build anywhere, and ardently desired that no more people should settle in the neighborhood; and, in general, infested the southern shore with a success worthy of a mythological dragon. Instead, therefore, of a fine hotel at the extremity of the Lake, commanding a view of its length, and situated in grounds properly picturesque, there is a house on one side of the end, looking across it to the opposite mountain, and forever teasing the traveller with wonder that it stands where it does.

The hotel is kept admirably, however, and the faults of position and size are obviated, as far as possible, by the courtesy and ability of the host. But the increasing throng of travel justifies the erection of an inn equal in every manner to the best. This year the little hamlet was but the "colony" of the hotel, and a mile across the Lake, on the opposite shore, was a small house for the accommodation of the public.

Lake George is a strange lull in excitement after Saratoga. Its tranquillity is like the morning after a ball. There is nothing to do but to bowl or to sit upon the piazza, or to go fishing upon the Lake. It is a good place to study fancy fishermen, who have taken their piscatory degrees in Wall and Pearl-streets. Most of the visitors are guests of a night, but there are also pleasant parties who pass weeks upon the Lake, and listen to the enthusiastic stories of Saratoga as incredulously as to Syren-songs; to whom Saratoga is a name and a vapor, incredible as the fervor of a tropical day to the Russian Empress in her icy palace; parties of a character rare in our country, who do not utterly surrender the summer to luxurious idleness, but steal honey from the flowers as they fly....

Lake George is a simple mountain lake upon the verge of the wilderness. You ascend from its banks westward and plunge into a wild region. The hills that frame the water are low, and when not bare—for fires frequently consume many miles of woodland on the hillsides—covered with the stiffly outlined, dark and cold foliage of evergreens. Among these are no signs of life. You might well fancy the populace of the primeval forest yet holding those retreats. You might still dream in the twilight that it were not impossible to catch the ring of a French or English rifle, or the wild whoop of the Indian; sure that the landscape you see, was the same they saw, and their remotest ancestors.

FREDRIKA BREMER

Conversations with Washington Irving

November 5, 1849

...There was a whole crowd of strangers to dinner at Mr. Hamilton's, among whom was Washington Irving, a man of about sixty, with large, beautiful eyes, a large, well-formed nose, a face still handsome, in which youthful little dimples and smiles bear witness to a youthfully fresh and humorous disposition and soul. He is also said to have an unusually happy temperament and a most excellent heart. He has surrounded himself with a number of nieces (he says he cannot conceive of what use boys are in this world) whom he makes happy, and who make him so by their affection. They say he has the peculiar faculty of liking everything which he possesses, and everything that seeks his protection. He is an optimist, but not a conceited one.

He was my neighbor at table, and I did not blame him for becoming sleepy; nor did I feel responsible this time when people told me that he was accustomed to be sleepy at big dinners, at which I certainly am not surprised. But the dinner to-day was not one of those long and tedious ones; besides, he visibly endeavored to make the conversation interesting and agreeable; and I, too, did my best, as you may easily suppose, but we did not succeed very well.

In the afternoon I begged him to allow me to take a profile likeness of him; and, in order that he might not go to sleep during the operation, I asked Angelica Hamilton to sit opposite him and talk to him. The plan succeeded excellently. The handsome old gentleman now became wide awake, loquacious and lively, and there was such vivacity in his smile, and so much fun in all the merry dimples of his countenance, that it is my own fault if I have not made one of the best and most characteristic portraits that have ever been taken of this universally beloved author. I am glad to have

From *America of the Fifties: Letters of Fredrika Bremer,* published by The American-Scandinavian Foundation, New York, 1924. Reprinted by permission of The American-Scandinavian Foundation.

it to show to his friends and admirers in Sweden. Washington Irving invited me and my friends to his house for the following day, and in the forenoon I paid him a visit. His house or villa, which stands on the banks of the Hudson, resembles a peaceful idyll; thick masses of ivy clothe one portion of the white walls and garland the eaves. Fat cows graze in a meadow right before the window. Within, the room seemed full of summer warmth and peace, and gave the appearance of something living. One felt that a cordial spirit, full of the best sentiments of the soul, lived and worked there. Washington Irving, although possessed of the politeness of a man of the world, and with abundant natural good temper, has nevertheless some of that natural shyness which so easily attaches itself to the author of the better and more refined type. The poetical mind, through its intercourse with the divine spheres, is often brought into disharmony with clumsy earthly realities. To these belong especially the visits of strangers and the forms of social intercourse, such as we employ in good society on earth, and which are shells that must be cracked if one would get at the juice of either kernel or fruit. But that is a difficulty for which one often has no time. A portrait which hangs in Washington Irving's drawing-room, and which was painted many years ago, represents him as a remarkably handsome man with dark eyes and hair—a head which might have belonged to a Spaniard. He must have been exceptionally handsome as a young man. He was engaged to a young lady of rare beauty and excellence; it would have been difficult to meet a handsomer pair. But she died, and Washington Irving never again sought another bride. He has been wise enough to content himself with the memory of a perfect love and to live for literature, friendship, and nature. He is a sage without wrinkles or gray hair. Irving was at this time occupied with his *Life of Mahomet,* which will shortly be sent to press.

EARL CONRAD

Harriet Tubman

Although the time of Harriet Tubman's beginning as a slave is without certainty the *times* are not; and that is more important to the understanding of this woman than the detail of a date.

From *Harriet Tubman* by Earl Conrad. Published by Associated Publishers, Washington, D. C., 1943.

She was born during he dark and starless night of slavery, probably in the year 1820. The place of origin was Bucktown, a village of a few hundred persons, in Dorchester County, Maryland. Harriet was the property of a plantation owner....

...In the America of Harriet's grandparents, the Underground Railroad, of which Harriet became the guiding genius, was already taking root. On to the North, on to Canada. This became the primary thought of the blacks, uniting them, giving them a common aspiration. And at night, over special paths and with secret aid, they went....

Harriet never had a day of schooling. She was suddenly ripped out of infancy and placed in slave labor. At five she knew what it was to have a mistress, to keep house, to take care of a baby, to labor day and night, and to feel all of the callous injury that some indifferent white souls in the South of that time leveled upon their human fellows....

Harriet at the age of nine, for example, was hired out as a nurse and general houseworker. After slaving all day she was required to attend the baby at night. Her mistress was particularly cruel and whipped her as often as five or six times a day. When Harriet was nearly starved to death and was unable to perform her tasks she was sent home to her master....

By the time she was twelve or thirteen she had won a victory for she no longer had to work indoors. During the remainder of her slavery she farmed, wearing a bandana to protect her head from the sun; and her skirts, getting longer, brushed against the upturned earth. In the neighboring fields were her brothers and she could wave to them, or sing a song and hear an answering chant a moment later. She could go down to the cabin and get a drink and say a kind word to her mother or one of her little sisters, and if when she returned to her post in the field the overseer objected she jarred him with her defiance....

Harriet Tubman, the escaped slave woman, was...once more trampling upon the hated Fugitive Slave Law. Black as plumbago, her small, fierce carriage eloquent with strength like a creature of the wildwood, she was leading the citizens of the town of Troy, New York, teaching them how to deliver a body blow to slavery. Cool brisk the day, noon sunny the hour, and the time, April 27, 1860.

Her presence in that town might have been called accidental, but her leadership of the anti-slavery action was not. En route to Boston to meet with the Abolitionists...she stopped in Troy to visit a relative; a fugitive slave case had arisen during her presence and she organized the present demonstration. The fury of the Negro woman was the match struck to one of the fiercest outbreaks after John Brown's raid on Harper's Ferry and prior to the Civil War. The demand was that the fugitive mulatto, Charles Nalle, be seized from the hands of the Federal law and spirited away to freedom.

As the pack of cause-stricken anti-slavers swarmed into the street below the courtroom, and the pro-slavers crushed against them, political temperature and bodily heat mounted, and from the pavement the sun was blotted out. Harriet's brood was out there ready to live or die for Charles Nalle.

Eclipse of the business center became complete. The Trojans poured into the commercial area, many bearing arms that had been hanging on walls ever since the revolt from the British. Anxious eyes lifted to the second story of the drab, wooden building at State and First Streets where through the window, whose panes trembled from the tension below, the townspeople saw the figures in the slave case. Work stopped as all business closed in a spontaneous standstill. Keys turned in store doors. Running feet, clenched fists pointed toward the town center, now a marketplace, a man's life the article for sale, and the Northern law prepared to abide by its contract with the South.

At this minute General Tubman employed the effective ruse that she often used in her night-time operations on the Underground. Posted at the open door of the small courtroom, jackknifed into the crouch of a crippled and weak old lady, her intense ebon face covered by the strands of a shawl converted into a bonnet, and shielded by a nearby empty food basket which she maneuvered about her head, she whined to be admitted into the room. Being short she could posture decrepitude; but beneath this masked aspect of anility she was tensed as a tiger, and like a tiger, ready to spring.

...Holding faintly to the broad guard's coat lapel as if to touch him by kindness, smiling gently and lifting her sable brows so that lines appeared in her forehead, she transformed her normally vigorous appearance into the mask of an octogenarian. Anguished of eye, wizened of body, she clung to two strong colored women who feigned supporting her. The guard was touched and he fell silent....

Planting themselves at strategic spots in the throng, Abolitionists, Negro and white, enspirited the crowd, and one Negro, William Henry, who had never orated publicly before, discovered that he had a natural eloquence to hold a crowd.

...Bill Henry only said, "There is a fugitive in that office. Pretty soon you will see him come forth. He's going to be taken down South, and you'll have a chance to see him. He is to be taken to the depot, to go to Virginia in the first train."...

Soon the murmurings for a forcible rescue became a clamor for immediate action. At the courtroom door, moaning like some helpless wind lost in a forest, Harriet listened to the roar in the street and viewed the scene in court. She waited for the right instant, measured every slightest motion, each developing factor, and waved the basket, shield-like before her eyes.

She gazed incredulously at the witness from Virginia who was bringing the evidence against prisoner Charles Nalle. The Southern agent was the brother of the accused! A rare thing, but it happened sometimes; one could speculate that the agent was a free Negro or perhaps an especially favored slave of his master. The Virginian looked like the accused Negro; both were mulatto, but the testifying brother looked almost white.

The prisoner was about thirty, good-looking, intelligent of appearance, unnerved by his ordeal; and now he paced about before the tremoring window and looked down upon the whirlpool of friends and enemies. Perceiving that he had suddenly become a *cause célèbre,* and encouraged by the manifestation of sympathy that thundered from the marketplace, he weighed his chances for escape. The stake was high; the cost might be death. The fugitive Daniel had been sent back to slavery from Buffalo; Hamlet had been captured in New York after a grim pursuit; but Shadrach had escaped to Canada, spirited there; and Ellen Craft, beautiful quadroon, had successfully fled to England with her husband William Craft. He looked down into the throng and realized that he had odds; that the time was later than he thought; it was 1860 and the Fugitive Law was old and hated now; here in Troy was enough anti-slavery sentiment to give him a two to one chance. Others had lost; he might win; and win or lose, it was better than slavery. A daring thought placed itself in his forehead....

When, with a provincial majesty, the inevitable decision against Nalle was pronounced, as the guards began to squirm, and as Harriet's deep groan of protest suffused the room like a chant, Nalle leaped to action. He turned swiftly as a wheel, darted toward the window with a half dive, opened it with a fleet movement of his gray-white wrists, and stepped out on the ledge. As yells of welcome greeted him from the street, he twisted himself into position for a dangerous drop to the pavement.

"The crowd at this time numbered nearly a thousand persons," said the *Troy Whig*. "Many of them were black, and a good share were of the female sex. They blocked up State Street from First Street to the alley, and kept surging to and fro." Nor was it accidental that many of the anti-slavers were women; for women like the Negroes were on the high road, too, grasping for suffrage, seeing in the anti-slavery struggle a stepping stone to their own freedom, and so, throwing themselves into such struggle, into the bloody street scenes, into the great fugitive cases.

The guards soon bayed the prisoner; hands encircled his neck, his sprawling limbs, his whole body, and they hauled him back into the offices of the Commissioner and held to him like crabs to food. Aching for breath in their hard grasp, Charles Nalle subsided; and he looked for help to the swaying Negro women who filled the doorway with their bodies and their bursts of lament at his recapture.

Harriet had straightened up during the fugitive's attempted flight, and she was prepared to barricade the door if the law attempted to come through and go down the stairs to recover him.... Nalle had moved not quickly enough, she decided; so she resumed her patient crouch, moaning like a calm breeze that could not possibly whip up into anything stronger.

... While Attorney Martin Townsend for the prisoner hurried to a nearby office to appeal the judgment, the situation in the courtroom, presided over by Commissioner Beach, was stalemated; in here there was nothing but tension, two brothers glowering upon each other with a hate deep as death, an "old lady" waiting to rediscover her youth, an unnerved judge who peered outside at the expanding scene, the most historic in Troy, and the law grasping onto the convicted man's wrists with pressure that turned the mulatto's color white as newlaid paint.

As numbers spiral when they are multiplied so the crowd enlarged until the thousands merged and flowed, a great social and human tide. Suddenly there arose from the street a last desperate cry that cracked into the courtroom like a flame, *"We will buy his freedom. What is his master's price?"*

The Southern agent leaped to the rattling window, ready to strike a bargain. Money for flesh. Flesh for money. That was different. Flesh might not be higher than law, but money was.

"Twelve hundred dollars," shouted the Virginian.

Pools of citizens eddied with a new excitement as pouches flashed into the open and pledges loosed on the air. The well-to-do gave richly, and the poor heroically. Two hundred was mounted by three hundred more; a wave of notes and a jangle of silver lifted the sum to a thousand. Soon, like all tides that reach the shore, there was a mighty surf of final contribution.

"We have raised twelve hundred dollars!"

But the slaveowner's agent was avaricious, and he shouted back at the throng, *"Fifteen hundred dollars!"* ...

The anti-slavers pressed forward, ready to give their lives if need be in the name of Freedom.

Simultaneously Martin Townsend returned with an order calling for the fugitive's immediate appearance before the judge of the Supreme Court. A husky deputy sheriff presented the paper; the Commissioner read it; and there was no alternative for the law but to undertake to deliver Charles Nalle to the higher court at once.

Harriet unraveled some of the kinks in her slight body. As several guards and deputies manacled the prisoner and headed toward the door, ordering onlookers aside, she arose to her full height, which was not impressive, sent the basket reeling and bumping into a corner, magically dropped her aged appearance, and fleet-footed across the courtroom to the window. Her words, declaiming on the Troy air like some tonal bell in a hollow steeple, became the cue for the Abolitionists.

"Here he comes! Take him!"

She sped back to the door, with skirt flying and bonnet waving like a banner, glided down the stairway like a path of flame, and entered into the volcanic street, overtaking the guards with the demand that was nearest the heart of the North.

"This man shall not go back to slavery! Take him, friends! Drag him to the river! Drown him! But don't let them take him back!"

Adroitly Harriet gave directions to the battle. She wanted Nalle steered toward the river where by pre-arrangement a boat would whisk him across the cold water to temporary freedom in Albany County. As she shouted challenges and directions she locked her iron arms under the manacled bleeding wrist of Nalle, and began pulling him out of the lock-strong hands of his guards.

Oaken clubs and chisels struck against human heads and pistols blazed. Abolitionist, anti-slaver and sympathizer crushed with the pro-slavers and blood washed the Troy streets that afternoon.

"In the melee she was repeatedly beaten over the head with policeman's clubs, but she never for a moment released her hold, but cheered Nalle and his friends with her voice, and struggled with the officers until they were literally worn out with their exertions, and Nalle was separated from them. . . ."

When after long attack, and after the fighting throng had swept down the town's blocks toward the river, and when the power of the police and the pro-slavers was smashed, Harriet, still clinging to Nalle, broke away, dashed to the river front, and protected by a brave band of hurt and bleeding whites and Negroes, placed the prisoner in a skiff manned by a sympathetic ferryman.

Harriet, who had fought the enemy in scores of battles, knew his tactics, his reserves, his cunning. She foresaw the possibility of the recapture of Nalle on the other shore and rallied the anti-slavers for a trip across the river. As the *Troy Whig* described it: "Then there was another rush for the steam ferry boat; which carried four hundred persons and left as many more—a few of the latter being doused in their efforts to get on the boat."

The prisoner, who was almost unconscious from his injuries, himself having fought furiously, was captured as soon as he reached the other shore, and there he was rushed to Police Justice Stewart's office. The law threw up barricades and prepared to fight anew.

With Harriet Tubman in the forefront, the conflict became sharpest and bloodiest at this point. "Not a moment was lost. Upstairs went a score or more of resolute men—the rest piling in promiscuously, shouting and execrating the officers." Stones flew against the door, pistol shots came from the guards inside. There was a momentary retreat until someone shouted, "They can only kill a dozen of us—come on!" The citadel was stormed, amidst a hail of thrown stones and a returning theme of gunfire.

"At last," said *The Whig,* "the door was pulled open by an immense Negro and in a moment he was felled by the hatchet in the hands of Deputy Sheriff Morrison; but the body of the fallen man blocked up the door so that it could not be shut...."

Attorney Martin Townsend has said the last word. "...and when the men who led the assault upon the door of Judge Stewart's office were stricken down, Harriet and a number of other colored women rushed over their bodies, brought Nalle out, and putting him into the first wagon passing, started him for the West...."

HENRY JAMES

"Saratoga"

Its two main features are the two monster hotels which stand facing each other along a goodly portion of its course. One, I believe, is considered much better than the other,—less of a monster and more of a refuge,—but in appearance there is little choice between them. Both are immense brick structures, directly on the crowded, noisy street, with vast covered piazzas running along the facade, supported by great iron posts. The piazza of the Union Hotel, I have been repeatedly informed, is the largest "in the world." There are a number of objects in Saratoga, by the way, which in their respective kinds are the finest in the world. One of these is Mr. John

Published in *The Nation,* August 11, 1870.

Morrissey's casino. I bowed my head submissively to this statement, but privately I thought of the blue Mediterranean, and the little white promontory of Monaco, and the silver-gray verdure of olives, and the view across the outer sea toward the bosky cliffs of Italy. The Congress waters, too, it is well known, are excellent in the superlative degree; this I am perfectly willing to maintain.

The piazzas of these great hotels may very well be the biggest of all piazzas. They have not architectural beauty; but they doubtless serve their purpose—that of affording sitting-space in the open air to an immense number of persons. They are, of course, quite the best places to observe the Saratoga world. In the evening, when the "boarders" have all come forth and seated themselves in groups, or have begun to stroll in (not always, I regret to say, to the sad detriment of the dramatic interest, bisexual) couples, the big heterogeneous scene affords a great deal of entertainment. Seeing it for the first time, the observer is likely to assure himself that he has neglected an important item in the sum of American manners. The rough brick wall of the house, illumined by a line of flaring gaslights, forms a natural background to the crude, impermanent, discordant tone of the assembly. In the larger of the two hotels, a series of long windows open into an immense parlour—the largest, I suppose, in the world, and the most scantily furnished in proportion to its size. A few dozen rocking-chairs, an equal number of small tables, tripods to the eternal ice-pitcher, serve chiefly to emphasize the vacuous grandeur of the spot. On the piazza, in the outer multitude, ladies largely prevail, both by numbers and (you are not slow to perceive) by distinction of appearance. The good old times of Saratoga, I believe, as of the world in general, are rapidly passing away. The time was when it was the chosen resort of none but "nice people." At the present day, I hear it constantly affirmed, "the company is dreadfully mixed."

JOHN BURROUGHS

A River View

A small river or stream flowing by one's door has many attractions over a large body of water like the Hudson. One can make a com-

From *Signs and Seasons* by John Burroughs. Published by Houghton, Mifflin & Company, Boston, 1886. Taken from *John Burroughs' America.* The Devin-Adair Company, New York, 1951.

panion of it; he can walk with it and sit with it, or lounge on its banks and feel that it is all his own. It becomes something private and special to him. You cannot have the same kind of attachment and sympathy with a great river; it does not flow through your affections like a lesser stream. The Hudson is a long arm of the sea, and it has something of the sea's austerity and grandeur. I think one might spend a lifetime upon its banks without feeling any sense of ownership in it or becoming at all intimate with it: it keeps one at arm's length. It is a great highway of travel and of commerce; ships from all parts of our seaboard plow its waters.

The river never seems so much a thing of life as in the spring when it first slips off its icy fetters. The dead comes to life before one's very eyes. The rigid, pallid river is resurrected in a twinkling. You look out of your window one moment, and there is that great, white, motionless expanse; you look again, and there in its place is the tender, dimpling, sparkling water. But if your eyes are sharp, you may have noticed the signs all the forenoon; the time was ripe, the river stirred a little in its icy shroud, put forth a little streak or filament of blue water near shore, made breathing holes. Then, after a while, the ice was rent in places, and the edges crushed together or shoved one slightly upon the other; there was apparently something growing more and more alive and restless underneath. Then suddenly the whole mass of the ice from shore to shore begins to move downstream—very gently, almost imperceptibly at first, then with a steady, deliberate pace that soon lays bare a large expanse of bright, dancing water. The island above keeps back the northern ice, and the ebb tide makes a clean sweep from that point south for a few miles until the return of the flood, when the ice comes back.

After the ice is once in motion, a few hours suffice to break it up pretty thoroughly. Then what a wild, chaotic scene the river presents: in one part of the day the great masses hurrying downstream, crowding and jostling each other and struggling for the right of way; in the other, all running upstream again, as if sure of escape in that direction. Thus they race up and down, the sport of the ebb and flow; but the ebb wins each time by some distance.

If the opening of the river is gentle, the closing of it is sometimes attended by scenes exactly the reverse.

A cold wave one December was accompanied by a violent wind, which blew for two days and two nights. The ice formed rapidly in the river, but the wind and waves kept it from uniting and massing. On the second day the scene was indescribably wild and forbidding; the frost and fury of December were never more vividly pictured: vast crumpled, spumy ice-fields interspersed with stretches of wildly agitated water, the heaving waves thick with forming crystals, the shores piled with frozen foam and pulverized floes. After the cold wave had spent itself and the masses had become united and stationary, the scene was scarcely less wild. I fancied the plain looked more like a field of lava and scoria than like a field of ice, an eruption from some huge frost volcano of the north. Or did it suggest that a battle had been fought there and that this wild confusion was the ruin wrought by the contending forces?

No sooner has the river pulled his icy coverlid over him than he begins to snore in his winter sleep. It is a singular sound. Thoreau calls it a "whoop," Emerson a "cannonade" and in "Merlin" speaks of

the gasp and moan
Of the ice-imprisoned flood.

Sometimes it is a well-defined grunt—*e-h-h, e-h-h,* as if some ice god turned uneasily in his bed.

One fancies the sound is like this, when he hears it in the still winter nights seated by his fireside or else when snugly wrapped in his own bed.

One winter the river shut up in a single night, beneath a cold wave of great severity and extent. Zero weather continued nearly a week, with a clear sky and calm, motionless air; and the effect of the brilliant sun by day and of the naked skies by night upon this vast area of new black ice, one expanding it, the other contracting, was very marked.

A cannonade indeed! As the morning advanced, out of the sunshine came peal upon peal of soft mimic thunder; occasionally becoming a regular crash, as if all the ice batteries were discharged at once. As noon approached the sound grew to one continuous mellow roar, which lessened and became more intermittent as the day waned, until about sundown it was nearly hushed. Then, as the chill of night came on, the conditions were reversed, and the ice began to thunder under the effects of contraction; cracks opened from shore to shore and grew to be two or three inches broad under the shrinkage of the ice. On the morrow the expansion of the ice often found vent in one of these cracks; the two edges would first crush together and then gradually overlap each other for two feet or more.

This expansive force of the sun upon the ice is sometimes enormous. I have seen the ice explode with a loud noise and a great commotion in the water, and a huge crack shoot like a thunderbolt from shore to shore, with its edges overlapping and shivered into fragments.

When unprotected by a covering of snow, the ice, under the expansive force of the sun, breaks regularly, every two or three miles, from shore to shore. The break appears as a slight ridge, formed by the edges of the overlapping ice.

This icy uproar is like thunder, because it seems to proceed from something in swift motion; you cannot locate it; it is everywhere and yet nowhere. There is something strange and phantomlike about it. To the eye all is still and rigid, but to the ear all is in swift motion.

A fall of snow, and this icy uproar is instantly hushed, the river sleeps in peace. The snow is like a coverlid, which protects the ice from the changes of temperature of the air and brings repose to its uneasy spirit.

When the river is at its wildest, usually in March, the eagles appear. They prowl about amid the ice floes, alighting upon them or flying heavily above them in quest of fish or a wounded duck or other game.

I have counted ten of these noble birds at one time, some seated grim and motionless upon cakes of ice—usually surrounded by crows—others flapping along, sharply scrutinizing the surface beneath. Where the eagles are, there the crows do congregate. The crow follows the eagle, as the jackal follows the lion, in hope of getting the leavings of the royal table. Then I suspect the crow is a real hero worshiper. I have seen a dozen or more of them sitting in a circle about an eagle upon the ice, all with their faces turned toward him and apparently in silent admiration of the dusky king.

Of the Hudson it may be said that it is a very large river for its size—that is, for the quantity of water it discharges into the sea. Its watershed is comparatively small—less, I think, than that of the Connecticut.

It is a huge trough with a very slight incline, through which the current moves very slowly and which would fill from the sea were its supplies from the mountains cut off. Its fall from Albany to the bay is only about five feet. Any object upon it, drifting with the current, progresses southward no more than eight miles in twenty-four hours. The ebb tide will carry it about twelve miles, and the flood set it back from seven to nine. A drop of water at Albany, therefore, will be nearly three weeks in reaching New York, though it will get pretty well pickled some days earlier.

Some rivers by their volume and impetuosity penetrate the sea, but here the sea is the aggressor and sometimes meets the mountain water nearly halfway.

This fact was illustrated a few years ago, when the basin of the Hudson was visited by one of the most severe droughts ever known in this part of the State. In the early winter, after the river was frozen over above Poughkeepsie, it was discovered that immense numbers of fish were retreating upstream before the slow encroachment of the salt water. There was a general exodus of the finny tribes from the whole lower part of the river; it was like the spring and fall migration of the birds or the fleeing of the population of a district before some approaching danger: vast swarms of catfish, white and yellow perch, and striped bass were *en route* for the fresh water farther north. When people alongshore made the discovery, they turned out as they do in the rural districts when the pigeons appear, and, with small gill nets let down through holes in the ice, captured them in fabulous numbers. On the heels of the retreating perch and catfish came the denizens of salt water, and codfish were taken ninety miles above New York. When the February thaw came and brought up the volume of fresh water again, the sea brine was beaten back, and the fish, what was left of them, resumed their old feeding grounds.

According to Professor Newberry, that part of our coast that flanks the mouth of the Hudson is still sinking at the rate of a few inches per century, so that in the twinkling of a hundred thousand years or so the sea will completely submerge the city of New York, the top of Trinity Church steeple alone standing above the flood. We who live so far inland and sigh for the salt water need only to have a little patience, and we shall wake up some fine morning and find the surf beating upon our doorsteps.

The Friendly Rocks

I find there is enough of the troglodyte in most persons to make them love the rocks and the caves and ledges that the air and the rains have carved out of them.

The rocks are not so close akin to us as the soil; they are one more remove from us; but they lie back of all and are the final source of all. I do not suppose they attract us on this account, but on quite other grounds. Rocks do not recommend the land to the tiller of the soil, but they recommend it to those who reap a harvest of another sort—the artist, the poet, the walker, the student and lover of all primitive open-air things.

Time, geologic time, looks out at us from the rocks as from no other objects in the landscape. Geologic time! How the striking of the great clock, whose hours are millions of years, reverberates out of the abyss of the past! Mountains fall and the foundations of the earth shift as it beats out the moments of terrestrial history. Rocks have literally come down to us from a foreworld. The youth of the earth is in the soil and in the trees and verdure that spring from it; its age is in the rocks; in the great stone book of the

From *Under the Apple Trees* by John Burroughs. Published by Houghton, Mifflin & Company, Boston, 1916. Used with permission of the publisher.

geologic strata its history is written. Even if we do not know our geology, there is something in the face of a cliff and in the look of a granite boulder that gives us pause and draws us thitherward in our walk.

The rocks have a history; gray and weatherworn, they are veterans of many battles; they have most of them marched in the ranks of vast stone brigades during the ice age; they have been torn from the hills, recruited from the mountaintops, and marshaled on the plains and in the valleys; and now the elemental war is over, there they lie waging a gentle but incessant warfare with time and slowly, oh, so slowly, yielding to its attacks! I say they lie there, but some of them are still in motion, creeping down the slopes or out from the claybanks, nudged and urged along by the frosts and the rains and the sun. It is hard even for the rocks to keep still in this world of motion, but it takes the hour hand of many years to mark their progress. What in my childhood we called "the old pennyroyal rock," because pennyroyal always grew beside it, has, in my time, crept out of the bank by the roadside three or four feet. When a rock, loosened from its ties in the hills, once becomes a wanderer, it is restless ever after and stirs in its sleep. Heat and cold expand and contract it and make it creep down an incline. Hitch your rock to a sunbeam and come back in a hundred years and see how much it has moved. I know a great platform of rock weighing hundreds of tons and large enough to build a house upon, that has slid down the hill from the ledges above and that is pushing a roll of turf before it as a boat pushes a wave, but stand there till you are gray, and you will see no motion; return in a century and you will doubtless find that the great rock raft has progressed a few inches. What a sense of leisure such things give us hurrying mortals!

MARIETTA HOLLEY

Adventures at Various Springs

A few days after this Josiah Allen came in, an sez he, "The Everlastin' spring is the one for me, Samantha! I believe it will keep me alive for hundreds and hundreds of years."

Sez I, "I don't believe that, Josiah Allen."

From *Samantha at Saratoga* by Josiah Allen's Wife. Published by A. L. Burt Company, New York, 1887.

"Wall, it is so, whether you believe it or not. Why, I see a feller jest now who sez he don't believe anybody would ever die at all, if they kep' themselves kinder wet through all the time with this water."

Sez I, "Josiah Allen, you are not talkin' Bible. The Bible sez, 'all flesh is as grass.' "

"Wall, that is what he meant; if the grass wuz watered with that water all the time it wouldn't never wilt."

"Oh, shaw!" sez I. (I seldom say shaw, but this seemed to me a time for shawin'.)

But Josiah kep' on, for he wuz fearfully excited. Sez he, "Why, the feller said there wuz a old man who lived right by the side of this spring, and felt the effects of it inside and out all the time, it wuz so healthy there. Why, the old man kep' on a -livin' and a-livin' till he got to be a hundred. And he wuz kinder lazy naturally, and he got tired of livin'. He said he wuz tired of gettin' up mornin's and dressin' of him, tired of pullin' on his boots and drawin' on his trowses, and he told his grandson Sam to take him up to Troy and let him die.

"Wall, Sam took him up to Troy, and he died right away, almost. And Sam, bein' a good-hearted chap, thought it would please the old man to be buried down by the spring, that healthy spot. So he took him back there in a wagon he borrowed. And when he got clost to the spring, Sam heard a sithe, and he looked back, and there the old gentleman wuz a-settin' up and a-leanin' his head on his elbo, and he sez, in a sort of a sad way, not mad, but melancholly, 'You hadn't ort to done it, Sam. You hadn't ort to. I'm in now for another hundred years.' "

I told Josiah I didn't believe that. Sez I, "I believe the waters are good, very good, and the air is healthy here in the extreme, but I don't believe that."

But he said that it wuz a fact, and the feller said he could prove it. "Why," Josiah sez, "with the minerals there is in that spring, if you only take enough of it, I don't see how anybody can die." And sez Josiah, "I am a-goin' to jest live on that water while I am here."

"Wall," sez I, "you must do as you are a-mind to, with fear and tremblin'."

I thought mebby quotin' Scripter to him would kinder quell him down, for he wuz fearfully agitated and wrought up about the Everlastin' spring. And he begun at once to calculate on it, on how much he could drink of it, if he begun early in the mornin' and drinked late at night.

But I kep' on megum. I drinked the waters that seemed to help me and made me feel better, but wuz megum in it, and didn't get overexcited about any on 'em. But oh! oh! the quantities of that water that Josiah Allen took!

Why, it seemed as if he would make a perfect shipwreck of his own body, and wash himself away, till one day he came in fearful excited ag'in, and sez he, in agitated axents, "I made a mistake, Samantha. The Immortal spring is the one for me."

"Why?" sez I.

"Oh, I have jest seen a feller that has been a-tellin' me about it."

"What did he say?" sez I, in calm axents.

"Wait, I'll tell you. It has acted on my feelin's dretful." Sez he, "I have shed some tears." (I see Josiah Allen had been a-cryin' when he came in.)

And I sez ag'in, "What is it?"

"Wall," he said, "this man had a dretful sick wife. And he wuz a-carryin' her to the Immortal spring jest as fast as he could, for he felt it would save her, if he could get her to it. But she died a mile and a half from the spring. It wuz night, for he had traveled night and day to get her there, and the taverns wuz all shut up, and he laid her on the spring-house floor, and laid down himself on one of the benches. He took a drink himself, the last thing before he laid down, for he felt that he must have sunthin' to sustain him in his affliction.

"Wall, in the night he heard a splashin', and he rousted up and he see that he had left the water kinder careless the night before, and it had broke loose and covered the floor, and riz up round the body, and there she wuz, all bright and hearty, a-splashin' and a-swimmin' round in the water." He said the man cried like a child when he told him of it.

And sez Josiah, "It wuz dretful affectin'. It brought tears from me to hear on't. I thought what if it had been you, Samantha!"

"Wall," sez I, "I don't see no occasion for tears, unless you would have been sorry to had me brung to."

"Oh!" sez Josiah, "I didn't think! I guess I have cried in the wrong place."

Sez I, coldly, "I should think as much."

And Josiah put on his hat and hurried out. He meant well. But it is quite a nack for pardners to know jest when to cry and when to laff.

Wall, he follered up that spring, and drinked more, fur more than wuz good for him of that water. And then, anon, he would hear of another one, and some dretful big story about it, and he would foller that up, and so it went on, he a-follerin' on, and I a-bein' megum, and drinkin' stiddy but moderate. And as it might be expected, I gained in health every day and every hour. For the waters is good, there hain't no doubt of it.

But Josiah takin' 'em as he did, bobbin' round from one to the other, drinkin' 'em at all hours of day and night, and floodin' himself out with 'em, every one on 'em—why, he lost strength and health every day, till

I felt truly, that if it went on much longer, I should go home in weeds. Not mullein, or burdock, or anything of that sort, but crape.

But at last a event occurred that sort a sot him to thinkin' and quelled him down some. One day we sot out for a walk, Josiah and Ardelia Tutt and me. And in spite of all my protestations, my pardner had drinked 11 glassfuls of the spring he wuz a-follerin' then. And he looked white round the lips as anything. And Ardelia and I wuz a-settin' in a good shady place, and Josiah a little distance off, when a man ackosted him, a man with black eyes and black whiskers, and sez, "You look pale, sir. What water are you a-drinkin'?"

And Josiah told him that at that time he wuz a-drinkin' the water from the Immortal spring.

"Drinkin' that water?" sez the man, startin' back horrified.

"Yes," sez Josiah, turnin' paler than ever, for the man's looks wuz skairful in the extreme.

"Oh! oh!" groaned the man. "And you are a married man?" he groaned out mournfully, a-lookin' pitifully at him. "With a family?"

"Yes," sez Josiah, faintly.

"Oh, dear," sez the man, "must it be so, to die, so—so—lamented?"

"To die!" sez Josiah, turnin' white jest round the lip.

"Yes, to die! Did you not say you had been a-drinkin' the water from the Immortal spring?"

"Yes," sez Josiah.

"Wall, it is a certain, a deadly poison."

"Hain't there no help for me?" sez Josiah.

"Yes," sez the man, "you must drink from the Live-forever spring at the other end of the village. That water has the happy effect of neutralizin' the poisons of the Immortal spring. If anything can save you, that can. Why," sez he, "folks that have been entirely broke down and made helpless and hopeless invalids, them that have been brung down on their death-beds by the use of that vile Immortal water, have been cured by a few glasses of the pure healin' waters of the Live-forever spring. I'd advise you for your own sake, and the sake of your family, who would mourn your ontimely decese, to drink from that spring at once."

"But," sez Josiah, with a agonized and hopeless look, "I can't drink no more now."

"Why?" sez the man.

"Because I don't hold any more. I don't hold but two quarts, and I have drinked 11 tumblerfuls now."

"Eleven glasses of that poison?" sez the man. "Wall, if it is too late, I am not to blame. I've warned you. Farewell," sez he, a-graspin' holt of Josiah's hand, "farewell forever. But if you do live," sez he, "if by a miracle you are saved, remember the Live-forever spring. If there is any help for you it is in them waters."

And he dashed away, for another stranger wuz approachin' the seen....

...But Josiah Allen didn't die. And this incident made him more megum. More as I wanted him to be. Why, you have to be megum in everything, no matter how good it is. Milk porridge, or the Bible, or anything. You can kill yourself on milk porridge if you drink enough. And you can set down and read the Bible till you grow to your chair and lose your eyesight.

EDMUND PEARSON

Steamboat Annie of Nyack

This story comes from many sources, and it is possible that the process of accretion has touched it up, gilded here and there its gold, or tinted its lilies. The fundamental facts are, I believe, true, but there may well be other versions of the tale. I give it with no additions of my own, but as it has been told to me.

Many years ago there lived somewhere along this left bank of the river, between Nyack and Piermont, a family whose members attained a certain raffish distinction like that of some of the folk described in Mark Twain's books about the Mississippi. This would have been toward the end of the Hudson River's busy steamboating days. The family—for convenience they may be called the Golgans—were seldom found on the side of the angels: the men were notable drinkers, and the women celebrated for frailty. The eldest daughter had such a reputation along the waterfront that she acquired the title of Steamboat Annie. (She should not be confused with a fiction and cinema character of later years called Tugboat Annie.) On the river, the name of Steamboat Annie was known from Albany to New York, and, as Miss Marlene Dietrich, in one of her motion pictures, said of the notorious lady she was impersonating, "One is not called Shanghai Lee-lee for being acquainted with only *one* gentleman!"

Steamboat Annie had a sister, Clementine, a very young girl, who showed every indication of surpassing even the remarkable good looks of Annie herself. Well-disposed neighbors and friends who deplored Annie's journey along the primrose path were much concerned lest the younger girl should follow in these lamentable ways and become an even more startling sinner. At last, however, before any wrongdoing had been observed in the conduct of the younger sister, she vanished from the scene, and Nyack and its neighborhood saw her nevermore.

Years—perhaps twenty of them—passed by, and one day a lawyer from Rockland County was refreshing himself in a hotel bar in New York. It might have been the St. Denis, a resort of foreigners and also the home of many a literary romance. There stood next to the lawyer a gentleman of foreign speech and manner, and the two drifted into conversation. Said the foreigner, "Your city amuses me, ver' much! So much that three days 'ave gone by since I arrive, and I have done nozzing. I am a barrister, from Belgium. Perhaps you could tell me, M'sieu, do you ever hear of a place called Nee-ack?"

"Nyack?" inquired the other, amused. "I know it well. I live not far from Nyack."

"Zat is fortunate," replied the Belgian lawyer. "Perhaps you could tell me of zees lady?"

And he showed him a bit of paper inscribed "Miss Annie Golgan."

"Yes, I know her, too."

The Belgian was enraptured. They sat together, ordered two more of the same, and the story was told. The foreign barrister was in New York, and was going to Nyack, as administrator of a will. A lady, an American lady, a very, very beautiful lady, had died somewhere in France or Belgium. She had been in her lifetime so fortunate as to arouse the interest and enlist the favor of no less a connoisseur of beautiful ladies than Leopold II, King of the Belgians, the old gentleman who possessed the long white beard, and was at a later date the patron of the beautiful Mlle. Cléo de Mérode.

His Majesty had bestowed many gifts upon the beautiful American lady. Many, many gifts. There had been a *petite maison* near Paris, which, by the terms of the lady's will, had already been sold and converted into cash. There were beautiful jewels, there were gowns (*magnifiques!*), and there were other moneys and other objects of value and beauty. Now, she had bequeathed all this property to her sister, who was Miss Annie Golgan of Nee-ack, New York, Etats-Unis d'Amérique du Nord.

Would his polite American *confrère* be so good as to guide the Belgian lawyer to Miss Annie Golgan? The American, who had seen what was coming, admitted that he could do so, and would. The two lawyers had another drink; they made an appointment to meet on the day after the morrow. The Belgian was having too good a time to hurry, and he was going that evening with some friends, to visit "Conee" Island, which he understood was very amusing. They should meet again in the same hotel, when the European, bearing bequests, would be introduced to the heiress and affairs would be arranged, all correct and proper.

The Rockland County lawyer was a man of action. He missed no single step. He dashed to Nyack. He called on the town clerk, on a justice of the peace, and on Steamboat Annie. This lady was now a little past her youthful prime, but still a fine figure of a woman, and had retired, at least officially, from the active practice of her profession. She was living in modest but comfortable circumstances at some place along the old riverfront which had been the scene of her greatest glory.

And when, on the next day but one, the Belgian lawyer again met his *cher confrère* at the hotel, he was introduced not to Miss Golgan but, said the American, to "My wife."

The Belgian stared and gasped for only an instant. Then his face became ecstatic. He warmly shook the hands of both, embraced the bridegroom, and gurgled his appreciation of the prudence and wisdom which had been displayed.

The will was administered, the bequests were paid, the money—tens and tens of thousands of francs—was transferred into a very substantial number of dollars. Some of the objects left in the will of the deceased sister were decidedly bulky, and one very important item had to be kept in the carriage house. The Belgian sailed away, and all seemed to be set for happiness.

Not complete happiness, however. Nyack could hardly forgive and forget. There was the bride's own career, and there was—as soon as the story came to be gossiped about—the strange and alluring, but wicked, source of all this wealth. So for a while the lawyer and his wife suffered social ostracism. No one called; no one invited them to parties.

At the end of a year of this chilliness, however, there came a big jamboree, a fireman's ball, to which everyone in Nyack—everyone who *was* anyone—simply must be asked. There was an air of civic spirit about it, a feeling of get-together. And the hitherto excluded pair duly received an invitation. They resolved to do the firemen proud.

On the evening of the ball, the town had a treat. One part of the great bequest, one mark of the royal favor bestowed on Nyack's long-vanished daughter, Mlle. Clémentine, had never been shown in public, never seen the light of day. It was the one kept in the carriage house. It was a gilt coach—one of the minor state coaches—belonging to the ruler of that European kingdom and by him presented to his *chérie*. Its owners now hired four white horses to draw it, and seated inside, the lady wearing one of the most fetching of her sister's gowns and adorned with the regal jewels, Mr. and Mrs. Steamboat Annie were conveyed to the ball, through the streets of Nyack, in the golden coach of His Majesty the King of the Belgians.

A. J. LIEBLING

River Men

River men are born in places like Kingston and Athens up the Hudson. Kingston men usually are pilots. Engineers belong to Athens, which is pronounced Aythens. The river men are of an America which is not New York. They say "narthing" when they mean "nothing." Harbor men say "nuttin." The Mississippi is said to breed bombast, but Hudson River men have a gift of understatement which is a more effective medium for remarkable lies. This is known as the deadpan or London Times system of prevarication. The Hudson is a river where wise men spawn. Arrived at maturity they go down to the sea in towboats. Judge from this story of Captain Billy Barnett's.

"I remember when I was a lad," Captain Billy once told me—he's almost eighty now—"I shipped in the schooner Benjamin Akin, carrying bluestone from Roundout Creek to Mount Vernon. We had to pass up Eastchester Creek to deliver our cargo, and the old man had never been up there so he hove to and waited for a pilot.

"After a piece an old feller come along and 'Captain,' he says, 'are you in want of a pilot? I been taking vessels up this creek all my life and I never been on a rock yet.'

" 'I'll be damned if I believe you know where the rocks are, then,' says the old man, and he wouldn't have him. Along come another old feller. 'Ever been on the rocks?' asks the old man. 'Been on every goddam rock in the creek,' he says. 'You're the man for me,' says the old man. 'You got experience.'

"When I was a boy," Captain Barnett remarked on another occasion, "it snowed and it blowed and it hailed and it made ice. The old Norwich, of the

Cornell Steamboat Company was built in 1836 and she was the greatest icebreaker on the river. She had a cross-head engine like the original Clermont and a high bow, and she would run way up on the ice and crash down on it, and sometimes she would fall over on her side.

"Then she'd sort of shake herself and get up and come down on that ice like a terrier worrying a rat and she'd clear a course through twenty inches of ice like a man would eat a buckwheat cake. Yes, sir, she was a remarkable boat." The antithesis of a remarkable boat, in Captain Billy's language, is "a boat that couldn't draw a shad out of a net," or "couldn't draw the slack out of a line."

The Hudson made New York, for after the opening of the Erie Canal in 1825 * and before the completion of the railroads into the West, all the produce of the Lakes region came through the canal and down the Hudson. ... By the time the railroads got going New York had such a headstart on the other centres of regional culture that the city has been on the chinstrap since, tincanning a mile in front of the field and without a challenger in sight. Hudson River men even today like to remind New Yorkers that the Hudson gave our town its bust at the gate.

* The author is not responsible for dates. He relies upon local word-of-mouth tradition for all of them.

20TH CENTURY

CHARLES NORMAN

[*Two poems about Saratoga*]

A Poem in Praise

Let us praise the morning raining birdsong,
The leaves that move like mobiles in the light,
The light that falls from the leaves
Like water flowing over sand,
The wind and light in the leaves
Like water flowing over stone,
And the air that flows like light
Till light and leaves are one.

Let us praise birds on echelon,
The ballet of pigeons on gravel or grass,
And birds alone morning and evening—
The hummingbird in the columbine,
The scissor barn swallow snipping dusk,
Or the pheasant uttering its hoarse, hollow cry
Trumpeting that trees are spurting red,
That leaves are ripe as fruit,
And the hills as full of hunters
As fleas in a setter's ear.

The naming of simple things
Is both praise and pleasure:
Crocuses burst like firecrackers;
Sea lavender fills the shore with spray;
Clouds break on the high hills like surf;
The little hills are beavers on a bank,
And the plash of a wave on the beach
Is like the plunge of a diver.

In the glooms and greens of the wood,
Sycamores are scrawled in chalk,
Bare boughs are wisps of light,
Bare trees, pen scratches in the sky.
Bell notes ripple the still air
Like pebbles cast in ponds.
Rain swarms over the roof like bees;
But on arched highways gleaming in the rain,
Where lights of cars ride by like lights of ships,
Bright wheels whisper the sea's sound.

Finally, let us praise the moon
That turns green meadows into silver lakes,
And the sun that rises crowing like a cock,
Pecking the mist and growing, to become
A pride of lions in a lair of gold,
And goes down like a ship on fire
By burning shoals at day's end
Far away in a lagoon of air.

The Lake

Massed green and silences
Stand guard around the lake;
Maple and the pensive pine
Both shade and shadow make.

Through windows of the wood,
Glooms and gold are seen,
Long boughs where lightfall lies,
Massed silences and green.

Bright-thighed birch and beech
Crowd down upon the shore,
To wade out of the wood,
Loving the lake more.

The water lies so still,
It could be shadow there
Of the still, blue sky
And the still, white air.

Over its placid depth,
A single bird glides past;
Within its shaded deep
Lie fish like shadows cast.

The water is so still,
It lies like silence there,
The silence of the wood
That treads its soft air.

Thin as ferns and fronds,
The woodland settles down,
Drowned in that still pool,
Where stars will stream and drown.

—Yaddo, Saratoga Springs

EDITH WHARTON

The Willows

"It's here," Upton said.

Vance had jokingly offered to accompany Upton to the Willows, and help him to dust Miss Lorburn's rooms, so that Laura Lou should not miss the movies. But Laura Lou, flushing crimson, replied in a frightened whisper that it wasn't true, that she wanted to go to the Willows, that she always

From *Hudson River Bracketed* by Edith Wharton. Published by D. Appleton and Company, New York, 1929.

did go when her mother couldn't—so Vance hired a bicycle at a near-by garage, and the three cousins set out.

Upton stopped before a padlocked gate overhung with trees. A deep green lane led up to it, so rutty and grass-grown that the cousins, jumping from their bicycles, climbed it on foot. Upton pulled out a key, unlocked the padlock of the gate, and led the way in, followed by Vance and Laura Lou. The house, which was painted a dark brown, stood at the end of a short grass-grown drive, its front so veiled in the showering gold-green foliage of two ancient weeping willows that Vance could only catch, here and there, a hint of a steep roof, a jutting balcony, an aspiring turret. The façade, thus seen in trembling glimpses, as if it were as fluid as the trees, suggested vastness, fantasy and secrecy. Green slopes of unmown grass, and heavy shrubberies of unpruned syringa and lilac, surrounded it; and beyond the view was closed in on all sides by trees and more trees. "An old house—this is the way an old house looks!" Vance thought.

The three walked up the drive, their steps muffled by the long grass and clover which had pushed up through the gravel. When the front of the house was before them, disengaged from the fluctuating veil of willows, Vance saw that it was smaller than he had expected; but the air of fantasy and mystery remained. Everything about the front was irregular, but with an irregularity unfamiliar to him. The shuttered windows were very tall and narrow, and narrow too the balconies, which projected at odd angles, supported by ornate wooden brackets. One corner of the house rose into a tower with a high shingled roof, and arched windows which seemed to simulate the openings in a belfry. A sort of sloping roof over the front door also rested on elaborately ornamented brackets, and on each side of the steps was a large urn of fluted iron painted to imitate stone, in which some half-dead geraniums languished.

While Upton unlocked the front door and went in with his sister, Vance wandered around to the other side of the building. Here a still stranger spectacle awaited him. An arcaded verandah ran across this front, and all about it, and reaching out above it from bracket to bracket, from balcony to balcony, a wistaria with huge distorted branches like rheumatic arms lifted itself to the eaves, festooning, as it mounted, every projecting point with long lilac fringes—as if, Vance thought, a flock of very old monkeys had been ordered to climb up and decorate the house-front in celebration of some august arrival. He had never seen so prodigal a flowering, or a plant so crippled and ancient; and for a while it took his attention from the house. But not for long. To bear so old a climber on its front, the house must be still older; and its age, its mystery, its reserve, laid a weight on his heart. He remembered once, at Euphoria, waking in the night—a thing which seldom happened to him—and hearing the bell of the Roman Catholic church slowly and solemnly toll the hour. He saw the church every day on his way to school: a narrow fronted red brick building with sandstone trim, and a sandstone cross over the gable; and though he had heard the bell time and time again its note had never struck him. But sounding thus through the hush of the night, alone awake in the sleeping town, it spoke to his wakefulness with a shock of mystery.

The same feeling came over him as he stood in the long grass before the abandoned house. He felt in the age and the emptiness of it something of the church bell's haunting sonority—as if it kept in its mute walls a voice as secret and compelling. If only he had known how to pull the rope and start the clapper swinging!

As he stood there the shutters were thrown back from one of the windows on the ground floor, and Upton leaned out to hail him. "Hul*lo!* Laura Lou thought the ghosts had got you."

"They had—almost," Vance laughed. He went up to the window and swung himself into the room. Upton had opened all the shutters, and the afternoon light flowed softly in. The room was not large, but its ceiling was high, with a dim cobwebby cornice. On the floor was a carpet with a design of large flower-wreaths and bows and loops of faded green. The mantelpiece, richly carved, was surmounted by a mirror reaching to the ceiling; and here and there stood pieces of furniture of a polished black wood inlaid with patterns of ivory or metal. There were tall vases on mantel and table, their flanks painted with landscapes in medallion, or garlanded with heavy wreaths like those on the carpet. On the mantelpiece Vance noticed a round-faced clock guarded by an old man in bronze with a scythe and an hour-glass; and stiffly ranged about the room were arm-chairs and small seats covered with a pale material slit and tattered with age. As Vance stood looking at it all Laura Lou appeared from another room. A long apron covered her from chin to knees, and she had tied a towel about her head, and carried a large feather duster.

"This is where she always sat," she whispered to Vance, signalling to him to follow. The room she led him into was more sombre than the other, partly because the wistaria had stretched a long drapery across one of the windows, partly because the walls were dark and had tall heavy bookcases against them. In a bow-window stood a table with a velvet table-cover trailing its faded folds and moth-eaten fringes on the floor. It bore a monumental inkstand, a bronze lamp with a globe of engraved glass, a work-basket, and two or three books. But what startled Vance, and made him, in his surprise, forget everything else, was the fact that one of the books lay open, and that across the page was a small pair of oddly-shaped spectacles in a thin gold mounting. It looked as if some one had been reading there a few minutes before, and, disturbed by the sound of steps, had dropped the book and spectacles and glided out of sight. Vance remembered Laura Lou's fear of ghosts, and glanced about him half apprehensively, as if the reader of that book, the wearer of those spectacles, might be peering at them from some shadowy corner of the room.

As he looked his eye fell on a picture hanging above the mantelpiece—a crayon drawing, he thought it must be, in a bossy and ponderous gilt frame. It was the portrait of a middle-aged woman, seen in three-quarter length. She leaned on a table with a heavy velvet cover, bearing an inkstand and some books—the very table and the very inkstand, Vance perceived, on which the picture itself looked down. And the lady, past a doubt, was Miss Lorburn: Miss Lorburn in her thoughtful middle age. She had dark hair, parted in heavy folds above a wide meditative forehead touched with high-lights in chalk. Her face was long and melancholy. The lappets of her lace cap fell on her shoulders, and her thin arms emerged from the wide sleeves of a dark jacket, with undersleeves of white lawn also picked out in chalk.

The peculiar dress, the sad face, resembled nothing Vance had ever seen; but instantly he felt their intimate relation to all that was peculiar and unfamiliar in the house. The past—they all belonged to the past, this woman and her house, to the same past, a past of their own, a past so remote from anything in Vance Weston's experience that it took its place in the pages of history anywhere in the dark Unknown before Euphoria was. He continued to gaze up at the sad woman, who looked down on him with large full-orbed eyes, as if it were she who had just dropped her book and spectacles, and re-ascended to her frame as he came in....

He turned from the portrait and looked about the room, trying vainly to picture what this woman's life had been, in her solemn high-ceilinged house, alone among her books. He thought of her on winter evenings, sitting at this table, beside the oil-lamp with the engraved globe, her queer little spectacles on that long grave nose, poring, poring over the pages, while the wind wailed down the chimney and the snow piled itself up on the lawns. And on summer evenings she sat here too, probably—he could not picture her out of doors; sat here in a slanting light, like that now falling through the wistaria fringes, and leaned her sad head on her hand, and read and read....

...The steps and voices of his cousins had died away. The very afternoon light seemed to lie arrested on the page. He seemed to have been sitting there a long time, in this unmoving ecstasy, when something stirred near him, and raising his head he saw a girl standing in the door and looking at him....

...Then he saw that she was young, tall and pale, with dark hair banded close under her drooping hat. There was something about her, he saw also, that fitted into the scene, seemed to mark her as a part of it, though he was instantly aware of her being so young, not much older than himself, he imagined. But what were time and space at that moment?...

He flushed up, and for the first time looked at her with full awareness of her presence as a stranger, and an intruder on his dream. The look confirmed him in the impression that she was very young, though probably two or three years older than himself. But it might be only her tallness and self-assurance which made him think her older. She had dark gray eyes, deeply lashed, and features somewhat too long and thin in repose, but rounded and illumined by a smile which flashed across her face in sudden sympathy or amusement....

...His eyes followed hers about the crowded shelves. "I've never before been in a house with a library—a real library like this."

She gave a little shrug. "Oh, it's a funny library; antiquated, like the house. But cousin Elinor does seem to have cared for good poetry. When other ladies were reading 'Friendship's Garland' she chose Coleridge."

His gaze returned perplexed to her face. "Why do you call it a funny library?"

"Well, it's not exactly up-to-date. I suppose it's a fairly good specimen of what used to be called a 'gentleman's library' in my great-grandfather's time. With additions, naturally, from each generation. Cousin Elinor must have bought a good many books herself." She looked about her critically. "After all," she concluded with a smile, "the Willows is getting to have an atmosphere."

Vance listened, still perplexed. Her allusions escaped him—her smile was unintelligible—but he gathered that she attached no very great importance to the house, or to the books, and he dimly resented this air of taking for granted what to him was the revelation of an unknown world.

Involuntarily he lowered his voice. "It's the first time I've ever been in a very old house," he said, as if announcing something of importance.

"A very old house? The Willows?" The idea seemed a new one to her. "Well—after all, everything is relative, as what's-his-name said."

"Don't you call it a very old house?"

She wrinkled her dark eyebrows in an effort of memory. "Let me see. Father's great-uncle Ambrose Lorburn built it, I believe. When would that be?" She began to count on her fingers. "Say about 1830. Well, that *does* make it very nearly an old house for America, doesn't it? Almost a hundred years!"

"And the same folks always lived in it?"

"Oh, of course."... Again she surveyed the plaintive shadowy room. "I suppose," she mused, "the house will be getting to have an archaeological interest of its own before long. It must be one of the best specimens of Hudson River Bracketed that are left, even in our ultra-conservative neighbourhood."

To Vance she seemed still to be speaking another language, of which he caught only an occasional phrase, and even that but half comprehensible.

"Hudson River Bracketed?" he echoed. "What's that?"

"Why, didn't you know it was our indigenous style of architecture in this part of the world?" Her smile of mockery had returned, but he did not mind for he saw it was not directed against himself. "I perceive," she continued, "that you are not familiar with the epoch-making work of A. J. Downing Esqre on Landscape Gardening in America." She turned to the bookcases, ran her hand along a shelf, and took down a volume bound in black cloth with the title in gilt Gothic lettering. Her fingers flew from page to page, her short-sighted eyes following as swiftly. "Here—here's the place. It's too long to read aloud; but the point is that Mr. Downing, who was the great authority of the period, sums up the principal architectural styles as the Grecian, the Chinese, the Gothic, the Tuscan or Italian villa, and—Hudson River Bracketed. Unless I'm mistaken, he cites the Willows as one of the most perfect examples of Hudson River Bracketed (this was in 1842), and—yes, here's the place: 'The seat of Ambrose Lorburn Esqre, the Willows, near Paul's Landing, Dutchess County, N. Y., is one of the most successful instances of etc., etc.... architectural elements ingeniously combined from the Chinese and the Tuscan.'... And so they were! What an eye the man had. And here's the picture, willows and all! How lovely these old steel-engravings were... and look at my great-uncle and aunt on the lawn, pointing out to each other with pride and admiration their fairly obvious copper beech ...'one of the first ever planted in a gentleman's grounds in the United States.'..."

They bent their heads together over the engraving, which, as she said, reproduced the house exactly as Vance had just beheld it, except that the willows were then slender young trees, and the lawns mown, that striped awnings shaded the lower windows, and that a gentleman in a tall hat and a stock was calling the attention of a lady in bonnet and cashmere shawl to the celebrated copper beech.... Vance could not tell whether pride or mockery were uppermost in her comments on her ancestor's achievement. But he dimly guessed that, though she might laugh at the Willows, and at what Mr. Downing said of it, she was not sorry that the house figured so honourably in his book.

"There," she concluded with a laugh, "now you know what the Hudson River Bracketed style was like, and why uncle Ambrose Lorburn was so proud of his specimen of it."...

She disappeared in the spectral shadows of the drawing-room, and Vance heard her heels rapping lightly across the hall, and through unknown rooms and passages beyond. He sat motionless where she had left him, his elbows propped on the table, the book still open before him, his head pressed between his hands, letting the strangeness of the place and the hour envelop him like the falling light....

...He realized that instead of seizing the opportunity to explore every nook of it, he had sat all the afternoon in one room, and merely dreamed of what he might have seen in the others. But that was always his way: the least little fragment of fact was enough for him to transform into a palace of dreams, whereas if he tried to grasp more of it at a time it remained on his hands as so much unusable reality.

MARION EDEY

Where We Began

Many years later she went back to the house. There was our woods. That old stump was our apple tree. It was like looking through the wrong end of a spy glass: clear and distinct as ever but everything had unaccountably shrunk. She felt at the same time extremely large and extremely small. Taking advantage of a moment when there was no one in the library she drew out the magazine rack from its deep niche beside the fireplace and crawled with some difficulty into the dark recess which had at one time held both Noel and herself so comfortably. And running a remembering finger around the ledge at the back, found among several small withered secrets the most treasured secret of all, a sample box of beautiful

From *Early in the Morning* by Marion Edey.

pink pills given by Martha. They had faded almost white. Should she bury them in the melon bed? Should she take them away with her? Or eat them? In the end the box went back into its own tiny ring of dust.

No more summers at Danskammer. That Juggernaut, the brickyard, was inexorably coming nearer, leveling the Borrowpit, eating away the gravel bank, creeping toward the garden.

If the clock were turned back and if Noel were to come home—not singing, we trust, not plucking with unaccustomed thumbs the strings of a golden harp—we think he would look first to the welfare of the animals. And then with equal interest at his fruit trees and vines. And after that he would assuredly make his way down the hill and out along the small rocky point to the lighthouse which was for so many years an integral part of his daily life.

His Danskammer is over. The woods are edging in along the lane. A pheasant squawks in the orchard and woodchucks are at home in a garden tall with weeds. Below the churchyard, hylas shrill in April. The moonlight spreads like a fan over the graves and the pale river carries its trembling reflection. The wild geese follow the line of the water, flowing south on the wind of winter, a ribbon of pure beauty. The lighthouse is still there; but a lighthouse speaks only for itself and has only one thing to say: I am shining for you no longer.

Between sleeping and walking comes that moment of clarity which is like being born into a new day, pure and plain from top to bottom, all the riddles of life answered. Everything is clear now, as sharply defined as one of those charts of the muscles within an outline of the human body—asexual, or it might be with a fig leaf. Perhaps it is because we are living in history-making times that we feel shaken out of our groove—looking at life in the round.

What in the end can we bring from the past—a scene, a voice, a vision? Which words are true and which but half or wrongly remembered? Yet the over-all impression must be the right one: happiness, beauty and love.

Many years ago R. L. S. (not, from all accounts, the most orthodox of Christians) made a Thanksgiving prayer, often thought of and long remembered in the family.

Was it declaimed by Tusitala on the occasion of some glorious feast prepared in his honor by savage royalty? While the tropic stars blazed in a black velvet sky and the tropic wind rushed remotely through those strange treetops did he rise in his place, drinking a toast and pouring a libation? He must have glanced with affection along the row of dark-skinned friends;

and at his wife in her hollico and garland; and at the background of nearly-naked giants—freshly oiled and wreathed—each holding high a flaring torch to light the array of curious or delicious viands (no longer including long pig):

"...We thank Thee for this place in which we dwell; for the love that unites us; for the peace accorded us this day; for the hope with which we expect tomorrow....Courage and gaiety and the quiet mind...."

PHYLLIS McGINLEY

Small-Town Parade

DECORATION DAY

Below the lawns and picket fences,
  Just past the firehouse, half a block,
Sharp at eleven-five commences
  This ardent and memorial walk
  (Announced, last night, for ten o'clock).

Solemn, beneath the elmy arches,
  Neighbor and next-door neighbor meet.
For half the village forward marches
  To the school band's uncertain beat,
  And half is lined along the street.

O the brave show! O twirling baton!
  O drummer stepping smartly out!
O mayor, perspiring, with no hat on!
  O nurses' aid! O martial rout
  Of Bluebird, Brownie, Eagle Scout!

And at the rear, aloof and splendid,
  Lugging the lanterns of their pride,
O the red firemen, well attended
  By boys on bicycles who ride
  With envious reverence at their side!

The morning smells of buds and grasses.
  Birds twitter louder than the flute.
And wives, as the procession passes,
  Wave plodding husbands wild salute
  From porches handy to the route.

Flags snap. And children, vaguely greeted,
  Wander into the ranks a while.
The band, bemused but undefeated,
  Plays Sousa, pedagogic style,
  Clean to the Square—a measured mile.

Until at last by streets grown stony,
  To the gray monument they bring
The wreath which is less testimony
  To Death than Life, continuing
  Through this and every other spring.

THE CATSKILLS

19TH CENTURY

WASHINGTON IRVING

The Kaatskill Mountains

Whoever has made a voyage up the Hudson, must remember the Kaatskill mountains. They are a dismembered branch of the great Appalachian family, and are seen away to the west of the river, swelling up to a noble height, and lording it over the surrounding country. Every change of season, every change of weather, indeed every hour of the day produces some change in the magical hues and shapes of these mountains; and they are regarded by all the good wives, far and near, as perfect barometers. When the weather is fair and settled, they are clothed in blue and purple, and print their bold outlines on the clear evening sky; but sometimes, when the rest of the landscape is cloudless, they will gather a hood of gray vapors about their summits, which, in the last rays of the setting sun, will glow and light up like a crown of glory.

From *The Sketch Book* by Washington Irving. Published by G. P. Putnam's Sons, New York, 1822.

ORIANA ATKINSON

Freedom Ware

Up from the River, thirty miles back in the wilderness of the Catskills, the town of Atta was being born. Carved out of the mountainside

From *The Golden Season,* copyright 1953 by Oriana Atkinson, reprinted by special permission of the publishers, The Bobbs-Merrill Company, Inc.

by daring men riding west out of Connecticut, men already tired of the thin soil and stony farms of New England, this desolate, wildcat-ridden hill of York State had been changed into a homestead place. A man could stand on the trail above Atta and see the smoke from more than a dozen chimneys streaming upward into the bright blue sky.

It is a fine thing to be young in a young country. You could almost hear destiny on the march in the year 1803. The men and women of Atta were pretty puffed up over the progress they had made in ten short years. They had a sawmill now; nobody built log cabins any more. Newcomers had good slab houses. And a young fellow named Joe Haddock, up from Catskill, had opened a wagon-making shop—a crazy scheme, since the trail was not wide enough for even a cart.

"Kinda ahead of yourself," people said. "Got to have a road before you can start selling wagons."

Haddock didn't even bother to smile. "Never heard tell of the new Pike, did ye? Already started at the River and heading west fast. Going right dab through Atta. When she gits here I'll be waiting."

That was the spirit everywhere. Men hoped and believed and dared.

A fellow named Butts started a fulling mill—whatever *that* was. Well, it was a place where a woman could take her homespun and get it finished off as smooth as silk.

"Fine thing if a woman can't finish her own goods after she spinned and weaved it," men said scornfully. The women thought different. They were glad to be relieved of the tedious chore of shrinking and cleansing cloth, and the little fulling mill with its big spouts of steam and its tremendous irons had all the work it could do.

A couple of gristmills got into operation. Had patchy sledding at first, but they were looking to the time when the Pike would make it easy for crops to be brought to their doors.

There was a shingle factory; a blacksmith shop; and, best of all, a church, with its skinny steeple pointing to the heavenly home. There was no schoolhouse yet, but there was a school. Master Jordan and his wife Alice, from over Boston way, kept school in their big cabin at the turn of the trail, and eight children went to them every winter for learning.

The center and life of the whole community, however, was the Twin Cousins Inn, owned by a family named Ware. No need to go into all the ins and outs of how it got started. It was all more or less perchance, but it had been a roarer from the beginning. How could it help being, people asked, when one of the owners, Widow Gretchen Ware, was daughter to the great patroon Jan Von Smid? She had only to reach out her hand to bring it back full of gold. She was her father's cosset lamb, and he humored her in everything.

But if Jan Von Smid considered the tavern nothing but a play-toy of his Gretchen, the other owner, Luther Ware, a Yankee from Connecticut, was taking no guff from anybody, and that included the great patroon. The inn would stand on its own bottom, or Luther Ware wanted to know why.

He had been brought up in a hard school. His father, a tin peddler, had early taught his son the fundamentals of earning and keeping a shilling. Luther Ware, a handsome, upstanding black-bearded man of twenty, was now determined that the Twin Cousins should provide a living for him and his wife Content and daughter Freedom. And if the Widow Ware—she was no real kin, just widow of Potter Ware, cousin to Luther—if she was free-handed and lavish, the same could not be said of Luther, who knew how to cut corners and make a deal. The Dutch widow and the Connecticut Yankee made a good business team, probably because they were so different. Anyhow, they made a go of the tavern.

At three years of age Freedom Ware, only child of Luther and Content, was a dancing fairy of a child with dark silken hair that fell in a soft mane to her shoulders. Her eyes were deep blue and fringed with sooty lashes. She had an apple blossom of a face and a pale, soft mouth. Gretchen Ware, wealthy and loving, kept old Mistress Cunningham busy fashioning quaint gowns for Freedom. Even Biddy O'Brien, the kitchen drudge, an acid old hen, could not withstand Freedom Ware in a long silken dress held daintily high over deerskin shoes.

Many of the people of Atta were childless. Infants pined and died early in the bitter new country. Inflammation of the lungs, rickets, river fever and such swept many little ones away. And the hearts of the bereaved parents went out in pity and longing to the daughter of the inn. The rough men, hunters and trappers and movers who clumped through the Twin Cousins, acted as though Freedom was made of Venetian glass. They would kneel before her and thrust their dirty, grinning faces at her and growl, "Where'd ye get them big blue eyes?" and hand her an otter pelt or a wampum strip or some such trinket brought from miles away to please her. Many a tough old codger rode a long journey out of his way merely to catch a glimpse of Freedom and rode on, chuckling and nodding if he had so much as caught sight of her running through the taproom.

The new road being built to the West—the Susquehanna Turnpike—neared Atta, and to Freedom's permanent court were added Turnpikers and engineers and others connected with the making of the road.

It made Freedom's mother, Content Ware, uneasy and unhappy. She felt it unseemly for her daughter to be held on the laps of the men who came to the inn, cuddled in their arms and kissed by their bearded lips. Content was a parson's daughter, and she was full of grave doubts as to the decency of such goings' on, but the Widow Gretchen hooted her to scorn.

"Not a man of dem but would die for dot little maid," said hearty Gretchen. "Don't be so pooky. Let de child be." But Content shivered whenever she saw Freedom's arms around some trapper's neck or saw her cheerfully permitting some Tod-Noddy to blow down her neck or tickle her in the ribs.

Content complained to Luther. "I've told her a thousand times to keep out of the taproom. But she pays no heed."

Luther grinned amiably. He could not bring himself to object to the way his daughter was worshiped. It was as good as a dose of physic to see how everybody's face lighted up when the sound of Freedom's laughter went pealing through the house. Yet in spite of all the spoiling she got the little girl was gentle and modest. Perhaps it was because her mother constantly drilled such virtues into her. At any rate, Freedom was undisputed queen of Atta, and she had nothing but love and trust in her heart.

Content, at this time, was being whispered about. She "had something the matter with her"; she was childing. It was no longer fitting that she be seen among the patrons of the inn; she had to keep abovestairs, out of sight. And Freedom, usually a biddable child, chafed at the restriction of being always with her mother, plaguing to be back in the boiling activities of taproom and parlor.

"Now the devil fly away with that one!" grumbled Biddy O'Brien, shoving Freedom roughly aside. "It's a clout in the jaw she needs."

Everything was in a fine pudder when a neat catalogue from the Jordans solved all. Luther could read, but Content could do better, so she read aloud from the gold-and-white booklet:

"THE ATTA SEMINARY

"Philomel and Alice Jordan, Props.

"Course of Study will Include:

"Arithmetic, English Grammar, Literature, History, Penmanship, Deportment and Singing. Terms: Twelve weeks, more or less. Fee: $6 per pupil, cash or the equivalent in goods. Payable in advance, and no refunds given!"

"That's the ticket!" cried Luther. "We'll send the minx to school! We can swing it, all right, and it's the place for her."

Content sighed. "She's only a baby," she said. "They'll never take one so young."

"I'll talk old Jordan into it," said Luther. "He'll be glad of the money."

So Freedom became the youngest scholar of the Seminary.

The Turnpikers working on the trail waved to Freedom as she rode by on Old Red, the placid, ancient mare. Freedom did not deign to answer. She rode with cool dignity, sharing her great day with nobody. Just as Alice Jordan rang the big brass bell Freedom slid from the mare and walked bravely into the dooryard. But her first day at school had to be postponed.

Out of the mountains to the west came a faint drumming. The Turnpikers stopped work to listen. A small black speck appeared in the western sky, and the Turnpikers threw down their axes, leaped for horses and guns and shouted, "The birds!"

Before the men were mounted the passenger pigeons were overhead. With incredible speed the great flocks swept across the sky, and the light of the sun went out. In the eerie gloom the sound of wings was like a mighty wind. People came running to see, and the school children poured out of the cabin. Freedom, shaking with fright, burst into tears. This terrible movement of the birds happened every year, but she had never been away from home before.

"It's only the birds, children," cried the Jordans, but their voices could not be heard. They pushed and herded the youngsters into the cabin, shut the wooden blinds and barred the door. But two of the oldest boys unbarred it again and ran out to see the excitement. Then it was useless to try to keep the others. All except Freedom pounded out the door in the wake of the first two.

The everyday aspects of life were suspended. In a few minutes nothing existed save the one desperate need to fight and kill the birds. Against the unending heaven of pigeons rose the hysterical blood lust of the people.

Gunfire brought the passenger pigeons down by the dozens. Great nets, made and kept for this vast annual flight, were flung into the air by ten or twelve men, entangling a hundred or more birds at a cast and bringing them fluttering and squawking to earth. Then the children fell on them with sticks and stones and clubbed them to death. Freedom, catching sight of some of her schoolmates, ran to help. She got pigeon blood in her hair and on her face, and, like everyone else, she grew drunk with the excitement of slaughter.

Nothing that anybody did seemed to make any difference in the apparent number of birds. Hundreds of thousands, flying high, flying low, streamed like doom across the skies. Bird dung fell like rain. The twittering and chattering of the birds, a sound called *cooing* when a few of them murmured softly to one another in the leafy branches of the forest, was now harsh and thunderous; and when they settled on a tree the weight of their numbers stripped the branches and left but the splintered trunk standing stark in the wood. The myriad travelers complained and called. The scream of Johnny Taylor's sawmill many times magnified would have been pleasanter than the ceaseless din of the pigeons. Cattle stampeded and nobody cared; horses snorted and reared and ran away and their owners let them run. Men shouted, women and children shrieked. The kill went on.

Alice Jordan, sickened by the blood lust, withdrew with her husband to the cabin. "Why must everybody turn murderer?" she asked shakily.

Jordan smiled cheerfully. "My love," said he, "birds in such number are a menace to the human race. Slaughtered they must be if such as we are to endure."

Freedom reached home exhausted. She fell asleep while Content was stripping off her clothes and before she could be cleansed of blood and feathers. And although the flight continued for three days more, Freedom had had enough of it and went no more to the hunt.

When the last pigeon had disappeared toward the east Atta took stock of itself. Bonfires had been lighted everywhere, and pigeons were being shoveled in great heaps into the flames. Nobody could eat so many pigeons. Mounds of pigeon feathers lay drying in the sun, being cleaned for use in pillows and feather beds. Lice crawled everywhere, and people scratched themselves absent-mindedly as they went about their affairs. A stink of burning pigeon filled the air and turned people's stomachs. Everybody was sick of pigeon meat and pigeon smell and pigeon guts. They swore never to kill another pigeon. (But when the pigeons flew the next year, out came guns, nets and ropes as usual.)

Now school began in earnest, and the center of Freedom's life swung abruptly from home to school. She scarcely spoke to Luther and Content, stared blankly at all her former admirers and turned deaf ears to their entreaties to tell them about school.

Suz! she thought impatiently. What do they know? She felt sorry for them; she could not bother with them now.

But they refused to be put by so easily. Sweeny, the overseer who had been her particular favorite, boosted her, protesting, to the tavern table early one evening and said, "Come, now, Sissy, show us what you learn at school."

Freedom looked at the crowd of men coldly and sighed. She decided she might as well be done with it, so she made a curtsy as she had been taught, and in a thin, cool pipe she began to sing:

"Alas, and did my Saviour bleed,
And did my Saviour die?
Would He de-vote that sacred head
For such a worm as I?
For such a worm as I?"

There was a mutter of surprise and admiration. There came a dead silence and a sigh. Then thunders of hand clapping and foot stamping. One giant of a trapper pushed his old hat back on his graying curls and let his tears run down into his beard. "Blasted little pismire!" he shouted worshipfully. "Who ever heard the like?"

Freedom could not help feeling flattered. She made another curtsy. "I'll count for you," she told them kindly. And she chanted:

"I'll sing the 12-o.
Pray, what's the 12-o?
12 are the 12 apostles,
11 are the 11 employments,
10 are the 10 commandments,
9 are the 9 bright shiners,
8 are the gable rangers,
7 are the 7 stars in the sky,

"*And*," Freedom went on, drawing a big breath,

"6 are the proud blood walkers,
5 are the 5 thimbles in her bosom,
4 are the 4 gospel preachers,
3 are the 3 riders,
2 are the lily-white boys
Dressed all in green-o,

"*And*," said Freedom with a little jump,

"When a man is dead and gone he shall ever more
Be so."

And she made her final curtsy.

Men stared at each other in wonder as Sweeny lifted the little one from the table.

"Sounds kinda popish, don't it?" somebody muttered.

"Whatever the hell it is," said the gray-haired trapper, "that little polecat's as smart as they come."

No argument about that. Freedom waved good night and climbed the stairs to her mother.

JAMES FENIMORE COOPER

Leather-stocking Remembers When

..."I have travelled the woods for fifty-three years," said Leather-stocking, "and have made them my home for more than forty: and I can say that I have met but one place that was more to my liking; and that was only to eyesight, and not for hunting or fishing."

"And where was that?" asked Edwards.

"Where! why, up on the Catskills. I used often to go up into the mountains after wolves' skins and bears; once they bought me to get them a stuffed painter; and so I often went. There's a place in them hills that I used to climb to when I wanted to see the carryings on of the world, that would well pay any man for a barked shin or a torn moccasin. You know the Catskills, lad, for you must have seen them on your left, as you followed the river up from York, looking as blue as a piece of clear sky, and holding the clouds on their tops, as the smoke curls over the head of an Indian chief at a council fire. Well, there's the High-peak and the Round-top, which lay back, like a father and mother among their children, seeing they are far above all the other hills. But the place I mean is next to the river, where one of the ridges juts out a little from the rest, and where the rocks fall for the best part of a thousand feet so much up and down that a man standing on their edges is fool enough to think he can jump from top to bottom."

"What see you when you get there?" asked Edwards.

"Creation!" said Natty, dropping the end of his rod into the water, and sweeping one hand around him in a circle—"all creation, lad. I was on that hill when Vaughan burnt 'Sopus, in the last war; and I seen the vessels come out of the Highlands as plainly as I can see that lime-scow rowing into the Susquehanna, though one was twenty times further from me than the other.

From *The Pioneers* by James Fenimore Cooper. Published by Charles Wiley, E. B. Clayton, New York, 1823.

The river was in sight for seventy miles, under my feet, looking like a curled shaving, though it was eight long miles to its banks. I saw the hills in the Hampshire grants, the high lands of the river, and all that God had done or man could do, as far as the eye could reach—you know that the Indians named me for my sight, lad—and, from the flat on the top of that mountain, I have often found the place where Albany stands; and, as for 'Sopus! the day the royal troops burned the town the smoke seemed so nigh that I thought I could hear the screeches of the women."

"It must have been worth the toil to meet with such a glorious view."

"If being the best part of a mile in the air, and having men's farms and housen at your feet, with rivers looking like ribands, and mountains bigger than the 'Vision,' seeming to be haystacks of green grass under you, gives any satisfaction to a man, I can recommend the spot. When I first came into the woods to live, I used to have weak spells, and I felt lonesome; and then I would go to the Catskills and spend a few days on that hill, to look at the ways of man; but it's now many a year since I felt any such longings, and I'm getting too old for them rugged rocks. But there's a place, a short two miles back of that very hill, that in the late times I relished better than the mountains; for it was more kivered by the trees, and more nateral."

"And where was that?" inquired Edwards, whose curiosity was strongly excited by the simple description of the hunter.

"Why, there's a fall in the hills, where the water of two little ponds that lie near each other breaks out of their bounds, and runs over the rocks into the valley. The stream is, may be, such a one as would turn a mill, if so useless a thing was wanted in the wilderness. But the hand that made that 'Leap' never made a mill! There the water comes crooking and winding among the rocks, first so slow that a trout could swim in it, and then starting and running just like any creater that wanted to make a far spring, till it gets to where the mountain divides like the cleft hoof of a deer, leaving a deep hollow for the brook to tumble into. The first pitch is nigh two hundred feet, and the water looks like flakes of driven snow afore it touches the bottom; and there the stream gathers itself together again for a new start, and maybe flutters over fifty feet of flat-rock, before it falls for another hundred, when it jumps about from shelf to shelf, first turning this-away and then turning that-away, striving to get out of the hollow, till it finally comes to the plain."

"I have never heard of this spot before," exclaimed Edwards; "it is not mentioned in the books."

"I never read a book in my life," said Leather-stocking; "and how should a man who has lived in towns and schools know anything about the wonders of the woods? No, no, lad; there has that little stream of water been playing among them hills, since He made the world, and not a dozen white men have ever laid eyes on it. The rock sweeps like mason-work, in a half-round, on both sides of the fall, and shelves over the bottom for fifty feet; so that when I've been sitting at the foot of the first pitch, and my hounds have run into the caverns behind the sheet of water, they've looked no bigger than so many rabbits. To my judgment, lad, it's the best piece of work that I've met with in the woods; and none know how often the hand of God is seen in a wilderness but them that rove it for a man's life."

"What becomes of the water? in which direction does it run? is it a tributary of the Delaware?"

"Anan!" said Natty.

"Does the water run into the Delaware?"

"No, no: it's a drop for the old Hudson; and a merry time it has till it gets down off the mountain. I've sat on the shelving rock many a long hour, boy, and watched the bubbles as they shot by me, and thought how long it would be before that very water which seemed made for the wilderness would be under the bottom of a vessel, and tossing in the salt sea. It is a spot to make a man solemnize. You can see right down into the valley that lies to the east of the High-peak, where, in the fall of the year, thousands of acres of woods are before your eyes in the deep hollow and along the side of the mountain, painted like ten thousand rainbows by no hand of man, though not without the ordering of God's providence."

"Why, you are eloquent, Leather-stocking," exclaimed the youth.

TYRONE POWER

At the Mountain House

A stage was in waiting at the landing-place, which quickly took us to the town, where we took a carriage directly to the Mountain House, which we had marked from the river as the morning sun lighted it up, looking like a white dove-cot raised against the dark hill-side.

I will say nothing of our winding, rocky road, or of the glimpses we now and then had of the nether world, which "momentarily grew less," as,

From *Impressions of America, During 1833-35*, by Tyrone Power, Esq. Published by R. Bentley, London, 1836.

whilst halting for breath, we curiously peeped through the leafy screen, flying from the faded leaf and drooping flower of scorching summer, and finding ourselves once more surrounded by all the lovely evidences of early spring. I walked more than half way, and never felt less weary than when I rested on the natural platform, which, thrust from the hill-side, forms a stand whence may be worshipped one of the most glorious prospects ever given by the Creator to man's admiration.

In the cool shade we stood here, and from this eyry looked upon the silver line drawn through the vast rich valley far below, doubtful of its being the broad Hudson, upon whose bosom we had so lately floated in a huge vessel crowded with passengers; for this vessel we searched in vain; but, by the aid of a telescope, made out one of the same kind, which appeared to flit along like some fairy skiff on a pantomimic lake, made all radiant with gold and pearl.

How delightful were the sensations attendant upon a first repose in this changed climate, enhanced as these were by the remembrance of the broiling we had so recently endured! I never remember to have risen with feelings more elastic, or in higher spirits, than I did after my first night's rest upon the mountain....

A ride of some three miles brought us as close as might be to the spot (the Falls), and a walk of as many hundred yards presented to view a scene as well suited for a witch's festival as any spot in the old world....

With two others, I decided upon walking back, and pleasant it is to walk through these quiet wild-wood paths, where the chirps of the birds and the nestle of the leaves alone break in upon the repose. These mountains are everywhere thickly clothed with wood, save only the platform where the house is built; deer abound on the lower ridges, and the bear yet finds ample cover here. A number of these animals are killed every season by an indefatigable old Nimrod who lives in the valley beneath, and who breeds some very fine dogs to this sport.

I did promise unto myself that during the coming November I would return up here, for the purpose of seeing Bruin baited in his proper lair; but regret to say my plan was frustrated. It must be an exciting chase to rouse the lord of this wild mountain forest on a sunny morning, with the first hoar frost yet crisping the feathery pines; and to hear the deep-mouthed hounds giving tongue where an hundred echoes wait to bay the fierce challenge back, and to hear the sharp crack of the rifle rattle through the thin air.

NATHANIEL P. WILLIS

The Catskill Mountains

At this elevation you may wear woollen and sleep under blankets in midsummer; and that is a pleasant temperature where much hard work is to be done in the way of pleasure-hunting. No place so agreeable as Catskill, after one has been parboiled in the city. The cool woods, the small silver lakes, the falls, the mountain-tops, are all delicious haunts for the idler-away of the hot months, and, to the credit of our taste, it may be said they are fully improved,—Catskill is a "resort."

From the Mountain House the busy and all-glorious Hudson is seen winding half its silver length,—towns, villas, and white spires, sparkling on the shores, and snowy sails and gaily-painted steamers specking its bosom. It is a constant diorama of the most lively beauty; and the traveller, as he looks down upon it, sighs to make it a home. Yet a smaller and less-frequented stream would best fulfil desires born of a sigh. There is either no seclusion on the Hudson, or there is so much that the conveniences of life are difficult to obtain. Where the steamers come to shore (twenty a day, with each from one to seven hundred passengers) it is certainly far from secluded enough. No place can be rural, in all the *virtues* of the phrase, where a steamer will take the villager to the city betwen noon and night, and bring him back between midnight and morning. There is a suburban look and character about all the villages on the Hudson which seems out of place among such scenery. They are suburbs, in fact; steam has destroyed the distance between them and the city.

The Mountain House on the Catskill, it should be remarked, is a luxurious hotel. How the proprietor can have dragged up, and keeps dragging up, so many superfluities from the river level to the eagle's nest, excites your wonder. It is the more strange, because in climbing a mountain the feeling is natural that you leave such enervating indulgences below.

The mountain-top is too near heaven. It should be a monastery to lodge in so high; a St. Gotthard, or a Vallambrosa. But here you may choose between Hermitages, "white" or "red" Burgundias, Madeiras, French dishes, and French dances, as if you had descended upon Capua.

From *The Catskill Mountains and the Region Around,* Rev. Charles Rockwell, editor. Published by Taintor Brothers & Co., New York, 1867.

WILLIAM CULLEN BRYANT

The Cauterskill Falls

Midst greens and shades the Cauterskill leaps,
  From cliffs where the wood-flower clings;
All summer he moistens his verdant steps,
  With the sweet light spray of the mountain springs;
And he shakes the woods on the mountain side,
  When they drip with the rains of autumn tide.

But when in the forest bare and old,
  The blast of December calls—
He builds in the starlight clear and cold,
  A palace of ice where his torrent falls;
With turret, and arch, and fretwork fair,
  And pillars blue as the summer air.

For whom are those glorious chambers wrought,
  In the cold and cloudless night?
Is there neither spirit nor motion of thought,
  In forms so lovely and hues so bright?
Hear what the gray-haired woodmen tell
  Of this wild stream and its rocky dell.

'Twas here a youth of dreamy mood,
  A hundred winters ago—
Had wandered over the mighty wood,
  Where the panther's track was fresh on the snow;
And keen were the winds that came to stir
  The long dark boughs of the hemlock fir.

Too gentle of mien he seemed, and fair,
  For a child of those rugged steeps;
His home lay down in the valley where
  The kingly Hudson rolls to the deeps;
But he wore the hunter's frock that day,
  And a slender gun on his shoulder lay.

From *Poetical Works of William Cullen Bryant.* Published by D. Appleton and Company, New York, 1887.

And here he paused, and against the trunk
  Of a tall gray linden leant;
Where the broad, clear orb of the sun had sunk
  From his path in the frosty firmament;
And over the round dark edge of the hill,
  A cold green light was quivering still.

And the crescent moon, high over the green,
  From a sky of crimson shone;
On that icy palace where towers were seen,
  To sparkle as if with stars of their own;
While the water fell with a hollow sound,
  'Twixt the glistening pillars ranged around.

Is that a being of life that moves
  Where the crystal battlements rise?
A maiden watching the moon she loves,
  At the twilight hour with pensive eyes?
Was that a garment which seemed to gleam,
  Betwixt the eye and the falling stream?

'Tis only the torrent tumbling o'er,
  In the midst of those glassy walls;
Gushing, and plunging, and beating the floor
  Of the rocky basin in which it falls;
'Tis only the torrent, but why that start?
  Why gazes the youth with a throbbing heart?

He thinks no more of his home afar,
  Where his sire and his sister wait;
He heeds no longer how star after star,
  Looks forth on the night as the hour grows late;
He heeds not the snow-wreath, lifted and cast
  From a thousand boughs by the rising blast.

His thoughts are alone of those who dwell
  In the halls of frost and snow;
Who pass where the crystal domes upswell,
  From the alabaster floors below;
Where the frost-trees bourgeon with leaf and spray,
  And frost-gems scatter a silvery day.

And oh! that those glorious haunts were mine!
He speaks, and throughout the glen,
Their shadows swim in the faint moonshine,
And take a ghastly likeness of men;
As if the slain by the wintry storms
Came forth to the air in their earthly forms.

There pass the chasers of seal and whale,
With their weapons quaint and grim;
And bands of warriors in glittering mail,
And herdsmen and hunters, huge of limb;
There are naked arms with bow and spear,
And furry gauntlets the carbine rear.

There are mothers, and oh! how sadly their eyes,
On their children's white brows rest!
There are youthful lovers—the maiden lies,
In a seeming sleep, on the chosen breast;
There are fair, wan women, with moonstruck air,
And snow-stars flecking their long loose hair.

They eye him not as they pass along,
But his hair stands up with dread;
When he feels that he moves with that phantom throng,
Till those icy turrets are over his head;
And the torrent's roar as they enter, seems
Like a drowsy murmur heard in dreams.

The glittering threshold is scarcely passed,
When there gathers and wraps him round,
A thick white twilight, sullen and vast,
In which there is neither form nor sound;
The phantoms, the glory, vanish all,
With the dying voice of the waterfall.

Slow passes the darkness of that trance,
And the youth now faintly sees—
Huge shadows, and gushes of light that dance
On a rugged ceiling of unhewn trees;
And walls where the skins of beasts are hung,
And rifles glitter, on antlers strung.

On a couch of shaggy skins he lies,
  As he strives to raise his head;
Hard-featured woodmen, with kindly eyes,
  Come round him and smoothe his furry bed;
And bid him rest, for the evening star
  Is scarcely set, and the day is far.

They had found at eve the dreaming one,
  By the base of that icy steep;
When over his stiffening limbs begun
  The deadly slumber of frost to creep;
And they cherished the pale and breathless form,
  Till the stagnant blood ran free and warm.

GEORGE WILLIAM CURTIS

Catskill

July
The Mountain House

The "New World" is a filagree frame-work of white wood surrounding a huge engine, which is much too conspicuous. I am speaking, by-the-by, of the Hudson steamer; and yet, perhaps, the symbol holds for the characteristic expression of the nation. For just so flimsy and overfine are our social arrangements, our peculiarities of manner and dress, and just so prominent and evident is the homely practical genius that carries us forward, with steam-speed, through the sloop-sluggishness of our compeers.

A sharp-faced, thought-furrowed, hard-handed American, with his anxious eye and sallow complexion, his nervous motion and concentrated expression, and withal, accoutred for travelling in blue coat with gilt buttons, dark pantaloons, patent leather boots, and silk vest hung with charms, chains, and bits of metal, as if the Indian love of lustre lingered in the Yankee, is not unlike one of these steamers, whose machinery, driving it along, jars the cut glass and the choice centre-tables and crimson-covered lounges, and with a like accelerated impetus, would shiver the filagree into splinters.

From *Lotus-Eating: A Summer Book* by George William Curtis. Published by Harper & Brothers, New York, 1852.

Yet for all this the "New World" is a very pleasant place. It has a light, airy, open and clean deck, whence you may spy the shyest nook of scenery upon the banks, and a spacious cabin, where you do not dine at a huge table, with eager men plunging their forks into dishes before you, and their elbows into your sides, but quietly and pleasantly as at a Parisian café. What an appalling ordeal an American table d'hôte is! What a chaos of pickles, puddings and meats! and each man plunging through every thing as if he and the steamer were racing for victory. The waiters, usually one third the necessary number, rush up and down the rear of the benches, and cascades of gravies and sauces drip ominously along their wake. It is the seed-time of dyspepsia, and Dickens in that anti-American novel, which none of us can read without feeling its injustice, has yet described, only too well, an American ordinary.

Who can wonder that we are lantern-jawed, lean, sickly and serious of aspect, when he has dined on a steamer or at a great business hotel? We laugh very loftily at the Rhine dinners in which the pudding and fish meet in the middle of the courses. But a Rhine dinner upon the open, upper deck of the steamer, is quiet and orderly and inoffensive, while one of our gregarious repasts must needs offend every man who has some regard for proprieties and some self-respect.

—And Catskill?

Yes, we are rapidly approaching, even while we sit on deck and our eyes slide along the gentle green banks, as we meditate American manners and the extremes that meet in our characteristics. Beyond Poughkeepsie a train darts along the shore, rattling over the stones on the water's edge, and rolling with muffled roar behind the cuts and among the heavy foliage. So nearly matched is our speed, that until the locomotive ran beside us, I did not know how rapid was our silent movement. But there is heat and bustle and dust in the nervous little train, which winds along, like a jointed reptile, while with our stately steamer there is silence, and the cool, constant patter of the few drops, where our sharp prow cuts the river.

A little above Poughkeepsie the river bends, and the finest point is gained. It is a foreground of cultivated and foliaged hills of great variety of outline, rising as they recede, and ranging, and towering at last along the horizon, in the Catskill mountains. It was a brilliant day, and the heavy, rounding clouds piled in folds along the line of the hills—taking, at length, precisely their own hue, and so walling up the earth with a sombre, vaporous rampart, such as Titans and fallen angels storm. As we glided nearer, keen flashes darted from the wall of cloud, and as if riven and rent with its sharpness, the heavy masses rolled asunder; then more heavily piled themselves in dense darkness, fold overlying fold, while the startled wind changed, and rushed down the river, chilled, and breathing cold before the storm.

No longer a wall, but a swiftly advancing and devastating power, the storm threw up pile upon pile of jagged blackness into the clear, tender blue of the afternoon, and there was a wail in the hurried gusts that swept past us and over us, and the river curled more and more into sudden waves, which were foam-tipped, and scattered spray.

We were now abreast of the mountains, and far behind them the storm had burst. Down the vast ravines that opened outward toward the river, I saw the first softness of the shower skimming along the distant hillsides, moister and grayer, until they were merged in mist....

...The breeze was cool and strong as we landed at Catskill. We were huddled ashore rapidly, the board was pulled in, and the "New World" disappeared....

During the first eight miles of the inland drive toward the Mountain House, I enjoyed the prospect of six travellers, four stained leather curtains, and the two wooden windows of the door. It was not cool inside the coach, but without, the wind was in high frolic with the rain, and through the slightest crevice the wily witch dashed us with her missiles, cold and very wet. Then the showers swept along a little, and we threw up the curtains and breathed fresh air, and about three miles from the Mountain House, where the steep ascent commences, Olde and Swansdowne and I jumped out of the stage and walked. The road is very firmly built, and is fortunate in its material of a slaty rock, and in the luxuriance of foliage, for the tangled tree-roots hold the soil together.

The road climbs at first in easy zigzags, and presently pushes straight on through the woods, and upon the side of a steep ravine; the level-branched foliage sheering regularly down, sheeting the mountain side with leafy terraces. Between the trunks and down the gorges we looked over a wide but mountainous landscape, and as we ascended, the air became more invigorating with the greater height and the coolness of the shower. Two hours before sunset we stood upon the plateau before the Mountain House, 2,800 feet above the sea.

There is a fine sense of height there, but all mountain views over a plain are alike. You stand on the piazza of the Mountain House and look directly down into the valley of the Hudson, with only a foreground, deep beneath you, of a lower layer than that on which you stand, with its precipice of pine and hemlock. The rest stretches then, a smooth surface to the eye, but hilly enough to the feet, when you are there, to an unconfined horizon at the north and south, and easterly to the Berkshire hills.

Through this expanse lies the Hudson, not very sinuous, but a line of light dividing the plain. In the vague twilight atmosphere it was very effective. Sometimes the mist blotted out individual outlines, and the whole scene was but a silver-gray abyss, and the hither line of the river was the horizon, and the stream itself a white gleam of sky beyond. Then the distance and the foreground were mingled in the haze, a shining opaque veil, wherein the river was a rent, through which beamed a remote brightness. Or the vapors clustered toward the south and the stream flowed into them, flashing and far, as into a terrene cloud-land. All the country was chequered with yellow patches of ripe grain, and marked faintly with walls and fences, and looked rather a vast domain than a mountain-ruled landscape.

Whoever is familiar with mountain scenery will know what to anticipate in the Catskill view. The whole thing is graceful and generous, but not sublime. Your genuine mountaineer (which I am not) shrugs his shoulder at the shoulders of mountains which soar thousands of feet above him and are still shaggy with forest. He draws a long breath over the spacious plain, but he feels the want of that true mountain sublimity, the presence of lonely snow-peaks.

And as we always require in scenery of a similar class, similar emotions, there is necessarily a little disappointment in the Catskills. They are hills rather than mountains....

The Mountain House is really unceremonious. You are not required to appear at dinner in ball costume, and if you choose, you may scramble to the Falls in cowhide boots and not in varnished pumps. The house has a long and not ill-proportioned Corinthian colonnade, wooden of course, and glaring white. The last point, however, is a satisfaction from below, for its vivid contrast with the dark green forest reveals the house from a great distance upon the river....

A written placard around the house announced that dancing music could be had at the bar. But none wished to polk—and how music could be made in that parlor, which seemed to have been dislocated by some tempestuous mountain ague, remains a mystery to me. There are eight windows, and none of them opposite to any of the others: folding-doors which have gone down the side of the room in some wild architectural dance, and have never returned, and a row of small columns stretching in an independent line across the room, quite irrespective of the middle. It is a dangerous parlor for a nervous man.

REVEREND DR. MURDOCH

"The Spectral Looking-Glass"

"The Fata Morgana, seen so remarkably on the Straits of Messina, has been observed on the Catskills to perfection. The vision, as described in the text, was seen from the balcony of the Mountain House in 1845....

"...The wind rose from the north, lifting up the black cloud that had hung like a heavy sheet behind them, and was rolling it up like a scroll, so that the sun was coming out in a clear sky west of the mountain. On the flat rock were all the persons known to us, standing together on the verge of the cliff. When their attention was properly fixed, Teunis saw, for the first time, what he had heard the old hunters tell of, the *Geest Wolk Waren* —the Spirit of the Mist—seen only at rare times in these regions. There were huge masses of vapor passing in different strata, some of which were denser than others. That which was nearest to them was thin and transparent, reflecting all the objects which stood between it and the light thrown upon it from the clearer sky behind. It was indeed a moving mirror that slowly passed, as a panorama is unrolled before a company of spectators. There was, however, this difference between nature and art: the faces and forms of the persons looking on were the figures in the picture before them, taken instantly, and held up to them. Every one saw himself distinctly, and his nearest neighbor, only less vividly drawn. The whole was more like an artist's dream than a reality. It seemed as if they could have walked out and touched the picture, till a moment's reflection made them sensible that the whole was but a shadow. Teunis gazed first at his own outline, then on the tall, straight form of the Indian, who stood immovable. Behind the front group he saw those who had lain down on the laurel bed, and beside them several starting up in evident alarm. Others were rushing forward with curious and hasty looks of wonder at the strange sight; and around the place where hemlock branches had been woven into tents, some of the Indians were stooping, like Arabs when an alarm has been given caused by the mirage, when it has lifted the forms of an enemy above the level of their

From *The Dutch Dominie of the Catskills* by the Rev. Dr. Murdoch. Published by Derby & Jackson, New York, 1861.

sandy plains. Scarcely one of those present had seen the wonder before, and those who had heard of it were more inclined to regard it as a vision of a frightened imagination than a fact....

"The whole assemblage were awakened to the intensest eagerness. All were under an undefined feeling of superstition, as if what they saw was like the writing on the wall which the profane king saw, ominous of his own doom. The sheet-cloud went slowly by, figure after figure melting into thin air. It was affecting to hear each one tell, afterwards, how he felt an internal shivering as he saw his own body dissolving, before his eyes, into nothing.

"Soon the whole east was covered with the same black cloud as before, while the thin, white vapor, which had served as a reflector, was wheeled round to the south and settled against the sides of the hill, which rises bluffly, a few hundred feet higher than Flat Rock. There again it became a new mirror, but far different from what it was before. Each one, instead of himself, saw his nearest neighbor to the right of him. Fear and superstition gave place to curiosity, and then to frolic and fun. One, who had been the most cowardly of the crew, gave a caper in the air, which threw others into the same absurd attitudes, until an hundred more were seen dancing around and hallooing like madmen. Solemnly and silently the figures in the cloud mocked the fools outside."

EDMUND GILLIGAN

Seasons in The Vly

...'Cobus opened the door and looked out into the night. Beyond the roofs and walls of The Vly, beyond its square meadows, the eastern summits of the Catskills lay, dark surge against the sky, a barrow piled by giants. At hand, the yellow gleams of lamps poured clearly out of uncurtained windows: for in The Vly it was counted a discourtesy and a loss to shut out the eyes of friends or to hide the treasures of parlors. Beyond the white walls of the cottages, in which the windows shone like golden looking-glasses, he saw the somber, unlighted shapes and shadows of the barns; and beyond all these the forest began, a forest full of music:

From *Strangers in The Vly* by Edmund Gilligan. Published by Charles Scribner's Sons, New York, 1941. Reprinted by permission of the author.

Kill's echo, subtle tread of deer, horn rustles, sleepy twitters, murmur of pine needles, endlessly clashing. Folded lambs bleated, mares struck against their stalls, and heifers, uneased by the spring moons, lowed in their stanchions, adding a bass harmony to the grandeur of the Catskills theme. Beyond the surge, far above Wittenberg's towers of rock and crown of tossing hemlock boughs, the evening star, young Venus, crossed a bridge of cloud and cast her emerald beam down upon the boundless reach of the forest; and the star drew apart from our world, leaving behind the bridge of cloud, which then lost, in its upper part, that greenish hue. Presently it took on, in its lower part, a fiery color, cast forward by the yet unrisen moon. Then, to the east and to the west, stars appeared in sudden ranks and companies, until there were many gleaming and twinkling....

Now the eighth-month flowers bloomed and faded; the cherries fattened and the yellow porter apples pressed the boughs far down. The warblers and the song sparrows left off their sweet singing because moulting-time had come; and the summer flourished in corn fields and barley spray, and the summer waned upon the summits of the Catskills, where, amidst the grandeur of the hemlock forests, a lofty tree here and there turned slowly from green to gold. The nights began to lengthen and red moons shone. The West Wind blew more often than the South and high-sailing hawks came slanting down on the first green shoots of dawn. The Vly went the way of its centuries. Lambs cried louder in the folds and became ewes and rams; heifers went lowing by in herds and the oxen strained in the dim-lit forest. Children were churched, farmers' lads wed farmers' maids, and the ancient ones were carried to the long home....

The rain set in, wetted the earth an hour, then ceased. Clouds held off the break of day. Cocks crowed in vain. Crows, perched for an autumn convention, stared in dismay at yellow leaves whirling outward, earthward. Bitterly the birds cursed winter's approach and spoke in envious terms of the red-hackled cocks, who'd sing content in snug barns the winter long. Sweeps of rain spilled on the crests of Aaron Berg and on the meadows of Round Top, where the fading grass took on a last false touch of green. The pure liquor of the Kill became milky in the rain-rush. The trout pushed from the riffles to sandy places, there to whirl and spawn. A rare arc of yellow light streamed over the slumbering Vly, embraced its darkness with a fierce embrace, and faded. The myriad needles of the pine forests clashed and chanted a celebration of eternal green. Hemlocks and balsams joined in a moaning chorus. The gray day came, bearing the tatters of night. Mixing sweetly in the balsamic stream, there came a new and headier fragrance, born of green things passing into earth, thus to become green again in good time. Swallows leaped from the barn eaves and flew cheeping, flew so high that the blue sheen of the cock-birds gleamed again in the purer light. Notes of departure sped among the elder birds; notes of anxiety among the younger. Throughout the Catskills, in the coverts of Mount Solomon and in the caverns of Wildenberg, the wilderness inhabitants, having done with mating and upbringing, celebrated the close hour of wintry change, the hour of migration. And heifers lowed against their stanchions. Ewes bleated beseechingly. Even men's voices, now raised in the way of toil, seemed to have changed in the night; for the human heart, hearing the autumnal prelude, remembered the melancholy theme....

...The days tumbled swiftly down the mountainside, stayed a shorter time in The Vly, and made way for longer, sparkling nights. The Hunter's Moon and the Harvest Moon blazed beyond the Clove. The new Evening Star coursed in the southern sky and sank among lattices of black boughs, bare of leaves. Harvests were gathered and threshing done. All day long the scythes whistled in the hay fields. Ox-teams, blowing jets of cloud, turned into the forests at the crack of dawn. Men and beasts labored at the logs until moonset. Out of the smokehouses came the fragrance of hams and bacon at the curing, and cider presses, full of russet apples, added their bouquet. Boys and squirrels vied under the chestnut trees. In the early mornings, the red-winged blackbirds answered their marshals' cries, wheeled in long, bending columns above Pool Judith and began their southward pilgrimage. And one night, Elizabeth heard a wild goose call and a wild goose answer in the high passage....

...Ten nights later, Elizabeth, nursing her son by the fireside, heard a pelting at her window. She looked up and saw the snowflakes falling. In the morning, clear again, the hemlock boughs lay burdened. At noon, the snowfall began again. By night-time, winter had begun for The Vly; and its chimneys sent up sparky smoke all day long and far into the night.

20TH CENTURY

BROOKS ATKINSON

Smoke from a Valley Cabin

Although I had rented the cabin up-river as a place merely to visit occasionally in winter I was astonished to find how soon it began to assert authority of its own. Within a month it reduced me from free agent to servant, from master to student. Each time I visited it I found myself busier than before in accounting for all the changes in the landscape. At last I could feel Nature in my bones as a living force....

Four miles from the railroad and the main thoroughfare, the cabin appeared to be as remote from New York as the Catskills or the Adirondacks. As a matter of fact, it was about two hours journey from my apartment—fifty miles up the west bank of the Hudson River by railroad to Bear Mountain Station, in the Palisades Inter-State Park, and then four miles by auto to the backlands of the river hills. In the summer a vast horde of city vacationists swarmed through these woods, picnicked everywhere and bumped row-boats excitedly in Queensboro Lake. In the winter, visitors were less common than the birds. No one ever climbed those hills or patrolled the thick woods north of the water.

The cabin was set in a cleared field beside the brook, a one-room peak-roofed, shingled building with a tiny kitchen ell, plain and rather squalid. On all four sides rose modest hills, mountainous in contour and proportion. To the northeast a rambling lake in the rough shape of a cross lapped at the edge of rolling woods. A patch of hemlocks a few rods up the brook made

From *East of the Hudson* by Brooks Atkinson. Published by Alfred A. Knopf, New York, 1928. Reprinted by permission of the author.

grateful contrast with the prevailing hardwood trees and attracted a special group of the winter birds. What I enjoyed most were the variety of uninhabited country in all directions, and my proximity to the out of doors even when I was inside. Rabbits, squirrels, chipmunks, woodchucks, muskrats, phlegmatic skunks and an occasional deer wandered through the valley, sometimes timidly up to the kitchen door in search of scraps. Two colonies of beaver, introduced several years before, lived in houses in the lake. And only a reluctance to believe the improbable kept me from publishing one series of broad, flat, heavy footprints in the snow as the tracks of Bruin. According to a newspaper item, dated several days later, three bears had recently escaped from a neighboring park. Had one of them lumbered through the woods near camp? I liked to think that he had. It was no time of year for a bear to be roaming the frozen countryside, but it seemed like a neighborly thing for him to do....

IN HONOR OF A SHINGLED HAT

As a city-dweller I had hoped, as I say, to surprise Nature in her fleeting glories by living close to them on week-ends. Being a part of Nature the cabin set all those beauties before me, and I soon became sentimentally attached to it. Like the elms in the valley, it humbly bore the rain and the snow, it reflected the daylight and it cast a creeping shadow as the sun moved across the sky. I knew every caprice of the out of doors the instant it happened, for my winter retreat caught the natural impulse at once. Sometimes I knew without stirring from the fireside; the patter of rain, the gentle brush of snow, the uncanny howl of the North wind, the cracking of shingles on a cold night, needed no investigation. Sometimes I heard the muffled boom of the frozen lake as it wrestled with the warmth or cold—a deep-toned gong in the moonlight. When the fox sparrows began to sing in March I had only to open the door cautiously and listen to the Pan-pipe of the spring. I kept tabs on the season by regular expeditions to the lake across certain fields, through variegated woods, along the brook, over Round Hill, through an apple orchard. On each visit I relished what I saw, not only for its own beauty, but for its comparison with my last visit. These weekly changes in the fabric of Nature were the imponderable mysteries. Thus by May I had stolen time to see the leaves drop and the new ones expand, the ice form, thicken, and disappear; and nearly all the birds I had seen migrating South in the autumn I greeted upon their return in the spring. I saw a November frost before sunrise, a magnificent spectacle; I was treated to a long snow storm in February, white and untrammeled to the horizon;

and I was outdoors in April to hear the new birds salute the dawn. In December I saw icy ledges on Bear Mountain gleaming like precious jewels in the moonlight. I was always newly surprised by the brilliance of the universe at night. I felt the warmth of the day and the chill of the night as quickly as any part of the valley. For eight months I felt every turn of the season in my bones or I sniffed it in the air. Indeed, it seemed to me that my capacity for feeling increased tremendously with each visit, and that nothing could happen outdoors without leaving, however faintly, its impress on me.

HEARTH AND STOVE

To write of my winter trips appreciatively, however, was to celebrate the supernatural wonders of the hearth. The humble fires in my cabin fairly dominated that corner of New York State with their beneficence inside and their curls of smoke outside, beseeching the gods "to pardon my clear flame." Of the two fires the open hearth was the more spectacular with its brave show of color and coals; but the ugly barrel stove supplied the heat I needed and performed the major business of civilization....

THE RHYTHM OF THE SEASONS

By good fortune I happened to be at the cabin on one perfect day in each season—one day so characteristic as to be the apotheosis. Many days were indifferent to the season's splendor; they were too warm and sluggish in the autumn, or too crisp in the spring. But on the three ideal days of autumn, winter and spring I fancied that I reflected within myself the colored mood of the landscape and felt in my blood the throb of the universe.

Each season was vibrant with beauty. I felt none of the poetaster's melancholy about the autumn. After the leaves had fallen, clean and crackling under foot, the woods were full of light, the views widened through bare branches, the evergreens bathed the eye more soothingly than ever and the structural design of the deciduous trees was revealed as perfect symmetry. Shorn of its summer verdure the shagbark cut against the sky like an etching; its sharp network of twigs and branches seemed almost acid-bitten. I felt that the season was not merely dying, but preparing its rebirth with submission and composure. The tree sparrows had come down from the north for their winter sojourn, apparently in the best of spirits. Fox sparrows and white-throated sparrows were scratching contentedly in the leaves. Two flights of rusty blackbirds winged south in such numbers that they seemed to cut off the light like a fleeting cloud. Pushing through the fields and woods and watching the birds everywhere I found myself looking forward to the next seasons—anticipating the crystalline beauties of the winter landscape and regarding the swamps in terms of the spring migration. As the old year faded the new year lay waiting the summons. Everywhere the beech-tips were rolled tightly, ready for the encouragement of warm sunshine. The same wind that whirled the dead leaves through the woods distributed the seeds in the fields. The roots of spring were thus deep in the autumn. For November was courier of May. When I went out to the wood pile with a lantern after supper, the nipping air foretold, not so much the death of Nature, as the coming of a glorious season in which every field and hill would be newly transfigured. After this perfect autumn day I found myself instinctively facing forward, towards the new, not only confident but eager.

WINTER AT ZERO

My emotions had not led me astray. For the perfect week-end of the winter redeemed every promise. During the preceding night the thermometer had dropped below zero where it hung without much variation for two days. The morning was clear, crisp and invigorating. Although I kept the fire roaring in dangerous fury, the cabin was never actually warm. At the warmest time the surface of the bucket of water skimmed over. A patch of snow about seven feet from the fireplace never melted all the time I was there. But I was generally comfortable and I fancied myself extremely well sheltered.

The outdoors was glorious. Conscious of the tingling cold I felt a kinship with everything—with the crusted snow, the sparkling ledges on Bear Mountain, the restless, hidden lake, the muffled brook flowing under huge covers of glittering ice. Every bird note sounded the universal theme. The hairy and downy woodpeckers, blue jays and chickadees seemed vividly alive. Chickadees scampered through the bare branches and followed me, *deeing* with curiosity and excitement, as I made the usual rounds. But the perfect expression of this dynamic season was the activity of a flock of rosy and gray birds in a hemlock tree beyond. I had heard their sweet call-note some distance away. All at once I saw them clinging to the cones, tearing out the seeds, swirling off for no accountable reason, round and round and back again—a whirligig of animation. Wanderers from the far north, they were white-winged crossbills whom I had seen once or twice in the mountains. What dashing and accomplished birds they were! How spontaneous! Like true vagabonds they were enjoying themselves completely. I could never anticipate their next movement. One of them dropped to the brook and flew timidly over the black, turbulent water. Then others came down, one by one, splashes of warm color against the snow; and after a time the brookside became a carnival of chattering crossbills perching on the snow and ice and hovering over the water. Only two or three of them, it seemed to me, mustered up courage enough to dip. But they all took a fling at the sport. I stood in the snow, watching them, until my fingertips began to tingle. Then I raced back to the fireplace.

The moon was full that night. After supper I visited the lake and woods again, occasionally disturbing a rabbit in the thicket. The light was softer than by day and the woods were full of mysterious shadows lying gently on the snow. In general, the winter season was self-sufficient—a complete state, an entity. I could hardly remember when the lake was open. Winter dominated every sense; I could not add to it, take away from it or withhold myself. I could not play truant by dreaming of balmier days. Every sensation seemed complete and final, and beyond human equivocation.

WHEN THE ICE BROKE UP

When spring came I was there to extend the official greeting of Queensboro Valley. For several days even the city had been softening unaccountably. When I reached the cabin at noontime the temperature was 50, the air warm, the haze gentle and pastel-colored; and the sun was gradually working out of the clouds and creating, single-handed, a fine spring afternoon. The brook, now almost free of ice, roared vigorously. Pussy willows enlivened the swampy woods. Everywhere there was the sweet content of natural release. While I was indoors, impatiently cooking lunch, I knew that the early birds would be back; and in my mind I checked off the most likely ones—song sparrows, red-winged blackbirds, robins, bluebirds and meadowlarks. After lunch I found chickadees, goldfinches and one song sparrow in the hemlock woods, but they were all wearing their winter manners. On the way to the lake I found song sparrows in every thicket. Finally I heard one singing—olit, olit, olit, chip, chip, chee, char, chewiss, wiss, wiss—the first spring serenade. Although at the same time I heard the red-winged blackbirds stuttering a few rods ahead, I was satisfied with the song sparrow completely as though the season had kept its vows to the letter and need offer no further proof of divine guidance. Suddenly the warm warble of a bluebird melted the air in the south. As I turned to look for him the air everywhere began to flow with the strains of bluebird melody, and presently fifteen or twenty birds fluttered into the north. They were gone before I could focus my glasses. If there had been anything tentative about the song sparrow, the bluebirds now clinched the season definitely. With their dancing, buoyant passage, spring flushed and expanded, as though they had sprinkled the air with a magic compound while they hurried along, fertilizing the country over which they flew. They were the appointed deliverers.

I still needed the assurance of their brilliant color. Lo! when I turned my back to the road I saw bluebirds everywhere. Ten minutes before there had not been one; they had just arrived. Like returned vacationists they were examining every nook of the land—flying from twig to ground to telegraph wire to fence post in numbers hard to estimate. At last I saw a male spread his wings to reveal their loveliest color. At least for that moment he was the center of the universe. All along the road for a mile the soft air danced with their flecks of summer sky, bursting on my arid vision like a sign from God in a barren land. They were not pagan birds; they were the distilled foam of heaven dripping from twig to grass, and as they sang the air quivered with mellifluous sound. Thus, before my eyes, the miracle of spring was accomplished. Again I felt like one whom the gods had signally honored.

By Sunday morning, of course, the intensest excitement was over, and the bluebirds had enraptured the land. During breakfast I left the door open to hear their warble as they adorned the trees near the cabin. Other migrants had come in during the night. On the way to the Lake I saw the robins and the meadowlarks. In an open bay, between margins of thin ice, six male American mergansers were courting two of their ladies. They dove bravely under the cakes of ice, swam passionately here and there; and occasionally they half-rose from the water to reveal their enchanting salmon bellies. I enjoyed them. But the bluebirds had released the floods of spring with their "slant blue beams down the aisles of the woods." And I was thoroughly content in their company.

THE HOUNDS OF SPRING

During the remaining weekends of my tenancy, life streamed through my little valley in a mighty flood of rejoicing and expectation—of hopes born in the warm south and blown northward on the blossoms of the season. Although I had sworn to play no favorites, to study the texture of each season impartially and to transcribe its symbols without prejudice, I found myself dissolved by the spring—saturated until nothing of myself remained untouched by "the first fine careless rapture" of Nature's awakening. Now the green began to edge the woods with color, the violets, bloodroot, arbutus, and wild geranium sweetened the ground, and the birds went by in a mysterious wave of motion until every thicket, field and glade rang with song.

Lounging on a hill behind the cabin one March evening I heard bluebirds, song sparrows, juncos, redwing blackbirds, bluejays, crows, meadowlarks, and the fragile, luminous aria of the fox sparrow—all these songs simultaneously so that it was difficult to distinguish them as individual voices. Individually they were bird music, "splendors pouring through the air." Collectively they were the divine summons to spring like the ringing of many vesper bells in a mountain village. Long before our ancestors travelled this country, these birds made their way north each spring through this tiny valley in response to the mighty forces that governed them; and long after we were dead they made the same journey each year and serenaded the valley in the same pure tones. How did they know when to come or where to go? Why did they follow the same courses? None of us knew. But to quiet every worldly alarm it was sufficient to know that they did come. When the bluebird failed to leap out of the sky, when the bloodroot no longer pushed through the dead leaves, then it would be time to stitch up our ascension robes for immediate and serious action.

THE TACONICS

18TH CENTURY

HENRY NOBLE MacCRACKEN

William Prendergast, Agrarian

[1765]

An agrarian is one who advocates by agitation or political dissension a redistribution of the system of land tenure in the direction of greater equality. Alone among the "rioters" of '66 William Prendergast stands out as the true agrarian because of his single-minded devotion to the farmers' cause. He never bought nor advocated the purchase of Indian deeds. He had never paid rent, and had no personal grievance. He never advocated, as did the Connecticut radicals, the cancellation of all debts. On one occasion, as a conspicuous example, he paid off a small debt at a country store, while leading his followers against the landlords. He wanted one thing only: justice for the farmer; reform of the courts, an unprejudiced judiciary, and a land tenure inviolable so long as a fair rent was paid and the farmer treated the land well; with no more cruel evictions by a conspiracy of sheriffs and landlords.

In a word, William Prendergast was a crusader, fighting for a cause every item of which has been enacted into law in England since 1875, and most of which has been won in these States, where more than a third of the land is held in tenancy. Prendergast is a hero of the farmers' cause, and deserves to be remembered by some monument in our famous county.

From *Old Dutchess Forever!: The Story of an American County* by Henry Noble MacCracken. Published by Hastings House, New York. Copyright 1956 by Henry Noble MacCracken. Reprinted by permission of the author, Casperkill Press, Poughkeepsie, New York.

Where did Prendergast find his principles and his practice? In Ireland, his native country, where Presbyterian Protestants like him suffered almost as cruelly under the Anglican tyranny as did the Catholics. So heavy were the taxes, and so harsh the penalties, that only two courses were open to men who refused to conform, outlawry or emigration. Prendergast probably tried first the one and then the other. Certainly his friend and neighbor, John Kane, had done so. "Kane was Prendergast's good friend," Seth Lovely testified, "for he was his countryman and also traded with him a hundred (pounds) a year." On one occasion, when the mob fell to quarreling as to who should occupy the house from which a "replaced" tenant had been forcibly evicted by them, Kane's advice was asked. "Damn it," cried Kane, "you will bring yourselves to nothing yet by having so many disputes among yourselves." He never knew but one mob succeed yet, he went on, and that was in his own country; they did not go on contending, but what they did, they did quickly. "They destroyed or tore down gardens and made Gentlemen get out of their coaches and swore them on their knees."

It was Kane, not Prendergast, whose fiery eloquence fired the mob. Simon Lovel testified: "If it had not been for Kane's persuasion the mob would never have risen." Neither in the field nor in the "Notes" of his trial is there any suggestion that Prendergast was an orator. What is quoted of him is succinct and pithy.

His role in the conspiracy was rather like that of Brutus. A man of integrity, quiet and law-abiding, well-liked by his neighbors—so the testimony ran.... It was Dr. Joseph Crane who like Cassius persuaded our Brutus "to go over to Van Wyck's as an advocate of the mob before the Congress."...

A committee of Samuel Munroe, Benjamin Weed, John Ferriss, Isaiah Bennet, Jermiah Fowler, and Daniel Palmer were chosen. An office was set up at the house of Edward Rice, and an underwriting trade "to insure the lands at 25%," drawn up by Samuel Johnson as Attorney. But although the association had agreed to assume charge of further selling of leases, Samuel Munroe "continued to take Bonds to himself", while Joshua Baker, "an Incendiary", offered to take them at eight shillings the lease.

Such is the picture of the troubles in Philipse Patent. Our source is not too trustworthy. It is our old friend ex-Rev. Peter Pratt, who will be remembered as the first minister of Sharon, who had apparently gone into business along the Oblong. By his own testimony it was he who wrote out the leases for Daniel Nimham. He became an informer and spy for Beverly Robinson, who received from him ten documents, among others, which Robinson in turn sent to Attorney-General Kempe as material to set up the trial of Munroe for disherison and maintenance.... All these documents, save the last written before March 1765, show clearly by the fact of omission that William Prendergast was no party to the early agitation.

What brought Prendergast into the fight, and with him his adviser John Kane, was probably the cruel evictions and the forced one-year leases carried forward ... in the summer of 1765. It is this action and not those of a year later, to which Asa Spalding referred so feelingly in his "Historical Narrative" of Nimham's case. If so, then Spalding was only echoing and exploiting the wave of indignation that swept over the county and its Connecticut border. One can imagine now John Kane's fiery eloquence, no doubt exceeding that of his grandson James Kent, that spirited the mob up to the point of violence.

As early as April of '64, Moses Northrup had joined Munroe and Willcox in guaranteeing the validity of Indian deeds, for which, or a similar action, Robinson had expelled him from his lease along the Oblong. It was this "gore" on which Munroe and Willcox lived, as Prendergast lived in the "debateable" Philipse-Beekman gore. Such dry details must be insisted upon, as showing how completely the so-called "anti-rent" period was initially a question of title rather than of rent.

Prendergast, however, was perfectly clear in his own mind as to his course of action. Asked what his purpose was, he replied quietly: "to restore poor people to their possessions". He never varied....

In Westchester County active proselyting went on, so that by the following spring mobs were ready for riot, and some of their number had been arrested in April. The situation had become so serious that Governor Moore issued a proclamation against them, naming Prendergast among a group of a half-dozen agents from Dutchess at work in Westchester in expelling replacers. By June Connecticut farmers of Wallingford were bold enough to demand a moratorium on debt actions.

But these, though undoubtedly linked up with the Prendergast mob, found no leader like him. He first took "office" in November, 1765. The Dutchess lawyer Moss Kent, who had married John Kane's daughter, testified to the effectiveness of the "General Combination" among them. He had read on November 12, 1765, a paper ("advertisement") "inviting all persons having regard to their Tenements (tenures) to assemble in a few days to do justice to 'em." Their motive was that of Prendergast, "that none should be arrested for debt; that they would stand with lives and fortunes by each other; that they would suffer none of their party to be arrested for what they did as a mob; to resist all officers of justice; and that none should agree with landlords till the whole did. The combination existed in all the counties to support each other."...

At Malcolm Morrison's tavern on November 19, 1765, Kent watched Prendergast enter the room and walk about. He had already "opened his Commission" the week before, and had told Kent his purpose was "to restore the people turn'd out of possession". Now, however, for the first time he "swore he would head the mob".

On November 21, Gideon Prindle at Fredericksburgh (Patterson) watched a hundred farmers march past his door on their way from Towners to Morrison's. They were headed by Samuel Munroe, his son Daniel, Isaac Perry, Philip Philipse (no relation, I think, of the "heirs") and William Robellier. "Samuel Munroe took William Prendergast by the shoulders and told him he must be the captain or leader. Prendergast at first declined, but it being insisted on by Samuel Monroe and two or three others, he told them if he must be their captain they must obey him and do no mischief, nor abuse any person, but be very civil: and told them to fall in line and follow him to Sam Towners tavern."...

Thus the die was cast....

Our Captain next appeared at Westchester, with several of his lieutenants. Riots followed in the lower county against Van Cortlandt and others. Cooperating with them, Prendergast went to New York to rescue two Westchester tenants. They were halted at Kingsbridge, where the leader made a law "that recalcitrant officials who persisted in serving warrants or in spying on the tenants should be dragged and ridden on rails." Soon after his return Justice Peters fell in his way, and with a subordinate was given the works. Half strangled with the mud and sore from his ride on a rail, he had to swear on a Bible produced by Prendergast that he would give no evidence against his captor.

The New York march had produced alarm in the city. Governor Moore ordered out the militia, and commanded the rioters to disperse. In face of these actions, the local Sons of Liberty saw no reason to risk their necks, and Prendergast, who had proposed the march to his committee, and who expected a general uprising to join him, returned in great disappointment. He called his men Sons of Liberty, but the men of York were after the British, not the landlords, some of whom were their leaders....

...Blood would have blood, and guerilla warfare would follow. Livingston had some experience of this when...he went to arrest Prendergast and found him, sword in hand, at the head of his company. He drew off in good order....

Captain Prendergast, however, had lost heart, as did Brutus before Philippi. His captains quarreled among themselves for command. His Twelve Men disputed his authority. The mob went here and there at will. Worst of all, radicalism was rising and violence was spreading. The Prendergast code was forgotten. The attack was now on all law. The Sons of Liberty had disowned him....

On June 28, the Twenty-eighth Regiment marched off for the South Precinct. Everything was in disorder there. Prendergast had gone, apparently to his home near Quaker Hill. A few followers were with him, according to Peter Terry. Apparently he had marched from Fishkill after the Militia had been disbanded there. Stephen Crane told Terry they were on their way to Quaker Hill to meet the regulars....

Of the fight at Quaker Hill we have no direct report. D. Akins testified that two days before the fight he had told Prendergast that the Regulars would come; he had replied they should never get across the mountains. But apparently he never was able to carry out an ambush on the West Pawling Mountain such as he planned. He was caught at Pawling without a shot, and his troop dispersed. Taken to York to prison, he was brought back for trial at Poughkeepsie.

There, from July 29 to August 14, the Supreme Court under Judge Horsmanden held a special session. Prendergast's trial took only twenty-four hours. Many other rioters were tried, but his was the only one on the charge of high treason. He was convicted and sentenced to be hanged with the usual pretty details customary in British law for traitors. A recommendation to the King's mercy was included in the jury's verdict, and joined by the judges in their sentence.

The "Notes" on the trial, taken by a reporter who leaned toward the side of the King, and the News reports of Weymann's Gazette contrast with the report in the Weekly Gazette, which dwells on the sufferer, the fairness of the judges, and particularly on the newsworthy and unprecedented participation in the trial of Mehitabel Wing Prendergast, the defendant's wife....

Of Mehitabel, who at this moment shares our attention with the despairing Prendergast, the Post Boy wrote in glowing terms. The whole item must be quoted, in order to understand how completely our poor William was overshadowed by Mehitabel.

"At the Special Court of Oyer and Terminer which began at Poughkeepsey on the 29th of July, and held till the 14th August, for the Trial of Persons concerned in the late Riots in Dutchess County, several indictments were found, one for high treason, one for burglary, a large number for Riots, a few for Assaults and batteries and other trivial Offences.

"William Prendergast, after a Trial of 24 Horus, wherein every reasonable Indulgence was allowed him, was by a Jury of some of the most respected Freeholders, found Guilty of High Treason: ('tis said in this, they differ'd from the opinion of the Court, and were sent back, but persisted in their Verdict.) He was sentenced and ordered to be executed on Friday, the 26th of September Instant. Several of the Rioters, more or less according to the Nature of their Offenses, two stood in the Pillory, and two were ordered to Imprisonment for a Trial. They all expressed much Penitence, protested against such Riotous Proceedings for the Future, and exhorted the Bystanders to take Warning.

"The Sheriff of Dutchess County, Mr. James Livingston, has offer'd a Good Reward to any Person Inclin'd to assist at the Execution of Prendergast, and has promis'd to disguise them so that they shall not be known, and secure them from Insults.

"(We hear that on the Trial of Prendergast, the Behavior of his wife was very remarkable, and greatly attracted Notice of the Audience. During the whole long Trial, she was solicitously attentive to every particular; and without the least impertinence, or Indecorum of Behavior, sedately anxious for her Husband, as the Evidence open'd against him she never failed to make every Remark that might tend to extenuate the Nature of the Offence, and put his Conduct in the most favorable Point of View; not suffering one Circumstance that could be collected from the Evidence, or thought of in his favour, set out for York, to solicit a Reprieve, and tho' above 70 miles, returned in three Days, with Hopes of success—the Prisoner having been recommended by the Court and Jury to the King's Mercy. In short the whole Behaviour of this unhappy woman was such, as did Honour to her Sex and the Conjugal State.)

"When the terrible Sentence was pronounced upon the Prisoner, he utter'd an ejaculatory Prayer to God for mercy, with such Earnestness, and looked so distress'd, that the whole Audience, even those least susceptible of Compassion, were melted into Tears."

The Prendergasts returned to Pawling after the trial. No objection to his tenancy came from the Philipse heirs. In 1771 William obtained title, and in 1774 completed purchase in fee for £137. Quitrents still hampered him, however. The first represented the original Philipse quitrent of twenty shillings on the first patent; the second was based on the Colden formula of two shillings sixpence for each hundred acres, and was assessed on 4725 acres of the second patent. Thus by 1784, according to the reckoning of Humphrey Slocum, "yeoman" of Pawling, when Prendergast sold the farm to him, he was indebted in the sum of £62. 16s. 10d. This was one-third of the quitrents for fifteen and twenty-five years respectively. Morris and Robinson shares being confiscated, and quitrents abolished by law on such estates, only a third remained to pay.

But Prendergast, as stated in this document, had removed to "Scatacook", near Saratoga. Slocum's bill may have had something to do with our hero's trek to the west, for he certainly would have died rather than pay a cent for quitrent. He joined the great migration, at one time getting to Kentucky.

The family finally settled on the southern end of Lake Chautauqua, where his son James is celebrated as the founder of Jamestown. There was good stock in the family. The history of New York would have contained brighter pages if all its Irish Presbyterians had married all its Quaker maids. There were not enough Mehitabel Wings to go round....

19TH CENTURY

HENRY NOBLE MacCRACKEN

Thoroughfare of Freedom

Wild grapes and self-sown wheat
  And then the Golden Door—
Newcomes, starved in the ships—
  What were they seeking for?
What made their axes sing,
  Their ox-teams tug and strain?
What hopes quickened their heart,
  And soothed the throbbing pain?
What shall we make of it,
  This fair and friendly land?
Will the old folks recall,
  Their children understand?

As others saw us.

Not all English tourists visited the States in order to abuse them, nor was there any general conspiracy of abuse. A perusal of some of these observations shows that Dutchess County was very kindly remembered in the journals of our guests. Perhaps, the Highlands, the River, and the countyside were a refreshing change from bustling New York and its cuspidorean palaces. Perhaps it was, that in most cases Dutchess was the first American landscape they saw. Jaded eyes find fault; the wide-awake find something

From *Blithe Duchess: The Flowering of an American County from 1812* by Henry Noble MacCracken. Published by Hastings House, New York. Copyright 1958 by Henry Noble MacCracken. Reprinted by permission of the author, Casperkill Press, Poughkeepsie, New York.

strange and beautiful in every new turn of the road. And, perhaps, Dutchess really was as lovely as they said it was.

The Scotsman who went by night up the Hudson and was wakened by a collision between his steam boat and an obtrusive schooner could hardly be blamed for some caustic remarks. The schooner's bowsprit pierced his cabin wall, and came to rest directly above an old gentleman in the lower berth.

But when the schooner swung around and withdrew its beak, good-nature returned, and the view of the green shores was "almost perfect." The charm of Hyde Park, where our Scot visited Robert Emmett, nephew of the hero, was beyond cavil. He did not blame Mr. Emmett for preferring his farm and garden to New York. He left Jacob Harvey impressed with a personality of benevolence.

Dr. Hosack's place, near by, was most often visited and praised. The tourists, like caterpillars, were already laying down for themselves a little Ariadnean thread to guide them in their sight-seeing in the new republic, and hospitable Dr. Hosack came first. Our Scotsman enjoyed his drive from Poughkeepsie Landing with his tolerant host (his adjective) though he did not approve the hideous zigzag fences along the turnpike. The powerful carriage horses carried him safely by them, however, and soon the bald and rugged summits of the Catskills rewarded him.

He confided two impressions to his journal that night: the vast American barber-shop on the steam boat, and the manners of the Americans at table. "Each man seemed to devour under the uncontrollable impulse of some sudden hurricane of appetite, to which it would be difficult to find any parallel beyond the limits of the zoological garden."

Another Scotsman, also visiting Dr. Hosack, thought the Hudson "one of Nature's felicities." As for the grounds (now in the Vanderbilt Mansion park) "poet or painter could desire nothing more beautiful." Everything was in its proper place. Add anything to the mountain, and the River would be diminished.

Mr. J. G. Buckingham was more practical in his inspection. He, too, noted the pretty country-seats, and even stopped at the far-famed Catskill Mountain House. But his admiration was reserved for the Poughkeepsie Screw Factory, "where mathematical precision in all its parts make the product likely to supersede every other kind of screw in use."

Francis Lieber, the agrarian Reformer, praised the American farmer. "I have never received a stupid answer from a farmer." But he objected to the excesses of the American revivals.

The traveler Shirreff, on his return from travels in Dutchess and her neighbors, could no longer wear his clothes when he unpacked them in New

York. Even the chairs were too small; he had to sit on a sofa, so plenteous had been the Hudson fare. This brings to mind the Fat Girl of the curious Ezra Stiles, who saw her at Nine Partners. At nineteen she weighed 432 pounds. Dutchess was dangerous in those days, and she has not much improved.

Alexander Mackay examined the public schools in his "Western World." Gideon Hawley had been at work. "If we spent at the same rate," wrote this frank Briton, "it would cost us ten times as much as it does." But he added, "their scientific acquirements are attained at the cost of their accomplishments." A puzzling thought, until we reflect that he was referring to our social gifts.

Fidler told how his River captain crossed and re-crossed the bow of the rival boat, until the exasperated competitor rammed him. The crash was tremendous, but both boats reached Albany in safety. He found time to note that "the Dutch, who are not renowned for taste or elegance, have contrived, wherever they locate themselves, to select and appropriate the most beautiful and fertile places." Nature, of course, must take the blame. Fidler also thought long upon the gap he observed between the really respectable and the other classes. "The former are as much in advance of the country's civil institutions as are the latter in arrears."

Not meeting, or not venturing to meet, many people in their travels, the tourists, then as now, were reduced to discussion of their meals. Stuart thought his breakfast at Fishkill one of the best he ever ate. But he was surprised to see his driver served at an adjoining table in the general dining-room, and eating exactly the same meal.

At Red Hook each guest had four eggs for breakfast. Women served them, though a little boy of color did the honors at Fishkill.

He was pleased when preserves of peach and pear appeared, and the landlord told him to take all the apples he could carry away from the orchard. Always abundance, always unostentatious hospitality. He missed the hearty way in which the British host pressed food upon his guests. In Dutchess no talk of food or praise of wine seemed welcome. Americans simply fell to.

Hugh Duffie, the Irish liveryman who drove him up the Hudson shore, was entirely satisfied with the rate of hire that had been stipulated. An extraordinary occurrence for the seasoned European traveler, who had braced himself for the usual altercation.

"Fibbleton," in his burlesque travel diary, had great fun with American politics: "Coots," "Quids," "Bucktails," "Highbinders" and "Highminders" were the butts of his harmless jesting.

The worthy Sir Augustus John Foster, Bart., in "Jeffersonian America," was moved to contemplate the superior blessings of aristocracy. "For I hold that men are as distinctive in race as horses." This accounted for the superior cultivation of Rensselaer and Livingston estates. He noted that Tom Paine had resided somewhere near Poughkeepsie on the North River. He was relieved to find that Tallmadges could be traced back to a respectable English family. Yet "I cannot quite call Americans the sons of European immigrants." Something new and different had been added, thought this authority on human heredity.

Perhaps it was the steep climb up Quaker Hill on a hot summer day in 1799, that moved Friend John Griffith to be somewhat critical of his American brethren. He found them plain and becoming in their outward garb, but dry and formal in the true light. "The word went forth like a flame of fire against the wood, hay, and stubble. Truth had great dominion that day." There followed a "close service" at Nine Partners, and a painful afflicting at Oswego.

Hodgson found Poughkeepsie "principally a Dutch town, as is very evident in the construction of the buildings, and the figures of the men and women; the former of smaller, the latter of ampler dimensions than are common in America." He enjoyed the ride to New York, "far wilder than the Trossachs." He found "a surly landlord, but a good room." The American landlord often took a dim view of those who treated him as an inferior.

John Lambert enjoyed his voyage upriver on a big River sloop. The singing on board was objectionable, because it kept him awake. What would we not give today for some old Hudson chanties? The captain, Elihu Bunker, turned out to be a plain religious sort of man, and everyone enjoyed the debate which ensued between a parson and a rationalist. There was time to open one's mind on a Hudson sail.

Lambert thought well of R. R. Livingston for shifting the ignominy of the Purchase of Louisiana upon Jefferson's shoulders. Wealthy Easterners, he noticed, feared that the addition of so much land to the national domain would ruin the sale of their own farms.

Bristede, a more foreseeing man, believed the West would soon outvote the East, but urged the Erie Canal, all the same. With it "the State of New York would soon in itself become a powerful empire." The city of New York would then become the greatest emporium in the world.

In the light of such good-natured comments as these—I have suppressed none that have crossed my way—the battle of words over English belittlings suggests that Paulding and the other defenders of America were a bit thin-skinned. The English tourists brought with them their own temperaments, and usually toured too fast to see much beyond the surface. But there was little hostility. Mrs. Trollope, who went broke, and Basil Hall, who squatted with his whole family upon his resentful hosts, were exceptions.

What they missed, of course, was the sense of history. Americans for a hundred years or more were sensitive about this lack. Some of them, like a well-known industrialist, thought it was bunk. Others apologized for our barrenness. Then our novelists got to work even before our historians. Cooper gave us the Indians before anyone else did. Irving forestalled a history of New Netherland with his delightful sketch. But today we are beginning to see that in each unit of each part of our land there is already a history in the stage of record, ready for the writer.

Dutchess has been a thoroughfare, always. The great River passed her door, the King's Highway threaded her valleys. Men crossed the County along the Salisbury Pike and the Fishkill road, and the Dutchess Turnpike to Poughkeepsie. These were the ways of the pioneers, many of whom sojourned for a generation or two, giving tone to the towns. Companies marched away to the French wars, and regiments to the Revolution, 1812, 1861, 1898, 1917, 1941, 1950.

The County has been a thoroughfare of ideas. Of tolerance toward the Indians, Quakers, and many others who did not conform. Of law, studied and practised as livelihood to make living useful. Of neighborhood as the principle of society as against rank. Of initiative, originality, invention. Of sport, recreation, and frolic, of good times. And always, a thoroughfare of freedom, for none of these could thrive without it. The State and National Constitutions, here written or debated, dealt with freedom, and their adoption hung upon that point. And here a President passed his youth, who concerned himself with four freedoms. Here he learned his political primer. But long before him, before rail or paddle-wheel, our farmers stood for their fields and freedom of organization.

When the railroad came upon us, our tourists passed us by. All they knew of Dutchess was the cry, "twenty minutes for refreshments," at the genteel restaurant of Mr. Johnson in the Poughkeepsie station. Sports writers week-ending in Dutchess at the river races, and correspondents following President Roosevelt back and forth between Hyde Park and Washington were extremely myopic in their views, which do not bear repetition. A picture of a county fair, done as a bucolic exercise by a non-farmer, adorned a metropolitan weekly a few months ago. No one else has shown the very body of our time its form and pressure.

We have no stage to show it to us. No poet, essayist, philosopher. Only the historian, and the journalist, who writes history day by day, have worked together to preserve what they have found to be the color and feel of a county.

ANNE COLVER

Old Bet

FOREWORD

There was a real Old Bet. She landed in America, from far across the sea, in 1808, and was owned by the real Mr. Hachaliah Bailey of Somers, New York. A live "ely-phunt" was an unheard-of curiosity to Americans of that day, and Old Bet became the star attraction of Mr. Bailey's menagerie exhibit. In summer seasons they traveled from town to town, always at night, the elephant always walking, through New England as far north as Camden, Maine. A wooden statue of Bet and the Elephant Hotel, named in her honor, are still landmarks on the pleasant village green of Somers in northern Westchester.

A.C.

When the schooner *Seven Seas* sailed into New York one fair spring morning in the year 1808 with a rich cargo of ivory, she carried just two passengers....

The captain had listed them in the ship's log: *One boy. Name: T'wan-Ka Baker Clark, age 10, relatives unknown. One elephant. Name: Old Bet, age ditto, relatives ditto.*

A boy and an elephant, who had grown up together on the coast of Africa, landing in New York without family or friend between them! The captain frowned and rubbed his whiskered chin and squinted through his spyglass and wished for the hundredth time he'd never brought them as passengers at all.

It was old Mauna who had persuaded the captain. Mauna was chief of a native village where the captain traded for ivory. "The boy's parents came from America as missionaries," Mauna said gently. "They taught us and they were our friends. They even named their son in our language—T'wan-Ka which means Sturdy One. Now they are dead of fever and T'wan must go back to his own people."

All very well, the captain had harrumphed impatiently, but who *were* the lad's people? What relatives had his father and mother left?

It was a mystery, old Mauna admitted. Floods had swept the village and carried off all T'wan's father's books, all his mother's letters. Even the carved chest with her precious keepsakes from America. "The boy himself was too young to remember," Mauna sighed. "All the more reason why you will want to take Old Bet too. Away from our village, the elephant will be T'wan's only friend."

The captain had wanted no such thing. A homeless boy was bad enough. But take the great cumbersome heathen beast on his ship he would not!

Or so he thought. Until Mauna, who was wise as well as gentle, had said he could not trade the captain his best ivory after all—*unless* the captain would agree.

The captain had agreed. And he had to admit his passengers had been no trouble on the voyage. The lad was quiet and helpful, and the elephant had excellent elephant manners. During the worst storms there hadn't been a whimper out of either one.

Still he wondered whether anyone in all the crowded city of New York would welcome one boy with relatives unknown.

And one elephant, *ditto*....

At noon next day flags flew on Broadway from Battery Park to the brand new City Hall in honor of Bet's parade. People crowded the curb and hung out of shop and office windows for their first sight of the strange foreign beast.

A band led the parade. They wore bright blue coats and played sometimes on key and sometimes not, sounding very enthusiastic either way. Next came the city's best fire engine of red with shining brass, pulled by white horses that snorted and pawed the cobblestones. A group of sailors from different nations followed. Mr. Bailey had gathered them up along the waterfront and invited them to march. They did, with pleasure, arms about each other, singing sea chanties in a dozen languages. Then there was an Irish marching society, with harps and green jackets, and a group of Scottish Highlanders, bagpipes in full cry.

Mr. Bailey and Patty rode in a carriage draped in red, white and blue. And last of all, escorted by Mayor De Witt Clinton's own guard of honor, ambled Old Bet herself.

Tom [as the Baileys called T'wan] walked beside her, wearing a new vest and breeches and elegant russet leather boots. Patty had made him get a proper haircut, and he marched head up, feeling altogether different and very fine....

All the way to the village of Somers, where the Bailey family lived, Tom wondered how Mr. Bailey's wife would feel about having a new boy and an elephant added to the household so suddenly. His first sight of Mrs. Bailey made him realize she wasn't a person who spent much time worrying. Tom thought perhaps having a menagerie show in the family made the Baileys take unexpected things cheerfullly.

"I saw in the papers you'd bought an elephant," Mrs. Bailey said. She came across the yard from the brick farmhouse. Patty's two little sisters, Clarissa and Melissa, ran ahead. They had hair as fluffy and yellow as new chicks.

Mrs. Bailey took one look at Old Bet. Then she turned to give Tom a nice sensible handshake. "I'm certainly glad you came along to take care of her." She glanced up at Bet's bulging grey side and smiled. "I was afraid I'd be expected to cook for an elephant."

CHARLES DICKENS

Lebanon; The Shaker Village

After breakfasting at Whitehall, we took the stage-coach for Albany, a large and busy town, where we arrived between five and six o'clock that afternoon, after a very hot day's journey, for we were now in the height of summer again. At seven we started for New York on board a great North River steamboat, which was so crowded with passengers that the upper deck was like the box lobby of a theatre between the pieces, and the lower one like Tottenham Court Road on a Saturday night. But we slept soundly, notwithstanding, and soon after five o'clock next morning reached New York.

Tarrying here only that day and night to recruit after our late fatigues, we started off once more upon our last journey in America. We had yet five

From *American Notes for General Circulation* by Charles Dickens. Published by D. Appleton and Company, New York, 1872.

days to spare before embarking for England, and I had a great desire to see "the Shaker Village," which is peopled by a religious sect from whom it takes its name.

To this end we went up the North River again as far as the town of Hudson, and there hired an extra to carry us to Lebanon, thirty miles distant, and of course another and a different Lebanon from that village where I slept on the night of the Prairie trip.

The country through which the road meandered was rich and beautiful, the weather very fine, and for many miles the Kaatskill Mountains where Rip Van Winkle and the ghastly Dutchman played at ninepins one memorable gusty afternoon, towered in the blue distance, like stately clouds. At one point, as we ascended a steep hill, athwart whose base a railroad, yet constructing, took its course, we came upon an Irish colony. With means at hand of building decent cabins, it was wonderful to see how clumsy, rough, and wretched its hovels were. The best were poor protection from the weather; the worst let in the wind and rain through wide breaches in the roofs of sodden grass, and in the walls of mud; some had neither door nor window; some had nearly fallen down, and were imperfectly propped up by stakes and poles; all were ruinous and filthy. Hideously ugly old women and very buxom young ones, pigs, dogs, men, children, babies, pots, kettles, dunghills, vile refuse, rank straw, and standing water, all wallowing together in an inseparable heap, composed the furniture of every dark and dirty hut.

Between nine and ten o'clock at night we arrived at Lebanon, which is renowned for its warm baths, and for a great hotel, well adapted, I have no doubt, to the gregarious taste of those seekers after health or pleasure who repair here, but inexpressibly comfortless to me. We were shown into an immense apartment, lighted by two dim candles, called the drawing-room, from which there was a descent by a flight of steps to another vast desert called the dining-room. Our bedchambers were among certain long rows of little whitewashed cells, which opened from either side of a dreary passage, and were so like rooms in a prison that I half expected to be locked up when I went to bed, and listened involuntarily for the turning of the key on the outside. There need be baths somewhere in the neighborhood, for the other washing arrangements were on as limited a scale as I ever saw, even in America; indeed, these bedrooms were so very bare of even such common luxuries as chairs, that I should say they were not provided with enough of anything, but that I bethink myself of our having been most bountifully bitten all night.

The house is very pleasantly situated, however, and we had a good breakfast. That done, we went to visit our place of destination, which was some two miles off, and the way to which was soon indicated by a finger-post, whereon was painted, "To the Shaker Village."

As we rode along, we passed a party of Shakers, who were at work upon the road, who wore the broadest of all broad-brimmed hats, and were in all visible respects such very wooden men, that I felt about as much sympathy for them, and as much interest in them, as if they had been so many figure-heads of ships. Presently we came to the beginning of the village, and alighting at the door of a house where the Shaker manufactures are sold, and which is the head-quarters of the elders, requested permission to see the Shaker worship.

Pending the conveyance of this request to some person in authority, we walked into a grim room, where several grim hats were hanging on grim pegs, and the time was grimly told by a grim clock, which uttered every tick with a kind of struggle, as if it broke the grim silence reluctantly, and under protest. Ranged against the wall were six or eight stiff high-backed chairs, and they partook so strongly of the general grimness, that one would rather have sat on the floor than incurred the smallest obligation to any of them.

Presently there stalked into this apartment a grim old Shaker, with his eyes as hard and dull and cold as the great round metal buttons on his coat and waistcoat,—a sort of calm goblin. Being informed of our desire, he produced a newspaper wherein the body of elders whereof he was a member had advertised but a few days before, that in consequence of certain unseemly interruptions which their worship had received from strangers, their chapel was closed to the public for the space of one year.

As nothing was to be urged in opposition to this reasonable arrangement, we requested leave to make some trifling purchases of Shaker goods, which was grimly conceded. We accordingly repaired to a store in the same house and on the opposite side of the passage, where the stock was presided over by something alive in a russet case, which the elder said was a woman, and which I suppose *was* a woman, though I should not have suspected it.

On the opposite side of the road was their place of worship,—a cool, clean edifice of wood, with large windows and green blinds, like a spacious summer-house. As there was no getting into this place, and nothing was to be done but walk up and down, and look at it and the other buildings in the village (which were chiefly of wood painted a dark red, like English barns, and composed of many stories like English factories), I have nothing to communicate to the reader beyond the scanty results I gleaned the while our purchases were making.

These people are called Shakers from their peculiar form of adoration, which consists of a dance performed by the men and women af all ages, who arrange themselves for that purpose in opposite parties; the men first divesting themselves of their hats and coats, which they gravely hang against the wall before they begin; and tying a ribbon round their shirt-sleeves as though they were going to bleed. They accompany themselves with a droning, humming noise, and dance until they are quite exhausted, alternately advancing and retiring in a preposterous sort of trot. The effect is said to be unspeakably absurd; and if I may judge from a print of this ceremony which I have in my possession, and which I am informed by those who have visited the chapel is perfectly accurate, it must be infinitely grotesque.

They are governed by a woman, and her rule is understood to be absolute, though she has the assistance of a council of elders. She lives, it is said, in strict seclusion in certain rooms above the chapel, and is never shown to profane eyes. If she at all resemble the lady who presided over the store, it is a great charity to keep her as close as possible, and I cannot too strongly express my perfect concurrence in this benevolent proceeding.

All the possessions and revenues of the settlement are thrown into a common stock, which is managed by the elders. As they have made converts among people who were well to do in the world, and are frugal and thrifty, it is understood that this fund prospers, the more especially as they have made large purchases of land. Nor is this at Lebanon the only Shaker settlement; there are, I think, at least three others.

They are good farmers, and all their produce is eagerly purchased and highly esteemed. "Shaker seeds," "Shaker herbs," and "Shaker distilled waters" are commonly announced for sale in the shops of towns and cities. They are good breeders of cattle, and are kind and merciful to the brute creation. Consequently Shaker beasts seldom fail to find a ready market.

They eat and drink together, after the Spartan model, at a great public table. There is no union of the sexes, and every Shaker, male and female, is devoted to a life of celibacy. Rumor has been busy upon this theme, but here again I must refer to the lady of the store, and say that if many of the sister Shakers resemble her, I treat all such slander as bearing on its face the strongest marks of wild improbability. But that they take as proselytes persons so young that they cannot know their own minds, and cannot possess much strength of resolution in this or any other respect, I can assert from my own observation of the extreme juvenility of certain youthful Shakers whom I saw at work among the party on the road.

They are said to be good drivers of bargains, but to be honest and just in their transactions, and even in horse-dealing to resist those thievish tendencies which would seem, for some undiscovered reason, to be almost inseparable from that branch of traffic. In all they hold their own course quietly, live in their gloomy, silent commonwealth, and show little desire to interfere with other people.

This is well enough, but nevertheless I cannot, I confess, incline towards the Shakers, view them with much favor, or extend towards them any very lenient construction. I so abhor and from my soul detest that bad spirit, no matter by what class or sect it may be entertained, which would strip life of its healthful graces, rob youth of its innocent pleasures, pluck from maturity and age their pleasant ornaments, and make existence but a narrow path towards the grave; that odious spirit which, if it could have had full scope and sway upon the earth, must have blasted and made barren the imaginations of the greatest men, and left them in their power of raising up enduring images before their fellow-creatures yet unborn, no better than the beasts; that in these very broad-brimmed hats and very sombre coats—in stiff-necked solemn-visaged piety, in short, no matter what its garb, whether it have cropped hair as in a Shaker village, or long nails as in a Hindoo temple—I recognize the worst among the enemies of Heaven and Earth, who turn the water of the marriage feasts of this poor world, not into wine, but gall. And if there must be people of innocent delights and gayeties, which are a part of human nature,—as much a part of it as any other love or hope that is our common portion,—let them, for me, stand openly revealed among the ribald and licentious: the very idiots know that *they* are not on the Immortal road and will despise them and avoid them readily.

20TH CENTURY

EDNA ST. VINCENT MILLAY

Steepletop

1

Even you, Sweet Basil: even you,
Lemon Verbena: must exert yourselves now
  and somewhat harden
Against untimely frost; I have hovered you and
  covered you and kept going
  smudges,
Until I am close to worn out. Now, you
Go about it. I have other things to do,
Writing poetry, for instance. And I, too,
Live in this garden.

2

Nothing could stand
All this rain.
The lilacs were drowned, browned
  before I had even
  smelled them
Cool against my cheek, held down
A little by my hand.
Pain
Is seldom preventable, but is
  presentable
Even to strangers on a train—

But what the rain
Does to the lilacs—is something
  you must sigh and try
To explain.

3

Borage, forage for bees
And for those who love blue,
Why must you,
Having been transplanted
From where you were not wanted
Either by the bee or by me
From under the sage, engage in this
  self-destruction?
I was tender about your slender
  tap-root.
I thought you would send out shoot after
  shoot
Of thick cucumber-smelling, hairy leaves.
But why anybody believes
Anything, I do not know. I thought I
  could trust you.

BOOK TWO

The Adirondacks

The St. Lawrence

Adirondacks

INTRODUCTION TO BOOK II

THE HIGH wooded peaks of the Adirondacks were more rugged and dramatic than the Catskill Mountains. Bold Samuel de Champlain found them impressive and challenging as he and his Indian allies paddled from the St. Lawrence River, up the Richelieu, and through the firefly-ridden night, up the length of the lake which has been named for him. Historians have found his one shot from an arquebus, which killed three Mohawk chieftains, perhaps the most important event in the competition between Britain and France for control of Canada and its neighboring lands to the south. Its result was a lasting enmity toward France on the part of the powerful Confederacy of the Iroquois Indians.

Most mountain ranges have provided such isolation as to give their inhabitants distinctive characteristics. The Adirondacks are no exception, and authors have found much to write about describing the landscape and the human "characters" who dwell there. Residence among the lonely hills has encouraged eccentricity, independence, originality. It is quite natural then that Book Two offers a gallery of portraits of people on whom the mountain landscape has worked its influence.

THE ADIRONDACKS

17TH CENTURY

MORRIS BISHOP

The Fourth Voyage: Lake Champlain

The Richelieu was broad and bland. The Indians assured Champlain that in his shallop he could sail up it to the Lake of the Iroquois. (Perhaps there was a misunderstanding; or perhaps they were tempting him on.) But when Champlain reached the roaring rapids at Chambly, he found no passage for his shallop and no possibility of cutting a road for it through the dense woods. "I was particularly sorry to return without seeing a very large lake, filled with beautiful islands, and a large, beautiful region near the lake, where they had represented to me their enemies lived. Having thought it over well, I decided to proceed thither in order to carry out my promise and also to fulfill my desire." The "desire" is the lust of the explorer, to see the yet unseen, first of any men of his race.

Champlain called for volunteers. Two stepped forward; their names we do not know. The others quailed at the prospect of the adventure; "their noses bled," says Champlain. He let them go, sending them back to Quebec in the shallop.

Now (it was July 12) the sincere warriors, white and red, held a review above the Chambly Rapids. There were twenty-four canoes with sixty Indians, a mingling of Hurons, Montagnais, and Ottawa Algonquins. Champlain and his two Frenchmen carried, for all their baggage, their heavy arquebuses, powder, match, and shot. They wore steel corselets, half armor. (You may see an authentic example in the museum at Fort Ticonderoga.)

Champlain had an old soldier's interest in the routine of the warpath.

On making camp, the Indians built wigwams and felled trees for a barricade. The riverbank was left open, to permit escape by canoe. The chief sent three canoes upriver to scout for evidence of the enemy. "All night long they rely upon the explorations of these scouts, and it is a very bad custom; for sometimes they are surprised in their sleep by their enemies, who club them before they have time to rise and defend themselves. Realizing this, I pointed out to them the mistake they were making, and said that they ought to keep watch as they had seen us do every night, and have men posted to listen and see whether they might perceive anything, and not live as they were doing like silly creatures. They told me that they could not stay awake, and that they worked enough during the day when hunting."

So these Indians were at the same time stoic and soft, grim-purposed and capricious, cunning and silly, like the rest of us.

On the march, a troop of scouts went first, watching for the marks on trees which were messages from friends or indications of enemies. The main body followed; parties of hunters fanned out on the flanks.

Every night the *pilotois,* the medicine man, was called upon for augury. He built a wigwam covered with beaver-skin. "When it is made, he gets inside so that he is completely hidden; then he seizes one of the poles of the tent and shakes it, whilst he mumbles between his teeth certain words, with which he declares he is invoking the devil, who appears to him in the form of a stone and tells him whether his friends will come upon their enemeis and kill many of them. This pilotois will lie flat upon the ground, without moving, merely speaking to the devil, and suddenly he will rise to his feet, speaking and writhing so that he is all in a perspiration, though stark naked. The whole tribe will be about the tent sitting on their buttocks like monkeys. They often told me that the shaking of the tent which I saw was caused by the devil and not by the man inside, although I saw the contrary.... I often pointed out to them that what they did was pure folly, and that they ought not to believe in such things."

In accordance with the forecasts of the oracle, "the chiefs take sticks a foot long, one for each man, and indicate by others somewhat longer their leaders. Then they go into the wood, and level off a place five or six feet square, where the headman, as sergeant-major, arranges all these sticks as to him seems best. Then he calls his companions, who approach fully armed, and he shows them the rank and order which they are to observe when they fight with the enemy. This all these Indians regard attentively, and notice the figure made with these sticks by their chief. And afterwards they return from that place and begin to arrange themselves in the order in which they have seen these sticks. Then they mix themselves up and again put themselves in proper order, repeating this two or three times, and go back to their camp, without any need of a sergeant to make them keep their ranks, which they are quite able to maintain without getting into confusion."

The trouble with this sort of battle practice, which used to be called in our own army a "dry run," is that it may be totally forgotten in combat.

On July 13 the party paddled cautiously up the broad Richelieu. The hunters brought in abounding game: stags, fallow deer, fawns, roebuck, bear. By nightfall the party stood where the waters broaden out, at or near Rouses Point, to form a shining lake.

Champlain and his two companions were the first known white men to set foot on the soil of New York State.

Now for two weeks (if Champlain's chronology is at all exact, and indeed it is often sadly at fault) the party felt its way prudently south along the lake. Champlain noted the beautiful islands and rivers. His mention of a grove of chestnuts places him in Burlington, Vermont, for there alone are they known to have stood by the lake. He observed to the eastward "very high mountains on the tops of which there was snow." This is amazing indeed. Perhaps, say the commentators, he was deceived by white marble outcroppings on the Green Mountains. Still, an experienced explorer should not have been so easily deceived.

He was still a little credulous. The Indians gave him the piglike snout of a five-foot garfish. Some, they said, are eight or ten feet long. This fish "shows marvellous ingenuity in that, when it wishes to catch birds, it goes in amongst the rushes or reeds that lie along the shores of the lake, and puts its snout out of the water without moving. The result is that when the birds come and light on its snout, mistaking it for a stump of wood, the fish is so cunning that, shutting its half-open mouth, it pulls them by their feet under the water." It couldn't have been a crocodile?

Champlain looked across the lake to the blue humps of the Adirondacks. The Indians told him that there they would meet their enemies. They would pass a rapid ("which I afterwards saw"); then they would enter another lake, ten leagues long [Lake George], then go by land two leagues to a river [the Hudson], which descends to the coast of Norumbega, adjoining that of Florida.

This information is pretty accurate. Champlain's knowledge of Algonquin and the Algonquins' knowledge of French were sufficient for the communication of geographical facts.

Now, as the party was in hostile territory, it traveled by night, hiding by day in the deep woods. The Indians asked Champlain anxiously about his dreams. In fact, he says, he dreamed that he saw the Iroquois drowning in a lake; he tried to rescue them but was prevented by his companions, who said the Iroquois were all bad men and should properly drown. This dream gave great encouragement to his allies.

For Champlain it was an intoxicating journey. He was stirred by the beauty of the summer nights on this lovely lake, winding among monstrous mountains. He watched the strange fireflies, drawing bright lines in the velvet darkness; he heard the enormous purr of unknown insects, happy in the heat. This lake, he determined, would be his own. He would call it by his own name.

At ten o'clock on the evening of July 29, the invaders, paddling softly southward, came to a cape on the westward shore. It was, almost certainly, the rounded promontory below Fort Ticonderoga, rich with its memories of later wars. Some spots on this earth seem destined to be battlefields; they smell of blood.

Out of the dark came loud shouts and cries. It was a war party of Mohawk Iroquois, heading north in their heavy, clumsy, elm-bark canoes.

The Iroquois, recognizing their inferiority on the water, pulled in to shore and immediately built a barricade, chopping down trees "with the poor axes they sometimes win in war, and with stone axes."

The invaders lay off the shore, tying their canoes together with long poles.

Two Iroquois canoes paddled out for a parley, "to learn from their enemies whether they wished to fight, and these replied that they had no other desire, but that for the moment nothing could be seen and that it was necessary to wait for daylight in order to distinguish one another. They said that as soon as the sun should rise, they would attack us, and to this our Indians agreed."

This then was the etiquette of warfare: a parley and an agreement on the hour of battle. This war had much of the character of an organized sport. The later wars, for commerce and survival, had no such courtly air.

All night the Iroquois danced on the shore. The allies in their canoes sang songs of insult. Both sides shouted boasts of victory and scurrilous depreciation of the opponent, as in the ritual of modern baseball.

In the first dawn the allies went ashore unhindered by the Iroquois. It was no doubt thought unsporting to interfere with a landing operation. The three Frenchmen with their arquebuses were carefully hidden from the enemy's view.

The allies formed in battle array. At the agreed time the Iroquois marched solemnly out of their barricade. There were two hundred of them, strong, robust men. They outnumbered the allies by more than three to one.

"They came slowly to meet us with a gravity and calm which I admired; and at their head were three chiefs. Our Indians likewise advanced in similar order, and told me that those who had the three big plumes were the chiefs, and that there were only these three, whom you could recognize by these plumes, which were larger than those of their companions; and I was to do what I could to kill them. I promised them to do all in my power, and told them I was very sorry they could not understand me, so that I might direct their method of attacking the enemy, all of whom undoubtedly we should thus defeat; but that there was no help for it, and that I was very glad to show them, as soon as the engagement began, the courage and readiness which were in me.

"As soon as we landed, our Indians began to run some two hundred yards toward their enemies, who stood firm and had not yet noticed my white companions who went off into the woods with some Indians. Our Indians began to call to me with loud cries; and to make way for me they divided into two groups, and put me ahead some twenty yards, and I marched on until I was within some thirty yards of the enemy, who as soon as they caught sight of me halted and gazed at me and I at them. When I saw them make a move to draw their bows upon us, I took aim with my arquebus and shot straight at one of the three chiefs, and with this shot two fell to the ground, and one of their companions was wounded who died thereof a little later. I had put four bullets into my arquebus. As soon as our people saw this shot so favorable for them, they began to shout so loudly that one could not have heard it thunder, and meanwhile the arrows flew thick on both sides. The Iroquois were much astonished that two men should have been killed so quickly, although they were provided with shields made of cotton thread woven together and wood, which were proof against their arrows. This frightened them greatly. As I was reloading my arquebus, one of my companions fired a shot from within the woods, which astonished them again so much that, seeing their chiefs dead, they lost courage and took to flight, abandoning the field and their fort, and fleeing into the depths of the forest, whither I pursued them and laid low still more of them. Our Indians also killed several and took ten or twelve prisoners. The remainder fled with the wounded. Of our Indians fifteen or sixteen were wounded with arrows, but these were quickly healed."

So at Ticonderoga, on the green shore of Champlain's lake, was fired the first musket shot in a war that was to continue, in effect, for two hundred years.

The battle was won, as, we are told, wars are usually won, by the New Weapon. This new weapon was to transform completely the wars of red men and white, and red men and red. The battle of Ticonderoga was fought by two massed groups in close order. We shall not see such another. The Indians soon threw away their useless shields, revised their tactics, and resorted to a strategy of raids and surprises.

What we have seen was a Stone Age battle, half war, half sport. It was a noble dance of death, a bloody ballet, performed according to accepted rules. Champlain, with his new weapon, violated the rules.

The resentment of the Iroquois was bitter. (The resentment is always bitter on the part of those "unfairly" defeated by mechanization, air raids, atomic bombs, bacteria.) Champlain's arquebus inspired among the Iroquois a tradition of French treachery never to be forgotten.

18TH CENTURY

FRANCIS PARKMAN

1842 Journal

July 15th, [*18*]*42.* We crossed the boundary line to Chatham, the first New York village. The country was as level as that about Boston. We passed through Kinderhook and Schodack—or however else it is spelled—and at half past six saw the Hudson, moping dismally between its banks under a cloudy sky, with a steamboat solemnly digging its way through the leaden waters. In five minutes the spires and dirt of Albany rose in sight on the opposite shore. We crossed in a steamboat and entered the old city, which, indeed, impressed us at once with its antiquity by the most ancient and fish-like smell which saluted our shrinking nostrils, the instant we set foot on the wharf. We have put up at the Eagle Hotel—a good house. Nevertheless, we are both eager to leave cities behind us.

July 16th, Caldwell [*Lake George*]. This morning we left Albany—which I devoutly hope I may never see again—in the cars, for Saratoga. My plan of going up the river to Ft. Edward [1] I had to abandon, for it was impracti-

From pp. 44-48 and 50-51 *The Journals of Francis Parkman,* edited by Mason Wade. Copyright 1947 by Massachusetts Historical Society.
Reprinted with the permission of Harper & Row, Publishers, Inc.

[1] Fort Edward is near Glens Falls, New York, on the upper Hudson. A stockade fort was first built on this site—long known as the Great Carrying Place because it was the chief portage on the Hudson–Lake George–Lake Champlain–Richelieu water route—by Colonel Francis Nicholson in 1790 and was named after him. Another fort, first known as Lydius after a Dutch settler and later as Fort Edward after the Duke of York, was built here by General Phineas Lyman of Connecticut in 1755, and was sometimes called Lyman's Fort. Its occupation by General Webb halted Montcalm after the French capture of William Henry in 1757. Fort Edward was also the goal of Marin's French and Indian raid earlier in the same summer. See *Half-Century,* I, 140; and *Montcalm and Wolfe,* II, 173, 205-7.

cable—no boat beyond Troy. Railroad the worst I was ever on; the country flat and dull; the weather dismal. The Catskills appeared in the distance. After passing the inclined plane and riding a couple of hours we reached the valley of the Mohawk and Schenectady. I was prepared for something filthy in the last mentioned venerable town, but for nothing quite so disgusting as the reality. Canal docks, full of stinking water, superannuated rotten canal boats and dirty children and pigs paddling about, formed the foreground of the delicious picture, while in the rear was a mass of (of) tumbling houses and sheds, bursting open in all directions; green with antiquity, dampness, and lack of paint. Each house had its peculiar dunghill, with the group of reposing hogs. In short, London itself could exhibit nothing much nastier.[2] In crossing the main street, indeed, things wore an appearance which might be called decent. The car-house here is enormous. Five or six trains were on the point of starting for the north, south, east, and west; and the brood of railroads and taverns swarmed about the place like bees. We cleared the babel at last, passed Union College,[3] another tract of monotonous country, Ballston, and finally reached Saratoga, having travelled latterly at the astonishing rate of about seven miles an hour. "Caldwell stage ready!" We got our baggage on board, and I found time to enter one or two of the huge hotels.[4] After perambulating the entries filled with sleek waiters and sneaking fops, dashing through the columned porticoes and enclosures, drinking some of the water and spitting it out again in high disgust, I sprang onto the stage, cursing Saratoga and all New York. With an unmitigated temper, I journeyed to Glen's Falls, and here my wrath mounted higher yet, at the sight of that noble cataract almost concealed under a huge awkward bridge, thrown directly across it, with the addition of a dam above, and about twenty mills of various kinds. Add to all, that the current was choked by masses of drift logs above and below, and that a dirty village lined the banks of the river on both sides; and some idea may possibly be formed of the way in which the New Yorkers have bedevilled Glen's. Still the water comes

[2] Parkman first visited London two years later, but he was familiar with Dickens' accounts of it.

[3] Union College, which grew out of the Schenectady Academy (1784), was chartered in 1795.

[4] Saratoga Springs was a favorite summer camping ground of the Iroquois, particularly the Mohawks, who were attracted to the place by the medicinal springs long before white men visited the region. The district was the scene of several conflicts between the French and English and their Indian allies. In 1693 a French expedition was defeated by Governor Benjamin Fletcher and Peter Schuyler. In 1745 the settlers were massacred by French and Indian raiders. The battle of Saratoga during the Revolution was fought about five miles southeast of the present village. The first lodging house for visitors to the springs, a log cabin, was built in 1771, and by 1830 the place had become one of the most popular American resorts.

down over the marble ledges in foam and fury, and the roar completely drowns the clatter of the machinery. I left the stage and ran down to the bed of the river to the rocks at the foot of the falls. Two little boys volunteered to show me the "caverns," which may be reached dry-shod when the stream is low. I followed them down amid the din and spray to a little hole in the rock which led to a place a good deal like the Swallows' Cave, and squeezed in after them. "This is Cooper's Cave, sir; where he went and hid the two ladies." They evidently took the story in *The Last of the Mohicans*[5] for Gospel. They led the way to the larger cave, and one of them ran down to the edge of the water which boiled most savagely past the opening. "This is Hawkeye's Cave: here's where he shot an Indian." "No, he didn't either," squalled the other, "it was higher up on the rocks." "I tell you it wasn't." "I tell you it was." I put an end to the controversy with two cents.

Dined at the tavern, and rode on. Country dreary as before; the driver one of the best of his genus I ever met. He regaled me as we rode on with stories of his adventures with deer, skunks, and passengers. A mountain heaved up against the sky some distance before us, with a number of smaller hills stretching away on each hand, all wood-crowned to the top. Away on the right rose the Green Mts., dimly seen through the haze, and scarcely distinguishable from the blue clouds that lay upon them. Between was a country of half cultivated fields, tottering houses, and forests of dwarf pines and scrub oaks. But as we drew near, the mountain in front assumed a wilder and a loftier aspect. Crags started from its woody sides and leaned over a deep valley below. "What mountain is that?" "That 'ere is French Mounting"—the scene of one of the most desperate and memorable battles[6] in the Old French War. As we passed down the valley, the mountain rose above the forest half a mile on our right, while a hill on the left, close to the road, formed the other side. The trees flanked the road on both sides. In a little opening in her woods, a cavity in the ground, with a pile of stones at each end, marked the spot where was buried that accomplished warrior and gentleman, Colonel Williams,[7] whose bones, however, have

[5] In Fenimore Cooper's *The Last of the Mohicans* (Ch. 6-9) Hawkeye, Uncas, and Chingachgook hide Cora, Alice, Duncan Heywood, and David in these caverns while fleeing from the Mingoes. Cooper was Parkman's favorite novelist.

[6] The skirmish of Rocky Brook, which is referred to in the text, took place on the morning of September 6, 1755, when the French and Indians under Baron Dieskau and Le Gardeur de St. Pierre ambushed a portion of Sir William Johnson's forces, under the command of Colonel Ephraim Williams and Lieutenant Colonel Whiting. After the initial French success in this skirmish, they were defeated at Lake George by Johnson, and Dieskau was wounded and taken prisoner.

[7] Colonel Ephraim Williams (1714/5-55), who came to Stockbridge, Massachusetts, with his family in 1737 from the Connecticut Valley, commanded the line of frontier outposts known as the Massachusetts Forts, which ran from Fort Dummer in Vermont

since been removed. Farther on is the rock on the right where he was shot, having mounted it on the look-out—an event which decided the day; the Indians and English broke and fled at once. Still farther on is the scene of the third tragedy of that day, when the victorious French, having been in their turn, by a piece of great good luck, beaten by the valorous Johnson[8] at his entrenchment by the lake, were met at this place on their retreat by McGinnis,[9] and almost cut to pieces. Bloody Pond,[10] a little, slimy, dark sheet of stagnant water, covered with weeds and pond-lilies and shadowed by the gloomy forest around it, is the place where hundreds of dead bodies were flung after the battle, and where the bones still lie. A few miles farther, and Lake George lay before us, the mountains and water confused and indistinct in the mist. We rode into Caldwell, took supper—a boat—and then a bed.

July 17th, Caldwell. The tavern is full of fashionable New Yorkers—all of a piece. Henry and myself both look like the Old Nick, and are evidently

---

to Fort Massachusetts near Williamstown, where he usually resided. In 1755 he commanded the 3rd Massachusetts, in Johnson's army, and headed the detachment sent out from the main camp at Lake George to intercept Dieskau's lines of communication with South Bay. Early in the engagement at Rocky Brook he was shot through the head, when he mounted a rock to reconnoiter. He was buried near the spot where he fell, at the foot of a huge pine beside the military road linking the lake and Fort Edward. His grave was later marked with a boulder inscribed E.W. 1755. He made provision in his will for a free school at Williamstown, which in 1793 became the college called after him. There is a tablet to his memory in the Williams Chapel. See *Montcalm and Wolfe,* I, 301-4, 309-15.

[8] Sir William Johnson (1715-74), who was born in Ireland, came to America in 1738 to take charge of the New York estates of his uncle, Admiral Sir Peter Warren. He was appointed Indian agent in 1744 and obtained remarkable influence over the Iroquois. In 1755 he became Superintendent of Indian Affairs, and was also made major general in command of the expedition against Fort Frédéric (Crown Point). Braddock's ill-fated march against Fort Duquesne and Shirley's expedition against Fort Niagara were part of the three fold plan of this campaign. Johnson intended to build a fort at the head of Lake George, proceed up the lake and capture Carillon (Ticonderoga), and there await the rest of his army before attacking Fort Frédéric. But news of Dieskau's flanking attack by South Bay on Fort Edward forced him to give battle at Lake George on September 5. For his victory he received the thanks of Parliament, a baronetcy, and £5,000. He has been criticized for not following up his success and moving against Carillon and Fort Frédéric as originally planned, but it was late in the season and his army had been rudely handled before it won its triumph. See *Montcalm and Wolfe,* I, 296-329.

[9] Captain William McGinnis (?-1755) of Schenectady commanded the detachment from Fort Edward which encountered French stragglers at Bloody Pond, after the battle at the lake. During this final action of September 5, 1755, McGinnis was hit in the head by a ricocheting ball, but continued in command until the end of the fray. He died two days later. See *Montcalm and Wolfe,* I, 319-20.

[10] Bloody Pond, two and a half or three miles south of Johnson's camp at Lake George, was the place where two hundred men from Fort Edward under Captains Folsom and McGinnis fell upon the French and Indian stragglers and drove them to their boats at South Bay, after capturing their baggage and ammunition. The name of the pond commemorates the unceremonious burial in its waters of the victims of the fray.

looked upon in a manner corresponding. I went this morning to see William Henry.[11] The old fort is much larger than I had thought; the earthen mounds cover many acres. It stood on the southwest extremity of the lake close by the water. The enterprising genius of (of) the inhabitants has made a road directly through the ruins, and turned bastion, moat, and glacis into a flourishing cornfield, so that the spot so celebrated in our colonial history is now scarcely to be distinguished. Large trees are growing on the untouched parts, especially on the embankment along the lake shore. In the rear, a hundred or two yards distant, is a gloomy wood of pines, where the lines of Montcalm [12] can easily be traced. A little behind these lines is the burying place of the French who fell during that memorable siege. The marks of a thousand graves can be seen among the trees, which, of course, have sprung up since. Most of them have been opened, and bones and skulls dug up in great numbers. A range of mountains towers above this fine forest—Cobble Mt.—the Prospect, &c., the haunt of bears and rattle-snakes. The ruins of Ft. George [13] are on a low hill of lime-stone a short distance southeast of William Henry—of stone, and in much better preservation than the other, for they are under the special protection of Mr. Caldwell,[14] the owner of the village; but they have no historical associations connected with them. I noticed some curious marks of recent digging in William Henry and asked an explanation of an old fellow who was hoeing corn in a field close by. He said that some fools had come up the lake with a wizard and a divining

[11] The first fortification at the head of Lake George, consisting of embankments of gravel surmounted by logs, was built by Sir William Johnson in 1755 and named by him after the commander in chief, the Duke of Cumberland, younger son of George II, the victor of Culloden and the loser of Fontenoy. The site was an unfortunate choice, being swampy and easily commanded from the surrounding hills. The fort was captured by Montcalm on August 9, 1757, and most of its garrison were massacred by his Indians, who refused to abide by the terms of capitulation. The French burned the fort, which had been greatly strengthened since 1755, and stripped it of munitions and supplies.

[12] The Marquis de Montcalm (1712-59), who came to America as commander in chief in 1756, sent Rigaud de Vaudreuil to reconnoiter William Henry in March 1757, and then himself besieged it in form in the following August with 8,000 men. Landing at Artillery Cove on August 3, he opened trenches and parallels, and bombarded the fort, which surrendered six days later. His lines ran from Artillery Cove to within a few hundred yards of the fort, around the southwest corner of the lake. See the plan, "Siege of Fort William Henry, 1757," in *Montcalm and Wolfe,* II, 183.

[13] Fort George, a short distance southeast of William Henry, was surveyed by General James Abercromby and his engineer Montresor in 1758, but was not built until the following year under Amherst. It was solidly constructed of masonry on the hill which had formed part of Johnson's camp in 1755 and of a division of Munro's forces in 1757. The capture in 1759 of Carillon and Fort Frédéric on Lake Champlain eliminated its usefulness, and only one bastion was completed.

[14] William Caldwell was the son of General James Caldwell, an Albany merchant, who acquired 1,595 acres of upstate New York land in 1787.

rod to dig for money in the ruins.[15] They went at midnight for many successive nights and dug till day light. I undertook to climb the Prospect—three miles high, without a path. I guided myself by the sun and summits of the mountains, and got to the top almost suffocated with heat and thirst. The view embraced the whole lake as far as Ty [Ticonderoga]. All was hazy and indistinct, only the general features of the scene could be distinguished in the dull atmosphere. The lake seemed like a huge river, winding among mountains. Came down, dined, and went to church. The church is a minute edifice, with belfry and bell exactly like a little school-house. It might hold easily about sixty. About thirty were present—countrymen; cute, sly, sunburnt slaves of Mammon; maidens of sixty and of sixteen; the former desperately ugly, with black bonnets, frilled caps, peaked noses and chins, and an aspect diabolically prim and saturnine; the latter for the most part remarkably pretty and delicate. For a long time the numerous congregation sat in a pious silence, waiting for the minister. At last he came, dodged into a little door behind the pulpit, and presently reappeared and took his place, arrayed in a white surplice with black facing. He was very young, and *Yankee ploughboy* was stamped on every feature. Judge of my astonishment when he began to read the Episcopal service in voice so clear and manner so appropriate that I have never heard better even in Boston. He read the passage in Exodus—quite appropriate to the place—beginning "the Lord is a man of war." In his sermon, which was polished and even elegant, every figure was taken from warfare. One of Montcalm's lines ran northwest of the tavern toward the mountains.[16] Two or three years ago, in digging for some purpose, a great quantity of deer, bear, and moose bones were found here, with arrows and hatchets, which the tavern keeper thinks mark the place of some Indian feast. The spikes and timbers of sunken vessels may be seen in strong sunlight, when the water is still, at the bottom of the lake, along the southern beach. Abercrombie [Abercromby] sunk his boats here.[17]

[15] The legend of treasure buried at William Henry, probably at the time of its surrender to Montcalm in 1757, is referred to in Hoyt's *Antiquarian Researches,* which is quoted in Van Rensselaer, *Battle of Lake George,* 69.

[16] This was probably one of the trenches of Montcalm's siege works. See *Montcalm and Wolfe,* II, 192 & n.

[17] General James Abercromby (1706-81), called "Nambycromby" by the provincials for his excessive caution which bordered on poltroonry, came to America in 1756 and superseded Shirley and Webb in command of the army, being supplanted in turn by the Earl of Loudoun. In 1757 he commanded the second brigade in the Louisbourg Expedition, and in 1758 he became commander in chief on Loudoun's recall. He led the unsuccessful expedition of that year against Carillon (Ticonderoga), with Lord George Howe as his second-in-command. After the latter's death at Trout Brook the campaign became a dismal failure, with Montcalm hopelessly outwitting Abercromby. After his disastrous attack on Carillon, Abercromby retreated to the head of Lake George, and burned his boats in the general panic.

There are remains of batteries [18] on French Mt. and the mountains north of it, I suppose to command the road from Ft. Edward. This evening visited the French graves. I write this at camp, July 18th. Just turned over my ink-bottle and spilt all the ink....

Wednesday, July 20th. Entered the Narrows this morning, and rowed among all the islands and along all the shores. White trailed a line behind the boat, by which means he caught a large bass. Scenery noble, but mists still on the mountains....

...The water was a dark glistening blue, with lines of foam on the crests of the waves; huge shadows of clouds coursed along the mountains. The little islands would be lighted at one instant by a stream of sunshine falling on them and almost making their black pines transparent, and the next moment they would be suddenly darkened and all around the glittering with a sudden burst of light from the opening clouds. We passed under Black Mt., whose precipices and shaggy woods wore a very savage and impressive aspect in that peculiar weather, and kept down the lake seven miles to Sabbath Day Pt. High and steep mountains flanked the lake the whole way. In front, at some distance, they seemed to slope gradually away, and a low green point, with an ancient dingy house upon it closed the perspective. This was Sabbath Day Pt., the famous landing place of many a huge army.[19] We noticed two abrupt mountains on our left, and steering under them, found them the most savage and warlike precipices we had yet seen. One impended over the lake, like the stooping wall of an old castle; its top was fringed with trees, which seemed bushes, from the height, and great fragments of broken rock were piled around its base. We ran our boat on the beach of Sabbath Day Pt. and asked lodging at the house. An old woman, after a multitude of guesses and calculations, guessed as how she could accommodate us with a supper and a bed, though she couldn't say nohow how we should like it, seeing as how she war'nt used to visitors. The house was an old, rickety, dingy shingle palace, with a potatoe garden in front, hogs perambulating the outhouses, and a group of old men and women engaged in earnest conversation in the tumble-down portico. The chief figure was an old grey-haired man, tall and spare as a skeleton, who was giving some advice to a chubby old lady about her corns.

"Well, now," said the old lady, "I declare they hurt me mighty bad."

[18] These batteries may have been part of Montcalm's siege works.

[19] Parkman's enthusiasm for historic spots here led him into rhetorical excess. Sabbath Day Point was merely the scene of the ambush of Colonel Parker's scouts by the partisan Corbière and his Indians on July 26, 1757, and a stopping place of Abercromby's army on July 5, 1758, as it moved against Ticonderoga.

"I'll give you something to cure them right off."

"What is it? I hope it a'nt snails. I always hated snails since I was a baby, but I've heered say they are better for corns nor nothing else at all." . . .

FRANCIS PARKMAN

Campbell of Inverawe

The ancient castle of Inverawe stands by the banks of the Awe, in the midst of the wild and picturesque scenery of the Western Highlands. Late one evening, before the middle of the last century [18th], as the laird, Duncan Campbell, sat alone in the old hall, there was a loud knocking at the gate; and, opening it, he saw a stranger, with torn clothing and kilt smeared with blood, who in a breathless voice begged for asylum. He went on to say that he had killed a man in a fray, and that the pursuers were at his heels. Campbell promised to shelter him. "Swear on your dirk!" said the stranger, and Campbell swore. He then led him to a secret recess in the depths of the castle. Scarcely was he hidden when again there was a loud knocking at the gate, and two armed men appeared. "Your cousin Donald has been murdered, and we are looking for the murderer!" Campbell, remembering his oath, professed to have no knowledge of the fugitive; and the men went on their way. The laird, in great agitation, lay down to rest in a large dark room where at length he fell asleep. Waking suddenly in bewilderment and terror, he saw the ghost of the murdered Donald standing by his bedside, and heard a hollow voice pronounce the words: "Inverawe! Inverawe! blood has been shed. Shield not the murderer." In the morning Campbell went to the hiding place of the guilty man and told him he could harbor him no longer. "You have sworn on your dirk," he replied and the laird of Inverawe, greatly perplexed and troubled, made a compromise between conflicting duties, promised not to betray his guest, led him to the neighboring mountain (Ben Cruachan) and hid him in a cave.

In the next night, as he lay tossing in feverish slumbers, the same stern voice awoke him, the ghost of his cousin Donald stood again at his bedside, and again he heard the same appalling words: "Inverawe! Inverawe! blood

From *Montcalm and Wolfe* by Francis Parkman, published by Little, Brown and Company, Boston, 1884.

has been shed. Shield not the murderer!" At break of day he hastened, in strange agitation, to the cave; but it was empty, the stranger had gone. At night, as he strove in vain to sleep, the vision appeared once more, ghastly pale, but less stern of aspect than before. "Farewell, Inverawe!" it said; "Farewell, till we meet at TICONDEROGA!"

The strange name dwelt in Campbell's memory. He had joined the Black Watch, or Forty-Second Regiment, then employed in keeping order in the turbulent Highlands. In time he became its Major; and, a year or two after the war broke out, he went with it to America. Here, to his horror, he learned that it was ordered to the attack of Ticonderoga. His story was well known among his brother officers. They combined among themselves to disarm his fears; and when they reached the fatal spot they told him on the eve of the battle, "This is not Ticonderoga; we are not there yet; this is Fort George." But in the morning he came to them with haggard looks. "I have seen him! You have deceived me! He came to my tent last night! This is Ticonderoga! I shall die today!" And his prediction was fulfilled.

JOHN PELL

The Capture of Ticonderoga

The rendezvous was Hand's Cove. A mile north of the promontory of Ticonderoga, on the eastern shore of Lake Champlain, it forms in early spring a natural harbor entirely hidden from the Fort across the Lake. Gershom Beach, a Rutland blacksmith, had been sent to rouse the Green Mountain Boys in the north (he is said to have covered sixty miles in twenty-four hours), and all night they poured in to the appointed place. The moon was in the last quarter, but, after it rose, full enough to show trees as shadows darker than the ground....

The selection from *Ethan Allen* by John Pell, copyright 1929, is reprinted by permission of and arrangement with Houghton Mifflin Company, the authorized publishers.

Toward morning an officer wearing the scarlet coat of the Connecticut Governor's footguards, mounted and accompanied by a servant, reached Hand's Cove, found Ethan with the other officers, introduced himself as Captain Benedict Arnold, and produced a commission from the Cambridge

Committee of Safety to enlist four hundred men and reduce Ticonderoga. He was a handsome, proud-looking man who seemed perfectly confident that the Green Mountain officers would hand over their men to him—although he had already demanded the command from the Board of War, at Castleton, and had been refused. As Mott had informed him, the men, when they enlisted, were promised that they would be commanded by their own officers. Nevertheless, early in the morning, Arnold hurried forward to Hand's Cove and there again insisted that he should have the command. The men threatened to go home unless they could have their own officers.... Ethan and Easton soothed them by promising that Arnold wasn't going to have the command, and pointing out that even if he did the pay would be the same. But the men said they would damn the pay, they were not going to be commanded by anybody but their own officers.

A compromise was found which satisfied both Arnold and the men. There is no documentary evidence of its terms, but unquestionably Arnold was allowed to march at the head of the column, beside Ethan....

There were now more than two hundred men gathered on the shores of the cove.... Leaving Warner in command of the rear guard, Ethan filled the two boats to capacity and started across the Lake in a southwesterly direction. It would be interesting to know what passed through his mind as he stood in the bow of the first boat watching for lights or moving shadows on the distant shore. It must have occurred to him that six hours from now the Continental Congress would meet at Philadelphia. Perhaps, as he listened to the patter of water dripping from the oars and the moaning of the wind, he wondered whether he was going to be acclaimed by Congress or hanged by the King. Perhaps he thought of what he would say when he demanded surrender of the Fort.

Landing just north of Willow Point, he ranged his men three deep on the beach and (as he remembered the occasion four years later) harangued them as follows:

> Friends and fellow soldiers, you have for a number of years past been a scourge and terror to arbitrary power. Your valor has been famed abroad, and acknowledged, as appears by the advice and orders to me from the General Assembly of Connecticut, to surprise and take the garrison now before us. I now propose to advance before you, and, in person, conduct you through the wicket-gate; for we must this morning either quit our pretensions to valor, or possess ourselves of this fortress in a few minutes; and, inasmuch as it is a desperate attempt, which none but the bravest of men dare undertake, I do not urge it on any contrary to his will. You that will undertake voluntarily, poise your fire-locks.

Every man raised his gun. Ethan gave the command to march and they started for the Fort. It was about three o'clock, still dark, but the sky was paling in the sky was paling in the east. Ethan and Arnold headed the column, both in uniform and wearing swords; but, whereas Arnold's was the uniform of a captain in the Connecticut Governor's footguards, Ethan's was an invention of his own designed for the unique position of Colonel Commandant of the Green Mountain Boys. It was modeled on a British Infantry officer's uniform; probably was a green coat with yellow or buff breeches and certainly had large gold epaulettes. The men were farmers dressed in their working clothes, hunting clothes or even Sunday clothes. They wore breeches of buckskin, linsey-woolsey, fustian, and plush. They wore woolen stockings, buckled shoes or moccasins, calico and silk waistcoats, beaver and felt hats, and bearskin caps. They carried rifles, blunderbusses, pistols, hangers, hunting-knives, and clubs.

Near the landing there was a road leading past the charcoal oven, the Pontleroi redoubt, and the well, skirting the east wall of the Fort to the ruined entrance in the south wall. Just opposite this break in the center of the south curtain of the main Fort there was a gate with a wicket, where a sentry was posted. He was probably dozing on a bench with an hourglass beside him. Ethan and Arnold were at the head of the column which swarmed through and over the break in the south wall. The sentry, awakened from his dream, saw in the pale gray light an enormous apparition rushing at him with a sword waving above its head. He had presence of mind enough to cock his musket and pull the trigger, but the flint flashed in the pan and the gun misfired. Taking to his heels, he ran through the long archway under the south barracks into the *place d'armes* and across it to a bombproof on the other side, shouting all the while to rouse the garrison. Ethan rushed after him, and the men, with Indian war-whoops, crowded through the wicket gate and climbed the walls of the bastions. Ethan ordered them to form a hollow square in the *place d'armes,* but after they had given three cheers their enthusiasm overcame their discipline, and, shouting 'No Quarter!' they rushed at the doors and stairways of the barracks.

The first soldier to emerge from the guard-room in the south barracks made a pass at one of the invaders with a charged bayonet, but Ethan, coming up just then, hit him over the head with the flat of his sword. The man's life probably was saved by a comb he was wearing in his hair. He begged for quarter, which Ethan granted on condition that he point out the Commandant's room. The soldier led the way to a stairway leading up the façade of the west barracks. With Arnold beside him and a crowd of his men at his back, Ethan started up.

A door opened at the head of the stairs and there appeared on the landing a man wearing an infantry lieutenant's coat and waistcoat, but holding his breeches in his hand. Ethan shouted some such phrase as 'Come out of there, you damned old rat!'—and, with Arnold at his side, began to climb the stairs, meanwhile demanding the surrender of the Fort at the top of his lungs. The man above motioned them to stop, and then asked by what authority they entered His Majesty's Fort. Ethan shouted: 'In the name of the Great Jehovah and the Continental Congress!' Reaching the top with his sword waving in the air, he told the breechesless officer 'that he must have immediate possession of the Fort and all the effects of George the Third'; adding that if this 'was not complied with, or that there was a single gun fired in the fort, neither man, woman or child should be left alive in the Fort.'

Finding that the officer whom he had been addressing (Lieutenant Feltham) was not the Commandant, Ethan started to break in the door, but Arnold restrained him. The door opened without his aid, however, and Captain Delaplace, the Commandant, fully dressed, stepped out. Realizing there was nothing else to do, he handed his sword to Ethan and ordered his men to be paraded without arms. Arnold told the British officers he had received instructions from the Cambridge Committee of Correspondence to take the Fort, and Ethan told them his orders were from the Province of Connecticut. Feltham was immediately locked up in the Commandant's room, with sentries before both doors, while Ethan and Arnold took Delaplace downstairs to order his men to lay down their arms. Meanwhile, the invaders had broken in the doors of the barracks and captured the regulars in their bunks. At Ethan's command they dragged the bewildered prisoners out and lined them up in the *place d'armes,* while their arms were all piled in a room guarded by a sentry. A guard was allotted to each prisoner and they were allowed to break ranks and return to their quarters. By now daylight was breaking, the rear guard was swarming into the Fort, and the men had discovered the captain's liquor. As Ethan afterwards remembered the occasion:

> The sun seemed to rise that morning with a superior lustre; and Ticonderoga and its dependencies smiled on its conquerors, who tossed about the flowing bowl, and wished success to Congress, and the liberty and freedom of America.

19TH CENTURY

CHARLES DUDLEY WARNER

Old Phelps

He was a true citizen of the wildernesses. Thoreau would have liked him, as he liked Indians and woodchucks, and the smell of pine-forests; and, if Old Phelps had seen Thoreau, he would probably have said to him, "Why on airth, Mr. Thoreau, don't you live accordin' to your preachin'?" You might be misled by the shaggy suggestions of old Phelps's given name —Orson—into the notion that he was a mighty hunter, with the fierce spirit of the Berserkers in his veins. Nothing could be farther from the truth. The hirsute and grisly sound of Orson expresses only his entire affinity with the untamed and the natural, an uncouth but gentle passion for the freedom and wildness of the forest. Orson Phelps has only those unconventional and humorous qualities of the bear which make the animal so beloved in literature; and one does not think of Old Phelps so much as a lover of nature,—to use the sentimental slang of the period,—as a part of nature itself.

His appearance at the time when as a "guide" he began to come into public notice fostered this impression,—a sturdy figure, with long body and short legs, clad in a woollen shirt and butternut-colored trousers repaired to the point of picturesqueness, his head surmounted by a limp, light-brown felt hat, frayed away at the top, so that his yellowish hair grew out of it like some nameless fern out of a pot. His tawny hair was long and tangled, matted now many years past the possibility of being entered by a comb. His features were small and delicate, and set in the frame of a reddish beard, the razor having mowed away a clearing about the sensitive mouth, which

From *In the Wilderness* by Charles Dudley Warner. Published by Houghton Mifflin and Company, Boston, 1884.

was not seldom wreathed with a child-like and charming smile. Out of this hirsute environment looked the small gray eyes, set near together; eyes keen to observe, and quick to express change of thought; eyes that made you believe instinct can grow into philosophic judgment. His feet and hands were of aristocratic smallness, although the latter were not worn away by ablutions; in fact, they assisted his toilet to give you the impression that here was a man who had just come out of the ground,—a real son of the soil, whose appearance was partially explained by his humorous relation to soap. "Soap is a thing," he said, "that I hain't no kinder use for." His clothes seemed to have been put on him once for all, like the bark of a tree, a long time ago. The observant stranger was sure to be puzzled by the contrast of this realistic and uncouth exterior with the internal fineness, amounting to refinement and culture, that shone through it all. What communion had supplied the place of our artificial breeding to this man?

Perhaps his most characteristic attitude was sitting on a log, with a short pipe in his mouth. If ever man was formed to sit on a log, it was Old Phelps. He was essentially a contemplative person. Walking on a country road, or anywhere in the "open," was irksome to him. He had a shambling, loose-jointed gait, not unlike that of the bear; his short legs bowed out, as if they had been more in the habit of climbing trees than of walking. On land, if we may use that expression, he was something like a sailor; but, once in the rugged trail or the unmarked route of his native forest, he was a different person, and few pedestrians could compete with him. The vulgar estimate of his contemporaries, that reckoned Old Phelps "lazy," was simply a failure to comprehend the conditions of his being....

If the appearance of Old Phelps attracts attention, his voice, when first heard, invariably startles the listener. A small, high-pitched, half-querulous voice, it easily rises into the shrillest falsetto; and it has a quality in it that makes it audible in all the tempests of the forest, or the roar of rapids, like the piping of a boatswain's whistle at sea in a gale. He has a way of letting it rise as his sentence goes on, or when he is opposed in argument, or wishes to mount above other voices in the conversation, until it dominates everything. Heard in the depths of the woods, quavering aloft, it is felt to be as much a part of nature, an original force, as the northwest wind or the scream of the hen-hawk. When he is pottering about the camp-fire, trying to light his pipe with a twig held in the flame, he is apt to begin some philosophical observation in a small, slow, stumbling voice, which seems about to end in defeat; when he puts on some unsuspected force, and the sentence ends in an insistent shriek. Horace Greeley had such a voice, and could regulate it in the same manner. But Phelps's voice is not seldom plaintive, as if touched by the dreamy sadness of the woods themselves.

When Old Mountain Phelps was discovered, he was, as the reader has already guessed, not understood by his contemporaries. His neighbors, farmers in the secluded valley, had many of them grown thrifty and prosperous, cultivating the fertile meadows, and vigorously attacking the timbered mountains; while Phelps, with not much more faculty of acquiring property than the roaming deer, had pursued the even tenor of the life in the forest on which he set out. They would have been surprised to be told that Old Phelps owned more of what makes the value of the Adirondacks than all of them put together, but it was true. This woodsman, this trapper, this hunter, this fisherman, this sitter on a log, and philosopher, was the real proprietor of the region over which he was ready to guide the stranger. It is true that he had not a monopoly of its geography or its topography, though his knowledge was superior in these respects; there were other trappers, and more deadly hunters, and as intrepid guides; but Old Phelps was the discoverer of the beauties and sublimities of the mountains; and when city strangers broke into the region, he monopolized the appreciation of these delights and wonders of nature. I suppose, that, in all that country, he alone had noticed the sunsets, and observed the delightful processes of the seasons, taken pleasure in the woods for themselves, and climbed mountains solely for the sake of the prospect. He alone understood what was meant by "scenery." In the eyes of his neighbors, who did not know that he was a poet and a philosopher, I dare say he appeared to be a slack provider, a rather shiftless trapper and fisherman; and his passionate love of the forest and the mountains, if it was noticed, was accounted to him for idleness....

Phelps loved his mountains. He was the discoverer of Marcy, and caused the first trail to be cut to its summit, so that others could enjoy the noble views from its round and rocky top. To him it was, in noble symmetry and beauty, the chief mountain of the globe. To stand on it gave him, as he said, "a feeling of heaven up-h'isted-ness." He heard with impatience that Mount Washington was a thousand feet higher, and he had a child-like incredulity about the surpassing sublimity of the Alps. Praise of any other elevation he seemed to consider a slight to Mount Marcy, and did not willingly hear it, any more than a lover hears the laudation of the beauty of another woman than the one he loves....

...Phelps was the ideal guide; he knew every foot of the pathless forest; he knew all wood-craft, all the signs of the weather, or, what is the same thing, how to make a Delphic prediction about it. He was fisherman and hunter, and had been the comrade of sportsmen and explorers; and his enthusiasm for the beauty and sublimity of the region, and for its untamable wildness, amounted to a passion. He loved his profession; and yet it very soon appeared that he exercised it with reluctance for those who had neither ideality, nor love for the woods. Their presence was a profanation amid the scenery he loved. To guide into his private and secret haunts a party that had no appreciation of their loveliness disgusted him. It was a waste of his time to conduct flippant young men and giddy girls who made a noisy and irreverent lark of the expedition....

I recall the bearing of Old Phelps, when, several years ago, he conducted a party to the summit of Mount Marcy by the way he had "bushed out." This was his mountain, and he had a peculiar sense of ownership in it. In a way, it was holy ground; and he would rather no one should go on it who did not feel its sanctity....The bare summit that day was swept by a fierce, cold wind, and lost in an occasional chilling cloud. Some of the party, exhausted by the climb, and shivering in the rude wind, wanted a fire kindled and a cup of tea made, and thought this the guide's business. Fire and tea were far enough from his thought. He had withdrawn himself quite apart, and, wrapped in a ragged blanket, still and silent as the rock he stood on, was gazing out upon the wilderness of peaks. The view from Marcy is peculiar. It is without softness or relief. The narrow valleys are only dark shadows; the lakes are bits of broken mirror. From horizon to horizon there is a tumultuous sea of billows turned to stone. You stand upon the highest billow; you command the situation; you have surprised Nature in a high creative act; the mighty primal energy has only just become repose. This was a supreme hour to Old Phelps. Tea! I believe the boys succeeded in kindling a fire; but the enthusiastic stoic had no reason to complain of want of appreciation in the rest of the party. When we were descending, he told us, with mingled humor and scorn, of a party of ladies he once led to the top of the mountain on a still day, who began immediately to talk about the fashions! As he related the scene, stopping and facing us in the trail, his mild, far-in eyes came to the front, and his voice rose with his language to a kind of scream.

"Why, there they were, right before the greatest view they ever *saw,* talkin' about the *fashions!*"

Impossible to convey the accent of contempt in which he pronounced the word "fashions," and then added, with a sort of regretful bitterness,—

"I was a great mind to come down, and leave 'em there."...

It is only by recalling fragmentary remarks and incidents that I can put the reader in possession of the peculiarities of my subject; and this involves the wrenching of things out of their natural order and continuity, and introducing them abruptly,—an abruptness illustrated by the remark of "Old Man Hoskins," which Phelps liked to quote, when one day he suddenly slipped down a bank into a thicket, and seated himself in a wasps' nest; "I hain't no business here; but here I be!"

The first time we went into camp on the Upper Ausable Pond, which has been justly celebrated as the most prettily set sheet of water in the region, we were disposed to build our shanty on the south side, so that we could have in full view the Gothics and that loveliest of mountain contours. To our surprise, Old Phelps, whose sentimental weakness for these mountains we knew, opposed this. His favorite camping-ground was on the north side, —a pretty site in itself, but with no special view. In order to enjoy the lovely mountains, we should be obliged to row out into the lake: we wanted them always before our eyes,—at sunrise and sunset, and in the blaze of noon. With deliberate speech, as if weighing our arguments and disposing of them, he replied, "Waal, now, them Gothics ain't the kinder scenery you want ter *hog down!*"

It was on quiet Sundays in the woods, or in talks by the camp-fire, that Phelps came out as the philosopher, and commonly contributed the light of his observations. Unfortunate marriages, and marriages in general, were, on one occasion, the subject of discussion; and a good deal of darkness had been cast on it by various speakers; when Phelps suddenly piped up, from a log where he had sat silent, almost invisible, in the shadow and smoke,—

"Waal, now, when you've said all there is to be said, marriage is mostly for discipline."...

The sentiment of the man about nature, or his poetic sensibility, was frequently not to be distinguished from a natural religion, and was always tinged with the devoutness of Wordsworth's verse. Climbing slowly one day up the Balcony,—he was more than usually calm and slow,—he espied an exquisite fragile flower in the crevice of a rock, in a very lonely spot.

"It seems as if," he said, or rather dreamed out,—"it seems as if the Creator had kept something just to look at himself."

To a lady whom he had taken to Chapel Pond, a retired but rather uninteresting spot, and who expressed a little disappointment at its tameness, saying,—

"Why, Mr. Phelps, the principal charm of this place seems to be its loneliness,"—

"Yes," he replied in gentle and lingering tones, "and its *nativeness*. It lies here just where it was born."...

Old Phelps used words sometimes like algebraic signs, and had a habit of making one do duty for a season together for all occasions. "Speckerlation"

encounter before leaving on his climacteric errand—Roberta announcing that because of the heat and the fact that they were coming back to dinner, she would leave her hat and coat—a hat in which he had already seen the label of Braunstein in Lycurgus—and which at the time caused him to meditate as to the wisdom of leaving or extracting it. But he had decided that perhaps afterwards—afterwards—if he should really do this—it might not make any difference whether it was there or not. Was she not likely to be identified anyhow, if found, and if not found, who was to know who she was?

In a confused and turbulent state mentally, scarcely realizing the clarity or import of any particular thought or movement or act now, he took up his bag and led the way to the boathouse platform. And then, after dropping the bag into the boat, asking of the boathouse keeper if he knew where the best views were, that he wanted to photograph them. And this done—the meaningless explanation over, assisting Roberta (an almost nebulous figure, she now seemed, stepping down into an insubstantial rowboat upon a purely ideational lake), he now stepped in after her, seating himself in the center and taking the oars.

The quiet, glassy, iridescent surface of this lake that now to both seeemed, not so much like water as oil—like molten glass that, of enormous bulk and weight, resting upon the substantial earth so very far below. And the lightness and freshness and intoxication of the gentle air blowing here and there, yet scarcely rippling the surface of the lake. And the softness and furry thickness of the tall pines about the shore. Everywhere pines—tall and spearlike. And above them the humped backs of the dark and distant Adirondacks beyond. Not a rower to be seen. Not a house or cabin. He sought to distinguish the camp of which the guide had spoken. He could not. He sought to distinguish the voices of those who might be there—or any voices. Yet, except for the lock-lock of his own oars as he rowed and the voice of the boathouse keeper and the guide in converse two hundred, three hundred, five hundred, a thousand feet behind, there was no sound.

"Isn't it still and peaceful?" It was Roberta talking. "It seems to be so restful here. I think it's beautiful, truly, so much more beautiful than that other lake. These trees are so tall, aren't they? And those mountains. I was thinking all the way over how cool and silent that road was, even if it was a little rough."

"Did you talk to any one in the inn there just now?"

"Why, no; what makes you ask?"

"Oh, I thought you might have run into some one. There don't seem to be very many people up here to-day, though, does there?"

"No, I don't see any one on the lake. I saw two men in that billiard room at the back there, and there was a girl in the ladies' room, that was all. Isn't this water cold?" She had put her hand over the side and was trailing it in the blue-black ripples made by his oars.

"Is it? I haven't felt it yet."

He paused in his rowing and put out his hand, then resumed. He would not row directly to that island to the south. It was—too far—too early. She might think it odd. Better a little delay. A little time in which to think—a little while in which to reconnoiter. Roberta would be wanting to eat her lunch (her lunch!) and there was a charming looking point of land there to the west about a mile further on. They could go there and eat first—or she could—for he would not be eating to-day. And then—and then——

She was looking at the very same point of land that he was—a curved horn of land that bent to the south and yet reached quite far out into the water and combed with tall pines. And now she added:

"Have you any spot in mind, dear, where we could stop and eat? I'm getting a little hungry, aren't you?" (If she would only not call him *dear,* here and now!)

The little inn and the boathouse to the north were growing momentarily smaller,—looking now, like that other boathouse and pavilion on Crum Lake the day he had first rowed there, and when he had been wishing that he might come to such a lake as this in the Adirondacks, dreaming of such a lake—and wishing to meet such a girl as Roberta—then——And overhead was one of those identical woolly clouds that had sailed above him at Crum Lake on that fateful day.

The horror of this effort!

They might look for water-lilies here to-day to kill time a little, before—to kill time . . . to kill, (God)—he must quit thinking of that, if he were going to do it at all. He needn't be thinking of it now, at any rate.

At the point of land favored by Roberta, into a minute protected bay with a small, curved, honey-colored beach, and safe from all prying eyes north or east. And then he and she stepping out normally enough. And Roberta, after Clyde had extracted the lunch most cautiously from his bag, spreading it on a newspaper on the shore, while he walked here and there, making strained and yet admiring comments on the beauty of the scene—the pines and the curve of this small bay, yet thinking—thinking, thinking of the island farther on and the bay below that again somewhere, where somehow, and in the fact of a weakening courage for it, he must still execute this grim and terrible business before him—not allow this carefully planned opportunity to go for nothing—if—if—he were to not really run away and leave all that he most desired to keep.

And yet the horror of this business and the danger, now that it was so close at hand—the danger of making a mistake of some kind—if nothing more, of not upsetting the boat right—of not being able to—to—oh, God! And subsequently, maybe, to be proved to be what he would be—then—a murderer. Arrested! Tried. (He could not, he would not, go through with it. No, no, no!)

LOUIS C. JONES

The Most Haunted House

"Seems there was a young couple who were in the antique business. They had an old station wagon and they'd go back up into the mountains and buy up all the old chairs and cribs and tables and dishes and glassware they could pile in the car and bring it back to their shop in Fort Edward. They would fix them up a little and sell 'em to summer visitors for five or six times what they paid for 'em. Sometimes they'd be back in the mountains two or three days before they'd get a load. They made a kind of vacation out of it.

"This time I'm telling you about they'd been back up in Washington County, north of here, and they'd been three days going over the little mountain roads. They had a good pile of stuff lashed on all over the back and top as well as the inside. Churns, beds, a saddlemaker's bench, and I don't know what all. It got dusk and they were close to lost when their lights began to flicker. The road was very steep and rocky and had a lot of nasty turns in it, so they decided to put up at the first farmhouse that would take them in.

"They could just about see a big boulder that jutted out so that the road had to turn sharp around it, and there on the other side was a little farmhouse with a light in the window. So Mr. Kraft—that was his name, Wilbur Kraft, my cousin knows him well—he pulled the car over to the well-worn tracks of an old driveway. He knocked on the door and when an elderly couple came to the door he explained how he and his wife were looking for a place to stay and asked if these folks would put them up for the night.

"The old couple looked at each other for a minute and then they told Mr. Kraft that they didn't have much room, but they guessed it could be arranged, if the Krafts would take them as they were and not expect anything special. So Mrs. Kraft came in and the four of them sat around the little living room talking. The old folks said their name was Butler and they had lived there a long time and they told the Krafts stories about the old days on the mountain and how different things were from what they used to be.

"Mrs. Kraft kept looking around the room to see if there was any antiques they could buy off the old folks. Over in one corner she sees a kidney-shaped marble-top table. Would the Butlers be willing to sell it? No, they were very partial to that; it had been a wedding present and they wouldn't feel they could sell it.

"After a little while Mr. Kraft said he thought they would go to bed now and could he pay for their lodging right then so's they could skin out early in the morning and get on home.

"Mr. Butler said, 'We talked this over when you went out to get your wife and we agreed that you would be our guests and that you were to pay us nothing.' They argued about it politely for a spell and then they all went to bed.

"About five o'clock the Krafts got up and dressed and came downstairs on their tiptoes. He went over to the corner and put a silver dollar on the edge of the marble-top table they had been admiring the night before and went out the door.

"They got the car started and drove down the mountain a couple of miles where they found a little town with a quick-lunch room open. They had some breakfast and while they were eating, the girl who waited on them got talking to them.

" 'Come far this morning?' she asks them after a while.

" 'No, we stayed a couple of miles up the mountain,' said Mr. Kraft.

" 'That so?' she says. 'Where'd you stay? I live up there and know just about everybody.'

" 'With a nice old couple named Butler,' says Kraft's wife.

" 'Butler? Butler? I never heard of anybody by that name on the mountain. Whereabouts do they live?' she wants to know.

"Well, they try to tell her and she remembers the place in the road but she's bound and determined there isn't a house within a mile of that place. Just then the boss comes into the argument and when he hears what it's all about, a funny look comes over his face.

" 'Mister,' he said to Kraft, 'you ain't tryin' to kid us, are you?'

" 'I don't know what you mean,' says Kraft. 'I'm telling the simple truth. We spent the night with a couple named Butler on the mountain at the place in the road where the big boulder sticks way out into the road. And the girl here says we didn't. It's a little silly, if you ask me.'

" 'That's what anybody would think, only there's more to it. The girl is right. There's not a house within a mile of the big boulder. But, Mister—and this is the funny part—thirty years ago there *was* a house right there and the couple who lived there *was* named Butler. They both died when the place burned down. I remember the night it burned like it was yesterday.'

"That settled matters; all four of them got in the boss's car and went back up the mountain, just to see for themselves. What do you 'spose they found? No house, that was clear enough, though they found the tracks in the grass where Kraft had parked his car. But they found the old foundation of the house, all overgrown with weeds and hollyhocks. There were charred timbers and places where the foundation had fallen in. The Krafts just stood there, bug-eyed, looking at the hole in the ground and then at each other. They started to go back to the car when Mrs. Kraft let out a little yip and fainted dead away.

"They got some water and brought her around after a bit. All she could say for a few minutes was, 'The marble top. The marble top!' Then her husband saw it too. Back in the corner of the foundation, in exactly the same position it had occupied in the room, was the kidney-shaped marble-top. The table was long since rotted away. But there on the edge of the marble was the silver dollar Kraft had left just a few hours before.

"Up in my country we call that the story about the most haunted house."

WILLIAM CHAPMAN WHITE

Adirondack Year

[*Three of Mr. White's twelve psalms to the marching months.*]

March... March means a dozen promises of warmth, and winter's end betrayed by nightfall as the temperature sinks low again. How so much mischief and disappointment and general orneriness can be put into thirty-one days is hard to understand.

March days get into men's moods. If political scraps have been simmering in the villages, and most villages have them, they boil in March. Neighborhood quarrels, parental arguments, schoolroom spats turn up more frequently. If young married couples have been running into squalls, this is the month they can break into tempest. This is the month farmers walk restlessly a dozen times a day to the barn to check on what they checked on an hour before and spend more than one evening figuring if it wouldn't be smart to sell the farm. Nothing's really wrong with politician, family, parent, child, bride, farmer, or farm. It's only March. This is the month when the smart people, at least those who are solvent, try to get out of town to the South and meet the spring coming North.

In March a man congratulates himself on having come through the winter without a cold and thereupon comes down with the worst in three years. March is the month when a man figures he can get by without another tank of fuel oil and thus spare the budget. Along comes subzero cold and here's the fuel-oil truck and there goes the budget. As lovely a morning as the year brings can turn up, with a soft south wind, with the sound and sign of moist earth and of frost leaving the ground. By noon it has become a howling winter day, with snow flying, cars skidding, and drifts piled up in the garden where just four hours before flower shoots were showing a first fresh green.

By day the roads run water but at night are frozen hard again. The back roads have icy ruts that can slip a car over to the ditch in a twinkling. Mud covers sidewalks and street. A driver, innocent of the rides of March, can go

From *Adirondack Country* by William Chapman White. Published by Duell, Sloan & Pearce, New York, Little, Brown & Company, Boston, 1954. Reprinted by permission.

along happily with his window open, to get a tidal wave in his face from a passing car. The mud is tracked into the house by small fry and onto living-room rugs. The children mill around, their skis and skates useless in the mud; every indoor activity has been tried a hundred times and all are boring.

The sun comes out bright again. Temperatures stay above freezing for a night and a man asks hopefully, "Now?" He need not ask. The next day everything is frozen tight again. New icicles form on the roof, new snow falls. Again the cry of March in the Adirondacks rises: "How long, how long?"

Village unemployment rolls are now at their highest. The number of visitors on the streets is zero. Heavily loaded lumber trucks come highballing along the roads, bringing the winter cut out as fast as possible, sometimes driving around the clock, coming through lonely back roads at 3 A.M., skidding down ice-covered hills with ten tons of big logs aboard. A skid and an overturned truck and all the work of loading has to be done again, to say nothing of an injured driver in the hospital.

If the Conservation Department has declared an open season beaver trappers head for the dams in the backwoods. Rabbit season has closed. Winter fishing is over as the lake ice becomes treacherous in the succession of warm and cold days. Fishermen bring out their trout equipment, clean it, repair it, clean it again. A bright afternoon may even lure them outdoors to practice a few casts, but a shift in the clouds can bring sudden snow and they retreat to the fire indoors, asking, "How long?" Frost leaves the ground, but nothing can be done in the resulting mud in farm land or garden. Tomatoes are started in seed flats near the kitchen stove. On a rare warm day, with the temperature near fifty, house plants may be set outdoors for a few hours. The wind shifts, plants come indoor, the sky darkens, and it snows, and all that is left is to cry "How long?"

March brings one new activity and one cheerful note. Adirondack people watch the weather closely in the first weeks, or even at the end of February, waiting for the first sign of "sugar weather," bright sunny days to set the sap running fast in the maples, and cold crisp nights. Most years have them, but sugaring has been spoiled or shortened many a time by a March that stays cold, sleety, and sunless until it is too late to make decent syrup.

The Adirondack country has a large lore about maple tapping. The first hole each year should be breast-high on the south side of a tree, and if a second hole is made later in the season that goes on the north. The largest flow is obtained by tapping on the side bearing the most branches or over the largest root. The richest sap comes from the layer near the bark; deeper bores give less syrup and of darker color and less value.

When sugaring time comes, from Deer River to Chateaugay, from Poke O'Moonshine to the Kayaderosseras, men work fast. A few people make sugaring a big business; they may have as many as three thousand trees in their sugar bush, pipes to run the sap down from the grove to the evaporators, and gauges and gadgets to tell just when the sap has boiled down enough and is fit for syrup and for sugar. The average Adirondack farmer who has a few trees knows little of this industry. He looks on them not as a source for profit but for pleasure. As long as he has the strength to carry the sap buckets to the boiler he knows that he will not have to eat "pancake syrup" that is 99 percent cane sugar or glucose with a touch of artificial maple flavor added. He usually makes enough syrup for his own family, but if the sap runs well he may have a few gallons to give to friends.

His is hand labor. By hand he bores the holes in the trees, inserts the metal spouts, and hangs the buckets. Twice a day he collects the thin, watery sap, and, in pails that hang over a yoke on his shoulders, he lugs it to a shallow pan over a wood fire. There it boils and the room fills with a steam that has a cottony flavor. Never must that fire go out, day or night, as it boils down the forty gallons of sap for every gallon of syrup. The farmer knows when the syrup is thick enough, not by gauge or gadget, but by holding it to the light as his grandfather did, by testing it on snow where the thin liquid crackles gold, or, if he has a real genius for sugar making, just by the way it smells.

Once sugaring time was a time for celebration. The last day of sugaring saw dancing and singing at the sugar house and, of course, sampling of the newly made sugar. Now and then "snow parties" do take place these days, with singing and dancing in the kitchen by the stove and the chief point of the party, eating "wax on snow." A snow party needs only neighbors, a Sunday-school class, or a class from a rural school, some pails and buckets filled with snow, and a kettle of thickening sap boiling on the kitchen range. The routine is simple. The guests take a soup plate filled with snow, pour a few tablespoons of hot syrup over it, and watch it cool and harden to taffy. Then the mass is rolled up on a fork and eaten. That is a sweet dish. The Adirondack people—and nothing better proves their hardiness—add two unchanging items to a snow party: salted crackers and sour pickles. A party of twenty can put away a couple of gallons of syrup, a gallon of pickles, and pound after pound of crackers in one evening.

Sugaring time is usually over by March 20 and still the winter may hold.

If a man looks to the hills he will see the first of a pink film spreading over the distant ones. The maple branches, seen against the sky, show swelling buds. The first robins are on the soggy lawns, the first crows are calling over the sodden fields. Rain water stands in puddles on the lake ice. Slogging along in mud, in the stronger sunlight, a man asks as he looks up in the clear-washed sky, "How long?" Then it snows. Standing at his window and considering a winter world from which all promise of freedom has been snatched away, a man can wish desperately, "If only the wind would shift to the south!"

Another cold day rises. Noon is bright but frosty. The sunset is muted and gray and heavy clouds roll in from the west. The thermometer starts down. At dusk it stops well above zero. The barometer falls slowly. Suddenly the windows on the south side of the house begin to rattle in a fresh breeze. Over the woods comes the quiet sigh of freshening wind. Rain begins to trickle on the window panes. If a man goes outdoors for a moment he can feel something new, fresh, and alive in the washed air. Through the night comes a new sound, of water dripping from the eaves, water running over the icebound land. For the first time in weeks the night promises a temperature above freezing and rain that will not slacken. As a man opens the windows and feels a touch of comparative warmth in the air he can say triumphantly, "South wind!" He may even feel he's helped to bring it, just by watching and hoping.

In a day or so the sheet of snow in the woods and the remnants in the fields begin to shrink, first over the banks and slopes, then under the heavy trees and finally in the open places. The hummock of snow on the ridge turns out to be a forgotten stump, a rock, or a large pine downed by the winter wind. The woods look messy and untidy, full of the raw scars of winter. The leaves of last season still hang on the beech. The tips of the cedars are brown with winterkill, but a May breeze will brush that off. Although the world around is a drab world, on the distant mountain slopes the winter black of the spruces and pines lighten into a first green, and over the stand of birch and alder thickets there is the first misty pink of life in the branches. The spruce buds, ready since last August, are fat and their sheaths are almost broken through. Over the whole land is new odor, the clean fresh smell of raw earth.

The snow is off the lake ice and rain ripples the puddles. In a few places the lakes are "making water"—rifts show in the ice where there is current underneath. The open water flashes in the sun and the colder water sinks to the bottom. The brooks are broken loose again and the water rushes by the ice that may still overhang the banks.

The silence of winter is gone. There is sound everywhere, wet gurgling sound, of water running from field and woods, in roadway gutters, from every slope, down every hill. Water gushes from fields, from woods, and from springs that will be dry long before June. Water oozes from the ground as the frost comes out, and the earth is a muddy place. One sound is still missing, of the lakes lapping at their shores, but that will soon be heard. More sun and more rain, and lake ice, slowly thinning, will darken to a dirty gray then change to a thin skin of long ice crystals that will rise and fall on the windswept water like a rubber boat. The sharp wind of a late April day will finish the job and free the water. Patches of ice will break off and move fast across the lake, to end on the shore in a continuous tinkle of breaking crystals. The lakes will be blue and wind-tossed once again.

No people walk the woods these days. The lumbermen are gone, their tote roads a mass of mud. In the remote hills the bears waken from sleep and move out into the open glades with their cubs, nuzzling in the brown grass for a trace of anything fresh and green. Deer begin to move from the balsam swamps up the slopes, nibbling at the hemlocks as they pass. The fawns that floundered in a snowy world can move free now—those that survived February—and bound ahead through the leafless brush and the stands of maple whips. The sounds of the lonely world are wet sounds, of soggy squashy mud, but high overhead the crows cry and the blue jays call from the old maples. Only on the distant shining peaks is the world unchanged. The snow and ice will stay there through May.

So, hour by hour, the woods come again to life. The change is not a sudden one, worked overnight as by the rise of one great curtain. Rather, a hundred voile curtains mask what is to be and rise one at a time to reveal just a bit more of what is to come. What they reveal is the coming of one of the miracles of the land—an Adirondack spring.

And many a man will say, gratefully, that these are the best days of the Adirondack year.

June... As everywhere else in the land, it goes too fast.

The greens of June have no precise naming. The buttery green of new spruce shoots, the blackened green of old spruce, the silvered green of the undersides of poplar leaves in a June breeze are one with the ruddy green of maples, the metallic green of raspberry leaves, and the sunlit green of new cedar. With them is the gray-bearded green of young poppy leaves, the feathery green of young tamarack, the waxed green of young pea shoots and the whitened green of young iris, the translucent green of a lawn after a June shower and the feathered green of a young hayfield under the first hot sun. Nearby are the leathery green of primrose leaves and the white-green of the new fern fronds. And what are the precise names for the velvet green of fresh moss beneath the hemlocks, the paper green of young birch leaves, the purpled green of asparagus as it comes from the earth, the rubbery green of tulip foliage, and the dusted green of Indian paintbrush now flourishing in the meadows?

Looking at the heat haze over the hills on this solid green world, it is difficult to believe that four months ago the woods were gaunt and black, the hills snow-covered. The change to the rich maturity of June is always a surprise. From one year to the next a man forgets how thick the green carpet grows on the floor of the world and how bright with flowers, how avidly the maple saplings reach for the sky, how daintily the foam flower floats in the slightest wind. Yet as June races by, the signs of spring recede with it. Already the spring fullness of the brooks and lakes has gone. Rocks show in stream bottoms and the lake levels fall to their summer mark.

As a man stands and looks at the woods in blossom and at his young garden he feels that the frost must be past, but Adirondack people always expect a frost in early June. It may come but it is rarely harsh. More likely are occasional days with downstate heat and the first of the few breathless hot nights when the lake lies still under the moonlight, the water beetles skate about in silly circles, and a battery of insects storms the window screens.

The fresh-washed sense of spring is still in the air. The alders bud late in the brookside thickets, a kingfisher darts and poses over the water, and a woodpecker hammers its own rhythm on a distant apple tree. The first of the mountain thunderstorms comes swift and hard in its impact; Adirondack lakes blow up to whitecaps and spume in a moment. Mosquitoes grow smarter and find the slightest chink in the screen. The tent caterpillars do their miserable job on wild cherry and apple trees. Markers are put atop roadside trees to guide airplanes spraying against assorted insect invasions.

Daisies plate the open places. The ruddy orange of Indian paintbrush colors the meadows. Hay grows fast. Potatoes are well up and the farmer wonders what their price will be at harvest. Blueberries start to fill out and raspberries are in flower in the woods. Deer come down to the gardens by night. Grackles nest near the house and evening grosbeaks come now and then from their hidden nests to the feeding places. The woods are alive with warblers, kinglets, thrushes, and juncoes. Fishing slows down as June dries the trout streams.

The coming of people that began at the end of May is full flood by the end of June. Businessmen begin to ask the vital Adirondack question: "Will this summer be ahead of last year?" The first climbers try the high peaks. The first canoers appear on the lakes and rangers have the overnight lean-tos ready for them. Every week end the townspeople are out at their camps by the lake shores on state land. The first city cowgirls sit shakily on dude-ranch horses. State camps are open. The first campers pitch their tents and build their smudges at night to keep away the punkies and the no-see-ums. The last days of school drag as slowly as anywhere else, but in the afternoons the kids are at the beaches and do not seem to notice that the water is still too cold for comfortable swimming.

At children's summer camps painters, carpenters, and caretakers work long days. They patch holes in roofs that were hit by falling branches in a winter wind and rebuild the corner of the dock that the winter ice wrecked. They haul off fallen trees. They paint boats, put out the safety floats at the swimming place, set up new diving boards, clean up the tennis courts, and repair tables, chairs, and bunks. The many jobs all have a sense of things-about-to-happen. Lake shores that have long been silent will soon echo the calls of a hundred kids. Lake waters, unbroken by a diving body or a canoe paddle, will foam and splash. A familiar cry will sound in the brush: "Johnny, the mail's in!"

As the caretaker finishes a last paint job he talks to his helpers about the kids of last year. "Remember the boy who learned to hoot like an owl and used to wake up the whole camp at two every morning? And that one from New York who ate enough for six men—I remember he used to put maple syrup and sugar on his baked beans. And the girl who got a rope around a porcupine and wanted to take it home for her baby brother? And the one who put water in the truck's gas tank on the last day because he didn't want to be driven to the railroad station? Oh, brother, were they something! I wonder if they'll all be back this summer?"

He puts his paintbrush down for a moment and looks across the empty lake. "Things have been peaceful around here for ten months now and that's long enough."

September The flickers now gather in flocks on the lawn and the swallows by the roadside. In the morning they are gone. It is like that with the summer people. On one day lakes are alive and noisy, camps are filled, and every tourist cabin taken. A day or so after Labor Day and most people are gone. Some private camps may stay open for hunting season. Some hotels keep open for another month. Yet two of the best Adirondack months are ahead. As the Adirondack people say, on a hot September afternoon with a warm wind raising whitecaps on the lakes, "We keep the best weather for ourselves."

As the old-timers leave they wonder if there will be another summer in the Adirondacks for them. As the hotel help and even many of the visitors leave they say regretfully, "If only there were some way to make a living up here the year around." For the first time in months empty parking places appear on village streets.

All the house guests are gone. For the first time in months no one needs to apologize for the bad weather or to answer a guest's question, "Does it always rain?" Neighbors drop in and talk leisurely. They entertain one another as they had no time to do in summer. By midwinter only pleasant memories about last summer's guests will be left. In no time a man will be saying to his wife, "It's pretty quiet, isn't it? June will be here before we know it and we ought to start asking a few people up for their vacations before they make other plans."

At the state camp sites, trailers are again hitched to cars. Gear is stowed and good-bys said, with promises to return the next year or to meet in Florida in the next month. By mid-September the last of the trailers is gone. Porcupines that have sniffed at the salty smell of trailers, based the previous winter by the Florida sea and now headed back to it, move about the camp sites without concern. Nosy deer come from the woods and take over the lake shore once more. The camp caretaker puts up the bars on the entrance road and heads off to a village for the winter. His hard work now begins: figuring how to get even more camp sites for next year around the rigid border of a lake that is already plotted out to the last inch.

Many odd-shaped crates arrive at the express offices. They are filled with little trees, sent out for reforesting purposes by the Conservation Department from the state nurseries. They cost nothing but the transportation. On some of these September days many men walk, if they walk at all, with backs like ironing boards. Setting out baby trees may be setting out roots to the future, but only those who have put in a thousand trees six feet apart each way know that the forests of the future are started not only with seedlings but with grunts and backaches. The trees won't amount to much for some years. The man who plants them on a sunny September day may never live to see their glory. But he plants today with a calm assurance that trees will still be growing in the land twenty-five years from now. His children may walk the woods he has made.

Farmers are busy in September. Potato vines have browned and the crop must be dug. Most Adirondack farmers use mechanical diggers, but picking potatoes still needs hand labor. Many a farmer's wife makes spare money now by working in the fields for the large growers, bending over a thousand times a day and following down the field after the digger. Winter preparations begin. Wood must be cut, screens removed, the last house repairs made before the first cold wind comes.

In the store windows hunting equipment replaces fishing gear. Conservation trucks drive back roads and stock streams with fish. Men walk the woods to look hopefully for deer tracks and to make a mental note of where to hunt in a few more weeks.

On the lakes a stronger wind streaks foam across the water. Algae, working since the end of August, fill some lakes with a gray cloudiness that soon passes. Maple seeds spiral down on the lakes and the waves wash them into scaly piles on the sandy shores. The lakes, so busy just a few weeks before, are empty, except for a loafing loon and a few sheldrake ducks that are chasing whatever it is that lures a sheldrake. On the rocks in the middle of some lakes young gulls try their wings. In back streams beavers labor fast against the approaching cold. Their dams are repaired. Every animal in the colony works harder to get in the winter's food supply of poplar logs and to anchor them firmly at the bottom of the water beyond the reach of ice.

Meadows and pastures are rusty, marked with the seed heads of golden rod and fireweed. In open places in the woods ladies' tresses and rattlesnake plantain are among the last flowers to bloom. Day by day more single maple branches turn color, then suddenly an entire tree. It may be a small one by a road or a large one in the meadow that goes first; there is no order to it except that the same early tree is usually early each autumn. Against the reddening of the woods, particularly noticeable at a distance, the spruces begin to darken. Birches fade and give a springlike yellow-greenness to the hillsides. The unobtrusive English ivy over the rocks, unnoticed all summer, turns a flaming red. Pine needles begin to brown and fall, showering down to provide slippery walking in smooth places. Lilac leaves crisp at the edges. Fat bear, their cubs gone their own way long ago, may come through the rusty bracken of a deserted farm to search out the old apple trees and a last meal of the year.

As days stay warm, nights grow chilly. A few maple leaves begin to fall; that, the Adirondack people say, means frost within a week. The first frost usually holds off until about September 15. The day of the first frost commences bright and clear. The heat of summer is gone but its sparkle remains. A breeze rises in late morning. The afternoon has a close warmth that makes any thought of approaching frost almost ridiculous. By evening the sunset fills the sky. The temperature falls from the sixties to the low forties, almost as fast as a leaf twirls down from a tree. At dusk, mist comes off the land in wisps of thin batting and the temperature continues to drop. At night everything is very still and the long leaves of the late corn are quiet. By bedtime the temperature is in the thirties, the stars are as bright as in deep winter, and the night air has a fresh crackle. The gardener lies abed, remembering the crops still out in the garden, and he hopes. The chill of the night air through the window cuts sharply through those hopes.

Next morning tells the story, but not at once. A heavy dew can mask for a little while any damage done. By mid-morning cucumber and squash leaves are up at the edges, wrinkled and black. Tomato leaves are shriveled. Only the root crops are left untouched, and all in one night. The gardener turns to the garden to clear up the debris. The day after the frost is even clearer, more sparkling, almost springlike. The next ten days and nights may even be hot. As a gardener pulls up the blackened squash vine he has a chance to think of next year's garden. Next year, maybe, the frost will hold off until October.

As the month ends the woods race to their climax of color. Another heavy frost sets the distant mountain peaks shining white against the high blue sky. At sunset they turn lilac. The reds on the hillsides below deepen under the violet of the early twilight. The evening wind carries more chill in the earlier darkness. But the days come warm and clear, in a world where the mounting color on the hills spreads like fire.

ROBERT F. HALL

The Betwixt and Between Season

Being an essay on the betwixt and between season after Autumn departs and before Winter comes

Lewis, New York. Chauncey Blinn, our township superintendent of roads, sat in the hall on election day and squinted through the window at the gray clouds. "They say it'll be a tough winter and I believe it," he said.

Leamon Cross, a farmer from over towards Stowersville, nodded glumly. "Can't have it open every winter," he said.

From the *Warrensburg–Lake George News, Warrensburg,* New York.

The mood of Chauncey and Leamon is typical of this season in the Adirondacks. It is an attitude of cheerless resignation and is as inevitable at this time of the year as the shortening daylight and the long angle of the sun.

For here we have not four but five seasons. The fifth is the brief period after election day when autumn has departed and winter, with no doubt in her mind as to the certainty of her coming, is content to be vague about the exact date.

There are frosty mornings when the thermometer on my woodshed registers four or five degrees below freezing. But it is not the stimulating, nippy chill of autumn. There is a foreboding dampness about it. The mist which gathers around the peaks of Hurricane and Jay will leave their upper slopes white with snow and there will be flurries before noon if the sun doesn't break through.

But because it is not yet winter, the clouds will usually part and by the time Mrs. Dickerson, the mail carrier on our route, has traversed half of the five miles between Elizabethtown and Lewis, the frost will have melted and everyone (whistling by the graveyard) is saying what a fine day it is.

Of course it can't be a fine day for very long, either. This isn't October; it is well into November. The hope of an Indian summer which beguiles football fans and gay drivers of convertibles a couple of hundred miles to the south, isn't for us. That hope vanished from these parts with the last golden leaf of the aspen in our meadow. Here, at this season, we count it a blessing if the day which was fine at noon hasn't turned wintry by dusk.

So preoccupied are we with preparations for winter, putting up storm windows, laying in fuel supplies, banking dirt and leaves around the base of the house, that we are seldom conscious of the somber beauty which hangs about the mountains, forests and meadows.

The flaming colors are long gone but there is a suggestion of red and gold still in the brown leaves on the forest floor or along the roadside. A ray of sunlight pushing now unopposed into the depths of the woods will lift this color into the atmosphere.

This is the magic moment for the paper birches, and their white bark shines more brightly than at any other time of the year.

In the woods, the limbs of all but the evergreen conifers are bare, and it is now possible to locate the nests of the songsters who eluded you last summer. Near the farm houses, only the tough old apple trees are clinging to their withered leaves. Almost everywhere, the color scheme is brown, but it is a warm brown which remembers, if it does not reflect, the hues of autumn.

There are partridge and grouse in the woods, but around the house the chickadees are taking over. Although there is still food in the woods, they now come each morning and noon to your bird-feeding stations for easy-to-get suet or sunflower seeds. You can take them or leave them now, but in a few short weeks they will be the only sign of life in the vast, white winter.

In the village, the human chickadees who don't go south for the winter, are pursuing their tasks purposefully if not cheerfully. The summer visitors have gone, and with them an important source of our income. It seems too early for the meetings of merchants and hotel operators to plan the campaigns for next summer's tourist trade, and that is fortunate because our seasonal negativism would produce nothing constructive.

The village streets are quiet until three o'clock when the school busses roll through with homeward-bound children. The town comes to life again at five when the final mail of the day is distributed. For a few minutes there is commotion around the post office as cars drive up.

But this is not the season of sociability. Greetings are exchanged without enthusiasm. Someone may mention that it's getting colder. But there is no prolonged chatting in the post office lobby. The box-holder spins the little combination, slams the lid shut and hurries out to his car. Darkness is settling upon the village and as he departs, he switches on his headlights.

The temptations of hunting no longer war with the obligations of husbandry. Our local hunters have either "got their buck" or put away their deer rifles in discouragement. If the woodshed hasn't yet been filled, the rains or snows which make mountain roads impassable will make you regret your tardiness.

A farmer used to figure his fuel needs at fifteen to twenty cords of wood. Since a cord is 4 x 4 x 8 feet, that adds up to a pretty large woodpile. But these days, it's a rare farmer who hasn't converted to kerosene, fuel oil or bottled gas for at least a part of his heating and cooking needs.

He will still use seven or eight cords for his fireplace and for the kitchen range because the women folk are partial to wood fires in the cooking stove on a cold morning. It takes five eight-inch trees to make a cord, which is another way of saying that for each family, some thirty-five to forty trees must be felled.

This would be a more serious chore if it were not for power-driven chain saws now used to fell the trees and saw them into suitable lengths for fireplace or stove. To fill my shed Red Boyd came over last Saturday after finishing his week's work cutting pulp wood and logs for the lumber company. Red was conscientious about the trees he cut with his chain saw. He by-passed the saleable white pines. He scorned the poplars, "poppies" as we call them, for their poor heating quality. And true woodsman that he is, he chose the dead, or dying, the twisted or gnarled, for my firewood.

Like Thoreau who was warmed first by the splitting of the stumps in his bean field, Red could work up a sweat, even in this damp chill, by the effort of manipulating the heavy chain saw. Working by the hour, Red determines for himself the timing of his smoke breaks.

Squatting on his haunches, he rolls a cigarette and drinks from a can of beer which he has opened with one corner of his double-bitted axe.

Red tells me that fifteen years ago he left his native mountains in North Carolina to travel with a circus as a roustabout and then as a strong man. During the four normal seasons of the year Red has never doubted his wisdom in settling here in the Adirondacks. But now, with autumn gone and winter approaching, he has doubts.

"It does get pretty cold here," Red said.

At this season there are no optimists.

"Oh, it's time for a real cold winter," 79-year-old Dean White concedes.

Perhaps it will be like 1935 when the thermometer stayed so low for so long that when the mercury reached zero, it was considered a nice day.

"In 1888, I helped my father tap the old Philo Estes sugar bush," says Dean. "The snow was so deep my father had to chop the snow around the maple trees to make a place to hang the sap bucket. And when the snow melted, I wasn't able to reach up to the bucket.

"We used to be snowed in about November 10 to a level of four feet," Dean says. "On New Year's Eve of 1894 there was a thunderstorm for an hour. Then the weather turned off cold and next morning there was eight inches of ice over the snow. The farmers drew their hay to the barn on the ice crust. They didn't bother with gates. They just took the top rail off the fence and drove right over."

As spring is the season of hope, this, then, is the season of premonition, of a sense of impending hardships. It is a time for unending chores, for labor, for resignation.

The mood of the residents will continue through the increasing cold and the countless brief flurries until that magic morning when we awake to find the whole countryside white with the first big snow of the season. The air will be clear and cold. As a people, we will stamp our boots in the snow and briskly rub our hands, and smile at each other with a cheerfulness we haven't known in weeks.

"Isn't it a fine day?" everyone will say.

THE ST. LAWRENCE

19TH CENTURY

FLETCHER PRATT

Sword of the Border

Fate tried to conceal him under one of the most common of names; Time, by pitching him into the most unmilitary period in the history of our peaceful republic; his parents, by bringing him up as a Quaker; the commanding general of the U.S. Army, by reporting him as the most stupid and insubordinate officer under his command; and the government by giving him neither men nor horses nor guns. Yet he saved our northern frontier twice; he won one of the most desperate battles in American history, and with raw militia at his back he broke the veterans who stood unwavering before Napoleon. Not Sheridan nor Longstreet nor Mad Anthony Wayne more furiously rode the whirlwind. Gentlemen, I give you General Jacob Brown, the best battle captain in the history of the nation.

A pleasant-faced man with rather sharp features and curling hair looks at us out of his portraits; there is a keen eye, an erect carriage, and a skeptical line to the mouth. He was born into a family Quaker for many generations, in Bucks County, Pennsylvania, a month after Lexington, son of a prosperous farmer who fished in the troubled waters of commercial speculation in the years following the Revolution and lost all his money. His education, says a man who knew him young "was accurate and useful as far as it went, without aspiring to elegant literature or mere speculative science." He supplemented it by reading everything he could lay his hands on, and when the family fortunes shipwrecked at the time of his eighteenth birthday, young Jacob Brown easily fulfilled the requirements for becoming a country schoolteacher, a trade which he followed for three years.

At that period the Ordinance of 1787 had recently gone through and the West was opening to ambition. Brown went to Cincinnati and had enough mathematical equipment to get a post as a surveyor. It is interesting to note that he followed Washington in this profession; and that biographies of such otherwise diverse captains as Frederick the Great, Napoleon, and Julius Caesar speak of the "surveyor's eye"—the sense of distance and direction possessed by these men. Perhaps there is here some clue to the secret of leadership in battle.

Yet Jacob Brown was still far from battles and the thought of battles when he came east again after two years of failure to make his fortune in Ohio, and secured the position of head of the New York Friends' School. The life does not seem to have afforded enough scope for his intellectual activity, which was considerable; he left the post to take one as Alexander Hamilton's secretary. The table conversation at that house must have frequently turned on the Revolution and its military history; at all events we are told that it was at this period that Brown began to read Quintus Curtius and the strange military-philosophical works of the Maréchal de Saxe. His commercial fortunes also improved about this time, and in 1799 he bought "several thousand acres" of land near Watertown, N.Y., and formed there a small settlement which he called Brownville.

As the squire of the district and county-court judge, he was elected colonel of the local militia in 1808, apparently less because he was thought able to command a regiment in war than because his big estate and comfortable house made a good spot to hold the quarterly drinking bout which passed under the name "militia exercises." He was politically active at the period ... and his appointment as brigadier general in the state service by Governor Tompkins in 1811 was in the nature of a reward for services rendered at the polls, and not because he had shown military ability....

The American military and naval base on Ontario was Sackett's Harbor at the eastern end, faced across the lake by the British base of Kingston. Winter building had given the United States command of the water, but instead of striking at the enemy base, Chauncey commanding the fleet, and Dearborn the army, decided to trot off to the western end of their little inland sea for an attack on the Niagara frontier and Toronto, then called York. Lieutenant Colonel Backus, of the "Albany dragōons," was in charge of a small detachment and a hospital at Sackett's. He should have been in general charge, but Brown was a landed proprietor of considerable substance, and Dearborn, a toady if there ever was one, asked the latter to take charge of the post if any emergency arose.

Fortunate blunder! For the British learned of the American preoccupation at the wrong end of the line and Sir George Prevost, governor of Lower Canada, came down on Sackett's Harbor with all the force he could muster. He had a fleet, not large by any absolute standard, but of overwhelming power in relation to the defense; for a landing party he had some 600 Lobster-back regulars and 300 marines and sailors. The British sails were visible in the offing on the evening of May 27, but the airs fell light and baffling, and they could not close. All that night and the succeeding day messengers were out rousing the countryside. When the morning of the 29th came up, sunshiny and hot, Brown was at Sackett's and in command. He had 400 regulars, invalids, of whom half were sufficiently convalescent to fight; a regiment of Albany cavalry, 250 strong, who fell in line dismounted, and 500 militia, whose experience was limited to the quarterly keg-tapping aforementioned.

The only place where a landing could be made was on a spit west of the town, where a broad beach led some distance toward the line of barracks that formed the outer boundary. Along these buildings Brown deployed the regulars under Backus, with a couple of guns. He posted the militia at the landing point behind a gravel bank. Cowpens was the obvious model, where Morgan, of the famous Rifles, had placed his militia in the front line, sure they would run, hopeful they would not do so till they had delivered a couple of telling volleys.

Colonel Baynes, of the British 100th Regiment, led the landing party and advance; his report speaks of a "heavy and galling fire, which made it impossible for us to wait for the artillery to be landed and come up," so that he had to charge, out of hand and with infantry only, against the gravel bank. In fact, the "heavy and galling fire" was a single and ragged volley; as soon as the militiamen found their guns empty they became obsessed with the fear the British would be among them before they could reload, and vanished into the woods on their left.

The attackers cheered and came on; the fleet warped in and began to cannonade the flank of the battle line of regulars. The naval lieutenant in charge of the building yard, foreseeing that they could not hold out long, set fire to everything, so that Backus' tiny group fought with the town and dockyard blazing in their rear and double their strength of enemies closing on their front. They fought well; but the British got a lodgment at one of the barracks and prepared to sweep out the line; Backus was mortally wounded, Brown nowhere to be seen.

As a matter of fact, he was off in the woods, addressing the militia in somewhat un-Quakerly words. "Victory!" he was shouting, waving his sword, "Victory! Will you let the regulars claim your credit?" and rode on among them, gathering a little group and then a big one.... Just as Sir George Prevost reached out to grasp his own victory, the militia suddenly came storming out of the forest into his flank, with fixed bayonets and Brown at their head. They did not fire a shot; simply yelled in answer to their leader and flung themselves through a scattering volley into the British regulars from whom they had run not half an hour before. Colonel Baynes ordered a precipitate retreat, covered by the ships. He had lost 259 men, nearly a third of the force, and Prevost, when criticized for not countermanding the retirement order, pointed out with some energy that he was in an excellent position to lose everything if he stayed.

The armies were diminutive, but the results prodigious; certainly the victory saved Sackett's Harbor and probably the whole northern frontier. In the then existing state of affairs, it is difficult to see how the United States could have recovered from the loss of their one good base on the lakes. For Sackett's Harbor was the point through which went all the supplies for Oliver Perry, who had not yet fought the battle of Lake Erie, and for Harrison, who had not yet driven the British from Detroit. Secretary of War Armstrong, greatly impressed by Brown's rare talent for making militia fight, rewarded him with a snap promotion to brigadier general of the United States Army and the command of one of the four brigades being organized for the "conquest of Canada" that fall....

...In those lugubrious fall months while the high generals wrangled over this plan and that, their men dying like flies under pouring rains and "lake fever" (whatever that was), Brown's brigade had fewer men on sick report than any other, and was the only one that kept its strength. Why? We have one flash of insight into his methods. Alone among the brigade commanders he made his men build proper huts with fireplaces, drainage, and clean latrines. They worshiped him....

...And nobody but Brown ever thought of leading militia in a charge against veteran Scots, or would have got away with it had he done so.

There was, in short, some ineluctable secret of leadership, something in Brown's presence and manner, that made green country boys fight like the devil, and it would be worth a good deal to know that secret. But it would be silly to account for Brown's success on this basis alone. Scott complained of the general's ignorance of tactics, yet Brown's major tactics were, on the whole, better than Scott's. At Chippewa Scott's plan of a crescent resting on the river with the right wing supported by artillery was good; yet Brown had a better one—to hold hard in the center, bring Ripley in on the left and knock Riall's whole column into the Niagara. At Lundy's Lane Scott conceived the classical plan of breaking down a flank, the flank where the enemy thought himself the strongest; but it was Brown who saw that the big British battery in the center would queer any flanking sweep while it stood, and that its fall would entail the wreck of the whole line—he saw it in an instant, in the darkness of the night, in the midst of the battle. Again, at Sackett's Harbor it would have been easier and more normal for Brown to bring his rallied militia in on the line where the regulars were holding—but no, he had to lead those troops, already once broken, in a cold-metal charge against Prevost's sensitive wing. The essence of Brown's concept may be expressed by saying that while Scott played, and played well, to beat the enemy, Brown meant nothing less than his destruction at every stroke.

This suggests, then, that major tactics is something innate and not to be learned; all these ideas came out of Brown's own head, without benefit of military education. One would expect the same native genius to make him a good strategist also; but oddly enough this turns out to be his weak point.

Then there is another suggestion in Brown's career, perhaps even more important. The fact that the general's political influence in his home district was an influence of affection makes it clear that he treated the tenants of his estate much as he later treated the soldiers who fought so well for him—that is, with an attention to their physical well-being even rarer then than it is now. It was not only Scott's drill that made the men of Lundy's Lane follow their Quaker up the hill; it was those comfortable huts and the fight the general had made to provide good food and good clothes.

Yet neither these nor any other details can be tortured into a Jacob Brown formula. His secret was the secret of all great leaders, and what man can discover that?

T. WOOD CLARKE

The Grande Dame of Great Bend

The ship *Bellone,* chartered especially by Le Ray to bring to America settlers for his land development scheme in northern New York, landed September 24, 1816. Among the passengers was Jenika de Feriet. Le Ray seems to have induced her to give up her original plan of joining her brother in New Orleans, and to accompany him and his daughter to their

From *Émigrés in the Wilderness* by T. Wood Clarke, published by The Macmillan Company. New York, 1941.

home. The party headed north, and for several years Madame de Feriet remained at Leraysville as the guest of Le Ray and the companion of the Countess de Gonvello.

During her sojourn with the Le Rays she occupied a small house on the estate. In June 1823 there was a fire in this house, and Madame de Feriet lost some of her furniture. It may be that it was this small fire which was the basis of the general belief that the Le Ray Mansion burned in that year.

In 1820 she purchased from her host a large tract of land on the great bend of the Black River and, at the hamlet which still retains her name, began building a twenty-thousand-dollar mansion. While the construction was in progress she took occasion to make the tiresome trip to New Orleans to visit her brother. She remained in Louisiana from October 1821 to May 1822. The intense heat and the prevalence of fevers, however, displeased her and she was glad to return to the north to oversee the building of her new home.

This house, to which she gave the name of "The Hermitage," was ready for occupancy in the spring of 1824. It stood on a low hill overlooking a ford of the Black River about two hundred yards away. The house was built of gray stone. It was surrounded by a wide veranda. The great front door with its brass knocker was on the side of the house away from the river. To it, a circular driveway led through the dense woods. The main floor consisted of four immense rooms, each with its wide stone fireplace. The windows were in the shape of Gothic arches, and a window seat the width of the thick walls was placed at each. The reception rooms were in the front of the house, while the dining room looked out on the series of terraces which led down from the veranda to the river. There was an extensive conservatory, containing orange and lemon trees, and a well planned garden in which bloomed plants imported from various parts of the world. Outhouses were used for a kitchen and for the servants, none of whom lived in the mansion.

The house was fitted with furniture of beautiful design, mostly imported from France. The owner's musical taste was shown by the presence of what was said to be the first grand piano to be found in northern New York, a Grecian lyre, a harp, and a violin. Her artistic taste was emphasized on the walls, where hung sketches in water colors by the owner herself. Some of these are still extant and show a talent distinctly above the ordinary.

Into this beautiful home Jenika de Feriet moved in the spring of 1824. Here she lived for fifteen years and, according to the French custom with unmarried ladies of middle age who owned their own home, assumed the title of Madame de Feriet. She entertained lavishly, was visited by the aristocrats in the neighborhood, and became intimate with the American landed gentry as well as the French. A splendid equestrienne, she rode for miles over the countryside, dropping in unexpectedly at the homes of her friends and neighbors. When social events of importance were held in Watertown, Madame de Feriet was sure to be present, arrayed in gowns of silk and brocade such as had never been seen in that country. It was said that these gowns were the relics of the days when she had been a lady-in-waiting to Queen Marie Antoinette. The belief in this was strengthened by a letter written after her return to France when she wrote: "Paris is no longer a court but a camp. I wander in the park where I once followed my beautiful Queen, and mourn for the days and friends that are gone." When, however, Mr. Kellogg investigated the subject he was informed by Pierre de Nòlhac, the greatest authority on Marie Antoinette, that he can find no record that Jenika de Feriet had been connected with the household of the queen. The letter may have been an artistic touch to help maintain a fiction which she knew had been current among her friends, but had never seen fit to deny.

Whether or not Madame de Feriet had been a lady-in-waiting on the queen, there is no question that she had a remarkable personality. A skilled musician, a competent artist, a versatile *littérateur,* a wit, and a woman of exceptional personal magnetism, she held social sway over the countryside in her miniature court at The Hermitage.

But with all her charm and ability to make others happy she was not happy herself. Soon financial worries became pressing. She had invested nearly her whole capital in her estate, expecting to rent out plots to settlers and live on her rentals. But the settlers did not come. Her estate was on the wrong side of the river from the highway. For a good part of the year the river was unfordable. Those wishing homes passed her by. To meet this, she built a wooden bridge across the Black River at the foot of her lawn, and a few years later replaced this by a bridge of stone arches. By this time, however, the Erie Canal had opened and settlers had been diverted westward.

As early as 1826, two years after she moved into The Hermitage, she asked her brother in New Orleans to try to sell her estate for her; and when he said that this was impossible in New Orleans she begged him to try to obtain a partner with money enough to tide her over her financial stringency. In this same year her letters begin complaining about the conduct of Vincent Le Ray. She apparently bought the property on the divided payment plan. These installments she had been unable to meet, and M. Le Ray has been making trouble for her. This seems to have led to an estrangement with the family with whom she had lived for four years. As the Le Rays were influential citizens and her nearest neighbors, this increased her sense of loneliness. By 1828 the property had been mortgaged. There was a large estate in France to be settled which would make her financially independent. As years dragged by and the settlement seemed no nearer consummation, her gloom increased. Her brother, also suffering from the widespread financial depression, could give her no aid. With the completion of her bridge in 1831 her hopes again rose. She started to build a village near The Hermitage to attract settlers. After she had sunk more money in this than she could afford, the houses remained untenanted.

By 1830 most of the other French aristocrats had returned to France, and when in 1832 the Le Rays departed she was left very much alone. Her solitude was at times broken by visits from her nieces and nephews from New Orleans. In 1824 her nephew Gabriel, seeking a better education than could be obtained in Louisiana, was sent to his aunt. He entered the academy at Lowville and for two years gave his aunt the pleasure of his company during vacations.

As the years went on, Madame de Feriet's finances grew worse and her loneliness and homesickness for France increased. Her brother kept urging her to sell her place and join him at New Orleans. Cash purchasers, however, were hard to find, and she refused the offers made her to exchange her beautiful home for speculative tracts of unsettled land. In 1836 she finally put her property on the market. As no purchaser was forthcoming and as her nostalgia was too much for her to stand, she decided to make another visit to her brother in New Orleans.

She started out on the long trip escorted by her maid, Hortense, who had come with her from France and faithfully shared her fortunes since. The incidents of the journey are well described in a letter to her other maid, Hortense's sister, Hélène, who remained behind: "Hortense must have told you how worried I was about the stage [which she probably took at Champion or Great Bend] which did not arrive until noon, to leave again at once. I had a place at the back, and the remainder was occupied by eight men, all strangers to this part of the state of New York; all young men, very common, and ignorant of any courtesy to women, laughing and jeering at random at absolutely everything. Only one was married, and he was of still less account than the rest; we know him very well, but no one is more ordinary or has less the appearance of a more evil person than he. In short, it was Prince Murat, who has been to The Hermitage with his uncle. When I recognized and saw the others he was with, I took good care not to make myself known nor to appear to know him, in fear that he should annoy me with some marked impertinence. It would be better that his rudeness should be inflicted upon a stranger than upon Madame de Feriet!

It was in this evil company that I journeyed until 7 o'clock in the evening, when we stopped at Leyden for supper. I had had nothing since breakfast, and the road was more and more detestable so that I was very tired and faint and vexed with everything. The whole night was horrible. I could not sleep and feared every instant that I should not be able to resist the jolts of that wretched vehicle. The rudeness of my companions continued: they did not, however, pay me the slightest attention. I went like this all the way to Utica, where we arrived yesterday Thursday, at 8:30 A.M. in a great rainstorm. I was exhausted with cold and with fatigue, and there was no one to take care of my baggage except myself. The rail-road would leave at 9 o'clock and I had no time for any rest. I called for a cup of coffee, and the people from the Tavern helped me to the Rail-Road where I was agreeably surprised to find good people in my car, who were polite and attentive to me.... The journey was pleasant on account of the variety of charming views—I had no more than found them ere they had swiftly passed, and this manner of traveling appears to me really a great improvement." In Albany, she visited in the home of Mr. Rufus King, of whose house and hospitality she speaks in the highest terms.

The journey was at last completed and Madame de Feriet spent a year with the families of her brother and her married nephews and nieces. She was urged to remain with them permanently, but did not like the climate and so in 1839 returned to The Hermitage. After spending over a year in straightening out her finances she decided that she could endure her loneliness no longer, and on July 15, 1841, drove to Lowville as the first step on the long trip back to the France towards which she had for twenty-four years been turning longing eyes.

In France another disappointment awaited her. Most of her friends were either dead or moved away. Lonely, poor, disheartened and ill, she did not long survive her return. A note in the diary of her maid Hélène which, as she had not returned with her, has been preserved among the treasured records of Jefferson County, states that Madame de Feriet died on May 6, 1843, at Versailles.

In 1871 the stately home which she had graced on the banks of the Black River burned to the ground. The ancient bridge of stone arches has been replaced by a modern span of steel and concrete. All that remains today to mark the site of The Hermitage, one of the beauty spots of the Northland, is a row of trees which lined the driveway, an old cellar completely obliterated by a modern house, and the name of the quiet but prosperous village, Deferiet.

CHARD POWERS SMITH

First Kiss

Ike Lathrop, second son of the Squire, awoke as planned to the sound of the big clock below stairs striking five. From the scratch of a squirrel's claws scampering over the roof, he knew it had frozen in the night. From the absolute darkness and a snug oppressiveness in the silence, he sensed that it was snowing. In the little rope bed beside his big one, his young brother Benjamin rolled over in sleep, and Ike's mind stirred to his duties as the nineteen-year-old, senior member of his generation in the house.

It was a Friday, thirteen days before Thanksgiving, in the year 1850, and Ike was to drive the four and a half miles down to the Falls to meet his elderly cousins Joel and Alvina who would arrive on the Utica stage at 7, along with Uncle Brandon, a lawyer in Utica and a frequent visitor, and probably sister Agatha and her husband from Oberlin, Ohio. The elderly cousins were coming all the way from the old homestead in Connecticut to visit the new homestead in northern New York. It was an important event for the family, and Ike's mother had asked him particularly to look nice when he met his cousins. Privately he considered it a piece of danged nonsense to rig up like a dude on a work-day, but he didn't want to disappoint his ma. "Clothes ain't but a custom," he considered as he lay in the darkness. "Best do the proper thing and not stew about it."

Ike nevertheless decided not to get into his new store suit. Best save that to cut a figure on Sunday. For today he'd pick out some old duds that had been dress-up once, though they might be a little patchy and too tight for him now. He'd put on his big brother John's one-time best buff pants; his own every-day boots; one of his new, plaited shirt-fronts; the newfangled bow tie John had brought him from New Haven last summer and which John had tied for him the once he had worn it; his old pink waistcoat and brass-buttoned green coat he could still squeeze into; and brother John's coonskin cap which was now virtually discarded and, though torn in the lining, less frayed externally than Ike's own....

... Ike stepped out of bed onto the cold floor. He groped for his wool stockings on the chest and pulled them on. He walked unerringly through the dark to the closet, picked up his every-day boots and, carrying them in his hand, tiptoed down the front stairs, through the little hall where the big clock beat in the darkness, and into the keeping-room. He kicked a chair that Octavia must have left there, and the agony of his big toe forced a "Consarn it" from him. "Good-morning, son," came his father's quiet voice through the door of the master's bedroom at the rear. Ike found the latch and opened the door noiselessly. "Mornin', pa—sorry I woke ye."

"It's right fresh out, Isaac, and you should take along a drop of spirits for your cousins Joel and Alvina. You will find the flask in the cupboard in the north parlor." "Yes, sir," said Ike, much dignified by this assignment of authority in the mature matter of alcohol. He heard his father dismiss him by rolling over in bed, and so closed the door....

...In spite of the horses' warmth it was cold in the barn; but Ike held to his plan of doing the early chores now so as to keep his clothes clean once he was dressed for the trip to the Falls.... [He] finished the horse chores quickly with a few passes of the brush, for he wanted time to dress as he had planned and he was shivering....

Hurrying back to the kitchen, he took the two big tin pails, one from the wooden sink and one from under it, and, opening the kitchen door, went through the courtyard with its woodpile looming in the lantern-light and out to the well again. His teeth were chattering while he filled the buckets, and an idea tempted him. "I mustn't take cold," he rationalized as he returned to the kitchen. Putting one bucket in its place in the sink beside the washbasin, he filled from the other the pot on the crane over the fire, set the bucket under the sink, swung the crane back over the fire, and paused in the throes of a moral decision. "I'm shiverin', ain't I," he thought, "right here by the fire?"

Although he figured his pa wouldn't mind, yet instinctively he listened for sounds from the master's bedroom or from the back stairs whence Octavia the hired girl might emerge any minute now. Then, convinced of the reasonableness of his intent, this six-foot-one, red-night-shirted youth seized the lantern, walked determinedly into the north parlor, opened the cupboard over the little fireplace, took out the big pewter flask, slid off the elliptical cup that fitted over it, unscrewed its stopper, poured himself out a minute drink of rum and swallowed it.

Although Ike had had his glass of grog on festive occasions for years, this was the first drink he had ever taken except as proffered by Pa, and it was his first taste of neat spirits. Unable to breathe, he rushed back into the kitchen, snatched the piggin and gulped water from the pail. When he stopped gasping he remembered an axiom of Master Lane the hired man—"A gentleman don't swill liquor like a hog." "Serves me right," said Ike in a dramatic whisper, then poured himself out a larger drink, filled it up with water and drank again, in nonchalant and solitary dignity.

Too late he heard the click of a latch. The door of the back stairs swung open and down stepped Octavia Samson, holding a candle high so that her billowy golden hair glittered, waving out from the part and down behind her ears, framing the long, flat cheeks, the pointed chin, the short, full mouth, the brown eyes wide apart and shining in the firelight like ebony.

Ike had often seen the dove-gray dress swelling out from the trim waist that needed no stays. But he hadn't seen the gold hair released from the mesh that usually confined it, nor the gay ribbon with the lilac rosette at the ear, nor, as she came down the last high step, the white silk stockings with black needlework, and the lilac rosettes on her slippers. Nor had Octavia ever seen Ike in the guise in which she now surprised him, the unstopped flask beside him, the empty evidence of guilt in his hand.... Each stood for a moment speechless, jaws dropping in astonishment.

Ike found his tongue first, his sense of guilt vanishing in admiration. "Tavie, ye're pretty as a picture!" he said, and colored faintly, for he was inexperienced in the matter of girls and this was his first compliment to womankind outside his ma and sister. Tavie dropped her eyes, then flashed up at him, "Ike, aren't you ashamed? What are you up to?" Manliness and rum restored the young sinner's composure. "It's colder'n blue crickets out this morning," he said casually, replacing the cup on the flask and screwing down the stopper. Then with the utmost bravado he walked to the row of wraps hanging on their pegs above the table on the south wall, carefully selected his own greatcoat, deposited the flask in its pocket with an air of authority, and strode magnificently into the darkness of the keeping room.

Immediately Tavie heard a chair falling and a full-spoken "god dang it." She seized the lantern he had left on the sink and rushed after him. "Here, Ike, you forgot your light. And you'd better hurry. It's almost five already." "Keerect, Tave," he said, then pressed a finger to his lips, and they both listened. Behind his door they heard the Squire snoring calmly. The big clock in the front hall announced five-thirty. Ike tip-toed up the front stairs two steps at a time, possessed by a combined sense of guilt and a tendency to giggle. Tavie returned to the kitchen, hesitated, reached a decision, ran to Ike's greatcoat, and carried something into the darkness of the north parlor. Then she went back to the kitchen, bore her candle into the north pantry, took down a plate, cup, and a tin of tea, slipped a ham from its hook, and began to slice it violently. "Tavie Samson, you're a silly fool," she said aloud.

Tavie was twenty-one and a graduate of Oberlin College, one of the few hundred women in the whole United States to be dignified by an A.B. degree. Indeed she had been second in her class, and was only helping her family's neighbors, the Lathrops, until her application for a teaching position in Oberlin should be honored. "Oh, why doesn't a letter arrive?" she thought desperately. During her summer vacation two years ago she had attended the Women's Rights Convention at Seneca Falls, where Mistress Lucretia Mott and Mistress Elizabeth Cady Stanton, especially the former, had elicited her worship, both leaders having corresponded with her since, and Mrs. Stanton having recently intimated that there might soon be a paid position for her somewhere in the ranks of the Cause. The Temperance lecturers at Oberlin, too, had taken an interest in her and she had sat on the platform in some of the Ohio villages. Oh, why didn't a letter arrive?—from anywhere! She had thought everything out, and her pa approved. America was the greatest country in the world, and in a few years every abuse would be swept away. Time enough after women were free and alcohol subjugated and prisons reformed and even slavery abolished, time enough then to think of marrying. Oh, why didn't a letter arrive? Slicing the ham, she narrowly missed cutting herself. "You're a silly girl," she said in an angry whisper—"Marrying forsooth!" Gradually she smiled a little, twisted smile. Her long face settled into its accustomed, tense calm, and Ike faded into the problem of breakfast.

In his room Ike, feeling the alcohol throbbing in his veins, held up the lantern and looked at himself long and searchingly in the mirror. "Steady, old man, steady," he said with solemnity....

With laborious precision Ike began to array himself as projected. The only mishaps were when one of the brass buttons on the sleeve of the green coat caught on the latch of the closet as he snatched it out and was left dangling; and when, being fully dressed and inspecting himself in the mirror, he threw out his chest for better effect and split his waistcoat up the back—but that wouldn't show under his coat.

He was proud of his achievement in neckwear. Having affixed the plaited shirt-front and attached the lofty "swaller-chocker" collar without accident, he tied round the latter his new and modish black satin bow tie which, being long enough to encircle his neck twice but now circling it only once, hung in two long loops and two long ribbons down inside his pink waistcoat.

The effects of his drink were wearing off. "There," he said, giving himself a last approving look, and a few more stitches gave way in the back of his waistcoat. Tavie came to the stairs and spoke softly, "Ike, what are you doing? You ought to be harnessing by now. Don't you want any breakfast?" Ike clumped down stairs. Benjamin jumped out of bed, retrieved the lantern his brother had left, snatched *The Plays of William Shakespeare* from the corner shelf, and climbed back into bed.

Tavie had set out the table before the fire, with a candle in the center of it and at Ike's place a thick slice of broiled ham and an enormous wedge of his favorite hickory nut cake. As he stepped into the room she shovelled the fried potatoes from the spider onto his plate, returned to the fireplace and lifted the tea-pot from the trivet. She glanced up and saw that he had struck an attitude for her appraisal, one hand propped against the door-frame and dangling the torn button, one foot thrown out over the other, the toe on the floor. She restrained a gasp at his array. His brow puckered between his big blue eyes that opened wide. She saw the essential combination that was Ike, in the pucker between the eyes the gentleness and sweetness that wanted her approval, and behind the eyes something at once lonely and frightening, something hard and challenging that she knew no woman would ever reach. She slopped the tea pouring it.

"Now hustle," she said, and, setting back the tea-pot on the trivet, ran up the back stairs with the lantern. Ike dumped some tea into his saucer to cool, and attacked the ham. When Tavie came back his cheeks were swollen with cake. She had needle and thread and knelt quickly beside him, sewing the dangling button on the cuff of his coat-sleeve. He finished the cake and the tea with his left hand.

"Now stand up," said Tavie. "That's a nice tie but you don't know quite how to manage it." As she untied his foolish knot she said, "When John tied it for you he wound it round twice, and I suppose he knows. Here, hold this." And while Ike held one end down she walked round him twice with the other, adjusting the satin band so a thin border of it showed above the green coat collar. While she looked up at him tying the bow she saw his big, gentle features lift into the quiet, long-dimpled smile that always seemed to understand everything and made him a person without age.

She gave the tie a final pat and stepped back, letting herself smile richly for once. Then she saw the pucker between his eyes and stiffened in panic. "Tavie," said his rich baritone as if from miles away, "I guess there'd be no wrong in my kissing ye." She felt suddenly strong and looked straight up at him from her glittering brown eyes. "You'll be sorry if you do, Ike." But he kissed her all the same, taking her by the shoulders and touching her lips so gently that she relaxed for an instant and found herself leaning against him. Then she drew back in fury at her weakness, and when she stared up at him his boyish face flushed red.

"Guess I'd best be off," he said lamely, and Tavie rushed to the wraps on the wall—"Here's your coat"—she threw it at him—"I put sugar for the horses in the pocket—Here's your tippet—Here's your mittens—Here's"—she paused with his wool cap in her hands—"I suppose you want John's coonskin—get out to the horses—I'll fetch it—I was going to mend the lining." She rushed up the backstairs. The clock in the front hall began to strike six.

Ike grabbed the lantern and ran out through the summer kitchen where in the second of his passing every familiar detail—the stove, the churn, the barrels of flour and meal, the sap-pails hanging from the ceiling, the three muskets on their pegs—seemed fresh and wonderful and important. The first thing he knew he had Dandy in place across the pole of the little family coach. As he was leading Mol out of the stall he suddenly stopped dead still. "Crimus, I kissed her," he thought. "I kissed a girl."

WALTER GUEST KELLOGG

The Garden Party

To all of the many who saw her for the first time that June day, she looked radiantly happy, radiantly lovely in her close-fitting gown of black velvet and her pearls and her white lace, with the funny little Neapolitan cap perched upon her gray hair, moving so adroitly, with such poise, such precision, among the crowd gathered in the Mansion grounds, but old Mr. Rosseel, leaning on his cane, knew differently. Lovely, indeed, she was, fitted to adorn just such a fine fête as this, but happy? Ah, she looked happy, undeniably happy, but— She was acting, that was all. For when Mr. Parish had gone a month before, she'd waved bravely to him as he'd driven off—and it was Mr. Rosseel who'd found her, fainted dead away, at the Mansion gate. And, well, Dr. Laughlin had forbidden the fête, yet— But Olds' brass band struck up, and he turned to them, stationed near the gardener's lodge.

A pretty band, distinctly an ornamental, almost a gorgeous band. Blue suits with white leather belts; blue caps with stern black visors, and white leather straps, and jaunty white cockades; the leader with his enormous busby and long baton. Cornets, trombones, glittering in the sun. A pretty band, blatant, sonorous, but not musical. Judge James had chanced to remark, "What this town needs is a good band." Ed Olds, about to start a cheese-factory, heard him and was impressed. Forgetting the cheese-factory, he started a band, instead. Also he forgot that Judge James had stipulated "a good band," and he started, merely, a band. Seven of the twelve bandsmen played by note, having no ear; the other five played by ear only. Once the seven got started, they played each quaver, demi-quaver, and curly-cue precisely, exactly, as written: the five ear-players each played the tune according to his best recollection of it, the more open-minded among them adding, here and there, an occasional note, flourish or incidental passage of his own. The composite result was less a tune than an interesting example of how differently one and the same thing can be seen by a dozen men. Upon the bass-drum was painted "E. Olds's Brass Band—Live and Let Live." A moral band, its high standards embodied in those four ringing words, a pretty, a neat, a decorative band, but not, Mr. Rosseel reflected, a good band. Ah, the bands he'd heard in the Place d'Armes in Brussels! From Madame Vespucci to the band, and now, wearied and tired of its brazen, thumping, discordant blatancy, he turned once more to the crowds swarming over the Mansion lawns, over the Mansion gardens, over and into the Mansion stables, and through the woods at the south. Swarming, indeed, into the Mansion itself.

Madame Vespucci's "Pic-Nic," as the *Journal* called it—her tea, supper, lawn-fête, garden-party, what you please—her farewell (but none knew it but Madame Vespucci, himself, and Mr. Parish, now on the seas) to the people of Ogdensburgh, who for eighteen years had held her almost beneath contempt, and only now were beginning to realize that she wasn't utterly of the devil's own doing. But 'twas no love of her that brought the grown-ups, he knew, but only a curiosity to look over the Mansion, and the gardens, and the stables, and the conservatory, and to see, at close range, the mysterious "shut-in-lady of the arbor," the wicked woman, the village Delilah, and to see her, moreover, bedecked in all her finery.

Just inside the gate stood a trellised arch with red and white carnations spelling out the words "Welcome, Children." Opposite this arch, on the other side of the garden, stood another heralding the admonition: "Children, Love One Another." No floral greeting was provided for the elders, and properly, thought Mr. Rosseel, for many of them, urged by an indomitable curiosity, had shoved their way in, unbidden. They were, nevertheless, not unwelcome. Nor did any motto in red and white counsel them to brotherly love; several whom he saw in the crowd hated someone else there with a large and venomous hatred that wasn't to be baulked by any frail device in flowers. "No," reflected Mr. Rosseel, "old Davis'd like to take an ax to Jim Robinson; and Robinson cherishes the same affection for Davis. But children—maybe such mottoes will do them good." The elders stood apart, watching the children at their games.

Tag, pom-pom-pullaway, ring-round-the-rosie, blind-man's buff, post-office; common enough, these were, but who but Madame would have thought of a Maypole, high in the center of the track, with its spreading, umbrella-like ribbons of pink, and orange, and white, and blue, glistening chromatically in the warm sun, as the varying circles of gaily dressed, spick and span, freshly scrubbed boys and girls wove and interwove them about the lofty blue pole? And who but Madame would have had the Punch-and-Judy show brought all the way from New York, with Signor Blitz, similarly imported, to operate it, and afterward, upon the raised platform, to do his magical tricks? And the ponies—and the dogs—all beribboned. And, hung from the trees, and the stone-wall, and the shrubbery, festive paper lanterns—Japanese lanterns—glowed colorfully over the faces, little and great, making the grounds—well, as Dr. Peters observed, "a paradise, Ma'am, a veritable paradise."

The elders stared at her, but the children barely noticed her, she was so helpful to them, so busy putting their feet the *right* way into the stirrups, so solicitous that even the tiniest tot shouldn't miss an instant, even, of the justly celebrated Signor Blitz. "Please," she would say, "remove the rabbit from the hat once more, Signor, for this baby could not see! Now! There is the rabbit, dear—a real, live rabbit right out of the gentleman's hat! Is it not wonderful?"

"This little girl here was crying, Ma'am," said Billy Craig, "because she couldn't see the Punch-and-Judy. Her little friend's been telling her about it—and she's that broken-hearted!"

"Ah, but she shall, she must!" cried Ameriga. "Inform the good Signor Blitz; he will oblige, I'm certain. Oh, she shall, she shall see Punch-and-Judy!"

Those curious, peeping, uninvited elders! How gracious, how urbane she was to them! Her friends, all of them, they might have been, as she passed so flittingly amongst them; welcome they felt, for welcome she made them feel.

"You know," remarked Margaret Bliss that night, "I'd never seen her in my life! I went there perfectly brazenly, unasked, to see a woman I'd heard of always. A wicked, an awful woman! And she couldn't call me by name, for she didn't know it; she didn't presume and she wasn't forward, and yet she talked to me awhile, when I was standing alone, and I felt I'd known her intimately, yet that I wanted to know her still more."

In the dusk, long white-clothed tables appeared, and marvelous chairs which unfolded. And scores of white-capped waitresses, bearing cakes, and candies, and ice-cream, and milk, and ginger-pop, and lemonade, and cornucopias with pull-mottoes, and fantastic paper hats. And Madame, in a blue paper hat, and, gathered about her, as she sat in a swing under the big elm, children listening to the wolf-story which she had heard, when a child, from her mother's lips, in a patio, in far-off Italy. Oh, so long, long ago! And then there were little packages in tissue with her card—"La Contessina Ameriga M. E. Vespucci," it read—with "Please do not open till to-morrow" written upon it—which William Houston carried that evening to three little girls who'd spent happy afternoons with her in the Mansion garden.

The chatter stopped; the laughter, the shouts of those hundreds of children died down, for the grown-ups, looking very grave, were motioning for silence. A little man in black, his eyes pleasurably atwinkle, was rising from his chair, walking toward an open space near the Punch-and-Judy show: the Reverend L. Merrill Miller, pastor of the Presbyterian Church.

The children didn't like it, for it interfered with their fun; it was too much like church. The elders, surprised at seeing him present, were so much the more surprised when he dignified and sanctified the occasion with speech that most of them didn't catch what he was saying, and had to content themselves with reading, in the *Journal's* account of it, that: "the Reverend Miller spoke words of approval and encouragement to the children, a few more expressive of their thanks to their generous hostess, and an invocation of Heaven's blessing upon them all." And many considered that it was very nice and big and broad-minded of him to speak so, and others there were who thought precisely the other thing, and even went so far as to absent themselves from church for several consecutive Sundays to mark their disapproval of it. But Madame liked what he said, and she told him so, and she thanked him, with tears in her bright old eyes.

It was over. The wall-gate opened and shut, opened and shut. Grown-ups left decorously, formally; riotous, romping children left, bowing, shouting, mumbling their thanks to her. She smiled, she waved to them, she kissed little mouths and cheeks, she hugged them, grimy and sticky, to her black velvet, to her pearls—she laughed. Elders.... But children, harum-scarum children she'd never see again, bright eyes, rosy cheeks, clutching her oranges greedily to their breasts. The wall-gate opened and shut upon them all.

As she turned, she faced the desolation of it—papers, orange-peel, gay little caps scattered over the green lawns. Servants rolling the napery, extinguishing the lights, righting, to some semblance, the tables, the chairs—

Once she, too, had come to a party. And now it was over.

"No, William, thanks. It's quite all right," she said, mounting the stone steps, leaning upon the wooden railing. "I'm quite all right. Everything's been ver' nice. Good night, and thanks to you all."

At four the next morning, Mr. Rosseel saw her off. She cried in his fat old arms.

"God bless you, Ma'am," he said.

Fat men, wiping their eyes with large bandanna handkerchiefs, look silly, particularly silly in the dawn, staring after a puffing, snorting, rackety, wood-smoke-belching, ridiculous old train.

"God bless you," he sobbed.

IRVING BACHELLER

The Ten Treasures

Tip Taylor was, in the main, a serious minded man. A cross eye enhanced the natural solemnity of his countenance. He was little given to talk or laughter unless he were on a hunt, and then he only whispered his joy. He had seen a good bit of the world through the peek sight of his rifle, and there was something always in the feel of a gun that lifted him to higher moods. And yet one could reach a tender spot in him without the aid of a gun. That winter vacation I set myself to study things for declamation—specimens of the eloquence of Daniel Webster and Henry Clay and James Otis and Patrick Henry. I practiced them in the barn, often, in sight and hearing of the assembled herd and some of those fiery passages were rather too loud and threatening for the peace and comfort of my audience. The oxen seemed always to be expecting the sting of the bull whip; they stared at me timidly, tilting their ears every moment, as if to empty them of a heavy load; while the horses snorted with apprenhension. This haranguing of the herd had been going on a week or more when Uncle Eb and I, returning from a distant part of the farm, heard a great uproar in the stable.

From *Eben Holden: A Tale of the North Country,* published by the Lothrop Publishing Company, Boston, 1900.

Looking in at a window we saw Tip Taylor, his back toward us, extemporizing a speech. He was pressing his argument with gestures and the tone of thunder. We listened a moment, while a worried look came over the face of Uncle Eb. Tip's words were meaningless save for the secret aspiration they served to advertise. My old companion thought Tip had gone crazy, and immediately swung the door and stepped in. The orator fell suddenly from his lofty altitude and became a very sober looking hired man.

"What's the matter?" Uncle Eb inquired.

"Practicin'," said Tip soberly, as he turned slowly, his face damp and red with exertion.

"Fer what?" Uncle Eb inquired.

"Fer the 'sylum, I guess," he answered, with a faint smile.

"Ye don' need no more practice," Uncle Eb answered. "Looks t' me as though ye was purty well prepared."

To me there was a touch of pathos in this show of the deeper things in Tip's nature that had been kindled to eruption by my spouting. He would not come in to dinner that day, probably from an unfounded fear that we would make fun of his flight—a thing we should have been far from doing once we understood him.

It was a bitter day of one of the coldest winters we had ever known. A shrieking wind came over the hills, driving a scud of snow before it. The stock in the stables, we all came in, soon after dinner, and sat comfortably by the fire with cider, checkers and old sledge. The dismal roar of the trees and the wind-wail in the chimney served only to increase our pleasure. It was going dusk when mother, peering through the sheath of frost on a window pane, uttered an exclamation of surprise.

"Why! who is this at the door?" said she. "Why! It's a man in a cutter."

Father was near the door and he swung it open quickly.

There stood a horse and cutter, a man sitting in it, heavily muffled. The horse was shivering and the man sat motionless.

"Hello!" said David Brower in a loud voice.

He got no answer and ran bareheaded to the sleigh.

"Come, quick, Holden," he called, "it's Doctor Bigsby."

We all ran out then, while David lifted the still figure in his arms.

"In here, quick!" said Elizabeth, opening the door to the parlor. "Musn't take 'im near the stove."

We carried him into the cold room and laid him down, and David and I tore his wraps open while the others ran quickly after snow.

I rubbed it vigorously upon his face and ears, the others meantime applying it to his feet and arms, that had been quickly stripped. The doctor stared at us curiously and tried to speak.

"Get ap, Dobbin!" he called presently, and clucked as if urging his horse. "Get ap, Dobbin! Man'll die 'fore ever we git there."

We all worked upon him with might and main. The white went slowly out of his face. We lifted him to a sitting posture. Mother and Hope and Uncle Eb were rubbing his hands and feet.

"Where am I?" he inquired, his face now badly swollen.

"At David Brower's," said I.

"Huh?" he asked, with that kindly and familiar grunt of interrogation.

"At David Brower's," I repeated.

"Well, I'll have t' hurry," said he, trying feebly to rise. "Man's dyin' over——" he hesitated thoughtfully, "on the Plains," he added, looking around at us.

Grandma Bisnette brought a lamp and held it so the light fell on his face. He looked from one to another. He drew one of his hands away and stared at it.

"Somebody froze?" he asked.

"Yes," said I.

"Hm! Too bad. How'd it happen?" he asked.

"I don't know."

"How's the pulse?" he inquired, feeling for my wrist.

I let him hold it in his hand.

"Will you bring me some water in a glass?" he inquired, turning to Mrs. Brower, just as I had seen him do many a time in Gerald's illness. Before she came with the water his head fell forward upon his breast, while he muttered feebly. I thought then he was dead, but presently he roused himself with a mighty effort.

"David Brower!" he called loudly, and trying hard to rise, "bring the horse! bring the horse! Mus' be goin', I tell ye: Man's dyin' over—on the Plains."

He went limp as a rag then. I could feel his heart leap and struggle feebly.

"There's a man dyin' here," said David Brower, in a low tone. "Ye needn't rub no more."

"He's dead," Elizabeth whispered, holding his hand tenderly, and looking into his half-closed eyes. Then for a moment she covered her own with her handkerchief, while David, in a low, calm tone, that showed the depth of his feeling, told us what to do.

Uncle Eb and I watched that night, while Tip Taylor drove away to town.

The body lay in the parlor and we sat by the stove in the room adjoining. In a half whisper we talked of the sad event of the day.

"Never oughter gone out a day like this," said Uncle Eb. "Don' take much t' freeze an ol' man."

"Got to thinking of what happened yesterday and forgot the cold," I said.

"Bad day 't be absent minded," whispered Uncle Eb, as he rose and tiptoed to the window and peered through the frosty panes. "May o' got faint er sumthin'. Ol' hoss brought 'im right here—been here s' often with 'im."

He took the lantern and went out a moment. The door creaked upon its frosty hinges when he opened it.

"Thirty below zero," he whispered as he came in. "Win's gone down a leetle bit, mebbe."

Uncanny noises broke in upon the stillness of the old house. Its timbers, racked in the mighty grip of the cold, creaked and settled. Sometimes there came a sharp, breaking sound, like the crack of bones.

"If any man oughter go t' Heaven, he had," said Uncle Eb, as he drew on his boots.

"Think he's in Heaven?" I asked.

"Hain't a doubt uv it," said he, as he chewed a moment, preparing for expectoration.

"What kind of a place do you think it is?" I asked.

"Fer one thing," he said, deliberately, "nobody'll die there, 'less he'd ought to; don't believe there's goin' t' be any need o' swearin' er quarrelin'. To my way o' thinkin' it'll be a good deal like Dave Brower's farm—nice, smooth land and no stun on it, an' hills an' valleys an' white clover a plenty, an' wheat an' corn higher'n a man's head. No bull thistles, no hard winters, no narrer contracted fools; no long faces, an' plenty o' work. Folks sayin' 'How d'y do' 'stid o' 'good-by,' all the while—comin' 'stid o' goin'. There's goin' t' be some kind o' fun there. I ain' no idee what 'tis. Folks like it an' I kind o' believe 'at when God's gin a thing t' everybody he thinks purty middlin' well uv it."

"Anyhow, it seems a hard thing to die," I remarked.

"Seems so," he said thoughtfully. "Jes' like ever'thing else— them 'at knows much about it don' have a great deal t' say. Looks t'me like this: I cal'ate a man hes on the everidge ten things his heart is sot on—what is the word I want—?"

"Treasures?" I suggested.

"Thet's it," said he. "Ev'ry one hes about ten treasures. Some hev more—some less. Say one's his strength, one's his plan, the rest is them he loves, an' the more he loves the better 'tis fer him. Wall, they begin t' go one by one. Some die, some turn agin' him. Fin's it hard t' keep his allowance. When he's only nine he's lost eggzac'ly one-tenth uv his dread o' dyin'. Bime bye he counts up—one-two-three-four-five—an' thet's all ther is left. He figgers it up careful. His strength is gone, his plan's a failure, mebbe, an' this one's dead an' thet one's dead, an' t'other one better be. Then 's 'bout half ways with him. If he lives 'till the ten treasures is all gone, God gives him one more—thet's death. An' he can swop thet off an' git back all he's lost. Then he begins t' think it's a purty dum good thing, after all. Purty good thing, after all," he repeated, gaping as he spoke.

He began nodding shortly, and soon he went asleep in his chair.

20TH CENTURY

HENRY BESTON

The St. Lawrence

Under a vast land sky, milky-pale with a universal tissue of cloud, the great fresh-water sea rolls before the west wind towards the narrowing and approaching shores which begin the river. The pale waves of Ontario diminish as the wind crowds them into the St. Lawrence, and a thunderstorm of early afternoon touches the dark American green of the nearer woods with silver and a veil of rain. Save for the gulls who follow beside the ship, there seem few birds.

In its great departure, the river is itself something of another lake, flowing in vague and enormous motion to the east. Indeed the whole rhythm of the landscape has an eastward resolution, with its tree shapes and its tree boughs streaming backward, and the river itself moving eastward below both current and wave. Shores of fields and hardwoods in their midsummer greenery presently gather a blacker and old-fashioned wildness, and the stream surprisingly becomes a whole inland sea of fanciful isles and archipelagoes. The Thousand Islands (the phrase has touched the American imagination) are here for the counting. Some are mere rocks emerging from the stream, poising one resolute small tree in a crevice of grey stone, some are rural felicities of field and tree with the river as a moat, others are solitaries set apart, each like a lonely star. The houses which crown them are the comfortable houses of a comfortable past, but here and there one ventures into a realm of turreted and shingled castles which is fairy land as the American fancy of the seventies and eighties saw it with perhaps a little help from

The van Bergen Overmantel, shown in detail above and in entirety below, is the earliest-known American painting of the kind. In addition to being a decorative panel installed over the fireplace in the very farmhouse in the center of the composition, the picture shows the owner, Marten van Bergen, his wife and children, slaves, Indian neighbors, livestock, and the layout of the farm buildings. It is also a landscape, showing the mountains and forests of the Catskills with a surprising amount of temperament.

Artist unknown; about 1735. Leeds, Greene County. Oil on panel; 18″ x 84½″.

ALL PAINTINGS IN THIS FOLIO ARE FROM THE COLLECTION OF THE NEW YORK STATE HISTORICAL ASSOCIATION, COOPERSTOWN

Major General Frederick William Augustus von Steuben, a distinguished and idealistic German officer who, like Lafayette, volunteered to help the birthing of the new Republic. He was notably successful in training of troops and army management. Several states granted him lands, but he retired to those at Steubenville, N.Y.

Ralph Earl, 1786

Oil on canvas; 48½″ x 40″.

Joseph Brant, who served the Crown as a chief of the Iroquois during the Revolution, as seen by the solidly conventional Albany portraitist, Ezra Ames, in 1806, when Brant's greatest concerns were peaceful co-existence and Christianizing of his people.

Oil on canvas; 30½″ x 24½″.

Red Jacket, Seneca patriot and orator, at the beloved falls of Niagara. The little oil sketch was made in New York City in 1827 by Robert W. Weir, a young artist who was to become professor of drawing at West Point.

Oil on wood; 9″ x 7½″.

The Murder of Jane McCrea was a popular atrocity story of the Revolution and continued to be a favorite theme of New York artists well into the 19th Century. This example is one of two versions by John Vanderlyn.

Oil on canvas; 33½″ x 26⅛″.

TOP LEFT: *The Escape of Israel Putnam* from the Indians took place in 1755 on Woods Creek, one of the many adventures during the French and Indian Wars and the Revolution that endeared that spirited hero to the American imagination. Artist unknown, formerly attributed to Asher B. Durand.
Oil on canvas; 18″ x 21½″.

BOTTOM LEFT: *Washington's Headquarters, Newburgh,* is the first historic building in America set aside for preservation by a government agency, in this instance the State of New York in 1850. First the printmakers and after them hundreds of naïve painters found this combination of history, patriotism, and landscape irresistible.
Anonymous. c. 1855.
Oil on canvas; 13½″ x 18″.

ABOVE: An accurate record of history. *Seneca Veterans of the War of 1812,* including such leaders as Cornplanter, Two Guns, and I-Like-Her, gathered at that favorite Indian place of rendezvous for many years, Niagara Falls. Owned by Mrs. Eugene Brown, Scottsville; loaned to the New York State Historical Association. Now attributed to William Page, c. 1820.
Oil on panel; 23″ x 30″.

Thomas Bronk (1767-1862), a slave in the Averell family, who lived into the Civil War, becoming one of the most respected citizens of Cooperstown. Like many New York slaves, whose freedom came as early as 1827, he chose to remain in the town where he had long worked.
Artist unknown.
Pastel; 30″ x 21″.

Laura Hall is a girl of only 19, whose severity reflects the temper of the times and the tendency of the artist, J. Brown, to show his subjects in dour mien. A year after this portrait was painted, in 1808, Laura married Ambrose Kasson. The painting was long held as a family heirloom by the Kasson family of Utica.
Oil on canvas; 72″ x 36″.

FACING PAGE: *Robert Fulton,* perfecter of the steamboat, inventor, entrepreneur, and artist, as seen by the beloved President of the Royal Academy, our own Benjamin West. This 1806 portrait, done in London, shows in background Fulton's explosive naval mines, which he tried vainly to sell to various foreign governments.
Oil on canvas; 35¾″ x 28″.

DeWitt Clinton, governor of the State and powerful backer of the Erie Canal, is one of about two dozen leading American citizens captured in plaster life masks by John H. I. Browere. The secret of his process did not come down to us, but the busts survived and have been cast in bronze.

James Fenimore Cooper, the novelist, through whose work, perhaps more than any other, the United States became known in Europe. This little-known portrait dates from about 1830. Attributed to J. J. M. Achille Deveria.

Watercolor; 4¾″ x 4½″.

Otsego Hall, Cooperstown, built by William Cooper, the novelist's fathér, in 1798 as a straightforward brick structure. The building was remodeled by James Fenimore Cooper in 1834 with the advice of his friend, the artist-inventor Samuel F. B. Morse, using an appliqué of crenelations in the style of the Gothic Revival.

Detail of watercolor signed "CTE."
10¼″ x 19⅛″.

Mrs. William Cooper, mother of the novelist, with her beloved servant Joseph Stewart ("Governor"). Mrs. Cooper is seated in the large entrance chamber of Otsego Hall, shown when it was still in good Federalist style. Her son described the room minutely in Chapter V of *The Pioneers.*

Watercolor by "Mr. Freeman," 1816. 17½" x 21½".

View from Apple Hill, Cooperstown, not many rods from Otsego Hall, showing the beginning of the Susquehanna River and the prospect of Otsego Lake, Cooper's "Glimmerglass."

Samuel F. B. Morse, about 1829 — Oil on canvas; 32½″ x 39¾″.

Scene on Lake George from Cooper's *The Last of the Mohicans,* by Thomas Cole, founder of the Hudson River School. Signed and dated 1827, the painting is an early and magnificent example of the fruitful marriage of art and letters in New York. Oil on canvas; 25″ x 35″.

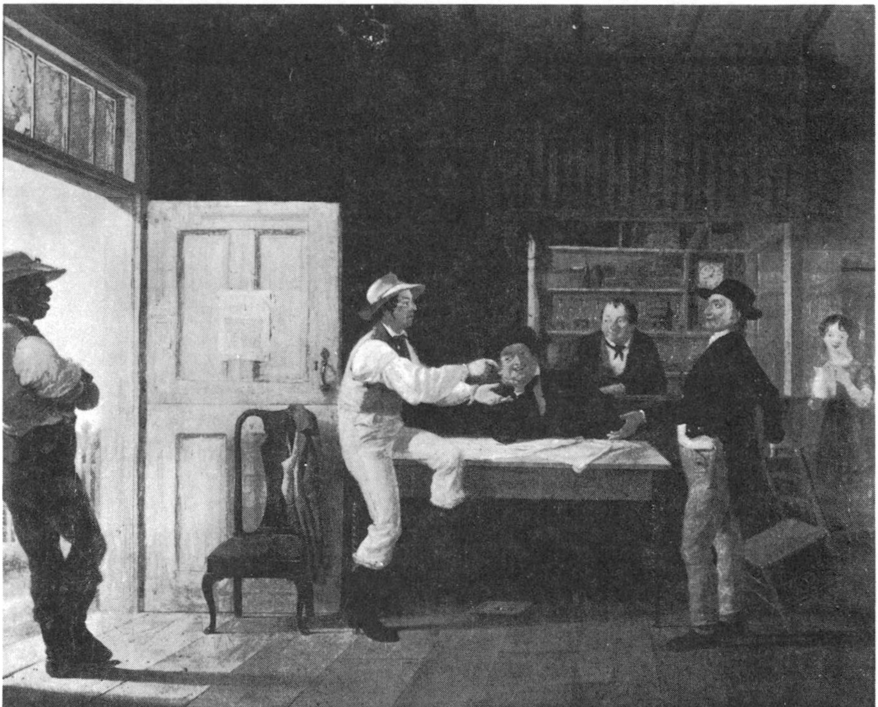

TOP LEFT: Scene from a dramatization of Cooper's novel *The Spy,* first produced in 1822. *The Spy* was the first novel to romanticize the Revolution in New York, and the scenes move back and forth across Westchester County. The picture is signed and dated 1822, by William Dunlop, artist, playwright, theatrical manager, and historian. Oil on canvas; 22″ x 27″.

BOTTOM LEFT: *Politicians in a Country Bar,* an utterly timeless subject, painted by James Clonney in 1844, probably in Otsego County. The painting is an enlargement of a tiny watercolor Clonney presumably made on the spot.
Oil on canvas; 17⅛″ x 21⅛″.

ABOVE: *The Turkey Shoot,* a scene from Cooper's *The Pioneers.* Most of the characters are visualized in the slick, artificially dramatic style so popular in the 19th Century, but the figure of Leatherstocking is *sui generis* and somehow called upon a freer, stronger, more imaginative vein in the artist.
Tompkins H. Matteson, 1857. Oil on canvas; 36⅛″ x 48″.

Justice's Court in the Backwoods is a document of frontier village life and law. The cobbler-justice, an ideal figure, is very real to the artist, whose neighbor he probably was. Tompkins H. Matteson, the painter, lived much of his life at Sherburne in central New York. This large and busy picture well repays a close look, for here is the standard cast of characters for many a village comedy and tragedy.

Oil on canvas; 31¾″ x 44″.

The Cider Mill is a portrait of one of the pleasanter old-time industrial scenes, and emphasizes how the various aspects of living intermingled in early days. Age and youth, people and animals, work and play are juxtaposed, and the senses of sight, touch, taste, and smell are tickled into sympathetic memories.

William T. Carlton (1816-1888).
Oil on canvas; 29″ x 36″.

Kept In is a sensitive yet unsentimental study of a schoolgirl of the 1880's. This small portrait is one of the most beloved by the public of all the collection at Fenimore House, Cooperstown. The artist lived and painted at Cragsmoor in the Shawingunk Mountains, south of the Catskills. Negro children were often favored subjects.
Edward L. Henry Oil on canvas; 13½" x 17¾".

Mrs. McCormick's General Store, Catskill, New York, showing juvenile delinquency, 1844. Alburtis D. O. Browere (son of the artist who did the life mask of DeWitt Clinton) painted the everyday life around him. Some of the buildings shown here are still standing. Oil on canvas; 20½" x 25".

F. Scott Smith, born in 1853, may have been four or five on the summer's day when some anonymous artist painted him and his patriotic dog. Notice the local militia drilling in background, preparing for the war soon to come.

Oil on canvas; 49″ x 39½″.

TOP: *Marimaid.* How this mermaid and the one on the facing page, perhaps deriving from the same source, or one from the other, happened to find themselves in the Catskills in the early 19th Century is a puzzle. This picture was done by Mary Ann Willson, an eccentric Greene County painter of the period.

Watercolor; 13″ x 15½″.

RIGHT: All too few early New York inn signs have survived. The weathering on this Catskill-area *Mermaid* leads us to think she may have welcomed travellers at some tavern. Primitive she may be, but she has style and a vital design that defies time and weather.

Oil on wood; 27½″ x 22⅝″. c. 1825

The Horse with the Longest Hair in the World, attributed to a Dr. Dorr in Chatham, New York. Shown at summer fairs in the 1880's, the horse wintered in Chatham, his mane and tail carefully wrapped in burlap bags.

Oil on canvas; 18″ x 24″.

Dexter, beloved racehorse of the last century, when Saratoga and Goshen were the most fashionable racing and trotting tracks in America. Drawn in India ink with touches of sepia, after a lithograph issued by Currier & Ives in 1865.

21¾″ x 27½″.

Poughkeepsie, New York, about 1870. J. M. Evans, an otherwise unknown primitive artist, signed this large panoramic view of the town. The specificity of the painting is strikingly characteristic of American folk art.

Oil on canvas; 29″ x 43″.

Steamer Niagara Passing Fort Washington Point, 1845, by James Bard. This artist and his twin brother, John, produced several hundred such crisp steamboat paintings. The detail of scenery and people lent beauty and amusement to the precise ship paintings. Oil on canvas; 36″ x 56″.

Pitsford on the Erie Canal—a Sultry Calm. A fine stipple technique is used in this and other "atmospheric" views of New York State, prepared by the artist for an ill-fated publishing venture. This view shows a scene near Rochester.
George Harvey, 1837. Watercolor; 8⅜" x 13⅝".

An ingratiating *View of the Hudson Near West Point* by James M. Hart of Albany, signed and dated 1859. A minor master of the Hudson River School at his calmest and most pastoral.

Oil on canvas; 19″ x 26″.

The Mohawk Valley, about 1850. The painting's details—the two artists, the active farm, the railroad train, the river, hills, and forests—invite the eye and soul. Such vistas appealed greatly to visitors from abroad, as here to the English-born artist, Robert Havell, Jr., who engraved many of Audubon's birds.

Oil on canvas; 36″ x 50″.

Thomas Cole's *View on the Schoharie*. Hudson River School, 1826. This "School" was commonly said to have begun in 1825 when three of young Cole's landscapes were discovered in a New York shop window by John Trumbull, William Dunlap, and Asher B. Durand. This painting shows "wild nature" in the tradition of Salvator Rosa. The other basic mood of the Hudson River School, harmonious with the work of Claude de Lorraine, is found in Durand's pastoral scene on the facing page.

Oil on canvas; 31½″ x 41½″.

Hudson River, Looking Toward the Catskills, 1847, by Asher B. Durand, is in a mood quite opposite to Cole's *Schoharie*. It exemplifies the other major groupings of ideas with which the Hudson River painters occupied themselves, the nobility and richness of God's work, considered in a pastoral setting. Durand, the leading engraver in America, turned only in middle age to the unfamiliar techniques of oil. His virtuosity is revealed here.

Oil on canvas; 46″ x 62″.

Main Street, Sharon Springs, about 1845. This painting is by marine artist James E. Butterworth. Oil on canvas; 30″ × 54″.

The snowy isolation of winter, seen in *The Holmes Homestead, Delaware County,* is still characteristic of many upstate New York farms.
Artist unknown. Oil on board; 12½″ x 18½″.

Poestenkill, in Rensselaer County, is recorded here by the local taxidermist, woodcarver, and constructor of wooden shadowboxes for flowers. Poestenkill looks much the same today.
Joseph H. Hidley, 1862. Oil on wood; 26″ x 38″.

Cider Making in the Country records one of the best-loved parts of the farmer's year, especially in an area so proud of its fine apple crops as New York State. The artist painted the scene for Currier & Ives in 1863, and an extremely popular lithograph was made from it.
George Henry Durrie. Oil on canvas; 35⅝″ x 54″.

George Mastin of Finger Lakes Country hired artists in 1845 to paint a portable art show, of which these two very large religious scenes were a part. Like many a Renaissance artist in Europe, this unknown country painter gave a most contemporary quality to *Adam and Eve* and the group around Christ in *Christ Blessing Little Children*. The children in the picture below are even wearing dresses of the period.

Both paintings are 7′5″ x 10′10″, and were designed to be rolled and carried in a box in the back of a wagon.

Whig Banner of the 1844 Cayuga County Campaign for Henry Clay, as painted by a sign, carriage, and landscape painter of Auburn, New York.

Terence J. Kennedy.
Oil on canvas; 66″ in diameter.

Tennyson. Currents stir in the seeming lake, flowing visibly between the isles: the river is gaining strength. At the water's edge, on polished shelves of stone, gatherings of the common tern stand massed in feathered whiteness, sheltering from the wind.

These waters might cover the entire earth so much do they seem without definition or bound. A narrow passage ultimately leads from them into the next great phase of the stream.

It is the York State St. Lawrence, the river with Ontario and Britain to one side, and the United States and Congress and the presidents to the other. To the Canadian north are old farms and fields with willows bordering their shores and silvering in the wind. Here and there, in crannies of the bank under a decorum of leaves, are old-fashioned cottages playful with architectural gingerbread, and from time to time appear small rustic towns whose houses and trees seem to have been planted together in some Canadian moment of the mid-Victorian mood. The landscape reflects a way of life less hurried than the American. Town halls have even something of a British propriety, and the bells in the brick churches strike noon with a measured and English air.

Across the stream, under the same inland light, the same level distances of grassland and trees fall back from the yellow earth of the New York shore. The farms seem more scattered and uneven and are farther from the river, towns count for less, and there are more groves of elms standing green beside the bank. It is not the landscape of the shores, however, which now seizes upon the imagination of the traveler. For thirty miles he has been following a great and single channel direct as some vast canal, a line of water drawn across a part of North America as it might be across the face of Mars. So evenly between its banks does it keep its average width of a fair two miles that the long, natural perspective has even something of an artificial air; one might be in the presence of some great work of the ancient and mysterious America of the Mound Builders. Looking westward from Prescott in Ontario one sees a surprising sight at the far end of the fairway. It is a sealike horizon on a river, a level line of water and sky suspended in space between the substantiality of parallel shores, themselves vanishing over the rounding plunge of earth.

Flat wavelets speckle the channel, flicked from the current by the inland breeze. Eastward and ahead, vast steps in the rush of the river downhill from the lakes, lie the great rapids, the roar of their narrow caldrons, long slopes, and wider seas of fury soon to break upon the listening ear.

Only the strong current, eddying in deep mid-channel and flowing like a long and hastening ripple past the banks, carries a hint of what is presently to come. The river has quickened pace into new country, an open tableland of grass and gravel down whose yellow banks glacial boulders have here and there rolled to the water's edge; the great main channel is over and done; ahead, level islands of the stream's own making bar and turn it in its gathering and meandering rush. It is farming land, and there are cattle on the islands, black-and-white Holsteins feeding under the willows and the grovelike beauty of the elms. A touch or two of industrialism on the Canadian side, and the beginning there of the canal world does not change the character of the landscape or the emphasis of its way of life. The river, which at Prescott and Ogdensburg was a pale and inland blue, has in this yellower earth gathered a tinge of green.

Lake freighters coming and going to Montreal have gone into the canals. Slow dignities of hulk and painted iron, they move along the separate water, their stacks visible in the distance above and through the trees.

The islands are now close at hand, lying in the stream like hindrances in a corridor, and confusing the descent with turns and passages about and between their steeper-growing banks. Alongside, the water is now plunging forward in a rush, boiling up from below in circles like huge lily pads expanding. Two rapids which are little more than a new and fiercer hurrying under the keel pass by without drama of sight or sound. More rapids follows and a long rush at whose far end a growing roar overflows into the blue and casual day.

A shudder, a strange motion downhill into a vast confusion and a vaster sound, and one is in the pool which is the climax of the rapids of the Long Sault. So steep is the winding rush downslope into the pool and out of it along a furious curve that the rims of water close along the banks stand higher than the tumult in the pit, and one passes, as it were, through banks of water as well as banks of land. Currents and agitations of wind, rapids of the invisible air, enclose the ship in a leap, scurrying the deck with their small and wild unrest. In the caldrons all is giant and eternal din, a confusion and war and leaping-up of white water in every figure and fury of its elemental being, the violence roaring in a ceaseless and universal hue and cry of water in all its sounds and tongues. The forms of water rising and falling here, onrushing, bursting, and dissolving, have little kinship with waves at sea, with those long bodies of the ocean's pulse. They are shapes of violence and the instancy of creation, towering pyramids crested with a splash of white, rising only to topple upstream as the downcurrent rushes at their base. Lifted for an instant of being into a beauty of pure form and the rising curve, they resemble nothing so much as the decorative and symbolic waves of the artists of Japan.

Enclosing the pool, in a strange contrast of mood, stands an almost sylvan scene, a country shore of grass and trees and a noontide restfulness of shade.

A bold turn of a gravel promontory, and one escapes out of the caldron into a broading reach of calmer water. Widening, widening to a lake, the river achieves an afternoon peace, and there comes slowly into view a landscape so much part of the old beauty of the past, a landscape so poignantly and profoundly American, that time seems to have stood still awhile above the river.

It is the landscape of Fenimore Cooper and Leatherstocking. Only canoes and bateaux should be using these miles of wide and peaceful water. Another lake has come into being; the Lac St. François; a stretch some twenty-five miles long by some half a dozen wide. Across this placidity of milk, this quiet of steel engraving, the level shores seem farther away than they really are, and beyond their dreamlike fields and distant, unsubstantial woods blue mountains rise like painted shapes of the older line and mood. Even the few islands in sight are the islands one sees in the older American prints, each one trailing off downstream with a submerged spur from whose tall grasses the red-winged blackbirds rise. All sign and show of industrial perversion has melted from sight. It is the America of Audubon, the country of the *Last of the Mohicans.*

BOOK THREE

The Mohawk Valley

The Erie Canal

The Erie Canal Locks at Lockport

INTRODUCTION TO BOOK III

THE MOHAWK RIVER is more democratic than the lordly Hudson, more comfortable than the high-angled Adirondacks, more homely and peaceful than the swift-running St. Lawrence. The Mohawk Valley is sometimes steep and rocky, sometimes wide and gentle, allowing room for action. Its adventurous history has proved this. It offers leisure for humor. It has been furnishing rural anecdotes for generations. Yet it has an almost psychic atmosphere—a mysterious magic quality which many an author has recognized.

As for that man-made river, the Erie Canal, it adds to the westward journey across the state which the Mohawk starts. For years a commercial treasure, it has also been a humorsome delight—Clinton's Ditch, The Big Giddap! The Horse Ocean. Few York State authors have failed to pay it homage, both historically as the "Way West," and humorously as a water alley of tall tales, colorful figures and burlesque adventures.

THE MOHAWK VALLEY

PANORAMIC VIEWS OF THE VALLEY

CODMAN HISLOP

Upstream

This is Te-non-an-at-che, "the river flowing through mountains," the Mohawk, along whose banks France failed to win great allies in the fight to dominate America, and England lost her key battle to hold the Thirteen Colonies. This river and its valley are worth knowing.

This is the river that cut a gate through the rock wall of the Appalachian Plateau, the only entrance into the Western Plains between Georgia and the St. Lawrence Valley. Let your imagination dwell on that one fact for a moment. As tides flow over the land, so, too, did streams of men flow north from the Atlantic seaboard up the forested basin of the Hudson to the Mohawk Valley, and then west into the Genesee country, the Great Lakes country, and the seemingly limitless America beyond.

Struggle and battle on a hundred levels took place to possess this river valley. To possess it meant to possess America. No? Look at your map. Follow the Mohawk west. From Cohoes, where it joins the Hudson, to Rome one hundred miles inland, where the New York State Barge Canal continues on to Lake Ontario and Lake Erie, you climb, step by step, up the twenty locks of the canal until you stand 420 feet above the Mohawk's level at the Hudson. At Rome the river makes an abrupt right turn to the highlands country of the Delta Reservoir, one of the huge canal control basins. Up and north it goes to a junction with the Lansing Kill. Not "Lansing Creek," mind you. The Dutch word "kill" has hung on the Mohawk country. Here in a narrow valley you find the river and the kill different only in name. The Mohawk now dwindles west and north again until it recedes at last to its source on the lonely reaches of Mohawk Hill, 1,800 feet above sea level.

But there's none of the river's poetry in altitudes and mileages. Listen rather to the music in the names of the streams that drain into the river from the western Catskills, and the lowlands of the Adirondacks. Say them out loud.

> The Maquas, the Mohaugs, the Mohawk, many and one,
> Depending on your angle and when you were born.
> Our creeks and kills belong to us and to none else;
> The Chuctanunda, Potash Creek, Burch,
> Briggs Run, Kayaderosseras, the Sandsea Kill,
> Schoharie, Otsquago, Alplaus and the Stony;
> Garoga, Canajoharie, the Sauquoit and the Flat;
> They all make one river, friend,
> The Maquas, the Mohaugs, the Mohawk, many and one,
> Many yet one, compounding a thousand streams
> That drain these hills....

New York's two greatest rivers, the Hudson and the Mohawk, join about a mile below the falls of the latter, at Cohoes. Green Island, Van Schaick Island, and Peebles Island break the Mohawk here into four arms. North of the upper arm is the town of Waterford. From here, like a great vein, runs the New York State Barge Canal, outgrowth of the empire-building Erie Canal. Here are the first locks of that tremendous inland waterway that connects the Atlantic Ocean with the Great Lakes. Opposite Cohoes and Van Schaick Island is the north end of the city of Troy, and south of Green Island is an ugly huddle of houses and tenements, on the site of the ancient Dutch community of Watervliet.

Rather than river's end, let this be, for us, river's beginning. Men have always looked upstream when they came to the Mohawk, for upstream was west. Let us head west, then, with that low-lying barge, the *Seneca,* heavy with gasoline, as it climbs the first water-stairs on its way to ports on the Great Lakes.

The once-renowned falls at Cohoes, which the canal by-passes, are now for most of the year a poor trickle of water, for the river here is drained into power flumes for the benefit of the factories that crowd around the last few miles of the Mohawk's course. The river winds northwest from the falls between shadowing low palisades until it enters a gentle country, farmers' country, with cedar groves along the banks and fields flowing south and north in soft curves. Now the *Seneca* passes the south shore town of Niskayuna and the north shore towns of Half Moon and Crescent. Soon it twists into a deep gorge east of Rexford, or Aqueduct, as the village is sometimes known, for here the old Erie Canal was carried from the south to the north shore of the Mohawk on a great stone bridge that gave Rexford its nickname. From the high palisades here, just east of the river's great bend at Schenectady, you can see a reach of water as lovely as any in America. West is the Dutchman's "Groote Vlachte," the Great Flat, and on beyond is the high, bold line of the Helderbergs and the Princetown Hills, walling in what Schenectady's first settler, Arendt Van Curler, called "the most beautiful land."

It takes seven canal locks to raise the *Seneca* upstream beyond the Mohawk rapids, and on into the Rexford gorge. There's quiet river sailing for quite a way, now.

That wide, water-filled ditch bordering the north bank of the Mohawk at the "Aqueduct" is all that is left here of the old Erie Canal. The wonderful, unmortared stonework of the Scotch stonecutters is still there, but the bawling "canawlers," shouting at their mules, untangling towlines, drinking, and yarn-swapping in the town's barnlike hotels, they are all gone.

Our barge soon passes Schenectady, "the place-beyond-the-pine-plains," today quieting down from the rush of war. Here are the sprawling plants of the General Electric Company and the American Locomotive Works, and, far older than either of them, the gray, ordered buildings of Union College. Schenectady is still full of Dutch names and there are Dutch houses here, rare now in America, crowded together in the lower part of the city, on streets that were once laced tight by a high, wooden stockade. Here one segment of the frontier of America ended, really, until the Revolution cleared the way for large-scale settlement of the Indian country.

South of Schenectady the river swings in a great bend again west, through meadowlands that have been farmed since they were made available to settlers by Holland's Dutch West India Company, and the Mohawk Indians, into whose old hunting grounds our barge now moves against the stream and the prevailing west winds.

The *Seneca* passes Scotia, whose name implies that its first settler could not forget his native Scotland; it passes the vast navy storage depot, as the hills north and south begin to crowd the fields of the Groote Vlachte. Eight miles beyond Schenectady, on the south shore of the river, is Rotterdam Junction, a railroad center, elbowed close to the riverbank by the Pattersonville Hills.

By the time our barge has reached Amsterdam it has climbed ten of its lock-stairs on its way to the Great Lakes; it is now about thirty-six river miles from the Hudson and 254 feet above it. Slowly this town, famous for its rug factories, is trying to take some of the beauty that goes into its looms and weave it into its pattern of crowded, factory-colored streets.

Just beyond Lock No. 12 the *Seneca* pushes through waters that flow out of the mouth of the Schoharie Creek. You're in Mohawk country now. Down the wind, out of the night, above the pulse of the *Seneca*'s diesels, the ear in tune can hear the far sounds of the frontier, of Johnson's "Blue Eyed Indians" on their ugly business of murder in the cabin clearings, shouts of the rivermen, poling their bateaux west, the sounds of musket drill in the shadow of Fort Hunter, and, faintly, the bell of Queen Anne's chapel. Schoharie Creek drains historic country.

Strong engines pushing gasoline west in a slow, easy trip stop only long enough to let the waters from upstream gather in the locks. Gently, up the gray stone walls of the lock our barge rises and then moves west again. Stair by stair, it climbs these colossal steps until it comes to the highest of them all, on the threshold of the gateway the river has opened through the plateau to the Great Lakes beyond.

First, though, as it rises to the higher levels, it passes Canajoharie, "the pot that washes itself." Here is a clean-scrubbed village on the river's south shore, where the Beech-nut Company adds to the foodstocks of the nation. Palatine Bridge, on the north shore, is a part of the German Flats country into which the eighteenth-century Palatines moved, and where they put down roots the frontier raids of the Indian wars and the Revolution were never to unearth. Fort Plain and St. Johnsville slip by as the *Seneca* heads for Lock No. 17, at Little Falls, the giant step up which the waters of the Mohawk lift our barge more than forty feet. Here, in strange contrast to the town's name, once roared the vast falls of the prehistoric Mohawk, grinding out a channel whose high palisades now close in on both shores of the river.

River, highways, and railroads bottleneck here. Here, somehow, the eastern slope of the nation seems to have tapered gently up to a thin pass beyond which lie the ever-widening plains. Look at your map again. Now it should be clear to you how much the Mohawk has meant to America. The colonial power that controlled this river controlled America. The names of some of its towns still begin with "Fort." Buried under the streets of other towns, west to the Great Lakes are the kitchen-middens of ghost forts. Here once was a line of armed camps whose function was to act as a dike to hold back the French tide, poised for more than a hundred years to sweep through the Mohawk Valley, down the Hudson to New York, drowning Englishmen wherever it found them.

West of Little Falls at Rome was Fort Stanwix, later Fort Schuyler. If, during the American Revolution, the English force under Barry St. Leger had been able to push east down the valley, burning and pillaging, as they had planned, and then to have joined forces with Burgoyne, it is possible that all of our heroes of those days would have been hanged, and remembered only as the leaders of a rabble in arms.

Slowly, low in the water, the *Seneca* moves to the heavy rhythm of its engines, past Little Falls, through the gateway to the west.

The mountains move south and north and our barge follows the canal channel through farmlands that were once vital to the larder of the Northern Revolutionary army. Herkimer, Mohawk, Ilion, Frankfurt, which we now pass on the way to Utica, revolve today about the Remington Arms and Remington-Rand factories. In them, and in many of the great plants that now bid for the valley's workers, new loyalties and alignments of men have been taking shape for many years. The right to farm Mohawk land is no longer the issue. Arguments and battles over property rights have turned into contests over the right to work and the conditions of work.

At Utica the *Seneca* has moved more than a hundred miles west from the Hudson and has climbed a little over four hundred feet. The river east to Frankfort and west to Rome is now really a canal, and the Mohawk is a captured stream in a huge man-made channel. Utica, almost at the geographical center of New York State, spreads out on a wide plain bordering the old south shore of the Mohawk. Here once met the Iroquois trails that ran north up the Black River Valley toward Canada, south into the rich Susquehanna Valley of Pennsylvania, and east and west between the Hudson and the Great Lakes. The highways out of Utica still follow these old forest paths.

Utica, if one thinks of the valley towns and cities to the east, is a new city. Its first merchant arrived as late as 1790, to capitalize on the growing throngs of settlers moving into the "western lands." Today its wide streets prove that its growth began well after the stockade period. Great fountain elms, which are the glory of the Mohawk Valley, line Utica's streets. Overhead there is often a veil of smoke to mark the city as the home of dozens of industries making everything from textiles to machine guns.

Fourteen miles west of Utica you could see, if you were standing on the south side of our barge, a tall gray stone shaft not far above the old shore line of the river. Someone among the crew might tell you it was the Oriskany Battle Monument, though, more likely, he would shrug his shoulders and go off on some important business. There, Nicholas Herkimer and his undisciplined Palatine neighbors stopped England. There, the Continentals' success at Saratoga was made possible and a free United States became something more tangible than the paper domain decreed by the Declaration of Independence.

West of this historic ground lies the great Oriskany Swamp, today a rich bottom land crowded with truck gardens; it, too, fades east as the *Seneca* glides into Rome.

Now look at your map again. Through this peaceful, elm-walled city walk and ride the ghosts of empire builders. Here the great highway of the Mohawk ends. Here was the Wood Creek "carry" and then Wood Creek, down which colonials ferried their trade goods to the "far Indians" of the Lakes country. For our barge carrying gasoline to the cities of the Great Lakes the fact is marked only by the disappearance of the river's winding, almost empty channel, which here bends north to the Adirondack highlands country.

The *Seneca,* however, pushes on west in its man-made channel, still carried on the canalized waters of the river that has brought it to Rome, 128 miles inland from the Hudson, 420 feet above the entrance to its first lock a Waterford.

It all seems so easy now. There is the nasal honk of the Twentieth Century Limited as it pounds west out of the valley on the New York Central tracks. Train after train, they pile past Rome, east and west, night and day, on one of the world's tightest schedules. West and east on the valley's arterial highways roar the cars and trucks whose life depends on the cargo of such barges as the *Seneca.* It all seems so easy. Up from the Atlantic as you like, by road or rail or by river, north with the Hudson to the Mohawk. And then west. There are no seams in this travel pattern. Through the Mohawk Valley you can go now, at whatever speeds suit your convenience; ten miles an hour through the canal's river and lake channels, six miles an hour through the canal's man-made links, up to fifty miles an hour on the river's north- and south-shore highways, seventy and more if you ride the Century.

And so through Rome, and out of the valley, into the west.

So easy? Look at your map. What did we have to begin with before "Clinton's Ditch," the old Erie Canal, began to make things easier? Before the Iron Horse began to scare his flesh and blood predecessor out of the traces; before we became Americans? We had only the river. But what the Mohawk has meant to America! It was Te-non-an-at-che, the "river flowing through mountains," the river that cut the only gate through a rock wall rearing from Georgia to the St. Lawrence. Possessing it was not easy. Developing it to please the ambitions of each new generation has not been easy....

T. WOOD CLARKE

The Valley Itself

The extraordinary rise in power of the Iroquois nation was to a great extent due to the dominating location of their home country. The story of the making of the Mohawk valley, a process extending over untold millions of years, while fascinatingly interesting to the geologist, cannot be told in its wealth of detail here. Its geography, however, must be understood.

The Mohawk River is the largest tributary of the Hudson, its deep and narrow valley stretching for a hundred miles from Schenectady to Rome. In its formation, working back through the soft Ordovician shales, between the hard Adirondack igneous rock on the north, and the Helderberg escarpment on the south, it beheaded the Susquehanna River and its tributaries, such as the Chenango and the Unadilla. The result was that, instead of rising as they originally did, in the Adirondacks, these rivers now have their headwaters only a dozen or so miles south of the Mohawk.

With the subsidence of the ice at the end of the glacial period the enormous Iro-Mohawk River swept through the valley, cutting through rock barriers, and scouring out a channel two miles wide and two hundred feet deep in the alluvial deposits of glacial Lake Amsterdam. This divided the valley into three sections.

Stretching westward from Little Falls the valley widens until at Rome it merges with the broad flat plains, the bottom of Lake Iroquois of post-glacial days, extending level and fertile all the way to Buffalo. From Little Falls to the two rugged cliffs projecting into the valley a few miles west of Fonda, known as the Noses, the banks slope more gradually and the bottom is flat and rich. East of the Noses, past Fonda and Amsterdam, the sides again become steeper and the bottom narrow. East of Schenectady the river turns north and then east and flows through a flat sandy country to empty into the Hudson at Cohoes. This lower section of the river has little geological or historical connection with the valley proper and, in descriptions of the Mohawk valley, is usually ignored.

Thus from Schenectady to Rome the Mohawk valley consists of high hills

From *The Bloody Mohawk* by T. Wood Clarke. Published by The Macmillan Company, New York, 1940. Reprinted by permission of the publisher.

to north and south, with wide fertile plateaus at their bases, and, in the level bottom, a dry river channel averaging two miles wide, with a small stream flowing through its center. West of Rome is the extensive, rich, flat land that made up the bottom of Lake Iroquois, known as the fruit country. This is bounded on the north by Lake Ontario, on the west by the Niagara River, and on the south by the Finger Lakes. Near the southern end of this plain begin the many tributaries of the west branch of the Susquehanna and of the Ohio. Into the Mohawk valley from the north come the valleys of the East and West Canada creeks and the Sacandaga River, while to the south are the Oriskany and Sauquoit valleys, the Ilion Gorge, the Otsquago, the Canajoharie, and the Schoharie creeks.

It will thus be seen that in a day when the chief means of travel was by birchbark canoe, the inhabitants of the Mohawk valley and the flat lands to its west held a strategic position of great strength. They lived in a flat, fertile plain on the low banks of rivers, or lakes, or, if they wanted sites of greater defensive power, they moved to plateaus several hundred feet above the water. If they wished to attack enemies in New England, or down the Hudson, the Mohawk offered a broad highway. If their foes dwelt in Pennsylvania, Maryland, or Delaware, a short carry to Otsego Lake or to the Chemung gave them a clear course by way of the Susquehanna to the south and east. A short trip through the Finger Lakes or up the Genesee River led to the Allegheny, the Ohio, and the Mississippi. To the north and west the blue waters of Lakes Ontario and Erie, reached through the Genesee River, the Irondequoit Creek, or the Seneca River, or Oneida Lake and the Oswego River, invited exploration and silent approach. If the St. Lawrence was to be the place of attack, it could be reached through Lake Ontario, the West Canada Creek and the Black River, or the Sacandaga River, Lake George, and Lake Champlain.

The occupants of such a region, if strong, brave, and ambitious, might well become the Roman Empire of America. And they did.

When later, however, the whites occupied the valley of the Mohawk and the raiding Indians were on the warpath, these same natural roadways, converging on the valley from all points of the compass, left the inhabitants exposed to attack from so many directions that their position was weak indeed. From north, south, east, or west the silent savage might descend upon the unsuspecting burghers, like a devastating tempest from a clear sky.

18TH CENTURY

JAMES THOMAS FLEXNER

The Iroquois Federation

Gradually Johnson cleared a high mental plateau from which he could see the wide topography of his situation. He saw the Mohawk River flowing, not only in its physical channel, but westward until a visionary extension of its waters rippled over the huge central valley of the continent, broke against mountains so distant they were known only to hearsay and dream. Eastward, the Mohawk seemed to move in a shining current through the dark Atlantic, until at last it lapped the thrones of England and France and washed them into conflict. For the river that moved through Johnson's dooryard was a key to a new empire over which the two old empires yearned. Rarely had destiny placed a man in so important a spot at so important a time.

The long Appalachian mountain range, which, as it roughly paralleled the Atlantic Ocean, marked the limits of British settlement, broke only twice to allow water communication with the North Central plain. The St. Lawrence River gave the Canadian French easy access to the Great Lakes and the whole center of the continent; Johnson's river, on a less lavish scale, did the same for the English. Sloops sailed up the Hudson from the ocean to the Mohawk; smaller boats moved past Mount Johnson to a marsh which was one of the most strategic spots in North America, for water flowed from it in two directions: some to New York harbor, some to the Great Lakes. Vessels which had been carried the short distance overland from the Mohawk were propelled by the current to Wood Creek and thence on the Onondaga River to Oswego on Lake Ontario. This was roughly the route of the Erie Canal that was to make New York the greatest city in America.

During more than a century, the French had used their waterway to explore millions of acres, to erect trading posts and Jesuit chapels. However, the Dutch and the English had ventured only occasionally on theirs. Exertion was for them unnecessary, since they had touched off in the wilderness one of those nationalistic explosions that bloody and change history.

Probably during the sixteenth century, five related Indian nations had fled into what is now northern New York from some Algonquin conqueror, and had stockaded themselves in a long, diffuse line on hills. These refugees were in no unusual situation—American prehistory was a slow churning of tribes, the vanquished receding from the victor—but the Iroquois had, after their defeat, made an amazing move. In a hunting culture, where every nation is automatically at war with every other, they had formed a federal government.

Whether the Iroquois League was established, as legend tells us, at a single constitutional convention attended by supernatural beings, or was the result of evolution, it was given permanence by being a carefully worked out expansion of the customs of the individual tribes. Thus the Iroquois territory was thought of as a long house, with each nation occupying a room around its own fire. One door opened on the Hudson: the Mohawks were the keepers of this door. Next, as the trails weaved westward, came the Oneidas, the Onondagas, the Cayugas, and, at the other door on the Genesee, the Senecas. Although the main council fire burned in the central chamber of the Onondagas, the Mohawks, who were reputed to have initiated the federation, remained the leaders of what was now called the Five Nations.

(By Johnson's time, the League was sometimes also called the Six Nations, for in 1710 the Tuscaroras, who had fled from white penetration in North Carolina, were taken in. They were, however, allowed no representatives of their own at Onondaga, being spoken for by the Oneidas, on whose territory they were quartered and whose "children" they were considered.)

The fifty sachems on whom executive, legislative, and judicial responsibility rested operated on three levels: As members of the Onondaga Council, they governed the League; they presided over their own nations in local affairs; and they were dignitaries in their personal clans, which helped cement the alliance since the clans extended beyond the boundaries of the individual nations. Every such means toward coherence was necessary, for the League, although it functioned more effectively than today's United Nations, was like it a union of states that had not abandoned their individual sovereignties. No Iroquois nation could be coerced by the others; all decisions of the Onondaga Council had to be unanimous.

When in 1609 the first Dutch ship sailed up the Hudson to the Long House's eastern door, the League had suffered no major trials; it was still passive on its defensive hilltops. But the warriors came down to exchange gifts.

It was a meeting of spring and autumn in the evolution of man, and if the result was to be tragedy for the younger culture, that was at first not evident. The two economies fitted neatly together. Unlike the Englishmen who were flocking into territories to the north and south, the Dutch were happy in their native land: They sent to New Netherland, not a flood of homesteaders, but a trickle of traders. The Dutch burghers coveted, not the Iroquois hunting grounds, but the products of Indian hunting. They imported cheaply from Holland goods that the Indians were enchanted to receive in exchange for furs which brought in Europe tremendous prices. Everyone was pleased, and, to keep the lucrative trade under strict control, the Dutch West India Company, which governed New Netherland, gave Albany a monopoly, and opposed any settlement in the Mohawk Valley that would clog that vital highroad of supply.

Before the white man came, the Iroquois were evolving toward an agricultural economy, their women supplementing the achievements of the hunters by cultivating ever larger fields of corn. Their society was a solid unit—but like that of all other Indians who were exposed to European goods, it was soon pulled into a shape that could not stand by itself. The collection of furs as a cash crop placed a new emphasis on the ancient tribal preoccupations with the chase and the warpath, but discouraged agriculture—the corn fields shrank—and handicrafts. The Indians lost most of their traditional skills in shaping wood and bark and clay, in shooting arrows: they became dependent on manufactured kettles and beads and paint and knives and—most grievous for their future power—guns and ammunition. These things they could not learn to make themselves, for their men were now more than ever convinced that all occupations were womanly except hunting animals—and man.

War soon became a necessity for the Iroquois, since in their eagerness for European manufactures they decimated the game in the Long House. To secure furs elsewhere, they enacted, between 1640 and 1685, a saga of conquest. Although they never boasted more than 2,500 warriors, they overran tribes occupying a huge territory that extended north to Hudson's Bay, south to the Carolinas, west as far as the Mississippi, and east to the white frontiers. In their pride, the Iroquois insisted that in the human race they alone were "men," and so great became their reputation for invincibility that, if a single Mohawk were discovered near a New England tribe, the cry, "A Mohawk! A Mohawk!" would echo from hill to hill, "upon which they all fled like sheep before wolves, without attempting the least resistance."

ROBERT W. CHAMBERS

Too Old to Change?

For the first time in my life, I saw a trace of physical decline in my guardian.

"At sixty," he said, as though to himself, "strong men should be in that mellow prime to which a sober life conducts."

After a moment he went on: "My life has been sober and without excess —but hard! very hard! I am an old man, a tired old man."

Looking up to meet my eyes, he smiled, watching the sympathy which twisted my face.

"All these wars! All these wars! Thirty years of war!" he murmured, caressing the belts. "War with the French, war with the Maquas, the Hurons, the Shawnees, the Ojibways! War in the Canadas, war in the Carolinas, war east and west and north and south! And—I am tired.

"I have worked with my hands," he said. "This land has drunk the sweat of my body. I have not spared myself in sickness or in health. My arms are tired; I have hewn forests away. My limbs ache; I have journeyed far through snow, through heat, from the Canadas to the Gulf—all my life I have journeyed on business for other men—for men I have never seen and shall never see—men yet to be born!"

There came a flush of earnest color into his face. He leaned forward toward me, elbow resting on the table, hand outstretched.

"Why, look you, Michael," he said, with childlike eagerness, "I found a wilderness and I leave a garden! Look at the valley! Look at this fair and pretty village! One hundred and eighty families! Three churches, a free school, a courthouse, a jail, barracks—all built by me; stores with red and

From *Cardigan* by Robert W. Chambers. Published by Harper & Brothers, New York, 1901.

blue swinging signs, bravely painted; inns with the good green bush aswing! Might it not be a Devonshire town? Ah—I forgot; you have never seen old England."

Smiling still, kind eyes dreaming, his head sank a little, and he clasped his hands in his lap.

"Lad," he said softly, "the English hay smells sweet, but not so sweet as the Mohawk Valley hay to me. This is my country. I am too old to change where in my youth I took root among these hills. To transplant me means my end."

The sunlight stole into the room through leaded diamond-panes and fell across his knees like a golden robe. The music from the robins in the orchard filled my ears; soft winds stirred the lace on Sir William's cuffs and collarette.

Presently he roused, shaking the dream from his eyes.

"Come!" he said, in a voice that held new vigor. "Life has but one meaning—to go on, ever on, lad! 'Tis a long doze awaits us at the journey's end."

..."Look, Michael. Should war come betwixt King and colonies, neither King nor colonies should forget that our frontiers are crowded with thousands of savages who, if adroitly treated, will remain neutral and inoffensive. Yet here is this madman Cresap turning the savages against the colonies by his crazy pranks on the Ohio!"

"But," said I, "in his blindness and folly, Colonel Cresap is throwing into our arms these very savages as allies!"

Sir William stopped short and stared at me with cold, steady eyes.

"Michael," said he, presently, "when this war comes—as surely it will come—choose which cause you will embrace, and then stand by it to the end. As for me, I cannot believe that God would let me live to see such a war; that He would leave me to choose between the King who has honored me and mine own people in this dear land of mine!"

He raised his head and passed one hand over his eyes.

"But should He in His wisdom demand that I choose—and if the sorrow kills me not—then, when the time comes, I shall choose."

"Which way, sir?" I said, in a sort of gasp.

But he only answered, "Wait!"

Stupefied, I watched him. It had never entered my head that there could be any course save unquestioned loyalty to the King in all things.

Feeling as though the bottom had fallen out of something, I sat there, my fascinated eyes never leaving Sir William's somber face.

What, then, were these tea-hating rebels that Sir William should defend them at breakfast and in the faces of half a dozen of His Majesty's officers?

I knew little of the troubles in Massachusetts save that they concerned taxes, and I had little sympathy for people who made such an ado about a shilling or two.

Some of these thoughts may have been easily read in my face, for Sir William said, with some abruptness:

"It is not money; it is principle that men fight for."

I was startled, although Sir William sometimes had a way of sounding out my groping thoughts with sudden spoken words which made me fear him.

"Well, well," he said, laughing and rising to stretch cramped limbs, "this is enough for one day, Michael. Let the morrow fret for itself, lad. Come, smile a bit! Nay, do not look so sober, Mickey. Who knows what will come? Who knows—who knows?"

JOHN TEBBEL AND KEITH JENNISON

Revolution in the Valley

...Early in September, a few weeks after the Wyoming Massacre, Brant and his Senecas struck in another quarter, this time in the Mohawk Valley itself. Brant led 150 braves and 300 Tories in a dawn assault on German Flats, a pretty little village where Herkimer, New York, now stands. Fortunately, the inhabitants, who expected the attack, had enough warning to remove themselves to safety, but their homes and barns were reduced to ashes and their horses, cattle, and sheep were driven back to the Indian town of Unadilla, fifty miles away.

Such a brutal onslaught invited revenge, and the settlers took it on October 8. It was the story of German Flats in reverse. The Indians, being warned, fled hurriedly, leaving corn, dogs, cattle, and furniture. Their homes —no wigwams, but stone and frame houses—were burned, except for one unaccountably spared, along with a sawmill and a grist mill.

Now the Senecas were outraged, but autumn was drawing to a close, and they were on their way to winter quarters at Fort Niagara when they encountered Captain Walter Butler, John's son, with 200 Rangers, bent on

From pp. 122-130 *The American Indian Wars* by John Tebbel and Keith Jennison.

mischief in Cherry Valley, a village about fifty miles west of Albany, near Otsego Lake. This town, whose fort had been the product of Lafayette's professional direction, was defended by the 7th Massachusetts regiment, under Colonel Ichabod Alden. Neither the Colonel nor his men knew anything of Indian warfare, which is the only way one can excuse Alden's carelessness in failing to put a guard on an old Indian trail, one of three accesses to the village.

Along that trail, in the early morning of November 11, came Butler and Brant, with their Tory and Indian contingent. There was a heavy fog to cover them, and under its protection they began to attack houses, dividing the work among them. In one house alone they massacred the owner, his mother, wife, brother, sister, three sons, a daughter, and sixteen soldiers billeted there. Before the morning's bloodshed was done, thirty innocent villagers were murdered and every house in the village burned. The fort, thanks to Lafayette's skill and care in building it, was too strong to be taken.

That was virtually the end of the year's depredations; but as soon as the weather grew warm again in the spring of 1779, Brant was on the warpath once more, burning, pillaging, and scalping. It had been said that Brant disclaimed any responsibility for the bloodshed at Cherry Valley, but no one believed him, especially when it was well known that his Senecas, in close league with the Butlers, were continuing to ravage the villages of the Mohawk Valley and of nearby Pennsylvania.

So thorough and widespread had these depredations become by late spring that the alarm of the whole border was communicated to General Washington himself, who saw that if the New York and Pennsylvania frontier were abandoned, the Hudson Valley itself would be once more endangered. Plainly, a counteroffensive against the Indians of the Six Nations would have to be mounted at once.

Washington planned the strategy himself, giving the execution of it to Major General John Sullivan, a mercurial Irishman who never lacked dash and daring. The supreme commander's orders were unequivocal. He called for "the total destruction and devastation of their settlements and the capture of as many prisoners of every age and sex as possible...." He wanted the country of the Six Nations not to be "merely *overrun* but *destroyed*."

The campaign to accomplish this was to be three-pronged. Sullivan was to lead a column up the Susquehanna to the New York border, while General James Clinton struck across the Mohawk Valley down Otsego Lake and the Susquehanna, and Colonel Daniel Brodhead was to direct an advance from Pittsburgh up the Allegheny. Altogether there were nearly 4000 men involved in the counteroffensive, the largest frontier army to be put in the field.

It was a spectacularly successful campaign. Sullivan's and Clinton's forces met as they had planned, built a fort at Tioga, and late in August took the offensive. They had first to defeat a small army of Indians and Tories who took a stand near the present Elmira, New York. Brant's Senecas and Butler's Greens did their best, but at last they had to give in to superior numbers. When it was over, the white men demonstrated themselves to be as savage as the savages. A young New Jersey lieutenant wrote in his journal that they found the bodies of two dead Indians whom they "skinned from their hips down for boot legs; one pair for the Major and the other for myself."

Then Sullivan's army moved down the valley, through the country of the Senecas, Cayugas, and Onondagas, laying waste the country with great thoroughness. They cut down orchards and burned the grain. They burned the Indians' houses with abandon, the fine ones and the hovels alike. In one village every house was burned but one, which was left standing for the benefit of an old squaw and a crippled boy who had been left behind. Other soldiers, full of youthful spirits, fastened the door of this house from the outside and set the building afire, burning the helpless inmates to death.

By October 15, Sullivan considered his work completed and wrote home to John Jay, then President of Congress, that he had destroyed forty towns, 160,000 bushels of corn, and an unknown but vast quantity of vegetables. In all the country of the Six Nations, he reported, one town remained standing. The only part of his assignment he had failed to carry out was the collection of prisoners as hostages. There were a few he might have taken, but their mutilated bodies lay in the dead villages.

...But the government's success against the Indians was only to be measured in the statistics of physical destruction. For one thing, Sullivan's failure to take prisoners meant that the Indians had succeeded in preserving their numbers virtually intact, as had the Tories. This offset the undeniable fact that the Iroquois had sustained a severe blow as the result of Sullivan's campaign, which had not only considerably lowered their military reputation but had discouraged them more than any other reverse they had suffered. As they contemplated their burned villages, they must have seen in the ruins the twilight of the Confederacy.

By virtue of his campaign, Sullivan had deluded himself and the government into believing that the Indian troubles were over. Washington's comfortable estimate in October, 1779, that the red men were "disconcerted" and "humbled" only emphasized that even this great leader did not really understand the Indians, a failing he shared with his fellow commanders, British and American. By contrast, the Tory leaders understood them very well, neither underestimating nor overestimating their value as allies.

The evidence that Sullivan had failed in his success was the flaming border itself, from the Mohawk to Kentucky, which was in turmoil until the end of the Revolution. More immediately, Brant had needed only the winter to recover from the autumn's disaster before he was ready to fight again, although it had been a terrible season for the Indians. They huddled in Fort Niagara under British protection, utterly destitute; without the aid and comfort of their redcoat allies, they would have perished. Consequently, they emerged in the spring feeling closer than ever to the British, and filled with a raging desire to revenge themselves on the Americans who had devastated their lands.

The motives of the Tories in carrying on the fight were more obscure, especially in the case of the Butlers and the Johnsons, who were certainly not moved by undying loyalty to the king. It would have been as much in their ultimate interest to side with the Americans if all they wanted was to retain their rich lands in the valley. The conclusion is inescapable that they were much more adventurers than they were British patriots.

In Brant, however, they had an exceptional leader who not only was fighting for the cause of the Indians but loved the king as well. He had been raised as a British subject, in a manner unknown to Iroquois chiefs—or to any Indian chief, for that matter. A good deal of this he owed to Sir William Johnson, who had been a most loyal subject of His Majesty in spite of his Irish origin. Johnson had recognized early the superiority of the young Mohawk and seen to it that he was educated in English at a school in Lebanon, Connecticut. There the founder of Dartmouth College, Dr. Eleazar Wheelock, was his tutor and worked with him in the translation of religious books into Mohawk. Eventually Brant went to England, where Romney painted his portrait, James Boswell entertained him, and he was presented at court.

Nevertheless, Brant remained an Indian and went home to be a leader of his people. He could hardly help being intensely loyal to the British, however, and believed sincerely that the British interest was the Indians'. He was loyal to the Johnson family, too. Not only had he worked closely with Sir William and later served as Guy Johnson's secretary, but his beautiful sister Molly had become William's wife, at least by Indian law and probably by civil law as well, and had given him eight children.

As the real leader of the Tory-Indian border war against the Americans,

Brant was fighting hard for both the British and his people. He was capable, almost in the same breath, of English civility and the most primitive savagery, but it was the savagery by which he was remembered.

In retrospect, it is sad to see so much ability wasted. Not only had Brant been unable to resist Sullivan, but when he emerged again in April of 1780, with his heart full of vengeance, he was the leader of a cause doubly lost. His British allies were no longer a threat from Canada or from the northwest. The Confederacy was a broken instrument. Tories and Indians together could still spread terror and bloodshed, but there was no hope of any significant action. It could only be a war of hatred in the Mohawk Valley.

With John Johnson, Brant continued to sweep up and down the Valley, burning and destroying, until the fall of 1781, when an American expedition under Colonel Marinus Willett, a thoroughly experienced frontier fighter, defeated a Tory and Indian force at Johnstown and pursued the survivors relentlessly all the way to Oswego. That, for all practical purposes, ended the war along the Mohawk.

...With the decisive battle of Yorktown, peace had come to the nation in fact if not officially.

...But there was peace, nevertheless, and to all the combatants it meant something different. For the British regulars, it meant that they could go home and leave the troublesome colonies to the Americans. They left behind their posts in the northwest and Canada and the south an encircling ring of potential trouble for the victors.

For the frontiersmen, peace meant that they could go back to their burned cabins and ruined fields and begin the process of settlement all over again, resuming their inevitable westward march.

For the Indian, peace meant that he was free to go back to his devastated villages or anywhere else as long as it was not to territory the white man wanted for himself. Now he stood alone, bereft successively of his powerful French and British allies, facing the naked power of a new nation from which he had learned to expect nothing but deception, hostility, and aggression, whose ablest and wisest leaders had advocated exterminating him.

The Indian did not know it, but the era of Manifest Destiny had begun.

Epilogue

...In 1960 the courts sanctioned another in the endless succession of land grabs, taking a large portion of Iroquois land for the benefit of a power project. For a while the newspapers were full of letters to the editor, protesting the action. None was more pointed, or more poignant, then one written by a young Indian private first class in the American Army, printed in the New York *Herald Tribune* of March 14, 1960. Private Mitchell L. Bush, Jr., wrote:

"Where will it end? Regarding the loss of land by the Seneca and the Tuscarora members of the Iroquois Confederacy, we have seen once again, as we have seen so many times since the white man arrived on this continent, an Indian nation which has been forced to part with its share of Mother Earth. In these times, however, the situation is different. The Indian is now a civilized American; therefore, there has been no bloody battle as in the days of old. Instead, the Indian has followed the white man's trail to the courts—but for what? Only for the loss of money used to hire attorneys (money which could have been spent for tribal improvement) and the heart-sickening verdict of the Supreme Court.

"That the United States could be so two-faced appalls me—we send our officials on good will trips all over the world and we aid less fortunate countries financially, but we do not intend to allow the continent's own indigenous people (we, the Amerindians) to live in a manner we might choose. The United States government is of the people, by the people, and for the people; therefore, we must conclude that the majority is against us—but why?

"We, the Amerindians, are content to be Indians and preserve our ancient ways of life while living like the average American as best we can. Why must you, the people, be so determined to end this by taking our land and forcing our inclusion in the American melting pot? As an Onondaga Indian of the Iroquois Confederacy, I speak with experience. Take a look at an aerial view of my own reservation and what do we see—a maze of power line, salt line, gas line and water line rights of way, a dam covering a couple of hundred acres, a four-lane highway bisecting the northeastern quarter, and a whole section missing for some unknown reason!

"The Iroquois had contributed much to early America. Were it not for us (the Iroquois), the United States might not be a democracy, for democracy was unknown in the European countries from which you came, but democracy was in full flourish here on this continent. The Iroquois Confederacy has survived for nearly 400 years through all kinds of war and strife, why must you call for its end by scattering to the four winds the land on which we live?

"How far have we come since the first white man landed? Where, indeed, will it end?"

WALTER D. EDMONDS

Adam Helmer's Run

Adam combed his hair as he lay in the green filtered sunlight. The woods were dim with the September haze. The August heat was continuing; but it was better to be hot than to lie out in the rain.

His first sight of the Indians came so abruptly that he knew it would be impossible to warn the men beyond him. There were forty Indians, he judged, Mohawks too, coming up the trail at a dogtrot. That many meant surely that there were flankers out. He heard them now. Whatever force it might be, it was coming fast.

At last what everyone had feared had come to pass, and Adam had allowed himself to get caught like a fifteen-year-old boy on his first scout. He knew that there was only one chance of those three fools getting away; and he knew also that someone would have to get away if German Flats were to be warned in time. Adam did not hesitate. He rolled over on his knee and took the leading Indian a clean shot right under the wishbone. Then, while they milled, he charged straight down the slope and over the trail and up the opposite bank. He made it so fast that the first shots the Indians had at him he was dodging through the scrub.

The musket fire crackled like dry sticks, and the stink of black powder reached out in the still air so that he smelled it as he ran. But he paid no attention to the shooting and yelling on the trail. He dodged into some heavier timber, and wheeled down the bank again. He had judged his course exactly. He hit the trail three hundred yards ahead of his first crossing, just beyond a bend.

He ran lightly, listening to the surge of voices behind him. Up at the lodge a sudden feeble burst of three shots sounded, then more yells. The damned fools hadn't had the sense to cut and run when he gave them the diversion. He knew as sure as he knew which end of himself he ate with that the three men were dead. It left him alone to carry the warning into German Flats.

German Flats lay twenty-four miles to north and he knew he had probably the pick of Brant's Indians on his trail, men who could run eighty miles through the woods between sunrise and noon. But Adam knew that he could run himself, and he knew that he would have to run on an open trail and that once the Indians discovered that, they would know he would stick to it. They wouldn't have to be bothered with tracking.

He eased up slightly, listening behind him. The first surge of yelling had overshot the eastern ridge; now it returned. It would be only a minute before they brought his tracks down to the trail. He began to put on a little pressure to make the next bend; but just before he rounded it he heard the war whoop slide up to its unhuman pitch and a wild shot cut the air high over his head.

His wind had come back from that first foolish burst up and down the ridge. He lengthened his stride. His yellow hair, fresh-combed and beautiful, whipped up and down on his shoulders like a short flapping blanket. His mouth opened as he reached his full pace and he took the slight grade with the bursting rush of a running buck deer.

The Indians had stopped yelling. At the end of the next straight stretch Adam flung a look over his shoulder and saw the first brave running bent over, going smooth and quick and soundless. The Indian knew that Helmer had seen him, but he didn't lift his gun. He wasn't carrying a gun. He had only his tomahawk, which was a great deal more deadly if he could pull up within forty feet.

The Indian must have been gaining, Adam thought, or else he was the leader of a group, following the old Mohawk dodge of sprinting to make the fugitive travel at top speed. The others would take a steadier pace; but as soon as the leader tired another man would sprint up. By keeping pressure on the fugitive in this way they could run down any man in four or five hours plain going. Adam would not only have to keep ahead of the press, he would have to run the heart completely out of them.

He sprinted himself now; not blindly, but picking his next easing point beforehand; he knew the trail, every stone and root of it, from Edmeston to German Flats, as well as he knew Polly Bowers. His easing point would be the ford over Licking Brook. A half mile.

At any time it was worth while to see Adam run. He was the biggest man in the flats, six feet five in his moccasins. With his mass of yellow hair he seemed yet taller. He weighed close to two hundred pounds, without an ounce of fat on him.

He began to draw away from the Indian as soon as he started to sprint. Glancing back again, he saw that the Indian had straightened up a little. He got the feeling that the Indian's face was surprised. Probably the Indian fancied himself as quite a runner. Maybe he was champion of some lousy set of lodges somewhere. Adam could have laughed if he had not needed his wind, but the laughter went on in his inside, sending the blood into his hands. His head felt fine and clear. He figured he had gained thirty yards on the Indian when he hit the brook.

He jumped the ford. It was too early to risk wetting his feet and going sore. But as he cleared the water, he threw his rifle from him. It splashed into the pool below the ford and sank. Now that his hands were free, Adam began unlacing his hunting shirt. He got it off. By the time he came to the big butternut tree, he had wrapped his powder flask and bullet pouch in it, and he threw it over a small clump of witch hobble. Then he tightened his belt and stuck his hatchet into the back of his belt, where the handle would not keep smacking against his legs.

He was now naked from the waist up. The wind of his running felt good on his chest, cooling the sweat as it trickled down through the short golden mane. He was a wonderful man to see; his skin white as a woman's except for his hands and face, which were deeply tanned. He was feeling fine and going well. He felt so fine that he thought he might almost let the leading Indian pull up and maybe chance a throw at him with his tomahawk. He eased a little, enough to see the Indian. When the buck appeared behind him, Adam saw that he was a new man. He was taller, and his face was painted black and white instead of red and yellow as the other's had been. He did not come quite so fast, but Adam's trained eye saw that he had better staying power. Adam decided then and there that he would put all ideas of a quick fight out of his mind. The Indians meant real business.

For the next four miles the chase continued with only a slight variation of the pace, Adam adapting himself to the man behind. He was beginning to feel the pressure, but he was running with greater canniness. He kept his eyes glued to the trail now. He did not dare risk a blind step. His ankles wouldn't hold up as well if he lit on a rolling stone or a slippery root. He had the feeling very definitely that the race was reaching a climax, and though he ran strongly, strong enough to lick any man in the flats at a hundred yards straightaway this minute, he knew that these Indians were good.

His breathing was still excellent. He had no fear of giving out; he could run till sundown, he thought; and then it came to him that it would be a fact, if he managed to clear the Indians, that he would hit the flats just about sundown. Even while he ran, he reasoned it out that Brant must have figured on reaching the valley at dark and striking in the morning. Adam wondered what would happen when Brant knew that the word had gone ahead of him. He doubted whether Brant could get up his main body anyway much before sunset. But it didn't matter much. The only thing in the world Adam could do was to reach the flats. If he got there first some people could get into the forts.

His eyes kept checking on his landmarks and he realized that Andrustown was only a mile, or a little more, ahead. He must have outdistanced most of even the first pursuit. He expected there would not be more than half a dozen who could have held on as long as this, and if that were so they would have to be sending up another man pretty soon. And they would all begin bearing down at the same time.

Adam figured that if he could get through Andrustown clearing he might better take to the woods, for he would have gained as much time as anyone could on the main body.

As he chanced a backward glance, he saw that the Indians were going to try to run him down now. The new man was there and it was evident that he was their best man. He was not tall. He was thickset and had thick short legs. He was entirely naked except for ankle moccasins and breech clout and he was oiled and painted and rather light-colored. He looked like a Mohawk. He wore three feathers. It seemed impossible that he could have kept up with the rest, just to see him at first, for he had a belly that showed out in front. But his belly did not bounce at all. After a minute Adam thought it must be an enlarged place where he kept his wind.

The Indian's legs moved with incredible rapidity. He had already taken his tomahawk from his belt as if he were confident of being able to haul up on the white man. That gesture gave Adam the incentive he needed. He was enraged, and he took his rage out in his running. When the Indian entered the clearing, Adam was already down past the black ruins of the houses and going away with every stride. It was the greatest running the Indian had ever looked at. He knew he was licked, and he started slowing up very gradually. By the time Adam hit the woods, the Indian had stopped and sat down by the roadside.

When Adam looked back from the woods the Indian wasn't even looking at him. He was all alone in the clearing and he was futilely banging the ground between his legs with his tomahawk. Adam knew he had made it. He did not stop, nor even let down quickly on his pace. All he had to race now was time. He would have laughed if he could have got the breath for it. Time? Time, hell!

They saw the runner coming down the long hill, his body glistening with sweat and reflecting red from the low-lying ball of the sun. He was coming hard. The sentry in the spy loft of Fort Herkimer saw men come out of houses as the runner passed. Then the men ran back into the houses. Before the runner was out half-way over the flat land, the family of the first house he had passed had their horse hitched to the family cart in front of the door and were piling their belongings and children into it.

The sentry let out a yell.

"It's Helmer!"

In the yard an officer stopped on his way out.

"Helmer?"

"Yes, Adam Helmer. He's running hard. He ain't got his gun. He ain't got his shirt on." He paused, looked out again, and then bawled down once more. "He looks pretty near played out." His voice flattened. "I reckon it's Brant."

"What makes you think so?"

"The people are coming in after him."

Without another word the officer went round the corner of the blockhouse on the run for the church. It was Colonel Bellinger. The sentry heard the whang of his feet on the rungs of the belfry ladder.

Bellinger was now in the steeple. He was yanking the canvas off the swivel. The brass barrel glinted in the sunset. Bellinger stood back, waving the match.

The gun roared. One shot.

All over the valley it brought people outdoors to stare at the church steeple. Before dark they were thronging towards the forts by road and river. Those who had already reached Fort Herkimer stood in front of the church and stared at Helmer's naked chest. It was whipped with branches, the white skin welted and bloody. But Helmer was breathing easily again. He had never, he thought, felt finer in his life.

CODMAN HISLOP

Letters from the Valley

Oneida Woods
July 25, 1787

Dear Father and Mother and Brothers,

Sally and the baby arrived three weeks ago from Albany, where I left them in June with the Campbells. They came up the Mohawk

River in Eben Campbell's bateau as far as Old Fort Schuyler where they staid with the Widow Damuth until I could borrow Mr. White's cart and fetch them here. I was favored when Sally married me. She's a brave girl to leave Middletown and her father's fine house for this Indian country. We're living with Mr. Hugh White above the Old Fort on the road to the Carrying Place for the Lakes until Sunday next when he and his boys and Mr. Wetmore, who lives near by, are going to help me raise our cabin. Sally's to be with Mrs. White all the time learning what she can. I wonder at her, pounding out corn in Mrs. White's samp mortar. Yesterday she made her first bread in a bake-kettle, hung over the fired logs we're clearing from Mr. White's pasture. Mrs. White said she'll teach Sally to use our gun. She said a woman could do the teaching better than I could, and if there were bears in our tract Sally had better know how to shoot. Nobody has said very much about the Indians yet, but Mr. White goes to a lot of trouble to feed them and sleep them when they come here, which is almost every day.

I've been here in the Oneida Woods now almost two months. If it hadn't been for father's letter to Mr. White and then all he and his boys did for me I would have gone back down river and home to New Hampshire in time for harvest. I just can't tell you what this country's like. You remember the stories Captain Hardy told about it, when the Massachusetts levies went with General Clinton in the war for Independence up the Mohawk and then through the Seneca villages, almost to Fort Niagara? He said it seemed like walking forever through an empty, dark world of trees where the sun stopped in the upper branches, where the lakes were cold as Nantuckett water and as big as a Massachusetts county. He said if they ever got roads beyond the frontier at the carrying place at Fort Stanwix all of New England would be over to settle. He was right about the country, but it will be a hundred years before they can get roads to the Lakes through these forests. Mr. White's place and the other settlements on the Mohawk at old Fort Schuyler and Dean's Patent, just beyond Fort Stanwix, are about as far west as anyone in his right mind would dream of going for years. Once we get our land along the Mohawk cleared it will be fine, though, for we've got rich land, near Mr. White's place on Sauquoit Creek which is just about the best mill site I ever saw. He says he thinks the location here may in time become the biggest mill center in the Mohawk Valley, and that Old Fort Schuyler below us will be our "port," for the Mohawk River above it is too shallow most of the summer for heavy boating. Anyway, we're almost all New Englanders in this new country, and the land is pretty nearly flat. There's no piling stones in the corner of every field you clear, for which I praise the Lord. Mr. White thinks about 200 Yankees have come into the

Oneida Woods west of the Germans on the middle Mohawk since he got here four years ago. If he keeps writing letters back to Connecticut and sending his neighbors samples of his potatoes and wheat and oats he'll double the population in the next five years. He has the green thumb.

If it hadn't been for Mr. White I'd have bought some of General George Washington's land. I don't say it isn't good land, but it's away south of the river, five or ten miles back from it on the Indian path that goes toward the Oneida village. They say that the General and Governor Clinton got it amazingly cheap from Colonel Willett who was in command at Fort Stanwix toward the last of the war, but they want up to two pounds, six shillings, York currency an acre for it, and the only way you could get to one of the lots would be on a blaze trail. It will be some time before the General and Governor Clinton sell off all of their 6000 acres. Mr. White says Mrs. Herkimer, widow of the famous General Herkimer who was killed at the fight on Oriskany Creek close by us, says General Washington and the Governor tried to buy the curative springs at Saratoga, and the carrying place beyond us at Fort Stanwix. I don't think the springs would have amounted to much, but they could have done well at the carry, for the trade through there for the Lakes country and Canada will get heavy in time. The generals seem to have got most of this upper Mohawk River land. General Schuyler and three of his friends own most of the flats around Old Fort Schuyler. Colonel Willett and Governor Clinton and General Washington have land, and they say General Steuben is to have 16,000 acres for his services in the war. None of the New York soldiers can take up any of their military grants west of Fort Stanwix because the Indians claim the land, though in time the Indians will be pushed out, Mr. White says.

For a long time, I guess, we're going to have to lean on these fumigating "Vans" down the river from us. I never saw people more set in their ways. They're poor farmers, though their bottom lands along the Mohawk River are so rich they can't help but get a crop. Most of them who were driven out by the Tory raids during the war are back now on their farms, though they've got very few cattle yet, and meat just can't be bought.

They don't seem to like Yankees. I rode from here forty miles down to the grist mill at German Flats and they wouldn't even say "good afternoon." When I asked the miller's boy to hold the reins of Mr. White's horse until I could get the sack down he just looked at me and said, "Who was your servant last year?" The mill Mr. White, Mr. Wetmore and Beardsly are building is almost finished, and I'll be glad when it's done, for there will be one less reason for trying to get on with these Germans.

The whole river from Schenectady to Herkimer's and the Flats is Dutch and German. They've been on the river for better than a hundred years and they've done little more than carve out farms along the flats. They've got a cart road up both sides of the river from Schenectady, though the one on the north shore is far better until you get to Walrath's Ferry, east of Fort Dayton, where you have to ford the river and then go up the south side around Little Falls. Of course there are no bridges over the Mohawk, and until there are, most of the freight will have to be boated up and down stream. The river's too shallow and the rifts are so bad you can't ferry any more than a two-ton load at a time. Sally was ten days getting herself and the baby and the furniture from Albany to Old Fort Schuyler, and Eben Campbell said at that they made good time because the rains had given them seventeen inches of water at the rift narrows. It took six yoke of oxen to get their bateau around the carry at Little Falls. Mr. White says if they ever get a canal around Little Falls and one across the carrying place at Fort Stanwix, these Mohawk Dutch will begin to see things happen along the river that will make their eyes pop. Canals and bridges will bring in Yankee families and we'll be glad to see them here. Sally says the seven log cabins in Mr. White's neighborhood hardly make a town.

Mother would never like Mr. Van Horne's store down at German Flats. He sells more grog and rum than anything else. His prices are high, but he sells everything from peace warrants to check handkerchiefs. One Dutchman drank up four nips of rum and cider while I was waiting to get Mrs. White's order filled, and paid two shillings sixpence for it. What a waste. A whole quart of spirits costs the same, and I took one back for Mr. White, against sickness. I got him a pound of pigtail tobacco for a shilling, and turned in three certificates for wolves he killed, for which I got three pounds. I bought four ells of corduroy for twenty-four shillings, which Sally says is high, one ell of blue shalloon, three shillings sixpence, enough leather for one pair of shoes, seven shillings. Father will yell when he sees that price, but you can hardly find a hide west of Fort Hunter. You can buy Indian shoes for three shillings twopence, but they are no good in the stump fields. Mr. Van Horne told me he'd pay good prices for all the ginseng I brought in. He said he didn't hold with it himself, but the heathen Chinese thought it was a cure for the plague. He said if I didn't have cash he'd take his pay in spinning, or carpentry, or playing the fiddle for dancing. You can see why mother would never take to these Dutchmen.

Sally is worried because we have no church up here, but I tell her churches and schools have to wait on housebuilding and clearing the fields. The Methodists send a circuit rider through to Dean's Patent sometimes and our Congregationalists are talking about organizing. We have a religious society of sorts now. We'll have churches and preaching soon, and enough to show the Dutchmen God's way.

We can't wait to get in our own cabin. It will be a hovel style, and one room, but it will do until I can get crops and flax in, and money ahead for the house we want. I've got four acres cleared now and Sally says I should stop work long enough to let her sew up the tears in my tow breeches and wash the smell of log burning out of my hair. While it's daylight I'll be in the woods and when Sally doesn't hear my axe it will be time for her to come complaining.

Mr. White sends his regards to all of you with this and wants father to know he's never been sorry he left Middletown. I've written more than I meant to, but your letter said James was talking about coming out to the Oneida Woods. We will all be glad to have him come, but he should know it is hardly thrifty country for a schoolmaster. If he means to turn farmer, good. Those of us who talked liberty and then fought for it in the war live it here. The trees are the only things that hem us in, and we've got our axes.

Sally sends love,
as does your son and brother,
Eliphalet Stark

Whitestown, Herkimer County
June 15, 1797

Dear Brother Ephraim,

Yours came by the mail-stage today. I'm glad you've sold the home place, now that father and mother have gone. I'm happier still that you and Elizabeth have decided at last to leave New Hampshire and try our western country. You both must come here to Whitestown directly from Alworth, and plan to stay with us until you decide what you want to do... we have room here in the new house, and Sally will not take "No" in this matter.

Your route to Albany is best by way of Springfield, Massachusetts. From there to Schenectady you'll take either Mr. Beal's or Mr. Hudson's stage, though I recommend Mr. Beal's, and a stop overnight at his fine tavern in Schenectady, which, by the way, the driver will probably call "Snacady," and a dirtier place on God's footstool you never saw. There's a a new college there, Union College, under the celebrated Jonathan Edwards, the Younger, who organized our Congregational churches here in Whitestown. Call on the Doctor and tell him you are interested in finding a Parish among our New England people.

Mr. Beal's stage will bring you on to Canajoharie, I trust you stop on the way at Pride's for breakfast; he keeps tavern in what was one of the great Tory houses, Guy Johnson's "Park." There's no finer stop on the river. The Whitestown coach may be a day or two late leaving Canajoharie, but Shepherd runs a good house there. If you have a long delay betwen (sic) stages, hire a wagon and go on to Little Falls, that is, if you and Elizabeth can abide more sight-seeing.

I want you to walk along the towpath of the Inland Lock Company's canal there for two reasons. First, because you'll see God's handiwork as you never saw it before. What river and what giant waterfall cut through those rocks and left those vast pot-holes high above the canal and the Mohawk that flows there today? I've heard the natives say in Little Falls that Mohawk disproves the story of Creation, for no river, they swear, could have cut through those rocks in 5,000 years. You'll hear much of doubting of the Bible in this new country, Ephraim, where there's a tavern and grog to be had for every mile of road.

And I want you to see the Inland Lock and Navigation Company's canal. Twenty-five hundred feet of it were cut through solid rock. That's the canal that's doubled the value of my land and every acre of land from here to Lake Erie. You'll see the new Durham boats locked around the falls where in the old days we dragged the bateaux around them with oxen. The Durham boats, Ephraim, carry up to 20 tons of goods! You'll know what that means when you get here, and see John Post's store at Old Fort Schuyler outfitting the wagons for the Genesee country. Durham boats can go right on now into Wood Creek through the new canal at Fort Stanwix and on into the Seneca rivers. Look at the canal a long time, Ephraim. It's like a vein pouring fresh blood into this young land. Some people are predicting a canal that will connect the lakes with the Atlantic Ocean, but I doubt that.

You remember when I came here and bought land from Mr. Hugh White, who knew father in Middletown? And I thought General Washington's land was too far back from the Mohawk River for settling? Ephraim, it's God's miracle worked before our eyes and you're coming just in time to partake of it! The General's lands are better than half settled with New England families. Instead of the Oneida Woods we have Yankee towns west, south and north of us by the dozens. They button onto the Genesee Road that now runs from Old Fort Schuyler through the Military Grants and into the heart of the richest farm country in the world, I'd guess, where Mr. Phelps and Mr. Gorham bought millions of acres from Massachusetts. New England families are going west from here better than a thousand a year. Someone told me that in three days last winter 1200 sleds were dragged up State Street hill in Albany, headed for new towns in Herkimer County, and on west of us, too. The year I came here, Ephraim, and began cutting my farm out of the woods, Mr. White was honored by having all the land west of old Fort Schuyler called "Whitestown." Our twenty-one cabins then stretched from the Old Fort to Dean's Patent, on Wood's Creek. We kept our children close to the cabins because we were afraid of bears and wolves, and we never knew what the Indians would do when they got drunk. Then Governor Clinton bought up most of the Indian lands west of Fort Stanwix for the State, and now we see Oneidas and Brothertown Indians often enough, but they're little trouble, and a feeble shadow of the people who were here when the Dutch and the British first came to the Mohawk Valley. Mr. Kirkland, who has been a preacher to the Oneida Indians since before the war, tells me the Mohawk Indians were the terrible ones, but they've been gone since the first year of the war, and are going to stay in Canada on lands the British have given them for the murdering they did along the Mohawk. The Yankees have taken care of the wolves, bears and Indians, Ephraim, and we'll build the Lord's Temple yet, build it out of these great trees. We've got iron in the hills of some of our towns, enough for the Temple gates, and we'll soon be weaving our own cloth along our mill streams for the banners, and making our own plow-shares. But we need more men of God, like yourself, Ephraim.

I despair of these Dutchmen and Germans in the old towns down the river. They resent Yankees more and more. In spite of their petition against us, Judge White and the rest of our New England families were able to cut Herkimer County out of their Montgomery County about six years ago. They still take their spite out against us at Militia Musters, but we're beginning to out-vote them, and soon we'll have our companies, and officers who speak English you can understand.

There's no bustle or enterprise among them, though I must except a Dutchman like General Schuyler who heads the Inland Lock Company, and some of the Durham boat builders in Schenectady. The German Flats farmers are already beginning to find out that their part of the valley is having a harder and harder time competing with our New Englanders when it comes to working the land. If there ever is a canal from the Hudson River straight across the state to the Great Lakes, the Mohawk Valley Dutch will have to find something else to raise besides grain, for the Genesee country will become the breadbasket for New York.

I'm enclosing a copy of our "Western Centinal" which Judge White suggested I send. There's Yankee push and go for you. Whitestown had this newspaper before any of the Dutch towns thought of starting one. If there is any thought in your mind that the Oneida Woods is still the far west, disabuse it by reading the "Centinal's" advertising. The farms for sale along the new Genesee Road here have framed houses on them. Log Cabin country is now out on the Military Grants and in the Genesee Valley. We've got sawmills and grist mills, oil mills for flax seed, fulling mills, a chair factory, tailoring establishments, and stores as well stocked as any down the Mohawk. Parker's mail-stage advertisement means more to me then the rest, for I used to walk the forty miles from here to German Flats nine years ago. But we've got things here, Ephraim, which I hope men like you will come prepared to fight. Every store and tavern sells rum, and the boatmen on the river grow worse each season. And there's a dancing school at New Hartford. Some of the new women powder their hair, and the cursing at the docks and taverns is worse than it was among the troops.

Come as soon as you can, Ephraim, and add a new congregation to this western country. We've begun a New Jerusalem. Come, and help us to finish it.

Sally sends love, and know your young nephew would if he were here, but we keep him boarded out at the Hamilton-Oneida Academy in Clinton which Mr. Kirkland started some four years back. There's strong discipline there.

Your brother
Eliphalet Stark

MARQUISE DE LA TOUR DU PIN

Country Life

My butter had become very popular. I arranged it carefully in little rolls formed in a mould marked with our cipher, and placed it attractively in a very neat basket upon a fine serviette. It was for general sale. We had eight cows which were well fed, and our butter did not feel the effects of the winter. My cream was always fresh. This brought me in every day quite a little money, and the sledge-load of wood also sold for at least two dollars.

Our slave, Prime, although he did not know how to read or write, never-

From *Recollections of the Revolution and the Empire,* published by Brentano's, New York, 1920.

theless kept his accounts with such exactitude that there was never the slightest error. He often brought back some fresh meat which he had bought at Albany, and, upon his return, my husband, from his report, wrote out the sum of the receipts and expenditures.

Property like ours was generally burdened with a small rent which was paid either in grain or in money. Our farm paid to the patroon, Van Rensselaer, twenty-two pecks of corn, either in kind or in money. All of the farms in his immense estate, which was eighteen miles wide by forty-two miles long, were held under the same conditions.

One of our neighbors at Albany, Monsieur Dejardin, had brought from Europe a complete suite of furniture, and, among other things, a fine library of a thousand or fifteen hundred books. He loaned these books to us, and my husband or Monsieur de Chambeau read to me during the evening, while I worked....

A propos of the springtime, it is interesting to recount with what promptitude it arrived in these parts. The latitude of forty-three degrees then made itself felt and resumed all its empire. The northwest wind, after having prevailed throughout the winter, ceased suddenly during the first days of March. The southerly breezes commenced to blow, and the snow melted with such speed that the roads were transformed into torrents during two days. As our dwelling occupied the slope of a hill, we were soon free from our white mantle. During the winter, the snow, three or four feet deep, had protected the grass and the plants from the ice. Therefore, in less than a week, the fields were green and were covered with flowers, and an innumerable variety of plants of every kind, unknown in Europe, filled the woods.

The Indians, who had not appeared during the entire winter, began to visit the farms. One of them, at the beginning of the cold weather, had asked my permission to cut some branches of a kind of willow tree which had shoots, large as my thumb and five or six feet long. He promised me to weave some baskets during the winter season. I counted little upon this promise, as I did not believe that Indians would keep their word to this degree, although I had been so informed. I was mistaken. Within a week after the snow had melted, my Indian came back with a load of baskets. He gave me six of them which were nested in one another. The first, which was round and very large, was so well made that, when filled with water, it retained it like an earthen vessel. I wished to pay him for the baskets, but he absolutely refused and would accept only a bowl of buttermilk of which the Indians are very fond. I was very careful not to give my visitors any rum, for which they have a great liking. But I had in an old paste-board box some remnants (artificial flowers, feathers, pieces of ribbons of all colors and glass beads, which were formerly much in vogue) and I distributed these among the squaws, who were delighted with them....

Although all joy had disappeared from our household, it was none the less necessary for us to continue our work, and we encouraged each other, my husband and I, to find distraction in the obligation under which we were not to remain a moment idle. The harvest of the apples approached. It promised to be very abundant, for our orchard had the finest appearance. We could count upon the trees as many apples as there were leaves. The autumn before we had essayed what is known at Bordeaux as *une façon*. This consists in turning over with a spade a square of four or five feet around each tree, something which had never been done there before. The Americans indeed have no idea of the effect which that produces upon vegetation; but when, in the springtime, they saw our trees covered with blossoms, they looked upon us as sorcerers.

Another act brought us great reputation. Instead of buying for our cider new barrels made of very porous wood, we succeeded in finding at Albany several casks which had contained Bordeaux and also some marked *cognac* which were well known to us. Then we arranged our cellar with the same care as if it were to contain wine of the Médoc. We borrowed a cider mill to crush the apples. A horse twenty-three years old which General Schuyler had given me was hitched to it. Here is the story of this horse which I have not previously recounted:

The horse had carried him through the war, and the General wished to let him die a happy death. It seemed as though he had almost reached the end of his days, when our negro, Prime, saw him in the pasture dragging one foot after the other and reduced to skin and bones. Prime requested me to ask the General to give me the horse, which he did with pleasure. He had been a magnificent pure-blooded animal, but he no longer had any teeth. Prime had much difficulty in leading the poor beast the four miles which separated the pasture from our stable. Every day he gave him a mixture of oats and boiled corn, hay finely cut up, carrots and so on. This fodder in abundance restored to the fine animal the vigor of his youth. At the end of the month I could mount him every day, and soon at a little gallop he carried me even to Albany without making a false step. They refused to believe that he was the same horse. This display of skill greatly increased the reputation of Prime.

But to return to our apples. The cider mill was very primitive. It consisted of two pieces of channelled wood which fitted into each other, and was turned by our horse attached to a pole. The apples were fed into a hopper, and when the juice had filled a large tub, it was taken to the cellar and poured into the casks.

The whole operation was very simple and, as we had very fine weather, this harvest was a charming recreation. My son who rode the horse during the day was convinced that without him nothing could have been done.

When the work was finished, we found ourselves provided with eight or ten barrels to sell, in addition to what we had reserved for ourselves. Our reputation for honesty was so great that people had confidence that we would not put any water into our cider. This enabled us to sell it at double the ordinary price, and all was sold at once. As for that which we had reserved for ourselves, we treated it exactly as we would have done with our white wine at Le Bouilh.

The crop of corn followed that of the apples. This crop was very abundant as it is the one which succeeds best in the United States where it is indigenous. As you must not leave the ear covered with the husk more than two days, we brought together all of our neighbors to finish the harvest quickly on the spot. This is what is called a "husking bee." We began by sweeping the floor of the barn with as much care as though we were going to give a ball. Then when night arrived, we lighted several candles and the people assembled, about thirty in all, black and white, and set themselves to work. One of the party did not cease to sing or to tell stories. Towards the middle of the night we served to each one a bowl of hot milk which we had previously mixed with cider. To this mixture you add five or six pounds of brown sugar, if you are prodigal, or an equal amount of molasses, if you are not, then spices, such as cloves, cinnamon and nutmeg. Our workers drank to our very best health the contents of an immense washboiler filled with this mixture, with which they ate toast. At five o'clock in the morning, when the weather was already quite chilly, they left us in good spirits. Our negroes were often invited to these gatherings, but my negress never went. When all of our crops had been harvested and garnered, we commenced to work our land and to undertake the labors which precede the winter. Under a shed was piled up the wood which was to be sold. The sleds were repaired and repainted. I bought a large piece of coarse blue and white checked flannel to make two shirts for each of my negroes. A tailor was employed by the day at the farm to make them coats and well-lined caps. This man ate with us because he was white. He would certainly have refused if we had asked him to eat with the slaves, although they were incomparably better dressed and had better manners than he. But I was very careful not to express the least remark upon this custom. My neighbors acted in this way, and I followed their example and in our reciprocal relations I was always careful not to make any allusion to the place which I had formerly occupied on the social ladder. I was the proprietor of a farm of 250 acres. I lived in the same manner as my neighbors, neither better nor worse. This simplicity and abnegation gave me more respect and consideration than as if I had wished to play the lady.

I never lost a moment. Every day, winter and summer alike, I was up at dawn and my toilette did not take long. The negroes before going to their work assisted the negress to milk the cows, of which we had eight. During this time, I was busy with skimming the milk in the dairy. The days we made butter, two or three times a week, Minck remained to turn the handle of the churn, a task which was too difficult for a woman. All the rest of the making of the butter which was quite tiresome was my task. I had a remarkable collection of bowls, spoons, wooden spatulas, which were the work of my good friends the Indians, and my dairy was considered the cleanest and also the most elegant in the country.

This year the winter came very early. During the first days of November, the black curtain which announced the snow commenced to rise in the west. As we would have wished, there followed eight days of bitter cold, and the river in twenty-four hours was frozen to the depth of three feet before the snow began to fall. When it began to snow, it fell with such violence that you could not see a man at the distance of ten paces. Prudent people took care not to hitch up their sleighs to mark out the routes. This work was left to those who were more in haste, or to those whose business compelled them to go to the city or to the river. Then before venturing upon the river, we waited until the passageways to descend upon the ice had been marked by pine branches. Without this precaution, it would have been very dangerous to venture on the ice, and every year there were accidents caused by imprudence. The tide before Albany and as far up as the junction of the Mohawk rises several feet and the ice often does not remain upon the water.

Our winter passed like the preceding one. We frequently went to dine with the Schuylers and the Van Rensselaers, whose friendship never changed. Monsieur de Talleyrand, who was again living at Philadelphia, had been able to recover in a very singular manner certain articles which belonged to me: a medallion portrait of the Queen, a casket and a watch which had been left me by my mother. He knew from me that our banker at The Hague had advised me that he had placed these articles in the hands of a young American diplomat (I have forgotten his name, fortunately for him) with the request that he should arrange to send them to me. But although

Monsieur de Talleyrand had done his best, he had never been able to put his hand on this person. Finally one evening, when calling upon a lady of his acquaintance at Philadelphia, she had spoken to him of a portrait of the Queen which Monsieur —— had procured at Paris and which he had loaned her to show to some of her friends. She wished to know from Monsieur de Talleyrand if the portrait was good. Hardly had he looked at it before he recognized that it belonged to me. He took possession of the medallion and informed the lady that it did not belong to the young diplomat. Then he went at once to find the latter and, without any preamble, demanded from him the casket and the watch which the banker at The Hague had confided to him with the portrait. The young man was much embarrassed and ended by restoring all of these articles, which Monsieur de Talleyrand sent to us at the farm.

19TH CENTURY

THOMAS MOORE

To the Falls of the Mohawk

"From rise of morn to set of sun,
I have seen the mighty Mohawk run;
And as I marked the woods of pine
Along his mirror darkly shine,
Like tall and gloomy forms that pass
Before the wizard's midnight glass;
And as I viewed the hurrying pace
With which he ran his turbid race,
Rushing, alike untired and wild,
Through shades that frowned and flowers that smiled,
Flying by every green recess
That woo'd him to its calm caress,
Yet, sometimes turning with the wind,
As if to leave one look behind!
Oh! I have thought, and thinking, sigh'd—
How like to thee, thou restless tide!
May be the lot, the life of him,
Who roams along thy water's brim!
Through what alternate shades of woe
And flowers of joy my path may go!
How many an humble, still retreat
May rise to court my weary feet,
While still pursuing, still unblest,
I wander on, nor dare to rest!
But, urgent as the doom that calls
Thy waters to its destined falls,

I see the world's bewildering force
Hurry my heart's devoted course
From lapse to lapse, till life be done,
And the last current cease to run!
Oh, may my falls be bright as thine!
May Heaven's forgiving rainbow shine
Upon the mist that circles me,
As soft as now it hangs o'er thee!"

Thomas Moore at Cohoes—1804

CHESTER HARDING

My Existography

At the age of fourteen, my father moved to the western part of New York State, into Madison County, then an unbroken wilderness. Now began my hard work and harder fare. Our first business was to build a log-house, and to clear a patch of ground, and fit it for seed. I had two brothers older than myself, the oldest of whom was a chair-maker by trade, and made common flag-bottomed chairs for the neighbors. By this means we could get an occasional piece of pork, some flour and potatoes; whilst my father and his other boys wielded the axe,—that great civilizer.

We finished the house, and in the spring we had a few acres felled and ready for burning. We planted corn and potatoes amongst the blackened stumps; fortunately, the crop needed no labor beyond that of planting. Before the season was far spent, we were all down with chills and fever. We managed somehow to live through that year, which was the hardest we had ever seen. I grew strong, and was distinguished for my skill in using the axe. I could lift a larger log than any one else, and, in short, at eighteen was considered a prodigy of strength. Our means for intellectual development were very scant. Our parents would sometimes read the Bible to us, the only book we had in the house; and occasionally we were blessed with a visit from some itinerant preacher, when the whole forest settlement would meet in some large building, either the school-house or a barn, and listen to his divine teachings. At nineteen I changed my mode of life. I began to think

From *My Existography* by Chester Harding. Published by Houghton, Mifflin and Company, Boston, 1866.

there might be an easier way of getting a living than by cutting down and clearing up the heavily timbered forest, and worked one winter with my brother at turning stuff for chairs.

About this time war was declared between the United States and Great Britain. A military spirit was aroused throughout the whole of western New York, and I imbibed as much of it as any one. I had become a distinguished drummer, and had drummed for pay, until I was obliged to do military duty. My brother, next younger than myself, was one of the first to enlist in the service for one year. The troops were soon called to active service at Oswego. After six months he was anxious to return home. I offered myself, and was accepted as a substitute. As he was a drummer, I could easily fill his place.

Nothing of importance broke in upon the monotony of camp-life until mid-winter, when we were ordered to prepare three days' provisions, and to march next morning for Sacket's Harbor. The snow was very deep, and the weather cold; yet the days of our march were holidays, when compared to camp-life. We committed many depredations on our way, such as stealing chickens, or, on rare occasions, a pig. I was on the rear section of the column one day, and with another soldier had fallen so far behind that we had lost sight of the troops. Being uncertain which of two roads to take, we applied at a house which was near, for directions. "Oh!" said the woman, "you have only to follow the feathers."

Sacket's Harbor was threatened with an attack by the British. They had a considerable force in Canada, nearly opposite; and the lake at that point was completely frozen over. We were constantly drilled, and kept in readiness for an attack. We had several alarms, and were often drummed out at midnight to face the foe; but he was only found in the imagination of the frightened sentinel.

Sickness now began to thin our ranks. Every hour in the day some poor fellow would be followed to Briarfield; and the tune, "Away goes the merry-man home to his grave," played on returning from the burial, was too often heard to leave the listeners indifferent to its notes. My turn came at last, and I was taken down with the prevailing disease, dysentery; but my lieutenant took me to his own quarters, instead of sending me to the hospital. He was my neighbor, and in this instance proved himself to be one in the Scripture sense. Had I gone to the hospital I should probably have shared the fate of nearly all who went there, and have been carried to Briarfield. As soon as I recovered sufficient strength to get home, I was discharged, as my time of service was nearly up.

I suffered intensely on my way home. I was thinly clad, without overcoat or gloves. I started from camp with a lad who was taking back a horse that an officer had ridden to Sacket's Harbor: he was warmly clothed and of a very robust make. We traveled on, until I began to feel a good deal fatigued. We at last came to a house where we had been told we could find accommodation. We arrived there just at dusk, and, to our dismay, were told by the master of the house, that he could not keep us, and that he had nothing on hand for either man or beast to eat. I was six miles to the next house and the road lay on the beach of the lake, exposed to the piercing winds which blew over it. We started off, I on foot as before, while the boy was mounted. I had to run to keep warm. At length we came in sight of a light; but what was our dismay to find an open river between us and it! I shouted to the utmost capacity of my lungs, but could get no response. What was to be done? Nothing, but to return to the shelter we had left an hour and a half before. I started back at the same speed I came; but, before we had gone half the distance, my strength gave out, leaving me no other alternative but to mount the horse with the boy. I soon found myself getting very cold, and a strong desire to go to sleep came over me. I looked at the thick clumps of evergreen that stood by our path, and thought seriously of lying down under one of them to wait until daylight. The boy was crying, and begged me to keep on, saying, "If you lie down there, you will freeze to death," which would indeed have been inevitable. I yielded to his entreaties, and we finally reached the house we had left three hours before. The boy was not much frozen, but I was badly bitten. My face, hands, and thighs were stiff. After a good deal of rapping and hallooing, the door was opened. The man of the house had been used to such scenes, and knew well what to do. He put my feet into cold water, at the same time making applications to my face, ears, and legs. Mortal never suffered more acute pain than I did through that sleepless night. I experienced the truth of our host's statement with regard to provisions. The next day at noon, we started again on our perilous journey, having been assured that we were mistaken about the river being open. Traveling more leisurely than we had done the previous night, we reached the river again; and, owing to the intense cold, it was covered with a thin coat of ice, but not thick enough to bear a man in an upright position. I got a long pole, and, by putting myself in a swimming posture, reached the opposite shore in safety, though it was frightful to feel the ice, not much thicker than a pane of window-glass, bending under me. At the house I was told that the crossing was half a mile back. I recrossed the river; and, retracing our steps a mile, we found a blind road leading over the bluff, which soon took us in safety to a comfortable house, where we found enough to eat for ourselves and our horse. The next day I started for my home, where my sufferings were soon forgotten. I speedily recovered, and went to work with my brother. We had a contract for drum-making from the United States, which gave us employment all the following summer.

Early in the fall of this year I embarked in a new business. A mechanic had invented and patented a spinning-head, which was thought to be a great improvement upon the old plan. I accepted an offer he made me to sell the patent in the State of Connecticut. The only thing in the way of my making a fortune was the want of capital. However, "Where there's a will, there's a way." I soon contrived to get a horse and wagon, and five or six dollars in money, besides a quantity of essences, such as peppermint, tansy, wintergreen, etc. With this fit-out I launched forth into the wide world in pursuit of fortune. There is no period in the history of a young man which awakens so many of the finer feelings of his nature as that when he leaves his home, and for the first time assumes the position and responsibility of an independent man. All the joyful recollections of that home he is about to leave, no matter how humble it is, rush with overwhelming force upon his susceptible heart. I started with all the firmness and resolution I could call to my aid; yet if my mother could have looked into my eyes, she would have seen them filled with big tears. I jumped into my wagon, whipped up my horse, and was soon out of sight of what, at that moment, seemed all the world to me.

I managed, in view of my small stock of money, to get along without drawing largely upon it. I often bartered my essences for a night's entertainment, and was going on swimmingly, until I came to a small town on the banks of the Mohawk. I stopped to bait my horse; and, as I was about to start, a man with a bundle of clothing in his hand wanted to get a ride as far as the next town, for which he would give me twenty-five cents. I, of course, was glad to avail myself of his offer. We had traveled perhaps a mile, when we overtook two men by the roadside, in violent dispute about a pack of cards. One was very drunk. My new friend proposed that we should stop and inquire into the rights of the case: so I pulled up. The drunken man was contending that he had won a quarter of a dollar of the other; whereupon he proceeded to show us how it was done. He had bet that the top card was the jack of clubs, and was willing to bet again that the top card was the jack of clubs; at the same time showing, as if by accident, that it was on the bottom of the pack. My friend bet him a quarter that it was not on the top, and won. He fixed his cards again very clumsily, as he was very drunk. I bet, and won. I bet a half next time; so did my friend: we lost. We now accused him of having two jacks in the pack, and my friend examined the pack, but found only one; and that he managed to drop into the bottom of the wagon, and covered it with his foot. The cards were again shuffled. We had no scruples about betting on a certainty, as it was to get our money back, so we each bet a dollar, but lost. In some mysterious manner the card had been taken from under the foot. There was nothing to be done but to bear this loss as well as I could; and we started on, very sad. My companion had lost every cent he had in the world. He had a loaded whip, worth two or three dollars, that he urged me to buy. In pity for the poor fellow I gave him his price, when he suddenly recollected that he had left something at the tavern, and must go back. He soon overtook the two worthies we had just left, and all three joined in a hearty laugh. My eyes were instantly opened. I clenched my new whip, determined to go back and thrash the scoundrels; but as they were three to one, I finally thought better of it. I firmly believe that, if I had gone back, I should have killed one of them at least with my loaded whip. I traveled on, not much in love with myself. I bore the loss of the money better than I did the way in which it was lost. This lesson has never been forgotten. I finally reached Connecticut, the field of my future operations. I returned with more money than I started with, and had a surplus of fifty or sixty wooden clocks and several watches, which I had taken for the patent in different parts of the State.

Near the close of the war, my brother (younger than myself) and I went into the cabinet and chair manufactory in Caledonia, a small town in Livingston County, New York.

At this juncture I happened to meet with Caroline Woodruff, a lovely girl of twenty, with handsome, dark eyes, fine brunette complexion, and of an amiable disposition. I fell in love with her at first sight. I can remember the dress she wore at our first meeting as well as I do those beautiful eyes. It was a dark crimson, woolen dress, with a neat little frill about the neck. I saw but little of her, for the family soon moved to a distance, forty or fifty miles. Though she was absent, however, her image was implanted too deeply in my heart to be forgotten. It haunted me day and night. At length I took the resolution to go to see her; which was at once carried out. I set out on foot, found her, and proposed, and was bid to wait a while for my answer. I went again, in the same way, and this time had the happiness to be accepted; and three weeks after, she became my wife, and accompanied me to my home. We had hardly reached it before I was sued for a small debt, which I could not meet: in short, business was not very flourishing, and we were much embarrassed.

To relieve myself I went into an entirely new business,—that of tavern-keeping. Here I paid off some old debts by making new ones. Matters, however, did not improve: on the contrary, creditors grew more clamorous and threatening. Nothing could strike me with more horror than the thought of being shut up in Batavia jail. At that time the barbarous practice of imprisonment for debt was in full force. My mind was made up. On Saturday night I took leave of my wife and child, and left for the headwaters of the Alleghany River. As soon as the river opened I took passage on a raft, and worked my way down to Pittsburgh.

CHARLES DUDLEY WARNER

A New "Vision of Sin"

[*Charles Dudley Warner is now remembered chiefly for his collaboration with Mark Twain on the post-Civil War satire called* The Gilded Age. *Primarily an essayist, Warner wrote many volumes of pleasant contemplations on life and nature. He was a graduate of Hamilton College and his* Backlog Studies, *published in 1872, contains a whimsy purporting to be a reminiscence of his college days. Since his collaboration with Twain occurred in the following year, scholars have suspected that his description of attending his own funeral might well have given Twain the idea for the famous scene in which Huckleberry Finn is present at his own obsequies.* Carl Carmer]

In the winter of 1850 I was a member of one of the leading colleges of this country.... I was an incessant and indiscriminate reader of books. For the solid sciences I had no particular fancy, but with mental modes and habits, and especially with the eccentric and fantastic in the intellectual and spiritual operations, I was tolerably familiar. All the literature of the supernatural was as real to me as the laboratory of the chemist, where I saw the continual struggle of material substances to evolve themselves into more volatile, less palpable and coarse forms.... I walked, as it seemed, from the solid earth onward, upon an impalpable plain, where I heard the same voices, I think, that Joan of Arc heard call to her in the garden at Domremy. She was inspired, however, while I only lacked exercise.... I cannot deny that I had seen something of the world, and had contracted about the average bad habits of young men who have the sole care of themselves, and rather

From *Backlog Studies* by Charles Dudley Warner. Published by James R. Osgood & Co., Boston, 1872.

bungle the matter. It is necessary to this relation to admit that I had seen a trifle more of what is called life than a young man ought to see, but at this period I was not only sick of my experience, but my habits were as correct as those of any Pharisee in our college, and we had some very favorable specimens of that ancient sect....

In the winter ... I made an effort to give up the use of tobacco,—a habit in which I was confirmed, and of which I have nothing more to say than this: that I should attribute to it almost all the sin and misery in the world, did I not remember that the old Romans attained a very considerable state of corruption without the assistance of the Virginia plant.

On the night of the third day of my abstinence, rendered more nervous and excitable than usual by the privation, I retired late, and later still I fell into an uneasy sleep, and thus into a dream, vivid, illuminated, more real than any event of my life. I was at home, and fell sick. The illness developed into a fever, and then a delirium set in; not an intellectual blank, but a misty and most delicious wandering in places of incomparable beauty. I learned subsequently that our regular physician was not certain to finish me, when a consultation was called, which did the business. I have the satisfaction of knowing that they were of the proper school. I lay sick for three days.

On the morning of the fourth, at sunrise, I died.

The sensation was not unpleasant. It was not a sudden shock. I passed out of my body as one would walk from the door of his house. There the body lay,—a blank, so far as I was concerned, and only interesting to me as I was rather entertained with watching the respect paid to it. My friends stood about the bedside, regarding *me* (as they seemed to suppose), while I, in a different part of the room, could hardly repress a smile at their mistake, solemnized as they were, and I too, for that matter, by my recent demise. A sensation (the word you see is material and inappropriate) of etherealization and imponderability pervaded me, and I was not sorry to get rid of such a dull, slow mass as I now perceived myself to be, lying there on the bed. When I speak of my death, let me be understood to say that there was no change, except that I passed out of my body and floated to the top of a bookcase in the corner of the room, from which I looked down. For a moment I was interested to see my person from the outside, but thereafter I was quite indifferent to the body. I was now simply soul. I seemed to be a globe, impalpable, transparent, about six inches in diameter. I saw and heard everything as before. Of course, matter was no obstacle to me, and I went easily and quickly wherever I willed to go. There was none of that tedious process of communicating my wishes to the nerves, and from them to the muscles. I simply resolved to be at a particular place and I was there. It was better than the telegraph.

It seemed to have been intimated to me at my death (birth I half incline to call it) that I could remain on this earth for four weeks after my disease, during which time I could amuse myself as I chose.

I chose, in the first place, to see myself decently buried, to stay by myself to the last, and attend my own funeral for once. As most of those referred to in this true narrative are still living, I am forbidden to indulge in personalities, nor shall I dare to say exactly how my death affected my friends, even the home circle. Whatever others did, I sat up with myself and kept awake. I saw the "pennies" used instead of the "quarters" which I should have preferred. I saw myself "laid out," a phrase that has come to have such a slang meaning that I smile as I write it. When the body was put into the coffin I took my place on the lid.

I cannot recall all the details, and they are commonplace besides. The funeral took place at the church. We all rode thither in carriages, and I, not fancying my place in mine, rode on the outside with the undertaker, whom I found to be a good deal more jolly than he looked to be. The coffin was placed in front of the pulpit when we arrived. I took my station on the pulpit cushion, from which elevation I had an admirable view of all the ceremonies, and could hear the sermon. How distinctly I remember the services! I think I could even at this distance write out the sermon. The tune sung was of the usual country selection,—Mount Vernon. I recall the text. I was rather flattered by the tribute paid to me, and my future was spoken of gravely and as kindly as possible,—indeed, with remarkable charity, considering that the minister was not aware of my presence. I used to beat him at chess, and I thought, even then, of the last game; for, however solemn the occasion might be to others, it was not so to me. With what interest I watched my kinsfolk and neighbors as they filed past for the last look! I saw, and I remember, who pulled a long face for the occasion and who exhibited genuine sadness. I learned with the most dreadful certainty what people really thought of me. It was a revelation never forgotten.

Several particular acquaintances of mine were talking on the steps as we passed out.

"Well, old Starr's gone up. Sudden, wasn't it? He was a first-rate fellow."

"Yes; queer about some things, but he had some mighty good streaks," said another. And so they ran on.

Streaks! So that is the reputation one gets during twenty years of life in this world. Streaks!

After the funeral I rode home with the family. It was pleasanter than the ride down, though it seemed sad to my relations. They did not mention me, however, and I may remark that, although I stayed about home for a week, I never heard my name mentioned by any of the family. Arrived at home, the teakettle was put on, and supper got ready.... They discussed the sermon and the singing, and the mistake of the sexton in digging the grave in the wrong place, and the large congregation. From the mantelpiece I watched the group. They had waffles for supper,—of which I had been exceedingly fond, but now I saw them disappear without a sigh.

For the first day or two of my sojourn at home I was here and there at all the neighbors', and heard a good deal about my life and character, some of which was not very pleasant, but very wholesome, doubtless, for me to hear. At the expiration of a week this amusement ceased to be such, for I ceased to be talked of. I realized the fact that I was dead and gone.

By an act of volition I found myself back at college. I floated into my own room, which was empty. I went to the room of my two warmest friends, whose friendship I was, and am yet, assured of. As usual, half a dozen of our set were lounging there. A game of whist was just commencing. I perched on a bust of Dante on the top of the bookshelves, where I could see two of the hands and give a good guess at a third. My particular friend Timmins was just shuffling the cards.

"Be hanged if it isn't lonesome without old Starr. Did you cut? I should like to see him lounge in now with his pipe, and with feet on the mantelpiece proceed to expound on the duplex functions of the soul."

"There—misdeal!" said his *vis-à-vis*. "Hope there's been no misdeal for old Starr."

"Spades, did you say?" the talk ran on. "I never knew Starr was sickly."...

And so the talk went on, mingled with whist-talk, reminiscent of me, not all exactly what I would have chosen to go into my biography, but on the whole kind and tender, after the fashion of the boys. At least I was in their thoughts, and I could see was a good deal regretted,—so I passed a very pleasant evening. Most of those present were of my society, and wore crape on their badges, and all wore the usual crape on the left arm. I learned that the following afternoon a eulogy would be delivered on me in the chapel.

The eulogy was delivered before members of our society and others, the next afternoon, in the chapel. I need not say that I was present. Indeed, I was perched on the desk, within reach of the speaker's hand. The apotheosis was pronounced by my most intimate friend, Timmins, and I must say he did me ample justice. He never was accustomed to "draw it very mild" (to use a vulgarism which I dislike) when he had his head, and on this occasion he entered into the matter with the zeal of a true friend, and a young man who never expected to have another occasion to sing a public "In Memoriam." It made my hair stand on end,—metaphorically, of course.... Once launched upon my college days, Timmins went on with all sails spread. I had, as it were, to hold on to the pulpit-cushion. Latin, Greek, the old literatures, I was perfect master of; all history was merely a light repast to me; mathematics I glanced at, and it disappeared; in the clouds of modern philosophy I was wrapped, but not obscured; over the field of light literature I familiarly roamed as the honey-bee over the wide fields of clover which blossom white in the Junes of this world! My life was pure, my character spotless, my name was inscribed among the names of those deathless few who were not born to die!

It was a noble eulogy, and I felt before he finished, though I had misgivings at the beginning, that I deserved it all. The effect on the audience was a little different. They said it was a "strong" oration, and I think Timmins got more credit by it than I did. After the performance they stood about the chapel, talking in a subdued tone, and seemed to be a good deal impressed by what they had heard, or perhaps by thoughts of the departed. At least they all soon went over to Austin's and called for beer. My particular friends called for it twice. Then they all lit pipes.

...So far as I could see, everything went on as if I were or had never been there. I could not even see the place where I had dropped out of the ranks. Occasionally I heard my name, but I must say that four weeks was quite long enough to stay in a world that had pretty much forgotten me. There is no great satisfaction in being dragged up to light now and then, like an old letter. The case was somewhat different with the people with whom I had boarded. They were relations of mine, and I often saw them weep, and they talked of me a good deal at twilight and Sunday nights, especially the youngest one, Carrie, who was handsomer than any one I knew, and not much older than I. I never used to imagine that she cared particularly for me, nor would she have done so if I had lived, but death brought with it a sort of sentimental regret, which, with the help of a daguerreotype, she nursed into quite a little passion....

But time hastened.... One day, while Carrie played (for me, though she knew it not) one of Mendelssohn's "songs without words," I suddenly... moved from the house, floated in the air, rose higher, higher, by an easy, delicious, exultant, yet inconceivably rapid motion. The ecstasy of that triumphant flight! Groves, trees, houses, the landscape, dimmed, faded, fled away beneath me. Upward mounting, as on angel's wings, with no effort, till the earth hung beneath me—a round black ball swinging, remote, in the universal ether. Upward mounting, till the earth, no longer bathed in the sun's rays, went out to my sight,—disappeared in the blank. Constellations, before seen from afar, I sailed among. Stars, too remote for shining on earth, I neared, and found to be round globes flying through space with a velocity only equaled by my own. New worlds continually opened on my sight; new fields of everlasting space opened and closed behind me.

For days and days—it seemed a mortal forever—I mounted up the great heavens, whose everlasting doors swung wide. How the worlds and systems, stars, constellations, neared me, blazed and flashed in splendor, and fled away! At length—was it not a thousand years?—I saw before me, yet afar off, a wall, the rocky bourn of that country whence travelers come not back, a battlement wider than I could guess, the height of which I could not see, the depth of which was infinite.

... Before me rose, a thousand feet in height, a wonderful gate of flashing diamond. Beside it sat a venerable man, with long white beard, a robe of light gray, ancient sandals, and a golden key hanging by a cord from his waist. In the serene beauty of his noble features I saw justice and mercy had met and were reconciled....

I humbly approached, and begged admission. St. Peter arose, and regarded me kindly, yet inquiringly.

"What is your name," asked he, "and from what place do you come?"

I answered, and, wishing to give a name well known, said I was from Washington, United States. He looked doubtful, as if he had never heard the name before.

"Give me," said he, "a full account of your whole life."

I felt instantaneously that there was no concealment possible; all disguise fell away, and an unknown power forced me to speak absolute and exact truth....

"Have you been accustomed," he said, after a time, rather sadly, "to break the Sabbath?"

I told him frankly that I had been rather lax in that matter, especially at college. I often went to sleep in the chapel on Sunday, when I was not reading some entertaining book. He then asked who the preacher was, and when I told him he remarked that I was not so much to blame as he had supposed.

"Have you," he went on, "ever stolen, or told any lie?"

I was able to say no, except admitting as to the first usual college "conveyances," and as to the last an occasional "blinder" to the professors. He was gracious enough to say that these could be overlooked as incident to the occasion.

"Have you ever been dissipated, living riotously and keeping late hours?"

"Yes."

This also could be forgiven me as an incident of youth.

"Did you ever," he went on, "commit the crime of using intoxicating drinks as a beverage?"

I answered that I had never been a habitual drinker, that I had never been what was called a "moderate drinker," that I had never gone to a bar and drank alone ... and for months before my demise had refrained from liquor altogether. The holy man looked grave, but, after reflection, said this might also be overlooked in a young man.

"What," continued he, in tones still more serious, "has been your conduct with regard to the other sex?"

I fell upon my knees in a tremor of fear. I pulled from my bosom a little book like the one Leporello exhibits in the opera of Don Giovanni. There, I said, was a record of my flirtation and inconstancy. I waited long for the decision, but it came in mercy.

"Rise," he cried; "young men will be young men, I suppose. We shall forgive this also to your youth and penitence."

"Your examination is satisfactory," he informed me, after a pause; "you can now enter the abodes of the happy."

Joy leaped within me. We approached the gate. The key turned in the lock. The gate swung noiselessly on its hinges a little open. Out flashed upon me unknown splendors. What I saw in that momentary gleam I shall never whisper in mortal ears....

"Stop! one moment," exclaimed St. Peter, laying his hand on my shoulder; "I have one more question to ask you."

I turned toward him.

"Young man, *did you ever use tobacco?"*

"I both smoked and chewed in my lifetime," I faltered, "but"—

"THEN TO HELL WITH YOU!" he shouted in a voice of thunder.

ARTEMUS WARD

High-Handed Outrage at Utica

In the Faul of 1856, I showed my show in Utiky, a trooly grate sitty in the State of New York.

From *Artemus Ward: His Works, Complete.* Published by G. W. Carleton & Co., New York, 1875.

The people gave me a cordyal recepshun. The press was loud in her prases.

1 day as I was givin a descripshun of my Beests and Snaiks in my usual flowry stile what was my skorn & disgust to see a big burly feller walk up to the cage containin my wax figgers of the Lord's Last Supper, and cease Judas Iscarrot by the feet and drag him out on the ground. He then commenced fur to pound him as hard as he cood.

"What under the son are you abowt?" cried I.

Sez he, "What did you bring this pussylanermus cuss here fur?" & he hit the wax figger another tremenjis blow on the hed.

Sez I, "You egrejus ass, that air's a wax figger—a representashun of the false 'Postle."

Sez he, "That's all very well fur you to say, but I tell you, old man, that Judas Iscarrot can't show hisself in Utiky with impunerty by a darn site!" with which observashun he kaved in Judassis hed. The young man belonged to 1 of the first famerlies in Utiky. I sood him, and the Joory brawt in a verdick of Arson in the 3d degree.

PIERREPONT B. NOYES

"Children's House"

I was born in 1870 in that socially radical nineteenth-century experiment called the "Oneida Community," and its protecting arms not only sheltered me but held me incommunicado from outside association and influences until I was ten years old. We Community children lived in a little world bounded on all sides by walls of isolation. We believed that outside those walls were philistine hordes who persisted in religious errors and social formulas under which they sinned and suffered. When I was a child, the word "outside" was a word of taboo.

The story of the Oneida Community begins in the 1830's when my father, John Humphrey Noyes, then a student in the Yale Theological Seminary, made what he always called his "Great Discovery."

From his profound study of the New Testament, he had discovered, or believed he had, that Jesus Christ did not sanction lives of alternate sinning and repentance, but insisted on perfection here on earth. Being a man of strong convictions, my father insisted on preaching his new doctrine at the New Haven Free Church, in spite of threats of expulsion from the Seminary. However, he was graduated and ordained a minister of the Congregational Church.

Later his heresy led to cancellation of his license to preach.

My father's answer was typical. "I took away their license to sin, and they go on sinning; they have taken away my license to preach, but I shall go on preaching." This was no idle threat. During the next fifteen years he went about the country preaching "Perfectionism" and published several small magazines devoted to proving the soundness of his theology.

Granting the premise—that human perfection is possible—the steps in my father's argument, practical application of which grew into the Oneida Community, were relentlessly logical. First and most important: the ownership of personal property bred selfishness, and selfishness could not be tolerated by seekers after the perfect life. Following naturally after this, the ownership of women in marriage, my father said, created the "Family Spirit" which, in turn, elevated selfishness to a virtue. Therefore, his little group in Vermont adopted, first, communism of property and later a modification of the marriage system.

As might have been expected this original experiment in Perfectionism was sufficiently irritating to the citizens of the Vermont village where the Noyes family had long stood high in public esteem, but when rumors regarding John Humphrey Noyes's new social theory and practices were circulated, these citizens rose in righteous wrath and drove the Perfectionists from Putney. Later my father and his faithful followers trekked to central New York. There, other believers—the Burts, the Ackleys, the Nashes, the Hatches—had gathered for a practical experiment in his "Bible Communism," and they promptly invited him to become their leader.

On the Oneida Reserve, a tract of land in central New York opened for settlement when the Oneida tribe was removed to Wisconsin, the Oneida Community was born. This was in the year 1848. Its members (at one time they numbered more than three hundred and fifty) held all property in common, worked without wages for the common support, abolished marriage and, by attacking their problems with Yankee efficiency, lifted themselves from poverty to a comfortable prosperity, to thrive for more than thirty years.

Just as the search for perfection led to common ownership of property, and as common ownership of property led to the system of "complex marriage," so, in the late 1860's, theory and opportunity led to an experiment in eugenics. That was before the word "eugenics" had been coined, and my father called his system "Stirpiculture."

This is where I come into the picture. Of the fifty-four children born in the Community between 1869 and 1880 (of which I was one) the parentage of all but six was planned in advance by a committee. We were not born according to law and were not brought up by our parents. At the age of eighteen months we became members of the Community's "Children's House," where capable men and women devoted all their time to our care. I saw my mother once or twice a week. That was all, and even those visits were dependent upon avoiding excessive exhibitions of the "Mother Spirit." I loved my mother, but I do not remember that, save for brief rebellions, I suffered over this separation from her. With a score or more of playmates, my days were too full of work and study and sport to leave much room for emotional regrets. I was a very objective boy.

Memory tells me that our guardians were wise men and women. If there was no petting, there was also no harsh discipline and little regimentation. Although education was a major Oneida Community enthusiasm, our school periods were short. Work was another enthusiasm, which probably accounts for the fact that even as little children we were expected to spend an hour every day after lunch working at allotted tasks. Then at five o'clock came Children's Meeting. There "Papa" Kelly, the head of the "Children's House," read the Bible to us, and at least in theory, prepared us to be good Perfectionists. At other times we were left largely to ourselves. We played games, organized athletic contests, and roamed widely over the Community's huge domain, always charged to keep within certain rather liberal boundaries. We were outdoor children.

The "mothers" of the Children's House saw to it that we were properly dressed, served us with simple but attractive food, tried to teach us manners, cared for us in sickness and fed us sulphur and molasses every spring to eliminate winter poisons. The "fathers" built equipment for our sports, enforced the rules they had made, taught us religion and Perfectionism at Evening Meetings, and punished erring ones. Living under them all, mothers, fathers and teachers, I had, so memory tells me, a healthy and happy childhood.

And then, in 1880, came the shock. My father had grown old. A generation of young men and women who lacked the religious enthusiasm of the early Perfectionists had arrived at maturity; internal dissension was rife, and external pressure increasing. During 1879 the Community decided to abandon their radical social system, hoping thereby to salvage Bible communism and their religion, Perfectionism.

One year's experience, however, proved that communism of property was impractical when subjected to the strains of separate family interests. On January 1, 1881, the Community businesses were transferred to a joint stock company and the shares divided among the old members. The Oneida Community was at an end and the new corporation, The Oneida Community, Ltd., began its life.

20TH CENTURY

ARTHUR TRAIN

Horse and Buggy Lawyer

The sun was setting as Angus and I, pumping hard on our safety bicycles, crested Schoolhouse Hill above Pottsville, and coasted down the long descent to the town. Westward I could look for miles over the checkered, gold-drenched valley of the Mohawk, while to the north the bend of the river shone like a newly ground scythe under the purple barrier of the Broadalbin hills. As we dismounted beside the sagging veranda of the old hotel a pleasant-faced, middle-aged woman came out and began beating an immense brass gong with a padded stick, the reverberation from which rattled across the square and galvanized into life the single somnolent guest who sat tilted in a rocker with his feet upon the balustrade.

"That's Ma Best!" said Angus. "One of the finest women in the United States.—Hello, Ma! Meet my friend Eph Tutt. He's thinking of settling in Pottsville."

"I hope he's right in the head!" she laughed. "Anyhow I'll do my best to make him comfortable." And she did—for four long and fairly happy years.

After supper Angus and I strolled down street to give the place the once over. The Phoenix House, Angus said, had enjoyed a period of great prosperity during stagecoach days. It had been the change station on the last leg of the Albany run from Utica and in the big stable were fifty-six stalls, but with the coming of the railroad its glory had departed.

The single unpaved thoroughfare, arched by elms and maples, ended in a square surrounded by a neo-classic courthouse with squat Doric pillars, a white church with a Wren spire, a red brick block, and a row of wooden stores with parti-colored rectangular false fronts. The farmers who had driven into town in runabouts, gigs, and buggies for the evening mail were swapping yarns on the edge of the octagonal horse-trough. The clop-clop of hooves, the jingle of trace-chains, the creak of ox carts, the scent of hay and timothy, the shrill of locusts, the rusty, hesitating clang of the village clock, all reminded me of home. Already I had lost my heart to the little town, so like a Currier & Ives print of the 1850's. It looked like a good place to live. Whether it would prove an equally good place to practice law was another matter.

Next day Angus, having shown me his favorite pools on Chasm Brook, pedalled off to the Adirondacks, while I settled myself comfortably in a corner room at Ma Best's overlooking the square, for which, with meals included, she charged me $7 per week. Ma ran the hotel herself without assistance save for her daughter Betty, a smart girl of fifteen, Willie Toothaker, a toothless, freckled, red-headed urchin who was something of a mechanical genius, and Joe, a Negro boy who looked after the horses, handled the luggage and, since there was no electricity in the town, cleaned the kerosene lamps. Between them they did all the work and did it very well, except during such periods as the hotel was over-crowded owing to the circus or a trial term of the Supreme Court. There were rarely more than half a dozen guests, usually "drummers," and when Ma had washed up after supper I used to sit in her front room with its framed worsted mottoes and parlor organ and talk with her until bedtime....

I rented the Greek Temple for $5 per month, books and all, and nailed up my first sign—black letters on a white ground—on the horse-chestnut tree in front—"Ephraim Tutt—Attorney and Counsellor-at-law." All I needed was clients.

The town, although I did not realize it then, was a museum piece, more New England than New England itself. It had been settled in the early 1700's by Dutch and English pioneers, augmented a century later by less hardy adventurers who dropped—or perhaps fell after an extra heavy slug of "black-strap"—off their covered wagons on the great trek along the Mohawk Valley from the eastern seaboard to the west.... It lies on the south side of the Mohawk River, beneath a range of low hills through which run many streams—the largest, Chasm Brook, emptying into a lake half a mile in diameter known as Turtle Pond. The Indian trails and especially the Indian burying ground at Turkey Hollow are of more than local interest.

At that period there was little contact with the outside world. The town was 98 per cent Republican, but its chief interest in national politics arose out of the fact that President Grover Cleveland had been sheriff of nearby Buffalo. The Albany paper arrived on the early morning train, but the Pottsville Weekly Clarion, which appeared on Saturdays, contained only local items and was given over mostly to advertisements. There were four churches, all well attended, and a small hospital, but there was no public place of amusement and no liquor was sold. While Pottsville was the county town and the center of litigation, there seemed at the moment to be little need for my services.

I was a mature and presumably well-educated young man, who for years had studied such profound and esoteric doctrines as *"cy pres"* and "equitable conversion," yet not since my childhood had I heard a case tried in court. I did not know how to frame a complaint or answer, to draw a will or a lease, or even how to fill out a summons or subpoena. I was like some young lady who, having taken cooking lessons, could prepare a *"côtelette d'Agneau à la Soubraise"* but was unable to fry an egg. How was I ever going to learn? Luckily, between my advent in the town and my first employment as an attorney I had time to familiarize myself with the simpler forms in Judge Wynkoop's books and the more elementary sections of the Code of Practice and Pleading. I also made a daily habit of hanging around the justice's court.

My shingle swayed in the breeze for several weeks without flagging any clients, and I had plenty of time to explore the possibilities of the neighboring brooks. My new fellow townsmen were friendly but showed no disposition to beat a path to the door of my office, and I began to wonder what made them so shy of me. Did I, perhaps, look too young to be a lawyer? Then one day while poking about in Judge Wynkoop's closet I stumbled upon an old stovepipe hat and ivory-headed cane which must have been his. The hat was shabby and cracked, and the silk was so ruffed and worn that in spots it was almost bare, but it fitted me exactly. "Well," thought I, "it won't cost me anything to wear it and see what happens."

That evening I paraded around the square and, strangely enough, the very next morning acquired a client. He was a house painter named Hiram Watkins who six months before had consulted Dr. J. Otis Osgood, the town's leading physician, about a wen the size of a marble which had unexpectedly appeared in the middle of his forehead, greatly to the disadvantage of his appearance. The doctor had offered to remove the wen for the inclusive price of fifteen dollars, but since Watkins did not have the money and the doctor's office needed touching up, it had been agreed that the former should give it two coats of the right shade, after which the doctor should remove the wen. The painter had made an excellent job of it, but, to his dismay, when he had finished, the wen had disappeared.

Although gratified at what nature had thus performed free of charge, Watkins, who had spent over seven dollars in paint, felt that Dr. Osgood ought at least to compensate him for his materials. The doctor for his part maintained, reasonably enough, that he had not agreed to pay cash money for having his office renovated but only to remove a wen, and this he was ready to do. He even offered to remove any other wen Watkins might have upon his anatomy now, or hereafter, or to do the same thing for one of his relatives. Watkins, who had neither wen nor relatives, felt greatly aggrieved. He had laid his complaint before Mason who, since Dr. Osgood was one of his best paying clients, had shooed him out of his office. It was at this point that, convinced there was no such thing as justice in the world, he had observed me stalking about in Judge Wynkoop's stovepipe hat and, learning that I was a lawyer, he had decided to consult me.

It will be seen that a highly delicate question was involved. The doctor had profited by an undertaking which he was ready and willing to perform but which nature had intervened to render impossible. It was true that this was not his fault, but neither was it that of Watkins. While the law would regard the doctor's mere promise to remove the wen as a sufficient consideration to support a contract, it was clearly the intent of both parties that he should actually delete it in return for having Watkins paint his office. Would the law imply an understanding that, if he were prevented from paying for the paint job in the method agreed upon, he should do so in another? Although such decisions as I could find were against me, I nevertheless felt that in all justice Dr. Osgood should do something to recompense my client for his time and materials.

The issue had been hotly debated from every angle at the grocery store and around the village horse-trough, and the Rev. Gamaliel Drum, one of the local preachers, who never lost an opportunity to advertise his own sanctity by fulminating against the backslidings of others, had even gone so far as to deliver a sermon aimed at the doctor, based on Matthew 25:24; "I know thee that thou art a hard man, reaping where thou has not sown." As a result, on the morning of the trial the Justice Court was packed with eager townsfolk.

"Squire" Dow, who was to determine the issue, was the owner of the local Hay & Feed Store. It was one of his earlier cases—he had only recently been elected a justice of the peace—and he was anxious to make a good impression. For a similar reason so was I. It was the first time I had ever appeared at the bar in Pottsville; I was careful to do so in full regalia; and

I suspect that Judge Wynkoop's stovepipe hat and ivory-handled cane impressed the feed-store proprietor quite as much as my argument on the law.

The testimony of the parties having been given I addressed a fervent plea to the conscience of the court. My client, I urged, had not only squandered many hours which he might otherwise have devoted to his wife and children, but had paid out of his own pocket for the paint used to redecorate the doctor's office and increase the latter's earning capacity. The disappearance of the wen was clearly an act of God and thus the case, as the learned justice of course well knew, became one of "unjust enrichment" for which the law would furnish redress by applying the ancient doctrine of "quantum meruit." My argument was received with audible approval by the audience and since Dr. Osgood had not regarded the claim as of sufficient importance to justify the retention of counsel, Squire Dow delivered judgment in the following terms:

"If Doc Osgood don't pay Hi Watkins for this paint job, he'll be gittin' som'p'n fer nuthin' which, as Lawyer Tutt pints out, is agin' justice and ekkity. O' course if they had both knowed the wen might go away of its own accord they'd hev' planned accordin'. But as they didn't, the law will make sich arrangements for 'em. Figurin' Hi's time at fifty cents an hour and paint at wholesale rates with five per cent discount fer cash, my judgment is fer the plaintiff in the sum of fifteen dollars and thirty cents, without costs."

The news of this triumph of justice, if not of law, swept through the town and became the principal topic of conversation. Behold, I might have sat for months smoking my stogies in my small Grecian temple, when Presto! through the fortuitous combination of a wen, a paint job, a stovepipe hat and a few ambiguous Latin phrases I became locally famous. It was as if a minor mantle of Judge Wynkoop's had descended upon me—as indeed it had. From that day I took my place alongside Judge Tompkins, the Rev. Drum, Dr. Osgood, Lawyer Mason, and the rest of the elite as "Lawyer Tutt." God moves in a mysterious way. And when, a few weeks later, the wen suddenly reappeared upon Hi Watkins' forehead and the doctor, thereupon, promptly removed it for a fee of fifteen dollars and thirty cents, everyone perceived that "Squire" Dow's decree had received the approval of the Almighty and my reputation was enhanced accordingly. Thereafter I had no dearth of clients, although few were of the fee-paying variety....

In Somerset County every defendant brought to the bar had, to some extent at least, been already pre-judged by the community as a whole, including the trial jury sitting in the case, who, no matter how forcibly instructed to the contrary by the judge, in fact expected him to prove his innocence. There is far more lynch law in country districts than in cities where the jury rarely know, or have even heard of, the defendant. What is called "law" easily becomes "lawlessness." This probably cannot be helped, for usually once the "hue and cry" is raised a fugitive's rights are ignored. The instinct of the pack is aroused and the man hunt often results in a "legal" kill. Such a case was that of "Skinny the Tramp," where only by the grace of God was I able to establish the innocence of a man already convicted in the eyes of the entire countryside.

In a shanty on the hillside overlooking Turtle Pond lived Wilbur Drake, a harmless recluse known as "The Hermit of Turkey Hollow." He was reputed to be a miser and to have a cache of gold hidden on his premises, although his only visible possession of any value was a grandfather's clock which stood opposite the door. One afternoon he was found lying dead in his shack in a pool of blood, his fingers clutching a shining five dollar gold piece.

James Hawkins, accused of his murder, was an amiable half-wit called "Skinny the Tramp," who twice a year turned up in Pottsville for a week or so, camping in a clearing not far from the Hermit with whom he was on friendly terms. He was a half mystic, half rustic philosopher, popular with the townsfolk on account of his sweetness of disposition. Credulous, he implicitly believed that at the foot of every rainbow was a pot of gold.

On the afternoon of the murder a woodsman named Charles Emerson, who had been cutting pea-sticks a hundred yards or so from the Hermit's shanty, saw Skinny hurrying towards it. Shortly thereafter his attention was attracted by a shot from the cabin, on reaching which he found the Hermit dead upon the floor, amid the shattered fragments of an earthen crock. No one was in sight, but fancying that he heard a crackling in the bushes in the direction of the village, he ran as fast as he could along the tote road in pursuit.

At precisely four o'clock by the Western Union electric clock in Colson's Grocery, Skinny with a bloody handkerchief around his hand, which he explained he had cut in the woods, came in and ordered a glass of root beer. Emerson, yelling "Murder" at the top of his lungs, appeared fifteen minutes later. The hue and cry was raised and Skinny, who had disappeared, was apprehended in flight about a mile away and lodged in the village jail. He refused to answer questions, his shoes fitted the prints discovered under the Hermit's window, and there in his pockets were twenty glittering gold pieces of the same mintage as the one in the dead man's hand.

Hezekiah Mason, who had just been appointed district attorney of Somerset County, seeing in the case an opportunity to make a reputation, arranged for Skinny's indictment for the murder, and as I was the only other lawyer in town it fell upon my shoulders to defend him. My responsibility weighed on me heavily, and since my client would not open his mouth I, perforce, had to invent a defense—a dubious one at best. This was that if the crackling heard by Emerson in the bushes had been caused by the murderer, Skinny could not possibly be guilty because he could not have increased his start of a couple of minutes to fifteen in the course of a three-mile chase. The obvious answer to this was that the noise, whatever its nature, had been made by another person, or by some animal such as a deer.

The trial took place before Judge Tompkins, and it seemed as if all the inhabitants of the Mohawk Valley had crowded into the courtroom to make a Roman holiday out of what could be little else than a legal execution. The jury were a hard-boiled bunch of local farmers and tradesmen who, I felt, could not be swayed by anything save the evidence. Emerson was the first witness, and when he had finished there was obviously no doubt in their minds of my client's guilt. I noticed, however, that Mason had omitted to ask Emerson if he knew the exact time when he entered the Hermit's shanty. This placed me in a dilemma. If I put the question myself and the witness set an hour such as three fifty-five which would have made it impossible for Skinny to reach the grocery store by four o'clock, I would have gone far towards winning my case, but if he answered, as I expected, "three thirty" or "three forty" I would have driven one more nail in Skinny's coffin, for it would give him ample time to have got there. Yet why, I asked myself, had Mason failed to ask the question unless he knew in advance that the answer would be unfavorable to his side? Accordingly, although with much misgiving, I decided to chance it.

"Do you know what time it was when you reached the Hermit's cabin?" I inquired.

"I do," replied Emerson. "It was exactly four o'clock by the Hermit's clock."

Instantly a murmur swept the courtroom. The chief witness for the prosecution had established a perfect alibi for the defendant.

"That is all," I exclaimed triumphantly.

I expected Mason to go after him hammer and tongs, but he did nothing of the sort, and it at once became apparent why he had not done so. Calling the photographer who, with Emerson, had accompanied the sheriff to the cabin several hours after the murder, Mason introduced in evidence a picture of the interior showing the hands of the clock still pointing to four o'clock. It was thus apparent that the clock had run down and had no evidentiary bearing on the hour of the murder. Mason had tricked me into asking Emerson the time in order afterwards to blast his testimony to smithereens!

Had Mason offered no more witnesses the case would have been ended. But the sheriff was an important public officer and, since he had investigated the locus in quo, measured the footprints outside and searched the body, his evidence was essential to fill out the picture. His testimony having been given at some length, the prosecutor asked him what, if anything, he had found in the Hermit's pockets, and in reply he recounted a list of miscellaneous objects, including matches, pipe, fish-hooks, pins, etc., and a hundred dollars in bills. It struck me as peculiar that a Hermit should have such a large sum upon his person, and I asked the sheriff to produce it. This he did —twenty crisp new five-dollar bills, each stamped in red ink: "W. Gookin—Pottsville's Boston Store."

Suddenly I had a flash. Was there possibly a connection between the twenty bills on the Hermit's body and the hundred dollars in gold pieces found in my client's possession? If Skinny had murdered the Hermit for his money, why had he not taken the hundred dollars in paper also?

My client, still remaining mute, I called Gookin to the stand and asked him when he had last seen the bills in question. He replied that on the morning of the murder Lawyer Mason had come into his store, borrowed a hundred dollars from him and given his note in return. I had Mason sworn and asked him if what Gookin had said was true, and he hesitatingly admitted that it was. I then inquired what he had done with the money. He replied, still more reluctantly, that he had given it to James Hawkins, the defendant. By this time most of the spectators including Judge Tompkins, were on their feet.

"Why did you give the defendant this money?" inquired His Honor.

"Because he asked me for it. I'm trustee of a five thousand dollar fund of which he's the beneficiary and I pay him the interest twice a year."

Tompkins stared at him. That Mason should be prosecuting a man for whom he was trustee seemed, to say the least, strange. Obviously something besides murder had taken place in the cabin, and we hadn't yet got to the bottom of it.

Determined now to bring out every detail I recalled Emerson to the stand.

"Mr. Emerson," I said, "you have testified that when you entered the Hermit's cabin the hands of the clock pointed to four. When you returned with the sheriff two hours later did you notice that the hands still pointed to four?"

"I did."

"Didn't you realize that the clock had run down?"

Emerson shook his head.

"It was goin' all right when I went in," he said quietly. "When I lifted the Hermit's head an' looked in his face the shanty was quiet 'cept for three things. The fust was a kind of cluckin' sound the Hermit's breath made on account of the blood in his throat. He was jest passin' out; his eyes was half open but they didn't see none; I felt real creepy all alone with him dyin'. But what skeered me most was an enormous moth, the biggest I ever see, that was bumpin' agin' the glass of the winder tryin' to git out. I thought it would stun itself sure. The other thing was the tick of the clock. I saw the minute hand slip to four o'clock, and all of a suddint the hull shanty become still. The Hermit stopped breathin', the moth flew out of the door, an'—the clock stopped."

An eerie silence had descended upon the courtroom. Each of us felt as if he had been personally present in the shanty. But was it credible that the clock had stopped at the precise moment of the Hermit's death? Should I go on and try to clinch the hour in some other way? I decided in the negative. The alibi as it stood ought to be enough to raise a reasonable doubt of Skinny's guilt. Better leave well enough alone.

"That's all," I said.

Then Mason got up and asked scornfully:

"Do you expect us to believe that while you was holdin' a dyin' man's head in your hands you noticed a clock tick?"

Emerson steadily returned his glance.

"Whether you believe it or not, it's true. Anyhow, there can't be no doubt as to the time, because just at that minute the whistle down to Sampson's mill blew four o'clock."

Only after his acquittal did Skinny tell me his version of what had occurred. He had been sitting on the hillside after a shower and had noticed the arc of a rainbow which seemed to be resting on the Hermit's shanty. Running as fast as he could he had peered in the window. Sure enough, the Hermit was sitting at a table in front of a pile of gold pieces beside an earthen crock. Skinny had gone in and at his request the Hermit had good-naturedly exchanged twenty of the gold pieces for the one hundred dollars in bills Mason had given him. That was all he knew about it. When he heard that the Hermit had been murdered he had been seized with fright and run away. He, too, remembered that the clock was going when he went in and that it had then pointed to a quarter to four.

Six months later one of the Zingara Gypsies, who had been camping on the Pottsville fair grounds on the day of the murder, confessed in the death house at Sing Sing where he was awaiting execution for another homicide, that he had committed the crime.

I am not a mystic, but I am not ashamed to admit that the undisputed facts in this case give me pause. Could there have been some relation between the stopping of the clock and the Hermit's death? Cannot an inanimate object in some mysterious way absorb or partake of the personality of its owner? People twit me about my clothes, but who dare say that my old stovepipe hat and frock coat are not as much a part of me as my heart and lungs? I know that without them I should lose my virtue and be like Samson without his hair. And the big gray moth? Was it possibly a materialization of the Hermit's soul seeking its escape from earth? Is it mere superstition that leads to the opening of the windows of a death chamber? I give it up! No doubt there are things in heaven and earth undreamed of in our philosophy. But the older I grow the more I agree with what Skinny once said to me:

"There's two worlds, Mr. Tutt. One you kin see an' smell an' touch, and one that you ordinarily can't—each right alongside t'other. Everything's alive—rocks 'n trees 'n flowers, an' water an' fire, an' bugs, an' beasts, just same as folks—an' none of 'em ever die. Everythin' has a ghost—walking right along beside it all the time—only it's in that other world. But sometimes—dependin' on circumstances—you kin catch a glimpse of what's goin' on there and see 'em and hear 'em."

Well, maybe he's right. Anyhow I believe that the clock stopped when the Hermit died.

W. W. CHRISTMAN

The Pines

I planted pines upon the hill.
The soil was stony, sour and chill.
The lean land held a meager sod
Of tickle grass and goldenrod
And the most sanguine would forbear
To fit the soil for sowing there.

From *Songs of the Western Gateway,* published by Lewis Copeland Company, New York, 1930. Reprinted by permission of Lansing Christman.

With gnarled white arms spread high and wide
The birch trees lord the woodlandside,
And on the hills no man has tilled
The scarlet oaks are domiciled
With hemlocks lofty and benign,—
My hill, I thought, would grow the pine.

'Twas land my father cleared and earned,
His coulter cleft, his mould-board turned;
Old men declared that the hill top
In a wet year would yield a crop,
And so they gibed at me: "You ass!
You're not the man your father was."

Among the goldenrod my trees
Stood barely level with one's knees;
Two years passed by—they made no haste
And hardly reached the walker's waist:
Boys spring to manhood, but snail-slow
The years it takes a pine to grow.

I shall not wait till they are grown,
Nor reap the harvest I have sown:
Only the century-mocking crow
That girds my work shall see them grow
To noble trees, but I divine
Part of the fruitage of the pine.

I leave my harvest and good will
To red poll, siskin and cross-bill;
To every singing soul good cheer:
Some walker of the snow may hear
The ringing carol of the shrike
Where the first shafts of sunrise strike.

I give bequeath, devote, devise
Shelter to every bird that flies;
Harbor to all that walk or creep;
To the red fox a bed for sleep;
Table and roof for every guest
And place for dove and thrush to nest.

Years hence, some boy driving tranquil,
Slow cattle up the pasture hill,
In a spring morning dewy and sweet
When field sparrows stay his loitering feet
Shall see my pine spires tipped with sun
And hear the thrushes carillon.

Religion

Jeremiah Saddlemire
  To Baptist ways inclined,
While Jeremiah's helpmate
  Was of John Wesley's mind.

When Mrs. S. from worship came
  The good old man would say:
"Be keerful, little children,
  Run out o' doors and play,—
Your mother's been to church ag'in,
  She's full of hell to day."

Blenheim

Past the steep wild pastures
  And the banks that grow
Goldenrod and asters,
  Youths I used to know—
Sinewy youths in denim,
  Brisk at any game,—
With the maids of Blenheim
  To the hop fields came.

When the harvest ripened
  Not a lad would ask
What should be the stipend
  For his happy task.

Blenheim from *Songs of the Helderhills,* published by Harold Vinal, New York, 1926. Reprinted by permission of Lansing Christman.

Were not love and laughter
  Reckoned in the pay,
While the dances after
  Made the midnight gay?

Still the wild creek's prattle
  All the valley fills
And the lazy cattle
  Walk the sundown hills;
But time brews a venom
  Subtle, slow and sure,
Nothing grows in Blenheim
  As it grew of yore.

Hop fields are in clover,
  Corn, and pasture grass;
Dancing days are over
  For each youth and lass.
But one that was in denim
  Wishes he were still
Picking hops in Blenheim
  By Schoharie Kill.

CLINTON SCOLLARD

A letter and poem by Edmund Gosse was sent to Clinton Scollard when Gosse received a copy of Scollard's second book. The text was later included in the Introduction to Scollard's collected poems, The Singing Heart.

My dear Scollard,

I was very glad to get your letter and your beautiful little volume of poems. I think the latter show an advance on all your previous work, and for many of them there is the additional charm of the memory of the poet's own accents, so modestly and fervently put forth one pleasant evening over the fire in my rooms at Trinity. Since you have enriched your gift to me by putting in some very pretty rhymes, I must pay you back in doggerel. You may blot it out with an elegiac tear:

To Clinton S.

Crown your genius, proudly local!
Make Clintonian boskage vocal!
You are young and I am ageing;
Fights I've lost you still are waging.

Out of youth's pomegranate summon
Wine that's god-like, blood that's human;
What you are I but remember;
You're a fire and I—an ember.

You are leafy, I a pollard:—
Push the nectar round, dear Scollard!
Push it round, but as you quaff it,
Think of me, your friend and prophet,
Edmund Gosse.

Cricket

Cricket, chirring in the autumn twilight,
Little kinsman,
I, like you, the unknown path must follow
Into darkness,—
One day into darkness.
Would I might, with your ecstatic buoyance,
Fare forth singing!

Harding Hill

In Kirkland glen the snows are deep;
By Ely Brook no wanderer goes;
White as the new-washed fleece of sheep
The Post Street ways are lost in snows;
And the great north wind trumpets shrill
Amid the woods on Harding Hill.

I tarry lonely leagues afar
From these familiar scenes of white,
But here no sun, no vesper star—
A beacon on the marge of night—
Sheds fairer beams than those that fill
With light the woods on Harding Hill.

I hear the low-winged meadow-lark
Its limpid, liquid strain prolong;
Until the closing in of dark
I catch the echo of its song;
It bears me back: I hear the trill
Of thrushes upon Harding Hill.

So though I know the clutch of cold
Is rigid where the maples stand,
I am the boy who strayed of old
Along the rising valley land,
On summer twilights cool and still
Beneath the woods on Harding Hill.

JOHN COWPER POWYS

The Enchanted Landscape

The country here has the very look of the old romances that I love best. Those who love tapestry say its hills offer the same enchanted vistas as did the mediaeval backgrounds to the castles of the Gothic North. It is more like England, this district of upper New York, than any landscape I have yet seen in the whole of America. It is like Shropshire. It even makes me think of my native Derbyshire. Thus has the wheel come full circle and I am at Shirley again! In every direction narrow lonely "dirt roads" wind through far-away valleys and over remote hill-tops, leaving behind them, as their perspectives diminish, that peculiar thrill that seems to come down to us from generations, but which is so peculiarly hard to define. It is an impression that has to do with horsemen journeying, inn-lights beckoning, journeys' ends coming to lovers, to tramps, to hunters, to camp-followers, to adventurers, to the life-weary Dead. It is an impression that has to do with all those mystic omens of the day that are driven off like hunted wild-geese by such things as "filling station," sign-boards, cement highways, ginger-pop stalls, and "residential sections."

And, moreover, this vague sense of old-world romance, which I am trying to describe, is a completely different thing from the startling natural grandeur of virgin forests, great prairies, vast deserts and towering mountains. It can only appear under particular conditions in the history of any landscape and it requires a particular kind of landscape for it to reveal itself at all. These conditions are precisely fulfilled in the hilly regions of "up-state" New York of which I am speaking. The hills are not too high, the woods are not too continuous. Grassy slopes, park-like reaches, winding rivers, pastoral valleys, old walls, old water-mills, old farmsteads, old bridges, old burying-grounds give to the contemplative imagination that poetic sense of *human continuity,* of the generations following each other in slow religious succession, which is what the mind pines for, if it is to feel the full sense of its mortal inheritance. Where, moreover, by an incredible piece of luck I was allowed to settle, the actual earth-strata is peculiarly harmonious to my exacting taste. Grey slaty boulders lie in every direction, covered with the loveliest mosses and lichens, and intersected where the pines and hemlocks and birches grow by rich black earth-mould where the most delicate of wild flowers and ferns appear in their seasons.

The rocks of this countryside too, for the region lends itself to cattle and sheep rather than to grain-cultivation, have a peculiar and special beauty of their own, in that, along with their dark slaty masses, they present at intervals large fragments of a marble-like substance, white and glistening, where actual pieces of crystal can be detached, and where sometimes the most unimaginable green lichens spot the white surface. Nowhere, no! not in England itself, does the Spring, when she comes at last, after the terrific, snow-bound zero-frozen winters, bring with her a more fragile, a more miraculous enchantment than in this region.

I have come to know by heart, like the lovely lines of some unequalled poet, the familiar order of the appearing of these delicate tokens. First come the hepaticas, shy and dainty from within their dusky calixes, their brittle-drooping stalks covered with minute downy hairs: then the blood-roots, their white water-lily flowers protected so tenderly by their large-enfolding leaves: then the orchid-leafed yellow adder-tongues: then the golden marsh-marigolds, called, for some odd reason, "cowslips" in America; then the triliums, or wake-robins, purple-brimmed, like sacramental wine, and illustrating the doctrine of the Trinity before even Easter has come round: then, first of all the flowering shrubs, the white blossoms of the shadblow. The red flowers of one particular kind of maple are the earliest sign among the bigger trees: but when they have fallen on the grass there follow the yellow-green flower-tassels—washed with an indescribable "chinese-white" as you catch them against the blue of the sky—of the other maples. After the blood-roots and the adder-tongues are over it is possible to find rare patches of "bluets" in remote upland grass-swards and with the unfolding of fern-fronds on the outskirts of the woods come the airplane-shaped, vermeil-coloured polygala, a species of wild cyclamen. But I feel as if most vividly of all the flowers that Proserpina "let fall from Dis's wagon," there will return to my mind, waving in the warm wind against the grey rocks, when I am far from here, the nodding clusters of wild red columbine....

...One of the peculiarities of this region that so appealed to me is the number of old stone walls dividing the fields, walls built without mortar and bearing on the top of them sturdy beams of wood, laid cross-wise, without the use of nails. Around these ancient walls and around these tumbledown wooden fences have grown up, by the work of Nature rather than of man, tall hedges of choke-berry, thorn, and other white-blossoming bushes; and the presence of both stone walls and hedges gives this landscape, combined with the bare grassy uplands between the wooded hills, a look somtimes, especially in the winter, that stirs up in me feelings that must revert to far-away impressions of my Salopian ancestors of the Welsh Marches.

Walking over these hills I have tried to strip myself of any pride in my lecturing and my writing. I have tried to imagine myself as an eccentric "Old Man of the Hills," called by my first name with some grotesque addition. I think it is a pity that nowadays we leave all expressive nicknames to gangsters and gunmen. It is part and parcel of the de-personalising, de-individualising of an unimaginative age. In my lonely walks in these hills I tried to think of myself as "Loony John" and to keep my life-illusion free of literary self-consciousness. There is a deep wisdom in... affectionate and wanton nicknames....

The grand secret of enjoying yourself with a free heart is to get rid of ambition, rid of even the most trifling competitions with other poor devils. But we must have our pride; and we must have a very deep pride. We must have a pride is simply being ourselves outside and beyond any conceivable competition. Lucikly for me I have inherited from my father a towering pride; but not a pride in anything in particular.

This is the subject I used to meditate upon more than upon anything else as I walked and walked over these saxifrage-covered hills. There is no "trespassing" here as there is with us in England. These isolated "up-state" farmers are of a mixed Holland-Dutch, German-Dutch and English descent.... And so while they own their farms and have substantial savings in the banks they are the extreme opposite of English farmers. I can walk in this region if I can overcome the physical obstacles, in any direction, all round the compass! And my neighbours don't get in the least annoyed when they see me forcing myself over or under their fences. For the first time in my life I could, starting from my door-step, walk on my two feet *wherever I pleased*. And this applies to these people's houses, paddocks, gardens, bartons, enclosures, chicken-yards, farm-yards, door-yards. Just imagine what it would have been like at Burpham if I had suddenly inaugurated the custom of walking into people's yards and across people's gardens!...

...It is certainly my opinion that a man could not—go where he might—find kinder, more considerate, more indulgent neighbours than I have found in this region. As I have made clear, I have travelled over this vast country from north to south and from east to west; but I have never found any Americans equal to these Americans. They have, in these four years, completely changed my ideas as to what the American character can be. They come of "good stock" as people say in this country; but it must be partly the climate, with its deadly winters and comparatively cool summers, and partly some curious psychic quality arising from the peculiar blending of races among them—the German with the Dutch, and the English with the Dutch....

But here in these hills, with an "aura" around me of Mohawk chiefs, as formidable as any Owen Glendower, these hard-working descendants of old Dutch "Patroons" and old German and English settlers take me at my face value. I don't need to hide behind any un-mortar'd wall, or any criss-cross fence, to learn what my status is among such as eat bread upon the earth. *I am a man*. In the city I confess I fall below that level, and become a "guy." But here in "up-state" New York I feel I can say, even as the Lord of Hosts said to his questioner, "I am *that* I am."

LANSING CHRISTMAN

They Too Were Meadows

If I am not here when spring comes back
Once more, let the old stone wall beyond
The pasture go unrepaired this year;
Let the boulders tumble if they will;
Let the lichened stones heave and fall
When the frost goes out. I will not hear;
I will not see. Only the woodchucks,
Leaving their burrows after a winter
Of sleep, will witness the crumbling;
Only the hands of the sun and the wind
And the rain will feel; only the ears
Of the buck and the doe loping gracefully
Through the wild fields will hear.
Let the stones lie where they have fallen;
The boulders will press themselves firmly
Into the snugness and the warmth of grass,
In the peacefulness of the old meadow
Worlds away from the acres of steel and smoke.
  They too were meadows once, with grass,
  And lichened stones, and wild deer loping.

(*Household Magazine,* 1943)

Sorting Apples

Colors of an October harvest fill these barrels,
The reds and yellows of the Northern Spy
And the Baldwin. The shed is rich
With an October fragrance. It is November now;
There is a strange contrast when I look out
Upon the brown hills. These colors were of the hills
Before the frost and the wind and the rain
Spilled them to the ground. Now these same
Bright colors are of the shed. And there is
The flavor of a tender spring, of a mild summer,
And of crisp fall mornings, blended in one
Under the reddened cheeks.

(*Christian Science Monitor,* 1938)

THE ERIE CANAL

19TH CENTURY

WILLIS GAYLORD CLARK

A Trip on the Erie Canal

The contrast between the spacious cabins of the Hudson steamers and the low narrow boats on the canal is unhappily too striking. You will find captains or superintendents who verily believe that there are no other places on earth but Schenectady and Utica. They are stupendous persons on a small scale. The idea of having some fifty or sixty individuals, by compulsion, in their power every day, gives them a sense of their own importance which nothing can annul; and the air of grandeur with which they help you to a half-boiled potato or a stinted radish would befit princes. But do not offend them. On the contrary, cause them to believe that you suppose them incomparable; their fare rich beyond description; their charges no swindle; and that you have no exalted opinion of the new railroad to be open in August and destined to carry passengers three times quicker, and you will get the best they have.

At first when you embark all seems fair; the eleemosynary negro, who vexes his clarionet to pay for his passage, seems a very Apollo to your ear; the appointments of the boat appear ample; a populous town slowly glides from your view and you feel quite comfortable and contented. 'Things above' attract your attention—some pretty point of landscape, or distant steeple, shining among the summer trees. Anon, the scenery becomes tame and you descend. A feeling comes over you as you draw your first breath in the cabin which impels to the holding of your nose. The cabin is full; you have hit your head twice against the ceiling thereof, and stumbled

From the *Knickerbocker Magazine,* 1836.

sundry times against the seats at the side. Babies, vociferous babies, are playing with their mother's noses or squalling in appalling concert. If you stir, your foot treads heavily upon the bulbous toes of some recumbent passenger; if you essay to sleep, the gabble of those around you, or the noisy gurgle of a lock, arouses you to consciousness. By and by dinner approaches. Slowly, and one by one, the dishes appear. At long intervals—say five for the whole length of the boat—you behold tumblers arranged with two forlorn radishes in each. The butter lies like gravy in the plate; the malodorous passengers of the masculine gender draw nigh to the scanty board; the captain comes near to act his oft-repeated part as President of the day. Oh, gracious! tis a scene of enormous cry and scanty wool.

I was walking on the deck after dinner ducking my head every moment at the cry of 'Bridge!' when the captain joined me and began to relate the perils that he had encountered on the 'deep waters' over which we were gliding. "Last year—it was in the fall—this canawl was visited with a gale. For twenty-five minutes this very boat rested upon a sand bank caused by the entrance of a creek. Judge of my feelings at that awful moment! I was on the eve of sinking in despair, with no hopes of ever getting off, when deliverance came! A swell from the lock, a few rods above, lifted us from our fearful situation and restored us to safety and comfort."

The grand charm and scene of a canal packet is in the evening. If on your way from Schenectady to Utica, the sun goes down into the rosy west just after you leave that beautiful gorge in the Mohawk mountains, where you see the towering pines on one side, rising precipitously near three hundred feet above you, and on the other, the gentle river calmly gliding through the vale below—forming the only tolerable scene on the route. Well, you go below and there you behold a hot and motley assemblage. A kind of stillness begins to reign around. It seems as if a protracted meeting were about to commence. Clergymen, capitalists, long-sided merchants, green-horns taking their first experience of the wonders of the deep on the canawl, all these are huddled together in wild and inexplicable confusion. By and by the captain takes his seat and the roll of berths is called. Then, what confusion! Layer upon layer of humanity is suddenly shelved for the night. Boots are released from a hundred feet, and their owners deposit them wherever they can. There was one man who pulled off the boots of another person, so thick were the limbs and feet. Another tourist—fat, oily and round—bribed the steward for two chairs placed by the side of his berth, whereon to rest his abdomen. Sleep, you can not. Feeble moschetoes, residents in the boat, whose health suffers from the noisome airs they are nightly compelled to breathe, do their work to annoy you; and then, Phoebus Apollo! how the sleepers snore! There is every variety of this music from the low wheeze of the asthmatic to the stentorian grunt of the corpulent and profound. At last, morning dawns; you ascend into pure air with hair unkempt, body and spirit unrefreshed, and show yourself to the people of some populous town into which you are entering, as you wash your face in canal water on deck from a hand basin!

WALTER D. EDMONDS

Water Never Hurt a Man

He trudged with his hands tight fists in his pockets, his head bowed to the wind and rain. Ahead of him in the darkness, so that he could hear the squudge of their hoofs, the towing team bowed their necks against the collars. He could not see them in the darkness. When he lifted his face, the rain cut at his eyes; and when lightning split the darkness he shut his eyes tight and pulled his head closer into his coat collar, waiting blindly for the thunder. Once in a lull he looked back. He could barely make out the bow-lantern and the arrows of gray rain slanting against it. Between him and the light he caught glimpses of the towrope, dipped slightly between the team's heaves, and the roughened water in the canal. Somewhere behind the light his father stood by the rudder-sweep, his beard curled and wet, his eyes slits, sighting for the bank, John wanted to go back, wanted to tie-by for the night, wanted to be in the bunk with his head buried in the friendly, musty smell of the blanket, where the storm could not reach him. He had gone back once, but his father had reached for his belt, saying, "Go on back. Watter never hurt a man. It keeps his hide from cracking."

John had gone back to the team. They did not need his guidance. But it was his place to keep the rope from fouling if a packet boat coming their way signaled to pass. He was afraid of his father at night, afraid of the big belt and strong hands with hair on the fingers over the knuckles. He caught up with the plodding horses and let the rain have its way. At each stroke of lightning his small back stiffened. It was his first year on the canal and he was afraid of storms at night.

He had been proud that spring when his father said, "John's old enough to be a driver-boy; he's coming along with me and the *Bacconola*." He had showed his dollar to his brothers and sisters, first pay in advance, and his father had bought him a pair of cowhide boots from the cobbler when he came to the village. Later, when the frost was out of the mud, John would go barefoot.

He was proud of his father. In Westernville, with other small boys, he had heard the dock loafers talking about his father, George Brace, bully of the Black River Canal. In some strange way they had news of every fight his father fought a day after it happened. "George licked the Amsterdam Bully Wednesday mornin'. Lock fifty-nine. It tuk nineteen minits only." "George is a great hand. Them big ditch bezabors is learning about George." A stranger had said, "Wait till Buffalo Joe meets up with him." There was silence then. Buffalo Joe Buller, he was bully of the western end of the Erie. A pea-souper, a Canadian, he fought the Erie bullies down one by one, and when he licked them he marked them with his boot in the Canadian style. It had a cross of nails to mark the beaten man's face. "You wait," said the stranger.

Little John, listening, felt shivers down his back. But now, with the wind and rain, and the lightning tumbling the clouds apart, he forgot. They were on the long haul westward, to Buffalo, with ploughs aboard, full-drafted in Rome. They had had to leave three hundredweight on the dock.

He felt his muddy boots slip in the towpath. He heard the squelching of the horses. Squelch-squelch, a steady rhythm as they kept step. Once the lightning caught his eyes; and he had a clear view of trees beyond the canalside meadow, their budded twigs bent down like old women with their backs to the storm, and the flat, sharp wall of a canal house sixty yards behind him. He had not even seen it as he passed. The rain was finding a channel down his neck. It crept farther, bit by bit, with a cold touch. He could feel his fists white in his pockets from clenching them. His legs ached with the slippery going. They had had supper at six, tied up by the bank, and John had eaten his plate of beans. He had felt sleepy afterward, barely noticing his father's body bent over the dishpan. It was warm in the cabin, with the little stove roaring red-hot, and his small hat hanging beside his father's cap on the door.

He had been almost asleep when his father's hand shook him roughly, then tumbled him from his chair. "Get out, John. Them ploughs we've got has to get west for spring ploughing. We'll pick up Bob in Syracuse, then we'll have a better chance to rest. Get out now," and he had reached for his belt.

What did John care for the old ploughs anyway? But it hadn't then begun to storm, and he had gone, with a tired sense of importance. One had to keep freight moving on the old Erie. The old *Bacconola* always made fast hauls. He had been proud and shouted in a high voice to the tired horses and kicked one with his new boots.

But now he did not care about the ploughs. He wished the crazy old *Bacconola* would spring a leak in her flat bottom, so they would have to stop till the hurry-up boat came along and patched her up. He thought of her now, bitterly, with her scabs of orange paint. "Crummy old blister," he called her to himself and made names for her, which he said aloud to the horses in a shrill voice. He was only twelve, with all the bitterness of twelve, and the world was a hateful thing.

"God-damned old crummy bitch of a tub..." But the lightning caught him, and his throat tightened and he wanted to cry out under the thunder.

A water rat went off the towpath with a splash, and a frog squeaked.

He glanced up to see a team on the opposite towpath heading east. "Hey, there!" yelled the driver in a hoarse voice; but John was too tired to answer. He liked to yell back in the daytime and crack his whip. But he had dropped his whip a while back. He would get a licking for that in the morning. But he didn't care. To hell with the whip and the driver and Pa!

"Hey, there!" shouted the other driver, a voice in the rain. "All right, all right, you dirty pup. Eat rain, if you want to, and go drownd." The rain took the voice, and the boat came by, silently, noiseless as oil, with its bow light a yellow touch against the rain. The steersman gave a toot upon the horn, but the sound bubbled through the water in it, and the steersman swore.

They were still on the long level, alone once more. It must be midnight. If only the lock would show. In Syracuse, Bob would come. He took turns driving and steering and cooking—a little man with a bent shoulder who had dizzy spells once in a while.

At the lock John could sit down and rest and listen to the tender snarling at his sluices while the boat went down, and heaving at his gate-beam, while John's father heaved against the other. He was crazy, the lock-keeper was; all lock-keepers were crazy. John's father always said so. John had seen a lot of them in their week of hauling, but he did not see why they were crazy. They looked no different even if they were. He hoped the lock-keeper would be asleep, so it would take a while to wake him.

Squelch, squelch-squelch, squelch. The horses kept plodding. Suddenly John caught a break in the rhythm. One foot sounded light. He pushed his way up beside them against the wind and laid a wet hand against a side. He could not see, but the side felt hot and wet, and he got a smell of sweat. Yes, he could feel the off horse limping. Hope filled him. He waited till the boat came up where he was, a small figure, shrunk with cold. The boat's bow, round and sullen, slipped along, the bow light hanging over and showing an old mullein stalk in silhouette against the water.

"Pa!"

His voice was thin against the wind.

He saw his father's figure, rain dripping from the visor of his cap, straight and big, almighty almost, breast to the wind.

"Pa!"

The head turned.

"Hey, there! What you doin? Get on back, or I'll soap you proper!"

"Pa! Prince has got a limp in his front foot. Pa!"

The voice turned hoarse with passion. "Get on back, you little pup! Fifty-nine's just round the next bend. Take your whip and tar him, or I'll tar you proper."

John sobbed aloud. For a bare moment he thought of staying still and letting the boat pass on. He would run away and join the railroad. He would get run over by an engine there, just when things went well, and they would be sorry. He started to draw himself a picture of his body coming home in a black box, and his mother crying, and his father looking ashamed and sorry, and then the lightning made a blue flare and he saw the straight figure of his father ahead, on the *Bacconola,* which seemed struck still, a pill box in the flat country, and he was afraid and went running desperately, hoping he could get back to the team before he was missed.

He caught the horses on the bend and, lifting his face to the storm, saw the lock lanterns dimly ahead. And even then his ears caught, coming up behind him, the harsh blast of a tin horn.

He looked back and saw a light, two rope lengths behind the *Bacconola.* Even while he watched over his shoulder, he saw that it was creeping up.

"John!" His father's voice beat down the sound of rain. "Lay into them brutes and beat into the lock!"

He could imagine his father glaring back. If only he had not dropped his whip. He would have liked to ask his father for the big bull whip that cracked like forty guns, but he knew what would happen if he did. He shrieked at the horses and fumbled for a stone to throw. But they had heard and recognized the note in his father's voice, and they were bending earnestly against the collars. A sudden excitement filled John as his father's horn rang out for the lock. The wind took the sound and carried it back, and the other boat's horn sounded a double toot for passing. John yelled shrilly. The horses seemed to stand still, and there was an odd effect in the rain of the canal sliding under them inch by inch laboriously, as if with his own feet he turned the world backward.

Minutes crept at them out of the rain, and the lights of the lock did not seem to stir. Then John heard the squelching of the team behind his back. Little by little they were coming up, past the *Bacconola,* until he could hear them panting through the rain, and saw them close behind, behind dim puffs of steamy breath. He watched them frantically. Then the lightning came once more, a triple bolt, and the thunder shook him, and when he opened his eyes once more he saw the lock lanterns a hundred yards ahead.

At that instant the driver of the boat behind yelled, "Haw!" and the following team swung across his towrope and they were snarled.

The horses stopped of themselves, shuddering. They were old hands, and knew enough not to move, for fear of being thrown from the towpath. The boats came drifting on, placidly as water-logged sticks. The light of the following boat showed a dark bow coming up. John heard his father roaring oaths, and saw by the bow light of the other boat a tall, clean-shaven man as big as his father, crouched to jump ashore. Then both boats came in by the towpath, and both men jumped. They made no sound except for the thump of their shoes, but John saw them dim against the lantern light, their fists coming at each other in slow, heavy swings.

The strange team was panting close beside him, and he did not hear the blows landing. There was a pushing upward in his chest, which hurt, and his fists made small balls in the pockets of his trousers. The other boater and his father were standing breast to breast, their faces still, cut, stonelike things in the yellow light, and the rain walling them in. He saw his father lift his hand, and the other man slip, and he would have yelled, for all his cold, if the lightning had not come again, so blue that his eyes smarted. He doubled up, hiding his face, and wept....

A hand caught him by the shoulder.

"A little puny girly boy," said a voice. "I wouldn't lick you proper! Not a little girly baby like you. But I'll spank you just to learn you to let us come by!"

John opened his eyes to see a boy, about his own height, but broader built, squinting at him through the rain.

"Take off your pants, dearie," said the boy in a mock voice, digging in his fingers till John winced. "Joe Buller can handle your captain smart enough. Me, I'll just paddle you to learn you."

John, looking up, was afraid. He did not know what to do, but without warning his hands acted for him, and he struck at the square face with all his might. A pain shot up his arm, making his elbow tingle, and the boy fell back. John could feel the surprise in that body stock-still in the rain, and had an instant of astonished pride.

Then panic laid hold of him and he tried to run. But the other boy jumped on his back. They went down flat in the mud, the older boy on John's shoulders, pummeling him till his head sang, and forcing his face into the track, and crying, "Eat it, you lousy little skunk! Eat it, eat it, eat it, eat it!"

John could taste the mud in his mouth, with a salty taste, and he began to squirm, twisting his head to escape the brown suffocation. He heaved himself behind, throwing the boy unexpectedly forward, twisted round, and kicked with all his might. The boy yelled and jumped back on him. And again they went down; this time the boy bent seriously to business. And this time John realized how it was to be hurt. At the third blow something burst loose in his inside and he screamed. He was crying madly. The other boy was heavier, but John squirmed over on his back, and as the brown hand came down on his face he caught it in both his own and bit with all the strength of his jaws. The hand had a slippery, muddy taste, but in a second it was warm in his mouth, and there was a sick, salt wetness on his tongue. The boy struck him once in the eyes and once on the nose, but John held on and bit. Then the boy howled and tore loose and ran back. There was another stroke of lightning, and John saw him doubled up, holding his hand to his mouth; and he got stiffly up, turned his back to the thunder, and saw his father bent over the other boater, taking off his shoe.

John walked up to them. His father's face was bleeding a trickle of blood from the right eye into his beard, but he was grinning.

"I'll take his boot for a souvenir," he said. "How'd you come out, Johnny?"

"Oh, pretty good. I guess that other feller won't bother us no more," said John, examining the fallen man. He lay half-stunned, by the water's edge a smooth, big man, with frightened, pale eyes. And one crumpled arm was in the water. John's father looked at the man and then at the boot he had in his hand.

"I'd ought to mark him by the rights of it; but he ain't worth the work, the way he laid down. Who'd ever know his name was Buller?"

Buller.... John gazed up admiringly at his big father and studied how the blood ran from the outer corner of the eye and lost its way in the black beard, which the rain had curled. His father had licked the western bully proper.

"Hey, there!"

The hail came in a thin, cracking voice. Turning, they saw the lock-keeper, white-bearded, peering at them from under the battered umbrella he held with both hands against the wind. The tails of his nightshirt whipped round the tops of his boots.

"Hey, there, you. There'll be some down boats by pretty quick, so you want to hurry along now, while the level's right."

John was aware of his father standing looking down at him.

"Shall we tie-by where we be?" asked his father.

John felt pains coming into the back of his neck where he had been pummeled, and his knuckles ached.

"We can stay here a spell," said his father. "The storm's comin' on again. There'll be bad lightnin', I make no doubt."

As he spoke there came a flash, and John whirled to see if the other driver-boy was still visible. He was proud to see him sitting by the towpath, nursing his hurt hand. John did not notice the thunder. He was elaborating a sentence in his mind.

He made a hole in the mud with the toe of his boot, spat into it, and covered it, the way he had seen his father do at home on a Sunday.

"Why," he said, in his high voice, eying the old *Bacconola,* "I guess them poor bezabor farmers will be wantin' them ploughs for the spring ploughing, I guess."

"Me, I'm kind of tuckered," said his father, raising his shoulders to loose the wet shirt off his back. "And the rain's commencing, too."

John said importantly, "Watter never hurt a man; it keeps his hide from cracking."

His father jumped aboard. He took his horn and tooted it for the lock. John ran ahead and put back the other boat's team and cried to their own horses to go on. They took up the slack wearily, and presently little ripples showed on the *Bacconola's* bow, and the lantern showed the shore slipping back. On the stern, George Brace blew a blast for the lock. The old lock-keeper was standing by the sluices, drops of water from his beard falling between his feet.

The boat went down, and the horses took it out. Ahead, the team and the boy left the lantern light and entered once more the darkness. The rope followed. And once more the *Bacconola* was alone with its own lantern.

Presently, though, in a stroke of light, George saw his son beside the boat.

"What's the matter? Hey, there!" he asked.

"Say, Pa! Will you chuck me your bull whip here ashore? Them horses is getting kind of dozy. They need soaping proper."

"Where's your whip?"

"I guess I left it a while back. I guess it was in that kind of scrummage we had. I guess it needs a heavier whip anyhow. I guess a man couldn't spare the time going back for it."

"Sure," said George.

He reached down and took it from its peg, recoiled it, and tossed it ashore. The boat went ahead, slowly, with a sound of water, and of rain falling, and of wind.

WALTER D. EDMONDS

Death in Albion

It was good to see Bisbee again. All the way down from Gaines, Chad had been worrying about how they would manage to show in a small place against an establishment the size of the Menagerie. But the sight of Bisbee, quietly walking the white-nosed horse through the long shadows, inspired confidence. He looked just the same as the first time Chad had seen him riding up to the Yellow Bud porch—his long, horselike face was thoughtful, his clothes dusty from the road, and he sounded brimming with confidence.

"Heard about Caroline and Shepley's new act. A man came into the tavern just before I left to meet you. He told about it. He said it was beautiful. I deposited a dollar for him to drink with, and I guess he's still talking. Best advertising you ever heard."

Going through the village he pointed out to Chad the more interesting features, the female seminary, the log jail, the courthouse, with as much familiar pride as though he had lived in Albion since it was settled. There was Menagerie paper everywhere, but Chad saw none of their own. He asked Bisbee whether he had had much trouble.

"Not to signify, trouble. I didn't try to tack up again. I worked the newspapers. I had pieces in the *American* and the *Republican*. Part of it's about Carolina, how the big circuses have tried to buy her away." He rolled his segar over his lower lip. "'Only the high sense of honor, not surprising to those acquainted with this lovely star of the upper air, with which she regards her contractual obligations has made possible Albion's viewing of such unparalleled grace, modesty, and talent.' I saved her a copy. Thought she might like to preserve it."

Chad thanked him.

"There's our lot," Bisbee said as they crossed the canal. "It's small, but it's this side of the Menagerie's. They need acreage. I hear they show in three pavilions."

Chad eyed the lot unfavorably. It was low and it looked wet. And Bastock was dubious also. "We can't risk any soft bottom with this double act," he told Bisbee. "It's too dangerous."

"There's footing for the ring in the corner," Bisbee said, imperturbably, watching Bastock verify the fact.

"How about that big show? Won't they make us trouble?" Chad demanded.

"I don't think so," Bisbee said mildly. "I've handed out free passes to the town board and the sheriff. I gave the sheriff ten free passes in case he wanted to swear in some deputies. A man likes to hand out free tickets if they don't cost him anything. And I told him that Albion was probably the first town its size to have two shows running the same day. I said it was bound to get into the papers and advertise the town. He could see that." He drew on the segar. "I hear Oscar's been sick," he said to Huguenine, who had sat down on the top step of the treasury wagon to watch the erection of the round-top.

"Yep," said Huguenine. "He has. But I guess I've cured him. I gave him a bottle of that bathhouse water. It cost fifty cents but I guess it was worth it."

Oscar was lying down. When Joe took off the side blinds, however, he swung his head to face the mild south wind, his yellow eyes unblinking. He looked like a brownstone statue, except for the slight stirring of his stringy mane.

"You know," Bisbee said, "I've got to admire that cat. When I heard he was sick, I felt kind of sad."

"We all did," Mrs. Huguenine said. "And he's been so nice, in all the time we went through. It was a time, too, Mr. Bisbee. I give my word it was."

She climbed down the steps past her husband with the blankets in her arms and hung them over a tree limb to air.

"Oh, Caroline," she called. "Would you mind whisking them before you bring them in? I found a moth bug on them."

Caroline, holding the cream at the tent entrance, waved her hand in reply and smiled.

"Her and Chad have been sleeping in the wagon," Mrs. Huguenine explained to Bisbee. Her fat face puckered up with sentimental tenderness. "They're just like two loving-birds in it. And she's so neat and clean I love to have them. Doc told A. D. he had to sleep in houses till his back limbered. You feel the dew in here. But those two!" she rolled her eyes. "I guess they just love dew."

As Caroline entered the tent, Bisbee looked after her thoughtfully. "Yes, she's nice. So's Chad," he said cautiously. "I guess you can trust them."

Mrs. Huguenine bristled.

"I guess we can," she said indignantly.

Huguenine grunted.

"Chad knows a lot too," he said. "He's pretty near as good as I am."

"Well, he's different," Bisbee said tactfully.

"Maybe that's it. But he's run this circus pretty well," Huguenine said. "He acts responsible."

"Getting married does that," Mrs. Huguenine said. "A nice girl like Caroline settles a boy."

Bisbee nodded, lipped his segar, blew smoke, and followed it with slow strides towards the tent. He watched the practice with approval, made Bastock grin by nodding his head slowly, and went out through the performers' entrance to examine Oscar.

Chad and Joe were shutting him in for the night.

"How's he eating?" he asked Joe.

"Pretty fair. He didn't eat so good this morning. I think he's still gassy here and there," Joe said. He closed the blind against the wind.

An hour later, near dark, the practice was over, and Chad was carrying the blankets into the wagon when he heard Oscar roar.

He stopped short at the steps to listen. The lot was still, there was no sound even from the canal basin. Joe Duddy was in the village somewhere, and except for themselves only Bastock and Budlong remained. Maybe the lion had had a dream, Chad thought, or maybe he had imagined the sound. But Caroline appeared in the door to ask what was the matter with Oscar.

Then Oscar roared again, his voice filling the evening. In the succeeding silence they now made out the pad of his feet. Something had excited him.

"Here, take these blankets." Chad stuffed them through the door and hurried across the lot. The two skinners emerged from the tent at the same time. Bastock said, "I never heard him make no noise like that."

"Listen a minute."

Budlong's lean face was lifted.

Far down the road they heard an answering roar, faint and far away, but unmistakably a lion's.

"It's the Menagerie coming," Budlong said.

From the cage wagon they could clearly hear the pad of Oscar's feet. He was moving rapidly back and forth in the narrow space. They heard his hide rasp against the slats.

"That excitement ain't going to do him good," Budlong said. "Knew a man got excited on top of a flux..."

"Keep quiet," Bastock broke in. "Hear that?"

It was a sound that none of them had ever heard. High-pitched, weirdly jibbering, almost like laughter. It brought a light thud of feet and Caroline ran down to them.

"What is it? It's awful. I'm afraid."

"Better light a lantern," Bastock said. "Maybe light will quiet Oscar."

"This feller," Budlong said, "saw ghosts."

They put the lantern by the cage wagon so Oscar could see the light through the cracks, and he paused in his walking.

Chad said suddenly, "I'm going up to the lot. I bet it's a wild animal."

"I'm coming with you," Caroline said.

The idea relieved them all.

The roars had brought some people out of the village. They paused at Huguenine's lot, then hearing another blast from down the road, with a renewal of the high-pitched insane laughter, they moved ahead.

Chad, Caroline clutching his arm, went with them. In the darkness, with the increasing wind in their faces, it was almost like walking to the world's ending.

A man was standing by the bars, swinging a lantern. Into its light tramped four heavy grey horses, rolling the first tent wagon. As the laughter broke out close at hand, Chad raised his voice to ask the man what it was.

"Hyenas. They carry on like that before a storm. They always do. You can't stop them. They're crazy."

Behind them, towards town, Oscar started his roaring once more.

"That's a lion," said the road marker. "He's from that little one-horse rig down the road. He's probably smelled these hyenas."

It was a queer experience, the wagons hauling past into the lot, full of sound and inner movement, and a strange covering smell from the foreign animals one could not see. It impressed Chad, but he was more impressed by the team upon team of matched horses, all greys. In daylight, he thought, the sight of that caravan of greys tramping the roads would be something a man would remember. They made Huguenine's little assortment pitiful to think of.

He jerked Caroline's arm.

"We' better go back," he said.

They reported to the skinners.

Budlong said, "It does smell like a storm." He had lit a second lantern which he had inside the round-top. "Oscar quieted a few minutes ago. Probably smelling Africa worked him up."

"If it's going to storm, we better get him inside," Joe said.

In the soggy grass, the cage wagon was hard to handle. Even Caroline had to push. She bent her slim body between Chad and Budlong at the tail gate. The wind was blowing hard by the time they had wrestled the wagon through the performers' entrance, and Bastock said, "It's a real blow coming. We better lace the canvas before the wind gets underneath. It's lucky we're low down."

They worked fast lacing the flaps. Budlong went round the pegs, setting them all with the sledge, while Caroline carried a lantern for him. The wind was yanking her skirt, wrapping her. It felt warm for all its force. But it took her breath like a winter wind. The wild hyena laughter from the Menagerie lot whipped brokenly over her head, like torn leaves. The first roll of thunder broke just as the men finished work. She and Chad pelted for the treasury wagon through the first rifling drops of rain.

The thunder lasted only a short time. They watched from the window in the treasury-wagon door, seeing the round-top spring out at them and vanish in the lightning flashes. Great valleys appeared in it, and sudden bubbles. But it held.

Then as the rain gained force and steadiness, the wind settled to an even blow. The thunder rolled northward, faded, and died.

Chad lit their candle.

"It's all right," he told her. "It's a good thing we had the tent up, too, or the ring would be like mush by now."

In the close space of the wagon, all they heard was the rain. By the time they were undressed, that too had slackened; there was only the drip from the roof. Chad said suddenly, "I wish I'd taken another look at Oscar."

"He'll be all right, Chad. I'm sure he is all right. He'd quieted down before the rain came."

What Caroline said was true. Oscar had quieted down. He had stretched out, his nose to the crack through which the wind drew the scents of Africa. Joe Duddy found him that way in the morning, his worn old carcass unmoving. Joe looked a moment at the armpit tufts; it always seemed strange to him to find a creature haired the way a man was. Then he poked the mop handle against the slatted ribs. "Hey you, Oscar," he said. "Wake up."

Budlong wandered into the tent.

"What you doing to the cat, Joe?"

"Rousing him," Joe said. He poked again. It came over him then that Oscar wasn't breathing. "My God," he said. "Get Chad. Get the gaffer. And you better tell Bisbee."

"Tell him what?" asked Budlong.

"Oscar's dead."

It was a catastrophe far more serious, they realized, than Albany's defection. It seemed worse, because they had expected something of the sort to happen, and then their fears had been lulled.

"He was the only lion we had," Huguenine said miserably. "Now we ain't even got him."

Even Bisbee showed defeat.

"By Harry," he said. "I just don't like showing here without that cat act. I don't like doing it at all after all the stories I got printed in the paper."

"If we announce he's dead, there won't nobody come," Huguenine said.

Ike said, "Maybe if we screened the wagon in the back and put a strap round Oscar's neck, Joe could wiggle it to make him look alive. I could do a lot of things. Maybe I could put my head in his mouth, like Van Amburgh."

Bisbee shook his head.

"We'd lose all the seat space at the back of the tent," he pointed out. "We can't afford that, even if Joe made Oscar act up. But Joe couldn't. Have you looked at Oscar, Ike?"

"Not to study him," Ike admitted.

"Well, he's the deadest-looking lion you ever saw. You wouldn't believe a lion could look that dead. You could put a fireworks display in his inside and he would still look dead."

Ike gave it up. He sat down on the step of the treasury wagon, to which Bisbee, the Huguenines, himself, and Chad had adjourned. Over the lot by the entrance of the round-top, the other performers and the skinners stood in a group watching them.

"We couldn't buy a lion, maybe from the Menagerie?" asked Mrs. Huguenine.

"They wouldn't sell," Huguenine said in a despondent voice.

"If they did, they'd ask more than this entire show is worth," Bisbee said. "Besides, I don't know how Ike feels, but I wouldn't want to be the Modern Daniel with a brand-new lion."

Ike didn't bother to answer.

"I guess we're licked," said Huguenine. "Do we announce it, Bisbee? Or do we go ahead and take a chance?"

"You said yourself they wouldn't come in," Bisbee reminded him. "Not even a punk's going to pay to see a dead lion when he can see four or five live ones at the same price."

Chad scratched his head.

"I don't see that, Mr. Bisbee. You can't get so close to a live lion. But I don't see why we couldn't advertise Oscar being dead. Kind of a curiosity, see? Like seeing the mammoth's bones in Rochester. Lots of people can see a live lion." He began to warm up to the idea himself. "Hell, they can see four or five of them right here. But they won't have many chances to see a dead one. He's the only dead lion on exhibition in the United States."

"By God," said Bisbee. "Say in North America."

Chad grinned.

"The Western Hemisphere."

"The world," suggested Bisbee. "They may kill 'em in Africa, but they don't exhibit them in a cage wagon, I'll bet a hat."

"You might take a chance on the Universe while you're about it," Ike put in wearily.

Huguenine grunted.

"The United States sounds good enough for me. But it's an idea, Chaddy. That's something none of us else have had. Bisbee, can you get a poster drawed in time?"

"I'll do it myself, if I can't."

Bisbee was off.

He was back at noon with two huge sheets of heavy paper, announcing the exclusive exhibition of the only dead lion in captivity in the United States. The larger, to be fastened on the round-top itself, could be read from the road. The smaller, to be affixed to the cage wagon in the tent, announced that for an additional ten cents the spectator could have the unusual experience of entering the cage wagon with the lion and examining the king of beasts as closely as his curiosity impelled.

Bisbee was enamored of this refinement of Chad's idea. Before long he had worked himself up to the idea that the whole scheme had been his from the beginning. "Somebody like you puts the idea into my head, I don't know how, you don't know how, but there it is." He tacked the sign to the wagon himself. "There," he said, "you see if that don't draw them in."

It did. It was astonishing how many entered the cage at the end of the performance. It was as good a stand as the circus had enjoyed since Lyons. But all during the preceding performance, Chad, with the rest of the troupe, had been conscious of the dead, slitted eyes behind the cage-wagon bars. A dead lion might draw all right, but live lions lasted longer.

JOHN V. A. WEAVER

"Moonlight All the Way"

Gramma sits in the corner by the hearth,
Efficient-fingered, placid, and very deaf.
She knits and sews,
And does innumerable handy jobs.
She is a shadow in the shadows,
Contentedly remote,
Pleased to be noticed now and then
With shouted pleasant platitudes.
Ask her about the past.
Press her for facts.
What are facts?

Houses are facts, maybe.
And you and I are facts, and so is Gramma—
Perhaps.... And life's a fact.... Oh, yes,
And love, and work, and wedding-trips....
So is romance....

Canals are facts. I search for detailed facts
About canals.
Gramma has known canals.
She made her wedding-journey up the Erie.
Now for the facts.

"Oh, yes, the wedding was just after noon.
We drove to Utica, three wagons-full.
From Clinton, yes. Your Grandpa was named Clint,
You know." I knew. "The boat was waiting for us.
We got on board at early candle-lighting."

"The boat—how big was it?" I prod her gently.
She turns the matter slowly in her mind.

"Oh—pretty big. I guess it seemed lots bigger
Than what it really was. At least, at first.
It was so strange, you see, so strange and new.
There we were, setting out for the wilderness,
Two youngsters, leaving all our folks behind us,
And hardly any money to our name.
I wasn't scared—oh, don't think that. Why, Clint
Was strong and fine, and there was the job ahead,
And sixty acres homestead.... Still and all,
Some nights when he'd be talking to the captain,
I'd lie there, thinking over everything—
The walls would seem an awful ways away.
But I got used to it. And by the time
We got to Buffalo, the boat seemed smaller,
Lots smaller. It was our first home, you see."

A smiling silence,
Which I break patiently.
"How big? As big as canal-boats nowadays?"

"It's been so long since I saw the Erie—well—
I can't exactly figure. One thing's sure,
It was a whole lot bigger than the one
We took again at Cleveland. That was little."
I abandon the question of size.
"What did you use for power? Horses, or mules?
Or did men pull it?"

On this point she was positive, "Not men.
Horses, I think. Or—maybe it was mules.
But it wasn't men. There was only Clint and the captain,
And a funny, dried-up fellow that drove the mules—
Or horses.... Anyhow, he was a case.
Chewed tobacco, and never spoke a word,
Not even to the—animals.... The captain,
He liked to talk. He was a handsome man.
Not near as handsome as my Clint, but nice.
I can see all the three of them right now,
Dressed up for Sunday, in their flowered waistcoats.
Men don't know how to dress up nowadays.
Clint certainly looked stylish, with his hat—
A big grey beaver—and the heavy watch-chain,
All solid gold, that was. It was the only

Real valuable thing we had. And I,
I'd wear my shoes—silk shoes. My Clint made those.
He was a shoemaker by trade, you see.
A piece left over from my wedding-gown,
That's what he used. There's another in my scrap-book.
You saw it often. We made a pretty couple,
Going to church some place along the way.
That's what the captain was always saying—
'A pretty couple,' yes, that's what he said."

I let her rest after this long description.
I try a feeble joke; "And did you see
Niagara Falls?" But that's no joke to her.
The facts are what she clings to. Yes, the facts.

"Oh, no! We took a little sailing ship
The afternoon we got to Buffalo.
We didn't even stay to see the city.
It was a freighter. Not a passenger
But us. Five days it took us going to Cleveland,
Or was it six? I didn't like it much,
I can't remember. I was pretty sick.
It felt so good to get on a canal
Again—the little boat this time. We went
Up to a place called—well, now, I declare—
The name's just gone. It was real near Coshocton.
Only two hours by stage-coach. Then we went
Straight from Coshocton to our piece of land
Across the river, in a place called Roscoe.
Seems like the last part of the trip went quicker—
Quicker than up the Erie, oh, lots quicker."

A fact is peering 'round the corner.
I made a frantic grasp. "How fast? I mean
What speed did those canal-boats make per hour?"

Slowly she speaks, then gathers speed herself.
"Well—you can guess how fast a pair of horses
Could pull a good-sized boat. Or mules. I'd sit
Out on the back with Clint, up on the cabin.
The roof was flat. We didn't go so fast
We couldn't see the trees down in the water.
The willows hung so low you couldn't tell

Where leaves begun and water started in.
My, it was green. The middle west is lovely,
The loveliest place in all the world, in June,
Or anyway, we thought so then. The captain
Of the Ohio boat was a young boy,
Not quite as old as Clint. He was full of fun.
We'd all sit out there nights, he'd play the guitar.
He played it well. And all of us would sing.
Clint had the prettiest baritone! He'd roll
The verses out, and we'd join in the chorus.
The time went quick."

Once more I stab at specifications.
"How were the accommodations? Furniture good?
Beds comfortable?"

"I don't suppose you'd call them wonderful,
But they were good enough."

"Food? It tasted fine." That long, slow smile
Once more. "We didn't notice very much.
We were so happy, being let alone
On our honeymoon, and going off on adventure."

I grin. "I should say so. Now, tell me, Gramma,
How long did it take from Utica to Coshocton?"

She doesn't answer. I wonder if she heard.
In a mild yell I say the question over.

"How long? Why, just a month. Yes, just a month."

"A month!" Why, here's one concrete fact at last.

"A month to a day." She takes her glasses off,
And peers past me into the dark behind me.
Then, with conviction and simplicity
She adds her other fact, her fact of facts:
"Yes. And—it was moonlight all the way!"

WILLIAM HARLAN HALE

Journeyman

He walked the towpath along the Erie Canal most of the night in search of an eastbound line boat. Now and then, in the darkness of the flat country with its mist-laden clearings, he could hear the slow thud of tow-horse hoofs coming the other way along the path, then the mumble of voices or the twang of a guitar afloat, and finally the creak of the towline as a boat hove into shape: these were westbound freighters, carrying immigrants into the interior. Toward dawn, when he finally hailed a barge bound east with Buffalo grain for Albany, he found some of its roughneck passengers still drinking on the cabin roof. They joshed him and asked him if he hadn't been spending the night with a woman out on the soft banks. He hurried below for some sleep.

The barge was towed in August morning sunshine along the giant stone aqueduct over the Genesee at Rochester, a town which the canal had turned overnight into a city of flour mills and five-story warehouses that tapped the West and now served the East. Then trackless timberland enfolded the narrow cut again, and no noise rose but that of wild fowl in the cedar swamps. But next one heard grinding mills, and here was Syracuse—a lonely settlement "surrounded by a desolate, poverty-stricken, woody country, enough to make an owl weep to fly over it," Colonel W. L. Stone of the New York *Commercial Advertiser* had said of it a decade before, yet now rising into "noble ranges of buildings, and two or three large, tasteful churches." Cotton textile mills were humming at Utica, where passengers could dine richly at Baggs' Hotel or eat for ten cents at the Oneida Temperance House while waiting for the boat to start the haul into the Mohawk Valley. Here red-and-gold canal packets came the other way, bearing ladies under parasols. Traffic thickened; high ridges and romantic glens closed in; and now canallers could be seen rafting oak timber to Schenectady to help in building America's newest innovation—a steam railroad.

Horace Greeley left the boat at Schenectady rather than stay with it for the long, slow descent through locks into the Hudson. He struck over the hills

From *Horace Greeley: Voice of the People* by William Harlan Hale. Pubished by Harper & Brothers, New York, 1950. Reprinted by permission of the author.

on foot to Albany, walking through a countryside that had just been startled by a revolutionary occurrence. A few days before, on freshly laid iron tracks, a gleaming festooned locomotive named the De Witt Clinton had hauled a string of crowded cars from Albany on the first trial run of a passenger train in the North. First the stage-like coaches, each shackled to the next by chains, had started up with such a jerk that the first citizens of Albany were hurled out of their seats. Then the shower of boiler sparks had ignited their Sunday clothes and parasols, and when the De Witt Clinton pulled up short for water the cars had banged into one another again, throwing the smoldering guests into another heap. Farmers' horses along the way had taken fright and overturned their wagons. The inns were full of excited talk. But Horace Greeley hurried on without taking time to listen. He was bent on catching the first morning Hudson River boat to face his own future in New York.

HERMAN MELVILLE

"Canallers"

"Canallers!" cried Don Pedro. "We have seen many whaleships in our harbors, but never heard of your Canallers. Pardon: who and what are they?"

"Canallers, Don, are the boatmen belonging to our grand Erie Canal. You must have heard of it."

"Nay, Senor; hereabouts in this dull, warm, most lazy, and hereditary land, we know but little of your vigorous North."

"Aye? Well then, Don, refill my cup.... I will tell ye what our Canallers are...."

"For three hundred and sixty miles, gentlemen, through the entire breadth of the state of New York; through numerous populous cities and most thriving villages; through long, dismal uninhabited swamps, and affluent, cultivated fields, unrivalled for fertility; by billiard-room and bar-room; through the holy-of-holies of great forests; on Roman arches over Indian rivers; through sun and shade; by happy hearts or broken; through all the wide contrasting scenery of those noble Mohawk counties; and especially, by rows of snow-white chapels, whose spires stand almost like milestones,

From *Moby Dick or The Whale* by Herman Melville. Published 1851.

flows one continual stream of Venetianly corrupt and often lawless life. There's your true Ashantee, gentlemen; there howl your pagans; where you ever find them, next door to you; under the long-flung shadow, and the snug patronizing lee of churches. For by some curious fatality, as it is often noted of your metropolitan freebooters that they ever encamp around the halls of justice, so sinners, gentlemen, most abound in holiest vicinities....

"Freely depicted in his own vocation, gentlemen, the Canaller would make a fine dramatic hero, so abundantly and picturesquely wicked is he. Like Mark Antony, for days and days along his green-turfed, flowery Nile, he indolently floats, openly toying with his red-cheeked Cleopatra, ripening his apricot thigh upon the sunny deck. But ashore, all this effeminacy is dashed. The brigandish guise which the Canaller so proudly sports; his slouched and gaily-ribboned hat betoken his grand features. A terror to the smiling innocence of the villages through which he floats; his swart visage and bold swagger are not unshunned in cities. Once a vagabond on his own canal, I have received good turns from one of these Canallers; I thank him heartily; would fain be not ungrateful; but it is often one of the prime redeeming qualities of your man of violence, that at times he has as stiff an arm to back a poor stranger in a strait, as to plunder a wealthy one. In sum, gentlemen, what the wildness of this canal life is, is emphatically evinced by this; that our wild whale-fishery contains so many of its most finished graduates, and that scarce any race of mankind, except Sydney men, are so much distrusted by our whaling captains. Nor does it at all diminish the curiousness of this matter, that to many thousands of our rural boys and young men born along its line, the probationary life of the Grand Canal furnishes the sole transition between quietly reaping in a Christian corn-field, and recklessly ploughing the waters of the most barbaric seas."

☛ BOOK FOUR ☚

The Finger Lakes

East view of Seneca Falls village

INTRODUCTION TO BOOK IV

THE HAND to which are attached the seven or eight blue and watery fingers is as unnatural as the paws of a seven-toed kitten. This is the state's Lake Country, comparable in many ways to the Lake Country of England. Those who travel it have come to expect, however, prosperous farms with checkered fields running gently up from lake shores. The area has for many years been the habitat of writers, most of whom have been justifiably regional in their approach. "Justifiably" because of the many colleges which bring to their students an interest in literature and in their own roots and background. The country is so beautiful that it has inspired many legends from the Indian's mythology to the white man's folk fancies.

This is the country of the lonesome drum whose muffled beats have often sounded on hot summer days out of the mists that cover the lake waters.

THE FINGER LAKES

17TH CENTURY

ALEXANDER McGINN STEWART

The Eat-All Dinner

On the 17th of May, 1656, Fr. René Ménard embarked at Quebec with members of a colony who were setting out to make the first white settlement in New York State, west of the lower Mohawk Valley....

The northwestern end of the city of Syracuse, N.Y., touches the southeastern end of Onondaga Lake. A site which slopes gently to the lake on the northeast side was chosen by the pioneers for the head house of the colony....

A great council of the Indians soon assembled. Fr. Chaumonot, who had been on the ground from the year before, addressed the Indians with fascinating and pictorial language. In part of his speech he said "It is for the faith that I take in my hands this rich present and open my mouth to remind you of the pledges you gave at the time you came to Quebec to conduct us to your country." Among the archives of the Onondagas was a belt of beads 4 feet long with a cross at one end. General Clark of Auburn thought that this might have been the present given at the time. The site of this council and of the first white man's colony, west of the Mohawk River, is Central New York's Plymouth Rock. A park and monument, now marking this site, were dedicated on August 16, 1933. The site was identified by the late Reverend William Beauchamp, S.T.D. The well of salt water, shown to Fr. Simon Le Moyne, S.J., on his mission to the Onondaga in 1654, and since known as "the Jesuit's well," is now enclosed with a suitable wall, having an inscription explanatory of its historical importance....

From *René Ménard* by Alexander McGinn Stewart. Published by Heindl Print, Rochester, N. Y., 1934. Reprinted with permission.

Superstition made difficulties and dangers. White traders in the Hudson River region told an Indian customer that baptism caused people to vomit up the soul with the blood and that children baptized died of sorcery. A crazy Cayuga came for three nights into the chief's house looking for a chance to kill Fr. Ménard as a sorcerer. The chief caught him just in time to turn aside the fatal blow. This danger was not long past when a young warrior accused Fr. Ménard of being able to give life or death to whom he pleased and since he had baptized a sick man and caused him to die, instead of making him live, the young warrior threatened to kill Fr. Ménard....

A dying Huron had made known a plot to massacre all the Frenchmen. Remaining at Onondaga meant torture and death for everybody. Yet the ice was still in the rivers; how could they escape?

M. De Puys, executive head of the colony, had made an ingenious plan. A young man who had won the affections of the chief had been instructed to go to the chief and tell that he (the young man) had dreamed that the French had given a great feast to the Onondagas and that he also dreamed that terrible calamities would fall on the Onondagas if the feast was not held.

Dreams were absolute commands from the spirit world to the Indians. So all other plans had to be set aside in order that the Indians might obey the command of the dream. One of the requirements of the dream was that it should be an eat-all feast. No Indian was to refuse anything which was set before him. M. De Puys found that fifty-three men could not be carried in the canoes they had, so that two boats had to be built secretly in the colony house with Indians lolling at the door, whose slightest suspicion would cause a massacre.

The evening of the feast came and the highway where cars now pass rapidly, between Syracuse and Liverpool, then saw a strange sight. All the Indians in the village were ready for the eat-all feast. Frenchmen began passing out huge quantities of food. No Indian was allowed to rest from eating. Every finished portion was renewed immediately.

Meanwhile, jesters, musicians and jolly noise-makers, kept up a tremendous din. When the din was at its happiest and loudest the boats were taken to the lake, while the Indians on the other side of the house, were rapidly becoming paralyzed with food. Then came the anxious moment when the last of the Frenchmen entered the colony stockade on one side, passed quickly around and out the other side to the last waiting canoe. On the lake the canoes moved very slowly, lest the noise of the ice which the refugees had to break might betray them to torture fires and death.

On the river with the high water of spring to carry them and the fear of capture behind them, safety was sacrificed for speed. All hazards were taken at rapids and cascades.

Fr. Le Mercier's letter tells of going down frightful precipices in the river, of traveling all night and all the next day, of the mouth of the river being frozen and of four hours portaging through the dark woods, where every windfall of trees might form a fort from which the enemy might attack them. The maze of islands as they approached the outlet of the lake leading into the St. Lawrence River puzzled them.

They had no Indian guides. In the rapids on the St. Lawrence River it was possible for the men in one canoe to look into a space between two rocks and see a canoe upside down with three of its occupants out in the river, never to return again. The fourth man, clinging to the side of the canoe, was washed down through the rapids and rescued an instant before he also would have disappeared into the river.

Fr. Regueneau wrote "We landed at Montreal in the beginning of the night," the 3rd of April, 1658.

19TH CENTURY

SAMUEL HOPKINS ADAMS

Munk Birgo and the Carcagne

Against the admonitions of his wife, Grandfather had gone out walking in the March slush. In consequence—though he would never have given our step-grandmother the satisfaction of admitting it—he came down with a hard cold.

"Let me send for Dr. Ely, Mr. Adams," she urged.

"No such a thing," the old gentleman retorted. "It is no more than a pesky rheum. Hand me my antifogmatic."

Throughout the day he treated himself to frequent sips from the amber-hued bottle containing his favorite home remedy, Hop Bitters. He was still dosing when, the next afternoon, Jenny, John, Reno, Charles and I found him basking in the glow of his lyre-shaped Franklin stove. To the cheering alcoholic influence of the Bitters we owed, I am sure, the one story of the supernatural that we ever heard from his lips.

A Lake Ontario gale had been blowing for two days. A specially savage blast rocked the frame cottage, filling the dark afternoon with unearthly voices. Grandfather cocked an ear.

"Howls like the carcagne," he observed.

"What's that, sir?" I asked.

He put on his look of pretended incredulity. "You don't know what a carcagne is?" He swept the circle of our faces with his glance. "Not any of you?"

"No, sir," John answered.

The rest of us shook our heads in expectant agreement.

"Just as well, perhaps," said Grandfather. "Superstitions are not for the young."

"I don't mind ghosts," Charlie averred valiantly.

"Was it a ghost, Grandpa?" Jenny asked. "The carcagne, I mean."

"She, not it," he corrected. "No, not a ghost. You must understand that there is no such thing as a carcagne any more than there are ghosts."

"If there had been, what would it be like?" Charlie inquired insinuatingly.

"She was supposed to be a storm-hag with a wolf's head, a vampire's mouth, and a bat's wings."

"Oo-oo-oo!" said Charlie enjoyably and shrank perceptively as the wind echoed him.

"None but the lakers believed in her," the old gentleman continued. "They were a witch-ridden lot alongshore."

"Our lakers?" John asked. "Lake Ontario?"

Grandfather nodded. "Stout enough fellows in a storm or a ruckus," he said, "but scared of an owl in the dark. Say 'carcagne' to any one of them and he would spin you a tale to make a woodcat's whiskers bristle. All fahdoodle, as I have warned you. And yet—and yet"—his voice dropped to a ruminative murmur—"I have often wished that Munk Birgo could have lived to tell what he saw and heard that foul night of gale off Oswego Harbor."

Jenny's breath oozed forth in a softly tremulous sigh. "I don't think you ever spoke of Mr. Birgo before, Grandpa. Was he a friend of yours?"

"Of no man's," replied Grandfather.

"It's a funny name," John said. "Was he baptized that way, sir?"

"Baptismal water never touched him," said Grandfather. "It would have sizzled."

Everybody on the lake and ashore knew Munk Birgo for a man of evil in word and deed, Grandfather continued. He was part French, part Indian, and part (if loose talk was to be believed) something worse than either. When in liquor, he would scutter up a tree like a squirrel and shout, "I am Munk Birgo! There is fire in my blood and breath, and I can spit brimstone!"

"Could he, Grandpa?" Charlie asked in awe.

"I never saw him do so," was the cautious reply, "but many accredited him with strange potencies derived from his parentage."

Munk, by common report, had been born in a feverous hag's nest on a reed-encircled islet of the great Montezuma Marshes, Grandfather told us.

It was said that his mother was not a broom-witch but a fork-witch, which is one degree worse. Who Munk's father was, nobody inquired with too much particularity. Some said the Devil.

Munk's first commercial activity was as an owler out of Ogdensburg. No great harm in that, Grandfather said. Most Lake Ontario small craft did a bit in the contraband line—woollens, powder, rum and whatnot. But now Munk came by his sloop was a darker matter. He claimed to have sighted her from a low point off Sodus, unmanned, unrigged, and drifting toward a lee shore, but there was plenty of piracy on the lakes in those days, and few to put factious questions. At any rate when Munk turned up with his new sloop, her stern board had been scoured clean and bore the legend, in fresh-painted red-and-blue lettering:

Munk Birgo

His Fancy.

She was a sweet craft, in Grandfather's opinion, a bit walt perhaps, but trim, staunch and clover to handle, and could show her heels to the fastest revenuer between York State and Canada Shore.

"Then you saw her, sir?" John said.

"Once only," Grandfather replied. "She was pelting into Genesee mouth, full sail and both sheets made fast before fifty miles of gale, as foolhardy seamanship as ever I saw in my life. There stood Munk, tall and spare, black-a-vised and jaunty—well favored, too, in his dark way—with the tiller between his knees, singing the Devil's Anthem and beating time with a cemetery bone."

Having held the sheet of a sharpie's mainsail in Owasco Lake races, I deemed myself a nautical expert. "Do you mean he steered with his legs, sir?" I asked incredulously.

"Always," Grandfather said. "It was his special sea-trick. He had built a low steering platform aft, so that he could hold the tiller with his knees. It left his hands free to manipulate the sheets when a revenuer was to windward of him and he had to rely on sharp maneuvering. And," he added darkly, "he had need of all his trickery if half of what was said of him was true."

"What's a cemetery bone, sir?" Charlie asked.

The old gentleman hesitated. "Birgo was in a way of business that was spoken of under men's breath," he said.

"What was it? What business?" all four of us wanted to know.

"Anatomy," said Grandfather.

We others looked at John, who was our recognized expert in the often designedly obscure references of our grandfather. John blinked. "Did he teach it, sir?"

The old gentleman shook his head. "He practiced it. He was a resurrectioner, as the word went in those days."

"I know," John interpreted. "Body snatchers. They dug up dead people."

"What for?" Jenny asked, horrified.

"To sell," Grandfather answered. "It was a regular commerce."

The College of Physicians and Surgeons of Fairfield Seminary, in Herkimer County, needed cadavers for its students, Grandfather went on. There was another market in Albany, and a steady demand from New York City, where a subject in prime condition would fetch as high as fifty dollars. There was developed a nocturnal trade operated by bands of desperadoes who raided village churchyards and carted the bodies away. However, the countryside became aroused, and nightly patrols guarded both the shunpikes and the highroads against the "cad-wagons." It was when the roads had become hazardous for the operators of the business that Munk Birgo, so gossip ran, took up transporting their secret freight for them in his sloop.

The *Fancy* harbored in Oswego River mouth. Munk's avowed cargoes were salt from the Syracuse beds, grain, and now and again a run of fish.

"But when he sailed by night," the old gentleman said, "there was no manifest to tell what the sloop carried."

"Wasn't he ever caught, sir?" John asked.

Again the old gentleman hesitated. "Not by the law," he said.

"By—by the carcagne?" Jenny asked in a whisper.

A fit of coughing racked Grandfather's bent but still powerful frame. John poured a draught from the amber bottle, which the patient swallowed slowly and with appreciation. The paroxysm was appeased and the narrative was resumed.

"I will recount the story to you as it was told to me by a gypsy crone who was camped on the rocky point opposite the Oswego lighthouse on the night Munk Birgo was last seen," said Grandfather.

From then on, the narrator did not detract from his tale by warning us to disbelieve it. With a touch of histrionics, Grandfather gave himself over to the legend, which he told in the style and parlance of the gypsy herself.

All lake dwellers, so he prefaced the story, remember the great gale of 1829 that swept down one night out of a cloudless northeast. In local phraseology, it was fit to blow a bespoken boot off a wooden leg. Though it was mid-August a wintry chill was in the air. "Cold as Presbyterian charity," the gypsy woman had described it to her interested hearer.

The spears of an aurora were stabbing upward to the zenith. There was a wild whoobub of wind alow and aloft. The crested breakers that boomed upon the rocks spat electrons like thunderheads. All boats known to be out had come into harbor except one fishing smack, and a crowd stood on the slope above the docks, every eye watchful for her. At last she rounded the point, reefed down to the thirds, scuttering like a mink out of a henhouse, and fetched to against Saunders' dock. Her captain couldn't make the leap to the planking too soon; he craved solidity beneath his feet. His knees were shaking as he walked toward the people, and he looked like the Devil convicted of murder.

"Everybody safe inshore?" the captain asked, and when they told him that he was the last, he uncovered and said "God be thanked!"

The carcagne was out, he told the hushed crowd. Had he seen her, they asked fearfully. Nobody ever really sees her, he said—nobody that comes back in the flesh to tell of it—but he had glimpsed a dark patch swooping overhead, lighted by gleams of fox-fire redder than the aurora glow, and had heard a flutter of thick wings and smelled a whiff of corruption tainting the clean air. If it wasn't the carcagne...

Some of the crowd retreated toward their homes, but that was the ignorance of hoi polloi, Grandfather said, because, as all informed folk knew, the creature could not range overland, and they were safe enough on the hillside. Then, as the rumor spread, more inhabitants of the village came out, until all the slopes around the harbor were black with people. From the distant church tower came the strokes of twelve, Methodist time.

It was then that the citizens saw Munk Birgo strolling down the roadway that led to the small wharf where his *Fancy* was moored. He had been going from tap to tavern, and was unsteady on his pins. The Presbyterian preacher halted him.

"Surely you are not going out this night, Birgo?" he said.

Birgo cocked his chin. "Who says it?"

"For the sake of your sinful soul—" the minister began, but Munk Birgo stopped him with a spate of oaths.

"Do you know how much I value your spoopsy counsels?" Munk asked, and answered himself, "Not by the gizzard of a trifle. Not by the product of a quarter-cipher. Back to your humbox, parson!"

"You go to your damnation," the clergyman warned him.

"If all Hell yawned beyond the first line of breakers, go I would just the same," Munk said. "I have my own occasions, and I follow them."

"I know those godless occasions," the minister said, looking him in the eye.

"Then mind your own occasions, Reverend," Birgo said with a laugh. "I'll see you at sunup."

He swaggered down the wharf, jumped aboard, cast off, and, mounting the steering platform, took the tiller in his customary knee-grip. He was mouthing some broken rhythm. Most of those near enough to hear it stopped their ears. It was the Lord's Prayer backward, the gypsy woman had told Grandfather, and he went through it without hitch, gulp, or stutter.

"I am a Romany out of the true Egypt," she had said, "but those words would have burnt my throat to a cinder."

Settled into position, Munk touched neither sheet nor halyard to make sail. Nevertheless, the sloop veered smartly from the dock and set course for the open, missing the guardian rock at the river mouth by a thin hair.

At this, my nautical soul was stirred to protest. "How could she sail upwind under bare poles?" I demanded.

"I don't know," the old gentleman said. "Nobody knows. I am passing on to you the account as it came to me from the gypsy."

A small mist oozed out of nowhere and cloaked the sloop from human sight.

Oswego had little sleep that night. Some said that Munk Birgo had sailed out to keep tryst with the carcagne. Soberer opinion had it that he was transferring a shipment of anatomy for the resurrectioners, three of whom had lately been seen in the locality. The crowd on the hillsides settled down to wait the night out. They watched the northern lights shooting up and falling away. Strange sounds were heard from the upper air that were not of the storm, a high, mad wailing that had laughter in it, too.

With the first paling of the east, the gale turned gusty, then diminished and steadied to a fisherman's breeze. From the lighthouse, a voice shouted, "Sail ho!" All eyes swung to the north.

The sloop was coming in, moving faster than any man there had seen human craft move before. Mainsail, foresail and jib were trim and taut. Above and ahead, as if pointing the course, sped a thick, small cloud that at one moment took a hideous shape, and again became a formless blackness outrunning the breeze. The boat yawed, and shot between the lighthouse and the storm beacon, its deck so tilted that the crowds ashore could see the platform aft.

At that sight a shriek went up to split the moon. Those whose legs would serve them scrambled up the hillside and ran for the dear life and reason. Others cowered close to the ground with their cloaks over their heads. The minister thrust out his hands against the portent on the boat and prayed lustily.

Grandfather paused to cough, and John asked in a determined and manly voice, "What did they—I mean, what was in the boat?"

"The gypsy crone was too frozen with fright to look away," Grandfather resumed. "She recognized the—er—figure on the steering platform as Munk Birgo, but only because of the familiar attitude; it held the tiller between its knees." He took a slow swallow of the Invalid's Friend & Hope. "It was Munk Birgo's skeleton, picked bone-white," he said.

"Oh, my goodness!" Jenny quavered, ladylike even in shock.

Charlie's curiosity overbore his terrors. "Was it the carcagne that ate up Mr. Birgo?" he asked fearfully.

Grandfather's answer was to go on with the tale. The sloop, so the gypsy had told him, struck the guardian rock at the river mouth head-on with a splintering crash, slid off into the depths, and was nevermore seen, plank, strake, or gunnel. A mad hoot of triumph sounded through the air. There was the whirr of a strong wing-beat, and a trail of fox-fire and stinkstone sparks died away in the distance.

"So ended an evil life," Grandfather said solemnly.

Jenny rallied. "Grandpa, dear," she said, "you don't *believe* it was the carcagne, do you?"

"Certainly not," the old gentleman replied, all briskness now. "An idle tale, such as passes, lip to ear, wherever gypsies, tinkers, and other folk of the road gather over a fire-log. Discharge your minds of it."

"Yes, sir," said John. He stared out into the gloom which was deepening with uncomfortable rapidity. "I think we ought to be starting home."

Another violent blast shook the walls, tortured the thrashing boughs of the lilacs beyond the window, and passed on with a whistling wail. Grandfather tilted his head to listen with a frightening intentness.

"All huncamunca and fahdoodle," he mused. Then, with a sly insinuation he added, "Yet there are times, with a wildness such as this outside, when I find myself wondering what it was that piloted Munk Birgo's *Fancy* straight and true into Oswego Harbor on that night, fifty years and more past and gone."

EARL CONRAD

The Man in the Dungeon

It was the immortal hour in American life—the mid-1800s before the advent of the Civil War. Men and women were launched on a sea of reforms and they were making an inspiring history. They believed that what they were doing would produce an enduring imprint on the human consciousness thereafter. Words like "freedom," "mankind," "progress," were being given life. Causes were many and everywhere. Individuals believed that their efforts would prolong their personal identities long after their death. "Faith" was a word as powerful as the words "love" or "truth." A man with "faith" was a man of honesty and greatness and integrity, and a faithless one was doomed to go to some perdition of extinction.

America was growing and it was this attitude of new birth that was its essence.

It was in such an hour as this and in such a climate that a man named William H. Seward, destined to become Abraham Lincoln's Secretary of State, found himself, or plunged himself—as a man of faith—into one of the strangest and most meaningful purposes of that time.

In the 1840s they called the central part of New York State "the storm country." Cold Lake Ontario lay to the north, and the Canadian blasts drove across the lake and settled in the region where a half-dozen lakes stretched, taut and frozen, like fingers of a hand, on the countryside. Snow began falling late in November and there might be snow every day or so through March. The drifts were high and they could reach up to window levels, and in some rural spots to the eaves. The towns were vying for growth and commerce, and one of the larger villages, in 1846, was Auburn. It was then twice as big as Rochester to the west, and about the same size as Syracuse to the east. There were lakes all about Auburn, and close to the village was long lean Owasco Lake, a frozen mirror reflecting whatever colors the sky yielded.

Auburn was an antislavery and a suffragist center. Politics was a virtual

From *Mr. Seward for the Defense* by Earl Conrad. Published by Rinehart & Company, New York, 1956. Reprinted by permission of the author.

industry there, the Whig Party being strong. And in the center of the town lay the great gray stark structure known as Auburn Prison. Much of the town's life radiated about the prison, and from time to time events at the prison erupted and flowed through the villagers' lives.

The town was a whirl of hills which, one day early in February of this year, were deep with snow. It was two feet high along Genesee Street, the main street named after the Genesee Indians; and from the Exchange Building, where law offices and real estate men were located, the village looked harsh and cold, like a day for little business in the stores, a day to stay inside by the stoves.

On that morning, at eight thirty, the most prominent man in the village, William H. Seward, the lawyer, left his home on South Street, and trudged over the snow-covered slab sidewalks two hundred yards to his office in the newly built Exchange Building. There he was partner with David Wright, Christopher Morgan and Samuel Blatchford in the village's most flourishing law partnership. These were distinguished counsel, whose identities were known in Albany, New York and Washington.

When Seward arrived his clerk, Charles Parsons, greeted him. "Good morning, Governor."

Actually he was no longer Governor. But he had already been Governor of New York twice, his second administration ending in 1842. For the last three years he had been practicing law privately back in Auburn. But the title "Governor" clung to him as a token of respect, and no one called him otherwise, save Mrs. Seward who often called him "Henry" or, if people were about, "Mr. Seward."

The clerk held out a letter and said, "A prison guard brought this in first thing this morning. Said give it to you."

"Thank you, Charles." The clerk was one of several apprentice lawyers, who came from all over the region to learn law in Seward's offices.

Seward placed the note, which was inside an envelope, on his desk and didn't read it at once.

There were newspapers to look through swiftly, weeklies and the New York papers. Seward, a leader of the Whig Party, read his own recent criticism of the Democratic President Polk over the Mexican issue. The Whigs didn't want a war with Mexico that might strengthen the proslavery force, and Polk was drifting toward such a war. Seward noticed the latest on the Oregon question—where there was also a threat of war—this with England.

Then he turned to his own affairs, an issue or two before the Supreme

Court, a patent case, some small affairs about the village, which he delegated to his clerks.

Blatchford came in. Morgan and Wright entered later and went to their desks. The office hummed in the usual way, the cold entering the door each time it opened, and the large stove fuming away all full of coal and heat.

The clerk reminded the Governor of the note from the prison. He read it —a letter from a convict:

> Dear Governor Seward:
>
> I am under indictment for murder. I did murder James Gordon, but I had a reason for it. I don't have no money. I got no friends in this part. If someone dont hear my side of the story the court is going to hang me. I go to trial in two days. Governor Seward, I am please begging you to come see me and give me a chance.
>
> Yours respectfully,
> Henry G. Wyatt

Anything having to do with the prison sparked interest in lawyer Seward. When he had been Governor the problems of penology had fascinated him. Moreover, he didn't like what had come to be known as "the Auburn system" of imprisonment, a harsh system then spreading to most prisons in the nation.

He studied the note—such a personal appeal it was impossible not to do something about it.

The Governor decided to see the man at once. He reached for his black overcoat, his black hat—he dressed in a rich black most of the time—and he carefully put on boots, with leggings that rose to the knees.

"I'll be back soon, Parsons," he said.

Seward wasn't a handsome man. He wasn't always a graceful man either, and he hadn't an orator's smooth voice. People said his voice grated a bit. And, in spite of the expensive clothes he wore, he was sometimes a little careless of his physical appearance. But when the slight, middle-height, nervously energetic Seward stepped into the village streets, walking with power and an inner certainty, slogging through the drifts like his fellow townsmen, Auburnians leaped to life with alacrity and a respectful, "Good morning—*Governor*."

He strolled from his office in the Exchange Building down snow-covered State Street hill to the front entrance of the prison of the village. It gave the commercial section a somber character, and it cast a kind of shadow over the lives of the Auburnians. Some said the long gray walls, stretching for a quarter of a mile, took away from the natural beauty of the place; and that real estate in the neighborhood of the prison never would be too valuable....

Yet the presence of the prison was a source of philosophic uncertainty to Auburnians. Strange stories issued from the institution from time to time, strange stories of torture and insanity and mutiny.

Seward found Henry Wyatt on a stone floor in one of five dungeons beneath the north-wing cell block. He looked down at the manacled figure of Wyatt, who had murdered the inmate named James Gordon. He could barely make out the face of the convict in the dim lamplight. Wyatt's shackles clanked on the concrete.

The keeper told Wyatt, "Here's the Governor."

"Thank God, Governor. Thank God you came!"

"Maybe I can help ... what is it?"

"... Only to see, Governor, that I get a fair trial for this."

Wyatt was a white man with a dark stubble of beard. He was thin now, but before solitary he had been chunky and hard-set.

Seward stayed for an hour. He learned that Wyatt had been imprisoned for ten years on a burglary charge. But he had fallen into trouble with the convict, Gordon, who, trying to ingratiate himself, had told the prison authorities that Wyatt had murdered a man in Ohio and that out there they were looking for the murderer. Wyatt denied it, but the prison officials, trying to get an admission from him, beat him unmercifully. Then they put him into a small, dark and cold dungeon in the lower recesses of the prison. When he came out, he plunged one blade of a large pair of shears into Gordon. Wyatt reasoned that Gordon's stool-pigeon behavior, together with his lies, had got him punished and placed in solitary; it was also a threat to the other inmates. While in the dungeon he decided to kill Gordon; which was only justice, Wyatt told the lawyer.

Seward questioned him particularly about the prison punishments. Wyatt described the ball and chain and the yoke that offenders sometimes had to wear, and which he, Wyatt, had worn; also the cold shower taken in a bath to which he was confined by stocks and straps while water poured on him from a wide-nozzled sprinkler with a fall of about two feet. This hadn't forced a confession from him for a murder he said he knew nothing of, and then he was given "the cat." The cat was a club with six strands of leather at one end, each strand about fifteen inches long. Wyatt had received seventy-five lashes across the back.

Seward asked Wyatt what he had said to his tormentors. Had he protested? Wyatt told them, "It is hard for one white man to take off his shirt to be flogged by another." He also said, "For God's sakes, kill me at once, and not kill me by piecemeal." Prison Keeper Ulysses Doubleday ignored the protests and ordered, "Put it on him as long as he can stand it." Wyatt had not cried out as the lashes fell, but had borne them in silent agony until he toppled over unconscious.

Seward listened with horrified interest. He knew, as an ex-Governor, that the terrors of imprisonment and the barbaric practices then in wide use, particularly at Auburn, could drive men to homicide. When Auburn Prison had been first occupied, in 1819, the jailers had employed the *Newgate system* of handling inmates. Newgate was a prison in Greenwich Village, named after England's Newgate Prison. The convicts were kept in groups, in large pens, without labor—criminals of all ages and types—and it spawned evil. This had been modified and developed into the present *Auburn system,* or *silent system,* which many prisons copied. The procedure isolated one prisoner from the other. They were kept in separate cells at night, and during the day they marched in a curious in-time, lock-step fashion to and from meals, workshops and cells. They must walk with downcast eyes, not speak to each other, and they could not even face each other except if they had to at work. They wore zebra-striped black and white uniforms which would quickly identify them if they tried to escape. It was an efficient method of securing a maximum amount of hard labor.

The human body couldn't withstand such strictures, Seward knew. Such discipline made men "stir crazy," and the lawyer told Wyatt, "I'll see that you get competent counsel."

But as he left the prison and considered Wyatt's crude notions of self-justification, he decided to defend the man himself.

SAMUEL HOPKINS ADAMS

A Finger Lakes Boyhood

Summertimes I exchanged canalside life in Rochester for lake shore adventure in Cayuga County. This came about by the fortunate circumstance of my maternal grandfather, Samuel Miles Hopkins, D. D., buying a point on the east side of Owasco Lake, smallest of the five aquatic "fingers" which form a chain of beauty through the heart of Central New York. There I spent joyous vacation days with my Hopkins relatives and our friends from Auburn, the nearby city which assumed social proprietorship of the locality.

With the coming of summer to the lakes, the youth of the vicinity underwent a radical change of nature. We, who had been land animals, became not only lacustrine, but amphibian. When a new boy came among us he was subjected to an inquisition. The object was to determine his nautical status. The neophyte who could not handle himself as well on or in the water as on land, was out of luck. For, the length and breadth of the Finger Lakes, in the 1880's, aquatics were less a sport than a necessity.

Motor boats were, of course, far in the undreamed future. Steam launches were for millionaires; there were not a dozen on the five lakes. Oar and sail were the standard motive power. No road led to my Grandfather's place. The lake was our sole highway. A mile and a half away, on the opposite shore, the Southern Central Railroad was our medium of supplies and connecting link with the outer world.

The ordeal of a newcomer of the younger generation started with the key question:

"Can you swim?"

If he answered "No," he was sternly bidden to learn, it being indicated that this was not only a measure of self-preservation but also a preliminary to social recognition. The unfortunate ignoramus would be banished from boat and dock until he had learned the art. Once he had qualified in this respect he was examined as to his seamanship.

How would he handle a canoe in a storm? (This was a catch-question, the answer being, "Nobody but a darn fool takes a canoe out in a storm.") Would a flat-bottomed or a round-bottomed boat be safer in a seaway? (A "greeny" was likely to declare for the flat, because of its appearance of superior stability.) Did he row loose-oar or thole-pin? Could he feather? Was a smoothboard or a clinker-built slicker in the water? Then the final test: what did he know about sailing?

Rash, indeed, was the novice who based his pretensions on book-knowledge alone. (*The Boy's Book of Seamanship; How To Sail a Boat in Six Easy Lessons; 25 Cents.*) He might be able to identify a cleat, to distinguish between a halyard and a backstay, to tell how to reef, and to state glibly which tack had the right of way. But, unless he had actually handled tiller and sheet in a blow, he might better go inland and climb a tree than abide our test. For he would be cast adrift in our own private school-ship, appropriately called the *Tub,* and the result was invariably an inglorious grounding on the shore.

The pride of the Hopkins family was an eighteen-foot Sandusky sharpie. She was a lovely, lively little craft, two-masted, high-prowed, drawing less than a foot of water amidships, and stabilized by a deep centerboard. In the hands of experience, this is a safe type for the treacherous Finger Lakes weather, where vicious little gusts come sweeping down from the steep-hilled banks to undo any but the most vigilant expert. Our *Undine* was fast, too, and could show her wake to any competitor in the weekly races.

The sharpie was not for us Hopkins grandchildren, though we might ship as hands and haul the centerboard, or hold a sheet in light weather. Our personal navigation was limited to the rowboats and the *Tub.* This latter was a lumbering, snubnosed, flat-bottomed scow with a leg-of-mutton sail shaped out of one of Grandmother's discarded counterpanes, home-made leeboards, and a sawed-off oar for tiller. We learned about sailing from her.

As the senior of the male grandchildren, I was captain. By the time I was twelve and had handled the *Tub* for two seasons, I deemed myself capable of circumnavigating the globe. My confidence was not shared by my elders, and my control of the *Undine* was limited to a brief handling of the tiller while whatever senior was in charge was lighting his pipe. But the *Tub* had taught me much, and I picked up the rest by attentive observation, which proved to be fortunate. The great gale of 1883 gave me my opportunity.

This July storm was one of the worst three-day blows I have ever known. Owing to unexpected visitors over the week end, our camp larder had run low. Our natural emergency food supply was cut off: no fish would bite in that turmoil. We children brought in some mushrooms from the woods, and Grandfather shot a woodchuck, the fresh meat of which is preferable to starvation, but not greatly. On the fourth day of short rations, Grandmother addressed her husband.

"Samuel, we need bread."

"Yes, my dear."

"We are out of eggs, coffee, milk, bacon and other things that are spoiling in Ensenore station."

Grandfather held up a finger to the whistling gale and looked out across the mile of white spume between us and the far shore.

"It is blowing," he said conservatively.

"I didn't know that a Hopkins would stop for a little wind," she said.

"Quite so, my dear," he answered. He opened the door to the side room. "Come, my sons," he called. "Ensenore."

Uncle Jack and Uncle Woolsey rose from the cribbage board and reached for their caps.

I trailed along to the dock, in the vain hope of being allowed to ship. Grandfather merely remarked that it was no weather for small boys. I watched the *Undine* put out under a handkerchief of canvas on the foremast and rather less aft.

Two hours later she came in, yawing madly under mainsail alone. The foremast had carried away, a foot above the deck, in a wild squall that caught her before the sail could be dropped. The nearest shipyard was on Cayuga Lake, thirty miles away.

Back of the shore was the forest. With hatchet and saw we went mast-hunting. A hemlock of suitable girth and height was located, chopped down and trimmed. In less than two hours we had our improvised mast stepped, stayed and rigged. To the expert eye it appeared serviceable, but there was a flaw somewhere. It held on the next trip over to Ensenore and brought the *Undine* almost in on the return when, crack! And it was overside.

Tamarack is the favored local timber for masts in the lake country. A five-mile tramp to a tamarack bog yielded a likely-looking spar. It did not live up to its looks. Securely stepped and stayed, it bent with supple promise to several gusts—then snapped in tow. Again the *Undine* was a semi-wreck.

"If soft wood won't serve, hard wood may," Grandfather said.

He picked out a shagbark hickory sapling which was tough to fell and trim. It stood up.

Three days is the supposed limit for this type of storm. On the fourth morning the wind dropped, the sun came out, the gale was spent. That's what we thought, who should have known better the treacheries of Finger Lakes weather. Grandfather and Uncle Jack decided to take the morning train for Auburn, so Uncle Woolsey and I sailed them across before as sweet a breeze as a sailor's heart could wish. Having discharged our passengers and taken on cargo, we set out on the return trip. A cloud-bank formed with formidable swiftness in the north. The breeze whipped around and became a gale. Halfway home, my uncle handed me the tiller.

"I don't feel well," he said.

I have always thought that it was the aftermath of the woodchuck, though it may have been an over-age mushroom. In either case, my companion was reduced to total helplessness. The boat was mine to command, with two sails and a rudder to handle in the face of gusts which were rising to fifty-mile-an-hour velocity.

In a long lifetime, I doubt that I have ever felt an equally exhilarating sense of responsibility. For a long half hour I juggled the *Undine* up to windward. I coaxed her, I babied her, I eased her, and between squalls I drove her into the leaping assault of the head-waves.

Open navigation, I decided, was simple, but it could not be kept up indefinitely. My business was to bring my command into port. The problem was a tricky one. I had to put in as near shore as possible without smashing my centerboard upon the rocky bottom, then spin the boat about and nose her into the dock under her own momentum.

Looking up to estimate my distance, I beheld with dismay my grandmother advancing to the narrow and fragile planking which formed the outer span, followed by a bevy of female grandchildren. Now, if I misreckoned and bumped the dock too hard, the whole lot would be in the lake and I in disgrace forever.

I yelled to them to go back, but my voice must have been drowned by the wind. At that desperate moment I felt a grinding beneath my feet. Bottom!

To jam my tiller hard over was instinctive. The sharpie came up gallantly, but a cross-gust caught her and she made for the dock, head on, like a runaway freight car. I gave one last, despairing yelp, one last despairing shove to my tiller, and the prow swerved, missing the woodwork by a mouse's whisker.

When I came about, the dock was empty. The family had seen all they needed of my seamanship. Relieved of the anxiety of a wholesale immersion, I made a respectable landing at my second effort. The female contingent were too busy reviving my uncle to offer any comment at the time. The report must have been favorable, however, for a few days later, my grandfather said quite casually: "Samuel, suppose you and Winthrop (my younger cousin) take the sharpie over for the mail."

I can still see the astonished and envious faces of my contemporaries, gathered at Ensenore pier for the afternoon ceremony of meeting the 5:02, as I nonchalantly threaded the shipping (all manned by adults) and ordered my crew to "make her fast."

A week later I lost my hard-won reputation. Without informing any of us, Grandfather had rigged aloft from foremast to mainmast some sort of contraption which he called a vang. We were returning from Ensenore, I at the helm and Grandfather amidships when we were hit by a gust from the port quarter. It was the merest catspaw and should have made no trouble for the experienced mariner that I deemed myself. But when I eased up on the foresail it stuck. The interfering and unnoticed vang had caught and held the gaff. Over we went, a quarter of a mile from shore, in 150 feet of water.

Notwithstanding his seventy-odd years, the old gentleman, nimble as a spider, skittered up over the side of the slowly capsizing craft, and perched on the bottom, where I miserably joined him by swimming. Some carpenters, working on a barn roof, saw the mishap, came out in a flat, and we were ingloriously rescued. The *Undine* drifted ashore.

When next I showed my shamed face at Ensenore, the whole lake was aware of my disgrace. I was greeted by raucous hoots, saluted as "Captain Tipsytottle," treated to cries of "All hands stand by to abandon ship," and called by the fighting name of "landlubber." I was prepared to regret that I had not gone to the bottom, when Grandfather, like the fine gentleman he was, came to the rescue.

"I wish to hear no more contumelious remarks addressed to my grandson," he thundered in those tones which had made him a noted pulpit orator. "The accident was due entirely to my own carelessness. I have now to inform you all that Samuel will captain the *Undine* in next Saturday's regatta."

It was my day of restored glory. Alas! I did not live up to it. I misread the direction of an offshore puff, lost a twenty-rod advantage, and came in third. But, at least, my nautical status was established on a firm foundation.

Nowadays a score of cars come daily to the place that was my grandfather's and is now mine, bringing all the appurtenances of modern existence. Motor boats whizz past my dock. An occasional amphibian plane churns to a stop off my point. It is all very convenient. Life is far easier than in the old days. But it isn't half as much fun.

EDWARD NOYES WESTCOTT

A Hoss Trade

Mrs. Bixbee went on with her needlework, with an occasional side glance at her brother, who was immersed in the gospel of his politics. ... "Dave," she said, "d' you know what Deakin Perkins is sayin' about ye?"

David opened his paper so as to hide his face, and the corners of his mouth twitched as he asked in return, "Wa'al, what's the deakin sayin' now?"

"He's sayin'," she replied, in a voice of indignation and apprehension, "thet you sold him a balky horse, an' he's goin' to hev the law on ye."

From *David Harum,* by Edward Noyes Westcott. Published by D. Appleton and Company, New York, 1899.

David's shoulders shook behind the sheltering page, and his mouth expanded in a grin.

"Wa'al," he replied after a moment, lowering the paper and looking gravely at his companion over his glasses, "next to the deakin's religious experience, them of lawin' an' horse-tradin' air his strongest p'ints, an' he works the hull on 'em to once sometimes."

The evasiveness of this generality was not lost on Mrs. Bixbee, and she pressed the point with, "Did ye? an' will he?"

"Yes, an' no, an' mebbe, an' mebbe not," was the categorical reply.

"Wa'al," she answered with a snap, "mebbe you call that an answer.... I do believe you've ben playin' some trick on the deakin, an' won't own up. I do wish," she added, "that if you hed to git rid of a balky horse onto somebody you'd hev picked out somebody else."

"When you got a balker to dispose of," said David gravely, "you can't alwus pick an' choose. Fust come, fust served.... Now I'll tell ye. Quite a while ago—in fact, not long after I come to enjoy the priv'lidge of the deakin's acquaintance—we hed a deal. I wasn't jest on my guard, knowin' him to be a deakin an' all that, an' he lied to me so splendid that I was took in, clean over my head. He done me so brown I was burnt in places, an' you c'd smell smoke 'round me fer some time."

"Was it a horse?" asked Mrs. Bixbee gratuitously.

"Wa'al," David replied, "mebbe it *had* ben some time, but at that partic'lar time the only thing to determine that fact was that it wan't nothin' else."

"Wa'al, I declare!" exclaimed Mrs. Bixbee... "I'm 'mazed at the deakin."

"Yes'm," said David with a grin, "I'm quite a liar myself when it comes right down to the hoss bus'nis, but the deakin c'n give me both bowers ev'ry hand. He done it so slick that I had to laugh when I come to think it over—an' I had witnesses to the hull confab, too, that he didn't know of, an' I c'd 've showed him up in great shape if I'd had a mind to."

"Why didn't ye?" said Aunt Polly, whose feelings about the deacon were undergoing a revulsion.

"Wa'al, to tell ye the truth, I was so completely skunked that I hadn't a word to say.... Stid of squealin' 'round the way you say he's doin', like a stuck pig, I kep' my tongue between my teeth an' laid to git even some time."

"You ort to 've hed the law on him," declared Mrs. Bixbee, now fully converted. "The old scamp!"

"Wa'al," was the reply, "I gen'all prefer to settle out of court an'... I reckoned the time 'd come when mebbe I'd git the laugh on the deakin, an' it did, an' we're putty well settled now in full."...

"I wish you'd quit beatin' about the bush, an' tell me the hull story."

"Wa'al, it's like this, then, if you will hev it. I was over to Whiteboro a while ago... an' I seen a couple of fellers halter-exercisin' a hoss in the tavern yard. I stood 'round a spell watchin' 'em, an' when he come to a standstill I went an' looked him over, an' I liked his looks fust rate.

" 'Fer sale?' I says.

" 'Wa'al,' says the chap that was leadin' him, 'I never see the hoss that wa'n't if the price was right.'

" 'Your'n?' I says.

" 'Mine an' his'n,' he says, noddin' his head at the other feller.

" 'What ye askin' fer him?' I says.

" 'One-fifty,' he says.

"I looked him all over agin putty careful, an' once or twice I kind o' shook my head 's if I didn't quite like what I seen, an' when I got through I sort o' half turned away without sayin' anythin', 's if I'd seen enough.

" 'The' ain't a scratch ner a pimple on him,' says the feller, kind o' resentin' my looks. 'He's sound an' kind, an' 'll stand without hitchin', an' a lady c'n drive him 's well 's a man.'

" 'I ain't got anythin' agin him,' I says... 'but one-fifty's a consid'able price fer a hoss these days.'...

" 'He's wuth two hundred jest as he stands,' the feller says. 'He hain't had no trainin', an' he c'n draw two men in a road-wagin better'n fifty.'

"Wa'al, the more I looked at him the better I liked him, but I only says, 'Jes' so, jes' so, he may be wuth the money, but... I hain't got that much money with me if he was,' I says. The other feller hadn't said nothin' up to that time, an' he broke in now. 'I s'pose you'd take him fer a gift, wouldn't ye?' he says, kind o' sneerin'.

"Wa'al, yes,' I says, 'I dunno but I would if you'd throw in a pound of tea an' a halter.'

"He kind o' laughed an' says, 'Wa'al, this ain't no gift enterprise, an' I guess we ain't goin' to trade, but I'd like to know,' he says, 'jest as a matter of curios'ty, what you'd say he was wuth to ye?'

"Wa'al,' I says, 'I come over this mornin' to see a feller that owed me a trifle o' money. Exceptin' of some loose change, what he paid me 's all I got with me,' I says, takin' out my wallet. 'That wad's got a hundred an' twenty-five into it, an' if you'd sooner have your hoss an' halter than the wad,' I says, 'why, I'll bid ye good-day.'

" 'You're offerin' one-twenty-five fer the hoss an' halter?' he says.

" 'That's what I'm doin',' I says.

" 'You've made a trade,' he says, puttin' out his hand fer the money an' handin' the halter over to me."

"An' didn't ye suspicion nuthin' when he took ye up like that?" asked Mrs. Bixbee.

"I did smell woolen some," said David, "but I had the *hoss* an' they had the *money,* an', as fur 's I c'd see, the critter was all right.... I guess this ain't over 'n' above interestin' to ye, is it?" he asked after a pause, looking doubtfully at his sister.

"Yes, 'tis," she asserted. "I'm lookin' forrered to where the deakin comes in, but you jest tell it your own way."

"I'll git there all in good time," said David, "but some of the point of the story'll be lost if I don't tell ye what come fust."

"I allow to stan' it 's long 's you can," she said encouragingly ... "Did ye find out anythin' 'bout them fellers?"

"I ast the barn man if he knowed who they was, an' he said he never seen 'em till the yestiddy before, an' didn't know 'em f'm Adam. They come along with a couple of hosses, one drivin' an' t'other leadin'—the one I bought. I ast him if they knowed who I was, an' he said one on 'em ast him, an' he told him. The feller said to him seein' me drive up: 'That's a putty likely-lookin' hoss. Who's drivin' him?' An' he says to the feller: 'That's Dave Harum, f'm over to Homeville. He's a great feller fer hosses,' he says."

"Dave," said Mrs. Bixbee, "them chaps jest laid fer ye, didn't they?"

"I reckon they did," he admitted; "an' they was as slick a pair as was ever drawed to," which expression was lost upon his sister....

"Wa'al," he resumed, "after the talk with the barn man, I smelt woolen stronger'n ever, but I didn't say nothin', an' had the mare hitched an' started back. Old Jinny drives with one hand, an' I c'd watch the new one all right, an' as we come along I begun to think I wa'n't stuck after all. I never see a hoss travel evener an' nicer, an' when we come to a good level place I sent the old mare along the best she knew, an' the new one never broke his gait, an' kep' right up 'ithout 'par'ntly half tryin'; an' Jinny don't take most folks' dust neither. I swan! 'fore I got home I reckoned I'd jest as good as made seventy-five anyway."

"Then the' wan't nothin' the matter with him, after all," commented Mrs. Bixbee in rather a disappointed tone.

"The meanest thing top of the earth was the matter with him," declared David, "but I didn't find it out till the next afternoon, an' then I found it out good. I hitched him to the open buggy an' went 'round by the East road, 'cause that ain't so much travelled. He went along all right till we got a mile or so out of the village, an' then I slowed him down to a walk. Wa'al, sir, scat my —! He hadn't walked more'n a rod 'fore he come to a dead stan'still. I clucked an' git-app'd, an' finely took the gad to him a little; but he only jest kind o' humped up a little, an' stood like he'd took root."

"Wa'al now!" exclaimed Mrs. Bixbee.

"Yes'm," said David; "I was stuck in ev'ry sense of the word."

"What d'ye do?"

"Wa'al, I tried all the tricks I knowed—an' I could lead him—but when I was in the buggy he wouldn't stir till he got good an' ready; 'n' then he'd start of his own accord an' go on a spell, an'——"

"Did he keep it up?" Mrs. Bixbee interrupted.

"Wa'al, I s'd say he did.... He balked five separate times, varyin' in length, an' it was dark when we struck the barn."

"I should hev thought you'd a wanted to kill him," said Mrs. Bixbee; "an' the fellers that sold him to ye, too."

"The' *was* times," David replied with a nod of his head, "when if he'd a fell down dead I wouldn't hev figgered on puttin' a band on my hat, but it don't never pay to git mad with a hoss; an' as fur 's the feller I bought him of, when I remembered how he told me he'd stand without hitchin', I swan! I had to laugh. I did, fer a fact. 'Stand without hitchin'!' "...

"I guess you wouldn't think it was so awful funny if you hadn't gone an' stuck that horse onto Deakin Perkins...."

"Mebbe that *is* part of the joke," David allowed, "an' I'll tell ye th' rest on't. Th' next day I hitched the new one to the dem'crat wagin an' put in a lot of straps and rope, an' started off fer the East road agin. He went fust rate till we come to about the place where we had the fust trouble, an', sure enough, he balked agin. I leaned over an' hit him a smart cut on the off shoulder, but he only humped a little, an' never lifted a foot. I hit him another lick, with the self-same result. Then I got down an' I strapped that animal so't he couldn't move nothin' but his head an' tail, an' got back into the buggy. Wa'al, bom-by, it may 'a' ben ten minutes, or it may 'a' ben more or less—it's slow work settin' still behind a balkin' hoss—he was ready to go on his own account, but he couldn't budge. He kind o' looked around, much as to say, 'What on earth's the matter?' an' then he tried another move, an' then another, but no go. Then I got down an' took the hopples off an' then climbed back into the buggy, an' says 'Cluck' to him, an' off he stepped as chipper as could be, an' we went joggin' along all right mebbe two mile, an' when I slowed up, up he come agin. I gin him another clip in the same place on the shoulder, an' I got down an' tied him agin, an' the same thing happened as before, on'y it didn't take him quite so long to make up his mind about startin', an' we went some further without a hitch.

But I had to go through the pufformance the third time before he got it into his head that if he didn't go when *I* wanted he couldn't go when *he* wanted, an' that didn't suit him; an' when he felt the whip on his shoulder it meant bus'nis."

"Was that the end of his balkin'?" asked Mrs. Bixbee.

"I had to give him one more go-round," said David, "an' after that I didn't have no more trouble with him...."

"Wa'al, what's the deakin kickin' about then?" asked Aunt Polly. "You're jest sayin' you broke him of balkin'."

"Wa'al," said David slowly, "some hosses will balk with some folks an' not with others. You can't most alwus gen'ally tell."

"Didn't the deakin have a chance to try him?"

"He had all the chance he ast fer," replied David. "Fact is, he done most of the sellin', as well 's the buyin', himself."

"How's that?"

"Wa'al," said David, "...After I'd got the hoss where I c'd handle him I begun to think I'd had some interestin' an valu'ble experience, an' it wa'n't scurcely fair to keep it all to myself. I didn't want no patent on't, an' I was willin' to let some other feller git a piece. So one mornin', week before last ...I allowed to hitch an' drive up past the deakin's an' back....Wa'al, 's I come along I seen the deakin putterin' 'round, an' I waved my hand to him an' went by a-kitin'. I went up the road a ways an' killed a little time, an' when I come back there was the deakin, as I expected. He was leanin' over the fence, an' as I jogged up he hailed me, an' I pulled up.

" 'Mornin', Mr. Harum,' he says.

" 'Mornin', deakin,' I says. 'How are ye? and how's Mis' Perkins these days?'

" 'I'm fair,' he says; 'fair to middlin', but Mis Perkins is ailin' some—*as usyul,*' he says."

"They do say," put in Mrs. Bixbee, "thet Mis' Perkins don't hev much of a time herself."

"Guess she hez all the time the' is," answered David. "Wa'al," he went on, "we passed the time o' day, an' talked a spell about the weather an'... then I says: 'Oh, by the way,' I says, 'I jest thought on't. I heard Dominie White was lookin' fer a hoss that'd suit him.' 'I hain't heard,' he says; but I see in a minute he had...an' I says: 'I've got a road colt risin' five, that I took on a debt a spell ago, that I'll sell reasonable, that's as likely an' nice ev'ry way a young hoss as ever I owned. I don't need him,' I says, 'an' didn't want to take him, but it was that or nothin' at the time an' glad to git it, an' I'll sell him a barg'in. Now what I want to say to you, deakin, is this: That hoss'd suit the dominie to a tee in my opinion, but the dominie won't come to me. Now if *you* was to say to him—bein' in his church an' all thet,' I says, 'that you c'd get him the right kind of a hoss, he'd believe you, an' you an' me'd be doin' a little stroke of bus'nis, an' a favor to the dominie into the bargain. The dominie's well off,' I says, 'an' c'n afford to drive a good hoss.' "

"What did the deakin say?" asked Aunt Polly as David stopped for breath.

"I didn't expect him to jump down my throat," he answered; "but I seen him prick up his ears, an' all the time I was talkin' I noticed him lookin' my hoss over, head an' foot. 'Now I 'member,' he says, 'hearin' sunthin' 'bout Mr. White's lookin' fer a hoss, though when you fust spoke on't it had slipped my mind. Of course,' he says, 'the' ain't any real reason why Mr. White shouldn't deal with you direct, an' yit mebbe I *could* do more with him 'n you could. But,' he says, 'I wa'n't cal'latin' to go t' the village this mornin', an' I sent my hired man off with my drivin' hoss. Mebbe I'll drop 'round in a day or two,' he says, 'an' look at the roan.'

" 'You mightn't ketch me,' I says, 'an' I want to show him myself; an' more'n that,' I says, 'Dug Robinson's after the dominie. I'll tell ye,' I says, 'you jest git in 'ith me an' go down an' look at him an' I'll send ye back or drive ye back, an' if you've got anythin' special on hand you needn't be gone there quarters of an hour,' I says."

"He come, did he?" inquired Mrs. Bixbee.

"He done *so,*" said David sententiously.... "An' he rode a mile an a half livelier 'n he done in a good while, I reckon. He had to pull that old broadbrim of his'n down to his ears, an' don't you fergit it.... Wa'al, we drove into the yard, an' I told the hired man to unhitch the bay hoss an' fetch out the roan, an' while he was bein' unhitched the deakin stood 'round an' never took his eyes off'n him, an' I knowed I wouldn't sell the deakin no roan hoss *that* day, even if I wanted to. But when he come out I begun to crack him up, an' I talked hoss fer all I was wuth. The deakin looked him over in a don't-care kind of way, an' didn't 'parently give much heed to what I was sayin'. Finely I says, 'Wa'al, what do you think of him?' 'Wa'al,' he says, 'he seems to be a likely enough critter, but I don't believe he'd suit Mr. White—'fraid not,' he says. 'What you askin' fer him?' he says. 'One-fifty,' I says, 'an' he's a cheap hoss at the money.' "...

"What did he say?" asked Mrs. Bixbee.

" 'Wa'al,' he says, 'wa'al, I guess you ought to git that much fer him, but I'm 'fraid he ain't what Mr. White wants.' An' then, 'That's quite a hoss we come down with,' he says. 'Had him long?' 'Jest long 'nough to git 'quainted with him,' I says. 'Don't you want the roan fer your own use?' I says. 'Mebbe we c'd shade the price a little.' 'No,' he says, 'I guess not. I don't need another hoss jest now.' An' then, after a minute he says: 'Say, mebbe the bay hoss we drove 'd come nearer the mark fer White, if he's all right. Jest as soon I'd look at him?' he says. 'Wa'al, I hain't no objections, but I guess he's more of a hoss than the dominie 'd care for, but I'll go an' fetch him out,' I says. So I brought him out, an' the deakin looked him all over. I see it was a case of love at fust sight, as the storybooks says. 'Looks all right,' he says. 'I'll tell ye,' I says, 'what the feller I bought him of said to me,' I says, ' "that hoss hain't got a scratch ner a pimple on him. He's sound an' kind, an' 'll stand without hitchin', an' a lady c'd drive him as well 's a man." '

" 'That's what he said to me,' I says, 'an' it's every word on't true. You've seen whether or not he can travel,' I says, 'an', so fur's I've seen, he ain't 'fraid of nothin'.' 'D'ye want to sell him?' the deakin says. 'Wa'al,' I says, 'I ain't offerin' him fer sale. You'll go a good ways,' I says, ''fore you'll strike such another; but, of course, he ain't the only hoss in the world, an' I never had anythin' in the hoss line I wouldn't sell at *some* price.' 'Wa'al,' he says, 'what d' ye ask fer him?' 'Wa'al,' I says, 'if my own brother was to ask me that question I'd say to him two hundred dollars, cash down, an' I wouldn't hold the offer open an hour,' I says."

"My!" ejaculated Aunt Polly. "Did he take you up?"

" 'That's more'n I give fer a hoss 'n a good while,' he says, shaking his head, 'an' more'n I c'n afford, I'm 'fraid.' 'All right,' I says, 'I c'n afford to keep him'; but I knew I had the deakin same as the woodchuck had Skip. 'Hitch up the roan,' I says to Mike; 'the deakin wants to be took up to his house. 'Is that your last word?' he says. 'That's what it is,' I says. 'Two hundred, cash down.' "

"Didn't ye dast to trust the deakin?" asked Mrs. Bixbee.

"Polly," said David, "there's a number of holes in a ten-foot ladder." Mrs. Bixbee seemed to understand this rather ambiguous rejoinder.

"He must 'a' squirmed some," she remarked. David laughed.

"The deakin ain't much used to payin' the other feller's price," he said, "an' it was like pullin' teeth; but . . . after a little more squimmidgin' he hauled out his wallet an' forked over. Mike come out with the roan an' off the deakin went, leadin' the bay hoss."

"I don't see," said Mrs. Bixbee, looking up at her brother, "thet after all the' was anythin' you said to the deakin thet he could ketch holt on."

"The' wa'n't nothin'," he replied. "The only thing he c'n complain about's what I *didn't* say to him."

"Hain't he said anythin' to ye?" Mrs. Bixbee inquired....

"Wa'al, the day but one after the deakin sold himself Mr. Stickin'-Plaster I had an arrant three four mile or so up past his place, an' when I was comin' back, along 'bout four or half past, it come on to rain like all possessed. I had my old umbrel'...an' I sent the old mare along fer all she knew. As I come along to within a mile f'm the deakin's house I seen somebody in the road, an' when I come up closter I see it was the deakin himself, in trouble, an' I kind o' slowed up to see what was goin' on. There he was, settin' all humped up with his old broad-brim hat slopin' down his back, a-sheddin' water like a roof. Then I seen him lean over an' larrup the hoss with the ends of the lines fer all he was wuth. It appeared he hadn't no whip, an' it wouldn't done him no good if he had. Wa'al, sir, rain or no rain, I jest pulled up to watch him. He'd larrup a spell, an' then he'd set back; an' then he'd lean over an' try it again, harder'n ever. Scat my——! I thought I'd die laughin'. I couldn't hardly cluck to the mare when I got ready to move on. I drove alongside an' pulled up. 'Hullo, deakin,' I says, 'what's the matter?' He looked up at me, an' I won't say he was the maddest man I ever see, but he was long ways the maddest-*lookin'* man, an' he shook his fist at me jest like one o' the unregen'rit. 'Consarn ye, Dave Harum,' he says, 'I'll hev the law on ye fer this.' 'What fer?' I says. 'I didn't make it come on to rain, did I?' I says. 'You know mighty well what fer,' he says. 'You sold me this *damned beast,*' he says, 'an' he's balked with me *nine* times this afternoon, an' I'll fix ye for 't,' he says. 'Wa'al, deakin,' I says, 'I'm 'fraid the squire's office 'll be shut up 'fore you *git* there, but I'll take any word you'd like to send. You know I told ye,' I says, 'that he'd stand 'ithout hitchin'.' An' at that he only jest kind o' choked an' sputtered. He was so mad he couldn't say nothin', an' on I drove, an' when I got about forty rod or so I looked back, an' there was the deakin a-comin' along the road with as much of his shoulders as he could git under his hat an' *leadin'* his new hoss."... Aunt Polly wiped her eyes on her apron.

"But, Dave," she said, "did the deakin really say—*that word?"*

"Wa'al," he replied, "if 'twa'n't that it was the puttiest imitation on't that ever I heard."

"David," she continued, "don't you think it putty mean to badger the deakin so't he swore, an' then laugh 'bout it? An' I s'pose you've told the story all over."

"Mis' Bixbee," said David emphatically, "if I'd paid good money to see a funny show I'd be a blamed fool if I didn't laugh, wouldn't I? That specticle of the deakin cost me consid'able, but it was more'n wuth it."

20TH CENTURY

WARREN HUNTING SMITH

The Misses Elliot

There are certain people to whom the name "Geneva" suggests, not the home of the League of Nations, but a town in western New York. Residents of that town use its name with great complacency. If a stranger knows anything, he knows that a Geneva residence is a hallmark of distinction—and, if he doesn't, his ignorance merely exposes him. The old Geneva families came from the proudest stock in the country, and even the obscurest Genevans are somehow distinguished, and know how to live like individuals and not like a flock of sheep.

Two women were choice examples of this Geneva tradition. They weren't unusually handsome or talented; they certainly weren't rich; but they typified those pairs of unmarried sisters, who, like twin constellations, have illuminated Geneva's Main Street—that Great White Way of dazzling personalities. People still talk of the Griscom sisters (who were very good), or the Tibbs sisters (who were very queer), but no sisterly pair has made such inimitable conversation as the Elliot sisters.

They were named Primrose and Candida, names which had a somewhat virginal sound, appropriate to the one hundred and sixty-five years of celibacy which their two lives represented. The Elliots were landed gentry, though the ancestral acres had dwindled to a small and unproductive tract; they were also noted as a family for their wit. The aunts of Miss Primrose and Miss Candida contributed to the "tin-pail poetry" which sent an old kitchen pail banging from door to door on Main Street, accumulating dog-

From *The Misses Elliot of Geneva* by Warren Hunting Smith. Published by Farrar & Rinehart, Inc., New York, 1940. Reprinted by permission of the author.

gerel as it went. Even the most saintly Elliots became deliciously wicked when they had pen in hand and the neighbors in sight.

Their mother was a Miss McGregor, whose family originated in Scotland and ended in a big columned house on Main Street. The McGregors specialized in eccentricity and some of them overdid it. Old Miss Harriet McGregor, for instance, had been dead to the world several years before her actual death led Miss Primrose to remark that "We are *supposed* to be in affliction!"

Then there was Uncle Peter McGregor, a retired clergyman with matrimonial ambitions. He began by courting the Misses Bemis, who lived in an old farmhouse, and who, when their charms began to wane, received visitors by candlelight, in a darkened room—with "plumpers" in their cheeks. Uncle Peter proposed marriage to every girl on Main Street, and he proved conclusively that all Geneva's spinsters were spinsters by preference—not one of them chose to become Mrs. Peter McGregor! Uncle Peter wrote a treatise explaining the Book of Revelation, and sometimes appeared in the chancel with his ear muffs on.

A cousin by marriage was Mrs. James McGregor—a Protestant of Protestants. As someone said, "In those days we were all Low-Church, but the James McGregors were simply groveling!" Mrs. James would hold up her fan in church to preserve her eyes from glimpses of Popish ritual, and would linger in the vestibule until the processional cross had wended its Romeward way into the chancel.

Also there was Aunt Annabel, a precursor of the Prohibitionists, whose zeal for temperance was only abated by great old age and a doddering mind. There was Aunt Maria, who had eighty-one godchildren, and prayed for each one by name, every night. There was Aunt Tabitha, who tied strings to her cats so that she could catch them even when they climbed trees. There was Aunt Louisa who took her siesta under a pink veil to improve her complexion. There was Cousin Augusta who kept her baby chickens under a feather duster when the mother hen died.

The Elliots' spiritual ancestors were more important, however, than their lineal ones. The English race has been noted for its peppery old ladies, ever since the days of Queen Elizabeth, who was the most peppery of them all. You can read about them in any Victorian novel. You used to find them in inexpensive hotels in Brittany and Normandy, maintaining British frigidity among voluble foreigners; you could see them in every English country town, arguing with the vicar, and putting the squire in his place; you could find them in Charleston, Richmond, and Savannah, running boardinghouses and saying what they thought about the Yankees; you could get glimpses of them in New England villages, in old white houses under the elms. Above all, you could see them in English cathedrals, when the choirboys had disappeared down the dark aisles after evensong, and the organ fugue was punctuated by the tapping of canes from old ladies going home to tea.

It was said that Miss Primrose and Miss Candida refused their many suitors because they were afraid of perpetuating the family eccentricities. Nothing could be more unlikely; the Elliots were rather proud to be different from other people; the truth probably was that they were happier as they were. When you had once lived with an Elliot, living with a mere husband would have seemed very dull. Miss Agatha Van Bruggen said that she'd rather be kicked downstairs every day by a husband than remain an old maid, but the Elliots regarded Miss Agatha as a traitor to her sex—after all, she could have married their Uncle Peter, who never kicked anybody. People like Miss Agatha deserved a few kicks, but nobody would ever dare kick the Elliots!

Certainly the two sisters couldn't have had a better time. They had coming-out parties in the 1860's and were launched on the endless succession of dinners, dances, picnics, and sketching jaunts which were Geneva's chief diversions then. They had friends in all the eastern states, and they visited and entertained constantly. They didn't have much money, but in Geneva that doesn't matter.

To those of us who saw the Elliots only in their old age, their youth is hard to imagine. The perfect Geneva gentlewoman was such a finished product, that we forgot about her formative stages; she seemed to have sprung, full-grown, like Athena from the brain of Zeus. There was nothing girlish about the Elliots as I remember them. Miss Primrose was the shorter of the two, and stockier in build; she wore glasses. Miss Candida was taller, and slightly stooped, with ffuffy gray hair escaping from the confinement of her hat. Their clothes were rather old-fashioned, as befitted Geneva ladies of their type; even gentlemen, in Geneva, clung to old styles, and a man's parasol was still seen there in recent years, pursued by small boys shouting, "Hey, mister, it ain't raining!"

The golden age of the Elliot sisters started in their middle years when they retired to a many-gabled cottage, a little apart from the more pretentious mansions on Main Street. They designed it themselves, and made it so inconvenient that it remained vacant for years after they died. Here began that career of sparkling originality which made the Elliots a real Geneva institution. To be merely queer is no achievement, but to be brilliantly individualistic is a fine art which Geneva brought to perfection.

We were rather scornful, in Geneva, when well-meaning visitors compared our town to Cranford. Mrs. Gaskell's village was charming, we admitted, but most Genevans would have found it rather dull and prim. In Geneva we called a spade a spade, and we would have used a much earthier word if we could have found one—none of this middle-class prudery for us! When a bathing beauty performed in our midst, we said that she looked like a hussy with her clothes on, and looked even hussier with them off!

The Elliot sisters never minced their words. Their teamwork was excellent. Miss Candida supplied the gunpowder, and Miss Primrose exploded the fireworks. There would be a quiver of eyeglasses on Miss Primrose's emphatic nose, and out would come a sentence which would shatter the entire tea party. The collaborations of the two sisters were usually concealed, and Miss Primrose got all the credit for their masterpieces until her death left Miss Candida in possession of the field—and of most of the gunpowder.

People noticed that the Elliots' witticisms usually had a strong Biblical flavor. Somebody said that "to hear them talk, you'd think that God had given us the Bible just so that Primrose and Candida could make puns from it."

There was good reason, however, for this scriptural basis. The Bible supplied the two sisters with much more than puns. The Elliots were often fired with righteous indignation, and were at their fiercest in ecclesiastical disputes. They provided plenty of entertainment for their fellow townspeople, but they supplied a good deal of propaganda with it; it was the propaganda which gave cohesion to the entertainment, because a mere string of bon mots would have been pointless without the Elliots' crusades behind them. The two sisters stood up for the things in which they believed, and they seemed to think that divine aid was supporting them; their political and religious convictions were the backbone of their conversation and behavior. You had to respect them even while you laughed with them.

The Mayor of Geneva was almost routed from his office after the Elliots had seen the architect's drawings for the new city hall.

"We may not be architects," said Miss Candida, "but we know an ugly building when we see one!"

"We won't give any of our money to this municipal chicken coop of yours!" said Miss Primrose.

"If those plate-glass windows shed any light on the city administration, we'll approve of them," said Miss Candida.

"If your window washing is like your street cleaning, you'll see through a glass darkly," said Miss Primrose.

"You city officials always see through a glass darkly," said Miss Candida.

"Except when you assess us for taxes, and then you see through a magnifying glass!" said Miss Primrose.

As the dialogue progressed, the Elliots grew hotter and hotter, and every word sounded like a stone smashing one of the infamous plate-glass windows. The mayor almost had to call the fire department to extinguish the Elliots. There was something Olympian about their wrath; they didn't scowl and sputter like cross old women, nor did they raise their voices to a cackle; they merely stood in majesty, filling the air with crackling sparks of invective.

On their travels, they were Geneva's best ambassadors. "You have never heard of Geneva?" exclaimed Miss Primrose, "—then who *can* your friends be!" Though they had occasionally lived in other places, the Elliots wouldn't dream of saying that they were from Newport or Washington; the treachery of a Genevan who preferred to mention his Milwaukee origins aroused their loftiest scorn. Wherever they went, they were "the Misses Elliot of Geneva." At parties, they used to wear long kid gloves which enveloped them to the elbows in leathery armor. Hostesses found them stimulating but rather alarming; they left the impression that no place could be so well-bred or so terrifying as Geneva. To an adopted Genevan, Miss Primrose said:

"That happened before you were born—I mean, before you came to Geneva, because of course you weren't really born till you came here!"

"A woman who can pass muster in Geneva can pass muster anywhere!" they used to say.

In spite of such loyalties, they were full of sinister suspicions. They suspected the postman of stealing letters (their letters were well worth stealing, but the postman didn't know it), and so they took their mail "downstreet" to the post office. "There go the steam engines," a neighbor would say, on seeing the Elliot sisters puffing down the street, on a hot July afternoon, to post a letter. They quarreled with the cemetery commission over a burial lot; their ancestors had probably fought over castles and manors with the same feudal vigor which Miss Primrose and Miss Candida displayed over a few yards of cemetery turf.

Such tenacity, however, is in the true Geneva tradition. Genevans are apt to be greatly attached to worldly possessions, and one of the Van Bruggen sisters refused to mention her diamonds in her will, "because it would be too bad if she couldn't keep something for herself!" The other sister used to wear a sort of necklace of ancestral miniatures which she prized so highly that somebody suggested that she use it for a rosary. People's possessions often seemed to be the most important part of them; one gentleman's obituary devoted most of its space to the deceased's house, and merely referred to the late owner as a worthy occupant of the family mansion.

The Elliots, besides contesting the ownership of the cemetery lot, waged war on the local railroad company. They had bought shares of stock in it and got no dividends. Obviously the president of the company must be an embezzler. When they read in the paper that he had bought a new yacht, with red trimmings, they said that it had good reason to blush—it was named *The Dardanelles* but they called it *The Dividends*. Likewise their baker was suspected of conniving at a gas station near their house, and instantly their weekly order of a loaf of bread was canceled. They became embroiled with the Ladies' Book Club, that circulating library which, the Elliots said, circulated only in the opposite direction to their house. They resigned from the club with a great éclat, and so it was very awkward when a missing pair of the red-covered books was found amid snowdrifts on the Elliots' porch, one winter morning. Amazing things were always happening to them, and someone said that if you threw a leg of lamb out the window it would be sure to hit Miss Candida on the head. They installed a new lavatory in their house, and the plumber put the most essential fixture in a place where it couldn't possibly be sat upon—he probably couldn't imagine the Misses Elliot really using it.

At every great Geneva function, the Elliots took a prominent part. They went to a masquerade dressed as mother and daughter (Miss Candida, being younger, slimmer, and without glasses, was "daughter"); their arrivals and departures were significant moments at every party that they attended. They gave parties themselves, and it was a guest of theirs who used up fourteen starched white petticoats in one week's visit to Geneva; the Elliots' kid gloves were in evidence at even the simplest family gatherings. Their own parties were small ones (in that tiny house they had to be!) but the Elliots regarded large entertainments as almost vulgar.

"Party!" said Miss Primrose. "It was a town meeting!"

When they entertained guests at tea, the toast or the biscuits were sure to be slightly burned, and Miss Primrose would say "Have a burnt offering!" as she passed the dish. People hinted that the Elliots' toast was specially singed for the sake of that pun, or, perhaps, to prevent guests from eating too much, though the Elliots certainly weren't like the poor little Misses Griscom, who would invite you to share the drumstick of a chicken for lunch.

"Eat a good breakfast, Isabella," said Miss Evelina Scott to her sister, "you're going to the Griscoms' for lunch!"

The Elliots wouldn't have succeeded so well without the support of their fellow citizens. Some places would merely have resented their oddities; Geneva recognized them as artistic triumphs. Other towns might have ignored the Elliot ancestry and family portraits, but Geneva gave them proper homage. It also gave them competition, because there were plenty of people in town who were almost as odd, as aristocratic, and as tempestuous as the Elliots. Somebody once said to an Elliot cousin: "You know, I've met the strangest people lately, and they're all your relations!" It might have been said to almost anybody in Geneva.

When Miss Primrose went out to tea, she could expect to meet people before whom anybody but a true Genevan might well falter. When one woman declined an invitation because her false teeth were being fixed, and might drop out during a brilliant remark, her host answered that if he could be sure of the remark, he wouldn't care what else dropped with it. A real Genevan would hate to admit that her remarks weren't brilliant; she might occasionally overstep the bounds of truth, kindness, and decency, but those of brilliance she considered sacred. She might be completely ignorant, but a Geneva upbringing was the best sort of education for conversational purposes; if it didn't produce at least a sprinkling of wit, nothing else could. When people objected to what she said, she could reply that it was her business as a guest to be entertaining, and that they ought to be grateful, even if she sometimes insulted their friends and outraged their sense of propriety. When anything clever is repeated nowadays, old people can always remember having heard it years ago in Geneva.

The Elliots, therefore, had plenty of competitors in repartee; they had even more rivals in eccentricity. Geneva's garden of individuality produced many rare blooms; they flourished on each side of Main Street; their fragrance still lingers in the places where they were. Perhaps the choicest examples were the clerical ones. These were unusually numerous in Geneva; in fact somebody gave a clerical party in the '60's and overlooked several eligible guests. ("We forgot that they were clerical!" wrote the rector's daughter.) The Elliots' Uncle Peter was a rather humble member of this array of exotics; he attributed his oddities to the fact that he had had the measles and a stepmother when he was only three years old. One Geneva cleric retired from his labors to become a Passionist monk, and another should have retired (people said) to become sultan of a harem, although our dear old Miss Susie Griscom said that she had been his secretary for eight years, and he never made any improper advances to her!

In Geneva, you could do just as you pleased, with the reassuring knowledge that other people would probably outdo you. Miss Primrose and Miss Candida had their own way of doing things, and they followed that way without caring what other people might think about it. Even so had the saints of the church and the geniuses of art and science trod their solitary paths. The Elliots might not be saints or geniuses, and their paths certainly weren't solitary, but that made no difference. Other people might need such excuses, but, for Miss Primrose and Miss Candida, it was sufficient to be just "the Misses Elliot of Geneva."

The Misses Elliot and the Glorious Fourth

"I wish that those Revolutionary patriots didn't have such belligerent daughters," said the rector, one Fourth of July, after the Misses Elliot had been instructing him about the annual service for the Daughters of the Revolution. He was an object of suspicion because he suffered under the double handicap of being English and High-Church, and, to make matters worse, he was to be assisted by the college chaplain who was Canadian, by the sexton who was Scotch, and by a temporary organist who was English too. The Elliots felt that a patriotic service could hardly be in more unsympathetic hands, and they were arranging every detail beforehand, so as to leave no opportunity for sabotage.

"Last year, I'm sure that Dr. Tilton sang 'God Save the King' to the tune of 'My Country, 'Tis of Thee,'" said Miss Primrose. "This time we'll have the 'Star-Spangled Banner'—there's no English anthem to that tune!"

The Elliots gave the organist full instructions, and told him that if they caught him playing "Britannia Rules the Waves!" during the offertory, they'd have him deported to London. The Elliots might admire England on three hundred and sixty-four days of the year, but on the Fourth of July, they became its bitterest foe. They unfurled their flags with as much animosity as if they were waving red rags in John Bull's face.

Of course they hung out a flag in front of their own house, but there were other flags which were to be used to decorate the church. It wasn't enough to hoist a single emblem over the church door; the whole interior had to be decorated as if for a political convention. The sisters came pounding down the street like an army with banners, and proceeded to swathe the chancel in red, white and blue. The rector had a hard time getting into the pulpit across entanglements of bunting.

The Fourth of July service was the one service which the Elliots attended from beginning to end. At ordinary services, they would dash into the vestibule after the offertory because they resented seeing the congregation stand up at that moment. On Sundays, they usually left early because their maid was out, and they had to get dinner started.

"We call our pew Martha's Vineyard," said Miss Primrose, "because Martha in the Bible was busy with many things."

On the Fourth of July, however, the Elliots remained in eagle-eyed attendance during every moment of the service. It wouldn't do to dodge the offertory, and let the rector take advantage of their absence to sneak in a prayer for King George. As for their Fourth of July luncheon, it would have given them acute indigestion if, by leaving early, they had given the sexton a chance to spit on their American flags. The sexton had no intention of spitting on any flags, not being of the spitting persuasion, but the Elliots didn't trust him.

"That church flag looks as if it had been in the Battle of Bull Run," said Miss Primrose, "and don't tell me that moths made all those holes!"

Somebody remarked that the sexton must be the most powerful spitter in the country to be able to penetrate two thicknesses of bunting. Miss Primrose said that she didn't know about that, but there certainly were holes in the flag, with suspicious-looking stains around their edges.

"Perhaps he just flicks his cigarette ashes on it," she said.

The congregation was small, partly because the weather was very hot, and partly because many parishioners were afraid that if they attended, they might unconsciously do something which the Elliots would interpret as unpatriotic or High-Church.

"Why, if you even wore a red necktie on the Fourth of July," said the sexton, "those Daughters of the Revolution would think you were sympathizing with British tyranny!"

This time, things seemed to be going unusually well for the Elliots. They approved of the sermon almost as much as if they had written it themselves, and in fact they had dictated so many of its salient points that they might just as well have written it. The rector said that all he needed to do for a Fourth of July sermon was to write down some of the admonitions which the Elliots had been giving him during the previous week.

At the last moment, came disaster. The rector had to step over a flag-draped rail (there was no room to go around it), and a gasp of horror came from "Martha's Vineyard" when the Elliots saw that his heel caught in one corner of the sacred banner.

"Trampling on the flag!" hissed Miss Candida.

"He didn't need to go over that rail!" said Miss Primrose. "He could have blessed us just as well from the pulpit as from the altar, and I don't think that a blessing from someone who's trampled on the flag is worth much anyhow!"

When the service was over, the Elliots went out into the vestry room to tell the rector just what they thought about it all. He was wiping the perspiration from his forehead, for it was a very hot day, but the Elliots made him perspire a lot more.

"Maybe you Englishmen are in the habit of wiping your feet on your national banner," said Miss Candida, "but here in America, we respect our country's flag!"

They gathered up their desecrated decorations, and took them home again. The sexton offered to help, but his services were spurned. It was bad enough to have the rector trample on the flag—goodness knows what the sexton might not do to it! When the Elliots reached home, they examined the flag for traces of the rector's footprints.

"I'm sure his shoes were dirty," said Miss Candida.

"The whole building was dirty," said Miss Primrose. "That rail was so sooty that I told the sexton it looked as if he'd been decorating it for Ash Wednesday!"

The sexton himself said that he might just as well have been at the Battle of Bunker Hill as in Trinity Church on the Fourth of July, and that he supposed that the Daughters of the Revolution would be bringing firecrackers to church next year, but thank goodness Roman candles would be too High-Church for them!

Next year, the worm turned. When the Elliots came to arrange the annual patriotic service, the rector told them that he was going to be away during July.

"But who will take the service on the Fourth?" they asked.

"Dr. Dodge will be in charge while I'm away," said the rector. "You can talk to him about it."

Dr. Dodge was known to the Elliots only by reputation, but he was reputed to be the highest High Churchman within a radius of fifty miles, and they would just as soon listen to the Pope himself on the Fourth of July. They found so many faults with his sermon that it left them weak and speechless with indignation, and it hardly seemed worth while to fuss about anything so hopeless. The sexton, however, felt that for once the Fourth of July had been celebrated in a proper spirit of independence.

ROGER BURLINGAME

"Summer Devils"

How or when the summer devils began in Glenvil was never exactly known. The farmers hardly knew about it until they were in full swing in the middle nineties: Homer Burdett, driving his buggy down Oneida Street, noticed the different tilt to the parasols and the immensity of the balloon sleeves which no villager could have dared. Certainly these things did not belong to residents or their guests: Homer knew the residents and their house guests; when they ventured outside the walls of the estates they drove in carriages or rode horseback. He watched the parasols bobbing up and down, in and out of the stores, in and out of houses and announced that he would be goldarned.

"Yah," said Jake Sullivan the butcher, "them is the summer devils."

"How come?" said Burdett.

"Well, Homer, if you'd ever come down street you'd knowed. But you folks stickin' on your farms—I don't see how you stand it day in, day out, winter 'n' summer never seein' nobody—well, I say, if you'd of come down street to mix a little with us villagers, you'd knowed."

"Us on the farms works," said Homer. "Where do they live? Hotel?"

"Huh," said Sullivan, his lip curling down with scorn, "not them. Them soilin' their pretty dresses on the porches of the Glenvil Arrums? With all the drummers? No, Homer, you're clean out of the world out there. They lodges with my wife 'n' with May Baxter 'n' with Julie Flanagan 'n' with old Mrs. Higgins on Flanagan Street. Take, now, Mary Bryce, her's ben with my missis goin' on five year."

"I know her," said Burdett, "ben out to the farm makin' up to Mrs. Burdett and the kids, goldarn busybody. Wouldn't call her a summer devil exactly though, would you, Jake?"

"No, couldn't hardly call Mary a summer devil. No, you wouldn't hardly know what to call Mrs. Bryce. I wouldn't call her a busybody, neither, Homer."

"Um, got her nose in everywhere. This temperance 'n' cruelty to animals 'n' charity to folks don't need charity . . ."

"Does a lot of good, too, remember that. She was up a lot of nights with my Jane afore she died. That kind of busybody does a hull lot of good. I don't hold with temperance but yet I figure one saloon's enough for this here town 'stead of five outside of hotels."

1915

There were few automobiles in Glenvil in 1915. The old Cherry Valley turnpike, after it passed the Burdett farm, dodged the village elaborately: made, in fact, a half circle round it to the south, giving it quite a wide berth. No one knew why this had happened in the first place but, having happened, there was a coalition among the Van Huytens to keep it there. When the motor first raised its head as a menace, the Van Huytens sent lobbyists to Albany to prevent any short cut imperiling their beloved village with the horrible contraptions. Good heavens, wasn't it bad enough having two railroads?

The Van Huytens themselves (except the radical, Eldred) disdained motor cars. Eldred had to have one because he was a banker and had to get around. The others stuck to their dogcarts, surreys, runabouts, and coaches, and all of them except the Queen, Nick, and Hilda rode horseback.

So Woodie, as he trotted down Oneida Street with Mary, was undisturbed. Woodie didn't like automobiles either.

As she turned, at the end of Oneida Street, Mary saw a number of young people wandering out of the club with tennis rackets. They were sweet, inconsequential adolescents having nowhere to go, nothing to do, no purpose but to enjoy the long summer in this paradise. They would play a few sets of tennis, swim, eat, walk, swim again, dance, and go out in canoes in the moonlight. They loved in their light, cool way as they did everything; nothing seemed to go any deeper than their songs: *Oh, You Beautiful Lady,* and *Flow, River, Flow Down to the Sea;* beyond hand-holding in the dark and the rarest of shy kisses, they were utterly virginal. And yet the summer was never long enough for them. *That* they loved truly: the summer and Glenvil.

Most of them bowed to Mary; she watched them, smiling. The girls wore the simple, full dresses which Mrs. Irene Castle had caused to supplant the horror of the hobble: blue, pink, white, green, all expensive. The boys wore their eternal white trousers—two pairs a day. They were all delicious, Mary thought, no more to be taken seriously than the children in a Della Robbia frieze—these junior summer devils. She knew their names: Evelyn and Pauline Sutphin, the galumphing McMurtrie twins, Reggie Marsters who ate at Mrs. Sullivan's and nearly drove Mary distracted with his whistling of *Tipperary*—he stopped now between Good-by and Leicester Square to bow and smile and went on with his hands in his pockets: It's a long, long way. Mary used to laugh when summer devils brought her their children's problems: "But after all, my dear, they *don't* have to live on salt pork and soggy apple pie all winter!"

The Picnic

The heat lifted, at last, from the junction of the valleys and in the first week of August, a fine northwest wind made whitecaps on the blue lake. There was a series of electric days so vigorous and inspiriting that people could hardly contain their joy of being alive. The young played and swam and sailed themselves into a coma, the middle-aged became dangerously young and stood on the edge of folly, the old felt the sun, like a nostalgic fluid, warm about their bones. In the fields the burdened timothy bent low in the wind and the wind sang for the reaper. The corn was a high jungle, the tassels showered prolific pollen in a burst of love on the silk and the sheaths reddened at the secret growing of the ears. In a hundred barns the hay settled, filling the spaces below the rafters with an unbearable sweetness intoxicating to occasional lovesick youth which took refuge there in the cool afternoons. Beyond Pig Flats on the Augustus Road Jimmy Raymond looked at his steady golden vane against the blue, oiled and burnished his engine, trundled the old thresher from its shed to repair its belts, and in the valley of the creek a boy inhaled the first scent of greenings and laughed at the machine that crushed them.

It was these days that decided the Van Huytens to have a Picnic. This mid-summer event was spelled with a capital and it was no joke. The Bart Van Goghs, the social members of the tribe, were in charge of invitations. Margaret Van Gogh knew precisely whom to honor, whom to neglect, and whom to spite. This was important to the summer people for the Picnic in full career made quite a show as it paraded past the boarding houses and past the club and those who were not honored would do well not to show themselves to those who were.

It was decided to have the Picnic on Sanford's Ridge east of Augustus. As it was to be a large and rather inclusive picnic, it was not desirable to have it invade the privacy of the lake. The ridge, on the other hand, would provide a fine long drive and a good ride for the horsemen. Also it was geographically desirable. It was not, strictly, a ridge—the Connecticut Yankee, Sanford, had named it when sick for home amid the rolling lands—but a long hill running north and south. So its west slope provided, during supper, a superb sunset and, after the dishes were gathered up, the party could stroll across the summit and observe an equally spectacular rise of the full moon. And the Augustus Inn below, a quaint old tavern, said, erroneously, to derive from stagecoach days, supplied feed and stabling for the horses as well as hasty cocktails for the wilder males.

The Picnic would certainly provide less show, thought Mary Bryce, since the war had destroyed the count's tally-ho. He rushed to her, nevertheless, with an invitation to sit beside him in his dogcart which was almost as high. So Mary unpacked all her trunks and carefully sorted out a costume to do him honor and then, like a girl again under the various magic auspices, could hardly wait for the day.

1920

The spring of '20 seemed to come slower than other springs, perhaps because people were unusually eager for it. It was May before the ice was gone from the edges of the creek; mid-May before the last of the frost went out of the ground. Even then, nobody dared set out the frail tomato plants and people were watching the fruit trees warily. Warm days were liable to be treacherous, played tricks on the apples. Not that anybody made anything on apples any more, not unless you went into it in a big way. Henry Miles went into it in a big way, sending off carloads of crated Baldwins. Well, you had to do most everything in a big way, else you were sunk.

But the spring finally came and Glenvil was gay and animated. Farmers driving up and down Oneida Street stopped their Fords under the new maple leaves to talk, blocking the unexpected traffic behind them.

"Onions that high."

"Lose any stock?"

"Yah, one sow. Her was no good anyhow."

"Seen the new turnpike?"

"On my way down thar. I don't hold with it though."

"Me neither but thar's them that does."

"Thar's them that holds with a lot of things."

Oneida Street, after it crossed the creek, ran into a narrow and muddy detour round an abyss. In the abyss worked Italians with picks. They worked all the way east to Burdett's farm, hundreds of them, and at night red lanterns glowed along the edges. This was the new road that would cut off ten miles of the Cherry Valley Turnpike and bring thousands of cars through Glenvil to Ilium and the West. The villagers hung about watching the work, figuring the folks that would stop in at their stores.

"But, it'll take years."

"Naw, done before you know it. Before you can stock up."

"Asphawlt?"

"Naw, concrete!"

"Say, it'll change this old burg some, huh?"

"Time something did."

1924

Mary was up and out before the people in the next room were awake. She saw Mrs. Sullivan's sign: Tourists Accommodated, Chicken Dinners, on her way down the piazza steps. The house with its white paint was certainly neater than in the old crushed strawberry days. It was an ugly house anyway; it had started yellow with the filigree in brown and had turned strawberry in the early nineteen hundreds with the first summer-devil prosperity.

The sun was bright and hot on the washed trees. It was a lovely soft day. Half-way down Flanagan Street, Mary stopped. The old wooden high school was gone. In its place was a yard and well back from the street an enormous brick building with a cornice of white stone. Mary stood still to study it. It was so early that no one was in the yard. She tried to read the inscription which ran the length of the building on the cornice.

Presently a girl passed and Mary spoke to her.

"Will you read that for me?" she said.

"Yes, it says The Cyrus Jones Meachem High School, I don't know what CMXXII means.

"Oh," said Mary. "Nineteen twenty-two; so it's been there two years."

"I guess so. We came a year ago and it was very new then."

"I thought I didn't recognize you. I used to know most of the Glenvil people."

"Glenvil people? We're from Ilium. There's a lot of Ilium people here. Dad commutes."

"I see. I lived here for nearly thirty years. You may have heard of me. I'm Mary Bryce."

"I wouldn't know. We don't know the old timers. We know the Meachems of course, everybody knows them, and the Van Huytens."

"The Van Huytens. . . ."

"Yes, they're from Ilium too."

The school building was very impressive. Mary had protested so often in the board meetings against that old, ugly, wooden fire-trap of a high school.

She went on by the Higginses', the Grover Billingses', and the Applebys'. She thought of dropping in to see these people but of course it was too early. Mrs. Higgins had evidently not been so lucky in the tourist trade as Mrs. Sullivan, her old house was down at the heel. Mary passed the Presby church with the bronze soldiers' monument in front of it and then she was on Oneida Street.

It was tremendous. It had been widened, cutting into the lawns. It was concrete from curb to curb. Already the cars were flashing by, tourist cars bound for the West with baggage and tents strapped on behind; limousines, long open cars, little Fords and roadsters which Mary would always call runabouts. They all moved fast and purposefully as if their destinations were far away. Mary saw a Michigan and an Illinois license.

She looked west and saw the rows of old maples converge in the spot of blue where the lake was. They were the same trees and behind them stood the same houses: the Polks', the Baxters', the Jennings' and the Reillys', it was all the same except for the road and lovely but for the road and the noise of the cars. But Mary turned away from it and went east. Oneida Street as it ran into the center of the village was certainly astonishing.

The sidewalks were all new concrete. The big stone flags were gone. The high curbs built for the high rigs were low now; they had raised the street. At intervals, on both sides, were concrete posts with clusters of electric lights. Across the street from the window of Lawyer Green's office to the window over the old Candy Kitchen (more recently Susan Shane's) hung a tremendous banner, white, with the words in red:

WELCOME TO GLENVIL THE LAKE PARADISE.

Across the street where Reilly's grocery store had been, and including also the Chenango Saloon, was the Great Atlantic and Pacific Tea Company—they needed two store fronts for a name as long as that; next it, on the corner, Cobb's drugstore was now the United Cigar Stores. These places had stucco fronts over the painted brick. Polk's Furniture and Undertaking was still recognizable by the sign: Polk, Inc. Radios. Cars were coming in to the curbs now and arranging themselves obliquely. A policeman in a new uniform was regulating them. Mary shaded her eyes to look at him. It was Al Desmond, young brother of Paddy who had been sent to the State penitentiary for forging various Van Huyten names on checks. I'll speak to him later, Mary thought. But an uncertainly driven Ford came in parallel to the curb and Al came over.

"Can't leave it that way, Mr. Burdett," he said, "new rules."

Mary drove back over the lake road in the dark shade of the original woods, by the gate of the Mansion with its arms—the motto: *Ce que l'honneur exige* almost obliterated and the stone posts green with moss; by The Willows, dark and forbidding, by the gayer Van Gogh house and, suddenly, she was in a wide concrete thoroughfare with fast cars running by her. The new turnpike, the State road....

Here the aspect of everything was new. The summer-devil club was gone, its trees cut down and the space transformed into a park with benches and white drinking fountains. Children played there: one small villager was sailing his toy boat in the lake.

Next came an enormous house; ah, and quite good looking, too, in the conventional and dignified Georgian style. Well, after all, it might have been worse—much worse, thought Mary, remembering the derrick. And there was some very fine planting round it.

Then the club—her club—full of young people, mostly girls, looking so smart in their white tennis clothes and Helen Wills eyeshades that Mary wondered if they could really be villagers.

Beyond the club there was a stretch of unbroken woods: they were thin, you could see the lake through them but, thank heaven, Ruth had left them. Here! What a nice brick gate!

Mary drove through slowly on to the crunchy, blue gravel drive and stopped so suddenly that the car slid.

But it was beautiful!

It was brick and pure Dutch with a steep roof and enormous chimneys at the ends. It stood in the center of a clearing in the woods, almost a casual clearing, Mary thought, though it would look less casual when the lawns had grown deeper and smoother. The house stood sharp against the blue of the sky and the lake.

Mary got out and walked with a timidity that surprised her when she thought about it, to the door.

The upper half of the door was open and Mary looked through a wide paneled hall to another door that gave on a terrace and the lake. Evidently there were some young people on the terrace: she heard their voices remotely. But suddenly a single voice began to speak: a strange, metallic, unhuman voice that drowned out everything. It grew louder until it rang and echoed and resounded through the house and then it seemed eternal and inevitable like the voice of Destiny with no beginning or end. It held Mary so magnetized that she could not ring or go in or, in fact, move at all.

"And I repeat," the voice was saying, "that we stand today on the threshold of a new era; a new dawn undreamed of in the philosophy of our ancestors brightens the sky before us. The war is behind our backs, forgotten, the traditions of that moribund age which brought it to pass are fading into an obscure twilight; before us lies the land of promise awaiting us. Friends, we are coming out of chaos into order. For a time old morals were overturned and established convictions disturbed, but now clear young eyes are looking forward through the mists. They are seeing a new tolerance and a new freedom guided by science, they see the arts reborn—"...

ROMEYN BERRY

The Importance of Buckwheat

No one truly grasps the importance of buckwheat in the life of America until he starts these cold, winter mornings on a slice of dry toast and a cup of black coffee which have been falsely denominated "breakfast". On mornings when the snow creaks under foot, when the kitchen

From *Dirt Roads to Stoneposts* by Romeyn Berry. Published by Century House, Watkins Glen, N.Y., 1949. Reprinted by permission of the publisher.

windows are solid with frost and when teasing smells from the skillet waft through the chilly halls, I am inspired to suggest that the true symbol of America should be, not the eagle which embellishes our coins and public buildings, but rather a stack of hot buckwheat cakes surrounded cunningly by smoking sausages whose savory juices struggle ever in vain to unite themselves with the maple syrup which drools from the roof of the enticing mound.

I am informed and believe that the principal uses of buckwheat are to sustain the over-worked hen and to round out the winter breakfast of her owner. But possessing no hen and being denied (for a time) the gross pleasures of the breakfast table, it remains for me in monkish denial to get what buckwheat fun I can by jogging around on the dirt roads and watching the stuff grow. And when you aren't allowed to eat it, the decorative importance of buckwheat is not to be overlooked.

I realize, of course, that no farmer in his right mind plants buckwheat just for looks. Farmers plant buckwheat either because buckwheat is what they want to raise or because—by reason of their own delay or the failure of a previous planting—buckwheat has become the only possible crop. Nevertheless the plants of buckwheat make our hilltops, slopes and valley floors a far lovelier palette than they otherwise would be and the work of their hands gives joy to their fellow men from July until the snow flies.

Most crops move along on time and in step with the music of the changing seasons. Corn is planted in New York when it is planted in Massachusetts. It gets into the crib in Vermont just about the same time it reaches the same destination in New Jersey, Pennsylvania and New Hampshire. The flowering of the corn follows the seed time thereof, and the harvest the flowering, with the regularity of the stars in their courses. This is by no means true of buckwheat. Buckwheat can be planted most any time the farmer gets around to it and, in some cases, that's exactly when it is planted. And so in the late summer, from the same hill and at the same time, (if we include buckwheat planted not for grain but to be plowed under) it's possible to see on adjacent farms the blood-red stubble of the garnered crop on one, the glistening whiteness of the bloom on another and the pale green of the tender seedlings on a third.

A field of buckwheat flowering under the moon on a summer night may constitute beauty of the breath-taking sort, but it is a sight which is most fully appreciated by the person who has supped well and who can look forward with confidence to a hot, substantial breakfast. No one—no man, anyway—ever had beautiful thoughts on an empty stomach.

When the pinch of hunger grips a male person, his buckwheat dreams lead him out of summer nights and into warm, winter-morning kitchens. When I was a boy there used to be a brown, earthen-ware crock that stood back of the kitchen stove from November to April. It housed the buckwheat batter and it smelled to heaven. Those were the days when all boys were sound on the Bible,—however heretical their personal views on arithmetic, geography and spelling—and to me the buckwheat batter pot was another widow's cruse, for though I never saw anything put into it, a vast number of buckwheat cakes came out of it every morning with no diminution in the family's visible supply of batter. One took his miracles as a matter of course in the consulship of Grover Cleveland.

A second miracle occurred when, after a brief contact with the hot griddle, the sour corruption of the batter was changed to the inviting fragrance of the golden cake. Then the intelligent co-mingling of the buckwheat cakes, the maple syrup and the sausages followed by the hearty consumption of the same. His little stomach tight with such honest fuel and any boy would walk a mile to school against the fiercest tempest and through the most overwhelming snow drifts.

If our forefathers had been obliged to breakfast in the winter time on a slice of dry toast and a cup of black coffee, the race would not yet have progressed westward beyond the Hudson River. It might have produced an Emerson or two and perhaps a John Greenleaf Whittier—but no axemen or mule skinners. It was buckwheat cakes that laid the forest low, maple syrup crossed the plains and it was hot sausages that pierced the Rockies and drove the covered wagons to the bright Pacific strand.

No eagle is in any way responsible for the glory of America. It was buckwheat cakes that did the business and that fact should be emblazoned on our arms in the manner first suggested. And if our nation ever goes the way of Rome and Nineveh and Tyre—which God forbid—it will be because the people fell into the base practice of starting cold winter mornings on a cup of black coffee and a slice of dry toast and had the effrontery to refer to that sort of thing as "breakfast".

☛ BOOK FIVE ☚

Western New York

Niagara Falls

INTRODUCTION TO BOOK V

MUCH OF western New York is flat country comprising the wide plains that border Lake Ontario and a few miles along Lake Erie. It is a fertile land and its sandy soil has encouraged the growing of fruits and vegetables. The east-west highway, once called the Alluvial Way, was at that time the shoreline of Lake Ontario, but the water has receded now for a number of miles.

The Indian influence has been strong. The red man furnished many of the instruments and much of the wisdom that has characterized the successful agricultural development of the region. Many of its towns were given nautical titles—Spencerport, Brockport, Adam's Basin, Eagle Harbor—because they bordered the Erie Canal. Perhaps because they live so near to the Ohio border, the speech of the western New York people is characterized by the shorter A's and the distinct R's which prevail in the Middle West.

A great percentage of the population lives in the two great urban complexes—Rochester on the east, and Buffalo on the west. Niagara Falls has been its scenic treasure. Buffalo has drawn great numbers of emigrants from Europe; Rochester has been blessed by its philanthropists with cultural enterprises—but the bulk of the writings about this area has centered about the country communities and the small towns.

WESTERN NEW YORK

16TH CENTURY

JESSE CORNPLANTER OF THE SENECAS

The Origin of the False Faces

It was long, long time ago, when the earth was new, when the two brothers were contesting as to who would rule the world, just after they had played the gambling game of Bowl and Counters (on one side the Creator or Ha-wen-nih-yoh, and on the other side that of the Yeh-ken-sih or the older woman and the Evil-mind that is called Hah-nis-heh-ononh). It was with good fortune to all living things that the Ha-wen-nih-yoh won the Game by using the heads of the Chickadees. Then it was decided that the Ha-wen-nih-yoh was to rule, as he had made all things then about, that the Evil-mind did all he could to overthrow the good in all the work of his good brother. It was then that the Ha-wen-nih-yoh took a long walk to examine all the things that he had created, and he was going about, when he spied another man-being going about.

When that being met Ha-wen-nih-yoh, it said, "Where did you come from and what is your name?"

Then Ha-wen-nih-yoh replied thus: "I am going about examining all things growing about the earth. My name is Ha-wen-nih-yoh." Then Ha-wen-nih-yoh reversed the question by asking the man-being, "Since you asked me, I will now ask you, who might you be and from whence did you come?"

Then the man-being answered thus: "I am Sca-go-dyo-weh-go-wah, the spirit of the wind in motion. I go about the earth from one end to the other. I have great power. I came from the direction of the setting sun."

Again this man-being asked Ha-wen-nih-yoh what he was doing on earth. This is what he replied: "It is I who have created and completed the bodies of all mankind going about, also created all things that are growing hereabouts. Since you have stated that you have great power on earth, we might have a test of power right now."

At this the man-being called Sca-go-dyo-weh-go-wah held in his hand a huge rattle made of the shell of a Snapping-turtle, which he did shake with much force, that made such a noise, it scared all the animals nearby. He was trying his best to impress Ha-wen-nih-yoh of his great power; he was also making such a noise with his mouth. That only made the demand for test more urgent.

So Ha-wen-nih-yoh said: "Whoever can make that yonder mountain move, is the one that has the power. We will face away from it and at a command remain so, while the one showing his strength will command the mountain to move forward. At the length of a person's breath, then we shall turn around. So you will now do so."

And they both stood facing away from the mountain; then the man-being said, "You, yonder mountain, move towards us."

Then they turned and noted that it had move little. So Ha-wen-nih-yoh said it was his turn to show his power. They done the same thing again. At the command of Ha-wen-nih-yoh for the mountain to move up to them, the man-being heard some strange noise and turned around quick, forgetting the agreement of the test. As he did so, his face was so close to the cliff that he struck it with such force that his face was distorted, his mouth was drawn up one side and his nose was twisted. By that time Ha-wen-nih-yoh had turned around, and he also noted that the mountain was at their back; and then he saw that his friend, the man-being, had his face all twisted out of shape.

It was then that Ha-wen-nih-yoh spoke: "It was I, who have made everything here about,—I am the master of this place. I can create life. What has happened to your face, that it is so twisted now?"

Then Sca-go-dyo-weh-go-wah did say: "It is true that you are most powerful here on this earth; you are able to cause the mountain to move up to where we stood. By that reason, I am now as you see me. As we stood thus, I thought I heard a noise at our back and something seem to brush against me; so I turned around quick, forgetting our agreement. The cliff was just behind me. I struck my face so hard that it has distorted my face so. It is all as you say,—you are the creator here, and it is my own opinion to ask of you to let me be one of your helper,—if you should have mercy and let me help you. As the human race will dwell on this earth that you have created, I will be able to help the mankind that will live here in the future. It will come to pass that in time they, the people, will be troubled with visions and dreams. As it is now, I have certain amount of power or Ote-gonh in my flesh and being. I have infected with this Ote-gonh to all places that I have wandered. As I have now been the first to traverse this world now present, it is infected with my own power as I went about; so when the people who will dwell on this earth will go about, they shall be troubled with some sort of illness,—they shall have seen me, in vision or in dream.

"Then the people will cause to be made an image with my likeness; then will I aid the people with my own ceremony of healing; then will people go in the woods and carve a face of my likeness out of the Basswood tree, and true enough, my spirit will enter into that mask; then will I help your people by my power to cure sickness, I also will have power to control all wind in motion on this earth hereabouts. Then will mankind say as they will address to me, 'Our Grandfather, the mighty Sca-go-dyo-weh-go-wah, the great medicine man or healer of sickness.' Because the people will be as my own Grandchildren in the future. To my Grandchildren, I will not only cure sickness, but will be able to drive away strange and serious disease; also will be able to warn them of coming sickness, which they can easily avoid, providing they will fulfill my directions. In case of coming sickness or plague of serious nature, they will avoid all this by having their community be visited by the spirits of the Faces of 'Sca-go-dyo-weh-go-wah' to drive away all forms of disease. This will be done by men wearing my likeness, each to be dressed according to my manner of clothes. They shall go to all places of dwelling and go through every part of each home. At that time, there shall also be stationed at each spring of water a person wearing the medicine mask, who shall act as one that purifies their drinking water and thus free them from all things poison in their daily use.

"The leader of this society of Sca-go-dyo-weh-go-wah as they marches from lodge to lodge will carry with him our pole of hickory staff also striped with red paint; on it will be hung at the top small specimens of masks. As they go about on this mission, the leader will also sing our marching chant or 'Gah-nonh-eh-sh-wih.' As they enter each home, this leader will announce that the Sca-go-dyo-weh-go-wah are going house to house driving all known and unknown disease; that if there be someone in the place who wish to have the party give her or him any ceremony of curing, they can do so, if their own sacred tobacco is given as token for this ceremony; that there shall be the dance for the Faces alone, to be used after this curing ceremony, also another dance, which shall be called the 'Doorkeeper Dance' or 'Deh-yenh-sih-da-dih-ahs.' The dance for the Faces only shall be called 'Ho-di-gonh-sohs-gah-ah' or just their faces alone.

"In return for all these ceremonies, I will want as payment, a mush made from parched corn sweetened. Also at this big ceremony of driving the disease, there will be made a strong drink of Parched Sunflower Seeds boiled into strong drink for all to swallow as means of preventing sickness; this will be our own medicine to our grandchildren on earth. Every time anyone calls on us, we shall only hear through the medium of the sacred tobacco smoke and no other form. We are all over this great earth. As we travel all over, I have with me many other helpers who go about from one end of the earth to the other. I am very fond of 'Oyenh-gwa-onh-weh' or sacred tobacco; so every time your people desires my attention, all they have to do is to burn the tobacco, and in the smoke that wafts on send their message to me. I will hear their word every time.

"They must select out of their number one who will address to me. He must have this tobacco with him as he makes the speech,—the substance will be like: 'Now it goes up to you the smoke of the sacred tobacco. You who is fond of it, you of the Sca-go-dyo-weh-go-wah, you who goes all over the land from one end to the other, continue to listen as they direct their words to you. You have said that in the beginning you would be a Grandfather to the man-being on earth; that you would continue to help mankind providing they fulfill your wish; that you would always listen whenever they direct the word to you with the smoke of the sacred tobacco. Now also we give tobacco or Oyenh-gwa-onh-weh to your rattle of the Mud-turtle shell that you always carry with you. Now we give tobacco to your resting place, the giant pine tree with the limbs at the very top, where you rub your rattle as you go about,—this great pine tree which stands in the middle of the earth. Now we give tobacco to your staff which you use as a cane, the giant shell-bark hickory tree without the limbs. Now we give tobacco to your own song which you have said will be your own dance song. Now we ask of you to give your full power to restore to health one of your own grandchildren, by applying the hot ashes to the patient and then blowing the sickness away with your own breath. All this we ask of you with this tobacco which you value above all things.'

"This shall be the custom when mankind shall have societies of the Sca-go-dyo-weh-go-wah. All members shall compose of those who have been cured from sickness by the ceremony. This society shall be known as "Deh-yenh-sih-dah-de-ahs,' the 'Doorkeeper's Dance' and the 'Hoh-dih-gonh-sohs-gah-ah' or the 'Dance of the Faces only.' I am going to be your helper in this work that is ahead of you. You will depend on my help. I will be coming to the minds of the people that will dwell on this earth. They shall see me, in their visions. Then the people will make my likeness, and I shall give them my full powers to cure those that shall be afflicted with my own method of illness. It all depends on how they shall respect me and my dance. I shall be their friend and helper to those that repeatedly fulfill all my desires, that is—to put on the ceremony every little while, so I can have what I value most, the 'Oyenh-gwa-onh-weh' for my own enjoyment."

Thus spoke this man-being to "Ha-wen-nih-yoh." Then "Ha-wen-nih-yoh" spoke in this wise: "It shall be as you have offered. Everything that you suggested to me are very good. I shall accept your aid, and shall add to your power, so that in the future, when the earth hereabouts shall be full of mankind, you shall watch over my creation, the living mankind and all things created by me, for their well-being. You shall be on the alert for all evil-spirits that may come about, trying to do harm to my own people, the 'Onh-gweh-onh-weh,' of the earth. I have planted on earth your most valued of all gifts, the sacred tobacco, 'Oyenh-gwa-onh-weh.' They, the people, shall offer it to you as reward for your kindness to them, that the images of you, made from the Basswood tree, shall have as much power as I have myself. The people who shall carve my likeness shall give this offering at the tree, before the face is carved. Then the full spirit of the woodland, my spirit, shall enter into this mask. In case of any serious windstorm, you must watch for the signs of such storm. And when you see anything that may hurt or do harm to my own creation, the mankind, then you shall cause it to be made known to anyone whom you may choose, so they can comply to the proper precaution. You must ward off all elements that is capable to do them harm. All this I command you to do, to keep up as long as the 'Ong-gweh-onh-weh' shall live here on earth."

Thus was the agreement and acceptance of this spirit-of-the-Faces or Sca-go-dyo-weh-go-wah (often called Ga-gonh-sah as a common name) and Ha-wen-nih-yoh, later called the Creator or the Great Good Spirit, in the earlier days of this world, which is still functioning to this day. It is often mistaken by those that does not understand our belief, that this ceremony and the Sca-go-dyo-weh-go-wah is our religion,—which is a different thing entirely. He is our medicine man, but has no connection with our Spirit-world, as we call our Hereafter. Dah Neh-hoh....

18TH CENTURY

JAMES E. SEAVER

The White Woman of the Genesee
Mary Jemison, 1743-1833

I had then been with the Indians four summers and four winters, and had become so far accustomed to their mode of living, habits and dispositions, that my anxiety to get away, to be set at liberty, and leave them, had almost subsided. With them was my home; my family was there, and there I had many friends to whom I was warmly attached in consideration of the favors, affection and friendship with which they had uniformly treated me, from the time of my adoption. Our labor was not severe; and that of one year was exactly similar, in almost every respect, to that of the others, without that endless variety that is to be observed in the common labor of the white people. Notwithstanding the Indian women have all the fuel and bread to procure, and the cooking to perform, their task is probably not harder than that of white women, who have those articles provided for them; and their cares certainly are not half as numerous, nor as great. In the summer season, we planted, tended and harvested our corn, and generally had all our children with us; but had no master to oversee or drive us, so that we could work as leisurely as we pleased. We had no ploughs... but performed the whole process of planting and hoeing with a small tool that resembled, in some respects, a hoe with a very short handle.

Our cooking consisted in pounding our corn into samp or hominy, boil-

From *A Narrative of the Life of Mrs. Mary Jemison,* published by the American Scenic & Historic Preservation Society, 1925, and reprinted by permission of the society. First published in 1824.

ing the hominy, making now and then a cake and baking it in the ashes, and in boiling or roasting our venison. As our cooking and eating utensils consisted of a hominy block and pestle, a small kettle, a knife or two, and a few vessels of bark and wood, it required but little time to keep them in order for use.

Spinning, weaving, sewing, stocking knitting and the like, are arts which have never been practised in the Indian tribes generally. After the revolutionary war, I learned to sew, so that I could make my own clothing after a poor fashion; but the other domestic arts I have been wholly ignorant of the application of, since my captivity. In the season of hunting, it is our business, in addition to our cooking, to bring home the game that was taken by the Indians, dress it, and carefully preserve the eatable meat, and prepare or dress the skins. Our clothing was fastened together with strings of deer skin, and tied on with the same.

In that manner we lived, without any of those jealousies, quarrels, and revengeful battles between families and individuals, which have been common in the Indian tribes since the introduction of ardent spirits amongst them.

The use of ardent spirits amongst the Indians, and the attempts which have been made to civilize and christianize them by the white people, has constantly made them worse and worse; increased their vices, and robbed them of many of their virtues; and will ultimately produce their extermination. I have seen, in a number of instances, the effects of education upon some of our Indians, who were taken when young, from their families, and placed at school before they had had an opportunity to contract many Indian habits, and there kept till they arrived to manhood; but I have never seen one of those but what was an Indian in every respect after he returned. Indians must and will be Indians, in spite of all the means that can be used for their cultivation in the sciences and arts.

THOMAS MORRIS

The Universal Friend

Thomas Morris, son of Robert Morris, the financier of the Revolution, wrote the following account of Jemima Wilkinson and her community:

Prior to my having settled at Canandaigua (in 1792), Jemima Wilkinson and her followers had established themselves on a tract of land, purchased by them, and called the Friends' Settlement. Her disciples were a very orderly, sober, industrious, and some of them a well educated and intelligent set of people; and many of them possessed of handsome properties. She called herself, the "Universal Friend," and would not permit herself to be designated by any other appellation. She pretended to have had revelations from Heaven, in which she had been directed to devote her labors to the conversion of sinners. Her disciples placed the most unbounded confidence in her, and yielded, in all things, the most implicit obedience to her mandates. She would punish those among them who were guilty of the slightest deviation from her orders. In some instances, she would order the offending culprit to wear a cow-bell round his neck, for weeks or months, according to the nature of the offense; and in no instance was she known to be disobeyed. For some offense committed by one of her people, she banished him to Nova Scotia for three years, where he went, and from whence he returned only after the expiration of his sentence. When any of her people killed a calf or sheep, or purchased an article of dress, the "Friend" was asked what portion of it she would have; and the answer would sometimes be, that the Lord hath need of the one-half, and sometimes that the Lord hath need of the whole. Her house, her grounds, and her farms, were kept in the neatest order, by her followers, who labored for her without compensation. She was attended by two young women always neatly dressed. Those who acted in that capacity and enjoyed the most of her favor and confidence, at the time I was there, were named Sarah Richards and Rachel Milnin (Malin). Jemima prohibited her followers from marrying; and even those who had joined her after having been united in wedlock, were made to

From *History of Livingston County,* Lockwood R. Doty, editor, Jackson, Michigan, 1905.

separate and live apart from each other. This was attributed to her desire to inherit the property of those who died....

Among Jemima's followers, was an artful, cunning, and intelligent man, by the name of Elijah Parker. She dubbed him a Prophet, and called him the Prophet Elijah. He would, before prophesying, wear around the lower part of his waist, a bandage or girdle, tied very tight; and when it had caused the upper part of his stomach to swell, he would pretend to be filled with prophetic visions, which he would impart to the community. But, after some time, Jemima and her Prophet quarreled, and he then denounced her as an impostor—declared that she had imposed on his credulity, and that he had never been a Prophet....

When I first saw Jemima, she was a fine-looking woman, of a good height, and though not corpulent, inclined to embonpoint. Her hair was jet black, short, and curled on her shoulders. She had fine eyes, and good teeth and complexion. Her dress consisted of a silk robe, open in front. Her under dress was of the finest white cambric or muslin. Round her throat she wore a large cravat, bordered with fine lace. She was very ignorant, but possessed an uncommon memory. Though she could neither read nor write, it was said that she knew the Bible by heart, from its having been read to her. The sermon I heard her preach was bad in point of language, and almost unintelligible. Aware of her deficiencies, in this respect, she caused one of her followers to tell me, that in her discourses, she did not aim at expressing herself in fine language—preferring to adapt her style to the capacity of the most illiterate of her hearers.

OLIVER GOLDSMITH

The Cataract of Niagara, in Canada, North America

[*It has been said that facts meant little to Goldsmith. His concept of the geography of America in this passage is far from correct.* (See biographical note on page 539)]

This amazing fall of water is made by the River St. Lawrence, in its passage from lake Erie into the lake Ontario. The St. Lawrence is one of

From *The English Reader,* published by Hopkins and Seymour, 1803.

the largest rivers in the world; and yet the whole of its waters are here poured down, by a fall of a hundred and fifty feet perpendicular. It is not easy to bring the imagination to correspond to the greatness of the scene. A river extremely deep and rapid, and that serves to drain the waters of almost all North America into the Atlantic Ocean, is here poured precipitately down a ledge of rocks, that rises, like a wall, across the whole bed of its stream. The river, a little above, is near three quarters of a mile broad; and the rocks, where it grows narrower, are four hundred yards over. Their direction is not straight across, but hollowing inwards like a horse-shoe: so that the cataract, which bends to the shape of the obstacle, rounding inwards, presents a kind of theater the most tremendous in nature. Just in the middle of this circular wall of waters, a little island, that has braved the fury of the current, presents one of its points, and divides the stream at top into two parts; but they unite again long before they reach the bottom. The noise of the fall is heard at the distance of several leagues; and the fury of the waters, at the termination of their fall, is inconceivable. The dashing produces a mist that rises to the very clouds; and which forms a most beautiful rainbow, when the sun shines. It will readily be supposed, that such a cataract entirely destroys the navigation of the stream; and yet some Indian canoes, as it is said, have ventured down it with safety.

RED JACKET OF THE SENECAS

A Reply to a Missionary Agent, 1811

You say you want an answer to your talk before you leave this place. It is right you should have one, as you are a great distance from home, and we do not wish to detain you. But we will first look back a little, and tell you what our fathers have told us, and what we have heard from the white people.

Listen to what we say.

There was a time when our forefathers owned this great island. Their seats extended from the rising to the setting sun. The Great Spirit had made it for the use of Indians. He had created the buffalo, the deer, and other animals for food. He had made the bear and the beaver. Their skins served us for clothing. He had scattered them over the country, and taught us how to take them. He had caused the earth to produce corn for bread. All this He had done for his red children, because He loved them. If we had some disputes about our hunting ground, they were generally settled without the shedding of much blood. But an evil day came upon us. Your forefathers crossed the great water, and landed on this island. Their numbers were small. They found friends, not enemies. They told us they had fled from their country for fear of wicked men, and had come here to enjoy their religion. They asked for a small seat. We took pity on them, granted their request; and they sat down amongst us. We gave them corn and meat; they gave us poison in return.

The white people had now found our country. Tidings were carried back, and more came amongst us. Yet we did not fear them. We took them to be friends. They called us brothers. We believed them, and gave them a larger seat. At length their numbers had greatly increased. They wanted more land; they wanted our country. Our eyes were opened, and our minds became uneasy. Wars took place. Indians were hired to fight against Indians, and many of our people were destroyed. They also brought strong liquor amongst us. It was strong and powerful, and has slain thousands.

Our seats were once large and yours were small. You have now become a great people, and we have scarcely a place left to spread our blankets. You have got our country, but are not satisfied; you want to force your religion upon us.

Brother; Continue to listen.

You say that you are sent to instruct us how to worship the Great Spirit agreeably to his mind, and, if we do not take hold of the religion which you white people teach, we shall be unhappy hereafter. You say that you are right, and we are lost. How do we know this to be true? We understand that your religion is written in a book. If it was intended for us as well as you, why has not the Great Spirit given to us, and not only to us, but why did he not give to our forefathers, the knowledge of that book, with the means of understanding it rightly? We only know what you tell us about it. How shall we know when to believe, being so often deceived by the white people?

You say there is but one way to worship and serve the Great Spirit. If there is but one religion; why do you white people differ so much about it? Why not all agreed, as you can all read the book?

We do not understand these things.

19TH CENTURY

DE WITT CLINTON

Hibernicus on "Rattle Snakes"

LETTER XLI

Western Region, August, 1820

My Dear Sir,

I have had an opportunity of seeing the rattle snake, a serpent peculiar to America, and whose natural history is greatly involved in fable and mystery. Its venomous qualities have been somewhat exaggerated, and the antidotes against its poison have been much mispresented. It has a brown, broad head; the jaws are furnished with small, sharp teeth; four fangs in the upper jaw, incurvated, large, and pointed; at the base of each, a round orifice opening into a cavity, that near the end of the tooth appears again in form of a small channel; these teeth may be erected or compressed. When in the act of biting, they force out of a gland near their roots, the fatal juice; this is received into the round orifice of the teeth, conveyed through the tube into the channel, and thence with unerring direction into the wound.

Appended to the tail is a crepitaculum or rattle, a crustaceous substance composed of joints loosely connected; each distinct joint, or compartment, denotes a year of the life of the animal, and the number of joints indicates its age, after the third year, but according to some observers, after the second, and in the opinion of others, after the first year. Linnaeus has arranged the crotalus genus under four species, and his specific differences consists in

From *Letters on the Natural History and Internal Resources of the State of New York* by De Witt Clinton. Published New York, E. Bliss and E. White, 1822.

the number of plates of the belly and tail. The crotalus horridus, or common rattle snake, has, he says, 167 plates on the belly, and 23 belonging to the tail. In the common acceptation of the country, there are but two kinds; upland, which is large, and a small kind, which inhabits swamps. It was denominated by Nieremberg, an old author, domina serpentum.

The one I saw was caught near the cataract of Niagara. Charlevoix observed in his tour to the west, a great number in the vicinity of this celebrated place. They are said to have a den in a forest a few miles off, and there is also another den about 15 miles east of Lewiston, near the causeway. A small island near Grand Island, in the Niagara river, was called Rattle Snake Island, from the number which it formerly contained. Twenty-five were killed on it in one day, and none are now to be found there.

It is generally believed that they are devoured by hogs with impunity and with avidity; this is confidently denied; and again it is said that deer kill them by springing on them with collected feet. It is certain whatever may be the fact in these cases, that they disappear before population.

Venomous and dangerous as this animal is, yet a lady of fortune from Carolina carried about one as a pet. In the house where she boarded in New-York, her fellow lodgers were much alarmed one evening by observing several young rattle snakes about the rooms. It appears that they escaped through the holes of the case where the mother was confined, and where she had brought forth her young.

I believe that all venomous serpents come under the description of *ovi-viviparous;* that is, that the ova are hatched internally. A rattle snake was recently killed near the western canal, which had thirty eggs in it. This shows that they may have thirty young, although the general impression is, that their offspring cannot exceed twelve at one time. It is believed by many that the young retreat for security into the body of the mother, although this is confidently contradicted, as well in this case as in the case of the viper. That both are viviparous is certain.

Round Lake George, on the mountains, there are said to be at least 100 dens. There is one eight miles down the lake on East Mountain, and there are five others two miles from the head of the lake. There are two great dens within six miles of Ticonderoga—one at Rogers' rock, four miles from the foot of the lake; and the other about three miles off, on the east side of the lake. These snakes generally select a south eastern or sunny ravine on a mountain, for their hybernacula. They descend deep into the cavities of rocks, and look out for a position at the head of springs. The vulgar believe that they will not bite in the spring until they have tasted water, and that they have a king distinguished by a carbuncle, and "which, like the toad, ugly and venomous, wears a precious jewel in his head." This serpent frequently swims across lakes and rivers. Several persons dug for a den on the side of a mountain near Lake George, and after digging 15 feet they were arrested in their pursuit by a great rock, under which there were two holes large enough for a man to enter, from which ascended volumes of noxious exhalations, that were attributed to collections of snakes coiled together. They are eagerly sought after for their oil and gall, which are used in sprains and rheumatisms; and for their flesh, which has been applied in consumptions; and they are frequently destroyed by fires made accidentally, or for clearing the woods, and sometimes they bite with great fury at the flames. Owing to these causes their numbers are much diminished, and they are only preserved from extirpation by the fastnesses and deep recesses of the mountains.

During the late war, a detachment of the American army was encamped two miles north of Niagara, at a place called Snake Hill, which was greatly annoyed by rattle snakes. In order to keep them off, the tents were surrounded by boughs of the ash tree, which preventive, heretofore considered certain, was found unavailing.* Some were killed on the parade, and one morning a soldier shook two out of his blanket. This country is champaign, and there is no mountain nearer than eight miles.

Is it true that rattle snakes are killed every year on York-Island, about eight miles from the city, near the great strata of gneiss? I am told that some years ago a large one was found in a populous street of that city; and that it was supposed to have been lost by its keeper;—may it not have emigrated from its den on the island?

As soon as the warmth of the season will permit, this serpent evacuates his den, and travels at his leisure about eight or ten miles from it, where he continues until September, when he returns to his winter quarters, most terrifically furious and ferocious. He couples in August, and produces next June.

LETTER XLII

Western Region, August, 1820

My Dear Sir,

When the rattle snake intends to bite, he coils himself up like a cable, and then extending his head, throws his whole body forward with rapidity and fury at the object he intends to strike. Sometimes he makes a

* This notion may be traced back to Pliny, who asserts it in his Natural History. The Americans have derived it from their English ancestors, who believed in it, and perhaps it is now generally accredited in England. It is hardly necessary to say that it is entirely unfounded.

kind of singing noise, and when he rattles he does not mean to wound. All snakes are very irritable when in coition, and the crotalus is very dangerous from this period to the time of his hybernation.

I have already mentioned the failure of an experiment relative to the efficacy of white ash against the approaches of the rattle snake. I have been told of a rattle snake that had been kept in a cage eight months without food, and without any apparent diminution of bulk. Although furious when enraged, it is alleged, that he would not bite at a white ash stick. And it is asserted, that if you enclose this serpent by a circumvallation of white ash leaves and fire, that he will elect to make his retreat through the flames.* It is said that the juice of the leaves of the ash has been found efficacious against the bite of the coluber chersea, the asping of the Swedes, which like the prester of Lucan, kills by a horrible swelling of the whole human frame, and which inhabits only a particular district of Sweden among the willows. It is certain that there are districts of country in which rattle snakes are never seen while at no great distance they abound. For instance, they have never been known to inhabit the town of New-Berlin, in Chenango county, and yet they have been found about ten miles off, toward the mouth of the Unadilla. It is said that they avoid land timbered with beech and maple. Whether the cause arises from the timber or the soil which produces it may be a question. White oak land is preferred by them. The small species generally live in open swamps, and their bite is not considered so dangerous.

Some negroes killed 315 rattle snakes a few springs ago, by smoking them out of a den at the south end of Canandaigua Lake. There are many about Eighteen-mile creek, in Genesee county, where they inhabit the open ledges and fissures in the rocks, and there are dens in the mountains on the south side of the Mohawk river, at a place called the Nore, in Montgomery county. A great den exists on the east side of the Genesee river, near Rochester. In the spring they travel west, (as their heads are then found in that direction) ten or twelve miles, and scatter themselves over the low lands; and for this purpose they swim across the river. In autumn their heads are pointed to the east, as they return to their den. In August 1816, a monstrous rattle snake was killed at New-Mills, New-Jersey, which had eleven rattles, and was five feet long, and which was the only one seen for several years within many miles of that place: and some years ago, in the vicinity of Lake George, a whole den of rattle snakes migrated from one mountain to another. This was in the autumn, and was unquestionably done for a more secure and comfortable residence.

* This superstitious idea was refuted in a note to the last number.

Fancy has assigned to the lordly rattle snake an attendant, or minister, like the jackall of the king of the quadrupeds. This is a venomous viper, with a flat head, and a body coloured like the rattle snake. It has no crepitaculum, and is called the rattle snake's pilot.

I have been told, but I have had no opportunity of ascertaining the fact, that the rattle snake differs from all others, for that when skinned, the whole body becomes open to the back bone, and that no intestines are visible except the heart.

It appears that the rattle snake is not singular in the selection of his winter quarters. Thunberg speaks of a mountain, or rather a large single rock, in the Cape Colony, in Africa, called Slangenkof, (serpent's head) on one side of it is a large and deep crevice, which makes this rock remarkable, for every autumn the serpents go there and coil together, and come out in summer. The poison of the serpent has most power over those animals whose blood is the warmest, and the action of whose heart is the most lively; while on the contrary it is said not to be a poison to the serpent itself, nor to its fellows, nor in general to cold-blooded animals. I have heard this remark contradicted in relation to the bite of the rattle snake, although I believe it to be true of the viper tribe in general. A person saw two engaged in battle—at last one bit the other, which immediately retreated, and died in a few minutes. It was supposed that it went off rapidly for an antidote.

To show the rapidity of the bite, and the mortality of the venom, the following anecdotes were related to me: a man in pursuance of a common practice of killing snakes, took a rattle snake by the tail from under a log, and snapped off its head like the cracking of a whip; he was bit in the thumb, without knowing it, during this rapid operation, and died. Another one killed a rattle snake, and cut off the head about five inches long, and ordered a boy to bury it, not obeying the order fast enough, and being hurried in his work, the man took hold of the head, which turned round and bit him so that he died....

I am told that rattle snakes have been seen on Long-Island, and at Snake Hill, near Newburgh. There is a beautiful island called Diamond Island, containing about an acre of land near the head of Lake George, and it is said that it was formerly so overrun by rattle snakes, that travellers shipwrecked there were forced to lodge one night in the trees, and that the serpents were extirpated by hogs brought there for the purpose.

On the south side of a mountain west of this lake, and at the head of it, there is a large den of rattle snakes. At the village there lived a professional rattle snake catcher, who had taken in one season 1300, and who made a livelihood by selling the oil and the flesh, and by vending living ones for shows. He went out as usual, with a large basket covered with a carpet, and was found dead after an absence of some days. In carrying the basket, it is supposed that the covering fell off, and that one of his serpents bit him in the side, as he was much swollen, and there was found by him a rattle snake cut up, which it is presumed he had applied to the wound.

HARLAN HATCHER

Walk-in-the-Water

The long era of peace and prosperous commerce got under way rather promptly after the interruption of the War of 1812. Lake Erie, with Buffalo at its foot and Detroit at its head, became the center of activity on the Great Lakes....

There was also a rapidly expanding local trade on Lake Erie as the settlers continued to arrive, to hew out the forests and plant farms, homes and villages along the lake shore....

Obviously Erie was not a lake for rowboats. It needed seaworthy sails and the new steam engines to drive ships across her alternately still and storm-tossed waters. The *Walk-in-the-Water* was the first attempt to meet that need on Lake Erie. She was built in 1818 at Black Rock in the Niagara River for the Lake Erie Steamboat Company by the New York naval architect, Noah Brown, and his imported company of thirty ship carpenters. She was a trim, schooner-rigged, two-master with two giant, awkward-looking paddle wheels port and starboard amidships, and an incongruous smokestack forward. It is something of a question whether the sails were to augment the steam engine, or whether the steam was auxiliary to the sails. At any rate her schooner rig and her square foresail gave her a skimming speed before a good wind, and her engines failed to save her in her last big Erie storm.

Her maiden voyage was a sensation around Lake Erie. She was, indeed, an elegant ship. She carried on her taffrail a row of heavy carved work brightly painted in white, green and gold. Her figurehead was a bust of Commodore Oliver Hazard Perry. In good weather she carried a smart awning over the main and quarter-deck. She had no upper deck, but her quarter-deck was five feet above the main deck, and a companion door opened into the gentlemen's cabin. The mainmast ran down through this cabin, and was decorated with mirrors. Folding doors separated the gentlemen from the ladies' cabin aft. This cabin was lighted by six stern windows and a skylight. The below-deck space was too shallow to accommodate the boiler; about one-fourth of it extended above the main deck.

On Sunday, August 23, 1818, this fine ship was towed up the Niagara from Black Rock, with her engines running, by sixteen or twenty yoke of oxen. She could not put in at the Buffalo wharf because her eight-and-a-half-foot hold drew too much water for the shallow harbor. She stood outside at anchor and was tended by small boats. She took on sacks of mail and twenty-nine passengers for this first voyage, at a fare of $15 to Cleveland and $24 from Buffalo to Detroit.... Two days later, at nightfall, she triumphantly reached Fighting Island in the Detroit River.... She was met at the island by the mayor, his official family, and distinguished citizens. Then she steamed up the river lined with spectators, and with great ceremony came alongside the new wharf as her safe arrival was hailed by the firing of a gun. The wharf was jammed with welcoming citizens who looked on admiringly while Job Fish, megaphone in hand, stood on the fifteen-foot paddle box and directed the landing. Her voyage was a great success.

For three years she sailed on schedule back and forth across the lake, making money for her owners and carrying passengers speedily to the West. She made a few voyages also with United States troops and excursionists to Mackinac Island, and one voyage to Green Bay. James Flint took passage on her from Sandusky to Buffalo in October 1820, just a year almost to the day before she was lost in a storm that struck her off Point Abino. He left a graphic description of his trip.

"On the 14th I went on board the American steam-boat *Walk-in-the-Water,* a fine vessel of 330 tons burden, with two masts, and rigged, for taking advantage of the winds in the manner of sea-craft. The interior of this vessel is elegant, and the entertainment is luxurious. There were twelve cabin passengers of genteel and polite manners, and about an equal number of persons in the steerage; the whole indicating a degree of intercourse and refinement which I did not expect to see on Lake Erie.

"During the afternoon, and a part of the night, we experienced the most severe gale our mariners had felt on the lake. The swell rose to a great height, and occasionally immersed one of the wheels deeply, while the other was almost entirely out of the water, causing the vessel to heave and flounce very disagreeably. Most of the passengers were affected by the same kind of sickness, similar to that which prevails at sea ... the water appeared to be green, showing that its depth is considerable.... Altogether, the lake presents much of the phenomena of the ocean."

On the last day of October 1821 the *Walk-in-the-Water* sailed as usual from Buffalo in the late afternoon and with a good list of passengers aboard. The weather was dirty but not formidable. A storm came on and quickly increased to a gale. The big paddle wheels forced the ship on against the wind, but the seas rolled up angrily as evening fell. She was off Point Abino, a few miles from Buffalo, when the buffeting grew too severe for her light timbers to withstand. She lost headway and shipped water. The night was dark and the rain violent. The primitive boiler could not supply enough steam to run both the engine and the pumps at the same time.

Captain Rogers tried to turn around and head back to Buffalo. The storm whipped him off course and he lost his bearing. He dropped three anchors, but these only pulled his ship apart and let in more water. At four o'clock in the morning he called all passengers and told them he was about to run onshore. He then slipped the chain cable, cut the two ropes to the other anchors, and let his ship go with the gale. As she hit the beach on a swell the sound of breaking china and glass could be heard above the surf. Another swell fixed her in the sand not far from the mouth of Buffalo Creek. A sailor got ashore with a hawser which he secured from the ship to a tree. The passengers were then removed in the ship's boats. All were saved, but the ship, except for her engine, was a total loss....

Mrs. Thomas Palmer of Detroit, one of the passengers aboard the *Walk-in-the-Water* on that nerve-racking night, visited the wreck a few days later. She said that it lay broadside on, and that she "could almost walk around it dry shod, the sand had been deposited around it to such an extent. The oakum had worked out of the seams in the deck for yards, and the panel-work had become disjointed in many places." It was a pitiful ending for the first proud sailing steamer on the lake, but she was only one in a long list of ships that failed to survive the hazards of Lake Erie, as we shall have occasion to see.

FRANCES WRIGHT

A Trip to Niagara

Niagara, September, 1819

There is, it must be confessed, the strangest confusion of names in the western counties of this state that ingenuity could well imagine. In one district, you have all the poets from Homer to Pope, nay, for aught I know, they may come down to Byron; in another, you have a collection of Roman heroes; in a third, all the mighty cities of the world, from the great Assyrian empire downwards; and, scattered among this classic confusion, relics of the Indian vocabulary, which, I must observe, are often not the least elegant, and are indisputably always the most appropriate.

For the Roman heroes, bad, good, and indifferent, who in one district are scattered so plentifully, the new population is indebted to a land-surveyor, and a classical dictionary. Being requested, in parcelling out the lots, to affix a name to them, the worthy citizen, more practised in mensuration than baptism, shortly found his ingenuity baffled, and in despair had recourse to the pages of Lempriere.

There is something rather amusing in finding Cato or Regulus typified by a cluster of wooden houses; nor, perhaps, are the old worthies so much disgraced as some indignant scholars might imagine.

I met with one name on my route which somewhat surprised me, and which struck me as yet more inappropriate than the sonorous titles of antiquity, nor was I ill pleased to learn that it had occasioned some demur among the settlers. I thought that I had left *Waterloo,* on the other side of the Atlantic, in the streets, bridges, waltzes, ribands, hotels, and fly-coaches of Great Britain and Ireland. When objections were made to the founder of the little town flourishing under this appellation, the story goes, that he called to his aid the stream of water which turned the wheel of his mill, gravely affirming, that he had that in his eye, and not the battle in his thoughts, when he christened the settlement. "The name speaks for itself," said he, with a humourous gravity peculiar to his native district of New-

From *Views of Society and Manners in America* by an Englishwoman, published by E. Bliss and E. White, New York, 1821.

England—"*Water*-loo." If the name did not speak for itself, it was impossible not to let him speak for it; and so his neighbours turned away laughing....

The flourishing town of Rochester, strikingly situated, is seven years old,—that is to say, seven years ago, the planks of which its neat white houses are built, were growing in an unbroken forest. It now contains upwards of two hundred houses, well laid out in broad streets; shops, furnished with all the necessaries, and with many that may be accounted the luxuries of life; several good inns, or taverns, as they are universally styled in these states. We were very well, and very civilly treated in one of them; but, indeed, I have never yet met with any incivility, though occasionally with that sort of indifference which foreigners, accustomed to the obsequiousness of European service, sometimes mistake for it.

In the country, especially, service, however well paid for, is a favour received. Every man is a farmer and a proprietor; few therefore can be procured to work for hire, and these must generally be brought from a distance. Country gentlemen complain much of this difficulty. Most things, however, have their good and their evil. I have remarked that the American gentry are possessed of much more personal activity than is common in other countries. They acquire, as children, the habit of doing for themselves what others require to be done for them; and are, besides, saved from the sin of insolence, which is often so early fixed in the young mind. Some foreigners will tell you, that insolence here is with the poor. Each must speak from his own experience. I have never met with any.... I verily believe that you might travel from the Canada frontier to the gulf of Mexico, or from the Atlantic to the Missouri, and never receive from a *native born citizen* a rude word, it being understood always that you never *give one*....

At Rochester we dismissed our wagon; and the following morning, between three and four o'clock, once again seated in the regular stage, struck westward to the Niagara river....

The mode in which the contents of the post bag are usually distributed through the less populous districts, had often before amused me. I remember, when taking a cross cut in a queer sort of a caravan, bound for some settlement on the southern shore of Lake Erie, observing, with no small surprise, the operations of our charioteer; a paper flung to the right hand, and anon a paper flung to the left, where no sight or sound bespoke the presence of human beings.... "...when I don't find them ready, I throw the paper under a tree; and I warrant you they'll look sharp enough to find it; they're always curious of news in these wild parts;" and curious enough they seemed, for not a cabin did we pass that a newspaper was not flung from the hand of this enlightener of the wilderness. Occasionally making a halt at some solitary dwelling, the post bag and its guardian descended together, when, if the assistance of the farmer, who here acted as postmaster, could be obtained, the whole contents of the mail were discharged upon the ground, and all hands and eyes being put in requisition, such letters as might be addressed to the surrounding district, were scrambled out from the heap. ...On one occasion, I remember, neither man, woman, nor child, was to be found; the stage-driver whistled and hallooed, walked into the dwelling, and through the dwelling, sprang the fence, traversed the field of maize, and shouted into the wood; but all to no purpose. Having resumed his station, and set his horses in motion, I inquired how the letters were to find their destination, seeing that we were carrying them along with us, heaven knew where? "Oh! they'll keep in the country any how; it is likely indeed, they may go down the Ohio, and make a short tour of the states; this has happened sometimes; but it is a chance but they get to Washington at last; and then they'll commence a straight course anew, and be safe here again this day twelvemonth may be, or two years at farthest." ...

Forty miles from Lewiston, the ridge is broken for a considerable extent; and the log causeway, through a deep swamp that fills up the deficiency, is only to be crossed on foot. Fatigued and bruised as we by this time were, it was no easy matter to clamber over these cruel miles, which, though few, seemed eternal....

For the first forty miles, the road was, with some intermissions, bordered by a line of cultivation; or, where the plough had not absolutely turned up the soil, the axe was waging war with the trees. To this succeeded a stretch of forest; relieved at long intervals by the settler's rugged patch, smoking with burning timber, and encumbered with blackened logs.

A log road, or causeway, as it is denominated, is very grievous to the limbs; and when it traverses a dense and swampy forest, is not very cheering to the eyes; nor always is the travelling greatly more agreeable when, in lieu of the trunks of trees, you are dragged over their roots....

The settlers' fires have now scared away the wolves and bears, who, not five years since, held undisputed dominion in these unbroken shades....

The moon was up ere the dull level which we had so long traversed, was varied by the appearance of the ridge which is afterwards torn open by the Niagara. We ran along its base for some miles, on a smooth and firm road, which would have relieved our tired limbs, had they not now been too tired to be relieved by any thing. The chills of an autumnal night succeeding to a day of summer heat, had yet farther increased our discomfort when we entered the frontier village of Lewiston.

Alighting at a little tavern, we found the only public apartment sufficiently occupied, and accordingly made bold to enter a small room; which, by the cheering blaze of an oak fire, we discovered to be the kitchen, and, for the time being, the peculiar residence of the family of the house. An unusual inundation of travellers had thrown all into confusion. The busy matron, nursing an infant with one arm, and cooking with the other, seemed worked out of strength, and almost out of temper. A tribe of young urchins, kept from their rest by the unusual stir, were lying half asleep; some on the floor, and some upon a bed, which filled a third of the apartment. We were suffered to establish ourselves by the fire; and having relieved the troubled hostess from her chief encumbrance, she recovered good humour, and presently prepared our supper....

In the night, when all was still, I heard the first rumbling of the cataract. Wakeful from over fatigue, rather than from any discomfort in the lodging, I rose more than once to listen to a sound which the dullest ears could not catch for the first time without emotion. Opening the window, the low, hoarse thunder distinctly broke the silence of the night; when, at intervals, it swelled more full and deep, you will believe, that I held my breath to listen; they were solemn moments....

...Never shall I forget the moment when, throwing down my eyes, I first beheld the deep, slow, solemn tide, clear as crystal, and green as the ocean, sweeping through its channel of rocks with a sullen dignity of motion and sound.... You saw and *felt* immediately that it was no river you beheld, but an imprisoned sea; for such indeed are the lakes of these regions. The velocity of the waters, after the leap, until they issue from the chasm of Queenston, flowing over a rough and shelving bed, must actually be great; but, from their vast depth, they move with an apparent majesty, that seems to temper their vehemence, rolling onwards in heavy volumes, and with a hollow sound, as if labouring and groaning with their own weight.

A mile farther, we caught a first and partial glimpse of the cataract, on which the opposing sun flashed for a moment, as on a silvery screen that hung suspended in the sky. It disappeared again behind the forest, all save the white cloud that rose far up into the air, and marked the spot from whence the thunder came. We now pressed forward with increasing impatience, and after a few miles, reaching a small inn, we left our rude equipage, and hastened in the direction that was pointed to us.

Two foot-bridges have latterly been thrown, by daring and dexterous hands, from island to island, across the American side of the channel, some hundred feet above the brink of the fall; gaining in this manner the great island which divides the cataract into two unequal parts.... From its lower point, we obtained partial and imperfect views of the falling river; from the higher, we commanded a fine prospect of the upper channel. Nothing here denotes the dreadful commotion so soon about to take place; the thunder, indeed, is behind you, and the rapids are rolling and dashing on either hand; but before, the vast river comes sweeping down its broad and smooth waters between banks low and gentle as those of the Thames. Returning, we again stood long on the bridges, gazing on the rapids that rolled above and beneath us; the waters of the deepest sea-green, crested with silver, shooting under our feet with the velocity of lightning, till, reaching the brink, the vast waves seemed to pause, as if gathering their strength for the tremendous plunge. Formerly it was not unusual for the more adventurous traveller to drop down to the island in a well manned and well guided boat. This was done by keeping between the currents, as they rush on either side of the island, thus leaving a narrow stream, which flows gently to its point, and has to the eye contrasted with the rapidity of the tide, where to right and left the water is sucked to the Falls, the appearance of a strong back current.

It is but an inconsiderable portion of this imprisoned sea which flows on the American side; but even this were sufficient to fix the eye in admiration. Descending the ladder (now easy steps,) and approaching to the foot of this lesser Fall, we were driven away blinded, breathless, and smarting, the wind being high and blowing right against us. A young gentleman, who incautiously ventured a few steps farther, was thrown upon his back, and I had some apprehension, from the nature of the ground upon which he fell, was seriously hurt; he escaped, however, from the blast, upon hands and knees, with a few slight bruises. Turning a corner of the rock (where, descending less precipitously, it is wooded to the bottom) to recover our breath, and wring the water from our hair and clothes, we saw, on lifting our eyes, a corner of the summit of this graceful division of the cataract hanging above the projecting mass of trees, as it were in mid air, like the snowy top of a mountain. Above, the dazzling white of the shivered water was thrown into contrast with the deep blue of the unspotted heavens; below, with the living green of the summer foliage, fresh and sparkling in the eternal shower of the rising and falling spray.... The greater division of the cataract was here concealed from our sight by the dense volumes of vapour which the wind drove with fury across the immense basin directly towards us; sometimes indeed a veering gust parted for a moment the thick clouds, and partially revealed the heavy columns, that seemed more like fixed pillars of moving emerald than living sheets of water. Here, seating ourselves at the brink of this troubled ocean, beneath the gaze of the sun, we had the full advantage of a vapour bath; the fervid rays drying our garments one moment, and a blast from the basin drenching them the next. The wind at length having somewhat abated, and the ferryman being willing to attempt the passage, we here crossed in a little boat to the Canada side.... The angry waters, and the angry winds together, drove us farther down the channel than was quite agreeable....

Being landed two thirds of a mile below the cataract, a scramble, at first very intricate, through, and over, and under huge masses of rock, which occasionally seemed to deny all passage, and among which our guide often disappeared from our wandering eyes, placed us at the foot of the ladder by which the traveller descends on the Canada side. From hence a rough walk along a shelving ledge of loose stones brought us to the cavern formed by the projection of the ledge over which the water rolls, and which is known by the name of the Table Rock.

The gloom of this vast cavern, the whirlwind that ever plays in it, the deafening roar, the vast abyss of convulsed waters beneath you, the falling columns that hang over your head, all strike, not upon the ears and eyes only, but upon the heart....

The cavern formed by the projection of this rock, extends some feet behind the water, and ... when I descended within a few paces of this dark recess, I was obliged to hurry back some yards to draw breath....

From this spot, (beneath the Table Rock,) you *feel,* more than from any other, the height of the cataract, and the weight of its waters. It seems a tumbling ocean; and you yourself what a helpless atom amid these vast and eternal workings of gigantic nature! The wind had now abated, and what was better, we were now under the lee, and could admire its sport with the vapour, instead of being blinded by it. From the enormous basin into which the waters precipitate themselves in a clear leap of 140 feet, the clouds of smoke rose in white volumes, like the round-headed clouds you have sometimes seen in the evening horizon of a summer sky, and then shot up in pointed pinnacles, like the ice of mountain glaçières. Caught by the wind, it was now borne down the channel, then, re-collecting its strength, the tremulous vapour again sought the upper air, till broken and dispersed in the blue serene, it spread against it the only silvery veil which spotted the pure azure. In the centre of the Fall, where the water is the heaviest, it takes the leap in an unbroken mass of the deepest green, and in many places reaches the bottom in crystal columns of the same hue, till they meet the snow-white foam that heaves and rolls convulsedly in the enormous basin. But for the deafening roar, the darkness and the stormy whirlwind in which we stood, I could have fancied these massy volumes the walls of some fairy palace—living emeralds chased in silver. Never surely did nature throw together so fantastically so much beauty with such terrific grandeur.

BELLAMY PARTRIDGE

The First Case

At the time my father was admitted to the bar his knowledge of the law was entirely theoretical. He had never drawn a deed, he had never framed a complaint or an answer; indeed, he had never even filled out a summons or a subpoena.... At the time when he hung out his shingle and opened his office in Phelps he had tried only one case in his life—a little skirmish in police court in which he defended a janitor who was facing a charge of petty larceny.

Preparation for the bar in the sixties was much simpler than it is today. Academic requirements were practically nil. Nor were there formal examiners who made it a business to tangle up and trip, if possible, any youth who fondly imagined that he wanted to be a lawyer. Some local jurist was told off to examine a group of candidates, and he examined them according to his own fitness and his own ideas. If he happened to be a probate lawyer they were in for a severe quizzing on the law of wills, whereas if he was a criminal lawyer the questions were more likely to veer toward the distinction between manslaughter and murder, or the theory of reasonable doubt. And there were oral as well as written questions to test the candidate's fitness.

There was little or no supervision of the reading of a law clerk in those old days. The student was expected to read the commentaries of Kent and Blackstone and to familiarize himself with the works of Coke, Chitty, and Story, but there was no prescribed course of study such as is furnished by the law schools of today....

Business began coming to him from old Charley Hobson before my father had chairs enough in his office for the clients to sit down on. And within a week he had been retained as defense counsel in what turned out to be one of the locally famous cases of the season, though it never went further than the justice court. This case was the outgrowth of a desire on the part of the youth of the town to give the advent of the Fourth of July a suitable welcome.

For many years the arrival of the Fourth had been heralded by the lighting of a huge street bonfire on the bank corner. The preceding year, however, the boys had thoughtlessly built their fire so close to the curb that the heat from it had cracked a plate-glass window in the bank, and the Village Fathers had passed an ordinance forbidding all fires in the streets except for the burning of leaves and grass. The Solons had also taken the precaution of warning the merchants and storekeepers that if they should furnish the boys with the materials for a bonfire they would be held accountable for any damages that might result.

But, as was to have been expected, the youth of the town did not propose to have their patriotic zeal curbed by the ukase of Four Old Men, and as soon as night had fallen on the evening of the third they began to scout around for materials that would make a good bonfire. When they found the usual supply missing from the back doors of the stores, they enlarged the scope of their quest, with the result that when, on the stroke of twelve, the match was applied, the astonished villagers beheld on the bank corner a beacon fire, the like of which, both in brilliance and in aftereffects, had not been seen within the memory of the oldest inhabitant. It was such a bonfire as Chic Sale's "specialist" would have appreciated and enjoyed, for it was composed almost entirely of the small though useful structures of which that talented fabricator in wood was an acknowledged master builder.

Whoops of delight arose from the spectators as the flames went crackling upward through the well-seasoned wood which ignited with the speed of tinder boxes and burned with the roar of a forest fire.

Some of the buildings, as they burned, were neatly outlined, the doors, the oddly cut windows, the little wooden chimneys boldly etched in flame. High on top of the pile was a tidy red building with yellow trimmings which matched in color and architecture the barn of the Village President. Before the flames had reached this brilliant red-and-yellow apex of the pile, murmurings of regret were heard that it should have been given so important a position, only to be turned upside down. When, however, it became well ignited and the beholders saw how it burned in three tall pillars of fire reaching far into the sky—two large and one small—their lamentations died on their lips, and a laughter that was Jovian indeed burst in great tumult upon the midnight air.

As a bonfire it was a decided success, but there were, as I have intimated, reverberations. The Village Fathers were outraged, incensed, and insulted. They turned the minions of the law out with instructions to "get" the culprits, and before the end of the week there were arrests. Five young men, four of them scions of the best families, were arraigned before Lysander

Redman, a local justice of the peace, charged with malicious mischief and violation of an ordinance—and my father was retained to defend them.

He entered a plea of not guilty for his clients and called for a jury. This required an adjournment, and he took the youths and their fathers to his office for a conference. When the case came on for trial a week later, the Village Fathers showed how much in earnest they were by appearing in court with a prosecutor from Geneva and twenty witnesses. Some of the most indignant of the witnesses were those who had laughed the most loudly on the night of the fire....

The prosecution had no trouble in proving that all the defendants were on the scene on the night of the fire. Some of them were recognized as persons who had helped to draw the light wagon by which the fuel was brought to the location of the fire. Others were pointed out as members of the party who had piled up the materials in preparation for the conflagration. And one defendant was positively identified by an enraged citizen as the person who had sat on his chest to hold him down while the other boys had carried away certain inflammable parts of his freehold. No evidence was introduced, however, to show who had applied the match.

It was on this ground that my father moved for a dismissal of the complaint. Motion denied. Exception. He then announced that he would call no witnesses and was ready to present his case to the jury.

Though there had been some moments of hilarity during the trial, my father chose to regard his summary to the jury as a momentous occasion. It was his first opportunity to show his new friends and future clients what he was made of. He felt conscious of his youth and inexperience as he stood up before them; but he was unafraid, and he could not have been more serious if he had been addressing the Supreme Court of the United States. If people had come there expecting coarse jokes and broad humor they were doomed to disappointment. Never once did he refer even indirectly to the fuel of which the bonfire had been built. He confined himself strictly to the safe if humorless subject of patriotism. Were these young men to be punished, were they to have their records blackened and their characters besmirched because of a crime which was nothing more than excess of patriotism?

For a full hour he made the eagle scream. This was really no great effort on his part, since he still had fresh in his mind a Fourth of July oration that he had delivered in the little town of Irondequoit only a few days before, and he let the judge and the jury have the whole of it. Packed to suffocation, the Town Hall rang to the rafters with applause when he had finished.

The prosecutor had taken the case as the average lawyer takes justice court litigation. He regarded it as trivial and had made no particular preparation for it. He must have been somewhat surprised at the flight of eloquence displayed by his youthful opponent; but he disregarded it entirely and shouted with indignation over the uncontested evidence in the case. The good men and true, however, were not interested in uncontested evidence. Patriotism was much more important to them than a miscellaneous lot of carpenter's masterpieces, and after all the shouting was over they brought in a verdict of not guilty.

With fifty dollars in his pocket—ten from each defendant—my father walked home, feeling very much on top of the world. He laid the money on the table before my mother where they could both look at it and enjoy it—the first real money he had ever earned at his profession. There was never any other money like it. He remarked that it would pay for the new baby. It did, several months later, with twenty-five dollars left over.

The trial of this case brought my father welcome publicity, but it also brought him a nickname that was not quite so welcome. As he was going out of his front gate the next morning, two of the neighborhood boys went past. They touched their caps respectfully—a little too respectfully, he thought—and said, "Good morning, Judge." My father smiled as he returned their greeting. But he did not smile when the clerk in the post office said, "Well, Judge, I see you won your case."

My father did not look up from his mail. "Better be careful what you put on your bonfires in the future," he said and turned and walked out.

He resented the use of the title, since he felt sure that it was based on a desire to tease him. He hoped that the little joke would soon be forgotten. Perhaps it was. But the title stuck. There were little variations, of course. In time it became "the Judge" and after a good many years, "the Old Judge." And, ironically enough, at no time in his life was he actually a judge.

The trial of the bonfire case brought him something more important than a high-sounding nickname, however, and that was a realization of how abysmally ignorant he was about conducting a case in court. He realized, as he looked back on the trial, how fortunate he had been to have the Irondequoit speech to fall back on, and he shuddered as he recalled how awkward and ill at ease he had been in his questioning of both jurors and witnesses. The difference between doing a thing himself and watching somebody else do it became painfully apparent. And it was plain to him that he would have been floundering hopelessly had it not been for the example of his opponent, who was a lawyer of experience.

It was at this time that he recalled the oft-repeated advice of the old judge in whose office he had read law. "The justice court is the natural training ground for the young lawyer," he used to say. "It's the cheapest place there is to buy your experience. And if you can't try a small case well you can't try a big one any better."...

The lesson had gone home in no uncertain way, and it was my father's boast that for the next ten years he did not lose a single opportunity to try a case in justice court. Indeed, he never lost his relish for a keen bout before a justice of the peace.

"Have you got ten dollars?" I once heard him ask a prospective client with a cause pending in justice court.

"No."

"Have you got five?"

"No."

"Have you got any money at all?"

The fellow shook his head. "No—just a little change."

"Then how do you expect to pay your witnesses their fees?"

"They've promised to come anyway."

"All right, I'll take the case. Only, of course, I'll want to talk to those witnesses before they go on the stand."

During his first few years in practice he tried literally hundreds of these minor cases, some of them involving a total amount of no more than fifteen dollars. From the standpoint of cash it was not remunerative business, but in the matter of imponderables it was priceless. All the time he was schooling himself in the selection of jurors, the examination of witnesses, the tactful handling of the court, and the parrying with difficult counsel. It is well known among lawyers that the pettifogger is at his best in the minor courts. He has, indeed, almost ceased to exist in the courts of record. The lower courts in the larger cities are still infested with attorneys of a low order who wrangle and connive, coach witnesses, and even suborn if they dare, but as the bench improves and the bar tightens its regulations, they are being crowded out, or at least kept in hand.

In justice court, however, there is no way to cope with them. Anyone may practice there, and in almost every community there is a shrewd old codger, possibly an ex-justice, who, though not a member of the bar, knows all the tricks and pitfalls of justice court practice. A justice of the peace can make his rulings on the admission of evidence but cannot enforce them. The pettifogger knows this, and over the objection of opposing counsel and the ruling of the court he goes right ahead and introduces any evidence that he thinks will help him win the case. To meet one of the gentry on his own ground, an attorney must be alert and more than ordinarily resourceful. My father's method of fighting the pettifogger was to turn his own weapons against him if possible.

He was once called upon to prosecute a case of hog stealing in a distant corner of the county, far from the beaten track and miles from the railroad. After a long, muddy drive he found himself confronted by a fat, shifty-eyed old pettifogger and knew that he was in for trouble. Theft is never too easy to prove. Thieves are seldom caught in the act, and to prove them guilty, circumstantial evidence is nearly always necessary. My father had a strong case, however, and in spite of the most determined and exasperating opposition, aided and abetted in every possible way by the court, which favored the defense at every opportunity, he drove home his evidence.

After both sides had rested, the defendant's lawyer got to his feet and solemnly intoned to the six-man jury of farmers one Latin quotation after another. *"Nulli est homini perpetuum bonum. Qui desiderat pacem praeparet bellum. O quam cito transit gloria mundi!"*

The counsel for the defense rolled these under his tongue with relish, and the jury seemed much impressed. Then in a low, almost an injured tone he began a discussion of the "ridiculously inadequate" evidence that had been offered against his client. As he went on he gathered force and soon was shouting so that he could have been heard blocks away. But at the end he lowered his voice and fell once more into Latin. *"Ego cogito, ergo sum."*

After the defense counsel had seated himself my father rose and stood silent before the jury for a time. Then he began to intone in imitation of his opponent all the most common Latin phrases which came readily to mind. *"Sic semper tyrannis... multum in parvo... tempus fugit... e pluribus unum..."*

He paused, looking earnestly from one member of the jury to another. "That, gentlemen of the jury, is Latin. But," he shouted in a thunderous voice, "what has *Latin* got to do with it? This man was arrested for *stealing hogs—!"*

An outburst of laughter greeted this sally, and after that it was all over but the shouting. The defendant was held for the grand jury and eventually sent to Auburn, where he had a long time to reflect upon the maxims quoted by his learned counsel.

All the justices of the peace in a township have concurrent jurisdiction, and it is a favorable trick of the pettifogger to bring his suit before the justice least accessible to the defendant. The more isolated the place the better the pettifogger seems to like it. In an early case of my father's involving the sale of a threshing machine the defendant was summoned to appear before Justice Smith, a delightful old farmer who used to hold court in his own parlor among the framed mottoes on the wall and the wax flowers under glass. The stool of an Esty organ was used as the witness stand, and the opposing counsel sat at opposite ends of a sewing table. My father had brought with him a dozen or more threshing hands who were to be called as witnesses, but there was no room for them in the house, and they stood in the dooryard and listened to the testimony through the open windows.

When dinner time came the justice excused himself and retired to his own dining room to eat, leaving lawyers, litigants, and witnesses to sit in the parlor, where they could smell the tantalizing aroma of roasting meat, the pungent scent of pies baking in the oven. The case had not been completed at six o'clock, and the torture was repeated. There was no place within miles where they could go to eat; so they sat and suffered. The famished jurymen did not get the case until nearly nine o'clock, and at one minute after nine they were back with a verdict. My father never could remember which side won the case. That little detail was apparently not important enough to remain in his memory. But there was one thing he never could forget: the only person foresighted enough to bring his lunch was the pettifogger who brought the case.

During the early years of my father's practice there was hardly a week when he did not have horse cases to try. At that time the entire burden of rural transportation fell to old Dobbin. He pulled the plow and the farm machinery; he drew the crops to market; he hauled the buggies and carriages as well as the hacks and stages. Where a car or a tractor stands today there stood at that time a horse, or perhaps a team of horses.

A good horse, sound and well-broken, could be bought in those days for $100. For $50 a fair horse for work or general utility could be had. Usually these $50 nags were more than eight years old. After a horse has passed eight summers the condition of his teeth ceases to be an indication of his age. All that can be told is that he is more than eight years old. Nothing short of a high-blooded stepper would bring as much as $150. A good Morgan or a Hambletonian could be bought for that figure, and the books are full of cases in which a very ordinary critter would be sold as blooded stock. In almost every horse case the question of warranty would come up, a warranty as to age, breeding, disposition, or soundness.

With the passing of the horse, the justice court lost much of its color as well as its revenue; for swapping automobiles, even the kind that has the "heaves" and is knee-sprung, brings very little litigation into the justice court.

There was a famous old horse lawyer in Wayne County who had formerly been a Methodist minister but had fallen from grace and gone into law. He was a tall man, bald as an egg, with a long, bulbous nose that he used to stroke diligently whenever he was angry or perplexed. It was well to look out for yourself when old Luke Horton began to pull his nose. The old fellow was absolutely without ethics or principles, and he had a diabolical faculty for finding holes in the law through which a slimy malefactor could slip to safety.

When the ex-parson was around, no warranty, however ironclad, was safe unless it was in writing and nailed down. Old Luke's speech, which always had a strong nasal twang, was quick and jerky. In cross-examining he counted on confusing the witness by his speed, and he used to fire his questions with the rapidity and confusion of a corn popper. His summing up sounded like a mixture of prayer and Billingsgate. At times it was hard to tell whether he was addressing his remarks to the Squire or the Deity.

My father remarked once during a trial that he hardly knew whether to make his objections to this court or the one behind the Gates of Jasper.

"Either of 'em, Counselor," the parson snapped back. "One is as likely to give you hell as the other."

While he was acquiring the technique of pleading horse cases my father took some severe drubbings from Old Luke. But the time came when he could meet the old horse wrangler on his own ground at even money. After that the news of a horse case between them would bring the whole countryside into town. Both were good entertainers, and in addition to a sharply tried lawsuit the spectators were sure of some good laughs. As a result of his experience with horse cases my father became a real expert on the diseases of horses. Veterinarians dreaded to be cross-examined by him, for he could question a man on a simple ailment like spavin for two hours without repeating himself. He once completely nullified by his cross-examination of a noted horse trainer testimony that might otherwise have cost his client the loss of a race horse worth several thousand dollars.

There were those who made a business of horse cases, but to my father they were simply part of the day's work. He took them whenever they came along, just as he took every other kind of case. And at the end of five or six years of training in justice court he had rounded into a very competent trial lawyer, at ease in court, with a gift in the selection of juries that amounted almost to clairvoyance and an aptitude for handling witnesses that kept his cases unusually free from the exceptions that so often wreck an otherwise watertight verdict.

NATHANIEL HAWTHORNE

Niagara

It was an afternoon of glorious sunshine, without a cloud, save those of the cataracts. I gained an insulated rock, and beheld a broad sheet of brilliant and unbroken foam, not shooting in a curved line from the top of the precipice, but falling headlong down from height to depth. A narrow stream diverged from the main branch, and hurried over the crag by a channel of its own, leaving a little pine-clad island and a streak of precipice between itself and the larger sheet. Below arose the mist, on which was painted a dazzling sunbow with two concentric shadows,—one, almost as perfect as the original brightness; and the other, drawn faintly round the broken edge of the cloud.

Still I had not half seen Niagara. Following the verge of the island, the path led me to the Horseshoe, where the . . . broad [river], rushing along on a level with its banks, pours its whole breadth over a concave line of precipice, and thence pursues its course between lofty crags towards Ontario. A sort of bridge, two or three feet wide, stretches out along the edge of the descending sheet, and hangs upon the rising mist, as if that were the foundation of the frail structure. Here I stationed myself in the blast of wind, which the rushing river bore along with it. The bridge was tremulous beneath me, and marked the tremor of the solid earth. I looked along the whitening rapids, and endeavored to distinguish a mass of water far above the falls, to follow it to their verge, and go down with it, in fancy, to the abyss of clouds and storm. Casting my eyes across the river, and every side, I took in the whole scene at a glance, and tried to comprehend it in one vast idea. After an hour thus spent, I left the bridge, and, by a staircase, winding almost interminably round a post, descended to the base of the precipice. From that point, my path lay over slippery stones, and among great fragments of the cliff, to the edge of the cataract, where the wind at once enveloped me in spray, and perhaps dashed the rainbow round me. Were my long desires fulfilled? And had I seen Niagara?

Oh that I had never heard of Niagara till I beheld it! Blessed were the

From *The Dolliver Romance and Other Pieces,* published by J. R. Osgood and Co., Boston, 1876.

wanderers of old, who heard its deep roar, sounding through the woods, as the summons to an unknown wonder, and approached its awful brink, in all the freshness of native feeling. Had its own mysterious voice been the first to warn me of its existence, then, indeed, I might have knelt down and worshipped. But I had come thither, haunted with a vision of foam and fury, and dizzy cliffs, and an ocean tumbling down out of the sky,—a scene, in short, which nature had too much good taste and calm simplicity to realize. My mind had struggled to adapt these false conceptions to the reality, and finding the effort vain, a wretched sense of disappointment weighed me down....

Gradually, and after much contemplation, I came to know, by my own feelings, that Niagara is indeed a wonder of the world, and not the less wonderful, because time and thought must be employed in comprehending it. Casting aside all preconceived notions, and preparation to be dire-struck or delighted, the beholder must stand beside it in the simplicity of his heart, suffering the mighty scene to work its own impression. Night after night, I dreamed of it, and was gladdened every morning by the consciousness of a growing capacity to enjoy it.

JESSIE B. RITTENHOUSE

A Girl of the Genesee Valley

I was never too young to know that the old valley where I was born was beautiful. I can remember coming out of the house in the early morning and standing on a walk, lined with pink spirea, bleeding-heart, and lilies, to watch the sun put on its workaday light and roll the white mists to the hilltops. I could see the two tall Lombardy poplars at the foot of the terrace and the driveway between them; the great elm which stood at the left of the lawn, covering it with shade; the twin elms which grew upon the bank of the creek, arching over the deep pool below; and, beyond the white bridge spanning the creek, a boat drawn leisurely from lock to lock of the Genesee Valley Canal....

The selection from *My House of Life,* by Jessie B. Rittenhouse, copyright 1934, is reprinted by permission of and arrangement with Houghton, Mifflin Company, the authorized publishers.

...The orchard in May was a great pink tent, a flowery pavilion where one could smell the sweet air and hear the humming bees. There was no prohibition as to breaking the branches, since the apples in season were so plentiful we could not use them. Indeed, in the autumn, when the pickers had sorted the best for market, when several barrels had been put into the cellar and a load of the inferior grades drawn to the cider-mill, there were still enough that the poor families about us might come in and help themselves.

It was the same with the vineyard which my grandfather had planted on a sunny slope above the creek and from which he sold grapes in large quantities. There were the Concords, the muscadines, the Delawares, their luscious clusters, blue or red or amber, perfuming all the air. After we had disposed of what we could, and made a toppling load of them into wine, we could still remember the neighbors.

What delight it was to see the wine-press running with the scarlet juice, to watch it put into casks and stored in the cellar for medicinal purposes, or furnished to churches for the communion service! ...

'Here comes the boat!' may well be taken as the slogan of my childhood. There were two locks of the Genesee Valley Canal on the farm, the house being so placed as to give an unobstructed view of both. We could see the boat coming before it gained the lower lock and by taking to our heels could reach the spot before the gates swung open and the foamy water rushed in. Standing eagerly upon the edge, we would watch the boat rise higher and higher until it reached our level, the signal for us to jump on for our ride to the lock above. We seldom went empty-handed, but had provided ourselves, in anticipation of the moment, with cookies, fruit, or some other treat for those on board; for there was always a family on the boat, the man in charge and his frowzy wife who acted as cook and laundress. A washing was usually drying on the line and a baby or two running around, but there is no record that one of these hopefuls ever plunged overboard—so does Nature protect the undesirable. We were hailed with glee by these infants, owing to the cookies, and were in high favor with all on board, so that our delight was keen as we rode from lock to lock, often staying on until we reached one farther up the valley....

The dinner-table was set in the long old-fashioned dining-room and the best napery and silver had been brought out to grace an occasion momentous to me—my first excursion into the world. Not that my going would have been sufficient cause to bring out the white-and-gold china which had come down from grandmother or the best tablecloth or the small stock of solid silver, used only on state occasions, but the prettiest and youngest aunt, the aunt who still wore her hair in long curls down her back and who bore the charming name of Isabel Eddith MacArthur, was to return that day from a lengthy visit to us and her fiancé was coming to fetch her....

It was for him, then, that the table gleamed with the best napery and silver, for him that the white-and-gold china had been brought forth, for him that we had fricasseed chicken and dumpling, lemon pie, and many other things for which my mother was famous. It was a midday dinner, as we were to start immediately after for our long drive across country....

This was the first time I had ever seen the great elms on the 'flats' of the Genesee Valley, elms that would require the encircling arms of two men to span. These trees are among the largest in western New York, and the whole route is one of great beauty. Before reaching the flats, one passes the famous 'high-banks' where he can look down a deep gorge upon the river below....

I must have been ignominiously asleep when we reached the farm at nightfall, as I cannot remember the arrival nor the supper, but only of being put to bed in a large room, where I soon forgot everything until, long after as it seemed, I woke to hear a rushing about downstairs and to see a brilliant light reflected into the room. I jumped up and went to the window just in time to see my aunt and her lover and all the family at the farm running down the road toward the red light, which I knew must be a fire. It was at a neighboring farmhouse and I was left alone on the assumption that I would sleep. I could not run after them and they were too far to hear my call, so I stayed alone, standing by the window and watching the flames until they came back an hour or so afterwards.

This fright stamped the beginning of the visit upon my memory, but a far more indelible impression is left of the next morning when, dressed in one of my pretty new gowns, I came downstairs and went out into the yard. It was an exquisite summer morning and everything was suffused with a magical light, the light that irradiates the earth and air to the eyes of childhood. I can remember the sense of this light about me more vividly than the objects it touched, and it was so in all of my childhood. There were summer mornings in the old valley when I can still see myself standing looking away toward the hills and conscious only of being enveloped in a wonderful light, not sensing the objects within it. It is such an impression I carry away from the first morning upon my uncle's farm.

Indeed, I seem to recall very little of the visit and have introduced it because of the fact that it became the forerunner of other and more important ones, for my aunt was married in the autumn and set up a charming home in the little town of Conesus, whither I was bidden for the winter, to escape the long walk over the hills to the district school at home. We had fully a mile and a half to go over a bleak road which drifted level with the fences and it was necessary for father to get out the sleigh and break the roads much of the time in winter. In summer the road was beautiful, and I used to attend the district school during that period, as the year was then divided into two terms, but it was out of the question to struggle through the drifts in winter.

At Conesus there was a village school with several departments and I forged rapidly ahead; but it is not my studies that made the impression, but the delightful home where everything was so beautifully appointed and where there was so much love and cheer. My aunt had the touch of the artist in everything pertaining to a home and was also famous for her hospitality. I was allowed to entertain all the children I wished, and little parties were given me, with such cakes and ice cream as I have never since tasted. At Christmas there was a tree with presents, not only for me, but for all of my friends. No child could have had conditions more like a fairy tale than those which surrounded me from the time I was seven to thirteen years old, but in looking back upon it I recall more vividly getting hold of Dickens and Thackeray than all the parties at which I was allowed to play the small hostess.

RUDYARD KIPLING

Buffalo's Wheat Elevators

It was my felicity to catch a grain steamer and an elevator emptying that same steamer. The steamer might have been two thousand tons burden. She was laden with wheat in bulk; from stem to stern, thirteen feet deep, lay the clean, red wheat. There was no twenty-five per cent dirt admixture about it at all. It was wheat, fit for the grindstones as it lay. They maneuvered the fore-hatch of that steamer directly under an elevator—a house of red tin a hundred and fifty feet high. Then they let down into that fore-hatch a trunk as if it had been the trunk of an elephant, but stiff because it was a pipe of iron-clamped wood. And the trunk had a steel-shod nose to it, and contained an endless chain of steel buckets.

From *The Selected Works of Rudyard Kipling*. Published 1900.

Then the captain swore, raising his eyes to heaven, and a gruff voice answered him from the place he swore at, and certain machinery, also in the firmament, began to clack, and the glittering, steel-shod nose of that trunk burrowed into the wheat and the wheat quivered and sunk upon the instant as water sinks when the siphon sucks, because the steel buckets within the trunk were flying upon their endless round, carrying away each its appointed morsel of wheat.

The elevator was a Persian well wheel—a wheel squashed out thin and cased in a pipe, a wheel driven not by bullocks, but by much horse-power, licking up the grain at the rate of thousands of bushels the hour. And the wheat sunk into the fore-hatch while a man looked—sunk till the brown timbers of the bulkheads showed bare and men leaped down through clouds of golden dust and shoveled the wheat furiously round the nose of the trunk, and got a steam-shovel of glittering steel and made that shovel also, till there remained of the grain not more than a horse leaves in the fold of his nose-bag.

In this manner do they handle wheat at Buffalo. On one side of the elevator is the steamer, on the other the railway track; and the wheat is loaded into the cars in bulk. Wah! wah! God is great, and I do not think He ever intended Gar Sahai or Luckman Narain to supply England with her wheat. India can cut in not without profit to herself when her harvest is good and the American yield poor; but this very big country can upon the average supply the earth with all the beef and bread that is required.

20TH CENTURY

HENRY W. CLUNE

Linden Street

Living far back from a main road, in the center of a plot of some 20 acres of land, and with practically no neighborly intercourse, I sometimes wonder if the old spirit of neighborliness that gave such a distinct character to the average residential street before the advent of the motor car, the movie and other institutions of the present era that tend to take people out of and away from their homes, anywhere exists....

The pace of life today doesn't give much time for sitting on the front porch. The pace of traffic in the street doesn't permit kids to sit on the curb, just outside the nimbus of the street lamp, reviewing the day's events or planning for the future as we kids in Linden Street used to do every summer's night. The backyard, once the sanctified, inviolate area of retreat, domestic labor and entertainment of every home owner, where one might, if one wished, raise chickens, play croquet, sift ashes, paint screen doors, grow rutabagas, breed dogs, experiment in floriculture, beat rugs, dry curtains on frames, or cultivate plum trees, has generally given up its homely domestic functions to make room for the two-car garage.

We, in Linden Street, were a neighborly crowd in the old days. The railing of the front porch was the proper, the logical, open forum, each morning, when Mrs. So and So came out to shake the dust from a small rug and talk with her next door neighbor about her husband's lumbago, the price of eggs, little Tommy's colic, and weren't those tough boys, from down around Clin-

From *Seen & Heard* by Henry W. Clune. Published by *The Democrat and Chronicle*, Rochester, N.Y., 1933. Reprinted by permission of the publisher.

ton Avenue, who went hooting through the street at midnight, just too awful?

Supper over, of a summer's evening there was no feverish unrest until the front door was closed and locked and the entire household barged forth to go places and do things. Instead, the head of the house, more than likely, was to be found ensconced in his particular porch nook, trying to read the paper against the failing light of early evening, while the pleasant fumes of a mellow pipe filtered through the darkling fronds and creepers of a honeysuckle vine.

Life moved generally at a milder pace than it does today. People had time for friendly intercourse on front porches, in front parlors and over the backyard fence. Many of the social activities of the small group of neighbors in our section of the street were confined to the neighbors themselves. When someone entertained at a large party, everyone contributed a card table or extra silverware.

Once a year we held a backyard circus, "General Admission, 2 cents," which attracted spectators far outside the precincts of our little clan. Maloy's backyard, with chairs and benches tiered back eight or ten rows, offered the grandstand section; ours, because of its large swing, was converted into the arena. Distinctly, I remember the last of these affairs. Our chief performer on the trapeze that hung from the uprights of the swing was an attractive little girl, now grown to attractive womanhood. Under the influence of a famous aerialist of the day (Carmon, I believe she called herself), who had recently appeared at Cook's Opera House, and who prefaced her athletic exhibition by gracefully removing some of her dainty feminine accessories and tossing them into the audience, our star performer, resting easily on the bar of the trapeze, was calmly divesting herself of her outer clothing, in full view of the gaping multitude, when her mother rushed from a grandstand seat with the sharp adjuration, "Mary! Stop it! Get down from there—and keep your clothes on!" The interruption, it might be added, was exceedingly well timed.

The affairs of one household were often known to the members of several households. Kitchen recipes were freely exchanged, and during the canning season, our section of the street was pervaded with odors of chili sauce, mustard pickles and jellies of various fruits. If some new delicacy resulted from the experimentation of one housewife, she rushed next door with a sample and the recipe; although, with the culinary rivalry that existed those days, I sometimes heard it whispered that the recipes were often altered with deliberate, and slightly malicious intent, in the offering.

There were famed specialists in certain types of foods in our neighborhood. Saturday was always baking day. Waiting until her older son John had completed his Saturday morning cellar chores, I have often sat in the kitchen of Mrs. Tiefel's home and watched her deftly drop fat circles of white dough into an iron kettle of boiling fat. Three, four, five minutes, and her long handled fork would reach back into the kettle, spear a fried cake, and lift it to the stove rack, spread with brown paper, above. No one has ever made fried cakes any better. The crisp integument was golden brown and once your teeth reached through this a deliciously rich, a creamy substance gave surpassing delight to the palate. Just to sit there and catch the odors of those fried cakes was a treat; to be offered one, two—sometimes four or five—as they came, fresh and still warm from the drying paper, was an experience of boyhood that still, recalling it, brings moisture to my lips.

We formed the Linden Athletic Club in an abandoned chickencoop in Kies' backyard; we bought the largest giant fire-crackers at Plumb's store, at the South Avenue corner, and raised tin pans and tin cans high above the housetops long before respectable people had arisen on the morning of the Glorious Fourth. Once each year we hired a large carry-all, which Mrs. Tiefel, sitting erect on the front seat, arms spread wide like a chariot driver's, drove all the way to Kiefer's farm, in Henrietta, where we played all day in the barn and orchard and dined sumptuously with our elders (the men folk usually rode out in the evening on their bicycles) on fricasseed chicken and luscious biscuits; our coasting parties on Warner's Hill were the chief delights of winter.

Charlie Maloy's room was directly across from mine and our small writing desks were pushed close to the windows so we could see one another at work in our "offices" each evening. We had codes and signals; we held boxing matches in the cellar; foot races along the street; baseball games in the Ellwanger & Barry nursery, just over the back fence. I raised two bull terriers, and had a pair of rabbits, and once a skunk got under the Kies' porch, and the neighborhood was almost an impossible place in which to live until, by great dexterity and skill, the unwelcome visitor was driven from his strongly intrenched position. We dropped comic valentines on the porch of an irascible old man, and were caught, and sharply scolded, for laying a tick-tack against a spinster's window.

But we all hung together; Linden Street against the world! There were quarrels, and days when some of us passed without speaking. But these were comparatively rare and confined only to the younger members of the families. If anyone was ill the nearest neighbor brought over a smoking kettle of broth; our birthday parties followed a regular menu: Boston beans and steam sausages, and great quantities of cocoa with whipped cream. There were the Maloys, the Tiefels, the Dunbars, the Kieses, the Joneses, the Obergs, and others. Sleepy Linden Street, they used to call our thoroughfare. Perhaps it was. But a great street, withal; and a neighborly one.

Golden Plow

Henry Toothill, a mild mannered, soft-spoken little man of 81 years, who lives at 324 Plymouth Avenue South, dropped in the other afternoon to tell about the plow he once gold plated that won the gold medal at the first Chicago Fair, the Pan-American Exposition, and great exhibitions at Paris, Berlin and Tokyo.

For many years Mr. Toothill was proprietor of the Toothill Plating and Metal Arts Works at 119 North Water Street. He did the first plating ever used by the Eastman Kodak Company in the days when that gigantic industry was struggling for a start; he plated plumbing fixtures for Samuel Sloan & Co. and many other leading Rochester concerns. In those days, he said, he could plate almost anything, even a locomotive, if someone asked him to. One day a fellow came in and asked him if he could gold plate a full-sized plow.

Mr. Toothill thought the caller was joking. Replying in a spirit of jest he told him to send on the plow. A few days later the plow arrived and he realized that the whole thing was in dead earnest. It had come from the Syracuse Caill Plow Company, who wanted to feature it in the company's exhibit at the '93 World's Fair in Chicago. Mr. Toothill looked the plow over and shook his head. The plow was made of steel, and gold plating would not do too well on steel. A better idea, he said, was to cast a plow in bronze, on which the gold plate would hold.

The plow company acted on this suggestion, and Mr. Toothill coated the bronze plow with 24-karat gold. He plated the entire implement with gold, even the little gauge wheel in front, the colter, the clevis; everything, except the handles. These were made of black ebony. When the job was completed it cost $3,000 for gold alone and Mr. Toothill had spent a month at it.

The plow company people were tickled with Mr. Toothill's work, and after the plow had won its first gold medal at Chicago they permitted Mr. Toothill to display it in a store window in Rochester for a few days. Later it was put into the Pan-American Exposition, and afterwards it made a round of the big foreign shows, winning everywhere. In the end it was mounted on a mahogany base, covered with glass and retired to the Syracuse show rooms of the plow company. For all Mr. Toothill knows, it may still be there.

Mr. Toothill is an Englishman by birth, but an American by breeding. His father was a metal worker in Sheffield, England, who migrated to the American Sheffield, at Meriden, Conn. From there Mr. Toothill moved to Rochester, many years ago. He says "Toothill" is a good old English name that was given, years and years ago, to a street in London. Mr. Toothill knows the etymological significance of his name, which is a rare one in this country, but I have forgotten what he told me about this.

HELEN E. ALLEN

The Jumping Bass of Oak Orchard Creek

Time was when the jumping black bass of Oak Orchard Creek had tongues awagging over a wide area of western New York and even in more distant places. Many a hot argument took place between those who had seen the fish in action and people who did not believe their tales. But as the old-timers pass away and new families move into the community a new generation is arising which is woefully ignorant of the whole affair. Therefore when it appeared that old age was at last about to overtake the smith of Two Bridges, who was the central figure in these episodes, it seemed like a duty to posterity to hear again from his lips the true account of the antics of the jumping bass and record it in the annals of history.

It all began one lovely summer evening when John Podgers after a busy day at his anvil and forge, was enjoying a ride in his little canopy-topped steamboat. His cousin, whose name was also John Podgers but who was better known as Jim's John, was as usual running the engine. As frequently happened they had aboard some passengers from the nearby summer resort, Oak Orchard-on-the-Lake. These two couples had come to The Inn for a complete rest. An evening boat ride seemed like a peaceful way to bring to

From *New York Folklore Quarterly,* Summer, 1950. Reprinted by permission of the New York Folklore Society.

a close a quiet day. They had brought mandolins and banjos with them and languorously played and sang as they rode along. John said that the music sounded beautiful there on the water, and joy and contentment were complete as the boat glided smoothly along the tranquil stream and the evening breeze, soft as velvet, caressed their cheeks.

Suddenly the nocturnal harmony was shattered by a woman's scream and the clatter of mandolins dropped to the bottom of the boat! John looked around to see what had happened. The two ladies were crouched up on the seat. A big black bass was flopping about with the mandolins in the bottom of the boat. The ladies were moaning with terror but the men were too excited to notice.

"Will that fish jump out?" asked one.

"Well," John said, "he jumped in so I guess he'll jump out again if he feels like it."

At that the man made a lunge and grabbed it with both hands.

"I brought along fifty dollars' worth of fishing tackle and have been fishing for a week without getting a bite," he said. "This fish is not getting away!"

The ladies wanted to go ashore, but their husbands insisted that John take them up the creek again. The bass kept jumping and soon six big ones had landed in the boat. By this time the wives were in hysterics, so the men had to take them in.

One of the men found a pail in which to carry the fish and said to John, "Come up to the hotel with us, for no one will believe us when we tell this fish story."

At The Inn every one admired the bass. They weighed them and found that the six totaled eighteen pounds. But no one would believe that they had jumped into the steamboat. So John was engaged to take a bunch of men on a fishing expedition the next evening.

A jeering crowd of men boarded the boat and rode up and down the creek for a time without anything happening. But when it grew dark enough for the steamer's headlight to shine clearly out over the water, the bass started jumping and several landed in the boat. John chuckled to himself as the jeers changed to cheers, and when they went ashore each man tried to outdo the others in the tales he told of the leaping fish.

After that John and his steamboat were in great demand. Guests at the summer hotels, cottagers, neighbors, and people from nearby towns were out nearly every night. Usually the black bass were accommodating and put on a good show, besides providing many a delicious fish dinner, but sometimes there was great disappointment as friends or relatives were brought from a distance to see the piscatorial spectacle and nary a fish showed up.

One evening the Presbyterian minister was in the boat when a fish landed on the canopy top, flopped about for a minute, and then slid off the other side. When they went ashore the Reverend told his friends that now the bass had taken to jumping right over the boat.

A gentleman from the summer colony hired a fishing boat once and hitched it behind the steamer. Quite a crowd was out that night and John said that the black bass were in great jumping form. Every time one landed in either boat the men would yell, and there was great excitement to see which one would get the bigger catch. The steamboat won out and both together had fifty-two fish. A bushel basket would not hold them all. Of course, only a small proportion of the bass that jumped landed in the boats. John said that from his position in the bow, looking down the beam of the headlight, the fish were breaking water so fast that night that it looked as if the creek was boiling. It was a fantastic sight: the bubbling water, the many fish jumping just above the surface, and many more that leaped high and then came horizontally for a few feet, straight toward the light, with wet glistening bodies, fins and tails wiggling as if swimming through the air, and then dropped back into the water or into the boats.

The jumping bass of Oak Orchard Creek were the chief topic of conversation in this section for a while and their fame spread far and wide. This was one of the times when the building of a railroad from Batavia to Oak Orchard Harbor was being seriously considered. A Batavia newspaper derisively pointed out that it would be dangerous to build the railroad along the creek bank as the company had planned to do, for these precocious fish would probably jump through the train windows and injure the passengers.

A lawyer among the cottage crowd wondered if catching fish in this way might be breaking some game law. But another lawyer said to John:

"Don't worry about the law. You have a right to run your boat up and down the creek; and if those fool fish want to jump aboard, that's their lookout."

The incident that the old smith retold with the most relish occurred late in the summer. A gentleman from New York City was among the group aboard the steamer one evening and was greatly entertained by the leaping bass. He asked if he could engage John to take him out a week or so later.

"They will put me in a lunatic asylum if I go back to the city and tell this yarn," he said. "I must have a witness to bear me out."

One evening a short time later, John received word to come to Point

Breeze to pick up this man. He was accompanied by a very disgusted, large, elderly gentleman whom he introduced as his brother.

"Of all the crazy ideas," the older man sputtered as he came aboard, "dragging a busy man 'way out here from New York City to see a fish jump into a boat. I never in all my life heard such nonsense! Where shall I sit?" he continued, "I wouldn't want to interfere with any fish that wishes to come aboard."

"Sit where you please," John said. "The fish won't mind."

The brother sat down near the engine and watched Jim's John.

"These flying fish ever jump down the smoke stack and kick the fire out?" he asked sarcastically.

"Well, not yet," replied Jim's John.

The man who had engaged the boat was rather nervous. Having been blistered by his brother's wrath, he was very anxious for a lot of fish to jump aboard. But as he looked out over the smooth, shining surface of the water there was not even a ripple to indicate the presence of any fish.

The older brother took out his meerschaum pipe, caressed it fondly, and lighted up. It was a pleasant evening for a boat ride; a good smoke mellowed his mood, and presently he forgot about the fish and began to enjoy himself.

Suddenly there was a bellow of rage, a wild scrambling about, and a roar of laughter. A big bass had jumped right past the older man's head, showering him with water and knocking his pipe out of his mouth. The fish and the pipe were slithering about in the bottom of the boat while he was lunging around trying to rescue his precious meerschaum. His brother was laughing so hard the tears rolled down his cheeks.

After he had regained his pipe and composure he was as enthusiastic as his younger brother about the sport, and they kept John running the boat up and down the creek for several hours. Once they started, the fish jumped fast and furiously that night and the brothers got quite a haul.

That was about the end of the season. The next year the black bass of Oak Orchard Creek appeared to be more sophisticated and scarcely noticed the steamboat's headlight.

MRS. WINTHROP CHANLER

The Happy Valley

In the autumn of 1903 we went to stay with Major and Mrs. W. Austin Wadsworth in Geneseo for the opening meet of the Genesee Valley Hunt. Austin Wadsworth, owner of broad ancestral acres, kept a fine pack of English foxhounds. He was an old friend of my husband, who had long been an habitué of the hospitable Homestead and a member of the G.V.H. From Washington, Tuxedo Park, New York, or wherever we happened to be living, Wintie would, during the hunting season, take a night train that reached Geneseo or a neighboring station in time for the meet, would perhaps stay over for another "couple or three" gallops, and come home refreshed and rejoicing. "It is God's own country," he would say, and add ruefully, "but it is real country and you would not like it."...

In the days when Wintie went to Geneseo without me, Austin Wadsworth was unmarried and kept bachelor's hall at the Homestead. I had occasionally been invited, but I was loth to leave the babies, and Wintie, not sure that I should enjoy it, had never urged me to go along. Now Austin Wadsworth, who had become a Major during the Spanish War, had lately taken to himself a wife, the handsome Miss Elizabeth Perkins of Boston and Cotuit, a tall, spirited girl much younger than himself. He could not have found a more appropriate or a more devoted helpmate; she was—and still is, I am happy to say—a fine rider, a great lover of dogs, an enthusiastic gardener, initiated from childhood in the duties and interests, the pleasures and predicaments, of country life. She survived the Major, who died towards the end of the Great War, and brought up their only son, William Perkins, administering the estate until he was of age to take it over. William P. Wadsworth is now Master of the Genesee Valley Hounds, and long life to him!

The Homestead represents a century and a half of American tradition. The original structure was a blockhouse fortified against Indian raids, for the Genesee Valley was still the scene of Indian fighting when the Wads-

From *Autumn in the Valley* by Mrs. Winthrop Chanler. Published by Little, Brown and Company, Boston, 1936. Reprinted by permission.

worths first settled there, before the Big Tree Treaty put an end to hostilities. Much of the property was bought from the Indians, and the Wadsworths hold many of the original grants, made out on pelts. The blockhouse was altered and enlarged past all recognition, but the old solid timber walls are incorporated in the alterations, and when it came to wiring the house for electric lighting, their massive solidity presented the stolid defense planned against Indian aggression and gave much resistance to the peaceful attack of electricians.

The Wadsworths have always held their own in their country's history. The house is full of family portraits—a Revolutionary general and worthies of every sort. A well-stocked library contains Audubon's famous folios of birds and the noble army of classics which the present day seems to have so little use for. The whole place has the increasingly rare quality of having been a home for many generations of pleasant living. It has, since anyone in the Valley can remember, been the centre of cordial hospitality.

Austin Wadsworth was an accomplished horseman and breeder of horses. He kept a large stable of excellent hunters and his guests were royally mounted.

It was an amber-gold October morning; the hounds met before the Big Tree Inn on the unpaved village street. I rode Enid, a grand chestnut mare, spirited and kind, warranted an undefeated jumper, she and I both inwardly excited with that delicious tingle of eagerness and apprehension which horse and rider feel together before hunting. As a girl I used to feel it before a ball; the first good waltz with the right partner dispelled it. And so it is with fox-hunting. Once over the first jump, all your tremors are gone and the physical joy of living and riding is all you are conscious of.

The members of the Hunt were all strangers to me, but Wintie had long been a favorite with them and they were kind to his wife; I met that day people who have been my friends and neighbors ever since. This first meeting, on horseback, was very gay and informal. I have the impression that as we cantered side by side over the Oak Lot on our way to the covert, three or four of us burst into song. There were many bold riders in the field: the Wadsworths, Lords of the Manor, well represented by various branches of the family, among them the witty Jim Sam, something of a black sheep, who attached unforgettable nicknames to this and that member of the Hunt —"Red Haven Splits," "Angry Mat," "Little Potatoes" (are hard to peel), and many more.

From Buffalo came the tall Milburn brothers, of whom Devereux later won fame as a polo player and winner of international matches, and the whole tribe of Carys and Rumseys, sportsmen all and hard riders. There were six Cary brothers, most of them generally in the field.

The Carys originally came from Batavia, where they owned a handsome old house now converted into an Historical Museum. Long before I met them, the family had moved to Buffalo, where Dr. Charles, one of the six brothers, married a Rumsey, as did their only sister, Miss Evelyn Cary. The Rumseys owned houses and lands in Buffalo and the two families made a powerful clan. A whole chapter could easily be written about the Carys alone. When the youngest of the seven children was still a baby in arms they had all been taken to Europe by their parents, Dr. and Mrs. Cary, and had made the grand tour in a coach and four—their own four. Dr. Cary was a famous four-in-hand driver and drove himself, while the older boys rode the extra horses. At some wayside inn where they were putting up for the night, it was found that Baby Seward was missing. Someone then remembered that he had been put to sleep in the rumble of the coach. Search was made, lantern in hand, in the dark coach house, and the baby was found. This same baby grew up to be a great polo player. He is now a grandfather of grown children; I saw him last in the hunting field not many months ago. We pulled out together after we had both had enough....

On that first morning, we hunted the beautiful country north of Geneseo, great open fields for perfect galloping alternating with rides cut through primeval forests and steep adventurous scrambles up and down the gulleys and hogbacks, the Sugar Bush, the Big Woods, the Oxbow. In those days this part of the country was all fenced with timber—snake fences which had to be taken at the proper angle, and straight board fences where the top board was often broken by one or another of the riders and thus made easier for those who were not overbold. The landscape is lovely in every direction with rich variety of field and forest, wide pastures and wooded hills. The Genesee River meanders through it in endless curves and "oxbow" loops, bordered on either bank by fringes of woodland. The country is intersected by deep gullies cut by streams that swell to torrents in rainy seasons and wither to an imperceptible trickle during the summer.

I have now ridden over these banks and braes for thirty years, have cantered happily over the wide, open spaces, and their beauty never fails. As I write, my daughter comes in, flushed with the joy of a forty-five-minute run on the Home Farm Flats. "And, oh, Mummy, it was so beautiful. We were galloping as fast as we could and yet I could not forget how lovely the whole picture was." I know how she felt, how I still feel, for all my threescore years and ten, though now my love of riding has survived my hunting ardor, and I enjoy an easy canter more than a fast run.

I fell in love with the happy Valley on that bright October morning. I liked it indeed so well, and Wintie was so pleased with my liking it, that we have lived there ever since.

REXFORD G. TUGWELL

Buffalo

Buffalo, at the end of the century's first decade, was a small giant of a city, for the most part as ugly as the sin it sheltered. It flowered in the vast châteaux of Delaware Avenue and Chapin Parkway out of the east-side slums. The shops and stores of downtown—Main Street, Court Street, and Lafayette Square—were nothing remarkable but still able to furnish all the appurtenances of civilization. The city illustrated the best and worst of industrial America. It was pushing, inventive, and vigorous; but it was also disordered, corrupt, and hideous. Like Cleveland, Detroit, and Chicago, farther west on the Lakes, it was run by its businessmen; and its businessmen had no ambitions other than making money and retreating to their palaces with it.

Cereals from the northern plains and iron ore from the Superior ranges came plowing down the Lakes in the huge bulk carriers—hogbacks—and the Buffalo mills turned the grain into flour and feedstuffs and the ore into pig iron. In its harbor, heavy midwestern cargoes were transshipped to the Erie Canal or the East-going railroads; and in the hundreds of grimy, greasy slips of South Buffalo, canalboats were emptied into ships for passage West. The frontier industries slaughtered cattle and hogs, made soap and breakfast foods (Shredded Wheat, Quaker Oats, Force), ran mail-order businesses (Larkin), manufactured machinery and automobiles (Thomas, Pierce-Arrow), turned out paper, wallboard, cement, and lumber products. It reduced metals, fabricated steel and wire, and produced chemicals by the trainload.

All down the Niagara to the Falls, through Black Rock, the Tonawandas, La Salle, and on into the Falls city itself, the mills and factories smoked, steamed, and fumed through the days and flamed through the nights. The heavy clouds from their chimneys lay on the windward countryside like a blight. And it was there that the workers' company towns were built—endless rows of frame structures, half hidden in fumes, without gardens, without decent sanitation—a brownish swarming desert. But the industrial complex did turn out goods by the millions of tons, and they were shoveled or shoved into ships or freight trains and sent plowing or rolling away.

Around the Buffalo lake front and down toward Black Rock and the Tonawandas, the docks, piers, slips, and basins served vast warehouses, grain elevators, storage yards, and ore dumps. Even in summer, when at least the lake in the background was clear and blue, the whole waterfront had the look of having been shaken out of a gigantic bag and left to smoulder and rot in a swamp. In winter it was an arctic hell, half hidden in mist and smoke, the low clouds coming in on it from the west, everything crusted with dirty snow, dripping icicles, and sleet. Wandering through its mud flats, turning basins, and unloading slips was Buffalo Creek, most degraded of waterways, seeming to come from nowhere and ending in an obscene dispersal among rotting barges and rusting ships.

In those days this was the domain of W. J. Conners, universally known as Fingy, who was lord of the waterfront. The warehouses, mills, docks, and ships required a special breed of men, capable of enormous labors, indifferent to hardships, used to filth, and without thought for the future. Many of them were homeless; most of them illiterate, simple, savage, working hulks. It was to meet their requirements that the waterfront empire was maintained. The saloons, brothels, cheap eating places, pawnshops, flophouses—all the familiar businesses of such districts—functioned at the pleasure of the boss. Not too late in life he was a rich man; by then, too, he was a legend. More respectable citizens spoke of him in a shocked but half-humorous way, but they never gave him any real trouble. The empire lasted out his active years.

The waterfront blight crept up the streets into the city. Lower Main Street was becoming disreputable. This had been Grover Cleveland's favorite neighborhood, where for half a lifetime he had lived in furnished rooms and spent his leisure in saloons that now had degenerated into frowzy hangouts. What he had liked about them was the familiar company met in the elegance of mirrors, oil paintings, mahogany bars, and big armchairs around a card table where schooners of beer sat always at an elbow. In the noisy ease of saloons with sawdust on the floor Cleveland could really relax. They were elegant no longer. The mahogany was scarred, the chairs were rickety, and the company depressed. There were no more Clevelands.

A little farther east, Oak Street and its neighbors, as far north as Genesee, were given over to a red-light district where many of the establishments were generations old and maintained a kind of culture of their own. Their relationship with authority was an easy one. Corruption was an institution that no one expected to see disturbed. And Fingy Conners, piling up wealth, bought the Buffalo *Courier* and, when I was in high school, was building himself a green-tiled mansion at 1140 Delaware Avenue, spang in the middle of all the industrial aristocrats. He seemed not to know or not to care, having had the ambition so long, that the aristocrats were by then escaping into better-insulated suburban estates. They had limousines instead of coaches. They could travel farther from their homes to their Board rooms. And they could, they suddenly discovered, become country gentlemen. Delaware Avenue, at least its lower half, was already declining into a region of lesser uses—boardinghouses, professional offices, funeral parlors, shops, and clubs. The old mansions like that where Fillmore had lived, where McKinley had died in 1901, of which the merchants and factory owners had been so proud, were falling into strange ownerships and uses.[1]

When I knew it best Buffalo was certainly a city bursting with life and lusty growth, and its ugliness seemed no more than a natural accompaniment of this vigor. For the pushing and hauling was done by and for newly come immigrants from Ireland and Italy first, then from eastern Europe and the Near East. It was a peasant horde, a ghetto horde, translated without preparation to a completely strange environment. Many of its members did not even speak English, and they were well satisfied if they found jobs and earned a bare living. Their humility and disorganization would not last; but while it did, it was a situation made to order for political bosses and businessmen. These, like Fingy Conners, were Irish now, or German. The old families had retreated to the banks and insurance companies. The Scatcherds, the Rumseys, the Hamlins, and the Carys were no longer safely in control. The Germans owned the breweries, the distilleries, the bakeries, the stores and saloons; and soon they would be moving into the offices of company directors and financial enterprises.

St. Joseph's, a German-Polish Catholic cathedral, was being built—it was actually begun in 1910—in the old center of Protestant fashion, close to the new house Fingy was building. And next door the Seymour H. Knox mansion was to be the home of the presiding Bishop. Trinity Episcopal Church, once regarded as the appointed home of cultured religion, was left stranded

[1] The Conners family went on to become important in Buffalo's more exclusive commercial circles. A.W.J., Jr., was born in 1895 and went to Nichols preparatory school and Yale. He inherited the *Courier* and the *Enquirer* as well as other enterprises of his colorful father. He merged the Democratic *Courier* with the Republican *Express,* became vice-president of the Great Lakes Transit Corporation, a director of the Marine Trust, Sterling Engine, Maxson-Cadillac, and numerous other companies. He also became a member of the Saturn, the Buffalo, and the country clubs. W.J., III, served in World War II. Conners was by then a respectable name.

downtown, its heavy Gothic rapidly being demeaned by surrounding taxpayers shops and boardinghouses, its parishioners separated from it in distance more and more every year. Even the Germans were being visibly pushed by the Poles. The whole east side seemed to have been taken over by them. Buffalo was said to be the biggest Polish city in the world outside Poland, something the Germans, now in their third or fourth generation, spoke of with evident disgust. For the Poles were regarded as a raw and filthy people by the orderly Germans. And even the more easygoing Irish felt the competition and deplored the peasant manners of the newcomers....

Especially during the winter there was a succession of subscription balls got up by various school and other organizations. These were very formal. The ritual required full dress, the presentation of flowers, and transport in a horse-drawn coach—for these had not yet been supplanted by taxicabs for such affairs. And my memory calls up—pleasantly, I must admit—many a winter night, perhaps blizzardy and mean outside, when after dinner a most careful dressing began in our upstairs retreat. The aim was to be spotlessly turned out by about nine, when the coach was due. The flowers had been sent in the afternoon. The ride to the young lady's house took place in dignified stiffness—collars were high, clothes were tight, and the ensemble had at least to survive intact the entrance to the ballroom. The lady's house reached and the coachman told to wait, the pleasure of greeting her took place in the parlor. My standards were high; and my young women, descending the stairs in their evening gowns, corsage fresh, hair elaborately done, gold or silver slippers—and a bit of ankle—visible beneath the lifted flounces then so numerous, were really a delight, and I was often consciously glad that I could afford the paraphernalia required for such excursions.

The coach smelled a little of the livery stable, but for five dollars—as I recall—the Buffalo equipages were put at the disposal of customers until three or four in the morning, and if there was some smell, there was broadcloth and there were long springs to rock a couple of young lovers on their way home. The dancing or assembly halls were not too far, usually just over on the west side, and, arriving there, a pair of carefully got up newcomers became part of a rustling and glittering crowd. Evening clothes do wonders for women, and when they are young and happy women, with no more than the hazards of ordinary American life to look forward to, the beauty has a special quality. The girls I recall were rosy, full of grace, and warm; and young men are so constructed as to have no more than nominal resistance to such charms. At least I was.

Those were the days of waltzes and two-steps, with an occasional Virginia reel or Paul Jones. Cards, small folders with fancy cords, suitable to be kept as souvenirs, were made out for each dance, often sometime in advance. I should guess that many a grandmother's attic trunk still holds carefully tied bundles of these dance programs, evidence of conquests or disappointments, but anyway of excitements such as no one has in sober age.

The carefully arranged cards left little room for that sudden surge of mutual adoration which makes a boy and a girl find it urgently important to be together for more than one dance. But there were possibilities in a trading process that was a recognized procedure. So such emergencies could, within limits, be arranged for. There were one or two memorable occasions when I came back from such a party with a different partner from the one I had escorted so carefully there. My first had not been abandoned exactly, but an exchange had been arranged. This must have involved prodigies of bargaining effort, but the emotion inspiring it was an urgent one, and it overcame all difficulties. The sudden focusing of interest aroused by a hitherto unobserved grace of movement, a newly seen smile, or perhaps the glimpse of usually hidden charms revealed by a low-cut gown—something of the sort had been irresistible. Giving way to it and overcoming the obstacles to partnering was a satisfying activity. I never regretted the effort involved in such pursuits. As we creaked home in the big coach, kept from the freezing wind by robes and cushions, the world could seem centered in a moment and a place. A girl in his arms is heaven enough for any young man.

The girls of my youth seem to me to have been lovelier than those I see around me now. They have long since become grandmothers, as I have become a grandfather—one of those pursuits became that serious; but perhaps I am mistaken about this, merely aged. Still, I am under the impression that girls—ordinary girls, not athletes—got more exercise in those pedestrian times. And there was certainly less resort to beauty aids. They seem to me to have been healthier, to have had a higher bloom. They were plumper too, unless I am mistaken. For dieting was not yet fashionable, and curves were not regarded as deplorable. I expect my granddaughters will set me straight about this. But if they move through their world with half the grace their grandmother had, they too will be objects of delighted pursuit. What am I saying? Some of them already are.

I had no illusion about the quality of the society I moved in so pleasurably. It was not Buffalo's elite. There would have been, in fact, several grades between my circle and that of the Rumsey-Goodyear-Milburn-Schelkoff-Knox-Cary-Bissell set—the real Four Hundred. The city's annals are crowded with the extravagances of that upper class—not so spectacular in the years I write about as in the genuine Gilded Age, but still entertaining to read about. They seem incredible to a later generation; they seemed almost incredible to my own; still, they were not so far past as to be quite forgotten.

The society pages of 1910 must have reported only faded imitations of the events of ten or twenty years earlier. Surviving matriarchs were doubtless saying even then to their descendants that theirs was a stale and cheerless existence; things had been livelier and more colorful when the elite had really ruled the scene. A few times I touched the fringes of the then surviving social circle, but only at the larger charity balls and other such events. Often my coach passed those of the aristocracy along Delaware Avenue, and occasionally I made acquaintances who might have become friends; but actually I was happy with those I already had. I never, so to speak, moved up in the scale.

In the John T. Horton account of the society I have been speaking of there is a suitably sardonic account of the counterpart in Buffalo of the McAllister-Astor regime in New York. The show put on in pre-income-tax times, even in our provincial metropolis, was worthy of American ingenuity. And its vulgarity was an adequate counterpart of the way the wealth thus squandered had been acquired.

Buffalonian businessmen had no need to apologize to those in other parts. Their exploitation of their environment was total. They fought the workers with a vigor not equaled often in any other region, and they yielded to demands only at the end of riotous rebellions. They were the loudest of Americans in their appeals for tariff and other privileges; and the loudest, as well, in their support of the free competitive system. Their lawyers were among the nation's leaders in developing yellow-dog contracts, fellow-servant rules, evasions of the anti-trust acts, and blocks against welfare legislation. They were, to a later view, incredibly arrogant and selfish. And their society was no more than a fair representation of their view of their own importance. In my time the vulgarities were somewhat modified and the crudities damped down; there were boys in the family coming home from Yale and Princeton, where the elite was taught not to be ostentatious. But the attitudes were the same. A man's business was his own to run as he liked, workers were ungrateful when they made demands, and luxury was the necessary incentive to call out initiative. Also, the income tax was still nothing to worry about. There was plenty of money, and it was a public service to spend it.

If the Cary-Rumsey-Goodyear gilt was somewhat tarnished in the first decade of the century, it nevertheless had the authentic *nouveau riche* gloss. Some bloody battles had been fought, and some concessions had been made;

there was no longer quite the same confidence in superiority. But if it had been ten or fifteen years earlier that things had been at their best, they were still not too bad. There was no suffering—except a certain mental anguish, often voiced—along the avenue. The Waverly Balls had been discontinued, although they were still recalled with nostalgia. The last of these particular galas had, in fact, taken place in the home of Bronson Case Rumsey as long ago as 1898; they had been succeeded by less elaborate charades in more recent years. But there were still splendid entertainments in the châteaux and manor houses; the Charity Ball and even the 74th Regiment Ball were glamorous and elaborate. But perhaps it indicates the dimming refulgence of the really glorious era that a country boy could have gone to several of the more public entertainments for several years during his stay in Buffalo.

The season in Buffalo made the most of its wintry possibilities. The use of sleighs, like that of coaches in summer, was giving way to motorcars; but smart equipages, with peppery teams, were still commonly seen on the avenues; and in Delaware Park, just after the heavier snows, there was a show of jingling sleighs filled with fur-clad riders, rosy-cheeked in the cold. As a reminder of village childhood, I often saw boys running after these rigs with sleds to be hitched on behind. They shouted and tumbled under following horses' hoofs, but it was so much a custom that the danger was usually averted. It was not beyond the dignity of the drivers to accommodate themselves to small boys' demands. Those boys also had the park's hills for sledding and its lakes for skating. Winter at its best turned into something of a carnival. On certain evenings the city band established itself by the side of one of the lakes and played for the circling skaters. Those of us who were of a romantic age could use the ice as a ballroom floor; we danced on the glassy expanse, skates giving us a freedom mere feet could not match.

Winter, too, was a time for the theater. The Star and the Teck, as well as Shea's vaudeville, were then at their best. The Star was not new—it had been opened in 1888—but the gold paint had been freshened, and the plush draperies had been renewed; they were a deep rich red; and coming in from the wintry streets was agreeably warming. It was a small house, but it attracted week by week Broadway plays and musicals, very often with the original companies. How well I recall them! There was *The Merry Widow* with Fritzi Scheff, *The Red Mill* with Montgomery and Stone, and Raymond Hitchcock in successive comedies. The small theater was better suited to Wilde, Pinero, Shaw, and their contemporaries than to musicals, but we had both and liked them equally. Somehow, however, Strauss, Lehár, and Victor Herbert with their fragile and romantic gaiety seemed to have more appeal for me just then. I went nearly every week. Sometimes it was the larger Teck, instead of the Star. There, among others, I saw Clyde Fitch's *The City* and a beautiful performance of William Gillette in *The Blue and the Gray*.

The theaters were always full, as I recall. It was not yet fashionable to go South, away from the searching Canadian winds. And the castles on the upper west side were all open in the winter, their inhabitants home from Lakewood-on-Chautauqua, Niagara-on-the-Lake, or the hunting country in the Genesee Valley, where the vast holdings of the Wadsworth family were still intact; or even from places farther away—Saratoga, Newport, Bar Harbor, or the watering places of Europe. The social hegira was a summer phenomenon. In winter the fashionable folk all came home. Then for a few months the big houses bustled with activity, balls and entertainments went on night after night, the stables produced horses and fine equipages, and all the arts were patronized.

From some of this, at least, lesser folk might benefit. They might not have the front-row seats at the theater or the boxes at the great balls, but they could, in their appropriate degree, be present. It was all a life that most people—workers, tradesmen, and their families—might read or hear about with the same sense of remoteness that they might read or hear about the doings of European royalty. But it was not yet a time of persistent restlessness. There were occasional outbursts, especially when times were bad, and there was actual hunger or cold, and society went on with its customary gay schedule; but the welfare state was still far over the reformers' horizon, not even a realizable dream, so far as anyone could see. And the beneficiaries of unregulated capitalism were as yet not too much worried by intimations of change....

All during the nineteenth century, manufacture, mostly of semi-finished products, had been developing: pig iron (out in Lackawanna), brass, copper, wire, timber products (Tonawanda by 1880 was the biggest lumber port in the world), ships, locomotives, threshing and other farm machinery, and paper products, especially wallboard. The Union Bridge Company, at the time when the railroads were being extended most rapidly, was the largest of all the nation's bridge builders. Then of course there were the grain terminals and their subsidiary flour and feed mills which turned the produce of the prairies into flour for Easterners and feed for their horses and cattle. Presently, also, there came electric power from Niagara Falls and, almost at once, the electrochemical and similar industries. And the railroads themselves, centering in Buffalo from the South, the West, and Canada in the North, brought industry in a swelling volume.

The geographic reason for Buffalo's expansion was a cause also of the corruption which, if possible, was more degraded than that of other cities in that notorious age. What Lincoln Steffens had said of Philadelphia—that she was corrupt and contented—was not quite true of Buffalo. Her corruption matched any other city's, but her contentment was confined to the governing elite. There were occasional outbreaks of violent discontent. But since they were vigorously suppressed, they did not hinder growth. The city lay at the lower end of navigation on the Great Lakes, and it was a transfer station on the broad highway from the northern plains to the East. Even when the railroads took much of the older water traffic, they still ran along the level shores and through Buffalo on their routes to the East. The city was neither midwestern nor eastern but belonged somehow to both regions and perhaps it took the worst of each. From the Midwest came its grossness and crudity, its satisfaction in hugeness and in being tough and lavish; from the East came its love of money and its weakness for ostentation. There was sharp division among its classes, a division continually perpetuated by the inrush of foreigners, who for a generation would hardly dare think of themselves as the equals of their prosperous predecessors. Because they had come from the slums and villages of eastern Europe, their standards were primitive. A city whose houses and streets were untended, whose police were corrupt, and whose underworld throve, was not objectionable to immigrants. Such conditions might offend the Germans, but they were swamped by Poles; and matters went from bad to worse....

The Buffalo Club deserves a word for itself. It was actually a regional center of American capitalism at its time of most unlimited power. The club had not always been in the same place; by the time I knew of it, however, it had acquired the mansion of Stephen Van Rensselaer Watson, who had been the principal pioneering entrepreneur in the city's traction consolidations and who had died in 1880, leaving behind a vast house which even the fortune he also left to his descendants could not support, or perhaps they were not interested in such an establishment. At any rate, it went to the Club, and because it was centrally located and had a traditional magnificence, it was added to and embellished. "Here the magnificos foregathered in the complacent, jovial, sedate, and dignified manner of men who have immense reputations to sustain. Here they met to confer, consult, and converse on matters both grave and gay. Here they played at billiards or at sedentary games like poker, whist, and backgammon. Here they drank old wines, ancient brandies, and aged whiskies; and on great occasions they indulged a fancy for terrapin, lobster, venison, canvas-backs, and *pâté de foie gras*. The atmosphere of the place was tranquil; the decor rich, massive, and sombre, yet somehow contrived to heighten the *joie de vivre*. The place was one where Major Pendennis and Colonel Newcome would have been comfortable and at home...."

In that mansion, with its spacious rooms, its deep, rich rugs, its solid silver, its perfect service, momentous decisions were made, and all Buffalo knew that this was so. Ordinary citizens passing on the avenue looked at its high wrought-iron fence, its plate-glass windows, its expanses of brick, with a kind of awe. Politicos regarded its power and wealth with respect; workers hated its symbolism. It needed the pens of the muckrakers to expose its skeletons; but that exposure was mercifully withheld, as it was not from other institutions, and it survived sedately into my day, the home of wealth and power for all the region roundabout.

My father long aspired to membership, and presently he would be accepted. Then he too forgathered, perhaps a little timidly as a newcomer, with the others under the benign portrait of Cleveland or around the richly loaded tables. Other clubs—the Saturn, for instance, and the University—would drain off the socialite and typical collegiate product of the next generation. But the old Buffalo Club would remain what it had been from the first, the resort of the wealthy, powerful, uncontaminated conservatives of the business community.

Buffalo businessmen were remarkably successful in holding on to their positions and their perquisites. It was inevitable that they should be challenged by rising individuals in the new racial groups, but they took in enough of them to keep from being unseated. They kept control of the Boards and Finance Committees, and their sons came back from Yale and Princeton to replace them as they retired. Labor revolted once in a while; there was a permanent struggle for higher wages, shorter hours, and better working conditions. During depressions, desperation seized the unemployed; but the Buffalo Club conferees, meeting under the Cleveland portrait, plotting strategy in the leather armchairs and across the mahogany tables of the elite, always had the National Guard at their disposal. It was officered, usually, by their own sons, and when the police could not maintain law and order, the Guard was called on. The gains for labor in these years were so slow as to be almost invisible; an onlooker could see that changes were coming, but he could also see that none of them would come without strife.

The Club was also a place where members of the Bar, those at the very topmost levels, mingled in an easy atmosphere with their principal clients. It was, consequently, the place where policies were made on all the issues of importance to business. These members of the Bar saw to it that the local law school indoctrinated its students properly. Dean Daniels and his faculty were on the side of property and taught that latitude in acquiring it was necessary to the freedom of enterprise. That monopoly often resulted—paradoxically—was a point that was glossed over. That the Interstate Commerce Act was signed by their own Cleveland must have been a matter of sorrow to Buffalo lawyers, and that state regulation of the grain elevators was held by the courts to be constitutional must have given them a setback. But the Buffalo Bar was resourceful. It went on finding ways for its clients to do as they pleased in spite of legislatures and courts that sometimes acted perversely.

It is of some interest that the ancient fellow-servant doctrine had as persistent a life in the precincts of Buffalo as it can have had anywhere in its notorious history. Our historian tells at some length of the ways in which that doctrine was used to protect property interests against the attritions of workers who felt that their employers ought to be responsible for their agents. Not until the issue was settled in Federal courts did the Buffalonians give up. So also with the tariff. Throughout the old century, and on into the new, the industrialists had been importunate in their demands for protection. And attitudes on that issue often determined their generosity or lack of it in political campaigns; free enterprise, but not free trade!

Labor troubles; a latent class struggle; racial animosities—all these tended to merge. There were conservatives and there were radicals. No radical ever came through the doors of the Club. A man could retire there from the scenes of battle, confident that all those around him would be sympathizers. But if the elite clung together, so did certain other groups in Buffalo—the Germans, the Irish, the Poles, and the Italians had a natural tendency to hang together. Sometimes these national ties helped in the labor struggle, but more often it made animosities easily exploited by employers to their own advantage. The press and the pulpit were safely enough allied with the elite. If few of the clergy sat before the open fires in the old Watson mansion, their vestrymen and lay supporters did; and the newspaper proprietors, the Matthewses and the Butlers, could often be found there. And among them they served to keep opinion fairly well disciplined.

Only the Conners papers, the *Courier* and the *Enquirer* were unreliable. Fingy was a Democrat and even an influential one nationally; and if the papers could hardly be said to be radical, their yellowish tendencies often made them sympathetic to embarrassing exposures. There was more than a touch of Hearst in their attitudes. How capricious this could make them, there was reason to know; they took the lead in several unofficial investigations and on the whole were not trusted to be gentlemanly when good stories were scented.

This was Buffalo, which was now my second home. It was an ugly city, getting uglier every year. It was a polyglot city, with layers of new immigrants, each infiltrated with newer ones, until the last—the Poles—came in underneath to support the whole as common laborers in all the hard jobs of industry and transportation. But where could a boy have been in more intimate touch with the characteristic society of his turbulent nation? What I learned in Buffalo was certainly not mostly from the school I attended. It was from the friends I acquired, from the sights I saw, and from the deductions I could hardly help making....

Once school was over, early in the afternoon, we looked for something amusing to do, or rather we chose among many alternatives....One was Doc Blight's drugstore and soda fountain, where milk shakes, sundaes, and sodas were dispensed more regularly than prescriptions. Doc always treated students as though they were nuisances, taking him away from the serious functions of a pharmacist. Actually he was an incorrigible gossip, a more reliable school historian than any of the teachers. His chronicles were of a somewhat different sort than theirs would have been, but the accumulation became enormous.

It may be that the memory of me was less green in Doc's establishment than it might have been across the street at Guenther's saloon, if that business had not acquired a new proprietor. He had not made many alterations, however, and there seemed to be no more change than added patina and a heavier smell of the same sort I recalled so well. This was a blend of stale beer, tobacco smoke, and unwashed males. As before, the woodwork was darkened by smoke, the floor was sprinkled with sawdust, and there were poker tables with armchairs around them where customers carried their kümmelweckroll sandwiches and schooners of beer to be consumed at leisure. But the sandwiches were no longer a nickel, as they had been; and neither was the beer. There was, however, the same useful door at the back through which students could crowd as authority came in at the front. ...In the German neighborhoods of Buffalo it would have been hard to convince anyone that beer was bad for growing boys. And the real problem, as he knew well enough, was that there were no other recreation facilities of any sort. When I made my later visit, here was a new school with all sorts of improvements, and I had the impression that students were no longer steady customers at the saloon.

It was at Guenther's that we planned and organized our fraternity, half because about a dozen of us wanted in this way to seal our friendship, and half to express a rather sardonic view of high school affairs. We invented a fraternity of our own, I believe, because some of us, but not all, had been asked to join the local chapters of the two or three national high school fraternities then in existence. At any rate, we soon had an elaborate ritual, a pin, and clubrooms. For this last we rented a typical dentist's layout on the second floor of a taxpayer building at Main and Utica streets. In our rooms, furnished with secondhand chairs, tables, and a sofa or two, together with a gas heater, we loafed, had long conversations, and conspired against the adult world. Our retreat was uncomfortable, dirty, ugly—anything else of the sort—but it was our very own.

The energy, the sheer inventive output of that lively group, devoted entirely to the production of trivialities, would not be believed even if it could be described. Still, none of us ever regretted any of it. And actually I suppose much of it went to enlarge our interest in the world. For we often explored matters far beyond our competence or knowledge merely as an exercise in competitive cerebration. Some of us were thus familiarized with reaches of learning we had not heard of before, or at least had suggested to us much that we did not know. We had long sessions over politics and religion, for instance.... How could there be any question about the virtues of Republicanism, and why would anyone look beyond a genteel Protestantism? What was the use of discussing something you knew you would never do anything about? But there were some shockingly unorthodox opinions among the dozen of us, and they were aired for hours on end. It was sometimes obvious that the beliefs expressed did not run very deep and that the questions were not seriously raised. But it made for interesting conversation.

Mostly, of course, we talked about courses of conduct. Sexual ethics came in for repeated overhaulings. There were those whose professed attitude was crudely predatory. But they did not have it all their own way. There was a surprising dissent. But this endlessly fascinating subject did not monopolize our interest quite in the way it is supposed to do among males gathered together. I think our most interesting ventures had to do with the possibility of afterlife and even communication with the spirit world. And those of us who were skeptical, or who preferred to leave such matters to the priests or preachers, were still fascinated by attempts to invoke influences from some other where. We made tables jump by concentrating, and got answers to questions from imagined controls. We were puzzled, and we discussed the meaning of such phenomena at length; but we were at that happy age when it is possible to leave some matters up in the air, unanswered. We were neophytes in a complex world and we neither thought we knew all about it nor aspired to do so until in due time further evidence should become available.

PAUL HORGAN

How Dr. Faustus Came to Rochester

What there is about the Genesee Valley of upper New York state to invite witches, I don't know. It is a pastoral terrain, with low green hills, and lovely little rivers, and the frankest kind of houses, and almost no cattle with sinister deformities. Yet the metropolis of the region, Rochester, has a certain curious fame as the seat of occult influences. In the last century phenomena occurred which were afterward famous as the "Rochester Knockings," and by their means the Fox sisters became the founders of a spiritistic religion, which still flourishes; though it is said that one of the foundresses confessed on her death-bed that the "Rochester Knockings" were hoaxes. This did not lessen the zeal of her followers, who deplored that Sister was maundering toward the end.

And there have been other occult disturbances in Rochester. Something about the . . . land induces people to arise and prophesy and cock their ears toward the invisible powers. It is a lovely city, and anyone who has ever lived there will probably love it to the end of his days. It has a civilized inheritance from its great benefactor, Mr. George Eastman. It believes in education, and has a university. It believes in nature, and has beautiful parks. It believes in industry, and has model factories. It believes, or did once, in art, and underwent a renaissance. And, as I have already suggested, it believes in witches, and has had them. I am interested in describing an occult event that occurred one time during the Rochester Renaissance, in which the great sources of the town were all contributing to the same end, which was the production of opera in English at the Eastman Theater.

The American time was very happy for a renaissance. It was in the early half of the twenties. We were getting over the War and were still sensitive enough to use our imaginations. The arts seemed to be a happy outlet for that future civilization we were going to have, in which there would be no more killing and exhausting of a whole race. The first step toward the new Golden Age was culture, and *instant* culture. It was the time of Babbitt, and everyone remembers Babbitt's most charming trait, which was his receptivity to proposals that involved doing something new and honorable and hopeful with money. It seems now, ten years later, a little cruel of us to have laughed at Babbitt so much, when he was above all a kindly man, hellbent on doing something for somebody else.

Mr. Eastman, of course, was no Babbitt. He was a brilliant man full of respect for the exact things in this life. Art is inexact, but traditions had long ago indicated that art was valuable. As one of the most socially conscientious citizens we have ever known in America, Mr. Eastman sought ways constantly to share his wealth with his fellow-men.

He built the Eastman School of Music and gave it to the University of Rochester. Adjoining it was built the Eastman Theater, surely the loveliest theater in the country. And in the autumn of 1923—a very lovely season of copper smoke and crisp chill in the air—he mobilized at that theater the Rochester American Opera Company.

The Opera Company was established as the result of a conversation between "Mist-Eastman" and Monsieur Vladimir Rosing on a ship headed for Europe a few months before. Rosing was a small sturdy Russian with a beautiful tenor voice which had brought him celebrity abroad and a tour of this country. He couldn't believe that we had so little music of our own. He was positive America was dying for opera in all its inland capitals but didn't know it. How he would love to found a marvellous opera company—somewhere—which would give opera to Americans in English, and with fine ensemble! Rosing was always eloquent. He had a well-shaped head with short hair and a sensitive bony dome and deep little eyes. He was perhaps the most complete artist in his personality whom I ever knew. His charm, his talent, his earnestness, his passion, really, together with the excellence of his plan for Rochester, won Mist-Eastman, and he agreed to establish the opera company and back it for three years.

The operatic personality must be something born and bred into the bones of those who have it.

Rosing went across the country and listened to nine hundred singers from whom he picked about thirty as the nucleus of his troupe. They followed him to Rochester, and though those youngsters came from American institutions like church choirs, banks, embalming jobs, school teaching, store clerking, etc, they were all ready in that autumn to wear the mantles and the auras of Nordica, Caruso, Lehmann, the de Rezkes, and Mary Garden.

Rosing, whom we all called Val by now, had asked his friend Rouben Mamoulian to come from London to undertake the dramatic direction of the company and, giving up a contract with the Théâtre des Champs-Elysées in Paris, he came to Rochester. Ten years later, of course, he is one of the great men of the American theater. He was entirely different from Val. He was tall and dark, with open, speculative eyes very dark, behind pince-nez which he early discarded for American bone-rimmed spectacles. He was severe. He dressed superbly. He held himself and his affairs *en prince*. There was a dignity about him which everybody thought melancholy and romantic, and on him instead of on Val was showered responsive sympathy for the plight of the Russian exile after the Bolshevik upheaval. Rouben had deliberate manners that seemed to conceal the tragic experiences he had seen. He was remote and still friendly. He was as stern in rehearsal as a Russian Imperial army corps commander. His mind played charming lights through this attitude, and time and again the mark of his wit and his theater style would accent not only his work but his friendships. Val, on the other hand, was volatile, impulsive, never prepared in advance but always improvising, sometimes with genius; skating in his suede shoes across the rehearsal hall to show a position, he was like an inarticulate poet trying to translate his thoughts into a tongue he only heard but did not speak.

The two men were co-directors. Everybody admired them both very much, and very much relished their idiosyncrasies... Val carried dried cranberries and raisins in his pockets to eat. He wore two monocles until they got broken at rehearsal, after which he took to wearing horn-rimmed spectacles, which in a week were wrecked and mended with adhesive tape, string, hairpins, and glue.

Rouben always had a walking stick which he exchanged for a baton at rehearsals. He could give a marvellous impersonation of a conductor and a whole orchestra playing the overture to the "Barber of Seville," producing the illusion of the whole band and parodying both the music and the performance. The presence of the Russians—one a severe, wise, unemotional, intellectual artist, the other a vagrant of inspiration, credulous and appealing—gave the whole operatic atmosphere, already unreal enough, a soupçon of the fantastic.

Yet there was also a certain air of pioneering about the whole venture, and that was where the American virtue showed, I suppose. In the noble auditorium of the Eastman Theater the proceedings seemed full of promise and dignity, the wholeness of a beautiful idea; and the absurdities and discouragements were forgotten in the fact of production.

The scene is now set for my occult relation. As I remember it, the episode cannot be separated from the atmosphere which spawned it, or from the kinds of people upon whom it was to be visited. A Witches' Sabbath in Rochester in the time of the Renaissance had to have much to do with opera. After it all happened I remember how we would remark the earnest and whistling awfulness of having it happen as it did, to people like us, in the capital of the "Rochester Knockings."

Most actors and singers are surely the most superstitious people on earth. They become aware of their own strange powers early in life, and they know that whatever silver thread of destiny they can weave about people as artists, it is as nothing to the invisible background of magic which has given them that gift and which conceals another and more terrible power of which they are likely to remark, "No, it scares me to death. I'm afraid to play with it." Credulity is a great part of the makeup of the interpretive artist anyway. His very nature must be protean, and if he sings in opera he must be as charmed and impressed by the musty nonsense of "Rigoletto" as by the divine nonsense of Golaud.

II

In the middle of that winter, when snow lay over the city and there seemed to be an air of content, riches, and smugness about town, the opera company was preparing a production of Gounod's "Faust."

For weeks the rehearsals had been going on, and all departments had been co-ordinating their efforts toward the famous Thursday matinee which would see the curtain go up on our second triumph of the season. For most of the company it was touching but true that this was their first meeting with the Faust legend. Coming from the outland capitals where culture was worried out of its nooks by Women's Clubs, and the silent movies reigned instead of opera, our singers for the first time got an idea of what went on in Nuremberg so long ago, to the accompaniment of a sentimental score full of sweet charm and ingenuity that seem never to flag. There were fascinating lectures before rehearsal about the meaning of the Faust legend, and long intellectual arguments between the baritone from Oberlin College and the ex-embalmer basso from St. Louis as to whether Dr. Faustus ever really lived or not. There were lectures about the great interpretations of the Faust legend; American opera toiled on its way according to the technic of the college education. The work was very hard.

Mephistopheles always has the lion's share. The role was being prepared by George Fleming Houston, who was properly regarded as the Chaliapin of the company. He was—as he is now—tall and handsome with dark eyes full of sardonic charm. He was humorous and realistic and he could stop being a great golfer and a proper American to become a swell devil fired with perverse grace. He sang rehearsals full voice in a cloak. Mamoulian invented marvellous things for the cloak to do.

Until the opera got to the orchestra rehearsals, the singers were accompanied at the piano by the head répétiteur, Nicolai Slonimsky, who was learning English with my help by reading the novels of Charles Dickens. He was almost insolently efficient at his job. He used to come without the score of Faust but carrying instead a fat copy of *Pickwick Papers* which he propped up on the piano and, while accompanying the rehearsals with his hands on the keys, he would read Dickens, never missing either a note, a cue, a cut in the opera; or a word, a chuckle, or a trial pronunciation of a new word in the novel.

Val Rosing at rehearsal worked by the method of demonstrating to his players how to play. He could, with no suspicion of absurdity, do all the parts in the opera, shyly graceful as the virgin Marguerite, bustling nanny-goat as Martha, classic nurse, a Gothic satyr as Mephisto, and himself as Faust, passionate, credulous, fond of top notes, and inscrutably hasty.

Mamoulian created an understanding first, filling the actors' minds and willing them to know what they were doing. He seemed impersonal. He was serving a larger achievement than the company knew. If at the end of weeks, he said to an actor, "That's not bad," it was almost unbearable praise. One who earned it during "Faust" was the Marguerite, Cecile Sherman, a little Catholic girl with an adorable voice and a religious absorption in her role. She was preparing a moving study of the part.

Like people anywhere who work hard together, we found great friendships among our colleagues. Every evening after rehearsal we would gather and go to some restaurant for dinner, where we would sit for hours, playing games with pencils and paper or drawing caricatures. Many of the girls had apartments with kitchenettes where they fixed themselves meals. Most of the men ate downtown. The restaurant life of Rochester was a hardship. We would suddenly "awake" and jump to our feet, tired of the place we'd been sitting, and everybody would wonder what to do. One night Val said, "Let's go somewhere and have a seance."

"H'm," said Rouben.

"No, really, boy, dze most remarkable tsings!" insisted Rosing.

Miss Sherman, the soprano, seemed doubtful on religious grounds. It was explained by her friend, Mary Bell, of Texas, who sang Martha in the production, that it was just for fun. She needn't take it seriously. Peggy

Williamson was along. She and Val were in love and planning to be married. She proposed that we all go to her apartment and have the seance. George Houston murmured:

"There will nothing good come of it, mark me," and grinning in drollery, he led the way to the street where we found taxicabs in the snow and drove away.

We drove along streets that had street cars running, and the tracks were ice-blue in the light of the street lights. So many Rochester streets are gray all year round, board houses and cobblestones, and stiff high porches and odd angles at the street intersections, and against the night glow of downtown, residential roofs cutting the sky with old-fashioned silhouettes in sharp loomings.

Our two cabs arrived and we got out at the snowy curb. A street car came round the corner just then and its cold wheels whined on the steely curve of the tracks. A bluish arc light stood before Peggy's house and flickered. It was almost one o'clock. The streets were deserted, and the packed snow hushed the occasional late walker whose heels whimpered on the unmelting walks. We went into the house and up the stairs to the second-floor front apartment. Peggy turned on the light and let us get comfortable.

The room was like any furnished room. It had dark striped wallpaper, a hanging lamp with a ruby-and-emerald glass shade leaded together and fringed with white-glass beads. It had carved straight chairs of the Art Nouveau period, and two leather and mahogany arm chairs and a green plush and mahogany sofa. It was warm and substantial and without charm. The sofa sat back in a bay window that overhung the front porch and seemed right on the street. This was because the street lamp reached almost to the bay window's level, casting its bluish light through the lace curtains. Before the sofa stood a mahogany table.

The table was long enough for four people to sit at a side. It had two heavy drawers. Its legs were three or four inches in diameter, in the form of fluted columns that suddenly changed their nature and ended in brass griffons' claws, clutching solid brass balls. There was a solid mahogany shelf over an inch thick under the table. I should suppose the table weighed several hundred pounds.

On seeing it, Val exclaimed, "No, marvellous!" and began clearing off the top of it for the table-tipping seance.

Present were Val, Rouben, Peggy, George Houston, Mary Bell, Cecile Sherman, Guy Harrison, the conductor, who was amiably scornful, and myself.

III

"No, really, I do think this is nothing to *play* with," said Cecile.

"Nonsense, darlink," said Val. "I have had dze most maavellous in seance!"

She shrugged her shoulders and we sat down. We put our hands on the table top and, by stretching, touched little fingers to one another all the way round. Val bowed his head like a man in church, inviting inner communion by making the outward likeness of it. But in a second he raised his head and squinted.

"Dze light! Put out dze light! It must be daak for a seance!"

Peggy left the circle and snapped off the ruby-and-green lamp. Now there was a satisfactory glow on the ceiling from the street light.

"Now really!" said Guy, the conductor, in his brisk British. "Isn't this just a bit *too* much of a stage-set? Nobody can be expected to accept this!"

"Sshh! How do you expect dze spirits to come if you talk all dze time."

In the semi-dark then we sat together, patiently touching little finger tips and holding our peace. Because it was protracted, the silence, and because we were concentrated on a weird mission, the little sounds of our lives in that dark became funny and I wanted to laugh: Val making noises in his mouth with his tongue, as if eating the delicious atmosphere; Cecile breathing like a kitten next to me; Rouben's pipe, not burning, but anti-boredom; George's ghost of a tune which he hummed on the breath in his throat, and which managed to suggest that he was politely attending whatever Mr. Rosing's fancy might invite; the ticking of Guy's wrist watch, a sassy and skeptical sound taken from its owner's opinion in the dark; Mary Bell's tragic sighs, a suffering that was waiting to be enjoyed in a phantom rapport....

The street car came back, turned the corner again, and screamed vaguely on the ice.

"What can we ..." began George.

"Psst!" went Val, silencing him.

Val leaned down over the table and moaned. He grovelled in humble invitation, a priest of a midnight, backstreet cult, kissing his mahogany altar from Grand Rapids.

We exchanged glances round the table in the dark, our eyes grinning at his dramatics.

He moaned again.

The table moved.

It wafted itself delicately and slowly, slowly, that was what amazed us, in a slight tip and then it sat down again as if its fibers had never carried animate nerve messages.

"Oh my God!" whispered Cecile.

Val, sustaining his moan with his eyes squinted tight shut, said to the table,

"Who *a-r-e* you?"

Sharply Rouben broke the circuit and slapped the table.

"No, really, Val! Of all the . . . How do you suppose the table can answer you. 'Who are you!' when there is no system established? Do you suppose the table can say in a polite voice, 'I am Meister Albert Dupont, of Marseilles, France?"

"St!" went Val in hurt annoyance. "You have *ruined* it! Dze spirit will never come back now!"

"Perhaps not, but all this moaning, and who-are-you and *dying* does no good! . . . Suppose everybody lets me establish the system and ask the questions and we will read the answers back when they come in alphabet. Is that all right?"

"Da, da d'da," said Val impatiently, anxious to be back to his spirits.

Silence fell again with the effect of a light being turned out.

Val had resigned his premiership of the seance but not his anguish. He moaned and coughed in sympathy with the other world. Our world was silent and outdoors it was snowy, freezing. Lategoers must be hastening, their breaths plumy on the crystal air.

Suddenly the table rose and fell again.

"Psss!" warned Rouben in a whisper.

The table moved like the deck of a small excursion steamer, somehow taking us with it in the tilt of its wavy progress.

"My God," moaned Val.

"We are speaking to the spirit that moves this table," said Rouben in measured grave tones. "Will you speak to us? Answer *one* for yes and *two* for no."

The table tilted once, sharply.

"We will spell the alphabet aloud and you tip the table on the letter you mean," said Rouben. "Will you do that?"

The table tilted once, meaning yes.

"Who *are* you?" moaned Val incorrigibly.

The table wafted a little aimlessly and then rested dead. I must explain that this tipping sensation was perfectly discernible and, once you accepted the convention, not astonishing. It would pivot on two of its feet, lifting the other two off the floor about four or six inches. The levitation was full of motor energy. No one person at the table could have lifted the table as delicately as it moved, and all hands were aboveboard, and there were no places for knees to lift below.

"No, who-are-you, he is gone," said Rouben with toneless bitterness.

We sat again in silence and patience, for about ten minutes, I think. Again the human noises of simple occupancy seemed hysterically droll. Then suddenly the table quivered and arose and sat down again almost with a bang. We came into a tension and stared at one another. The table seemed like an animal, quiescent but charged with energy.

"Someone very strong is here," said Rouben.

"No, ask," hissed Val.

Rouben addressed the spirit and established the code.

"Will you spell us your name?" he said.

Bang, meaning yes.

"A, B, C, D, E, F," and at that the table tipped buoyantly.

"Pwa! such *strength,"* said Rouben before he started again.

"A" . . . and he got no farther.

He called letters until the table stopped him at U. He called again, and at S he was halted. Finally:

"F, A, U, S, T, U, S!"

"No, really!"

"Doctor Faustus!" groaned Val. "Is das maavellous!"

The table tipped yes, violently.

"Doctor Faustus, who lived so long ago in Nuremberg?" asked Rouben.

Bang.

"Then you really did live?"

Bang! a little annoyedly, I thought.

"And all the great poems and music are written about your life . . . ?"

Bang.

We were by now genuinely excited, for no matter what your opinion was, or your explanation was likely to be on the morrow, it was disturbing and outrageous to be visited by the ghost of the man whose musical biography you were busy producing in a theater. Cecile was trembling and her lips made a little pursed shape of prayer.

Rouben could look very solemn, and now did so, consulting my face.

I must emphasize that we were all much impressed and sharing the mystery.

"You are alive in the spirit?"

Bang!

"Have you been watching us to-night?"

Bang!

"Is it because we are staging the story of your life that you came to us to-night?"

Bang!

"Do you like the way we are doing it?"

Bang-*bang!* meaning no.

"Why?"

Spelling: NO TRUTH.

"You mean the facts of your life were not like that?"

Bang!

"Did Goethe tell the real story?"

Bang-bang!

"Did Marlowe?"

No.

"Did Boïto in his opera?"

No.

"Who has done so?"

Spelling: NO ONE. A pause. Then, LIFE IS OF THE SOUL AND SECRET.

A long pause.

We could think of little to say. Up to now we had been whispering questions to Rouben to ask Dr. Faustus, and he had conducted the seance with discretion and clarity. It took a long time, this spelling and tipping. We were hushed and the night seemed cracking with cold, the ice, and the invisible threads of current whose batteries we were.

"But he is so *like* Faust," Rouben murmured to us. "These answers, you see?"

The table moved as if to converse, reminding us.

"Will you tell us something of your life then?" asked Rouben.

VANITAS.

It staggered us. What could we say to such a soul?

"Then tell us something of your death?"

A pause. We thought he had left us. Then a slow bang and another wait. Rouben finally ventured to ask:

"Did you die a natural death?"

Bang-bang!

"Were you . . . murdered?"

Bang-bang!

"Did you kill yourself?"

Bang-bang!

"You did not die naturally; you were not murdered, and you did not commit suicide?"

Bang-bang! no!

"Then how?"

I WILLED TO DIE....

Again we stared at one another's faces. It was a strange statement, and the distinctions involved in it were the nice ones that a philosopher would likely relish. We collected ourselves then, and Rouben said:

"Would you tell us something about life in the other world where you are now?"

And I cannot say how gravely, with what portentous weight and repudiation the table of Dr. Faustus spelled out over many minutes the message:

WORDS DIE ON THE EDGE OF YOUR WORLD.

This finished us. We shuddered. The literary tone of this conversation with night was more terrifying than the classical spook tone would have been. Also, the fury and dominance of the personality that had the table in its use seemed to keep us at a pitch like wire.

The table became agitated. It spelled very rapidly, MUST GO.

"But will you come back to us again?" Rouben asked hastily.

Bang.

"When?"

THURSDAY.

"What time?"

But we knew what was coming. Cecile wailed.

AFTERNOON.

The first performance of *Faust* was to be on Thursday afternoon.

"Will you manifest yourself?"

Bang!

"How?"

LIGHTS.

There was a strange release now suddenly, as if a switch had been closed, and a current broken. Doctor Faustus was gone. We fell away from the table, now again a wooden object with its molecular pattern undisturbed, its physics again acceptable on the basis of its surface, and no longer terrifying for the inner life of its atomic fibers. Cecile Sherman jumped up from the table and flashed the light on us, and as we looked round and saw our faces and images of astonishment and strain we found it possible, no, necessary, to laugh at one another. It was almost three o'clock, and the world was still. Coming to ourselves, we began to assume the conventional attitudes of our several types. George "swore softly," like a man in a north-woods romance. Guy said, "Now really, who did all that wangling?" which offended Val deeply, for he was nodding his head and eating cranberries out of his pocket solemnly. Rouben said, "But how can you doubt? You heard what he said! It was his very quality!" Peggy and Cecile shivered and explained nothing. Mary Bell from Texas was safely through the emotional pull, and she grinned and narrowed her beautiful green cat's eyes skeptically.

"No, you see," said George suddenly, like a reasonable man, "what happens is that a current is established between us all, something that is powerful over matter, and working in unison like that, we have some force that actually does influence objects and move them. The subconscious must enter into it. We've been thinking *Faust* for days and weeks, and we all have imagination, and it wouldn't be hard for us to get the same rhythm of thought, you see. I think this was very interesting, and not at all spooky, and I for one am full of admiration for the way Rouben handled the thing and dictated those wonderful answers and wangled the table and kept it dramatically right. They say one strong personality in a group like this can dominate and make the telepathic message come out right. And so good night, good ones."

He stood up.

Cecile was beaming with relief and gratitude for his explanation. Val said: "Sto! *Why,* every time, must dze mystery and beauty of everytsing be talked out, in America! . . . Dze most extraordinary!"

He was furious.

Rouben looked calm and his calmness was withering.

"You are at perfect liberty to think anything you like," he said. "How could I handle that table all alone?"

"No, as George says," said Guy, "we all made it go, but you dominated and in a sense dictated, d'you see? Sounds perfectly reasonable to me, and enhances, rather than destroys, the romantic zip of the evening."

So in a quarrelsome mood the party broke up. We went our ways in the cracking freeze of before dawn, with our various opinions and beliefs much thought over. I thought George was very clever in his interpretation.

IV

The next day the story got round through the company, and seeped into the school of music and into the theater. We told about it at lunch at the Corner Club, and to all disputants Rouben disclaimed responsibility. The week passed quickly in the last fevers of rehearsal, costume try-ons, orchestra rehearsals, scene rehearsals, and light rehearsals. The stage was beautifully set by Norman Edwards. The light rehearsals lasted until very late, for several special effects had to be perfected. One morning as I left the theater it was paling into daylight, making me think of what the lights on our stage did in the prison scene, and then I remembered other effects, and the white eloquence of the cross of light which was projected on the stage floor in the church scene for Marguerite to kneel in, praying, while Mephisto deviled her from the outer darkness.

But hard as we worked, and sensible as we strove to be, there was always that lingering nervelike feeling that Doctor Faustus had left with us.

Thursday afternoon, January 15, 1925, the Eastman Theater began to fill up with a good audience about two o'clock. The great brocaded curtain was down, and the pale stone walls reflected on it the gold light of the huge chandelier. Backstage was pandemonium. I had to go there to help with morale, makeups, and atmosphere. There were vocalises sounding, and a couple of tantrums at devoted friends by singers of the afternoon who could hardly bear the wait before the curtain. Flowers came, and our directors made the rounds of the dressing rooms affectionately, and for them the singers were ready to die on the stage if need be. Presently the orchestra tuning up sounded from below. Ben Connolly, the stage manager, rang the fifteen-minute bell to all dressing rooms from the stage control board. We could only shake the final hand, kiss the powdered ear, murmuring "Nordica! De Reszke!" and go out front to take our seats, where we sat, Rouben, Val, Guy, myself, R. Eric Clarke, director general of the Eastman Theater, and a few other members of the production staff, and suffered as much as the singers until the curtain was up. When it went up, accumulating dark metallic folds in itself like a great thunder cloud, we heard the first words of the opera being sung, and we relaxed. It was a beautiful performance. There were many calls for the tenor and basso at the first-act curtain. The second act brought Sherman on, and she charmed everyone in a few notes. It is a thing you can feel, that sense of a theater full of people delighted with what they are seeing.

V

The church scene opened with everyone exhilarated. Even Mist-Eastman, sitting down there in the first row of the mezzanine chairs, wearing his little black skull cap, seemed to be happy at the proceedings. He was genuinely fond of music, and the stage picture was very pretty. It must have disturbed him when the cross of light on the stage floor where Marguerite was kneeling suddenly began to shiver and dance around the stage. It flashed like sunlight off a vagrant wave, and then it danced hither and yon like a capriciously played searchlight.

Cecile Sherman lost her cue. Her voice wavered. She was kneeling and she tried to rise, but went back to her knees again, and with a little birdlike call of hope, picked up her melody again and went on. George Houston came quickly forward as if she needed him. He stayed near her frozen in his immense cloak. Offstage the sound of the church choir's singing went on. The cross of light danced for a minute or so and then lay white again where it should have been.

But by that time we were backstage.

Rouben, Val and I, and I think Guy, went down to the basement and under the auditorium through the tunnel leading backstage. The scene was still playing when we got there.

"What moved that light?" demanded Val in a wild whisper of Ben, the stage manager.

"Nothin'!" he replied in an Irish rage. "You can go look! I got the projector over there on the other side of the stage enclosed by three flats, and Charlie was up on the prop-room steps to watch and see none of the chorus people got near to it. He said they didn't go near it."

We went round behind the backdrop and came to the projector lamp. It seemed undisturbed. There was plenty of clear space around it. Charlie, the prop man, was there.

"No," he said. "Nobody fooled with it."

The scene was finishing on stage.

It grew more and more eloquent. The singers were toiling for control, and, scared to death, they sang like morning stars. The curtain finally came down to the afternoon's peak of acclaim. We rushed on the stage. Cecile was trembling and ready to faint.

"Did you see it?"

"He *said,* 'Lights!' "

"Great God, when I saw that light begin to fly round . . . I thought I couldn't sing another note!"

The applause was rolling against the curtain like surf. Cecile was crying.

"I can't go out," she whispered.

"Come on, darling," said George. "It's all over. You sang like an angel."

The orchestra was crowding upstairs, and some of the men were asking what had gone wrong in the scene.

Other members of the company came backstage and their faces were white with wonder.

The curtain-hand pulled the rigging that opened the curtain a little way for calls, and George took Cecile out. She was still crying, but when she got out front she smiled and curtsied, and people thought it was from joy.

Meantime, "But do you suppose a truck went by in dze street backstage to make dze stage tremble," asked Val, "and dzat way dze lamp shook?"

Ben spat.

"Didn't see any other spots or olivets shivering all over the floor, did you, Mr. Rosing?"

They shrugged at each other.

There was nothing more to be said and the opera went on and ended in "triumph."

Later, I am sure, the directors were called into conference with Mist- Eastman over the merits and demerits of the production. He noticed everything, always. I wonder still what explanation they gave of the aberration of the lighting arrangements in the fourth act. He was one man with whom I don't think anyone could get very far talking about Witches' Sabbaths. I feel a little foolish even now at the implications this tale seems to pose. But in addition to saying, "Well, that's what happened!" I can say that there were no more seances.

ALDEN HATCH

The Wadsworths of the Genesee

The Wadsworths of the Genesee Valley are unique in that for five leisurely generations spanning 165 years they have lived on the land and by the land; and each generation, including this one, has given America at least one outstanding soldier or statesman.

This remarkable durability of the Wadsworths would seem to have a definite connection with their deep roots in the rich soil of their beloved valley. No matter how high they went or how far they traveled, the pull of the land brought them back. Indeed they considered the public phases of their lives as mere interruptions of their real occupation of farming. This was particularly true of the family's most eminent representative in our time, Senator James W. Wadsworth, Jr., even though he spent most of his life in the political arena.

Like most men of strong convictions and the integrity to uphold them, Senator Wadsworth was the center of a storm virtually all his life. Through forty-nine controversial years of public service he moved with imperturbable courtesy and an impish grin, never so much as swerving from the course he believed was right. Not that he always was right. Sometimes he was very wise, almost prescient; at others he seemed incredibly wrongheaded, as when he opposed woman's suffrage, and loosed the fury of half a million scorned women voters on his head.

But right or wrong everyone of both parties knew that what Wadsworth said Wadsworth truly believed. And they respected him for saying it even while they howled him down.

This makes Wadsworth sound like a poor politician. Actually he was a very good one. It is probable that no man of his time understood the devious techniques of that profession better; or could use them more effectively to promote the careers of other people. Never a President, he was a President-maker. It uncounted "smoke-filled rooms" including that most famous room of all at the Blackstone Hotel in Chicago, where on June 12, 1920, Warren G. Harding was picked for the Presidency—Jim Wadsworth, with the ninety-six votes of the New York delegation in his hip pocket, helped to sway the councils of his party.

Nor was he inflexible. He could connive with the best of them provided principle was not at stake. Also, he could forgive a good deal of skulduggery on the part of the Republican nominees for high office on the grounds of party loyalty, though he could not falsify himself to further his own career. Two things he put above party loyalty; principle and patriotism.

The politicians called Wadsworth lazy, because he did not devote his entire energy to politics. Though he served and fought in that arena with all his might, his first love was the land. This feeling comes out in the epitaph he wrote and had cut on the tomb of his father, who had also served his country in the Army and in Congress, and who also loved the land:

Soldier in the Civil War
Public Servant
Patron of Sport
Farmer All His Days

Well might they, son, father and grandsire, cherish their lovely land. Fifteen thousand fertile acres were theirs in the Genesee Valley, which lies some thirty miles south of Rochester in the best farming lands of northwestern New York. That urban sophisticate, the Bishop Prince de Talleyrand, described it in his American diary as "the fairest valley I have ever seen."

The Indians thought so, too. Long before the Frenchman—or the Wadsworths—came, the Senecas named it "Genesee"—"The Pleasant Valley." And pleasant it still is. Actually, it has changed very little in the past century or so. A traveler, who rode along the muddy road from Mount Morris to the sulphur springs at Canawaugus (Stinking Water) in 1825, describes the same vista that one sees today from the terrace of Wadsworth's beloved Hartford House.

The valley is a great shallow bowl of green and gold with a cloud-flecked lid of blue. Its almost circular sides are gentle hills marked in the ancient, rectangular pattern of agriculture; gold of wheat, dark green of corn; the paler green of turf that has grown unplowed for nearly two hundred years; and the striped brown and purple of rows of vegetables. Here and there wood lots vary the pattern while big red barns and small white houses point it up. The crests of the hills are forested, a tall stockade against the sky to keep the valley safe.

From his terrace the Senator looked westward across his flat rich bottom lands. They were big fields for New York State, mostly in grass. Because the pioneer Wadsworth brothers loved trees, they would never completely level a forest. When they cleared the fields they left great clumps of oak and walnut and elms. These stately survivals of the wilderness give the plain its unique graciousness. Under their shade the Senator's cattle stood belly-high in grass—western steers fattening for the market, or black and white Holsteins of the dairy herd. The little Genesee River, a mere crack in the plain, wandered erratically through the ordered fields. The whole wide vista was drenched in golden sunlight, the very essence of life.

No wonder, then, that the Senator, and now his son, Reverdy, always came home to his land. All these fruitful fields, fine crops, and fat cattle were here because their forefathers created this abundance. It was not their heritage alone, but a not insignificant part of the heritage of all Americans; the legacy of the pioneers, which they did not own, but held in trust for the generations of the future.

ARCH MERRILL

Old Legends Never Die

No mythical headless horseman galloped through western New York hollows. No Rip Van Winkle slept for 20 years in the Bristol Hills. But only because we had no Washington Irving to set down the tales. For this countryside is rich in legends.

This is old Indian country and the Indians felt its mystical quality. They wove picturesque folk tales about its great hills, its valleys, its rolling uplands, its lakes like fingers, its brawling streams, its tinkling waterfalls, its thundering cascades, its spring that caught fire. They peopled its glens and caverns with fabulous creatures and heard in them voices that were not of this world.

When the white men took over the old Indian land, they took over its legends, too. The settlers were mostly of the New England stock, but Yankees are not so prosaic and unimaginative as they seem. They perpetuated the old Indian legends, embellished them and created some of their own. They handed them down through the generations until they became firmly woven into the tapestry of our traditions.

So even today phantom boatmen glide over moonlit waters. Mysterious drums throb out of watery depths. A sad voice chants a death song at some Lover's Leap. Spectral hoofbeats echo along a lonely road and ghosts walk of night in long deserted places.

I

And there is the hill on which nothing ever grows. That is the barren mountain that towers above Canandaigua Lake, the legendary birthplace of the Seneca Nation. About it has ever clung the legend of the Serpent of Bare Hill.

That legend has several versions. This is one of them.

Long ago the Creator caused the earth to open and out of the side of a massive hill the ancestors of the Senecas came into being. For a time they

From *New York Folklore Quarterly*, Spring, 1957. Reprinted by permission of the New York Folklore Society.

lived in peace there. A boy of the tribe found a little snake in the woods. It was an unusual serpent for it had two heads. The boy took it home, made a pet of it and fed it the choicest deer meat. The thing grew to incredible size and its hunger knew no bounds. Its master could not obtain enough game for its voracious appetite. The people of the tribe came to fear it as a monster.

Finally, the great serpent encircled the hill and barred the gate with its opened, double jaws so that none could escape. Driven by hunger, the people tried to get away and, one by one, they were eaten by the monster. At last only a young warrior and his sister remained of all the People of the Hill.

One night the young brave had a vision. If he would fletch his arrows with his sister's hair, they would possess a fatal charm over the enemy. He followed his dream and shot his magic arrows straight into the serpent's heart. The reptile was mortally hurt and in agony writhed his way down Bare Hill, tearing out trees and flailing the earth until he finally slid into the lake.

As the snake rolled down the hill, he disgorged the skulls of the Senecas he had devoured. In the area have been found large rounded stones weirdly like human heads. And to this day nothing has ever grown in the path of the serpent down old Bare Hill. Its somber peak stands out above the rich and fruitful Vine Valley.

II

Many legends of the Red Men hover about that wanton Finger Lake, turbulent old Seneca. Out of Seneca's vast depths sometimes comes a strange thundering like the boom of hidden cannon or the beating of a great drum.

A legend of the "Land of the Lake Guns" which has lived through the years is that of Agayentah, the spectral Seneca warrior. Of all the braves, none was so tall, so powerful, so skillful in the chase, so brave in battle as Agayentah. One sultry Summer's day he went hunting along the lake "that has no bottom." The "Lake Guns" were booming, as they always do before a storm, and the young warrior took shelter under a big elm tree on the shore.

Suddenly there descended a dazzling lightning shaft and an ear-splitting crash. Tree and Indian went down together and together they floated out upon the lake. And they say that Agayentah, also known as "the Wandering Jew" or "the Wandering Chief," still rides his funeral barge around and around the lake, but only in the deathlike silence that precedes a storm—before Heno, the God of Thunder, looses his fiery bolts.

Generations of Hobart College men have preserved the legend and adopted Agayentah as their own. In 1896, Malcolm Saunders Johnson, a student who later became an Episcopal clergyman and a historian-composer, wrote for the campus paper, *The Echo,* these lines:

Often when the storm is coming
Sounds the voice of Agayentah.
Ever armed and on the warpath,
Roams his restless spirit ever
And his shout to battle calling
Echoes o'er the lake forever.

Now, when the men of Hobart face some especially critical test on the athletic field, they summon the spirit of Agayentah, the Seneca warrior, to lead them to Victory.

III

Still the voice of Mona-sha-sha
The benighted tourist hears
Where the falls of Portage thunder,
And its roof Glen Iris rears.

Many an Indian legend clings to Letchworth State Park, "where the falls of Portage thunder" in the Grand Canyon of the Genesee.

Long ago W. C. H. Hosmer, the Bard of Avon, New York, put the legend of Mona-sha-sha in rhyme. The verse quoted above is from his poem, "Voices of the Past," which he read at the last council fire in the old Seneca Council House in the park on October 1, 1872.

The poet introduced the story in this fashion:

When came the moon, to hunter dear,
Jonindch built his cabin ncar
Their boiling rapids, white with foam,
And brought with him his wife and child,
To gladden, in the dreary wild,
His temporary home.

The region round was full of game
But back each night Jonindeh came
With empty hands, though bow more true
No marksman of the nation drew.

As the days passed and the wild beasts and the forest birds continued to elude his arrow, the hunter's depression deepened and he believed that an Evil Spirit had cast its spell upon him. Morosely, he rebuffed all of his wife's attempts to cheer and console him.

Mona-sha-sha's heart was broken, for she believed she had lost her husband's love. One night, while he lay sleeping in the lodge, she lashed her baby to her back and crept into the woods. She reached the brink of a waterfall and from its hiding place she drew a light canoe. She paddled out into the moonlit current that grew ever swifter as it neared the cataract. The little boy clapped his hands in glee. Then Mona-sha-sha tossed her paddle aside and her frail craft shot like an arrow over the precipice and was lost in the maelstrom below.

When Jonindeh awoke from a troubled sleep, he listened in vain for his wife's morning song and the prattle of their babe. He searched the lodge. They were gone. He called and there was no answer. He rushed out and on the dewy grass he found Mona-sha-sha's footprints. They led him to the brink of the falls. There he found the canoe was missing.

Just then a white doe and fawn darted past him. "The spirits of the dead have passed, inviting me to follow," he cried, as he drew his hunting knife from his belt. He plunged the blade deep into his breast and staggering to the chasm, fell into the thunder water to join his wife and son.

It's far too sad a tale to be linked with such a beauty spot. But, after all, it's only a legend.

IV

The story of "The Silver Bullet" may be a legend. Maybe it really happened. You feel it did, when you hear Steuben County Attorney James S. Drake tell it, for Jim Drake is a rare storyteller, as well as a diligent collector of local lore.

It was in the pioneering time that John Teeple lived in the Town of Wayne within sight of three sparkling lakes, Keuka, Lamoka and Waneta. He was a substantial man among the settlers and was supervisor of his town. He had a daughter, Polly, who was the apple of his eye.

One day in the year of 1809, when Polly was sixteen years old, she was sent on an errand to a neighbor's house. She took her pet dog along. Their path led past the lonely cabin where the widow Slocum lived. The widow was an eccentric. Some said she was a witch. She had left the religious colony of Jemima Wilkinson, the Universal Friend, across Keuka Lake, to live by herself in the Town of Wayne.

Polly Teeple's dog howled long and lugubriously at the widow's cabin door. To the superstitious woman that howl was an omen of impending death. She came out of her cabin and, her voice quivering with rage as she pointed a long finger at Polly Teeple, she pronounced this curse on the hapless girl:

"Yes, I shall die—but you, Polly Teeple, shall never walk again."

Sure enough the girl sickened and took to her bed. She seemed to be paralyzed. John Teeple called in the best doctors, but they could do nothing. Finally, he consulted a clairvoyant and she told him how to break the curse: "Make an image of the widow Slocum in bread dough, then stand it against a basswood tree and at 125 feet pierce it with a silver bullet."

The dough image was made and Zenas Sackett molded the silver bullet and fired it at the required distance while more than 100 settlers, among them some of John Teeple's fellow supervisors, watched.

Zenas Sackett's aim was good. The silver bullet hit its mark. Then Polly Teeple rose from her bed and walked again.

That night they found the widow Slocum in the woods. Her body was hanging from the limb of a basswood tree.

V

Rochester's Sam Patch has leaped into the stream of national folklore. One of the chapters in a book, *Upstate, Downstate, Folk Stories of the Middle Atlantic States,* by M. (for Moritz) Jagendorf, is titled "Sam the Jumpin' Man."

It tells the familiar (to us) story of Sam's leaps that brought him fame and his one spectacular failure, that cost him his life on Friday, the 13th day of November, 1829, at the Upper Falls in Rochester.

Jagendorf departs from the traditional Patch story to conclude the chapter in this wise:

> Sam the Jumpin' Man swam and swam and swam until he came out in the China Sea where a New England sea captain who never told a lie said he saw him. Sam Patch was doing marvelous American deeds out there in the heathen lands. And for all I know, Sam may be still around some place jumping heights no man ever jumped from before.

And for all I know, Sam Patch is sleeping the last sleep right where they buried him on a windy March day in 1830—in the pioneer cemetery in old Charlotte, hard by the Genesee water that had conquered the greatest jumper of his time.

But folk tales are not necessarily historically accurate. For years after the finding of Sam's body by a farmer who was breaking the river ice to water his horse, legends sprang up that Patch was still alive and had been seen in various places. Like Banquo's ghost, John Wilkes Booth and Jesse James, "Sam the Jumpin' Man" was a long time dying.

There's a minor mystery connected with the Patch saga which has always intrigued me. When Sam came to Rochester he brought with him a pet black bear which he led around on a chain. On his first and successful jump over the Genesee Falls on November 6, 1829, Sam tossed the bear into the current ahead of him and Bruin swam safely to shore.

Sam made his second Rochester leap, his last on earth, at two o'clock on the afternoon of that ill-fated Friday the 13th. The bear was scheduled to jump at three o'clock. Of course, he didn't. But what became of him?

With apologies to M. Jagendorf, I would like to offer this sequel to the Sam Patch story:

> They say that whenever November 13 falls on a Friday, at the hour of three in the afternoon, a little black bear, dragging his chain behind him, trots along an old Indian trail in the Genesee gorge and mounts to a ledge above the cataract. He is poised as if to leap. Then he looks about him, whimpering piteously. Finally he creeps back in to the brush. The little black bear is looking for his master who never rose from the treacherous Genesee water that other Friday the 13th so long ago.

VI

Some years ago I thought I had latched on to a new and elegant legend. A barber, no longer living and whom I knew only as Sam, one day while he was trimming my luxuriant locks, told me this tale:

Around the time of the first World War he was working in the Northern Allegany County village of Fillmore. Living in the Genesee River town was a young section hand known to all as Patsy. Patsy had in his heart the music of his native Italy. He had a clear, sweet voice and he could play the mandolin.

Sometimes at night, after he had looked long upon the wine when it was red, Patsy would take his mandolin and climb out on the 155-foot high viaduct of the Erie Railroad cutoff which straddles the valley east of the village.

The people who lived nearby would hear the music of his voice and mandolin wafted down from the high bridge. They speculated each evening after the chores were done whether Patsy would come to the bridge that night. When they did not hear his serenade, they were disappointed.

One night when the harvest moon was shining and all was still, Patsy's song ended sharply—in the middle of a note. The neighbors did not think anything of it at the time. They figured maybe Patsy had dozed off.

The next morning they found his crushed body at the foot of the high bridge. His fingers still clutched the strings of his mandolin.

And ever since on moonlit nights in the harvest time, if you listen closely, you can hear elfin music floating down from the high bridge—Patsy singing as he strums his mandolin.

That's the way Sam the barber told me the story. He told it as Gospel truth. In those days I did not recognize a legend when I heard one. So in my blindness I checked up on the story down Fillmore way. I found nobody who had ever heard of Patsy or his untimely end, to say nothing of hearing his real or spectral music.

So I wrote off Sam the barber as a phony tipster. Now I know he really was a great creative artist. For legends are not made of such dull coarse stuff as facts. They are woven of the gossamer threads of fancy.

I should have let "The Legend of the Minstrel on the High Bridge" age in the wood a little longer. Legends need plenty of seasoning of time.

☛ BOOK SIX ☚

Southern Tier

Courthouse and other buildings, Owego

INTRODUCTION TO BOOK VI

ALTHOUGH THERE are fewer contributions from the area known as the Southern Tier, they are of unquestionable importance. The countryside itself is varied. Its rivers include the Chemung, the Unadilla, the Susquehanna. The names of the towns of Olean and Wellsville indicate that the oil fields of northern Pennsylvania had their counterpart across the New York border, but the Southern Tier has been richer in personalities than other comparable small areas. And Cornell University at Ithaca has since its beginnings been distinguished by nonconformists, independent scholars, geniuses in the fields of humor and practical jokes.

Elmira was once a cultural center of such magnitude that the editor has chosen a number of selections as a unit entitled "Elmira Anthology."

SOUTHERN TIER

18TH CENTURY

JUDGE COOPER

A Letter to William Sampson, Esq.

Sir:—I shall cheerfully answer the Queries you have put to me. The manly way in which you have challenged me, and the good sense you have shown upon a subject of which you can have no experience, and the object I preceive you have at heart, that of procuring information in a matter interesting to your countrymen, does you honor, and makes it a pleasure for me to satisfy so fair a curiosity....

It should be distinctly understood that the whole tract is open for settlement without any reserve on the part of the landlord, as nothing is more discouraging than any appearance in him of views distinct from the prosperity of the whole; and this would be evident if in the very outset he reserved any part in contemplation of a future advance, at the expense of the labor of the original settlers, to whose advantage these reserved tracts had not contributed. The reason is plain; the first difficulties are the greatest, and it is only by combination and coöperation that they can be surmounted. The more the settlers are in number, the more hands can be brought to affect those works which cannot be executd by a few; such are the making of roads and bridges, and other incidents to the cultivation of the Wilderness, which are impossible to individuals, but which numbers render practicable and easy.

Besides, he who comes to better his condition, by embarking in such an enterprise would find it no relief from his present poverty, to be doomed to a life of savage solitude; he will still desire the society of his species, and the

From *A Guide in the Wilderness* by Judge Cooper. Published by Gilbert & Hodges, Dublin, 1810.

ordinary comforts of life; he will look for some religious institution, some school for his children. There must be mechanics to build houses, and erect mills, and other useful or necessary purposes. Where there are a number of settlers, each bearing his proportion of the labor, and contributing to the expense, these things arise almost of course, but it would be very discouraging to a few scattered settlers to reflect that they were toiling under all the hardships and disadvantages of a new and arduous undertaking, whilst others, who had contributed nothing, should afterwards come in and reap all the advantages of their activity. The reserved tracts, therefore, serving only to separate from each other, and depriving them of the comforts of society, and of the advantages of coöperation, would be sources of just discontent, and the landlord who seemed to harbor the ungenerous project of trafficing with the future profits of their industry, and to give all his care to his own interest, without any sympathy with them, would become deservedly an object of distrust and jealousy; his influence would cease, and that confidence, which could alone animate and invigorate a difficult enterprise, once vanishing, nothing but failure could ensue . . .

You have desired to know something of my own proceedings, and since I am to speak of myself, can nowhere better introduce that subject than now, in proof of what I have asserted.

I began with the disadvantage of a small capital, and the encumbrance of a large family, and yet I have already settled more acres than any man in America. There are forty thousand souls now holding, directly or indirectly, under me, and I trust that no one amongst so many can justly impute to me any act resembling oppression. I am now descending into the vale of life, and I must acknowledge that I look back with self complacency upon what I have done, and am proud of having been an instrument in reclaiming such large and fruitful tracts from the waste of the creation. And I question whether that sensation is not now a recompense more grateful to me than all the other profits I have reaped. Your good sense and knowledge of the world will excuse this seeming boast; if it be vain (we all must have our vanities), let it at least serve to show that industry has its reward, and age its pleasures, and be an encouragement to others to persevere and prosper.

In 1785 I visited the rough and hilly country of Otsego where there existed not an inhabitant, nor any trace of a road; I was alone, three hundred miles from home, without bread, meat, or food of any kind; fire and fishing tackle were my only means of subsistence. I caught trout in the brook and roasted them on the ashes. My horse fed on the grass that grew by the edge of the waters. I laid me down to sleep in my watch coat, nothing but the melancholy Wilderness around me. In this way I explored the country, formed my plans of future settlement, and meditated upon the spot where a place of trade or a village should afterwards be established.

In May, 1786, I opened the sales of 40,000 acres, which in sixteen days were all taken up by the poorest order of men. I soon after established a store, and went to live among them, and continued so to do till 1790, when I brought on my family. For the ensuing four years the scarcity of provisions was a serious calamity; the country was mountainous, and there were neither roads nor bridges.

But the greatest discouragement was in the extreme poverty of the people, none of whom had the means of clearing more than a small spot in the midst of the thick and lofty woods, so that their grain grew chiefly in the shade; their maize did not ripen, their wheat was blasted, and the little they did gather they had no mill to grind within twenty miles distance; not one in twenty had a horse, and the way lay through rapid streams, across swamps or over bogs. They had neither provisions to take with them nor money to purchase them; nor if they had, were any to be found on their way. If the father of a family went abroad to labor for bread, it cost him three times its value before he could bring it home, and all the business on his farm stood still till his return.

I resided among them, and saw too clearly how bad their condition was. I erected a store-house, and during each winter filled it with large quantities of grain, purchased in distant places. I procured from my friend Henry Drinker a credit for a large quantity of sugar kettles; he also lent me some potash kettles, which we conveyed as we best could, sometimes by partial roads on sleighs, and sometimes over the ice. By this means I established potash works among the settlers, and made them debtor for their bread and laboring utensils. I also gave them credit for their maple sugar and potash, at a price that would bear transportation, and the first year after the adoption of this plan I collected in one mass forty-three hogsheads of sugar, and three hundred barrels of pot and pearl ash, worth about nine thousand dollars. This kept the people together and at home, and the country soon assumed a new face.

I had not funds of my own sufficient for the opening of new roads, but I collected the people at convenient seasons, and by joint efforts we were able to throw bridges over the deep streams, and to make, in the cheapest manner, such roads as suited our then humble purposes.

In the winter preceding the summer of 1789, grain rose in Albany to a price before unknown. The demand swept all the granaries of the Mohawk country. The number of beginners who depended upon it for their bread, greatly aggravated the evil, and a famine ensued which will never be forgotten by those who, though now in the enjoyment of ease and comfort, were then afflicted with the cruelest of wants.

In the month of April I arrived amongst them with several loads of provisions, destined for my own use and that of the laborers I had brought with me for certain necessary operations; but in a few days all was gone, and there remained not one pound of salt meat, nor a single biscuit. Many were reduced to such distress as to live upon the root of wild leeks; some more fortunate lived upon milk, whilst other supported nature by drinking a syrup made of maple sugar and water. The quantity of leeks they eat had such an effect upon their breath that they could be smelled at many paces distant, and when they came together it was like cattle that had been pastured in a garlic field. A man of the name of Beets mistaking some poisonous herb for a leek, eat it, and died in consequence. Judge of my feelings at this epoch, with two hundred families about me and not a morsel of bread.

A singular event seemed sent by a good Providence to our relief; it was reported to me that unusual shoals of fish were seen moving in the clear waters of the Susquehanna. I went, and was surprised to find that they were herrings. We made something like a small net, by the interweaving of twigs, and by this rude and simple contrivance we were able to take them in thousands. In less than ten days each family had an ample supply with plenty of salt. I also obtained from the Legislature, then in session, seventeen hundred bushels of corn. This we packed on horses' backs, and on our arrival made a distribution among the families, in proportion to the number of individuals of which each was composed.

This was the first settlement I made, and the first attempted after the Revolution.... It maintains at present eight thousand souls, with schools, academies, churches, meeting-houses, turnpike roads, and a market town. It annually yields to commerce large droves of oxen, great quantities of wheat and other grain, abundance of pork, potash in barrels, and other provisions; merchants with large capitals, and all kinds of useful mechanics reside upon it; the waters are stocked with fish, the air is salubrious, and the country thriving and happy. When I contemplate all this, and above all, when I see these good old settlers meet together, and hear them talk of past hardships, of which I bore my share, and compare the misery they then endured with the comforts they now enjoy, my emotions border upon weakness which manhood can scarcely avow.

GUY H. McMASTER

Captain Charles Williamson of Bath

Captain Williamson having, toward the close of the last century, fairly established himself at Bath, was the greatest man in all the land of the West. His dominion extended from Pennsylvania to Lake Ontario; a province of twelve hundred thousand acres owned him as its lord; Indian warriors hailed him as a great chief; settlements on the Genesee, by the Seneca and at the bays of Ontario, acknowledged him as their founder; and furthermore, by commission from the Governor of the State of New York, he was styled Colonel in the militia of the Commonwealth, and at the head of his bold foresters, stood in a posture of defiance before the Pro-Consul of Canada.

. . . His was no idle administration. It did not content him to sit in idle grandeur in his sumptuous log-fortress on the Conhocton, like a Viceroy of the Backwoods, feasting on the roasted sides of mighty stags, and eating luxurious hominy from huge wooden trenchers, with the captains of his host. Neither did he yield to those temptations which so often beset and overpower governors sent to administer the affairs of distant districts of the wilderness, who, instead of collecting tribute from the refractory aborigines, and keeping them well hanged, are forever scouring the woods with hounds, and beating the thickets for bears, to the great neglect of the Royal finances. He galloped hither and thither with restless activity—from Bath to Big Tree, from Seneca to Sodus, from Canadarque to Gerundigut, managing the concerns of his realm with an energy that filled the desert with life and activity. People heard of him afar off—in New England, in Virginia, and in Canada. The bankers of Albany and New York became familiar with his signature, Englishmen and Scotchmen were aroused from their homes and persuaded to cross the ocean for Genesee estates, and hearty young emigrants of the better sort—farmers and mechanics of some substance—were met upon their landing by recommendations to leave the old settlements behind them, and try their fortunes in Williamson's woods. Pioneers from below pushed their canoes and barges up the rivers, and men of the East toiled

From *History of Steuben County* by Guy H. McMaster. Published by R. S. Underhill & Co., Bath, N.Y., 1853.

wearily through the forest with their oxen and sledges. Not a few Virginian planters, with their great households, abandoned their barren estates beyond the Potomac, and performed marches up the Susquehanna valley . . . young-sters and young ladies making the journey gaily on horse-back, while the elderly rode in ponderous chaises, secured against catastrophes by ropes and props, and the shoulders of their negroes. . . .

Captain Williamson dwelt in his stronghold on the Conhocton, in high style, like a baron of old. All the expenses necessary to support the state which such a regent should maintain, were borne by the boundless fund which he controlled. Gentlemen from far countries came up to the woods on horse-back, and were entertained sumptuously. . . .

In 1796, Col. Williamson, by way of blowing a trumpet in the wilderness, advertised to all North America and the adjacent islands, that grand races would be held at Bath. . . . From Niagara to the Mohawk were but a few hundred scattered cabins, and in the south a dozen ragged settlements, contained the greater part of the civilized population till you reached Wyoming. But Col. Williamson did not mistake the spirit of the times. Those were the days of high thoughts and great deeds. On the day, and at the place appointed for the race and the proclamation, sportsmen from New York, Philadelphia and Baltimore were in attendance. The high blades of Virginia and Maryland, the fast-boys of Jersey, the wise jockeys of Long Island, men of Ontario, Pennsylvania and Canada, settlers, choppers, gamesters and hunters, to the number of fifteen hundred or two thousand, met on the Pine Plains to see horses run. . . . Men of blood and spirit made the journey from the Potomac and the Hudson on horse-back, supported by the high spirit of the ancients to endure the miseries of blind trails and log taverns.

The races passed off brilliantly. Col. Williamson himself, a sportsman of spirit and discretion, entered a Southern mare, name Virginia Nell; High Sheriff Dunn entered Silk Stocking, a New Jersey horse. . . . The ladies of the two dignitaries who owned the rival animals, bet each three hundred dollars and a pipe of wine on the horses of their lords, or, as otherwise related, poured seven hundred dollars into the apron of a third lady who was stake-holder. Silk Stocking was victorious. . . .

Colonel Williamson further embellished the backwoods with a theatre. The building, which was of logs, stood at the corner of Steuben and Morris streets. A troop of actors from Philadelphia, kept we believe, at the expense of the agents, entertained for a time the resident and foreign gentry. . . . The excellencies of the legitimate drama seem to have been harmoniously blended with those of the circus, and with the exploits of sorcery. We hear of one gifted genius who astonished the frontiers by balancing a row of three tobacco pipes on his chin, and by other mysterious feats which showed him to be clearly in league with the psychologists.

The race course and the theatre brought the village which they adorned into bad odor with the sober and discreet.... Colonel Williamson was inclined to hurry civilization. The "star of empire" was too slow a planet for him. He wished to kindle a torch in the darkness, to blow a horn in the mountains, to shake a banner from the towers, that men might be led by these singular phenomena to visit his establishment in the wilderness....

Baron Williamson's village bore a very undesirable reputation abroad—a reputation as of some riotous and extravagant youngster, who had been driven as a hopeless profligate from his father's house, and in a wild freak built him a shanty in the woods, where he could whoop and fire pistols, drink, swear, fight, and blow horns without disturbing his mother and sisters.... To suppose that Colonel Williamson's ambition was to be at the head of a gang of banditti who blew horns, pounded drums, fought bulls and drank whiskey from Christmas to the Fourth of July, and from the Fourth of July around to Christmas again, is an exercise of the rights of individual judgment in which those who indulge themselves should not of course be disturbed. It may be true that sometimes, indeed often, a horn or horns may have been blown upon the Pulteney Square, at unseasonable hours of the night in a manner not in accordance with the maxims of the most distinguished composers; it is not impossible that a drum or drums may have been pounded with more vigor than judgment at times when the safety of the republic, either from foreign foes or from internal seditions, did not demand such an expression of military fervor; it will not be confidently denied by the cautious historian that once or twice, or even three times, a large number of republicans may have assembled on the village common to witness a battle between a red bull and a black one: but from these cheerful ebulitions of popular humor, to jump to the popular conclusion that the public mind was entirely devoted to horns, drums and bulls, is a logical gymnastic worthy of a Congressman....

The story of the downfall of Backwoods Baron and his city, is a brief one. Ten years Col. Williamson lived on the Conhocton, and exhausted all chemistry in his experiments upon the possibility of turning a castle of rainbows into stone. His expenditures had been enormous, and the British proprietors began to grumble audibly. The towers of glass, which they once imagined they saw glimmering in the wildnerness, were scrutinized with profound suspicion. But whatever doubt there might be about the reality of those structures, as to one thing there could be no doubt at all. The greedy wilderness was swallowing the fortunes of the Pulteneys with as little gratitude as an anaconda. Hundreds of thousands of pounds had been thrown away to that monster, and like the grave it was yet hungry. To satisfy such a remorseless appetite one needed a silver mine, or a credit with the goblins....

He was a man of spirit, energy and ability. Prepossessing in person, free and frank in manner, generous and friendly in disposition, he is remembered to this day as a "fine fellow" by the farmers who were once young pioneers, and opened his roads and hewed his forests. A keen follower of sports, a lover of the horse, the rifle and the hound, he was accounted a man, by the rudest foresters. High-bred, intelligent, of engaging address, and readily adapting himself to the circumstances of all men, he was equally welcome to the cabin of the woodsman or the table of the Peer: and whether discussing a horse-race with Canisteo, a school project with Prattsburgh, or the philosophy of over-shot wheels with Bartle's Hollow, he was entirely at home, and pronounced opinions which were listened to with respect. His hale, prompt, manly greeting won for him the good will of the settlers, and gave him influence at the occasional assemblies of the citizens....

He had a gallant and impetuous way of doing what was to be done. Where he was, everything was kept stirring. The ordinary routine of a land agent's life had no charms for him. To sit in a drowsy office the live-long day, among quills, and maps, and ledgers, hearing complaints of failing crops, sickness, and hard times, pestered with petitions for the making of new roads and the mending of broken bridges, was unendurable. He must ride through the woods, talk with the settlers, awaken the aliens, show his lands to strangers, entertain gentlemen from abroad. By the pious and substantial settlers from the east, of whom there were many in the county, his tastes and practices were sternly condemned, but even these, while they were offended at his transgressions, and felt sure that no good would come of a state founded by such a Romulus, acknowledged the spirit and vigor of the man, and were willing to ascribe his failings partially to a military and European education.

He was dark of feature, tall, slender, and erect of figure. His habits were active, and he pleased the foresters by vaulting lightly to his saddle, and scouring the roads at full gallop....

In invading the wilderness, in hewing, burning, bridging, turning and overturning, till the stubborn powers of the forest were conquered, broken on the wheel and hanged up *in terorem,* like the rebellious in ancient warfare—in these he found excitement. To stand in the midst of the mountains, and hear the crashing of trees, the ringing of axes, and the rattling of the saw-mills—to see wild streams made tame, to see the continuous line of emigrant barges moving up the lower river, and to feel himself the centre of the movement, would brighten the wits of a dull man, much more invigorate one so wakeful as Col. Williamson. In his fine, dashing way, he would carry the wilderness by storm. Down with the woods; down with the hills; build bridges; build barns; build saw-mills, and shiver the forest into slabs and shingles—these were his orders, and they express the spirit of his administration. In this swashing onslaught his enthusiasm was fired. Besides, the money which he controlled, and the power which he wielded, made him a great man in the land. He was Baron of the Backwoods—Warden of the Wilderness—Hemlock Prince—King of Saw-mills. There was not a greater than he in all the land of the west.

19TH CENTURY

NATHANIEL P. WILLIS

Letters from Under a Bridge

"... This part of the country is not destitute of the chances of adventure, however, and twice in the year, at least, you may, if you choose, open a valve for your spirits. One half the population of the neighborhood is engaged in what is called *lumbering*....

The preparations for the adventures of which I speak, though laborious, are often conducted like a frolic. The felling of the trees in mid-winter, the cutting of shingles, and the drawing out on the snow, are employments preferred by the young men to the tamer but less arduous work of the farm-yard; and in the temporary and uncomfortable *shanties,* deep in the woods, subsisting often on nothing but pork and whiskey, they find metal more attractive than village or fireside. The small streams emptying into the Susquehannah are innumerable, and eight or ten miles back from the river the arks are built, and the materials of the rafts collected, ready to launch with the first thaw. I live, myself, as you know, on one of these tributaries, a quarter of a mile from its junction. The Owego trips along at the foot of my lawn, as private and untroubled for the greater part of the year as Virginia Water at Windsor; but, as it swells in March, the noise of voices and hammering coming out from the woods above, warn us of the approach of an ark, and at the rate of eight or ten miles an hour the rude structure shoots by, floating high on the water without its lading (which it takes in at the village below), and manned with a singing and saucy crew, who dodge the branches of the trees, and work their steering paddles with an adroitness

From *Letters from Under a Bridge* by Nathaniel P. Willis. Published by J. S. Redfield, Clinton Hall, New York, 1846.

and nonchalance which sufficiently shows the character of the class. The sudden bends which the river takes in describing my woody Omega, put their steersmanship to the test; and when the leaves are off the trees, it is a curious sight to see the bulky monsters, shining with new boards, whirling around in the swift eddies, and when caught by the current again, gliding off among the trees like a singing and swearing phantom of an unfinished barn.

At the village they take wheat and pork into the arks, load their rafts with plank and shingles, and wait for the return of the freshet. It is a fact you may not know, that when a river is rising, the middle is the highest, and vice versa when falling, sufficiently proved by the experience of the raftsmen, who, if they start before the flow is at its top, can not keep their crafts from the shore. A pent house, barely sufficient for a man to stretch himself below, is raised on the deck, with a fire-place of earth and loose stone, and with what provision they can afford, and plenty of whiskey, they shove out into the stream. Thenceforward it is *vogue la galère!* They have nothing to do, all day, but abandon themselves to the current, sing and dance and take their turn at the steering oars; and when the sun sets they look out for an eddy, and pull in to the shore. The stopping-places are not very numerous, and are well known to all who follow the trade; and, as the river swarms with rafts, the getting to land, and making sure of a fastening, is a scene always of great competition, and often of desperate fighting. When all is settled for the night, however, and the fires are lit on the long range of the flotilla, the raftsmen get together over their whiskey and provender, and tell the thousand stories of their escapes and accidents; and with the repetition of this, night after night, the whole rafting population along the five hundred miles of the Susquehannah becomes partially acquainted, and forms a sympathetic *corps,* whose excitement and *esprit* might be roused to very dangerous uses.

By daylight they are cast off and once more on the current, and in five or seven days they arrive at tide water, where the crew is immediately discharged, and start, usually on foot, to follow the river home again. There are several places in the navigation which are dangerous, such as rapids and dam-sluices; and what with these, and the scenes at the eddies, and their pilgrimage through a thinly settled and wild country home again, they see enough of adventure to make them fireside heroes, and incapacitate them (while their vigor lasts, at least), for all the more quiet habits of the farmer. The consequence is easy to be seen. Agriculture is but partially followed throughout the country, and while these cheap facilities for transporting produce to the seaboard exist, those who are contented to stay at home, and cultivate the rich river lands of the country, are sure of high prices and a ready reward for their labor.

Moral. Come to the Susquehannah, and settle on a farm.

...The raftsmen who "follow the Delaware" (to use their own poetical expression) are said to be a much wilder class than those on the Susquehannah. In returning to Owego, by different routes, I have often fallen in with parties of both: and certainly nothing could be more entertaining than to listen to their tales. In a couple of years the canal route on the Susquehannah will lay open this rich vein of the picturesque and amusing, and as the tranquil boat glides peacefully along the river bank, the traveller will be surprised with the strange effect of these immense flotillas, with their many fires and wild people, lying in the glassy bends of the solitary stream, the smoke stealing through the dark forest, and the confusion of a hundred excited voices breaking the silence.

...Adieu, dear Doctor! write me a long account of Vestris and Matthews (how *you* like them, I mean, for I know very well how I like them myself), and thank me for turning over to you a new leaf of American romance. You are welcome to write a novel, and call it "The Raftsman of the Susquehannah."

"When did I descend the Susquehannah on a raft?" Never, dear Doctor! But I have descended it in a steamboat, and that may surprise you more. It is an *in*-navigable river, it is true: and it is true, too, that there are some twenty dams across it between Owego and Wilkesbarre; yet I have steamed it from Owego to Wyoming, one hundred and fifty miles, in twelve hours—*on the top of a freshet.* The dams were deep under water, and the river was as smooth as the Hudson. And now you will wonder how a steamer came, by fair means, at Owego.

...A friend of mine, living here, took it into his head that, as salmon and shad will ascend a fall of twenty feet in a river, the propulsive energy of their tails might possibly furnish a hint for a steamer that would shoot up dams and rapids. The suggestion was made to a Connecticut man, who, of course, undertook it. He would have been less than a Yankee if he had not *tried.* The product of his ingenuity was the steamboat "Susquehannah", drawing but eighteen inches; and, besides her side-paddles, having an immense wheel in the stern, which playing in the slack water of the boat, would drive her up Niagara, if she would but hold together. The principal weight of her machinery hung upon two wooden arches running fore and aft, and altogether she was a neat piece of contrivance, and promised fairly to answer the purpose.

I think the "Susquehannah" had made three trips when she broke a shaft, and was laid up. . . . A month or two since, the proprietors determined to run her down the river for the purpose of selling her, and I was invited among others to join in the trip.

The only offices professionally filled on board were those of the engineer and pilot. Captain, mate, firemen, steward, cook, and chambermaid, were represented *en amateur* by gentlemen passengers. We rang the bell at the starting hour with the zeal usually displayed in that department, and, by the assistance of the current, got off in the usual style of a steamboat departure, wanting only the newsboys and pickpockets. With a stream running at five knots, and paddles calculated to mount a cascade, we could not fail to take the river in gallant style, and before we had regulated our woodpiles and pantry, we were backing water at Athens, twenty miles on our way.

Navigating the Susquehannah is very much like dancing "the cheat." You are always making straight up to a mountain, with no apparent possibility of escaping contact with it, and it is an even chance up to the last moment which side of it you are to *chassez* with the current. Meantime the sun seems capering about to all points of the compass, the shadows falling in every possible direction, and north, south, east, and west, changing places with the familiarity of a masquerade. The blindness of the river's course is increased by the innumerable small islands in its bosom, whose tall elms and close-set willows meet half-way those from either shore; and, the current very often dividing above them, it takes an old voyager to choose between the shaded alleys, by either of which you would think Arethusa might have eluded her lover.

My own mental occupation, as we glided on, was the distribution of white villas along the shore, on spots where nature seemed to have arranged the ground for their reception. I saw thousands of sites where the lawns were made, the terraces defined and levelled, the groves tastefully clumped, the ancient trees ready with their broad shadows, the approaches to the water laid out, the banks sloped, and in everything the labor of art seemingly all anticipated by nature. I grew tired of exclaiming, to the friend who was beside me, "What an exquisite site for a villa! What a sweet spot for a cottage!" If I had had the power to people the Susquehannah by the wave of a wand, from those I know capable of appreciating its beauty, what a paradise I could have spread out between my own home and Wyoming! . . .

It was sometimes ticklish steering among the rafts and arks with which the river was thronged, and we never passed one without getting the raftsman's rude hail. One of them furnished my vocabulary with a new measure of speed. He stood at the stern oar of a shingle raft, gaping at us, open-mouthed as we came down upon him. "Wal!" said he, as we shot past, "you're going a *good hickory,* mister!" . . .

We passed the Falls of Wyalusing (most musical of Indian names) and Buttermilk Falls, both cascades worthy of being known and sung, and twilight overtook us some two hours from Wyoming. We had no lights on board, and the engineer was unwilling to run in the dark; so our pilot being an old raftsman, we put into the first "eddy," and moored for the night. . . .

It was a still, starlight night, and the river was laced with the long reflections of the raft-fires, while the softened songs of the men over their evening carouse, came to us along the smooth water with the effect of far better music.

ELMIRA ANTHOLOGY

SAMUEL L. CLEMENS

Mark Twain's Courtship

In the beginning of February 1870 I was married to Miss Olivia L. Langdon, and I took up my residence in Buffalo, New York. Tomorrow * will be the thirty-sixth anniversary of our marriage. My wife passed from this life one year and eight months ago in Florence, Italy, after an unbroken illness of twenty-two months' duration.

I saw her first in the form of an ivory miniature in her brother Charley's stateroom in the steamer *Quaker City* in the Bay of Smyrna, in the summer of 1867, when she was in her twenty-second year. I saw her in the flesh for the first time in New York in the following December. She was slender and beautiful and girlish—and she was both girl and woman. She remained both girl and woman to the last day of her life. Under a grave and gentle exterior burned inextinguishable fires of sympathy, energy, devotion, enthusiasm and absolutely limitless affection. She was *always* frail in body and she lived upon her spirit, whose hopefulness and courage were indestructible. . . .

Perfect truth, perfect honesty, perfect candor, were qualities of my wife's

From pp. 183-190 *The Autobiography of Mark Twain,* edited by Charles Neider. Copyright © 1959 by The Mark Twain Company. Reprinted with the permission of Harper & Row, Publishers, Inc.

* Written February 1, 1906.

character which were born with her. Her judgments of people and things were sure and accurate. Her intuitions almost never deceived her. In her judgments of the characters and acts of both friends and strangers there was always room for charity, and this charity never failed. I have compared and contrasted her with hundreds of persons and my conviction remains that hers was the most perfect character I have ever met. And I may add that she was the most winningly dignified person I have ever known. Her character and disposition were of the sort that not only invite worship but command it. No servant ever left her service who deserved to remain in it. And as she could choose with a glance of her eye, the servants she selected did in almost all cases deserve to remain and they *did* remain.

She was always cheerful; and she was always able to communicate her cheerfulness to others. During the nine years that we spent in poverty and debt she was always able to reason me out of my despairs and find a bright side to the clouds and make me see it. In all that time I never knew her to utter a word of regret concerning our altered circumstances, nor did I ever know her children to do the like. For she had taught them and they drew their fortitude from her. The love which she bestowed upon those whom she loved took the form of worship, and in that form it was returned—returned by relatives, friends and the servants of her household.

It was a strange combination which wrought into one individual, so to speak, by marriage—her disposition and character and mine. She poured out her prodigal affections in kisses and caresses and in a vocabulary of endearments whose profusion was always an astonishment to me. I was born *reserved* as to endearments of speech, and caresses, and hers broke upon me as the summer waves break upon Gibraltar. I was reared in that atmosphere of reserve. As I have already said, I never knew a member of my father's family to kiss another member of it except once, and that at a deathbed. And our village was not a kissing community. The kissing and caressing ended with courtship—along with the deadly piano-playing of that day.

She had the heart-free laugh of a girl. It came seldom, but when it broke upon the ear it was as inspiring as music. I heard it for the last time when she had been occupying her sick bed for more than a year and I made a written note of it at the time—a note not to be repeated.

To-morrow will be the thirty-sixth anniversary. We were married in her father's house in Elmira, New York and went next day by special train to Buffalo, along with the Beechers and the Twichells, who had solemnized the marriage. We were to live in Buffalo, where I was to be one of the editors of the Buffalo *Express* and a part owner of the paper. I knew nothing about Buffalo but I had made my household arrangements there through a friend, by letter. I had instructed him to find a boarding-house of as respectable a character as my light salary as editor would command. We were received at about nine o'clock at the station in Buffalo and were put into several sleighs and driven all over America, as it seemed to me—for apparently we turned all the corners in the town and followed all the streets there were—I scolding freely and characterizing that friend of mine in very uncomplimentary ways for securing a boarding-house that apparently had no definite locality. But there was a conspiracy—and my bride knew of it, but I was in ignorance. Her father, Jervis Langdon, had bought and furnished a new house for us in the fashionable street, Delaware Avenue, and had laid in a cook and housemaids and a brisk and electric young coachman, an Irishman, Patrick McAleer—and we were being driven all over that city in order that one sleighful of these people could have time to go to the house and see that the gas was lighted all over it and a hot supper prepared for the crowd. We arrived at last, and when I entered that fairy place my indignation reached high-water mark, and without any reserve I delivered my opinion to that friend of mine for being so stupid as to put us into a boarding-house whose terms would be far out of my reach. Then Mr. Langdon brought forward a very pretty box and opened it and took from it a deed of the house. So the comedy ended very pleasantly and we sat down to supper.

The company departed about midnight and left us alone in our new quarters. Then Ellen, the cook, came in to get orders for the morning's marketing—and neither of us knew whether beefsteak was sold by the barrel or by the yard. We exposed our ignorance and Ellen was full of Irish delight over it. Patrick McAleer, that brisk young Irishman, came in to get his orders for next day—and that was our first glimpse of him.

It sounds easy and swift and unobstructed but that was not the way of it. It did not happen in that smooth and comfortable way. There was a deal of courtship. There were three or four proposals of marriage and just as many declinations. I was roving far and wide on the lecture beat but I managed to arrive in Elmira every now and then and renew the siege. Once I dug an invitation out of Charley Langdon to come and stay a week. It was a pleasant week but it had to come to an end. I was not able to invent any way to get the invitation enlarged. No schemes that I could contrive seemed likely to deceive. They did not even deceive *me,* and when a person cannot deceive himself the chances are against his being able to deceive other people. But at last help and good fortune came and from a most unexpected quarter. It was one of those cases so frequent in the past centuries, so infrequent in our day—a case where the hand of Providence is in it.

I was ready to leave for New York. A democrat wagon stood outside the main gate with my trunk in it, and Barney, the coachman, in the front seat with the reins in his hand. It was eight or nine in the evening and dark. I bade good-by to the grouped family on the front porch, and Charley and I went out and climbed into the wagon. We took our places back of the coachman on the remaining seat, which was aft toward the end of the wagon and was only a temporary arrangement for our accommodation and was not fastened in its place; a fact which—most fortunately for me—we were not aware of. Charley was smoking. Barney touched up the horse with the whip. He made a sudden spring forward. Charley and I went over the stern of the wagon backward. In the darkness the red bud of fire on the end of his cigar described a curve through the air which I can see yet. This was the only visible thing in all that gloomy scenery. I struck exactly on the top of my head and stood up that way for a moment, then crumbled down to the earth unconscious. It was a very good unconsciousness for a person who had not rehearsed the part. It was a cobblestone gutter and they had been repairing it. My head struck in a dish formed by the conjunction of four cobblestones. That depression was half full of fresh new sand and this made a competent cushion. My head did not touch any of those cobblestones. I got not a bruise. I was not even jolted. Nothing was the matter with me at all.

Charley was considerably battered, but in his solicitude for me he was substantially unaware of it. The whole family swarmed out, Theodore Crane in the van with a flask of brandy. He poured enough of it between my lips to strangle me and make me bark but it did not abate my unconsciousness. I was taking care of that myself. It was very pleasant to hear the pitying remarks trickling around over me. That was one of the happiest half dozen moments of my life. There was nothing to mar it—except that I had escaped damage. I was afraid that this would be discovered sooner or later and would shorten my visit. I was such a dead weight that it required the combined strength of Barney and Mr. Langdon, Theodore and Charley to lug me into the house, but it was accomplished. I was there. I recognized that this was victory. I was there. I was safe to be an incumbrance for an indefinite length of time—but for a length of time, at any rate, and a Providence was in it.

They set me up in an armchair in the parlor and sent for the family physician. Poor old creature, it was wrong to rout him out but it was business, and I was too unconscious to protest. Mrs. Crane—dear soul, she was in this house three days ago, gray and beautiful and as sympathetic as ever

—Mrs. Crane brought a bottle of some kind of liquid fire whose function was to reduce contusions. But I knew that mine would deride it and scoff at it. She poured this on my head and pawed it around with her hand, stroking and massaging, the fierce stuff dribbling down my backbone and marking its way, inch by inch, with the sensation of a forest fire. But *I* was satisfied. When she was getting worn out, her husband, Theodore, suggested that she take a rest and let Livy carry on the assuaging for a while. That was very pleasant. I should have been obliged to recover presently if it hadn't been for that. But under Livy's manipulations—if they had continued —I should probably be unconscious to this day. It was very delightful, those manipulations. So delightful, so comforting, so enchanting, that they even soothed the fire out of that fiendish successor to Perry Davis's "Pain-Killer."

Then that old family doctor arrived and went at the matter in an educated and practical way—that is to say, he started a search expedition for contusions and humps and bumps and announced that there were none. He said that if I would go to bed and forget my adventure I would be all right in the morning—which was not so. I was *not* all right in the morning. I didn't intend to be all right and I was far from being all right. But I said I only needed rest and I didn't need that doctor any more.

I got a good three days' extension out of that adventure and it helped a good deal. It pushed my suit forward several steps. A subsequent visit completed the matter and we became engaged conditionally; the condition being that the parents should consent.

In a private talk Mr. Langdon called my attention to something I had already noticed—which was that I was an almost entirely unknown person; that no one around about knew me except Charley, and he was too young to be a reliable judge of men; that I was from the other side of the continent and that only those people out there would be able to furnish me a character, in case I had one—so he asked me for references. I furnished them, and he said we would now suspend our industries and I could go away and wait until he could write to those people and get answers.

In due course answers came. I was sent for and we had another private conference. I had referred him to six prominent men, among them two clergymen (these were all San Franciscans), and he himself had written to a bank cashier who had in earlier years been a Sunday-school superintendent in Elmira and well known to Mr. Langdon. The results were not promising. All those men were frank to a fault. They not only spoke in disapproval of me but they were quite unnecessarily and exaggeratedly enthusiastic about it. One clergyman (Stebbins) and that ex-Sunday-school superintendent (I wish I could recall his name) added to their black testimony the conviction that I would fill a drunkard's grave. It was just one of those usual long-distance prophecies. There being no time limit, there is no telling how long you may have to wait. I have waited until now and the fulfillment seems as far away as ever.

The reading of the letters being finished, there was a good deal of a pause and it consisted largely of sadness and solemnity. I couldn't think of anything to say. Mr. Langdon was apparently in the same condition. Finally he raised his handsome head, fixed his clear and candid eye upon me and said: "What kind of people are these? Haven't you a friend in the world?"

I said, "Apparently not."

Then he said: "I'll be your friend myself. Take the girl. I know you better than they do."

Thus dramatically and happily was my fate settled. Afterward, hearing me talking lovingly, admiringly and fervently of Joe Goodman, he asked me where Goodman lived. I told him out on the Pacific coast. He said: "Why, he seems to be a friend of yours! Is he?"

I said, "Indeed he is; the best one I ever had."

"Why, then," he said, "what could you have been thinking of? Why didn't you refer me to him?"

I said: "Because he would have lied just as straightforwardly on the other side. The others gave me all the vices; Goodman would have given me all the virtues. You wanted unprejudiced testimony, of course. I knew you wouldn't get it from Goodman. I did believe you would get it from those others and possibly you did. But it was certainly less complimentary than I was expecting."

The date of our engagement was February 4, 1869. The engagement ring was plain and of heavy gold. That date was engraved inside of it. A year later I took it from her finger and prepared it to do service as a wedding ring by having the wedding date added and engraved inside of it—February 2, 1870. It was never again removed from her finger for even a moment.

In Italy when death had restored her vanished youth to her sweet face and she lay fair and beautiful and looking as she had looked when she was girl and bride, they were going to take that ring from her finger to keep for the children. But I prevented that sacrilege. It is buried with her.

In the beginning of our engagement the proofs of my first book, *The Innocents Abroad,* began to arrive and she read them with me. She also edited them. She was my faithful, judicious and painstaking editor from that day forth until within three or four months of her death—a stretch of more than a third of a century.

MAX EASTMAN

Mark Twain's Elmira

Jervis Langdon [father of Olivia, Mark Twain's wife]...lived about half his life as a country storekeeper, and one with a reputation for such fantastic acts of generosity parading in the guise of "simple justice" that you would hardly think he could get on at all.... When he got rich he did not alter these fantastic habits by a hair. When sued, for instance, by a prominent Philadelphia attorney, he gathered up and sent to him all the documents that would be of help to the plaintiff, saying that he wanted the case decided only on its merits.... He was an ardent abolitionist, and in days of wealth and poverty alike held his house and his pockets open to illegally escaping slaves. The story of his life was related by Thomas K. Beecher at a crowded memorial meeting held in the Elmira Opera House two weeks after he died, and it reads like a tale from the days of chivalry. Of Mr. Beecher's seventeen paragraphs in peroration, I will quote but six.

> To do humble tasks faithfully, with or without pay;
>
> To welcome partners when partners were needed, and leave them in sole possession, when they seemed to desire it;
>
> To serve employers so faithfully that the memory of the service remains indelible after the lapse of thirty years;...
>
> To befriend the friendless and champion the oppressed with the full measure of one man's resource, be the same large or small;
>
> To walk so generously that envy's self was silenced at sight of his prosperity, so many were sharing in it....
>
> In short, to have led a life of varied and amazing activity, through forty-five years, and at last to enter into rest, leaving upon earth not one voice to impeach his integrity, nor one acquaintance without regret for his going, nor one friend that is not proudly heart-stricken at loss of him;
>
> These, and things like these, were the ornaments and lessons of his life. I but gather them together as decorations for his memory.

That was the father of Olivia Clemens as seen by one of the most radical preachers of the time. Her mother was almost equally surprising, and she too

From *Heroes I Have Known: Twelve Who Lived Great Lives* by Max Eastman, published by Simon and Schuster, New York, 1942. Reprinted by permission of the author.

was celebrated by Mr. Beecher in a memorial sermon when she died. After reminding his audience that she and her husband had formed the head and front of the little group of abolitionists which split off from the Presbyterians in 1846 on the slavery issue, and formed the church in which he was speaking, Mr. Beecher continued:

> Forty-one years ago it was a costly matter to profess any interest in colored men, or disapproval of their enslavement, or to mention them in prayers. And when, in stormy times, a little company of Christians banded themselves together to form a new church in this community, it was an act which cost them social ostracism and contempt.... To women such ostracism is a distress, that can be bravely borne by them only who have found a better strength than *society*. Mrs. Langdon had this better strength. Though always weak in the flesh, yet she was strong and unflinching in generous courage and determination. The Langdon house, however small, had room in it for abolitionists—Garrison, Phillips, Quincy, Johnson, Gerrit Smith, Foster, Frederick Douglas. The family horse and purse were at the service of fugitives from slavery....

Olivia (Twain's) gospel, in so far as she learned it from the church in which her mother and father were the central social and financial force, was one of self-reliant revolt against forms and conventions as such. And if she suspected that Mark Twain had unorthodox views about religion, that could only have helped him to fit into the environment in which she had been born and reared. For her own mother was perhaps as unorthodox as anybody in Mr. Beecher's extremely free-thinking congregation.

"I have not concealed from you," he says in his memorial sermon, "nor have I proclaimed, that her views not infrequently diverged from those of her pastor."

That her views did not diverge in the direction of orthodoxy may be gathered from her answer to a question that he put to her upon her deathbed.

"No," she said, "it is all dark to me. It's like lifting a great stone and looking into a cave. But it will be as God wills and I shall be satisfied."

...That is not half the story of Mark Twain's extraordinary Elmira. The central figure in that Elmira, the dominant and molding intellectual and spiritual force, not only to Olivia Langdon, but in a large measure to Mark Twain himself, was this same eloquent and great Beecher whose words we have been reading—a man of more than Mark Twain's stature, you must realize, in the minds of those around them. Mr. Beecher did not call himself a minister of the gospel. He called himself "Teacher of the Park

Church"; and a whole rebel character and thought of life lay behind that choice. His thought was to live and be helpful in the community as a modern Jesus would, a downright, realistic, iconoclastic, life-loving Jesus, with a scientific training and a sense of humor and a fund of common sense. He was, in fact, a very eloquent preacher, more eloquent to a lucid listener than his famous brother, Henry Ward. But unlike Henry, and perhaps in part because of Henry's glibness, he did not believe in preaching. When he was invited to the Park Church in 1854 he replied with a letter laying down in almost imperious terms, as though putting all Christian churchdom on trial, the conditions upon which he would accept a call to any church.

> Do you remember that I do not think good can be done by a preacher's preaching? It must be by Christians working that good is done, if at all. ...Do you remember this, yes or no?

One Sunday Thomas somewhat unexpectedly substituted for Henry in his famous Plymouth Church, and when he rose in the pulpit a good number of the vast audience got up to go. He stopped them with his hand.

"Those," he said, "who came here to worship Henry Ward Beecher are excused. Those who wish to worship God will remain."

The man was masterful, humorous, poised upon himself although impetuous, and endowed with a supreme contempt for fame, money, and "success." He declined calls to our greatest metropolitan churches because he had "found love" in Elmira and created there a church in his own free-moving and magnanimous image. He belonged to the second Beecher brood, those with more integrity and less sentimentalism than the children of Roxana Foote. They all had genius; they all had unconventional and imposing force; they all had large-featured good looks and magnetism. He was the best-looking and the brainiest—possessing, according to old Lyman himself, "quickness, depth, and comprehension of discrimination surpassing almost any mind I have come in contact with"—and he had by far the most distinguished gift of expression. You rarely come upon a surviving sentence of his that does not have individuality and convey the impact of an edged and forceful mind. These, for instance, quoted in a pamphlet by an irate colleague:

> We do not care to argue, we simply assert that manly character cannot be developed in any human being who stands in fear of public sentiment. We make no account of it whatever among the instrumentalities which we use as a Christian pastor and teacher. When it opposes us, we defy it in the name of conscience. When it favors us, we regret the feebleness which such help entails upon manhood.

. . . As [Paxton] Hibben said, Thomas Beecher "voiced with least circumlocution what so many clergymen felt." Voicing without circumlocution was almost the essence of the man.

> Do you remember that while in good faith I profess to you that I am sound and evangelic in doctrine, yet I have no ambition to found, or foster or preserve a church as such? My exclusive aim is to help men as individuals to be Christians. No church prosperity dazzles me; no church poverty or adversity troubles me.
>
> Do you remember this, yes or no?
>
> Pardon my plain speech. Truth is at the bottom of all enduring love. Though I speak bold words, yet my heart is very tender and very tired and would fain rest in just some such place as Elmira.

Thus he approached his second parish, having been thrown out of his first for discovering a shady money deal among its leading members and threatening them with exposure if they did not quit. This little group of abolitionists in Elmira liked his abrupt but considerate advance notice of general rebellion against respectability and tradition. They accepted all his terms. "The next Sunday morning," writes Lyman Beecher Stowe, "amid the expectant hush of curiosity that always precedes the arrival of a new minister, there strode up the center aisle of the First Congregational Church of Elmira a tall, slender, handsome young man who, tossing a felt visor cap onto a chair, mounted the pulpit and opened the services. The tossing of that cap was an unconscious challenge to the traditionalists of the town which they were quick to accept."

In further challenge to the traditionalists, he made this announcement to his congregation:

> I cannot make pastoral calls. I am not constructed so that I can. But I am yours all times of the day and night when you want anything of me. If you are sick and need a watcher I will watch with you. If you are poor and need some one to saw wood for you I will saw wood for you. I can read the paper for you if you need somebody to do that. I am yours, but you must call me the same as you would a physician.

Adhering to that program, Mr. Beecher became as much a man of all work as a pastor to his congregation. He was a thoroughly trained mechanic and locomotive engineer, able to build a house and handle and repair anything from a ship to a railroad train, and he served his parishioners as carpenter, painter, paper hanger, clock and sewing-machine mender. For forty years he wound and set the Elmira town clock, keeping it in pace with the sun by means of observations made with his own instruments on famous East

Hill halfway up to Quarry Farm. He preached no doctrine but the fatherhood of God and brotherhood of man, and he walked about Elmira in ordinary and usually very old clothes like a workman, carrying when necessary a sewing machine or even a sofa on his back, and never taking off that cap with the big visor—never surrendering to the traditionalists. It was a railroad man's cap, or nearer that than anything else, and his head was so big that it had to be made to order by a special hatter. And the hatter—throughout the fifty years of its service as a symbol of his revolt against the traditionalists—was Olivia Clemens' exquisite and dearly beloved sister, Susan Langdon Crane! ...

Mr. Beecher was not only a man of all work; he was a man of all play. He was a skilled bowler and cricket player; he joined a whist club and organized a baseball team called the Lively Turtles, which scandalized the churchmen by not even taking baseball seriously. He sang college songs and played them on the church organ. He attended theaters, and played pool and billiards, and even installed a pool table in the church parlors. Although the original charter of his church declared for the "unfermented juice of the grape" in communions, and further affirmed that "no intoxicating liquors shall be used by the members," he strolled into a saloon when he felt like it and took a glass of beer. In fact, he made this a permanent revolution by installing his own private mug in a favorite saloon as others did in barbershops.

He ran a weekly column in the local paper—a pioneer in this field too—joining the politicians' battles with a sword of truth that slashed both ways and ... naming those who scandalized him by their proper names. The prohibitionists scandalized him with their straitlaced lies, and with the remark that this country is "too sunshiny and roomy" for all that ranting to be true, he took his public stand behind the liquor dealers. Still better, when he changed his mind on this in after years, he said that too. The extreme to which he dared to follow his conception of a Christian life is revealed in his befriending of a notorious prostitute, whom he finally, to the horror of his neighbors, took into his house and treated as a daughter until she gained her poise and married and went away.

It is needless to describe the raw hate aroused by these consummate blasphemies among the surrounding Apostles of Christ Jesus. Beecher and his church were regarded as a moral ulcer eating up the harvest of the gospel throughout the whole Chemung and Susquehanna valleys. When his Sunday-evening meetings grew too big for the old meetinghouse, and he crowned his sins by hiring the local theater, actually inviting in vast crowds to offer prayers to God in that Satanic edifice, the storm broke on this "Opera-House preacher" from all sides. He was expelled from the Ministerial Union and denounced from every pulpit in the city. He made no public answer to the fulminations of the ministers but embarrassed them in private with an extra-Christlike courtesy.

Jervis Langdon stood behind him like a rock. "My purse is open to you," he had said, "you can do more good with it than I can." And he now headed a movement to buy shares in the Opera House to ensure the future of this outrage. Mark Twain himself stood by him—not the Mark Twain you know, but just a well-known wit and travel writer who had married into the Langdon family. "Happy happy world," he wrote in the *Elmira Advertiser,* "that knows at last that a little congress of congregationless clergymen, of whom it never heard before, have crushed a famous Beecher and reduced his audiences from fifteen hundred down to fourteen hundred and seventy-five in one fell blow!"

When the crowds on Sunday morning overflowed the church also, Mr. Beecher further shocked the prelates by abandoning his church and meeting his congregation in a little public park outside the city. And to crown that crime he helped the street railway get special permission to run cars out to the park in violation of the Sunday laws, and he himself came out there to preach the gospel dressed in white ducks and a white felt hat.

Far deeper than these evidences of realistic good sense, two things distinguished Thomas K. Beecher from all other great American ministers. First, he was a man of science. I have described his accomplishments in practical astronomy and mechanics. They were linked with a theoretical passion which had all but diverted him from the ministerial calling and which kept him in the forefront of the march of scientific inquiry throughout his life....

The other thing which distinguished Mr. Beecher from all other men in the annals of our pulpit was the scope of his magnanimity, his absolute rejection, not of "angular sectarianism," but of all sectarianism whatsoever. He not only invited men of all denominations to become members of his church; he invited the members of his church to leave for no matter what trivial reasons of convenience and go and join some other. In his book *Our Seven Churches,* religious tolerance, a rare substance in any solution, is presented in pure essence....

> In at least five out of Our Seven Churches, except on rare occasions, a visitor has need to ask at the close of public worship the name of the church that has made him welcome. And all that saves the other two churches from a like uniformity is the necessity of one of clinging to a liturgy and in the other of holding fast to a dead language. There are many churches but one religion.

> ...This is my proposition: If a man loves all the churches, then it is proper for him to live with that church in which he can earn the most by doing the most....

All these wildly sensible acts and this greathearted thinking—in which, if you know anything about American churchdom of the period, you will recognize the outlines of a cultural revolution—culminated in 1872 in the raising of sixty-five thousand dollars to build a new church after Mr. Beecher's own heart. The sum was doubled by the Langdon family, and the new church, which extended through a whole block with entrances on two streets, was the largest in that region, as well as probably the most progressive in America.*

...The church had a kitchen equipped with china and silver for two or three hundred, "parlors" available to any who wished to use them, a free public library, pool and billiard tables, a dancing hall and children's "romp room" with a stage and the complete fittings of a theater. All this in 1873! There would be a "picnic supper" every week, and a "pay supper" every month. Every fourth Sunday would be children's Sunday, and the grown-up folks could stay at home or come and hear a "children's sermon." At other times the Sunday school would meet in the main auditorium following the morning service, and after a preliminary exercise in common, the children would march to gay music on the organ to their separate rooms and places of assembly. Mrs. Beecher remembered a Sunday back in the seventies when they marched to the tune of *Captain Jinks of the Horse Marines,* and I remember a day when our eccentric organist, George B. Carter, sent us skipping with a medley composed of *Onward, Christian Soldiers!* and *There'll Be a Hot Time in the Old Town Tonight.* Some shook their heads and smiled, but there was no indignant gossip; nobody was disturbed. A humorous informalism, a being at ease with your play instincts, was characteristic of all the Beechers—even austere old Lyman having been a brilliant performer of the double shuffle. It was equally characteristic of Mrs. Beecher—"my strong, courageous, energetic Julia," as he called her, "to whom belongs the credit for nine-tenths of the achievement of our long life in Elmira."

* In the book already cited, Lyman Beecher Stowe gives these statistics: "So this workman, teacher, and preacher built up in a town which grew, between the time he came in 1854 until his death in 1900, from eight thousand to thirty-eight thousand inhabitants, a church with not only this large and unique plant but with a membership which increased from fifty to seven hundred, with a Sunday School which came to number one thousand members of all ages from small children to their grandparents. The Sunday congregations of between thirteen hundred and fifteen hundred were made up not only of all denominations but of the unchurched and even agnostics. Traveling salesmen so routed their trips that they might be in Elmira over Sunday to hear Thomas K. Beecher preach."

Her energetic whims and impulses of geniality, and what might be called dynamic common sense, were uncontrollable by any feeling except the fear that she might really hurt somebody's feelings.

A word about Mrs. Beecher is essential to my theme because, among so many other things, she was Olivia's Sunday-school teacher. My mother, in a brochure called *A Flower of Puritanism,* described this most unusual Sunday-school teacher as combining a New England conscience with a Greek love of beauty and—she might have added—with a timeless sense of fun. She was a granddaughter of Noah Webster and, like old Noah, rich in whims and talents. She invented, one day when she was darning an old stocking, a species of rag doll which became celebrated for its plump and genial superiority to circumstance, and, by turning herself into a veritable factory for these "Beecher dolls," kept a lifelong stream of money pouring from her hands to charity. She made sculptures too and comic drawings and queer birds and beasts out of roots and autumn tassels, grotesque things that Mark Twain called Jabberwocks. These too she would auction off for charity, and on one occasion Mark Twain functioned as the auctioneer.

> My dear Mrs. Beecher: [he wrote] I have arranged your jabberwocks and other devils in procession according to number and rank on the piano in the drawing room and in that subdued light they take to themselves added atrocities of form and expression and so make a body's flesh crawl with pleasure.
>
> If I come down at midnight (with my usual dose of hot Scotch stowed) I shall very well be able to imagine I see them climbing about the furniture bearing their rigid tails high and inspecting everything with their calm, critical brass eyes.
>
> You have had a genuine inspiration, you have wrought it out not lamely, but to perfection. I shall hate to see any of these enchanting monsters going out of the house.... Make more; don't leave a root unutilized in Chemung county. But don't go to the last limit, that is don't breathe the breath of life into them, for I know (if there is anything in physiognomy and general appearance) that they would all vote the Democratic ticket, every devil of them.

When I think of Mrs. Beecher I see always the sweet and faithful firmness of the closure of her lips. And as I look, she jumps suddenly up to be on her way in endless labors for the suffering, sick, and ignorant with brisk, imperious, selfless energy. An admirer once said to her: "I love to see you pour coffee, because you do it with such indiscriminate fury!" With the same indiscriminate fury she would gather up the dishes after a meal, scrape them, and pile them to save labor for someone in the kitchen. "Your plate!" she would exclaim suddenly, stretching out a commanding hand to the astonished guest.

Mrs. Beecher was quite as headstrong as her husband in smashing through forms and conventions, and her rebellion was not only moral but aesthetic. She bobbed her hair in 1857, anticipating Irene Castle by about sixty years, and imparting to her beauty a quality as startling to her neighbors as though a cherub had alighted in their city. And she used to invade its stuffy parlors like a whirlwind, clearing out the mid-Victorian junk.

"Why do you have all those *little* things on that wall?" she would exclaim. "Don't you see how much better one big simple picture would look?"

To distinguish her yet more as a Sunday-school teacher of the "genteel female," Mrs. Beecher wore congress shoes with low flat heels. She kept up a kind of hilarious joy in her pupils too because she could not herself, with all her talents, learn a Bible verse by heart, not if she spent the week on it, and she was desperately honest about such things. Moreover, just as her Puritan morals were tempered with a pagan love of beauty, her New England piety was mingled with a wayward humor very much belonging to this earth. Once she said to Mr. Beecher at a meeting of Sunday-school teachers:

"I believe if we prayed *all night long* the way old-fashioned Christians did, we would really get what we prayed for!"

"Why don't you try it?" he said.

"Well, I wouldn't want to lose a night's sleep on an uncertainty."

On another occasion she and Mr. Beecher, hastening to an appointment at the reformatory, were held up by a long freight train, which suddenly parted exactly at the crossing.

"O, Tom," she cried, "I'm sorry I didn't pray, it would have been such a good answer!"

Mrs. Beecher and my mother were the closest of friends, and their friendship consisted largely of a voyage together, and in the company of Emerson and William Morris and Walt Whitman, beyond the confines of churchly ethics and religion. "She was eager to assimilate the results of scientific research in every field," my mother writes, and adds that "when any old doctrine that she could no longer hold was under discussion, she would say: 'But it was necessary in its time.'" I cherish the image of her sitting by my mother's hammock beside a brook reading aloud, with an expression of grim and yet joyful determination on her gentle features, the Calamus poems in Walt Whitman's *Song of Myself*.

MAX EASTMAN

The Hero as Parent

She was a Christian minister—the first woman ordained in the Congregational church of New York State, and she became the pastor of one of its large and famous churches. She was of medium height, with light-brown hair and green-blue eyes, a gently curving beauty both of face and figure. She wore in the pulpit a simple black robe of her own design which she called a surplice. It was pleated in front and made feminine by a little black lace in the opening at her throat. Her manner in the pulpit was as simple as her gown. She made few gestures, and never a motion that was not native to her. She had the two indispensable gifts of the orator, self-possession and a thrilling voice. When she rose to speak, you knew at once that she was in complete command of the situation, and you felt at ease. As there was nothing in the least degree mannish about her, you stopped bothering about whether she was a man or a woman. And when she began to speak, you were taken quiet possession of, first by the tones of her voice, and then by the surprisingly candid and wise and joyous, and often even humorous, things that she would say.

She believed in joy. As a freshman at Oberlin she had written a theme in which she advanced the theory that God himself *is* joy—a vast stream of joy surrounding all of us. And she believed in growing. She believed that the essential secret of a joyous life, no matter where you start from, is to be forever in a state of growth. These two beliefs, or instincts, comprise the essence of her teaching. They are at least what most distinguished it from the usual messages of those who put on black cloth as a mark of their profession. What also made her unforgettable was the undying gallant courage with which she carried into life whatever she believed.

Her father George Ford—grandson of a Henry Ford—had been a gunsmith in Peoria, Illinois, and a big boss around the house. He believed that woman's place is the home, and proved it by getting drunk frequently and making the home hell. She grew up, perhaps in consequence, with a quiet but firm belief that women ought to learn a trade. She decided while still

From *Heroes I Have Known: Twelve Who Lived Great Lives* by Max Eastman, published by Simon and Schuster, New York, 1942. Reprinted by permission of the author.

in high school—and that was in 1870 when such decisions were rare—that she was going to be economically independent. When Susan B. Anthony came to lecture in Peoria, this ambitious high-school girl introduced the famous suffragette, and did it with so much eloquence that, according to a clipping in my possession, her speech was "the talk of the town." What George Ford contributed to the talk on that occasion is not recorded.

At Oberlin, where she went to learn to teach, she fell in love with a theological student just graduating. And like many a feminist, she loved so hard that after one year of college she gave up her own career and married him. They settled in a parish in Canandaigua, near Rochester, New York, where she kept house for him, bore him four children, and helped him with his sermons—helped him almost like magic, for she could write so fluently and fast.

He needed help, for he had been a soldier in the Civil War and had come back with only one lung. When the youngest child was still a baby, that lung seemed to be giving out. He would come home after preaching, or even after prayer meeting, pale with exhaustion, hardly able to lift one knee after the other. When he gave up at last, he was so weak that she had to write his resignation for him. She found herself with five dependents and no means of support.

Well—she had always believed that women ought to do something. They ought to *be* something besides wives and mothers. Now Fate was saying: "Let's see you make good!"

There was a deserted church with a proud steeple but a leaking roof in the village of Brookton, not far from Ithaca. She persuaded the trustees to let her open the doors one Sunday, and invite the people to worship. The whole village came, of course, as they would to a side show to see a freak. But they came again the next Sunday, and the Sunday after that, for warmer reasons. Inside of a month the roof was mended, and the parish was paying her twelve dollars a week for her Saturdays and Sundays. In a little while she was called to a larger church in West Bloomfield, which provided her a commodious parsonage and a salary of eight hundred dollars a year. By that time, however, the fame of her eloquence was beginning to spread throughout all western New York, and she added to her income by giving lectures and by marrying and burying people in the surrounding towns. Although her knowledge of theology was only what she had picked up by helping her husband with his sermons, she had risen high enough in her profession by 1893 to be invited, from her little country parish, to address the World's Congress of Religions in Chicago.

All this was accomplished without the slightest affectation of importance.

Her sermons were so simply and directly spoken from her heart to yours that she seemed to have no art at all, but merely self-possession.

In one of them that she preached on "Children's Sunday," she began by telling the congregation of the hard time she had had finding a sermon. There seemed to be nothing around the house or out in the garden, or in fact anywhere in town. She finally went anxiously into the country and started down an old road through the woods looking for a sermon.

"I was walking very fast, and I know that the straight lines between my eyes were very deep, when all of a sudden I heard a voice. It was a slow, rather drawling voice, and it said: 'Why—don't—you—saunter?'

"It was the old road itself speaking.

"'I am a worker; I have no time for dallying,' I replied. And I quoted to the road a sentiment that had been printed on a little plate I used to eat from when I was a child: 'Dost thou love life? Then do not squander time. There will be rest enough in the grave.'

"The road laughed rudely, and said:

"'I suppose you think there's nothing worth while in a road but its end! That's where you and a lot of people get fooled! Believe me, no road has any end; what you call its end is only another beginning....

"'A lot of people in your church,' the road remarked at last, 'are so intent on getting to heaven that they haven't time to be good on the way. I'm afraid they will be turned back when they get there because they have no wedding garments on. You have to get your wedding garment, your immortality, as you go along, you know. If you do not find love and joy and peace on the road, they will not be waiting for you at the end....'"

That is the way she would preach.

"I could not help seeing that the old road was talking sense," she added, "and of course you can't help feeling respect for anybody who can quote Scripture correctly."

While still at Brookton she had been ordained by a ministerial council headed by Thomas K. Beecher, a more radical member of Henry Ward's family, who had established an undenominational church at Elmira, New York. Mr. Beecher was heretic enough to be proud rather than critical of her rapid flight over theological education. He said many times that she had preached the greatest sermons he ever heard. He loved her and watched her career with a father's pride. When his own strength began to fail he invited her, with the eager consent of his congregation, to join him in the pastorate of the Park Church at Elmira. She came with the understanding that her sick husband should help with the parish work. He helped increasingly and even soon began to do a share of the preaching. When Mr.

Beecher died in 1899, she and her husband were unanimously elected joint pastors of the Park Church.

Such was her public career.

My relation to her was a peculiar one: I was her youngest son. From the age of six to nine, I was the child of a woman who disappeared every Saturday and, after being a preacher and pastor for two days, returned on Monday to be my particular mother. To me at that time the arrangement seemed perfectly natural and all right. When some young lad in the neighborhood announced that he was going to be a minister, I piped up:

"You can't, you're a boy!"

I think many families would be happier if they didn't stick so tight together. Half the fun of loving people is having them come home after an absence.

Of course, my mother's energy was unusual, and I am not laying down any rules, but life for us children was richer and not poorer because of her public career. I never felt any lack either of mother love, or good housekeeping, or even of mending. I never saw a home that made me envious. She was, as my sister said, "the kind of mother that tucks you in and tells you a story, the kind that drags you to the dentist to have your teeth straightened." Perhaps her going away week ends put us on our mettle in a wholesome way not unlike that adopted in the modern schools. She would gather us on Saturday before she left, and tell us just how to meet any contingencies that might arise. I faced the situation, she used to tell me, with the imagination of an engineer.

"What shall we do," I said, "if a baby should be born?"

Later on, I found it a little painful to be marked out in this peculiar way among boys. It's bad enough to be one minister's son, let alone two! But what I suffered during the smart phase, the phase of trying to be *like* everybody else, was more than made up to me by her wise counsel in the hours of real ambition.

"Be an individual," she wrote when I was away at school. "Nothing you can gain will make up for the loss of your self. Conformity with the crowd is beautiful until it involves a sacrifice of principle—then it is disfiguring."

"Become interested in everything that is going on in the world, and train yourself to think about it. It's better to have your own thought, even if it's a mistaken one, than to be always repeating other people's."

"Life isn't really so hard when it is faced as when it is evaded. Keep yourself in good physical condition, and mind and soul will take care of themselves. Or is it just the other way round? I am puzzled sometimes about it!"

"Hold your head high—even if your heart is low—and look straight into everyone's face. It is much more important for you to stand up straight than to understand Latin."

RUSSELL LYNES

A Society for Truth and Beauty

The founder of Chautauqua, a young minister from Camptown, New Jersey, named John H. Vincent, had not the slightest idea when he laid out an outdoor map of the Holy Land in a grove of trees near his little church that he was starting a unique movement in mass education. His purpose was, quite simply, to brighten up the teaching of Sunday school and to show young men and women how to conduct Sunday school classes. He was gratified at the numbers that turned out to follow him about his map as he talked, and he decided that he might expand his work by providing courses by mail to those who lived too far away to come to Camptown. In this simple way Vincent introduced "correspondence courses" for the first time to American education. His audience grew rapidly. Several years later he suggested to a friend in Akron, Ohio, that he would like to have a two-week summer session at some appropriate place, and his friend, Lewis Miller, suggested a defunct camp at Lake Chautauqua, New York, of which he was a trustee. The first "summer school" (another new concept in American education) was opened at the lake in 1874 with forty young men and women, all very carefully chaperoned. By day they studied the Bible under the trees and during the evenings they sang songs by the shores of the lake to the light of campfires. The cost for the two weeks was $6 for each student. The food was good, the teaching excellent, the atmosphere eminently respectable, and the young people went away happy and filled with missionary zeal, not only for teaching the Bible, but for Camp Chautauqua.

It grew like wildfire. The two-week session was extended to two months, and the teaching of the Bible was expanded to the teaching of all sorts of "cultural" subjects. The camp grew into a tent city with thousands of tents and many more thousands of visitors who came from all over America. In the open air pavilions they sat enthralled by the wisdom and wit of statesmen and novelists, poets and humorists, critics and, of course, divines. There was scarcely a famous man or woman of the day who did not come sooner or later to speak to the audiences at Chautauqua. Six presidents of the United States lectured by the shores of the lake—Grant and Garfield, Theodore Roosevelt and Hayes, the martyred McKinley and the jovial Taft. Courses were given in science and philosophy and religion and music. The great singers and the great instrumentalists of the day and even a full symphony orchestra under the direction of Walter Damrosch gave concerts outdoors in "God's temple." Chautauqua became known as a university and by 1893 it was chartered by the State of New York to grant academic degrees.

Nothing so successful as this could exist for long without being imitated, and on the shores of lakes all over the country other Chautauquas, equally respectable and equally devoted to culture and uplift, were started to provide a haven for those who could not travel as far as upper New York State. By 1900 there were two hundred such centers of culture and propriety and, according to the Harvard philosopher William James who spoke at them, smugness. Hundreds of thousands of men and women flocked to the tent cities for their vacations and during the winter they pored over books selected from the seven hundred instructional or inspirational volumes that were issued under the Chautauqua imprint or read the *Chautauquan,* a monthly magazine.

REXFORD G. TUGWELL

Sinclairville

My own earliest recollections of school attach to a building at the end of the village common. It was conspicuous without being distinguished, square, many-windowed, red brick, with a worn and weedy yard. A range of wooden toilet facilities convenient to a back door hid at the rear; and a loud, if decidedly untuneful, bell swung in a belfry at the top. As we played games during recess, the sound of hammers on iron, as tires for wagons or shoes for horses were shaped on the anvils of a busy shop across the street, was a constant undertone; and the smell of burning hoofs, as shoes were fitted, was often pungent in the air. Besides a dozen houses, three churches also faced the common, the houses with well-proportioned doors and the churches in the classical white of the New England tradition, with graceful steeples and sensitively placed windows.

The rambling and shabby premises of the Prentice blacksmith shop, which was one of two in our village—my relatives, the Truslers, ran the other—where the old man worked with his two sons, all developed as only blacksmiths could be, with rippling muscles, deep chests, and slender waists, were an accepted part of the scene. The indeterminate yard with its litter of wagon wheels, discarded tires, and the other miscellaneous paraphernalia of the trade does not seem, as I look back, at all incongruous, facing the common, across the way from a church and several restrained white houses as well as the school. Nothing about it was offensive in the way the pretentious schoolhouse was, standing uncompromising and monstrous in the midst of so modestly executed a village.

But I suppose the attainment of such a building was the end of the usual long campaign, something planned for and wanted for a generation and finally managed after innumerable disappointments. It was in such a way that Americans got their better schools. And if, when it was built, it was ugly, I presume no one noticed if it served the purpose. It did have, at any rate, four lower rooms for grades and two large upper ones for high school; these were separated by a partition which slid back to make of the whole floor an auditorium.[1] There was a stage at one end, and this was something of a center for the intellectual improvement of the valley. On it graduates were presented with diplomas, of course, and from it we heard our principal's—or perhaps a distinguished visitor's—words of wisdom or caution several times a week and were practiced in the rituals of song and recitation, which would thus become forever familiar to all of us; but also it was used for lyceum lectures and entertainments. On winter nights, sleighs converged on the school, horses were blanketed, and families found places where they could listen to a lecture, a demonstration of popular science, or a group of singers or Swiss bell ringers. The lyceum course was supported by the sale of season tickets, so much the same audience appeared for each occasion. I recall that my father and some of his friends thought the entertainment label doubtfully deserved, and there were other occupations they would have preferred; but the ladies were firm and the men generally good-natured. I

[1] This school had been built in 1881 and so must have been about fifteen years old when I went to first grade. But it seemed ancient to me, perhaps because it actually was shabby from the first. The construction was cheap and it probably went to pieces fast. It was replaced about 1920, but until I was thirteen and we moved away I progressed one by one through its grades.

recall the familiar demonstration of steam rising from dry ice, one that was a sure hit for lecturers on popular science, and, in quite another cultural vein, a quartet of females who sang loudly and then produced a rack of tumblers on which they proceeded to play familiar tunes. I suppose there were addresses on public affairs and social problems—in fact, I know there were—but those I do not at all recall. Perhaps I was taken only to the entertainments and judged too young to appreciate the heavier fare. I suppose Sinclairville was too remote and too small to have had the important touring lecturers of the early century. But it will be recalled that this was a second occupation for Emerson, Alcott, and other popular philosophers as well as Dickens, Mark Twain, and other literary figures. Some of the important ones of the 'nineties may have come to Sinclairville, but I could hardly be expected to recall them. There can be no doubt that the school was an important center of life for all of us, old and young, and that its management and influence were matters of concern not only to the School Board, elected in warm contests each year, but to everyone in the community.

My mother's small schoolhouse and my larger one were both in the same valley near the center of Chautauqua County, at about the same distance from Fredonia to the north and Jamestown to the south. It was back over the hills from Lake Erie, which was west of us, and Chautauqua Lake, which was southwest. The valley was spacious enough to contain a life of its own, but not so large that any part was uncomfortably far from any other....

Ours was an authentic upland country; our winters, in consequence, were long and our summers brief. One of my half cousins used to say that the only trouble with the climate was that it never snowed in August. The considerably older cousin, George, who used to say this was a good-natured, easygoing fellow who was one of my favorites—the sort who always has time for a word with small boys and always thinks their dogs remarkable. He was, at the time I recall him best, the proprietor of a barbershop, and he used to make the observation about snow in August for its provocative effect on the old-timers who habitually sat chewing tobacco and gossiping in the row of armchairs against the wall of his establishment. Reacting, they would swear to recollections of times when it had snowed in August. Their citings of such antic occurrences he would then belittle as mere summer hailstorms on the Arkwright or Gerry hills—backcountry to us. This belittling would, naturally, induce protestations, corroborations, and elaborations. The matter would be come back to again and again, and a distant air of grievance would surround the later argument. It might go on for days.

The weather was certainly a favorite topic, but scarcely more so than such others as the sicknesses of neighbors, the farmers' crops, local improvements, the behavior or misbehavior of officials, the degenerate condition into which the younger generation was falling, and, in season, national politics. I can have been no more interested in oldsters' talk than most small boys would have been, but as I look back it seems to me that I witnessed a way of declining into age which was in most ways tolerable. The old men had lived to see their families disperse and perhaps lived on now with their wives in comfortable familiarity. The old house might be too big, but part of it could be closed off; there was no central heating. If the wife was gone too, they might live with children, contributing what they could from a small income of some sort. They were at least not alone, and life was easy and relaxed. These little daily gatherings in shops, along the sidewalks, on the hotel porch, or in the saloon were their last stretch of life. To pass it with familiars was a blessed thing. It cannot have been so agreeable to be dependent, but the households of those days were more elastic than they have since become.

Recollections were precious enough to be refined over and over and long drawn out, possibly even improved. They were exchanged in old and well-worn clothes, in equally well-worn chairs or on benches polished by long occupancy, and there were such sitting places everywhere.

This was the age, too, of the front porch. Every house had one, and some were broad and capacious, furnished with hammocks, rockers, and blooming plants. These, however, were the women's domain, except that in the evening the courting couples took them over. The men, old and getting old, preferred drifting together into little groups away from home, in a tolerant proprietor's store or shop where there was a big stove, inside the gristmill, where they liked the floury smells and could sit in a circle outside the center of activity, or, in summer, on the streets....

I should speak of Jake Evans, who was a kind of belated Daniel Boone. Nominally he ran a general store, but it was frequently closed at hours peculiar in the shopkeeping trade. When his door was locked we knew that he had gone fishing, or perhaps hunting, if the season was appropriate. It was he who took me on my first brook-fishing, coon-hunting, and squirrel-shooting expeditions, as he took every boy who wanted to go and was able to get away from his chores, or from school, or simply from his mother. Mothers disparaged association with him on principle, not only because he inducted us into blood sports and taught us irregular ways, but because he got along very well without a wife. He and his son ... carried on a sketchy, carefree existence in a clean little house, and this seemed to challenge the central position of women in that village and farm economy. It was they who tamed men to thrift and plodding husbandry—"kept their noses to the grindstone," Jake said—and the variety of faults they could find with Jake's behavior was remarkable.

But our mothers' disapproval did not prevent us from utilizing his ready talents as a teacher and leader. I have often thought what a tame and uninspired program the Boy Scouts have in comparison with the swinging tramps we had with Jake and the secrets of nature he disclosed to our receptive minds. He taught us how to handle gun, knife, and hatchet in pursuit of such wildlife as came under the heading of game. He knew their habits, their weaknesses (curiosity, for instance), and when they might be dangerous. He taught us patience and canniness and guile. When we had success he showed us how to make fires and prepare fish or animals for cooking. And sitting on logs around such fires, we heard much about the freer life and the more abundant game in the Tennessee mountains, whence, for reasons never made clear, he had come to our hill country. He asked no thanks but our company, and it never occurred to us that he was being extraordinarily kind. He was just one of the better arrangements of our environment, uncomplicated by any attempt to moralize or teach us anything we were not eager to learn. He must have been something like sixty when I was ten, but he covered an incredible mileage with his peculiar slouching stride. He saw animal trails where they were invisible to the uninitiated, and many a day he led us home at dark, exhausted and limp but happily certain of having put in a thoroughly valuable day.

The coon hunts by nights were a more highly organized affair and usually involved our fathers, since otherwise we would not have been allowed to go. I recall only a few. But they were high spots of boyhood. Starting out with Jake's three hounds (but there might be more; he always seemed to have litters of puppies in his storeroom between a vinegar barrel and a pile of soap-boxes) and with a few other men, we made straight for the swamp where the coons were at home. I presume Jake did not always find one, but I do not recall any failures. The dogs ranged widely for a while until their distant baying changed to yelps. This meant that they had treed an animal and we had only to catch up with them. The poor coon, peering down from his branch, was shot and, if time permitted, the dogs were started on another chase. There can be few such romantic memories for men to recall of their boyhood. The autumn forest, lit by flaring torches, the belling of the hounds, far away, then near, the suspense of wondering what animal had been treed—once it turned out to be a bobcat which snarled viciously; but such really wild creatures were very scarce by then. The coons merely looked bewildered, and if we had had a modicum of decency we should never have had the heart to shoot one. But the privilege of bringing down the victim was usually allowed the smallest boy, thus accustoming him to slaughter. He was never, I think, overcome with sympathy, but he often missed his shot because of excitement. I am afraid the hunting of helpless coons was stuff for a boys' paradise.

Sometimes there was meat enough from one of these hunts for a coon pie, made in a great dish, rich with sauce, and with thick biscuits on top. Otherwise they were roasted whole. The meat tasted to me much like the more usual squirrel and, if the truth has to be told, was too gamy for my youthful palate—boys never care much for flavorful food—but I always bravely ate my portion. I would not think of holding back merely because I was revolted. It was the end of, and the excuse for, a precious adventure.

Burt Smith, Earl Roberts, and I were inseparable—a curious trio, perhaps, but one that seemed natural to us. That I should have had for my earliest comrades a doctor's son and the son of a teamster seems now to illustrate a characteristic of that society which made it so inevitably a democracy. Probably my parents had little in common with those of Earl Roberts and they seldom associated, but I was never told that I ought not run around with Earl. I was fascinated by the Robertses' living arrangements. I realized later they were different from ours because the family was poor, but I never thought of it then. They were just different. I do recall thinking it was peculiar that they should eat bacon drippings on their bread instead of butter and that they should have no sheets on their beds. Their carpets had holes, their furniture was patched, and the house had that peculiar musty, sourish smell that so many farm homes had—the result, I suppose, of a scarcity of soap and hot water and of consequently flourishing molds. Earl was apt to brag that his father wore his long underwear all winter and plowed it under in their garden patch when spring came; and we were impressed—we must have been if I recall his saying so all those years ago. But we were not less good friends because of these peculiarities. We were free of each other's houses, and our joint enterprises did not suffer....

We played ball endlessly, when the weather was propitious, on the common or, when the grass there was too long or when the older boys preempted the playing space, in the wide road beside the Congregational church. We had a cramped but favored diamond there, irregular, dusty, and with the protruding roots of two old maples on either side of the street for first and third bases. It was, anyway, claimed by no other gang, and knowing all its peculiarities, we made allowances for them. Our balls more often than not were ones we had made ourselves by winding string around a rubber core (or a paper one if we were reduced to that), but we usually had a bat or two, treasured from year to year and put away carefully over the winter. This was the sandlot baseball which developed many professional players. None of us became so skilled, but the hours we spent at one-old-cat or in chosen sides, when we had enough for two teams of five or more, ought to have made professionals of us all.

But winter was the long season, and winter games were our most familiar ones. They were simple too. We did not skate often, because the snow was usually too deep on the ponds; but we did everything else that can be done in or with snow. Especially we skied and slid down the long hills on sleds that were almost part of us for months. We even dragged them to school and stacked them outside; I could slide much of the way home on mine, since there were two passable slopes on the way. On Saturdays we divided our time between sledding down the hills and catching tows, for that was the day when farmers came to town and traffic was heavy. It must have been customary to tolerate this minor nuisance; at any rate, we hitched rides in this way for hours on end, especially ones drawing us back up the hills so that we could escape that toilsome penalty for sliding down. We envied the older set who made evening parties of this sport. Allen and some of his friends made elaborate bobsleds, some of them ten or twelve feet long, and when the snow was deep and closely packed they borrowed horses to tow them to the top of Cobb Hill, and then, several couples packed closely, they slid all the way down through Main Street and sometimes even beyond the old stone house....

Nostalgia is probably bound to overcome any aged person with such a boyhood in his past, lived so securely in a somewhat isolated environment, and so intimately with a few satisfactory companions. It is a characteristic of this sentiment that it tends to stifle or obscure the unpleasant experiences, the unhappinesses, and the terrors of successive ages. Of these there were certainly many, and when I stop to recall them consciously they too come back with a like vividness.

HAROLD W. THOMPSON

Blind Sam, the Sailor

"And a fine day it is," said Blind Sam. "I can see well enough to know that. I remember you well enough, and your grandfather, old John Thompson. He had the prettiest cart I ever saw, but he would neither give nor sell it. It would have been just the thing, for my fish. I couldn't buy it now, even if he was alive, and I suppose he is not, unless he is a hundred and ten. I'm ninety myself and was just making a piece about it in case they should give me a stone." Sam stood up and cleared his throat:

Here lies the bones of Samuel Taylor.
In early life he was a sailor.
He sailed the world three times around
And fortunately has not been drowned.
    (But damn near.)
But his sight got dim, he could sail no more;
He finally landed safe on shore.
He's growing old and the end is nigh,
He's on the county farm to die.

"As you say, there is no hurry. Old John Thompson, cart and all, was in no hurry. You don't know where the cart is? It makes no odds. I've seen many changes, most of all in myself. You may remember that I would sometimes take a little too much? Well, sir, seventeen years ago on the twelfth of May—and I was only seventy-three—I says to myself one morning, 'Sam, here it is nine o'clock and you haven't had a drink.' So I dropped into a place at Dunkirk where they ignored the Prohibition Law, and I had one. It tasted bad. I stepped down the street and tried another. It tasted worse. Says I, 'Sam, I believe you've lost your taste for it.' I haven't had a drink since, that you could call a drink—a bottle of beer now and then. I made a piece about it, like one I heard long ago after I saw Lincoln lying at Buffalo. (I tried sailing the Lakes after that.) Well, here's the piece—some of it mine and some of it somebody else's, like all the songs we made at sea; this is Samuel Taylor up-to-date:

"Samuel, you look healthy now,
  Your dress is neat and clean,
You're never drunk about the streets.
  Tell us where you've been.

"Something must have happened;
  You used to look so strange.
Has MacClelland preached a sermon
  Has brought about this change?"

No, it was a voice, a warning voice
  That Heaven sent to me,
To take away the slavish curse
  From want and misery.

My money all was spent for drink,
  I was a wretched view,
I'd almost tired all my friends
  And tired their patience too.

For when I'd get arrested,
  And in drunken stupor lay,
And brought before Jim Prendergast
  Without a word to say,

And when he read the sentence,
  And would take no fine or bail,
The only thing was left for me
  Was *ninety days in jail.*

My friends with me grew weary,
  I was unhappy then;
I tired all their patience
  By getting drunk again.

Had this have been misfortune's end,
  How happy I'd have been!
But health with wealth declining,
  Dr. Seymour was called in.

He looked at me so serious,
  And answered me so plain,
"You've wrecked your constitution, Sam,
  By getting drunk again."

So in every heart there's some good
  Hidden in the dark,
If man would only take the pains
  To fan that vital spark.

So let this be a warning,
  Reflect while you have time:
It's folly to be jolly
  In drinking too much wine.

Sam stopped and looked thirsty; I felt that I should say something.

"You fool them all, Sam. They are all gone: Judge Prendergast and Doc Seymour and the Dominie."

"They are," Sam agreed. "Maybe responsibility is what killed them. I used to say to Dr. MacClelland, 'Reverend, you preached a grand sermon on Sunday; I can give you all the headings of it. It ain't your fault, but it didn't do me a damn bit of good.' He would say, *'How do you know, Sam?'* He hadn't gone to sea at twelve as I did.

"Was I ever wrecked? Why did you boys always ask that? . . . But I wasn't thinking of the wrecks. I was thinking of shipmasters like Old Bully Host * and the way he used to treat us lads. A nice man on shore, mind you, but a black devil at sea. That time out of San Francisco——

"I was steering—though I wasn't an able seaman. We had known from the minute we came on board that there would be hell to pay. The Old Man made every member of the crew lay his bag down on the deck, and then Host, he runs up and down on the bags with his heavy boots. That was to prevent our bringing drink aboard, he says, grinning. Well, as I say, I was steering. The Old Man swaggers up, and just as he comes beside me, he sees the young Swede. There's always one like the young Swede aboard. A fine-looking lad but mouthy. He had been complaining that he wasn't getting his pint and his pound—that's the way we called the legal rations. Somebody was making money on us.

" 'You, Swede,' says the captain, 'I hear you have been complaining that you haven't been getting your pint and your pound.'

" 'Yes, sir,' says the Swede, knowing in his heart that the old devil Host was the one who made the money by starving us.

* I have changed the name.

"The captain looks at him long and slow.

" 'Is your watch up?' says the captain.

" 'It is not, sir,' says the Swede.

" 'Then up to the mizzen top gaffs'l,' says the captain, 'and see what you can see.' (I think that was what he said; I don't remember the old names for things well, but he was sending him a hundred feet in the air.) Host stood there grinning till the Swede was aloft. Then he turned on me.

" 'Sam, you raynick?' he bellers. 'Where are you heading for?'

"I answered polite, giving my direction. We were headed for China.

" 'Why, damn you for a raynick,' says he, 'you're headed for San Francisco! Put her up in the wind!'

"I saw what he was about then; and he saw that I saw, and pulled out his revolver. I put her up as he said. The ship swung sharp and heeled as she turned. The Swede spun from a hundred feet aloft into the sea.

" 'Sam, you raynick,' says the Old Man, 'where are you headed? Do you want to take us to San Francisco?'

" 'Man overboard, Sir,' says I.

"He grinned and pointed his revolver. 'Put her back,' says he, 'or I'll be short *two* hands.'

"I swung her back—and we left the Swede alone in the sea."

We were quiet for a while. Then Bill said, "Sam, what is a raynick?"

"It's an expression," said Sam.*

"What happened to Captain Host?" I asked.

"We said nothing till we came home that voyage. Just outside San Francisco a feller came on that always asked whether the crew had any complaints. We had a committee ready for him. They kept us shut up for a long time till they could try Host. Oooooh my Goooooood, I wish I had some of the food they gave us! That's all of that story."

"No, it isn't," said Bill. "What happened to Host?"

"Oh, Host," said Sam. "They gave him a fine berth ashore with bigger pay than ever. A very nice man ashore was Host, though I've asked myself whether he said his prayers. He did things he ought not to have done."

"That sounds Episcopalian, Sam," I said.

"I don't claim to be an Episcopalian," said Sam. "Just a Christian that sings songs to people. But I have got a prayer. I made it up for myself, in a manner of speaking—like the piece about my drinking. (Queer how thirsty I used to get when I sang to people.)"

Sam stood up again. His shoulders were rounded a little, but he gave the

* Possibly the Dutch slang-word *roinek*, "red neck."

impression of being undefeated. His accent was refined, with a true cadence and love of words. He didn't shut his eyes.

"O Lord," he said, "teach me that sixty minutes make one hour. Teach me that sixteen ounces make one pound. Teach me that one hundred cents make one dollar. (Sailors never learn that.) Grant that I may lie down with a clear conscience, unhaunted by the faces of those to whom I have brought pain. Grant that I may do as I would be done by. *Deefen me to the jingle of tainted money and the rustle of unholy skirts.* (I haven't heard the jingle often, but I know about the other.) Blind me to the faults of others but reveal to me my own. And when I have done with this unfriendly world—not always unfriendly—let the ceremony be brief and the epitaph simple: *Here lies a man.* Amen."

We went through Sam's dormitory, very clean, with old men staring like silent penguins. Bill went to get the car. I kept thinking about Sam blowing the fish-horn; Sam selling shoestrings in summer, pretending to be stone-blind; Sam in that mine-explosion; Sam looking at the dead face of Lincoln; Sam treading the decks—*Sam, you raynick!* We were outside in the early autumn haze of the Chautauqua hills. You could almost smell the Westfield grapes over the ridge.

"Thanks for the pipe," said Sam. "Tell Mrs. Douglas I liked the peaches; she is a lady. They take care of us here all right. I used to slip away in summer, and they always let me come back. There's no disgrace in poverty, they say, but it's damn inconvenient. Next time I'll sing you *The Cumberland's Crew.* That cart of John Thompson's was the prettiest I ever saw, but he wouldn't part with it. We all have something we won't part with."

Bill was ready. I hated to leave Sam.

20TH CENTURY

THEODORE DREISER

Owego

. . . Owego appeared, a town say of about five thousand, nestling down by the waterside amid a great growth of elms, and showing every element of wealth and placid comfort. A group of homes along the Susquehanna, their backs perched out over it, reminded us of the houses at Florence on the Arno. . . . Then we entered the town over a long, shaky iron bridge and rejoiced to see one of the prettiest cities we had yet found.

Curiously, I was most definitely moved by Owego. There is something about the old fashioned, comfortable American town at its best—the town where moderate wealth and religion and a certain social tradition hold—which is at once pleasing and yet comfortable—a gratifying and yet almost disturbingly exclusive state of affairs. At least as far as I am concerned, such places and people are antipodal to anything that I could ever again think, believe or feel. From contemplating most of the small towns with which I have come in contact and the little streets of the cities as contrasted with the great, I have come to dread the conventional point of view. The small mind of the townsmen is antipolar to that of the larger, more sophisticated wisdom of the city. It may be that the still pools and backwaters of communal life as represented by these places is necessary to the preservation of the state and society. I do not know. Certainly the larger visioned must have something to direct and the small towns and little cities seem to provide them. They are in the main fecundating centres—regions where men and women are grown for more labor of the same kind. The churches and moral theorists and the principle of self preservation, which in the lowly and dull works out into the rule of "live and let live," provide the rules of their existence. They do not gain a real insight into the fact that they never practise what they believe or that merely living, as man is compelled to live, he cannot interpret his life in the terms of the religionist or the moral enthusiast. Men are animals with dreams of something superior to animality, but the small town soul—or the little soul anywhere—never gets this straight. These are the places in which the churches flourish. Here is where your theologically schooled numskull thrives, like the weed that he is. Here is where the ordinary family with a little tradition puts an inordinate value on that tradition. All the million and one notions that have been generated to explain the universe here float about in a nebulous mist and create a dream world of error, a miasmatic swamp mist above which these people never rise. I never was in such a place for any period of time without feeling cabined, cribbed, confined, intellectually if not emotionally....

...I contemplated a saloon which stood next door and on the window of which was pasted in gold glass letters "B. B. Delano." Thirsting for a glass of beer, I entered, and inside I found the customary small town saloon atmosphere, only this room was very large and clean and rather vacant. There was a smell of whiskey in the cask, a good smell, and a number of citizens drinking beer. A solemn looking bartender, who was exceptionally bald, was waiting on them. Some bits of cheese showed dolefully under a screen. I ordered a beer and gazed ruefully about. I was really not here, but back in Warsaw, Indiana, in 1886.

And in here was Mr. B. B. Delano himself, a small, dapper, rusty, red faced man, who, though only moderately intelligent, was pompous to the verge of bursting, as befits a small man who has made a moderate success in life. Yet Mr. B. B. Delano, as I was soon to discover, had his private fox gnawing at his vitals. There was a worm in the bud. Only recently there had been a great anti-liquor agitation and a fair proportion of the saloons all over the state had been closed. Three months before in this very town, at the spring election, "no license" had been voted. All the saloons here, to the number of four, would have to be closed, including Mr. Delano's, in the heart of the town. That meant that Mr. Delano would have to get another business of some kind or quit. I saw him looking at me curiously, almost mournfully.

"Touring the state?" he asked.

"We're riding out to Indiana," I explained. "I come from there."

"Oh, I see. Indiana! That's a nice little trip, isn't it? Well, I see lots of machines going through here these days, many more than I ever expected to see. It's made a difference in my business. Only"—and here followed a long account of his troubles. He owned houses and lands, a farm of three hundred acres not far out, on which he lived, and other properties, but this saloon obviously was his pet. "I'm thinking of making an eating place of it next fall," he added. " 'No license' may not last—forever." His eye had a shrewd, calculating expression.

"That's true," I said.

"It keeps me worried, though," he added doubtfully. "I don't like to leave now. Besides, I'm getting along. I'm nearly sixty," he straightened himself up as though he meant to prove that he was only forty, "and I like my farm. It really wouldn't kill me if I never could open this place anymore." But I could see that he was talking just to hear himself talk, boasting. He was desperately fond of his saloon and all that it represented; not ashamed, by any means.

"But there's Newark and New York," I said. "I should think you'd like to go down there."

"I might," he agreed; "perhaps I will. It's a long way for me, though. Won't you have another drink—you and your friends?" By now Franklin and Speed were returning and Mr. Delano waved a ceremonious, inclusive hand, as if to extend all the courtesies of the establishment.

The bartender was most alert—a cautious, apprehensive person. I could see that Mr. Delano was inclined to be something of a martinet. For some reason he had conceived of us as personages—richer than himself, no doubt —and was anxious to live up to our ideas of things and what he thought we might expect.

"Well, now," he said, as we were leaving, "if you ever come through here again you might stop and see if I'm still here."

BIOGRAPHIES

SAMUEL HOPKINS ADAMS

❧ Samuel Hopkins Adams began his career as a journalist. He first attracted national attention with articles exposing the frauds involved in the sale of patent medicines. Throughout his long life he was an avid student of the language of early Americans and the quality of our early national life. When he was in his mid-80's, his home on Owasco Lake was a favorite meeting place for literally hundreds of writers, painters, actors. His *Grandfather Stories,* published in 1955, proved all of his researches rewarding. It made easy and natural use of upstate New York incidents and told them in the language of their time. By the time of his death in 1958, Mr. Adams had written so many books that he could not remember the number of them.

HELEN E. ALLEN

❧ Helen E. Allen was born in Carlton, Orleans County, New York, and for more than sixty years lived on the family farm on Oak Orchard Creek. During the 1940's, Miss Allen's interest in local history led her to interview many elderly people who were descendants of the pioneers who settled Orleans County. "The Jumping Bass of Oak Orchard Creek" came from a group of pundits gathered under John Podgers' sign reading "Horse Shoeing Parlor" at the hamlet called Two Bridges. Many of Miss Allen's articles have appeared in the *Orleans Republican-American* and the *Albion Advertiser.*

MARGARET ARMSTRONG

❧ From the letters of her ancestors and their contemporaries, the late Margaret Armstrong selected passages which created charming pictures of the social life of five generations of Hudson River families. The life and letters begin at the end of the Revolution and end in the last decade of the nineteenth century.

Among her other books were a biography of the English actress, Fanny Kemble, and another of Fanny's friend (also the confidant of Shelley), the romantic Edward Trelawny. Both of these books Miss Armstrong wrote after she was seventy, and both were highly successful.

BROOKS ATKINSON

Brooks Atkinson (husband of Oriana Atkinson) was famous as a theater critic. He was an observant and poetic naturalist as well. His detailed and realistic calendar of the Catskill year is deserving a comparison with the essays of John Burroughs.

ORIANA ATKINSON

Oriana Atkinson writes of the early days of the Catskill country "thirty miles back from the Hudson." Two of her books, *The Twin Cousins* and *The Golden Season,* have as their background a lively, noisy tavern from which great caravans of settlers set out in covered Conestoga wagons along the great Susquehanna road for the western frontier. Mrs. Atkinson was the wife of the distinguished dramatic critic, Brooks Atkinson, who is also an eager naturalist and ornithologist.

IRVING BACHELLER

Though born at Pierpont, New York, Irving Bacheller made the wooded north country of his native state the background for many of his twenty-eight novels. His *Eben Holden* was the best known, and the title character became almost as popular among New York State readers as E. N. Westcott's David Harum.

ROMEYN BERRY

Romeyn ("Rym") Berry was for many years alumni secretary of Cornell University. He was also an articulate and greatly loved columnist, as well as a lawyer. For a short period some Cornell enthusiasts, believing that the *New Yorker* Magazine was in essence a provincial journal, succeeded in making him one of that magazine's editors. He was unhappy in the big city of New York and soon returned to his beloved Tompkins County, where he lived until his death.

HENRY BESTON

The style of Henry Beston's lucid prose has made him one of the most admired of American historians and essayists. His *The Outermost House* received enthusiastic praise and he has followed it with two other volumes of beautiful poetic content, *The St. Lawrence,* and *Northern Farm.*

MORRIS BISHOP

Morris Bishop, for many years Professor of romance languages at Cornell University, has contributed much light verse to American magazines. He was as widely known as a poet as he was for his scholarly studies in American history.

FREDRIKA BREMER

Soon after her arrival in America, little gray, blue-eyed, red-nosed Fredrika Bremer was a dinner guest at the home of James Hamilton, "the son of the general of that name, the contemporary and friend of Washington." There Fredrika was triumphant because elderly Washington Irving sat next to her at dinner and did not fall asleep as was his custom.

The famed Swedish novelist, whom Hawthorne called "maiden aunt to the human race," traveled in America from 1849 to 1851, noting her impressions for a volume called *Homes in the New World* (1853). Portions of these recollections were published in 1924 as *America of the Fifties,* under the editorship of A. B. Benson.

WILLIAM CULLEN BRYANT

William Cullen Bryant, a native of Massachusetts, first came to the world's attention with the publication in the *North American Review* of his most quoted poem, "Thanatopsis," in 1817. Eight years later Bryant became an editor of the *New York Review* and *Athenaeum* Magazine. And four years after that he became an editor of the New York *Evening Post.* He then carried on two careers, one as political essayist and the other as poet. He was a close friend of many members of the Hudson River School of painters and he was a great admirer of the American landscape of which he wrote with taste and enthusiasm.

ROGER BURLINGAME

Roger Burlingame, who has been a free-lance author since 1926, has devoted his writings mostly to non-fiction. In *Three Bags Full,* however, a novel published in 1936, he recreated the social life of three generations of a Finger Lake country family. No other novel with this background is so filled with authentic detail or so comprehensive in its scope.

JOHN BURROUGHS

John Burroughs sought early careers as a journalist, a bank examiner, and a treasury clerk in Washington, D.C. Then he settled down on a farm near the junction of Esopus Creek and the Hudson River and wrote in a simple and lucid style of his adventures as an observer of his wild life neighbors. His readers have ever since been charmed by his sunny philosophy and the warmth of his feelings for the rural world about him.

ROBERT W. CHAMBERS

Robert W. Chambers was a very popular American writer who alternated between producing books of cheap and sensational content and admirable historical novels. The most successful of his historical novels was *Cardigan.*

MRS. WINTHROP CHANLER

Mrs. Winthrop Chanler was the niece of Julia Ward Howe. She and her husband had found "country family" living in the Genesee Valley more congenial than that of Tuxedo Park and other resorts of American high society. Her residence in Rome during her early years resulted in an atmospheric autobiographical volume entitled *Roman Spring.* Her later volume, *Autumn in the Valley,* presented with equal charm the quality of life among members of the Genesee Valley Hunt and the "first families" of the area.

L. MARIA CHILD

An ardent abolitionist and editor of a weekly New York newspaper, the *National Anti-Slavery Standard,* Lydia Maria Child wrote historical novels, a book on the history of religions, and popular pamphlets devoted to causes of antislavery. She began her career as editor (1826-34) of a children's periodical, the *Juvenile Miscellany.* Her letters were published in 1883 by C. S. Furnace, with an introduction by John Greenleaf Whittier.

HENRY CHRISTMAN

A gifted son of the farmer-poet, W. W. Christman, Henry Christman made astonishing discoveries when he began his researches on the agricultural antirent revolts of the early 1840's against the abuses of the Hudson River manor lords. *Tin Horns and Calico,* published in 1945 by Henry Holt & Company, is at the same time the most colorful and the most comprehensive and authoritative account of the little-known, but highly significant, historical event.

LANSING CHRISTMAN

Lansing Christman, also a gifted son of William W. Christman, was a poet whose rhythmic products rival those of his father. In the daytime Lansing Christman worked at the radio station WGY in Schenectady, but in the evening he returned to the banks of the Bozenkill (Drunkard's Creek) whose foaming waters stagger through the slanting acres of the old Christman farm. Here he attended his crops and he wrote his verses between dinner and his early morning departure for Schenectady.

W. W. CHRISTMAN

William Christman was an upstate farmer in the Helderberg Hills. He grew successful crops on his hillside acres—children (nine sons and three daughters), farm produce, and poems. He had the temperament of the true poet and because of his children he had very strong opinions on education, which he made public by many letters to Albany newspapers.

WILLIS GAYLORD CLARK

Willis Gaylord Clark and his twin brother, Lewis Gaylord Clark, were born in Otisco, New York. In 1834 Lewis became editor of the *Knickerbocker Magazine* and Willis became a frequent contributor to a department called *Ollapodianna.* Willis died of consumption in 1841 and his brother, three years later, published his *Literary Remains.* Willis Gaylord Clark was an essayist, journalist and poet and he actively championed the cause of international copyright.

T. WOOD CLARKE

T. Wood Clarke was a central New York State historian who made the Mohawk Valley and the annals of the French émigrés who settled in northern New York his particular specialty.

DE WITT CLINTON

De Witt Clinton, a nephew of the first governor of New York State, George Clinton, himself succeeded to that governorship in 1817. Best known for his carrying through the project of the Erie Canal, he had many other interests including history, agriculture, art, and natural science.

HENRY W. CLUNE

Henry W. Clune, historian, novelist, and long beloved columnist of the Rochester *Democrat and Chronicle,* unearthed many a colorful character and incident in the life of the big city. He lived beside the Genesee River all his life and wrote the history of that stream in a volume of the Rivers of America Series.

ANNE COLVER

Anne Colver (maiden name of Mrs. Stewart Graff) wrote many books of Americana, some of them for children. Her Literary Guild selection, *Mr. Lincoln's Wife,* was one of the first distinguished studies of Mary Todd Lincoln and made Miss Colver a recognized authority on the Lincoln family.

EARL CONRAD

Earl Conrad chose many dramatic subjects out of the history of New York State for his books. His research has been detailed and the directness of his style has brought him praise from his fellow historians.

JAMES FENIMORE COOPER

In five of James Fenimore Cooper's adventure-filled novels appears the character, Natty Bumppo, variously known as Hawkeye, Pathfinder, Deerslayer, and Leatherstocking. This old woodsman, whose wisdom was obtained not from formal schooling, but from his experiences in the forests and on the streams of America, became the most widely known and greatly admired American fictional character in the world. Couched in the vernacular of his time, his sentences expressed a poetry inspired by the beauties of the American landscape, a philosophy drawn from a lifetime of American adventure and a panorama of the folk practices of the American people.

JUDGE COOPER

Judge William Cooper soon after the end of the Revolution took up several thousand acres in New York in what is now Otsego County. He encouraged settlement and in 1786 laid out Cooperstown. Here he moved his family in 1790 from New Jersey; later he built Otsego Hall, for many years the most stately residence in central New York. His *Guide to the Wilderness,* published in Dublin after his death, is made up of letters written to William Sampson, an Irish lawyer living in New York, and filled with advice about living on the then frontier.

JESSE CORNPLANTER

Winner of the Purple Heart in World War I was a tall, sturdy Seneca Indian of the Clan of the Snipe. Jesse Cornplanter was almost incredibly versatile —a craftsman, musician, actor, and teller of legends. As a representative of the Longhouse People (believers in the ancient religion of his tribe), he worked throughout his life for the preservation of the culture of the Iroquois. His book *Legends of the Longhouse* was written in the form of letters to a white friend, Mrs. Namee Henricks. Cornplanter died in March of 1957, a worthy descendant of his well-known ancestor, the Seneca Chief Cornplanter, who was a friend of General Washington.

J. HECTOR ST. JOHN de CRÈVECOEUR

Originally published in London in 1782, J. Hector St. John de Crèvecoeur's essays relate the social life and customs of life in the American colonies. The Normandy-born author became an American farmer in Orange County and undoubtedly influenced countless citizens to leave the oppressions and persecutions of eighteenth-century Europe for the new nation called America.

GEORGE WILLIAM CURTIS

Though the literary life of George William Curtis was interrupted by his activities as a reform politician, he was one of the group of Washington Irving's close friends who wrote easily and well. As occupant of the "Editor's Easy Chair" for *Harper's Magazine,* he proved an essayist of distinction.

DANIEL DENTON

Daniel Denton was an investor in the lands of New Jersey, Long Island and Staten Island. His *A Brief Description of New York Formerly called New Netherlands With the Places Thereunto Adjoining* was the first printed description in the English language of much of the country now known as the State of New York. Denton was one of the seventeenth-century settlers of the town of Jamaica, Long Island, to which he came with his father from Connecticut in 1644.

CHARLES DICKENS

Charles Dickens was already world-famous when he made his first visit to America in 1842. His *American Notes for General Circulation,* published in the same year, aroused widespread controversy and, since his attitude toward America was generally unfavorable, made him unpopular in many regions.

THEODORE DREISER

After the publication in 1900 of the grim and realistic novel, *Sister Carrie,* Theodore Dreiser continued with other serious novels until 1916, when he chose to write his amusing portrayal of the early days of the automobile. He was later to write other works, all of pessimistic nature, of which the novel *An American Tragedy* (1925), based on a true episode, was his greatest success.

MAX EASTMAN

Max Eastman in his early days combined his literary interest with insistence on his right to freedom of speech for his then unpopular political opinions. He devoted a long life to writing and many of his works have been important, among them *The Enjoyment of Laughter* and (especially) *Heroes I Have Known.* As a young boy he had the opportunity of observing a remarkable group of Elmira's creative people, among whom were his mother who was a famous preacher, Thomas K. Beecher, Mark Twain (Samuel Clemens), and his wife, Olivia Langdon.

MARION EDEY

Marion Edey, sister of Margaret Armstrong, was another member of perhaps the most gifted family of the Hudson Valley. In this remarkable group, the generation which included Margaret and Marion, and a third artist sister, Helen, also numbered the distinguished editor and writer, Hamilton Fish Armstrong, author of *Those Days.* The reading of *Five Generations, Early in the Morning,* and *Those Days* gives through reminiscences a profile of an American family such as is seldom achieved in literature.

WALTER D. EDMONDS

Walter D. Edmonds was justly famous as a chronicler of upstate New York life. His novels of life on the Erie Canal and his exciting book about the Revolution, *Drums Along the Mohawk,* have long been popular.

JAMES THOMAS FLEXNER

James Flexner, author of *Doctors on Horseback,* a study of the history of medicine in early America, has recently busied himself in the writing of a number of books narrating the history of American art and artists. Among these volumes are *America's Old Masters, That Wilder Image,* and *Light of Distant Skies.*

HAROLD FREDERIC

The novels of Harold Frederic were in his day regarded as highly realistic problem-novels. Among those which particularly illuminate the life of upstate New York were *In the Valley* (the Mohawk) and *The Damnation of Theron Ware.*

EDMUND GILLIGAN

Edmund Gilligan, who lived in Bearsville among the Catskills, created in his *Strangers in The Vly* a wild mountain legend more imaginative and poetic than the tales of Washington Irving had related in the previous century.

OLIVER GOLDSMITH

Oliver Goldsmith has been recently described by one biographer as a "miscellaneous" writer, by another as an author "to whom facts meant little." His interest in America was attested by his running away from Trinity College in Dublin with an impractical dream of coming here and later, after a serious disappointment, taking passage, then missing the boat. The source of his erroneous but vivid description of Niagara Falls is not based on personal observation. The fame and affection which he won during his lifetime rested on three immortal works, his novel *The Vicar of Wakefield,* his poem *The Deserted Village,* and his play *She Stoops to Conquer.* He was a close friend of the great Dr. Samuel Johnson and his circle. David Garrick, the most famous actor of his day, wrote a facetious epitaph for him:

Here lies Poet Goldsmith
For shortness called Noll,
Who wrote like an angel,
But talked like Poor Poll.

MRS. GRANT

The observant sympathetic mind of Anne Grant, Scottish governess at the home of the distinguished Schuyler family on the banks of the Hudson near Albany, found much of American life and customs delightful subject matter for her ready pen.

WILLIAM HARLAN HALE

William Harlan Hale, novelist, historian, journalist, brought his gifts to a colorful biography of the picturesque and temperamental and important nineteenth-century editor, Horace Greeley. Mr. Hale was himself editor of the magazine *Horizon* for a number of years.

MRS. BASIL HALL

Travelers to America early in the nineteenth century included the British naval officer, Captain Basil Hall, and his wife, Margaret Hunter Hall, "as snobbish an English blue blood as ever found Americans boorish." Their accounts gave valuable descriptions of life in America.

ROBERT HALL

Though born and educated in the Deep South, Robert Hall was for years the editor of the *Warrensburg-Lake George News,* in the small mountain town of Warrensburg. Mr. Hall had the knack of observation and poetic perception which has characterized many another country editor. His paper was eagerly awaited in the rural districts of the Adirondack Country.

CHESTER HARDING

Chester Harding, a "born artist," arrived at the pinnacle of his achievement the hard way. He was a typically resourceful frontiersman. Blessed with extraordinary height and physical strength, he became a woodsman, a farmer, a chairmaker, a saloonkeeper and a peddler. He liked to think of himself as an untutored artist, though, as the years of his career went on, he received excellent training from his contemporaries. His portraits in particular were very popular and he eventually obtained a considerable income from them. His autobiography, which he called *My Existography,* is an original and amusing account which gives a vivid and colorful image of the life of his time.

ALDEN HATCH

Alden Hatch made himself notable by writing many biographies of distinguished living people. Among these were Pope John XXIII, Prince Bernhard of the Netherlands, and Robert Briscoe, the Lord Mayor of Dublin. Mr. Hatch also did historical accounts of a number of well-known families. The first subject of this nature which he undertook was the Wadsworth family, long-time gentleman-farmer residents of the fertile acres beside the Genesee River.

HARLAN HATCHER

Harlan Hatcher, a noted educator who was President of the University of Michigan for a number of years, was also a writer of distinction. Born in Ohio, his books of Americana include *The Buckeye Country, A Pageant of Ohio, Tunnel Hill,* and *Patterns of Wolfpen.*

NATHANIEL HAWTHORNE

Nathaniel Hawthorne, like many another of America's most distinguished writers of the nineteenth century, looked upon Niagara Falls as a challenge to his descriptive abilities and inserted his prose picture of it in *The Dolliver Romance and Other Pieces.*

CODMAN HISLOP

Codman Hislop's *The Mohawk* was this Union College professor's contribution to the Rivers of America Series. Mr. Hislop went on to write a biography of Eliphalet Nott, wise and colorful president of Union College for sixty-two years.

MARIETTA HOLLEY

Marietta Holley, an astute upstate farm wife, under the pseudonym of Josiah Allen's Wife, won the hearty approval of a very wide public with her series of "Samantha" books. She created a female counterpart of such uneducated but wise and shrewd male characters as Josh Billings, David Harum, Artemus Ward.

PAUL HORGAN

A native of western New York, Paul Horgan spent a number of years in New Mexico and while there he wrote his *Great Rivers: the Rio Grande in North American History* which won the Pulitzer Prize in 1954. His writings on the city of Rochester, New York, where he served for three years on the production staff of the Eastman Theater, include essays in magazines and his novel, *The Fault of Angels*.

WASHINGTON IRVING

The sonorous and rhythmic prose of Washington Irving was the first work of an American author to become respected and admired in England. His enthusiastic interest in regional Americana, his sly and whimsical humor made him exceedingly popular in his own country. His regionalism, which centered about his home on the banks of the Hudson River, gave him such pride that he was able to say truly, "I thank God that I was born on the banks of the Hudson." He was nevertheless widely traveled, wrote many essays on English country life, studied the folklore of Germany (which greatly influenced his famous stories of "Rip Van Winkle" and "The Legend of Sleepy Hollow"), and his *Tales of the Alhambra,* inspired by his wanderings in Spain, gave him backgrounds for his romantic narratives.

HENRY JAMES

The subtle penetration of Henry James into the lives of *nouveau riche* Americans of the late nineteenth century created for the novelist a reputation as a master of technique. Educated in the United States and in Europe, he often depicted in his novels a contrast between the customs and mores of Europeans and Americans.

His essay on Saratoga, published in 1870 in the monthly periodical, *The Nation*, is one of his earliest prose works. Other writings included *The American* (1877), *The European* (1878), *Daisy Miller* (1878), *Washington Square* (1881), and a famous short story, "The Turn of the Screw."

LOUIS C. JONES

Louis C. Jones, Director of the New York State Historical Association at Cooperstown, was one of the country's major contributors to American folklore. He transformed his researches in this field into a number of well-written literary tales. His collections of these include, besides *Spooks of the Valley, Things That Go Bump in the Night.*

ROBERT JUET

Among the quarrelsome English and Dutch crew members sailing with Henry Hudson in 1609 in search of the northwest passage to China was a literate English officer, Robert Juet. The day-to-day journal kept by Juet for his employer (the Dutch East India Company) records impressions of the new land and encounters with natives living along the river banks.

For purposes of clarity his seventeenth-century spellings have been modified and repetitive navigational entries have been omitted.

WALTER GUEST KELLOGG

Walter Guest Kellogg was a resident of Ogdensburg who found the romantic subject matter of his novel about the Italian descendant of Amerigo Vespucci in the annals and the folklore of his home town.

RUDYARD KIPLING

While the distinguished English writer, Rudyard Kipling, was living temporarily in New England, he visited the grain evelators of the City of Buffalo and wrote soon afterward a description of them.

LA MARQUISE DE LA TOUR DU PIN

In 1795 La Marquise de la Tour du Pin, a refugee from the French Revolution, was living at her farm near Albany, New York. Her reminiscences of that year were written into her autobiographical *"Journal d'une femme de cinquante ans,"* first published in Paris in 1906. They were later published in a translation by Walter Geer in a volume entitled *Recollections of the Revolution and the Empire,* New York, 1920. No published memoirs give so detailed and entertaining a picture of country life among the Schuylers, the Van Rensselaers, and other well-to-do families of the Mohawk and upriver Hudson area.

A. J. LIEBLING

A. J. (Abbot Joseph) Liebling, who was one of a number of able reporters employed by the *New Yorker* Magazine, has here written a typical familiar essay reporting on the lives of the river men who live and work along the Hudson.

RUSSELL LYNES

Russell Lynes was an editor of *Harper's Magazine* and an historian of social customs and mores. His amusing and perceptive classifications of his fellow Americans were published in his book *Highbrow, Lowbrow, Middlebrow* and won him wide recognition. He also wrote the equally successful *The Tastemakers* and *The Domesticated Americans.*

HENRY NOBLE MAC CRACKEN

For many years the President of Vassar College, Henry Noble MacCracken turned his scholar's mind to the picturesque and dramatic history of the river country in which he has long resided.

PHYLLIS MC GINLEY

Phyllis McGinley's true observations of contemporary American life, her wit and gaiety and wisdom, made her one of the most beloved of American poets. She was also one of the most technically skillful, and in her serious poems, which are many, she achieved high reputation among American poets of philosophic and literary importance.

GUY H. MC MASTER

Guy H. McMaster was the author of an early history of a Genesee River area. His book, *The History of Steuben County,* was popular not merely for its content but for its lively style and his use of the contemporary vernacular. The excerpt used is much condensed, but all the words are the author's.

HERMAN MELVILLE

Herman Melville, one of the greatest novelists in the history of literature, included in his most praised book *Moby Dick* a description of the Mohawk River and the Erie Canal.

ARCH MERRILL

Arch Merrill found the field of local history very rewarding. He wrote many short volumes in which he has displayed the treasures that he has dug for in Rochester and the Lake Ontario, Ridge Road, Erie Canal and Southern Tier areas.

EDNA ST. VINCENT MILLAY

This very popular poet of the '20's, '30's, and '40's, found the inspiration for many of her references to natural beauty in her home in Austerlitz, New York (to which she moved in 1923). There the forests, hills and valleys, almost on the Connecticut border, gave Miss Millay a setting which resulted in much of her delicate imagery.

THOMAS MOORE

Thomas Moore was a very popular Irish poet. He visited America in 1803 and offended President Thomas Jefferson by his severely critical remarks. Jefferson later expressed his admiation for Moore's verses. Moore admired the American scenery and was inspired to write verses about it.

TOM MORRIS

Tom Morris, son of George Washington's friend, Robert Morris (who was a signer of the Declaration of Independence), came as a young man to western New York and lived in the town of Canandaigua. There he became acquainted with many an eccentric neighbor, including the Indian orator, Red Jacket, and Jemima Wilkinson, self-entitled the Publick Universal Friend.

THE REVEREND DR. MURDOCH

The Reverend Dr. David Murdoch, a clergyman, entered a widespread competition among American writers endeavoring to write the most effective description of the scene beheld from the porches of the Catskill Mountain House.

CHARLES NORMAN

Charles Norman, a modern classicist in the field of poetry, steadfastly clung to the great English tradition. His biographies of Marlowe, Shakespeare, and E. E. Cummings have won admiration, and his many volumes of verses have given him an established reputation.

PIERREPONT B. NOYES

Pierrepont B. Noyes was a son of the Perfectionist Prophet, John Humphrey Noyes, whose nine children were each born of a different mother. Pierrepont had many interests, among them the production of silver plate which had been one of the profitable businesses of the Oneida Community. Another favorite enterprise was literary and he wrote a reminiscence of life in the Children's House of the Community which his father founded and directed. Besides this book (entitled *My Father's House*), he was also the author of *A Goodly Heritage.*

FRANCIS PARKMAN

Francis Parkman devoted a life handicapped by illness to studies in early American history. Most literary of all American historians, his style was distinctive and beautiful. It has been said of him that he made poetry out of history.

BELLAMY PARTRIDGE

No writer has been more associated with the rural and small-town life of upstate New York than Bellamy Partridge. Much of what he wrote was from his firsthand knowledge of upstate people and upstate landscape, particularly in the area of Lyons, Clyde, Clifton Springs, and Phelps, where he was born. Among his very popular books of York State Americana are *Horse and Buggy Doctor, Country Lawyer, Big Family, Excuse My Dust.*

EDMUND PEARSON

Edmund Pearson won the attention of sophisticated readers by his retelling (with many a significant detail that had escaped the journalistic crime reporters) of sensational tales of murder in America.

JOHN PELL

John Pell, who lived most of his life in the Fort Ticonderoga area, did much research on the fort's history and on that of patriot Ethan Allen, with whom it is usually associated.

TYRONE POWER

Tyrone Power, Irish comedian who visited America in the early nineteenth century, wrote copious notes about the Americans he observed while on tour, traveling by stage, river boat and rail. He was the ancestor of the twentieth-century motion picture actor of the same name.

JOHN COWPER POWYS

The late English writer, John Cowper Powys, resided for a number of months in the Mohawk Valley and wrote in his autobiography about his visit there with the mysticism and delight in nature which characterized all of his works.

FLETCHER PRATT

The late Fletcher Pratt, during the course of his adult life, devoted his studies to the science of warfare. His historian friends used to visit his home in Greenwich Village to see him illustrate the strategy of naval engagements with the use of miniature battleships in the water of his bathtub. Mr. Pratt probably knew more of the planning and execution of the battles in American history than any other American, military or civilian.

RED JACKET

Red Jacket was renowned both among the Iroquois tribes and among his white contemporaries as an orator and poet. Though he was not regarded as a great warrior, he fought successfully with his mind and words against the white man's treatment of the Indian. He was strongly anti-Christian and he is reported to have said, "Brother, if you white people murdered the Saviour, make it up yourselves. We Indians had nothing to do with it."

JESSIE B. RITTENHOUSE

Jessie B. (christened Jessica Belle) Rittenhouse, one of the founders of the Poetry Society of America, wrote many volumes of verse and also took enthusiastic interest in her fellow poets. She compiled a number of anthologies of their work. Her first volume of criticism, *The Younger American Poets,* was published in 1904. Thirty years later her autobiography *My House of Life* was published. It contained several chapters on a young girl's growing up in the Genesee Valley. She was the wife of Clinton Scollard, the poet.

CLINTON SCOLLARD

Clinton Scollard, teacher, novelist, poet, was born at Clinton, New York, and for a number of years made his home there in a house near the foot of Harding Hill. In his two periods of teaching at Hamilton College, his rich voice, perfect diction, and his sensitive understanding made deep impressions on his classes. He was adept in the uses of such demanding verse forms as the ballade, the villanelle, and the sestina. His marriage to another American poet, Jessie Rittenhouse (see her *My House of Life* on page 426), proved most congenial.

JAMES E. SEAVER

James E. Seaver, an upstate New York clergyman, succeeded in obtaining the story of her life from Mary Jemison, a white woman who had been captured by Indians at the age of fifteen and who lived to be an important influence among the Indians of the Genesee Valley. Mr. Seaver's volume, *A Narrative of the Life of Mrs. Mary Jemison,* purports to be the autobiography of Mary Jemison and relates in considerable detail the facts of her successive marriages to two Indian chieftains and her good works in preserving a friendly relationship between Indians and whites.

CHARD POWERS SMITH

Chard Powers Smith, formerly a resident of Watertown, New York, used his detailed knowledge of the state's north country and his researches on the battle of Gettysburg to write a picturesque and powerful historical novel, *Artillery of Time.* The American critic, Lewis Gannett, wrote of it in the New York *Herald Tribune* at the time of its publication in 1939: "There's some mighty farm eating, some first rate hoss-swapping, the finest square dancing yet to appear in fiction form, a bit of sin and a lot of virtue, a thick slice of the Civil War and an interpretation of the essential conflict of America in the 1850's."

WARREN HUNTING SMITH

A native of Geneva, New York, Warren Hunting Smith was a scholar and researcher in the archives of Yale University. The little city of Geneva, sitting above Seneca Lake, has been fortunate in that Mr. Smith through his residence there was able to draw word portraits of two elderly maiden ladies, spirited sisters whom all readers of *The Misses Elliot of Geneva* look upon with delight. Almost every city has counterparts of these two, but not all have a literate and observant scholar to record their adventures.

ALEXANDER MC GINN STEWART

The late Alexander McGinn Stewart of Rochester, New York, made valuable researches in documents written by the Jesuit missionaries. Among these records were narrations of their adventures among the Indians, who often inflicted on them hardships, danger, and sometimes death. The place of the Jesuit settlement on the shores of Onondago Lake draws to it many visitors who have read in Mr. Stewart's prose the story of the "eat-all dinner" and the thrilling escape of the hosts from their murderous guests.

JOHN TEBBEL and KEITH JENNISON

Keith Jennison has been a writer of amusing non-fiction regional books such as *New York and the State It's In, Vermont Is Where You Find It,* and *The Maine Idea.* He has also been a well-known editor in various publishing houses. He is now retired and engaged in serious writing. He and John Tebbel, also a former editor, have written *The American Indian Wars,* which is given especial authority by the fact that Mr. Tebbel is of Indian ancestry.

HAROLD W. THOMPSON

Harold Thompson, long a Professor at Cornell University, became associated with his researches and his writings in the field of New York State folklore. His volume entitled *Body, Boots and Britches* is considered the most authoritative and comprehensive work on this subject.

ARTHUR TRAIN

Arthur Train's fictional character Ephraim Tutt was so cannily contrived that his readers could hardly believe that he did not exist. It was said of Tutt that he was "the best known of American lawyers," that he was "more typically true to the legal personality than life itself." Both the Mohawk and the Genesee valleys of New York State have claimed certain courthouses to have been the scenes of Tutt's activities. Mr. Train's development of the lawyer's character in *Yankee Lawyer, The Autobiography of Ephraim Tutt* is so filled with true historical figures and with historic detail that it is one of the most convincing of American fictional narratives.

REXFORD G. TUGWELL

Rexford Tugwell was a student of economics when he began his important adult career in the fields of economics and political science. In his autobiography, published in 1962, he returned in subject matter to his early years in the small towns of the Southern Tier, western New York and the city of Buffalo.

MARK TWAIN (SAMUEL LANGHORNE CLEMENS)

In the small anthology of Elmira profiles written by distinguished authors, none is more human, none more poignant than that written by America's great humorist, Mark Twain, about his courting of Olivia Langdon and his life with her after her father, having given permission for their marriage, gave the newlyweds a new house on Delaware Avenue in Buffalo.

ARTEMUS WARD

Artemus Ward was the pseudonym of Charles Farrar Browne. Browne's fictional character, Artemus Ward, was owner and captain of a canalboat on which he kept a museum of wax replicas of prominent people. The anecdote which Artemus told with regard to the visit of his canal craft to Utica, New York, proved so funny to President Abraham Lincoln that he insisted on reading it to his cabinet on a day when the news from the Civil War front was far from favorable.

CHARLES DUDLEY WARNER

Charles Dudley Warner was a widely known American essayist in the 1870's and '80's. He was a close friend of Mark Twain and collaborated with him on the novel *The Gilded Age* (1873). He was a lover of outdoor life; his *In the Wilderness* was published six years before he became an editor of *Harper's Magazine.*

JOHN V. A. WEAVER

John V. A. Weaver became well known as a poet shortly after his graduation from Hamilton College in 1914. His particular forte was the writing of poems in a language which he designated as American, the language of the city shopgirls and their male counterparts. The famous editor and critic, H. L. Mencken, admired his verses and published a number of them in the *American Mercury.* Since his death the actress Peggy Wood, who was his wife, has attracted large audiences by her readings of Weaver's poems and given them a renewed popularity.

EDGAR NOYES WESTCOTT

Edward Noyes Westcott turned his knowledge gained as a banker to good account by writing a novel about a banker. His *David Harum, A Story of American Life,* published in 1898, was so popular that, besides the Bible, it became the one permanent possession in every loyal New Yorker's library. It was dramatized both as a play and as a film (in which the late Will Rogers played David Harum).

EDITH WHARTON

These pages from the work of the distinguished American novelist Edith Wharton provide their own basis for selection in this anthology. The phrase "Hudson River Bracketed," originally descriptive of an architectural style, becomes symbolic of a period in the life of the aristocratic Hudson River families at the turn of the century.

WILLIAM CHAPMAN WHITE

William Chapman White was born in Reading, Pennsylvania, and his life as a scholar, a foreign correspondent, and in service during World War II took him to such various places as Russia, Poland, Germany and London. However, it was during the last years of his life in Saranac Lake, New York, that he wrote the many fine pieces about the mountain country he loved. They appeared as columns in the New York *Times* and the New York *Herald Tribune* for some five years. Mr. White also wrote *Adirondack Country* about his adopted upstate, and it is from this book that his observations on the seasons of his mountain home year are selected.

NATHANIEL PARKER WILLIS

Nathaniel Parker Willis was an exceedingly popular poet, essayist, and editor. He was very elegant and fashionable in his dress, rather too mannered in his behavior. His works are not read as much in the present as many of them deserve.

FRANCES WRIGHT

Frances Wright on an early visit to the United States lived for some months in Cooperstown, New York. Her writings about her upstate travels at that time were full of girlish enthusiasms and sentimentalities. Few of her companions then could have prophesied for her a career as a radical reformer and the founder of an unconventional community.

INDEX